What experts say about this book!

We found this book highly beneficial for our students. *Practice Tests for the SAT* is on our must-purchase list. Students will benefit from seeing first-hand how the SAT questions are constructed. Teachers will find this material useful in helping students to prepare for the SAT.

– Cathy Koehler
Librarian, Little Rock School District

Any book that can be used to prep students for the SAT is a necessary book for any American high school library and classroom. Students need all the advice and practice they can get, and this book makes a great addition to their prep resources. This book will be used in my classroom for any student planning to study in a US College or University.

– Zakri Banker
UESTC: Zhongshan Institute Educator

As all our students now take the SAT as a pathway to graduation, we have drastically had to increase our SAT prep in the classroom. It is wonderful to have an extra resource that not only provides sample problems but also gives explanations so kids can see where they went wrong and how the test takers think.

– Laura Dimmett
North Gibson School Corporation, University of Southern Indiana

Practice tests for the SAT is very useful for high school students.

– Laurie Kirkwood
Librarian, Beaver Falls Library

We would also like to thank these contributors for reviewing the previous and the current editions of this book.

- Dr. Aimee L. Weinstein, George Mason University
- Nina Guise-Gerrity, Private Tutor for SAT and ACT
- Chinu Vasudeva, Doyen-Ed
- Belle Hart
- Sophie D

VIBRANT
PUBLISHERS

PRACTICE TESTS
FOR THE
SAT®

2023

5 Full-Length SAT Tests

770 Practice Questions in total

Complete Practice for Reading,
Writing & Language, Math sections

Detailed Answers and Explanations
for all Questions

Second Edition

Practice Tests For The SAT®
Second Edition

Paperback ISBN-10: 1-63651-087-6
Paperback ISBN-13: 978-1-63651-087-3

Library of Congress Control Number: 2020937033

This publication is designed to provide accurate and authoritative information in regard to the subject matter covered. The Author has made every effort in the preparation of this book to ensure the accuracy of the information. However, information in this book is sold without warranty either expressed or implied. The Author or the Publisher will not be liable for any damages caused or alleged to be caused either directly or indirectly by this book.

Vibrant Publishers books are available at special quantity discount for sales promotions, or for use in corporate training programs. For more information please write to bulkorders@vibrantpublishers.com

Please email feedback / corrections (technical, grammatical or spelling) to spellerrors@vibrantpublishers.com

To access the complete catalogue of Vibrant Publishers, visit www.vibrantpublishers.com

SAT is a trademark registered by the College Board, which is not affiliated with, and does not endorse, this product.

Table of Contents

Dear Student,

Thank you for purchasing **Practice Tests for the SAT**. We are committed to publishing books that are content-rich, concise and approachable enabling more students to read and make the fullest use of them. We hope this book provides the most enriching learning experience as you prepare for your SAT exam.

Should you have any questions or suggestions, feel free to email us at reachus@vibrantpublishers.com

Thanks again for your purchase. Good luck for your SAT!

– Vibrant Publishers Team

ACT/SAT Books in Test Prep Series

Math Practice Tests for the ACT
ISBN:978-1-63651-085-9

SAT Math Practice Questions
ISBN: 978-1-63651-094-1

Winning Strategies For ACT Essay Writing:
With 15 Sample Prompts
ISBN: 978-1-63651-049-1

For the more updated list of books visit
www.vibrantpublishers.com

HOW TO GET THE MOST OUT OF THIS BOOK

This practice test book is designed to help you achieve as much of a real test experience as possible. By practicing with this book, you will be exposing yourself to the style and format of reading, writing and language, and math questions asked in the real SAT. At the same time, you will be gaining enough practice with the core content areas tested in the SAT. In this way, you will be increasing your familiarity with the SAT test format, as well as solidifying your knowledge of reading, writing and language, and math concepts. With this book, you will be able to save time, cut down on confusion, and increase your chances of scoring high on the real test day.

This book includes **5 full-length SAT tests** with a total of **770 practice questions** for thorough practice. Each question comes with detailed answer explanations that will help you to understand the logic behind a particular answer. This book also provides the difficulty level for all questions, which you can use to gauge your preparation level and get an idea of how ready you are to take the SAT.

Here are a few tips for getting the most out of your practice:

PRACTICE IN SIMULATED TEST CONDITIONS

For optimum practice, take the tests in quiet, unfamiliar settings, simulating the conditions of the actual SAT. This will enhance your performance, giving you the 'push' of pressure needed to perform well. You will also be able to understand how much time you take to complete each section.

ACTIVATE WHAT YOU KNOW

The concepts tested on the SAT are ones you have encountered all throughout middle school and high school. So all you need to do is solidify the concepts you are already aware of. Don't skip out on practicing concepts that you think are easy or that you know well; repetitive practice is the key.

REVIEW AND REVISE

The practice questions in this book have been constructed to be as similar to the real SAT as possible, in terms of format, difficulty levels, and content. Make use of the detailed answer guides given to understand the logic behind a particular answer, even the answers that you get correct. This will help you understand how the questions are structured, which will improve your accuracy in answering.

TIME YOURSELF

Get the most out of your practice by timing yourself according to the test timings given before each test. Check how you're progressing—are you eventually able to complete the tests in the given time? Remember, timed practice is key to familiarizing yourself with the actual SAT and minimizing confusion on the real test day.

MAKE EDUCATED GUESSES

Some questions are structured in a way that makes the answer obvious. Don't hesitate to make educated guesses for such questions instead of puzzling out the answer. However, do this only for questions you're very sure of.

SET A TARGET SCORE

Once you've taken the first few tests, you will be able to obtain an idea of your average score and how much it deviates from the score you need to obtain. Set a target score over and above the actual target score you want to receive and work towards attaining that.

PRACTICE, PRACTICE, PRACTICE

Once you've taken the first few tests, you will be able to obtain an idea of your average score and how much it deviates from the score you need to obtain. Set a target score over and above the actual target score you want to receive and work towards attaining that.

HOW CAN OUR PRACTICE BOOK HELP YOU BEYOND THE SAT?

The aim of standardized tests like the SAT is to test your readiness for college-level programs and graduate courses. The concepts tested on the SAT are not only needed for scoring well on the test, but are the fundamentals of the courses you will be learning in college and in graduate programs. The SAT is basically your window to your future, and practicing with this test book can help you become college-ready. If you prepare well for the SAT, you are essentially setting yourself up for success in your graduate experience and in life as well.

Get ready to score high on the SAT today!

SAT Overview

So, you've decided to take the SAT. At this point in your life, you probably have a lot of important decisions looming in front of you. What college would I like to attend? What do I need to get in? What classes should I be taking? What's a good GPA? Of course, you are also wondering about the SAT. This chapter provides an overview of the SAT as one of the data points considered for college entrance standards. It also provides the outline of the test, grading overview and some helpful hints to get you started. The most important first step is to know what to expect, so you can make the best-informed choices as you look forward to your exciting future. Congratulations on taking that first step.

What is the SAT

The SAT (Standardized Aptitude Test) is one of the two primary tests which colleges use to gauge whether or not you might be ready for college. It is a test that reflects the things you should have learned in middle school and high school and relies on strategic questioning to actively represent those skills and knowledge that are essential as you enter the world of college. But what is it really? The SAT is a measure of how well you can take what you learned and apply it to a timed testing environment. It shows how well you take tests and how well you do in a stressful situation. It does not, however, measure your intelligence. In fact, once you learn the tips and tricks of the test, one might argue it measures your testing ability more than what you know.

If that's what it is, why do colleges use it for a standard for admission? Colleges use this as a predictive analytic tool to try to figure out if you have the basic abilities required of a college freshman. They want to make sure you can comprehend reading at a level that is expected in your classes. Same with math: do you have a basic understanding of mathematical concepts so you can succeed not just in math class but in other required classes such as economics? Many colleges also want to see if you can write in a way that is conducive to the college classroom. Again, they are not testing whether or not you CAN write but whether or not you can follow instructions and apply what you read to create an essay that would be appropriate for the college classroom. Finally, they are assessing your ability to take lengthy, timed tests. This testing situation mirrors what you might encounter in your college classes. They want to make sure, when they check that box for YES, they will be admitting someone with the tools to succeed. Colleges and universities must report their success rates with students and if all their students drop out, because they are not prepared to succeed, then the college itself cannot succeed. That is one reason why the admission process is so rigorous.

Preparing for the SAT

Knowing all that, it is essential to understand the tips and tricks of this assessment. The SAT is a great vehicle to show what you know. It has recently been realigned with the current high school college readiness curriculum, so it does reflect what you have seen in your classroom. But like any other test, it requires preparation and planning to do your best. It is important to note that you can take the test more than once. It won't count against you to try again, and in the end, you can choose the test you would like to send to your chosen school. Some schools superscore, which means you can combine the best sections into one final score. (You can read more about that in the "Words to Know" section). All these options are handy, especially if test taking isn't one of your strengths, but the real goal should be to go into your first testing situation with a plan to succeed.

Here are some tips to prepare for that first testing day:

- Learn strategies, tips and tools
- Practice, practice, practice. The more questions you see; the better you will do
- Learn math and reading formulas
- Create a study group and learn from your friends

You also need to:

- Understand the purpose of the test

- Outline the standards and requirements of each section

- Learn strategies and practices that will help you do your best on the test

- And above all, know what to expect and develop a plan to succeed

On the day of the test here are some things to remember:

- Get a good night's sleep and relax. Remember it is not the end of the world if you don't have your best testing day. You can always take the test again.

- Have a good breakfast. It can be hard to eat when you're nervous, but make sure there's something in your stomach so you won't feel hungry later on.

- Gather your testing supplies. Take several sharpened number 2 pencils and your calculator (make sure it follows the guidelines set forth by the College Board).

- It is always smart to take a snack with you for your breaks. This will help energize you and keep you going.

- Don't forget your picture ID and your testing ticket. Make sure to double-check all the requirements on the College Board site. They will give you a detailed account of all the documents you need to bring.

Words to Know

College Board: The College Board is the manager of the SAT. This organization provides great resources to better understand the application process, the meaning of your score, and the components of the test.

Standardized: Standardized means the same for all. Everyone taking the SAT will be tested on standardized material. There is no truth in the old myth that a red cover is a harder version, or if you take the test in June, it's easier than if you take it in January. Whenever you take it, regardless of the color of your test, the content is the same.

ACT: This is a test similar to the SAT. When the SAT was redesigned, it became more aligned with the content of the ACT. Now the two tests are pretty similar. Both tests are equally important, and you should consult your colleges of choice to see which they prefer.

Data Point: You might hear the SAT mentioned as a data point. This means it is just one measure, one point of data that is used to predict whether or not you will be a good fit for the college or university. Remember, they are using a predictive analysis formula to find the best fit for their programs and campus mission. You'll notice that every institution rates data points differently so that those skills they value most will be the biggest data points to consider.

Old SAT vs. New SAT: In 2016, the SAT made some major changes to its format, grading formula and essay. For the first year that these changes were in place, students could choose which format they would like to take. However, now there is just one SAT. When you sit for the exam, you can be assured that everyone else sitting for the exam that day is receiving a similar version of the test.

Superscore: A Superscore is when after taking the SAT multiple times, you combine the best scores for each section to create the Superscore that you send to your school. For example, if you rocked the first math test but just bombed the reading, if you chose to take it again, and did great on the reading, your score could be composed of the math from the first test and the reading from the second. This sounds great, right? However, this is not a College Board thing. This is a school-to-school decision. You need to check with the schools you intend to apply to and see if they Superscore. If they do not, then you will use the total scores from each individual test. This is an important distinction.

Who takes the SAT

The typical test taker is a student planning to enter an undergraduate program in the United States or Canada. The SAT may be a requirement for admission, but it is important to check with your colleges of choice to see if they prefer the SAT or ACT. It is also essential to see if they require the essay. Typically, this test is taken in the 11th and 12th grade.

CONTINUE

Who gives the SAT

On the day of the test, your exam will be administered by trained proctors. They are employees of the College Board and they specialize in test security. They are not able to answer questions about the test but can answer your logistical questions such as where to take a break and when the test starts. They read their instructions from a script so the College Board can ensure that every test taker is receiving the same information. They are also responsible for watching for testing anomalies or misadministration issues.

The SAT is administered by the College Board. The College Board is an organization which writes, evaluates, and manages the registration for the exam. They are your one stop shop for anything you need to know about actually taking the test. You can register through their site as well as receive your final score. Once you register and choose your schools, the College Board will also send your scores directly to your schools of choice. They also provide a thorough explanation of your scores, so you can see your highs and lows and make plans for improvements, if you are considering retaking the test.

Remember, even though you may take the test at your high school, it is not your school that is responsible for the test. The College Board creates, grades, and secures all tests, so they can ensure test security. In other words, they can guarantee that you took the correct test with the correct results.

What is tested?

The SAT is divided into three sections:

- Reading
- Writing and language
- Math

Reading

The Reading test consists of 52 multiple choice questions and you have 65 minutes to complete it. You'll encounter passages or pairs of passages that are taken from the fields of literature, historical documents, social sciences, and natural sciences. The biggest advantage you have in this test is to choose the order you attack the passages. The best strategy is to practice. Your strategy will improve as you begin to understand your strengths and opportunities. That understanding comes with practice. For example, if you are good at historical documents, you might want to do that passage first and get it out of the way, so you can focus on the natural science passage that you know is a passage that will require more of your time.

You can also learn about question types and develop strategies for each one. The question types you will see include;

- Main idea/big picture questions
- Detail questions
- Inference questions
- Author's purpose and technique questions
- Vocabulary questions
- Analogy questions
- Data reasoning
- Use of evidence support

Each question type carries with it its own strategies and tips. The first step is to be able to decide which question type you are encountering. After you know what type of question it is, you can decide first what kind of answer you are looking for and next how to use the passage to find the answer. However, as you are deciding on these strategies, the clock is ticking, which is why practicing is essential.

Here are some quick tips to get you started:

- Know what to expect: format, time, expectations.

- Choose the order of passages.

- Read the passages in a way that makes sense to answer the questions. You don't have to necessarily read every word to answer these questions.

- Remember this is a passage-based assessment. They are not looking for what you think or what you know. Focus on what the passage says. That's all that matters.

- Save main idea questions for the last. By that time, you will have lived with the passage long enough to get the gist of what it is saying.

Writing and Language

You will have 35 minutes for the 44 multiple choice questions in this section. Questions cover grammar, vocabulary, and editing. You will start with four passages and work through the questions in context. What this means is that every question offers you a chance to practice real skills such as editing, choosing the best word, and reordering sentences. You will also be asked several reading comprehension questions mostly relating to topic sentences and details. Don't get too caught up in reading the passages but make sure as you are working through the questions, you have a general idea of what is going on in the passage. That makes it much easier to answer those tricky reading comprehension questions. You also may need to interpret graphics, so make sure you understand their role in the overall passage.

Math

The math section is divided into two parts with a total of 58 questions. Note that in the first section, you cannot use your calculator for the 20 questions. This section takes 25 minutes. The second section has 38 questions and lasts for 55 minutes. In this part, you can use your calculator.

The math section covers four main topics.

- Heart of Algebra

- Problem Solving and Data Analysis

- Passport to Advanced Math

- Additional Topics in Math

The most important thing in this section is to know what the question is asking. Make sure you have worked through all the steps to reach the answer the test really wants. Sometimes, not completing that last step or not converting inches to feet or pounds to ounces is the difference between a correct and incorrect answer. Also, read the word problems carefully. Use your reading strategies to find keywords and again, make sure you understand what type of answer is required. Finally, make sure you are able to use and apply the basic math formulas required for this test. The College Board website provides a comprehensive list of those formulas. Knowing what formula goes with what problem is a big first step towards math success.

Scoring

The SAT has two main scores: Evidence-based Reading and Writing and Math.

For each section, you can score between 200 and 800 points. A perfect final score is 1600.

Here are some terms to better understand your score:

Your **total score** is the sum of the Reading and Writing and Math sections. This can range between 400 and 1600. A **section score** is a score you receive on each of the separate sections: Reading and Writing and Math. Remember Reading and Writing are scored as one section. This can be helpful to students who have strengths in one of the sections but struggle in the other. They will eventually balance each other.

A **percentile** is a comparison between you and the rest of the students who took the SAT in the year of your test. This is a test that 11th and 12th graders can take, so you will be compared with all students, not just those students in your grade.

A **cross-test score** shows how you performed on select questions that represent knowledge in science and history. Finally, a **subscore** is reported as a number between 1-15 and it shows how you perform on basic knowledge questions that specifically relate to what you learned in high school. Topics include: a) Command of Evidence, b) Words in Context, c) Expression of Ideas and d) Standard English Conventions for Reading and Writing and Language tests and a) Heart of Algebra, b) Problem Solving and Data Analysis and c) Passport to Advanced Math for Math test.

The calculation of your overall score is a bit tricky. First, there is a raw score. A raw score is found through how many questions you got right. You are not penalized for skipping or guessing questions, but you should always attack each question with your best strategies. Then your score is "equated." What this means is basically your score is curved. The way the curve is determined is far more complicated than you need to understand to figure out your score, but here is the gist. The College Board takes all the tests and determines a high and low scoring range. Based on those highs and lows they set their scale. This scale tries to smooth out all the different testing situations, so everyone's curve is pretty much the same. The bottom line is that the curve never really makes that much difference in your final score. If you have a high raw score, you will have a high SAT score. So, the best strategy is to get as many right answers as you can.

Now that you know the basics you are ready to get started. The key is to practice and know what to expect. Good luck and get practicing.

Component	Time Allotted (minutes)	Number of Questions / Tasks
Reading	65	52
Writing & Language	35	44
Math	80	58
Total	180	154

Total Score
The redesigned SAT will report a total score that will be the sum of two section scores: (1) Evidence-Based Reading and Writing and (2) Math. The SAT total score will be reported on a scale ranging from 400 to 1600.

A Detailed Look at SAT-I	
Sections	A Detailed look at the Test Components
Reading	4 single passages plus 1 pair of passages; 500 to 750 words each, a total of 3,250 words; 10 to 11 questions per passage
Writing & Language	4 passages, 400 to 450 words each, a total of 1,700 words; 11 questions per passage
Math	1 No-Calculator Section: 25 mins - 20 questions 15 MCQ, 5 Grid-in 1 Calculator Section: 55 mins - 38 questions 30 MCQ, 8 Grid-in

No Test Material On This Page

SAT Practice
Test #1

It is recommended that you use a No. 2 pencil. It is very important that you fill in the entire circle darkly and completely. If you change your response, erase as completely as possible. Incomplete marks or erasures may affect your score.

	A B C D		A B C D		A B C D		A B C D
1	○ ○ ○ ○	14	○ ○ ○ ○	27	○ ○ ○ ○	40	○ ○ ○ ○
2	○ ○ ○ ○	15	○ ○ ○ ○	28	○ ○ ○ ○	41	○ ○ ○ ○
3	○ ○ ○ ○	16	○ ○ ○ ○	29	○ ○ ○ ○	42	○ ○ ○ ○
4	○ ○ ○ ○	17	○ ○ ○ ○	30	○ ○ ○ ○	43	○ ○ ○ ○
5	○ ○ ○ ○	18	○ ○ ○ ○	31	○ ○ ○ ○	44	○ ○ ○ ○
6	○ ○ ○ ○	19	○ ○ ○ ○	32	○ ○ ○ ○	45	○ ○ ○ ○
7	○ ○ ○ ○	20	○ ○ ○ ○	33	○ ○ ○ ○	46	○ ○ ○ ○
8	○ ○ ○ ○	21	○ ○ ○ ○	34	○ ○ ○ ○	47	○ ○ ○ ○
9	○ ○ ○ ○	22	○ ○ ○ ○	35	○ ○ ○ ○	48	○ ○ ○ ○
10	○ ○ ○ ○	23	○ ○ ○ ○	36	○ ○ ○ ○	49	○ ○ ○ ○
11	○ ○ ○ ○	24	○ ○ ○ ○	37	○ ○ ○ ○	50	○ ○ ○ ○
12	○ ○ ○ ○	25	○ ○ ○ ○	38	○ ○ ○ ○	51	○ ○ ○ ○
13	○ ○ ○ ○	26	○ ○ ○ ○	39	○ ○ ○ ○	52	○ ○ ○ ○

It is recommended that you use a No. 2 pencil. It is very important that you fill in the entire circle darkly and completely. If you change your response, erase as completely as possible. Incomplete marks or erasures may affect your score.

	A B C D		A B C D		A B C D		A B C D		A B C D
1	○○○○	10	○○○○	19	○○○○	28	○○○○	37	○○○○
2	○○○○	11	○○○○	20	○○○○	29	○○○○	38	○○○○
3	○○○○	12	○○○○	21	○○○○	30	○○○○	39	○○○○
4	○○○○	13	○○○○	22	○○○○	31	○○○○	40	○○○○
5	○○○○	14	○○○○	23	○○○○	32	○○○○	41	○○○○
6	○○○○	15	○○○○	24	○○○○	33	○○○○	42	○○○○
7	○○○○	16	○○○○	25	○○○○	34	○○○○	43	○○○○
8	○○○○	17	○○○○	26	○○○○	35	○○○○	44	○○○○
9	○○○○	18	○○○○	27	○○○○	36	○○○○		

It is recommended that you use a No. 2 pencil. It is very important that you fill in the entire circle darkly and completely. If you change your response, erase as completely as possible. Incomplete marks or erasures may affect your score.

	A B C D		A B C D		A B C D		A B C D		A B C D
1	○ ○ ○ ○	4	○ ○ ○ ○	7	○ ○ ○ ○	10	○ ○ ○ ○	13	○ ○ ○ ○
2	○ ○ ○ ○	5	○ ○ ○ ○	8	○ ○ ○ ○	11	○ ○ ○ ○	14	○ ○ ○ ○
3	○ ○ ○ ○	6	○ ○ ○ ○	9	○ ○ ○ ○	12	○ ○ ○ ○	15	○ ○ ○ ○

Only answers that are gridded will be scored. You will not receive credit for anything written in the boxes.

16, 17, 18, 19, 20 grid-in answer grids.

NO CALCULATOR ALLOWED

It is recommended that you use a No. 2 pencil. It is very important that you fill in the entire circle darkly and completely. If you change your response, erase as completely as possible. Incomplete marks or erasures may affect your score.

	A B C D		A B C D		A B C D		A B C D		A B C D
1	○ ○ ○ ○	7	○ ○ ○ ○	13	○ ○ ○ ○	19	○ ○ ○ ○	25	○ ○ ○ ○
2	○ ○ ○ ○	8	○ ○ ○ ○	14	○ ○ ○ ○	20	○ ○ ○ ○	26	○ ○ ○ ○
3	○ ○ ○ ○	9	○ ○ ○ ○	15	○ ○ ○ ○	21	○ ○ ○ ○	27	○ ○ ○ ○
4	○ ○ ○ ○	10	○ ○ ○ ○	16	○ ○ ○ ○	22	○ ○ ○ ○	28	○ ○ ○ ○
5	○ ○ ○ ○	11	○ ○ ○ ○	17	○ ○ ○ ○	23	○ ○ ○ ○	29	○ ○ ○ ○
6	○ ○ ○ ○	12	○ ○ ○ ○	18	○ ○ ○ ○	24	○ ○ ○ ○	30	○ ○ ○ ○

CALCULATOR ALLOWED

It is recommended that you use a No. 2 pencil. It is very important that you fill in the entire circle darkly and completely. If you change your response, erase as completely as possible. Incomplete marks or erasures may affect your score.

31 **32** **33** **34** **35**

Only answers that are gridded will be scored. You will not receive credit for anything written in the boxes.

36 **37** **38**

CALCULATOR ALLOWED

CONTINUE

Reading Test

65 MINUTES, 52 QUESTIONS

Turn to Section 1 of your answer sheet to answer the questions in this section

---

DIRECTIONS

Each passage or pair of passages below is followed by a number of questions. After reading each passage or pair, choose the best answer to each question based on what is stated or implied in the passage or passages and in any accompanying graphics (such as a table or graph).

Questions 1-10 are based on the following passage.

This passage is from Arlette Broncoth, *The Seamstress,* originally published in 1927.

It took me no more than a month to realise that I had made a grave error in both my choice of employment and my employer. In truth, in
Line such times as those, it was less a choice of which
5 employer to work for than it was a choice of whether to work at all. Mrs. Van Doren had had vacancies and that was all there had been to it. At the time it did not occur to me why that was always the case. Nobody likes to admit their own
10 foolishness, but, looking back, from the first day in Tenton I found my work an irritation. The job itself—stitching plain, workaday dresses from coarse broadcloth in colours as drab as my surroundings—was not difficult, but, oh, the
15 tedium! Each garment was so alike that even when assigned a new model, the design lacked such imagination as to be virtually indistinguishable from the last; even a double hem or an extra row of pin-tucking could have alleviated the boredom
20 for an hour or so, but even that was denied me. I am not wholly impatient, and realise that in order to make my own way in the world (as I had vowed I would do) and espouse the role of seamstress I would need to further my craft. Knowing that, I
25 could have borne the stagnation of my creative faculties; my imagination would not have begun to scream in the prison of my mind that there was more to this than the work that progressed beneath my restless fingers; I should have barricaded each
30 sigh and each escaping tear of loss and regret even as my desire for freedom grew. No, if that were all, I should have submitted to Fate's dictates, bowing to the will of her twin handmaidens, Duty and Humility; I should have cherished my dreams as
35 impossible flights of fancy from which my nights released me from the drudgery of the day. But my aversion to Mrs. Van Doren and her clear hostility toward me, evident from my first hour, began to grow, pressing me down into that well
40 called Despair. Each morning its weight pushed me further and further into the poisonous slurry and solitary darkness that lay at its bottom.

I cannot adequately express the woman's antipathy toward me, for it surrounded her
45 like a miasma. From the very moment of our acquaintance it seemed prompted by my merest glance or gesture. It grew with each dress I presented to her with which she was unable to find fault, no matter how hard she tried. She sneered at
50 my cultured tones and tutored bearing, and became irritated by my skilled workmanship, her mouth a thin, hard line and her small, close-set eyes no warmer than the polished jet beads she wore around her corpulent neck. Though I had done little to
55 deserve it, I knew the source of her dislike—a small, ugly, green-eyed creature—for in no case could she call herself my superior, save in years. I had skills equal to her own, and believe she suspected that I had a mental store that far surpassed hers.
60 I tried to keep it hidden, and, of a certainty, if she

could have found fault, ridiculed me in front of
the other women, held up my work as an example
of inadequacy, she probably would have hated me
less. Her malignity stalked my every move, but I
65 gathered my honor guard of Humility, Watchfulness
and Patience and never once did her arrows of spite
strike home.

That day, the end of March, I had received the
small envelope containing my precious wages,
70 startled by the joy it gave me. Not for itself, though
it would pay for my lodgings and provide enough
sustenance to keep me on the mortal plane (though
little more), but the sheer glee of knowing Mrs Van
Doren begrudged every cent of it, but was powerless
75 to prevent my having it. As I walked to my lodging
house, certain that the fire would have gone out and
that my evening meal would be spent alone, my
footsteps hammered out two incessant thoughts on
the cold, hard stone. "Dorothea, this torment must
80 end," said one. "How?" demanded the other. I pulled
out my latchkey, noting that no cheery glow greeted
me, and I resolved at that moment that every ounce
of my not inconsiderable will should be bent on
answering that question. How?

1

Which choice best summarizes the passage?

A) A young woman's experience of life begins in
hope but ends in despair.

B) A character reflects that her current job is
intolerable and considers why.

C) The conflict between a new employee and her
supervisor become increasingly bitter.

D) A character regrets a choice but determines to
stand by her decision.

2

The opening two sentences of the passage
primarily serve to

A) establish a chronology for the events that
follow.

B) suggest a foundation for Van Doren's position.

C) indicate the narrator's reason for repentance.

D) contextualize the narrator's current emotions.

3

Over the course of the passage, the narrator's focus shifts from

A) her dissatisfaction with her present position to a resolution that it must change.

B) anticipatory delight at making an independent living, to regret at her choice of career.

C) the specifics of the tasks that displease her to the reasons she displeases Van Doren.

D) a discussion of her work and its repetitiveness to the discomfort of her home and its loneliness.

4

The author's use of "poisonous slurry" and "solitary darkness" (lines 41-42) are intended to

A) encapsulate the narrator's fear of being confined.

B) reveal the narrator's increasing sense of isolation.

C) emphasize the narrator's utter dismay at her plight.

D) indicate that the employer had sinister intentions.

5

The passage most strongly suggests that Mrs. Van Doren's attitude is prompted by

A) exasperation with Dorothea's lack of skill.

B) envy of Dorothea's poise and ability.

C) contempt for Dorothea's aspirations.

D) impatience with Dorothea's complaints.

6

Which choice provides the best evidence for the answer to the previous question?

A) Lines 20-24 ("I am … craft")

B) Lines 47-49 ("It grew … tried")

C) Lines 49-51 ("She … workmanship")

D) Lines 55-57 ("I knew… superior")

7

At the end of the second paragraph, the author's use of a hunting metaphor mainly has the effect of

A) emphasizing the narrator's need to escape from an intolerable situation.

B) contrasting the behavior of Van Doren with that of the narrator.

C) suggesting that Van Doren was capable of physically harming Dorothea.

D) illustrating the superior position Van Doren holds over her workforce.

8

Based on the passage, Dorothea is best characterized as

A) quietly determined.

B) foolishly optimistic.

C) subtly aggressive.

D) superficially confident.

9

Which choice provides the best evidence for the answer to the previous question?

A) Lines 9-11 ("Nobody … irritation")

B) Lines 34-36 ("I should… day")

C) Lines 68-70 ("That day… me")

D) Lines 82-84 ("I resolved … question")

10

The passage indicates that when Dorothea receives her pay packet, she is pleased primarily because

A) she will have enough to pay for a few small luxuries.

B) her supervisor could not prevent her from receiving it.

C) she knows her work was good and she deserves it.

D) she owes money to her landlady for room and board.

Questions 11-20 are based on the following passage.

This passage is adapted from *A History of WomanSuffrage Volume I,* by Elizabeth Cady Stanton et al, first published in 1881.

As civilization advances, there is a continual change in the standard of human rights. In barbarous ages, the right of the strongest was the
Line only one recognized; but as mankind progressed
5 in the arts and sciences, intellect began to triumph over brute force. Change is a law of life and the development of society a natural growth. Although to this law we owe the discoveries of unknown worlds, the inventions of machinery, swifter modes
10 of travel, and clearer ideas as to the value of human life and thought, yet each successive change has met with the most determined opposition.

"Subjection to the powers that be" has been the lesson of both Church and State, throttling
15 science, checking invention, crushing free thought, persecuting and torturing those who have dared to speak or act outside of established authority. So entirely has the human will been enslaved that monarchs have humbled themselves to popes,
20 nations have knelt at the feet of monarchs, and individual self-reliance—the first incentive to freedom—has been lost. Obedience and self-sacrifice—the virtues prescribed for subordinate classes, and which naturally grow out of their
25 condition—are alike opposed to the theory of individual rights and self-government.

All these influences fell with crushing weight on woman; more sensitive, helpless, and imaginative, she suffered a thousand fears and wrongs where
30 man did one. Society, including our systems of jurisprudence, civil and political theories, trade, commerce, education, religion, friendships, and family life, have all been framed on the sole idea of man's rights and it is man who takes upon himself
35 the responsibility of directing and controlling the powers of woman.

The people who demand authority for every thought and action, who look to others for wisdom and protection, are those who perpetuate tyranny.
40 The thinkers and actors who find their authority within, are those who inaugurate freedom. Obedience to outside authority to which woman has everywhere been trained, has not only dwarfed

her capacity, but made her a retarding force in civilization. The elevation of women is hopeless
45 so long as they are taught that their condition is ordained: they have the power to block the wheels of progress. Hence, in the scientific education of woman, in the training of her faculties to independent thought and logical reasoning, lies the
50 hope of the future. Education frees the mind from the bondage of authority and makes the individual self-asserting.

The American Revolution—that great political rebellion of the ages—was based upon the inherent
55 rights of the individual. Perhaps in none but English Colonies could such a revolution have been consummated: England's people had defied monarchs and wrested from them many civil rights, which protected women as well as men. At its
60 outset, women were as active, earnest, determined, and self-sacrificing as the men, endowed with as lofty a patriotism as man, and fully understood the principles upon which the struggle was based.

Among the women who manifested deep
65 political insight, was Abigail Smith Adams, wife of John Adams. She early protested against the formation of a new government in which women should be unrecognized, demanding a voice and representation. In 1776, she wrote to her husband,
70 then in the Continental Congress, "In the new code of laws which I suppose it will be necessary for you to make, I desire you would remember the ladies, and be more generous and favorable to them than your ancestors. We will not obey any laws in which
75 we have no voice or representation."

Thus America started into governmental life freighted with the protests of the Revolutionary Mothers against being ruled without their consent. From that hour to the present, women have been
80 continually raising their voices against political tyranny, and demanding for themselves equality of opportunity in every department of life: Harriet Beecher Stowe, in literature; Angelica Kauffman, Rosa Bonheur, and Harriet Hosmer, in art; Mary
85 Somerville, in science; Dorothea Dix, in prison reform; Florence Nightingale and Clara Barton in the camp. All are part of the great uprising of women out of the lethargy of the past, and throughout global society there are similar minds
90 alive to the aggregated wrongs of centuries and inciting their overthrow.

CONTINUE

11

The central claim of this passage is that as civilizations develop systems of law and government,

A) free-thinking has been discouraged by both Church and State.

B) revolution and the desire for self-determination is inevitable.

C) both men and women must have an equal stake in their formulation.

D) the tyranny of one group requires the subjugation of others.

12

According to the authors, a fundamental difference between the modern age and barbarism is that

A) in the past, freedom of thought or challenges to authority resulted in persecution, whereas it is now applauded as progress.

B) in the past, systems of government were formulated by men for the benefit of men, but now they are for the benefit of all.

C) in the past, woman failed to protest their inequality or imprisonment of mind, but now they are unafraid to speak out.

D) in the past, physical strength imbued the holder with power, whereas the capacity to think and reason now holds sway.

13

Which choice provides the best evidence for the answer to the previous question?

A) Lines 2-6 ("In barbarous... brute force")

B) Lines 13-17 ("Subjection... authority")

C) Lines 30-34 ("Society... man's rights")

D) Lines 79-82 ("From that... life")

14

The passage suggests that the key to change is education primarily because it

A) prevents a mindset amongst men likely to retard civilization.

B) inaugurates freedom of thought and allows women to look within for authority.

C) teaches Church and State that individual self-reliance is the first incentive to freedom.

D) endows women with the patriotism capable of overthrowing tyranny.

15

As used in line 17, "established" most nearly means

A) customary

B) recognized

C) traditional

D) formal

16

The authors use the phrase "freighted with the protests of the Revolutionary Mothers" (lines 77-78) in order to suggest that

A) the country began under a burden of protests.

B) women are holding back the progress of society.

C) the government is hamstrung by ongoing dissent.

D) revolution is as unstoppable as a freight train.

17

The authors refer to Abigail Adams in paragraph 6 in order to

A) popularize a little-known fact about a famous figure in history.

B) foreshadow the listing of eminent women in history in the following paragraph.

C) offer support for a statement in the previous paragraph.

D) provide historical context to the discussion of the roles and rights of women.

18

A student claims that the struggle for women's suffrage is particular to America. Which of the following statements in the passage best contradicts the student's claim?

A) Lines 53-55 ("The American… individual")

B) Lines 57-59 ("England's… men")

C) Lines 76-78 ("Thus America… consent")

D) Lines 89-91 ("throughout… overthrow")

19

The primary development from the second to the third paragraph is from

A) those in authority as "the powers that be" to those under it as "subordinate classes."

B) the characteristics of culture and society to the mechanisms of government and trade.

C) the subjugation by the powers that be of the rights of people to how women have been even more subjugated than men.

D) the struggle for self-determination in the past to the struggle for self-determination now.

20

Based on the passage, with which of the following statements would the author most likely agree?

A) Suffrage is an inescapable right of citizenship.

B) Universal suffrage should rest upon universal education.

C) Women should never risk civil disobedience for their rights.

D) Only those who assume the burden of government should receive its privileges.

CONTINUE

Questions 21-31 are based on the following passage and supplementary material.

The following passage is from *A Different Kind of Invasion* by Sally Mewen, first published in 2017.

Nearly half of the plants on America's "endangered" list are under threat from alien invasive species. Some can be so vigorous that they cover thousands of acres of land. Various measures
5 have been tried to eradicate them, with varying success in terms of cost or efficiency. Physical removal is expensive because it means digging up every last piece of the plant with heavy equipment. Treatment with herbicides is tricky because toxins
10 can get into water systems or destroy native plants. Cutting creates tonnes of biomass that has to be removed or burned, and burning itself is both polluting and dangerous. Yet there may be a novel, (yet paradoxically traditional) solution: goats.

15 Brian Knox began raising goats for meat, but when he grew too fond of them to take them to the slaughterhouse, he set them to work on some invasive plants in one of his fields. Neighbors saw the results and began asking if they could borrow
20 the flock to remove plants like poison ivy and bittersweet. Knox has been successfully destroying non-native species by hiring out his goats for years now, and claims the goats enjoy the variety. "They like the magic of getting on the trailer when all
25 the food has gone and when the door opens again there's a whole new smorgasbord to eat."

Brian Cash runs a company that hires out a mixed herd in Georgia to clear infestations like the kudzu vine from people's properties. The vine
30 is a problem in the warm, damp climate of the southeastern region of the United States. Other invasive species like English ivy stop the animals' diet from becoming monotonous. Cash's customers find the experience fascinating and watch with
35 astonishment as the flock chomps pests to ground level in a matter of hours. To make sure vines are not tempted to grow back, Cash chops the roots with a chainsaw and uses a harmless growth inhibitor on what's left. He says he prefers to mix
40 sheep and goats because while the goats are more gastrically tolerant, the sheep are better behaved.

The concept of turning back to livestock grazing as a means of controlling plant growth is now being studied by universities and research groups, but
45 work relates to using goats on specific plants in specific places—not to all 50,000 invasive species. One study, for example, looked at an infestation of yellow star-thistle in the rocky canyons of Idaho. Allowing goats to graze the area seemed the only
50 available choice as the land was too rocky and remote to allow for herbicide spraying or cutting. The goats significantly reduced the incidence of the unwanted plant, but had to be quickly removed to prevent them from eating everything else as
55 well; goats lack discrimination. Another study looking at the eradication of spotted knapweed in the Pacific Northwest found that if goats grazed the land concerned after the plant formed buds but before it set seeds, that growth the following
60 year is significantly reduced. The motivation for the experiment was to use a natural means of eradication; the process took just half a day.

That raises an important issue. Goats have enormous appetites. Each animal needs 2-4 pounds
65 of biomass per day, and the more nutritionally deficient the fodder, the more they need to eat. Chewing up phragmites, a grass-like invasive reed, takes more energy and produces fewer calories than a nice clump of nutrient-rich alfalfa. That
70 means that using peripatetic livestock—primarily sheep and goats, although cattle and geese are contenders—may not be the panacea that these success stories suggest.

Research has also not investigated whether
75 the rent-a-flock method is feasible in terms of management. It has been working in Europe for some time, but farmers in Europe get payments for eradicating invasive species, along with help toward the cost of transporting livestock. Andrew Jenner,
80 writing in the *Modern Farmer*, is clear that this model would not work in the U.S.A. What would work, he claims, is hard cash when the customer is a municipality or the land involved is something the size of a large back yard, and a barter system when a
85 Texas-sized ranch is concerned. Cattlemen can't pay the thousands of dollars it costs to clear multiple acres over two or three visits, but they can provide winter fodder for goats in exchange for control of invasive species. It is an idea worth consideration,
90 especially since some invasive species, like tansy ragwort, are poisonous to cattle, but mere hors d'oeuvres to rampageous goats.

Figure 1

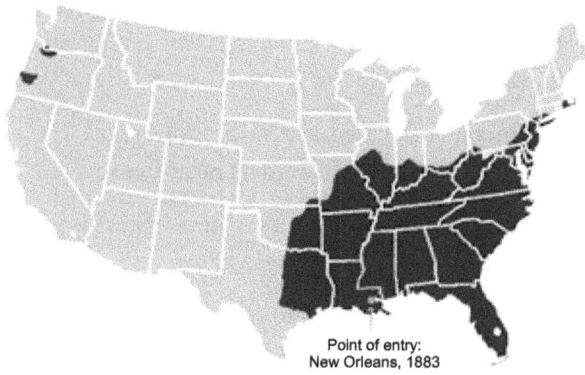

Point of entry:
New Orleans, 1883

Figure 2

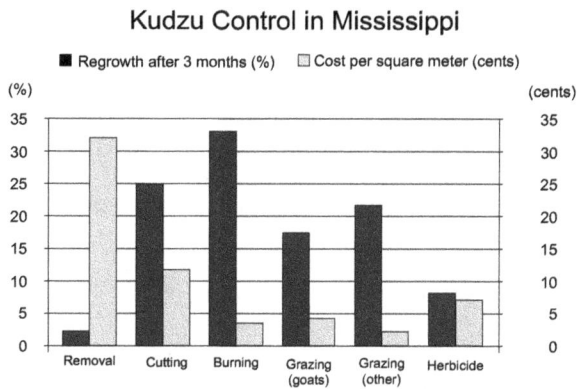

Kudzu Control in Mississippi

■ Regrowth after 3 months (%)   □ Cost per square meter (cents)

21

Over the course of the passage, the narrator's attitude shifts from

A) optimism that a solution to the issue of invasive plants has been found, to caution that it may not be as useful as expected.

B) concern over the threat to America's native species to relief that a natural solution to the problem has been found.

C) interest in the problem of controlling invasive species to appreciation of the utility of goats as a natural means of control.

D) admiring the enterprise of Brian Knox and Brian Cash to skepticism over the value of academic studies into single species control.

22

The author most likely includes the quotation in lines 23-26 in order to

A) ridicule the solution described.

B) cite a representative viewpoint.

C) present the issue from another perspective.

D) suggest an expert opinion on the matter.

23

Brian Cash's method of controlling invasive species differs from Brian Knox's in that

A) the former stumbled on the idea of using livestock for plant control whereas the latter made a deliberate choice.

B) the former used additional means to ensure plants were eradicated, while the latter used only livestock.

C) the former treated a number of different species of plants, while the latter generally dealt with a single species.

D) the former used only goats to control pest species whereas the latter used both sheep and goats.

24

The best evidence for the answer to the previous question is

A) Lines 15-18 ("Brian Knox ... his fields")

B) Lines 21-23 ("Knox has ... the variety")

C) Lines 27-29 ("Brian Cash ... properties")

D) Lines 36-39 ("To make ... what's left")

25

The passage's main conclusion strongly suggests that current research into the control of invasive species by goats is

A) inconclusive because of the volume of nutritional food the goats need to eat.

B) unlikely to solve the issue of invasive species because its focus is too narrow.

C) limited by the need to protect other plants in areas where the goats are grazing.

D) impractical because farmers in America are unable to pay for large scale eradications.

26

The best evidence for the answer to the previous question is

A) Lines 45-46 ("work ... species")

B) Lines 52-55 ("The goats ... as well")

C) Lines 64-66 ("Each ... to eat")

D) Lines 85-89 ("Cattlemen ... species")

27

As used in line 55, "discrimination" most nearly means

A) bias.

B) prejudices.

C) taste.

D) bigotry.

28

The primary function of the fifth paragraph (lines 63-73) is to

A) introduce cattle and geese as contenders for natural alien invasive species removal.

B) explain that goats cannot maintain a diet consisting entirely of nutritionally poor invasive species.

C) introduce the notion of bartering grazing pest species for supplies of winter fodder.

D) highlight the enormous amount of biomass goats can consume in a short amount of time.

29

Based on the passage, figure 1 most likely represents the spread of which invasive species?

A) Yellow star-thistle

B) Poison ivy

C) Kudzu vine

D) Spotted knapweed

30

Which choice states a relationship between re-growth and cost indicated by figure 2?

A) The most effective method of eradication is removal, but the costs are greater than all the other methods combined.

B) The least effective means of control in terms of cost-benefit is cutting because it is both relatively expensive and ineffective.

C) The cost of burning kudzu is relatively low, but the method is ineffective in controlling the vine as burning stimulates new growth.

D) While grazing by other animals costs less per meter than any other means of control, re-growth rates are higher than for goats because other grazers fail to pull out the roots.

31

Data in the figures support which of the following ideas from the passage?

A) Lines 29-31 ("The vine… United States")

B) Lines 42-46 ("The concept … species")

C) Lines 69-73 ("That means… suggest")

D) Lines 79-81 ("Andrew… U.S.A. ")

Questions 32-42 are based on the following passages.

Passage 1 is from The *Elements of Life* by Isabel Jeyn, first published in 2019. Passage 2 is based on *Atmospheric Chemistry* by Basil Melen, first published in 2015.

Passage 1

A century ago, two scientists, one from Russia and the other from Britain, both working alone, came up with the theory of chemical evolution.
Line Alexander Oparin and John Haldane suggested that
5 a reducing atmosphere could spontaneously create the building blocks of life on Earth: amino acids and sugars. It was a radical notion since a reducing atmosphere lacks oxygen. How could life exist without it?

10 Thirty years later at Chicago University in America, Stanley Miller, a graduate student, and Harold Urey, his supervisor, began experimenting with methane, ammonia and hydrogen, the gases believed to have comprised the Earth's atmosphere.
15 They put these in a tank with two electrodes, connected to a second tank containing water. The water was heated until vapour flowed into the chemical tank, and the current switched on to create sparks between the electrodes, simulating lightning.
20 Essentially, they were recreating in miniature the conditions believed to exist on Earth when life first began. After five days, they allowed the now slightly pink-coloured mixture to cool. On testing, it was revealed to contain no less than five amino acids and
25 other combinations of molecules used in building proteins.

The simple experiment has become the classic in terms of abiogenesis, or the production of organic life forms from inorganic materials, and began a
30 branch of science called prebiotic chemistry. Other experiments followed, with energy sources such as thermal energy, and including nitrogen and hydrogen sulphide, as many scientists believed life on Earth was kick-started by volcanic activity.
35 However, the underlying assumption of a reducing atmosphere remained unchallenged.

Until, that is, 2011, when Dustin Trail, Bruce Watson and Nicholas Tailby at Rensselaer Polytechnic Institute began conducting experiments
40 using zircon ($ZrSiO_4$). These told a different story.

Zircon, which contains tiny amounts of cerium (Ce), was produced by volcanic activity when the Earth was new, so samples from the Earth's crust are almost as old as the Earth itself. Cerium has two
45 forms: Ce^{4+} and Ce^{3+}. Under oxidizing conditions the cerium releases cerium dioxide (CeO_2), but under reducing conditions the mineral is stable and will not precipitate out in water, changing the Ce^{4+}:Ce^{3+} ratio. The three scientists created their
50 own zircon in the lab, adjusting the composition until the chemical signature matched that of ancient samples. What they found was that it contained the highly oxygenated form of cerium, suggesting that the atmosphere on Earth when life began was rich
55 in oxygen, far removed from the noxious quagmire previous studies suggested.

Passage 2

According to geologists, terrestrial planets generally have a primary atmosphere formed by the accretion of light gases, similar to that
60 around Jupiter. They are mostly hydrogen, a little helium and mere traces of everything else. Earth's atmosphere is different because our planet has a large mass and is close to the sun, giving it pulling power in terms of gravity. Because light gases like
65 helium (He) and hydrogen (H) have a small atomic mass, when they warm up, their velocity increases to the point where they can escape the planet's gravitational pull. On Earth, that left a combination of rocky materials like iron (Fe) and icy ones like
70 water (H_2O) and methane (CH_4) that combined to form the mantle and crust. As the icy materials warmed up, their gases were released to form a secondary, reducing atmosphere of 58% water vapor, 23% carbon dioxide, 13% sulfur dioxide, 5%
75 nitrogen dioxide, and 1% other gases. That water vapor condensed into oceans, which dissolved the carbon-dioxide-forming carbonate rocks.

Proving that was what happened on Earth billions of years ago has not been easy, but now
80 two scientists at the University of Washington, Bruce Fegley, a professor, and Laura Schaefer, his assistant, have done just that. Most icy materials remain in the outer solar system, but some reached Earth in the form of small rocky meteorites that
85 retain their chemical composition as they hurtle through space. Fegley and Schaefer examined

CONTINUE

masses of these chondrites—the small, icy, rocky meteorites that traveled to Earth from space—from different layers in the Earth's crust.Using computer
90 analysis, they figured out the mixture of gases each combination would have produced as the mini-meteorites interacted with each other. The result? A reducing atmosphere thick with methane (CH_4) and ammonia (NH_3), perfect for the emergence of
95 organic life just as Miller and Urey had claimed.

32

As used in line 7, "radical" most nearly means

A) thorough

B) belonging to the root of a word

C) revolutionary

D) fundamental

33

According to Passage 1, the theory that life on Earth developed from inorganic materials

A) was first proposed by two Americans working at Chicago University.

B) was accepted, although the conditions under which it took place were disputed.

C) relied on experiments producing amino acids under laboratory conditions.

D) was finally disproven in 2011 following experiments with cerium.

34

The best evidence for the answer to the previous question is

A) Lines 4-7 ("Alexander… sugars")

B) Lines 27-30 ("The simple… chemistry")

C) Lines 30-34 ("Other experiments… activity")

D) Lines 52-56 ("What they… suggested")

35

Trail, Watson, and Tailby's conclusions were based on the fact that

A) their samples of zircon were almost the same age as the Earth itself.

B) zircon is produced by volcanic activity.

C) they could produce multiple samples with varying $Ce^{4+}:Ce^{3+}$ in the laboratory.

D) cerium will not dissolve in water in an atmosphere lacking oxygen.

36

According to Passage 2, Earth's atmosphere lacks large quantities of light gases because

A) their atomic weights are too small to be attracted by Earth's gravity.

B) they accrete into primary atmospheres around planets like Jupiter.

C) they became trapped in chondrites in the earth's crust.

D) its proximity to the sun means they reach escape velocity.

37

The best evidence for the answer to the previous question is

A) Lines 57-60 ("According... Jupiter")

B) Lines 64-68 ("Because... pull")

C) Lines 71-75 ("As the... gases")

D) Lines 89-92 ("Using computer... other")

38

Passage 2 most strongly suggests that chondrites

A) begin to break down in the Earth's crust.

B) are a rare occurrence on Earth.

C) are classed as icy materials.

D) contain methane and ammonia.

39

As used in line 94, "emergence" primarily means

A) materialization

B) hatching

C) coming into existence

D) surfacing

40

Which choice best states the relationship between the two passages?

A) Passage 2 confirms a conclusion disputed in Passage 1.

B) Passage 2 presents support for a unpopular theory presented in Passage 1.

C) Passage 2 questions the experiments explained in Passage 1.

D) Passage 2 offers a means of reconciling the conflicting views in Passage 1.

41

The atmosphere described by the author in the final line of Passage 2 would likely be described by the author of Passage 1 as

A) an evolutionary condition.

B) a primary atmosphere.

C) a toxic swamp.

D) an assumption.

42

Oparin and Haldane would likely have responded to the Fegler and Schaefer's results with

A) dismay, because they contradict evidence produced by Trail, Watson and Tailby.

B) interest, because they confirm the presence of a reducing atmosphere.

C) delight, because they proved that life on Earth began without oxygen.

D) indifference, because the Washington team's experiments were based on chemistry, not biology.

CONTINUE ➡

Questions 43-52 are based on the following passage and supplementary material.

This passage is adapted from *Freeing the Freeways* by Lewin James, first published in 2018.

For anyone who spends hours stuck on the freeway in wall-to-wall traffic, the answer seems fairly obvious: build more roads. It is the answer
Line that city planners across the States have traditionally
5 turned to in projects such as the Los Angeles road improvement scheme and the expansion of the Katy Freeway in Houston. Both cost millions of dollars and the upshot was that congestion got worse. In the former, journey time doubled on
10 some commuter routes. For the latter, travel times increased by 55% in the evening rush hour and by a third in the mornings. It may be counterintuitive, but the answer to congestion could be reducing road capacity, not increasing it.

15 The reason for that is something called "induced demand," a term introduced in the 1960s by economists. It relates to the phenomenon that if more of a good is produced, more is consumed. In the same way, if more roads are provided, more
20 people are encouraged to drive. If more lanes are added to freeways, ultimately, they become just as congested as before.

Studying induced demand in terms of roads is not an exact science, however, because there
25 are so many variables. The local demographic, the economic background, alternative means of transport and how good they are in terms of quality or cost, and the decisions of hundreds of different individuals in dozens of different agencies all play
30 a part. What that means is that some people think the effects of induced demand are exaggerated, while others feel that road capacity in some areas needs to be increased regardless. The upshot is that the phenomenon has largely been ignored when it
35 comes to transport infrastructure planning. Instead, the fashion has been for toll lanes or congestion charges.

The advantage of these is that they can mitigate induced demand. This is evidenced by studies on
40 toll roads across America. The I-405 in Washington State uses variable pricing, so that if more people want to use a lane than its peak capacity for the rate of traffic (say 45 mph), the charge is raised until the demand drops off. The Department of Transport
45 says the result is no congestion, unlike on the I-5, where the fee on toll lanes is capped, making congestion a daily occurrence. Unfortunately, such schemes are unpopular with voters as they are imposed on rich and poor alike and are seen as a
50 form of indirect taxation.

In his book *Rethinking America's Highways*, author Robert Poole suggests that view is outmoded and that we need to regard the road network in the same way as every other utility. For other services
55 (electricity, or water, say), the consumer pays the provider directly. There is a transparent bill stating exactly how much the customer has used and what, precisely, they are paying for; use more, pay more. If improvement works are required (new under-street
60 cabling, say, or larger capacity pipes), which works are undertaken is decided on a need basis, not influenced by politics, and they are funded through capital markets, not out of takings from customers. Such measures would undoubtedly reduce demand,
65 but low-income families frequently live furthest from their places of work because they can't afford high-priced city housing, meaning the burden of paying for roads like a utility would fall most heavily on those least able to afford it.

70 Instead, freeway removal could provide the answer. In San Francisco, the 1989 Loma Prieta earthquake damaged the city's elevated Embarcadero Freeway, which carried around 100,000 people a day. It was replaced by a ground-
75 level 6-lane highway with broad sidewalks on either side. It only carries 45,000 passengers a day, but traffic flows more easily, the properties on either side are sought-after, and the neighborhoods through which it flows are more prosperous. This
80 is not an isolated example, and there are schemes afoot in other cities to reduce road capacity. They only work, however, in dense urban environments, with good public transport networks, and facilities for pedestrians and cyclists. What about elsewhere?

85 Traffic congestion will always prompt an emotional response, but whether the answer is building new roads or reducing capacity, there is nonetheless an underlying truth that the number of vehicle miles travelled year on year is increasing:
90 1.48 trillion in 1978 to 3.21 trillion in 2018. It seems Americans are simply just too attached to their cars. The only checks to this growth were in 1979 and

CONTINUE ➤

2008, which coincided with high oil prices. That seems to suggest that, with appropriate measures to
95 protect the poorest members of society, pricing our way out of congestion may be the answer after all.

Figure 1

The following chart shows the peak and freeflow travel times for ten different commuter journeys into Los Angeles and the average speed maintained.

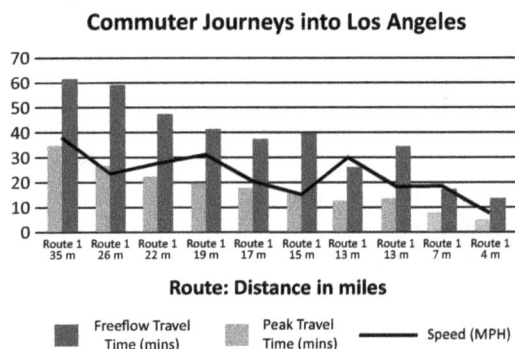

Commuter Journeys into Los Angeles

Route: Distance in miles

Freeflow Travel Time (mins)   Peak Travel Time (mins)   Speed (MPH)

43

The main idea of the passage is that road congestion in America is a complex issue that

A) is largely the result of increased road building.

B) can possibly be solved by financial means.

C) applies mostly to large cities with alternative transport options.

D) is insoluble as people love their cars too much.

44

As used in line 4, "traditionally" most nearly means

A) historically.

B) genuinely.

C) properly.

D) conservatively.

45

According to the author, induced demand is a phenomenon that

A) contradicts a widespread belief that congestion is the result of road building.

B) is rarely taken into account when road systems are being planned.

C) is understood by city planners and has affected their traditional solutions to traffic congestion.

D) can usually be mitigated by operating toll lanes with capped charges.

46

The best evidence for the answer to the previous question is

A) Lines 12-14 ("It may... increasing it")

B) Lines 20-22 ("If more... as before")

C) Lines 33-35 ("The upshot...planning")

D) Lines 44-47 ("The Department... occurrence")

CONTINUE

47

The author's attitude toward treating roads like other utilities is best described as one of

A) dismay.

B) delight.

C) disbelief.

D) disapproval.

48

The passage implies that road reduction schemes to ease traffic congestion have limited utility because they

A) only work in certain places with appropriate infrastructure.

B) are based on people's opinions rather than research.

C) are influenced by too many external factors to be reliable.

D) rely on funding from capital markets rather than revenue from users.

49

The best evidence for the answer to the previous question is

A) Lines 25-30 ("The local... a part")

B) Lines 58-63 ("If improvement... customers")

C) Lines 81-84 ("They only... cyclists")

D) Lines 90-91 ("It seems... their cars")

50

As used in line 78, "sought-after" most nearly means

A) in demand.

B) singled out.

C) precious.

D) on trend.

CONTINUE

51

The author of the passage would most likely consider the information in the chart to be

A) undoubtedly accurate but too lacking in detail to be truly informative

B) direct evidence for the central argument made in the passage.

C) representative of a perspective held by an authority cited in the passage.

D) a useful example of the effects of congestion in an urban area.

52

Which statement is best supported by the data in the chart?

A) The greater the length of journey, the greater the difference between peak flow journey time and freeflow travel time.

B) The shorter the length of journey, the greater the difference between peak flow journey time and freeflow travel time.

C) Average speed does not always correlate with distance from the city.

D) Road congestion in Los Angeles is a result of lanes added to the freeway entering the city.

STOP

If you finish before time is called, you may check your work on this section only.
Do not turn to any other section.

Writing and Language Test

35 MINUTES, 44 QUESTIONS

Turn to Section 2 of your answer sheet to answer the questions in this section

---

DIRECTIONS

Each passage below is accompanied by a number of questions. For some questions, you will consider how the passage might be revised to improve the expression of ideas. For other questions, you will consider how the passage might be edited to correct errors in sentence structure, usage, or punctuation. A passage or a question may be accompanied by one or more graphics (such as a table or graph) that you will consider as you make revising and editing decisions.

Some questions will direct you to an underlined portion of a passage. Other questions will direct you to a location in a passage or ask you to think about the passage as a whole.

After reading each passage, choose the answer to each question that most effectively improves the quality of writing in the passage or that makes the passage conform to the conventions of standard written English. Many questions include a "NO CHANGE" option. Choose that option if you think the best choice is to leave the relevant portion of the passage as it is.

Questions 1-11 are based on the following text that has been adapted from Sally Denshire's Autoethnography.

[1] Autoethnography is an alternative method and form of writing falling somewhere between anthropology and literary studies. Some social science researchers have an interpretive literary style and others have been trained to write in ways that use highly specialised vocabulary, that efface the personal and flatten the voice, or that avoid narrative in deference to dominant theories and methodologies of the social sciences. The complex relationship between social science writing and literary writing has led to a blurring 'between "fact" and "fiction" and between "true" and "imagined." Autoethnographers often blur boundaries, crafting fictions and other ways of being true in the interests of rewriting themselves in the social world.

1

The writer is considering deleting the underlined sentence. Should the sentence be kept or deleted?

A) Kept, because it shows the impact of autoethnography

B) Kept, because the sentence makes for an effective introduction to the passage

C) Deleted, because it ignores the fact that autoethnography is an anthropological method

D) Deleted, because it does not provide an effective introduction to the paragraph

[2] Yes, autoethnography is a contested field. [3] The introspective and subjective performances that are, to a greater or lesser extent, inevitable parts of the autoethnographic act still raise questions about the value of each autoethnographic account and which accounts are to be published and counted as research. Autoethnography [4] has beyond the writing of selves and although some of the early autoethnographies were written in an anthropological tradition, contemporary autoethnography is informed by a range of disciplines. Writers of these accounts address social questions of difference and becoming that may enable voices previously silenced to speak back.

[2]

Which choice best introduces the topic of this paragraph?

A) NO CHANGE

B) Autoethnography has revolutionized research.

C) There are no issues or concerns with the use of anthropology.

D) Autoethnography is a method that falls somewhere between anthropology and literary studies.

[3]

A) NO CHANGE

B) The introspective and subjective performances raise questions about the value of autoethnographic accounts as research.

C) The introspective and subjective performances that are, to a greater or lesser extent, inevitable parts of the autoethnographic act.

D) Autoethnography cannot be counted as research.

[4]

A) NO CHANGE

B) goes beyond

C) is going beyond

D) was beyond

[5] However, autoethnography contains elements of [6] autobiography, it goes beyond the writing of selves. Writing that crosses personal and professional life spaces goes further than autobiography whenever writers critique the depersonalizing tendencies that can come into play in social and cultural spaces [7] that has asymmetrical relations of power.

[5]

A) NO CHANGE

B) Each time

C) While

D) Whenever

[6]

A) NO CHANGE

B) autobiography:

C) autobiography;

D) autobiography -

[7]

A) NO CHANGE

B) that have

C) that will have

D) that are having

[8] In fact, different approaches in autoethnography can be characterized in terms of different relationships between the personal and the wider social and cultural world the writing seeks to enquire into. Ellis and Bochner (2006) have classified these differences in terms of 'evocative' and 'analytical' [9] approaches, where evocative autoethnography foregrounds the writer's personal stories and analytical autoethnography [10] does the opposite.

Autoethnography is usually written in the first person. An autobiographical defence of personal narrative in sociology will intentionally use the second person 'you' to address any charge of self-indulgence. Writing in the third person, as 'she' or 'he,' distances the self to become just another figure/character in the drama. This [11] is being a methodological decision so that the story becomes more fictive, a rationale drawn from collective memory work.

8
A) NO CHANGE
B) But
C) However
D) DELETE the underlined word.

9
A) NO CHANGE
B) approaches, and
C) approaches; indeed
D) approaches. Unfortunately,

10
A) NO CHANGE
B) connects to some broader set of social phenomena.
C) focuses on the writer's personal stories.
D) DELETE the underlined section.

11
A) NO CHANGE
B) was
C) is
D) will be

CONTINUE

Questions 12-22 are based on the following text that has been adapted from The Conversation's How the Partition of India happened.

(1)

[12] "Partition": the division of British India into the two separate states of India and Pakistan on August 14-15, 1947 – was the "last-minute" mechanism by which the British were able to secure agreement over how independence would take place. At the time, few people understood what Partition would entail or what its results would be, and the migration on the enormous scale that followed took the vast majority of contemporaries by surprise.

(2)

[13] Even before the 1940s, it had long argued for a unitary state with a strong centre; even though Congress was ostensibly secular in its objectives, organisations representing minority interests increasingly viewed this idea with suspicion, believing that it would entrench the political dominance of Hindus, [14] who made up about 80% of the population.

[12]

A) NO CHANGE

B) Partition –

C) Partition,

D) Partition. The

[13]

At this point, the author is considering including the following sentence:

"The main vehicle for nationalist activity was the Indian National Congress, whose best-known leaders included Mahatma Gandhi and Jawaharlal Nehru."

Should the writer make this addition here

A) Yes, because it provides information that helps clarify prior statements

B) Yes, because it provides an effective introduction for the following information

C) No, because it provides irrelevant information

D) No, because it would be more effective as a conclusion at the end of the paragraph

[14]

A) NO CHANGE

E) who are the majority

F) DELETE the underlined portion

G) who were biased against the minorities

(3)

The prospect of losing protection as independence drew closer worried more and more Muslims, first in parts of northern India, and then, after World War II, in the influential Muslim-majority provinces of Bengal and Punjab. In 1945-6, the All-India Muslim League, led by Muhammad Ali Jinnah, won a majority of Muslim votes in provincial elections. This strengthened the party's claim to speak for a substantial proportion of, but never all, the subcontinent's Muslims. 15

(4)

When Britain took India into the war without consultation in 1939, Congress opposed 16 them; large nationalist protests ensued, culminating in the 1942 Quit India movement, a mass movement against British rule.

15

Which choice provides the best conclusion to this paragraph?

A) NO CHANGE

B) Gandhi is called the father of the Indian nation.

C) Nehru was the first Prime Minister of India.

D) Then came World War II – and suddenly, the political stakes in India were considerably higher.

16

A) NO CHANGE

B) it's

C) its

D) it

17 For their part in it, Gandhi and Nehru and thousands of Congress workers were imprisoned until 1945.

(5)

Meanwhile, the British wartime need for local allies **18** gives the Muslim League an opening to offer its cooperation in exchange for future political safeguards.

17

A) NO CHANGE

B) Because of their role in the mass movement against British rule, Gandhi and Nehru and thousands of Congress workers were imprisoned until 1945

C) Those who opposed it were imprisoned.

D) DELETE the underlined portion

18

A) NO CHANGE

B) gave

C) that gives

D) that gave

19 In March 1940, the Muslim League's "Pakistan" resolution called for the creation of a separate "nation."

(6) 20

Historians are still divided on whether this rather vague demand was purely a bargaining counter or a firm objective. But while it may have been intended to solve the minority issue, it ended up aggravating it instead.

19

At this point, the writer is considering changing the underlined sentence to the following:

"In March 1940, the Muslim League's 'Pakistan' resolution called for the creation of 'separate states' – plural, not singular – to accommodate Indian Muslims, whom it argued were a separate 'nation.'"

Should the writer make this change here?

A) Yes, because it provides an effective transition.

B) Yes, because it improves clarity, tone, and voice of the sentence.

C) No, because it would be more effective as an introduction at the beginning of the paragraph.

D) No, because it eliminates relevant information.

20

To make this passage most logical, paragraph (6) should be placed:

A) before paragraph (3)

B) before paragraph (5)

C) where it is now

D) before paragraph (1)

21 Millions of people moved to what they hoped would be safer territory, with Muslims heading towards Pakistan, and Hindus and Sikhs in the direction of India. As many as 14-16 million people may have been eventually displaced, travelling on foot, in bullock carts and by train. 22

21

At this point, the writer is considering adding the following sentence:

"Partition triggered riots, mass casualties, and a colossal wave of migration."

Should the writer make this addition here?

A) No, because it provides information that interrupts the logical flow of the passage.

B) No, because it provides a more effective conclusion and should be placed at the end of the paragraph.

C) Yes, because it provides relevant information.

D) Yes, because it provides information that helps explain what comes next.

22

Which of the following most effectively summarizes the main point of the passage?

A) Colonialism has long-lasting effects.

B) The Partition of India and Pakistan caused a lot of bloodshed and strife.

C) The Partition of India and Pakistan is a historical event with complex causes, outcomes, and limitations.

D) The Partition of India and Pakistan is a really simple event to understand.

Questions 23-33 are based on the following text that has been adapted from Jules Odendahl-James' A History of U.S. Documentary Theatre in Three Stages.

Broadly conceived, American documentary theatre (also sometimes called docudrama, ethnodrama, verbatim theatre, tribunal theatre, theatre of witness, or theatre of fact) `23` was performance typically built by an individual or collective of artists from historical and/or archival materials such as trial transcripts, written or recorded interviews, newspaper reporting, personal or iconic visual images or video footage, government documents, biographies and autobiographies, and even academic papers and scientific research. `24`

`23`

A) NO CHANGE

B) were

C) are

D) is

`24`

At this point, the author is considering including the following sentence:

"The trajectory of American documentary theatre might be categorized under different moments of innovation."

Should the writer make this addition here

A) Yes, because it provides information that helps clarify prior statements

B) No, because it would be more effective as an introduction to this paragraph

C) Yes, because it provides an effective transition to the following paragraph

D) No, because it provides irrelevant information

The first moment of innovation in documentary performance is marked by the work produced under the auspices of the Federal Theater Project (1935-1939), particularly "living newspapers," [25] a form itself borrowed from agitprop and worker's theatre in Western Europe and Russia. While the content of these early American documentary plays was drawn from everyday life, particularly the experiences of first- and second-generation working-class immigrants, their form was [26] decidedly modernist, embracing collage, montage, expressionism, and minimalism in a symbiotic relationship with new forms of visual art, early cinema, and atonal musical compositions.

[25]

At this point, the writer is considering revising the underlined sentence to the following:

"a form which was influenced by related traditions from Western Europe and Russia."

Should the writer make this change here?

A) Yes, because it provides more effective support for the passage

B) Yes, because it improves language, clarity, and tone

C) No, because it provides inaccurate or unsupported information

D) No, because it provides redundant information

[26]

A) NO CHANGE

B) uniformly

C) finally

D) ultimately

(1) These plays were sometimes built with the input of `27` communities. Where artist-workers were stationed as part of FTP and the Works Progress Administration. `28` This tension between ethnographic content and modern or postmodern artistic form remains a hallmark of documentary performance, whether defined by features or practices. (2) But mostly artists crafted and performed them as an educative or cultural service, using techniques that may or may not have resonated with audiences who reflected the stories or characters depicted.

`29` If we mark the start of American documentary performance history in the early 1930s, it is easy to see the centrality of social and political crises to its content focus and aesthetic properties. On this timeline, the second key moment of development happens in the late 1960s, when the Civil Rights movement, the Vietnam War, global economic upheaval, and the newly dominant televisual mass media invited or compelled a new generation of theatre collectives to explore, employ, and explode the formal and aesthetic properties of documentary. `30`

`27`

A) NO CHANGE

B) communities; where

C) communities - where

D) communities where

`28`

To make this passage most logical, the underlined sentence should be placed:

A) NO CHANGE

B) after sentence (2)

C) before sentence (1)

D) after sentence (1)

`29`

The writer is considering deleting the underlined sentence. Should the sentence be kept or deleted?

A) Kept, because it provides an effective introduction to the following information

B) Kept, because it provides extensive information about the 1930s in America

C) Deleted, because it ignores what happened in the 1930s in America

D) Deleted, because it provides irrelevant information

These subjects 31 <u>were being</u> not wholly new to theatremakers. In the 19th century, artists in the emerging genres of naturalism and realism were also social reformers and took inspiration in both content and form from the lived experience and social/political struggles of "ordinary" people, their personal histories, and their environments.

30

At this point, the writer is considering adding the following sentence:

"Companies such as the Living Theatre, the Open Theatre, Bread and Puppet Theatre, Teatro Campesino, and the San Francisco Mime Troupe questioned dominant media and state narratives around economic and social oppression, democracy, equality, and the rule of law."

Should the writer make this change here?

A) Yes, because it helps clarify preceding information

B) Yes, because it provides an effective transition

C) No, because it would be more effective as an introduction at the beginning of the paragraph.

D) No, because it eliminates relevant information.

31

A) NO CHANGE

B) are being

C) were

D) are

But in the 1960s and '70s 32 , as traditional definitions of home, family, nation, and creation were contested with new fervor, energy shifted away from conventionally structured and produced plays and theatre spaces toward unbounded and unscripted events ("happenings") as well as highly controlled multimedia installations and durational work that tested 33 everyone's physical capacities. At the same time the impulse to craft a theatrical world from real lives, experiences, and places evolved into a rawer, distinctly autobiographical, artist-driven type of storytelling.

32

A) NO CHANGE

B) as

C) ; as

D) - as

33

A) NO CHANGE

B) artists' and audiences'

C) their

D) all

Questions 34-44 are based on the following text that has been adapted from Innovative Water Solutions' Rainwater Harvesting 101.

Rainwater harvesting is 34 collection the run-off from a structure or other impervious surface in order to store it for later use. Traditionally, this involves harvesting the rain from a roof. The rain collects in gutters that channel the water into downspouts and then into some sort of storage vessel. Rainwater collection systems can be as simple 35 as: collecting rain in a rain barrel or as elaborate as harvesting rainwater into large cisterns to supply your entire household demand. The idea of rainwater harvesting usually conjures up images of an old farm cistern or thoughts of developing countries. The reality is that rainwater harvesting is becoming a viable alternative for supplying our households and businesses with 36 water. It's not just for the farm anymore! There are many countries such as Germany and Australia where rainwater harvesting is a norm. Due to the green building movement, you will see rainwater harvesting systems become more popular here in America.

34

A) NO CHANGE

B) collecting

C) collected

D) collect

35

A) NO CHANGE

B) as, collecting

C) as - collecting

D) as collecting

36

A) NO CHANGE

B) water, and

C) water; however,

D) water. Although,

CONTINUE ➡

The collection of rainwater is known by many names throughout the world. [37] They ranges from rainwater collection to rainwater harvesting to rainwater catchment. [38]

We believe that rainwater harvesting is a viable technology in an urban setting. All that is necessary to take advantage of this resource is to capture the free water falling on your roof and direct it to a rainwater storage tank.

37

A) NO CHANGE

B) Their range

C) These range

D) The names ranges

38

At this point, the writer is considering adding the following sentence:

"In addition, terms such as roof-water collection or rooftop water collection are also used in other countries."

Should the writer make this addition here?

A) Yes, because it provides an effective transition to new information.

B) Yes, because it provides information that helps clarify prior information presented in the paragraph.

C) No, because it provides redundant information.

D) No, because it provides irrelevant information.

39 Directing this, you can take control of your water supply and replace all or at least a substantial portion of your water 40 needs, rainwater harvesting systems can be configured to supply your whole house and/or your landscape needs.

Rainwater harvesting is important for several reasons, but one of the biggest is the fact that we 41 tapped out water conservation gains inside our homes so we need to start looking outdoors for more opportunities.

39

A) NO CHANGE

B) By doing this,

C) Despite this,

D) Regardless of this,

40

A) NO CHANGE

B) needs; rainwater

C) needs. Rainwater

D) needs - rainwater

41

A) NO CHANGE

B) tap out

C) DELETE the underlined portion

D) are tapping out

The following graph shows the gains that have been achieved with our indoor water fixtures through the combination of governmental standards and innovation by fixture companies. 42 As you can see, we don't have much more room to go in terms of achieving more efficiency gains with our indoor fixtures. What's next... the 0.2 gallon per flush toilet? Probably not!

This phenomenon is known as the law of diminishing returns. So where will the next revolution in water conservation take place? We believe we offer services in the areas where this revolution will take place.

42

A) NO CHANGE

B) However,

C) Through this,

D) Despite this,

43

Which of the following provides the most effective support from Figure 1?

A) Dishwashers show the steepest increase in the progression of water conservation standards between 1960 and 2005.

B) Clothes washers show a decrease in water conservation standards between 1960 and 2005.

C) Clothes washers show the steepest increase in the progression of water conservation standards between 1960 and 2005.

D) Toilets show the steepest increase in progression of water conservation standards between 1960 and 2005.

You can essentially use rainwater anywhere you use tap water. The idea of using drinking water to flush our toilets and water our lawns is wasteful and irresponsible, especially in light of population growth and water shortages across the country. **44** Rainwater collection is a technique to green your home and to lessen your environmental footprint.

44

The writer is considering deleting the underlined sentence. Should the sentence be kept or deleted?

A) Kept, because it provides an effective transition between one concept and the next

B) Kept, because it is an effective conclusion to the passage

C) Deleted, because it interrupts the flow of the paragraph

D) Deleted, because it provides information that is not related to the passage

STOP

If you finish before time is called, you may check your work on this section only.
Do not turn to any other section.

Math Test - No Calculator

25 MINUTES, 20 QUESTIONS

Turn to Section 3 of your answer sheet to answer the questions in this section.

DIRECTIONS

For questions 1-15, solve each problem, choose the best answer from the choices provided, and fill in the corresponding circle on your answer sheet. **For questions 16-20**, solve the problem and enter your answer in the grid on the answer sheet. Please refer to the directions before question 16 on how to enter your answers in the grid. You may use any available space in your test booklet for scratch work.

NOTES

1. The use of a calculator **is not permitted.**
2. All variables and expressions used represent real numbers unless otherwise indicated.
3. Figures provided in this test are drawn to scale unless otherwise indicated.
4. All figures lie in a plane unless otherwise indicated.
5. Unless otherwise indicated, the domain of a given function f is the set of all real numbers x for which $f(x)$ is a real number.

REFERENCE

$A = \pi r^2$
$C = 2\pi r$

$A = \ell w$

$A = \dfrac{1}{2}bh$

$c^2 = a^2 + b^2$

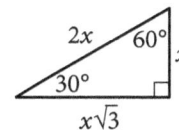

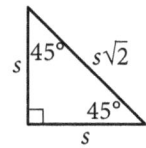

Special Right Triangles

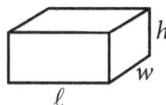

$V = \ell w h$

$V = \pi r^2 h$

$V = \dfrac{4}{3}\pi r^3$

$V = \dfrac{1}{3}\pi r^2 h$

$V = \dfrac{1}{3}\ell w h$

The number of degrees of arc in a circle is 360.

The number of radians of arc in a circle is 2π.

The sum of the measures in degrees of the angles of a triangle is 180.

1

When $x = 3$, what is the value of y in the function $3x + 3 = \dfrac{5y}{2}$?

A) 2

B) $\dfrac{16}{3}$

C) $\dfrac{24}{5}$

D) 5

2

If $\dfrac{5 + 3i}{1 + i}$ is rewritten in the form $x + yi$, where x and y are real numbers, what is the sum of x and y?

(Note: $i = \sqrt{-1}$)

A) 3

B) 4

C) 6

D) –6

3

Sally sold f fries and b burgers at her snack bar this weekend. If the price for fries is \$3.50 and the price for a burger is \$5.00, and there is no sales tax or tip, which of the following represents the total amount of money Sally made at her snack bar this weekend?

A) $5fb + 3.50$

B) $5b + 3.50f$

C) $3.50b + 5f$

D) $3.50fb + 5$

4

Daniel owns a website that sells tickets to live events. His website charges an initial, one-time fee for purchasing tickets through his website. The equation C = 29.99s + 14.99 represents the total amount, C dollars, that Daniel will charge per transaction of s tickets. What does the number 29.99 represent in the equation?

A) The price per ticket, in dollars.

B) The initial fee Daniel charges per transaction.

C) The total amount Daniel will make per transaction.

D) The number of tickets purchased in the transaction.

5

Which answer correctly simplifies expression $5x^2 + 4x - 15 - 2(x^2 + x - 1)$?

A) $3x^2 + 6x - 17$

B) $7x^2 - 6x - 17$

C) $3x^2 + 5x - 18$

D) $3x^2 + 2x - 13$

6

Martha is a math tutor who helps students prepare for tests. She charges $20 an hour for tutoring students one-on-one, but she charges $25 an hour for pairs of students studying with her in a small group. If Martha has 3 hours to tutor on the night before a test, what would be the difference in her profits if she were to tutor three pairs of students for an hour each vs. three individual students for an hour each?

A) $5

B) $15

C) $30

D) $45

7

The Law of Universal Gravitation can be represented by the formula $g = \dfrac{GM}{R^2}$ where g is acceleration due to gravity, G is a constant, M is mass, and R is the distance. Which of the following gives R in terms of g, G, and M?

A) $R = \sqrt{\dfrac{GM}{g}}$

B) $R = \sqrt{\dfrac{g}{GM}}$

C) $R = \dfrac{g}{GM}$

D) $R = \dfrac{gM}{G}$

CONTINUE ➡

8

If $\dfrac{x+4}{3} = 2$, then what is the value of $\dfrac{x+2}{(x-1)^2}$?

A) 2

B) 3

C) 4

D) 0

9

$$-x + 2y = -8$$
$$4x - y = 25$$

What is the solution (x, y) to the system of equations above?

A) $(-1, 6)$

B) $(6, -1)$

C) $(1, -6)$

D) $(6, -6)$

10

$$f(x) = (x - 4)(x + 2)$$
$$g(\text{x}) = 4x - 17$$

If $x > 0$, for what value of x is the statement $f(x) - g(x) = 0$ true?

A) -6

B) $\sqrt{3}$

C) -3

D) 3

11

Irene and Tabitha go out to lunch at a local restaurant. Irene's lunch costs $\$c$ and Tabitha's lunch costs $2 more than Irene's. If they split the bill evenly and both paid a 20% tip, which expression below represents the amount Irene paid for her lunch?

A) $1.2\,(c + 1)$

B) $1.2\,(2c - 1)$

C) $0.2\,(c + 1)$

D) $0.2\,(2c + 1)$

12

A line passes through points (2,1) and (−4,−2). What is the slope of the line that is perpendicular to the function formed by those two points?

A) −2

B) $\dfrac{1}{2}$

C) $-\dfrac{1}{2}$

D) 2

13

What is the value of x when

$$\dfrac{1}{(x+3)} = \left(x^2 - x - 12\right)^{-1}?$$

A) 3

B) 12

C) −4

D) 5

14

If $\dfrac{27^a}{3^a}$ and $a = \dfrac{1}{2}$ what is an equivalent value of the expression?

A) 3

B) 6

C) 9

D) 27

15

If $ax^2 + bx + c = (2x+1)(x-5) - 13$, then what is the value of $a+b+c$?

A) −25

B) 10

C) −12

D) 25

DIRECTIONS

For questions 16–20, solve the problem and enter your answer in the grid, as described below, on the answer sheet.

1. Although not required, it is suggested that you write your answer in the boxes at the top of the columns to help you fill in the circles accurately. You will receive credit only if the circles are filled in correctly.
2. Mark no more than one circle in any column.
3. No question has a negative answer.
4. Some problems may have more than one correct answer. In such cases, grid only one answer.
5. **Mixed numbers** such as $3\frac{1}{2}$ must be gridded as 3.5 or 7/2. (If $3\,|\,1\,|\,/\,|\,2$ is entered into the grid, it will be interpreted as $\frac{31}{2}$, not $3\frac{1}{2}$.)
6. **Decimal answers:** If you obtain a decimal answer with more digits than the grid can accommodate, it may be either rounded or truncated, but it must fill the entire grid.

Answer: $\frac{7}{12}$

Answer: 2.5

Write answer in boxes.
← Fraction line
Grid in result.
← Decimal point

Acceptable ways to grid $\frac{2}{3}$ are:

Answer: 201 – either position is correct

NOTE: You may start your answers in any column, space permitting. Columns you don't need to use should be left blank.

16

If $b^2 - \dfrac{1}{4} = 0$ and b is equal to all real numbers, what is the sum of all possible values of b?

17

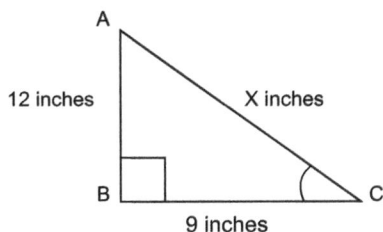

A

12 inches   X inches

B

9 inches

C

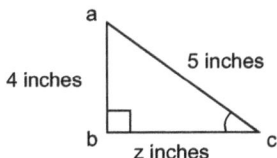

a

5 inches

4 inches

b   z inches   c

(Note: Figure is not drawn to scale)

Jen is choosing new tiles for her bathroom floor. She has two triangular options, triangle *ABC* and triangle abc, shown below. If Jen needs enough tiles to cover 540 square inches of floor in her bathroom, how many more tiles of triangle abc would she need to purchase if she chose that option over triangle *ABC*?

18

$$24x - 6y = 33$$
$$8x - sy = -12$$

For what values of s does the system of equations above have no real solutions?

19

If the sum of $x°$ and $y°$ is 90° and $sin\big(sin(x)\big) = \dfrac{5}{13}$,

what is the value of $cos\big(cos(y)\big)$? Express your answer as a fraction or as a decimal rounded to the nearest hundredth.

20

$$\sqrt{g+3} = f\sqrt{5}$$

If $f = 2$, what is the value of g?

STOP
If you finish before time is called, you may check your work on this section only.
Do not turn to any other section.

No Test Material On This Page

Math Test – Calculator

55 MINUTES, 38 QUESTIONS

Turn to Section 4 of your answer sheet to answer the questions in this section.

DIRECTIONS

For questions 1-30, solve each problem, choose the best answer from the choices provided, and fill in the corresponding circle on your answer sheet. **For questions 31-38**, solve the problem and enter your answer in the grid on the answer sheet. Please refer to the directions before question 16 on how to enter your answers in the grid. You may use any available space in your test booklet for scratch work.

NOTES

1. The use of a calculator **is permitted.**
2. All variables and expressions used represent real numbers unless otherwise indicated.
3. Figures provided in this test are drawn to scale unless otherwise indicated.
4. All figures lie in a plane unless otherwise indicated.
5. Unless otherwise indicated, the domain of a given function f is the set of all real numbers x for which $f(x)$ is a real number.

REFERENCE

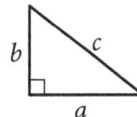 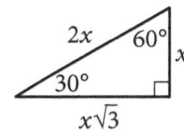 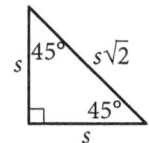

$A = \pi r^2$ $A = \ell w$ $A = \frac{1}{2}bh$ $c^2 = a^2 + b^2$ Special Right Triangles
$C = 2\pi r$

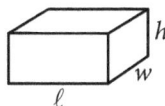 

$V = \ell wh$ $V = \pi r^2 h$ $V = \frac{4}{3}\pi r^3$ $V = \frac{1}{3}\pi r^2 h$ $V = \frac{1}{3}\ell wh$

The number of degrees of arc in a circle is 360.

The number of radians of arc in a circle is 2π.

The sum of the measures in degrees of the angles of a triangle is 180.

1

Which of the graphs below most closely represents the function $y = 2^x$?

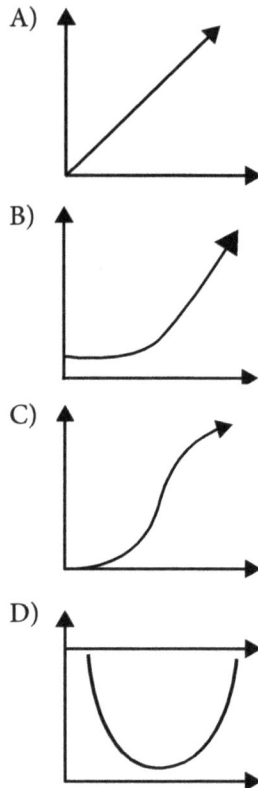

A)

B)

C)

D)

2

If y is 2 more than 3 times x and $x = \dfrac{1}{2}$, what is the sum of $x + y$?

A) $\dfrac{3}{2}$

B) 2

C) $\dfrac{7}{2}$

D) 4

3

Temperature on July 5th, 2005

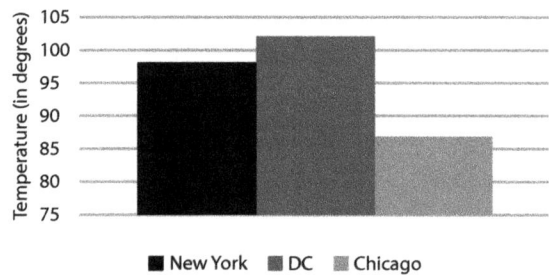

According to the graph above, what was the approximate average temperature of these three cities on July 5th, 2005?

A) 96

B) 105

C) 80

D) 90

Questions 4 and 5 refer to the following equation:

The formula to convert degrees Celsius to degrees Fahrenheit can be represented by the equation $\frac{9}{5}C + 32 = F$, where C is the temperature in degrees Celsius and F is the temperature in degrees Fahrenheit.

4

Which of the following equations represents C in terms of F?

A) $C = \frac{9}{5}(F - 32)$

B) $C = \frac{5}{9}(F - 32)$

C) $C = \frac{9}{5}(F + 32)$

D) $C = \frac{5}{9}(F + 32)$

5

If the temperature increases by two degrees Celsius, what would the equivalent increase be in degrees Fahrenheit? Round your answer to the nearest tenth.

A) 2

B) 1.1

C) 3.6

D) 35.6

6

If $|x + 3| = \frac{11}{5}$, what is the sum of all values of x?

A) $\frac{-4}{5}$

B) $\frac{-26}{5}$

C) 3

D) –6

CONTINUE

7

Jessica decides to drive across the country on a road trip. If the trip is 2,669 miles and she wants to drive at most 250 miles a day, how many weeks will it take her to complete the trip if she drives the maximum distance every day? Round your answer to the nearest tenth.

A)   1.5

B)   10.7

C)   2.1

D)   0.7

8

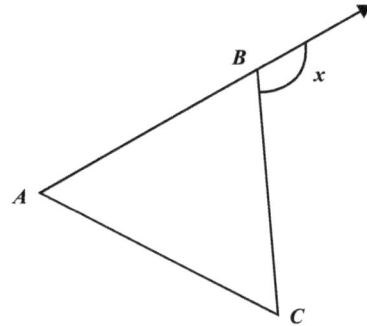

(Note: Image is not drawn to scale.)

If angle $A = 62°$ and angle $C = 51°$, what is the value of angle x?

A)   23°

B)   113°

C)   67°

D)   Cannot be determined

9

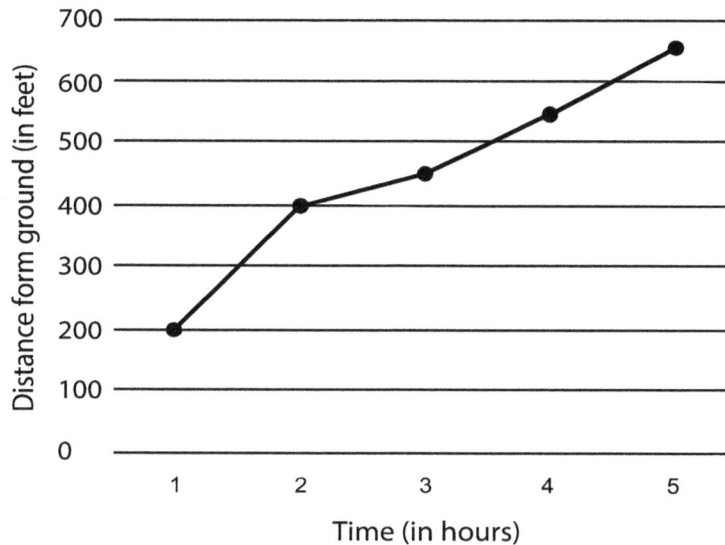

Lisa and Vivian hike a mountain one afternoon. The graph above shows their distance above ground level as they hike. In which interval do Lisa and Vivian hike at the slowest speed (in feet per hour)?

A) Between hours 1-2

B) Between hours 2-3

C) Between hours 3-4

D) Between hours 4-5

10

If $f(x) = \frac{3}{2}x + 2$ and $f(x) = 3$, what is the value of $(x)^{-1}$?

A) $\frac{3}{2}$

B) $\frac{2}{3}$

C) 3

D) 2

11

Student Population at Greendale School	
Grade	Number of Students
2nd	74
3rd	73
4th	81
5th	90
6th	75
7th	82

Based on the data in the table above, what grade would the median student be in at Greendale School?

A) 3

B) 4

C) 5

D) 6

12

If $x \geq 3$, which of the following equations is NOT true?

A) $2x \geq 6$

B) $4x + 2 \geq 14$

C) $\frac{6}{5}x \geq 21$

D) $\frac{1}{2}x - 2 \geq \frac{-1}{2}$

13

Mary has a jar of different flavored candies. She has 47 total pieces, including 16 chocolates and 17 peppermint flavored candies. If she also has a third type of candy, which are caramel flavored, what is the probability that Mary will NOT choose a caramel candy from the jar?

A) $\dfrac{16}{47}$

B) $\dfrac{17}{47}$

C) $\dfrac{14}{47}$

D) $\dfrac{33}{47}$

14

Two different math classes take the same math test. The median score for both classes is 84%, but the mean score for Class A is 80% and the mean score for Class B is 92%. Which statement below describes the relationship between the median and mean for both classes?

A) Class 1 most likely has a lower outlier score than Class 2.

B) Class 2 most likely has a lower outlier score than Class 1.

C) Class 2 and Class 1 have the same range in scores.

D) Class 2 and Class 1 have the same amount of scores above the median.

15

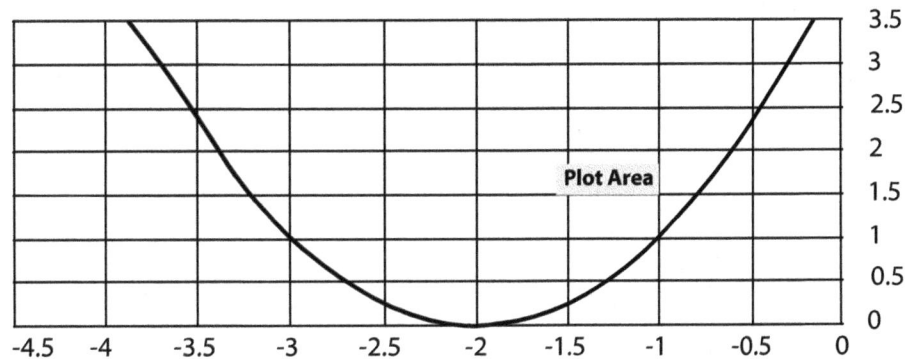

Function $g(x) = (x+2)^2$ is shown in the xy plane above. If $y = 3$ is also graphed on the same xy plane, for what value(s) of x is $g(x) = y + 6$?

A) 3

B) 4

C) $-5, -1$

D) $-5, 1$

16

A farmer's market is selling spots for their next event. They have 64 total square feet available for rent, with two options in size: 6 square feet (s) and 4 square feet (f). If the market rents out a total of 14 spots, which system of equations below represents the relationship between the number of 6 square feet spots sold and 4 square feet spots sold?

A) $6s + 4f = 14, s + f = 64$

B) $6f + 4s = 64, s - f = 14$

C) $6s + 4f = 64, s + f = 14$

D) $4s + 6f = 14, sf = 64$

CONTINUE

17

Cell Growth

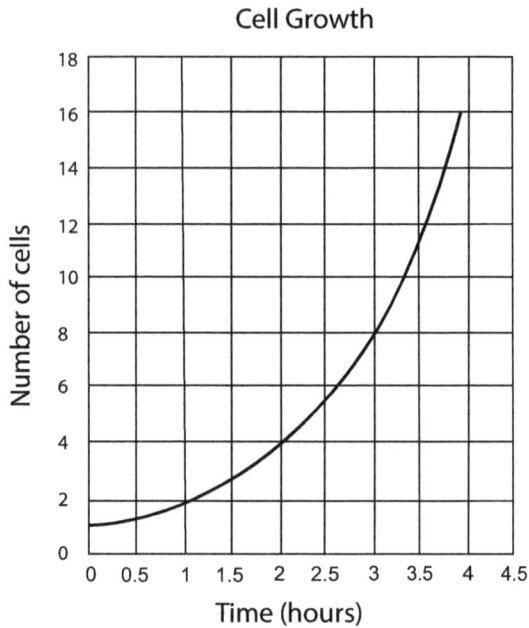

According to the data in the graph of $f(x)$ above, how many cells are present when $f(x)=1$?

A) 1

B) 2

C) 0

D) 3

18

What does the y -intercept represent in the graph to the left?

A) The total number of cells in the sample after 1 hour

B) The amount of time it takes to test the sample

C) The amount of cells present at 0 hours

D) The time when the sample stops multiplying

19

$$\frac{4}{5}x + by = 17$$

$$ax - 4y = c$$

If the system of equations above has infinitely many solutions, what is the value of $a+b+c$, if $b=2$?

A) −33.6

B) $\dfrac{-8}{5}$

C) −34

D) $\dfrac{-16}{5}$

20

	0-5 hours	6-10 hours	11-15 hours	Total hours
Grade 10	21	16	25	62
Grade 11	15	17	35	67
Total students	36	33	60	

According to the data in the table above, if you were to choose a student at random from grade 10, what is the probability that they studied at least 6 hours a night?

A) $\dfrac{32}{64}$

B) $\dfrac{16}{62}$

C) $\dfrac{17}{62}$

D) $\dfrac{41}{62}$

21

There was a sale on sofas at a furniture store for 60% off the original price of any sofa, with an additional 40% off your entire purchase if you purchase a matching armchair for a fixed price of $450. Which expression represents the final total of your purchase if you buy a sofa that is originally $s and an armchair for $a?

A)   0.4(0.6s + a)

B)   0.6(0.4s + 450)

C)   0.4s+0.6a

D)   0.24(s + 450)

22

If a circle has a center $(1,3)$ and a radius of $\sqrt{\dfrac{3}{10}}$, which of the following points is an endpoint of the circle?

A) $(\dfrac{13}{5},\dfrac{-3}{2})$

B) $(\dfrac{14}{5},\dfrac{3}{2})$

C) $(\dfrac{3}{2},\dfrac{-14}{5})$

D) $(3,1)$

23

The equation $-m^2 +27.5m = h$ represents the height h (in ft) of a hot air balloon m minutes after leaving the ground. If the hot air balloon is in the air for a total of 28 minutes before it reaches the ground again, which answer approximates the maximum height it reaches above the ground during that time?

A)   190 ft

B)   13 ft

C)   150 ft

D)   210 ft

Questions 24 and 25 refer to the following table:

Goose Population in the Four Major Cities of a State by the Season

City	Season			
	Spring	Summer	Fall	Winter
A	3740	2310	420	350
B	4762	1431	701	602
C	3621	709	300	174
D	4971	1200	673	500

24

What is the average number of geese in the state in the fall? Round answer to the nearest whole number.

A) 524

B) 407

C) 420

D) 561

25

Which season change below represents the largest change?

A) City A, spring to summer

B) City B, fall to winter

C) City C, summer to fall

D) City D, spring the summer

26

There is a "New and Improved" type of shampoo being sold at a convenience store. The bottle now says, "Now with 20% more shampoo per bottle!" If the original 20 oz bottle costs $15.99, and the new bottle costs $17.99, which bottle offers the best price per oz?

A) Original bottle

B) New bottle

C) Both cost the same

D) Cannot be determined

27

Number of Points	10	20	30	40	50	60	70	80	90	100
Jerome	2	1	0	1	3	0	0	1	1	0
Matilda	4	0	0	3	1	0	0	1	0	0

Jerome and Matilda are playing darts. There are 10 different point sections on the board and Jerome and Matilda have already played 9 of their 10 darts this game. The information is represented in the table above. If Jerome hits the 70 point spot on his final dart, what must Matilda score throw to beat Jerome?

A)   100

B)   90

C)   80

D)   Not possible given her current score

28

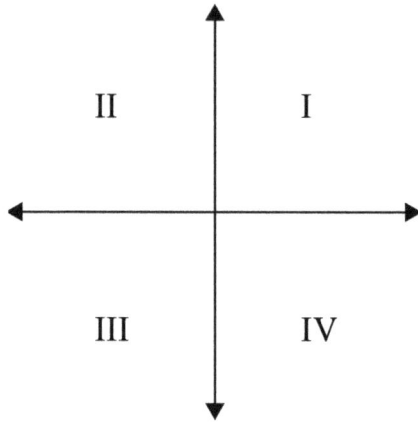

$$9x + y = -19$$

$$\frac{7}{4}x - 5y = \frac{3}{2}$$

For the system of equations above, in which quadrant does the solution lie?

A) I

B) II

C) III

D) IV

29

How many distinct solutions does the polynomial $(x^2 + 4x + 4)(x - 1) = 0$ have?

A) 0

B) 1

C) 2

D) 3

30

x	$f(x)$
-3	0
1	-16
5	0

Based on the table above, what are the coordinates of the vertex?

A) (16,1)

B) (1,–16)

C) (–1,16)

D) (2,16)

DIRECTIONS

For questions 31–38, solve the problem and enter your answer in the grid, as described below, on the answer sheet.

1. Although not required, it is suggested that you write your answer in the boxes at the top of the columns to help you fill in the circles accurately. You will receive credit only if the circles are filled in correctly.

2. Mark no more than one circle in any column.

3. No question has a negative answer.

4. Some problems may have more than one correct answer. In such cases, grid only one answer.

5. **Mixed numbers** such as $3\frac{1}{2}$ must be gridded as 3.5 or 7/2. (If $\boxed{3\,|\,1\,|\,/\,|\,2}$ is entered into the grid, it will be interpreted as $\frac{31}{2}$, not $3\frac{1}{2}$.)

6. **Decimal answers:** If you obtain a decimal answer with more digits than the grid can accommodate, it may be either rounded or truncated, but it must fill the entire grid.

Answer: $\frac{7}{12}$ — Write answer in boxes. — Fraction line — Grid in result.

Answer: 2.5 — Decimal point

Acceptable ways to grid $\frac{2}{3}$ are:

Answer: 201 – either position is correct

NOTE: You may start your answers in any column, space permitting. Columns you don't need to use should be left blank.

31

Chris drives 47 miles to work every morning. The drive usually takes him 45 min, but because of an accident on his usual route, it took him 50 min one morning. What is the difference in Chris' average speed from his usual trip vs. his day on the accident? Round your answer to the nearest hundredth.

32

A storage unit can store 100 cubic feet of storage. If boxes of dimensions 1 x 1 x 1 feet squared and 2 x 2 x 2 feet squared are put in the unit and there are 51 1 x 1 x 1 feet squared boxes in the unit already, what is the maximum number of 2 x 2 x 2 feet squared boxes that can fit in the unit?

CONTINUE

33

Applicants to State College

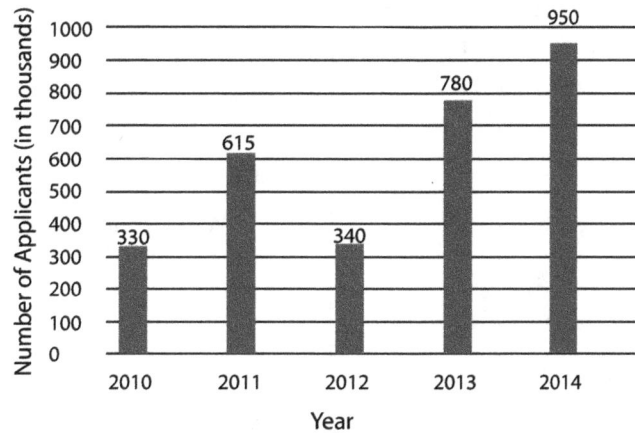

According to the graph above, what is the percent increase of applicants from 2010 to 2012? Omit the % in your answer.

34

Jerry is painting a fence around his yard. If the total surface area of the fence is 371 feet squared and a can of paint can cover 100 feet squared, how many cans of paint will Jerry need to buy if he wants to do two full coats of paint on his fence?

35

Cindy is choosing a piñata for a birthday party. The piñata she wants to buy is a sphere with a radius 7 inches. If she wants to fill the piñata with 1400 in^3 of candy, how much empty space will there be inside the piñata, in in^3? Round to the nearest tenth.

Questions 36 and 37 refer to the following information:

The equation $y = 3^x + 250$ represents the total cost of (y) of renting a car from Car Rental Company A for (x) days.

36

What is the cost of renting a car for four days?

37

The cost for renting a car from a rival company, Company B, can be represented by $y = 2^x + 300$. If you were to rent a car for three days, what would be the difference in cost between Company A and Company B?

38

$$f(b) = \frac{17}{(b+2)^2 - b(b-3) - 12}$$

For what value of b is the function $f(b)$ undefined?

STOP

If you finish before time is called, you may check your work on this section only.
Do not turn to any other section.

CONTINUE

No Test Material On This Page

Section #1 – Reading Test

#	Correct Answer	#	Correct Answer	#	Correct Answer	#	Correct Answer	#	Correct Answer	#	Correct Answer
1	B	11	C	21	A	31	C	41	C	51	D
2	D	12	D	22	C	32	C	42	C	52	C
3	A	13	A	23	B	33	B	43	B		
4	C	14	B	24	D	34	C	44	A		
5	B	15	B	25	B	35	D	45	B		
6	C	16	A	26	A	36	D	46	C		
7	A	17	C	27	C	37	B	47	D		
8	A	18	D	28	B	38	C	48	A		
9	D	19	C	29	C	39	C	49	C		
10	B	20	B	30	B	40	A	50	A		

Number of Correct Answers [   ] Reading Test Raw Score

Section #2 – Writing and Language Test

#	Correct Answer	#	Correct Answer	#	Correct Answer	#	Correct Answer	#	Correct Answer
1	B	11	C	21	D	31	C	41	D
2	A	12	B	22	C	32	A	42	A
3	B	13	B	23	D	33	B	43	C
4	B	14	A	24	C	34	B	44	B
5	C	15	D	25	B	35	D		
6	A	16	D	26	A	36	A		
7	B	17	A	27	D	37	C		
8	D	18	B	28	B	38	B		
9	A	19	B	29	A	39	B		
10	B	20	C	30	B	40	C		

Number of Correct Answers [   ] Writing and Language Test Raw Score

Section #3 – Math Test (No Calculator)

#	Correct Answer	#	Correct Answer	#	Correct Answer	#	Correct Answer
1	C	6	B	11	A	16	0
2	A	7	A	12	A	17	80
3	B	8	C	13	D	18	2
4	A	9	B	14	A	19	0.38
5	D	10	D	15	A	20	17

Number of Correct Answers [   ] **Math Test (No Calculator) Raw Score**

Section #4 – Math Test (Calculator)

#	Correct Answer	#	Correct Answer	#	Correct Answer	#	Correct Answer
1	B	11	C	21	B	31	6.27
2	D	12	C	22	B	32	6
3	A	13	D	23	A	33	3
4	B	14	A	24	A	34	8
5	C	15	D	25	D	35	36.8
6	D	16	C	26	B	36	331
7	A	17	C	27	D	37	31
8	B	18	C	28	C	38	1.14
9	B	19	A	29	C		
10	A	20	D	30	B		

Number of Correct Answers [   ] **Math Test (Calculator) Raw Score**

```
┌──────────┐  CONVERT  ┌──────────┐
│          │  ──────▶  │          │──────┐
└──────────┘           └──────────┘      │
Reading Test           Reading Test      │
Raw Score (0 - 52)     Score (10 - 40)   │
```

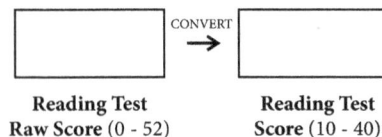

The following is a **Score Conversion Table** (Raw to Scaled) used by the College Board for an SAT® practice test available online. Although each SAT test is scored a bit differently, this table will give you an estimate of your score. Enter your raw scores in the appropriate boxes below, follow the conversion directions and know your estimated SAT scores for this test.

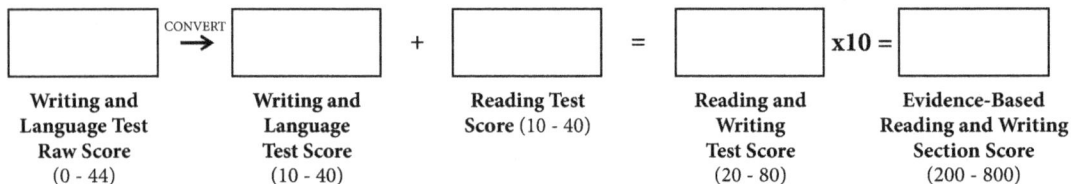

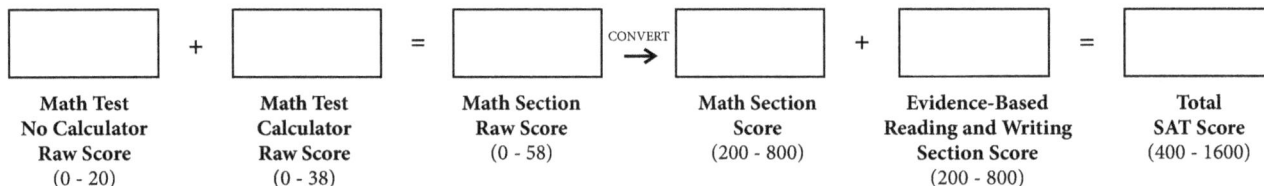

```
┌──────────┐  CONVERT  ┌──────────┐    ┌──────────┐    ┌──────────┐         ┌──────────┐
│          │  ──────▶  │          │ +  │          │ =  │          │  x10 =  │          │
└──────────┘           └──────────┘    └──────────┘    └──────────┘         └──────────┘
Writing and            Writing and     Reading Test    Reading and          Evidence-Based
Language Test          Language        Score (10 - 40) Writing              Reading and Writing
Raw Score              Test Score                      Test Score           Section Score
(0 - 44)               (10 - 40)                       (20 - 80)            (200 - 800)
                                                                                  ↓
┌──────────┐    ┌──────────┐    ┌──────────┐  CONVERT  ┌──────────┐    ┌──────────┐    ┌──────────┐
│          │ +  │          │ =  │          │  ──────▶  │          │ +  │          │ =  │          │
└──────────┘    └──────────┘    └──────────┘           └──────────┘    └──────────┘    └──────────┘
Math Test       Math Test       Math Section           Math Section    Evidence-Based       Total
No Calculator   Calculator      Raw Score              Score           Reading and Writing  SAT Score
Raw Score       Raw Score       (0 - 58)               (200 - 800)     Section Score        (400 - 1600)
(0 - 20)        (0 - 38)                                                (200 - 800)
```

Raw Score Conversion Table: Section and Test Scores

Raw Score (# of correct answers)	Math Section Score	Reading Test Score	Writing and Language Test Score	Raw Score (# of correct answers)	Math Section Score	Reading Test Score	Writing and Language Test Score
0	200	10	10	30	530	27	29
1	200	10	10	31	530	27	30
2	210	10	10	32	540	28	31
3	230	10	10	33	550	28	31
4	250	11	11	34	550	29	32
5	260	12	12	35	560	29	32
6	280	13	12	36	570	30	33
7	290	14	13	37	580	30	34
8	310	15	14	38	590	31	34
9	320	15	15	39	590	31	35
10	330	16	15	40	600	32	36
11	350	17	16	41	610	32	36
12	360	17	17	42	620	33	37
13	370	18	18	43	630	34	39
14	380	18	18	44	640	35	40
15	390	19	19	45	650	35	
16	400	20	19	46	660	36	
17	420	20	20	47	670	37	
18	430	21	21	48	680	37	
19	430	21	22	49	680	38	
20	440	22	22	50	690	39	
21	450	22	23	51	700	39	
22	460	23	24	52	720	40	
23	470	23	25	53	730		
24	480	24	25	54	740		
25	490	24	26	55	760		
26	500	25	26	56	770		
27	510	25	27	57	790		
28	510	26	28	58	800		
29	520	26	29				

1. **Choice B is the best answer.** The narrator admits that she finds her job "an irritation" (line 11) and a "tedium" (line 15) and reflects on the reasons she hates it, including "the stagnation of my creative faculties" (lines 25-26), but especially because of "my aversion to Mrs. Van Doren and her clear hostility toward me" (lines 37-38). She considers why Van Doren so dislikes her, and concludes it is because she is jealous (line 55) since "in no case could she call herself my superior, save in years" (lines 56-57).
Choice A is incorrect because the narrator begins with an explanation that she knew she had made a mistake after "no more than a month" (line 1) of employment. She is not hopeful at the start; rather, she is resigned, "submitted to Fate's dictates" (line 32). In the final paragraph she says to herself, "Dorothea, this torment must end" (lines 79-80) which suggests a new resolve and the beginnings of hope, rather than feelings of despair.
Choice C is incorrect because, although the narrator claims that "my aversion to Mrs. Van Doren and her clear hostility toward me, evident from my first hour, began to grow," (lines 37-39), the passage as a whole is not an escalation of the conflict between Dorothea and her supervisor. The narrator is able to avoid "her arrows of spite" (line 66) rather than get into arguments.
Choice D is incorrect because, although the first paragraph begins with Dorothea's admission that she has made a mistake in her choice of employer, she does not "stand by her decision" or "feel she must endure the situation." Instead, she determines that it must change (lines 81-86).

2. **Choice D is the best answer.** "Contextualize" refers to providing background information for an event. The sentences help explain the narrator's emotions because it shows that she realises she has made a mistake, but that she did not have much other choice. Without the sentence, the reader does not understand why she feels trapped, but does not quit.
Choice A is incorrect because we know that at the time in question it was "the end of March" (line 68) but the opening sentence doesn't tell us how long has elapsed between that first month and when Dorothea decides she has to change her life, so it doesn't establish the "chronology" or "time sequence" of what follows.
Choice B is incorrect because the opening sentence refers to Dorothea and establishes the "foundation" or "reason" for her current feelings, not those of Van Doren.
Choice C is incorrect because the sentences establish why the narrator laments her situation and wants to change it, but they do not show that she feels "repentance" or "sorrow for doing something wrong." She was not morally wrong; she just found a bad job.

3. **Choice A is the best answer.** The first paragraph explains why Dorothea is bored and stifled by the tedium of the job she took, while the second explains why she is miserable because of her supervisor's antipathy. However, by the third paragraph the narrator has made a resolution to find a way to escape her present position.
Choice B is incorrect because the passage doesn't begin with Dorothea's expectations that she will have a wonderful career. The first paragraph shows Dorothea's resolve "to make my own way in the world (as I had vowed I would do)" (lines 22-23), but already contains indications of her distress. The passage also doesn't end with regret, but with determination: "every ounce of my not inconsiderable will should be bent on" finding a way to change things (lines 82-83).
Choice C is incorrect because although the first paragraph mentions her work and its repetitiveness in detail in (lines 15-20) ("Each garment … denied me"), things which displease Dorothea, and in (lines 54-59) (Though I … hers") in the second paragraph she reflects on the reasons she displeases Van Doren, the overall shift in the passage is from what makes Dorothea miserable to her determination to change it.
Choice D is incorrect because the passage does begin by discussing the work Dorothea undertakes in (lines 12-14) ("The job… surroundings"), but it emphasizes that she could endure the work if it were not for the hostility of her employer. At the end of the passage, her home is described as unwelcoming (lines 71-77, "my lodging… spent alone"), but the focus is on her decision to change her entire situation.

4. **Choice C is the best answer.** The narrator explains that if it had only been the tedium of the work, she could have coped, but in (lines 35-39) explains that what makes her position intolerable is the toxic relationship between her and Mrs. Van Doren. It makes the narrator feel she is being forced deeper and deeper into a well of despair, and the quoted words reflect her "dismay" or "horror" at the position in which she finds herself.
Choice A is incorrect because although the well is a metaphor for the depths of misery into which Dorothea is plunged, (the "poisonous slurry" is Mrs. Van Doren's attitude and the "solitary darkness" is Dorothea's struggle

with her present situation), nowhere does the passage suggest that Dorothea has a literal fear of being "confined" or "imprisoned."

Choice B is incorrect because, although the expression "solitary darkness" suggests Dorothea's isolation, taken together with "poisonous slurry" it serves to emphasize Dorothea's increasing desperation over her plight. There is also no evidence that she feels "increasingly" or "more" isolated than at other times in her life.

Choice D is incorrect because, although the employer clearly harbours a dislike for Dorothea, the passage doesn't suggest that she intends to physically harm Dorothea in any way.

5. **Choice B is the best answer.** The narrator explains that Mrs. Van Doren "sneered at my cultured tones and tutored bearing, and became irritated by my skilled workmanship," (lines 49-51) and that she dislikes her because of "a small, ugly, green-eyed creature," (meaning jealousy) because "in no case could she call herself my superior, save in years."

Choice A is incorrect because Mrs. Van Doren is not "exasperated" or "annoyed" by a "lack of" or "no" skill in Dorothea's work. In fact, Dorothea claims in (lines 60-64) ("if she …less") that her employer would have hated her less if she *had* been a poor seamstress.

Choice C is incorrect because nowhere does the passage suggest that Mrs. Van Doren knows of any "aspirations" or "goals" that Dorothea might have.

Choice D is incorrect because, although the narrator complains to her readers that the work is tedious, that she's bored, and that Mrs. Van Doren is awful to her, she doesn't complain to her supervisor. In fact, she directly says, "I gathered my honor guard of Humility, Watchfulness and Patience" (lines 64-66) so Mrs. Van Doren has no cause to become impatient with her on that score.

6. **Choice C is the best answer.** The answer to the previous question is that Mrs. Van Doren's attitude is prompted by envy of Dorothea's poise and ability. Choice C says that Mrs Van Doren "sneered" or "showed contempt" because of Dorothea's "cultured tones and tutored bearing," which refers to "poise," and also at her "skilled workmanship." Therefore, Choice C shows that Van Doren's complaints were "prompted" or "spurred on" by these qualities in Dorothea.

Choice A is incorrect because this choice refers to Dorothea's desire to become a better seamstress, not to Van Doren's attitude.

Choice B is weak because (lines 47-49) refer to Van Doren's dislike growing "with each dress I presented to her with which she was unable to find fault" but not directly to Van Doren's jealousy.

Choice D is weak because it uses an analogy to personify Van Doren's jealousy at being not "superior" or "better" than Dorothea in any way. However, it does not specifically cite poise and skill as reasons for the jealousy.

7. **Choice A is the best answer.** (lines 64-67) refer to being "stalked" and to "arrows of spite," emphasising Dorothea's feelings of needing to escape like a wild animal being hunted down by a ruthless killer.

Choice B is incorrect because the focus of the hunting allusion is on the prey (Dorothea) rather than on Van Doren, so the author's purpose was not to emphasize differences between the two women.

Choice C is incorrect because the reference to hunting is metaphorical and does not have a literal meaning or suggest that Van Doren would actually have "stalked" Dorothea or shot arrows at her.

Choice D is incorrect because the hunting metaphor only shows the relationship of hunter to prey between Mrs. Van Doren and Dorothea. It doesn't include the workforce as a whole, and so cannot illustrate Van Doren's position in relation to it.

8. **Choice A is the best answer.** Although Dorothea admits she made a mistake taking the job, she also vows to make her own way in the world (line 22). She also shows a "quiet" or "private" quality by keeping her intelligence hidden (line 58). In the final paragraph, she resolves to find a way out of her present predicament.

Choice B is incorrect because, although Dorothea admits to making a mistake in the opening paragraph, she also claims she had little choice, and suggests a certain maturity rather than foolhardiness. She is also not portrayed as an especially "optimistic" or "cheerful" character, though she does have dreams and ambitions.

Choice C is incorrect because nowhere does the author characterize Dorothea as aggressive. In fact, she refers twice to "Humility" (lines 34 and 65) which is contrary to an aggressive attitude.

Choice D is incorrect because "superficial" or "surface" suggests that Dorothea lacks genuine confidence. She refers to "my not inconsiderable will" in (line 84), which suggests that she is actually very confident in her own

CONTINUE

abilities.

9. **Choice D is the best answer.** The answer to the previous question is that Dorothea is best characterized as quietly determined. In Choice D, Dorothea refers to applying her "not inconsiderable will" (line 84) to solve her problem. Therefore, she is "determined" or "resolute" about changing her situation.
Choice A is incorrect because it refers to Dorothea's irritation and feeling of foolishness, so it doesn't support the claim that Dorothea is quietly determined.
Choice B is incorrect because it emphasizes her frustration and lack of ability to stay with her job due to Mrs. Van Doren's hostility. Choice B therefore suggests that she plans to give up rather than emphasizing determination to achieve a different goal.
Choice C is incorrect because it refers to Dorothea's delight in being able to collect her wages and there being nothing Mrs Van Doren could do to prevent it, which suggests a certain smugness rather than determination.

10. **Choice B is the best answer.** The passage suggests that although Dorothea is glad of the money to support herself, it also refers to "the sheer glee of knowing Mrs Van Doren begrudged every cent of it, but was powerless to prevent my having it." (lines 73-75)
Choice A is incorrect because the passage explains that her wages "would pay for my lodgings and provide enough sustenance to keep me on the mortal plane (though little more)" (lines 71-73) which precludes the purchase of luxuries.
Choice C is incorrect because although she is aware of the quality of her workmanship (it's as good as her employer's, and her employer can find no fault with it) the passage doesn't say that she feels she especially deserves her wages. She is just pleased Van Doren can't stop her from claiming them.
Choice D is incorrect, because although the passage says the wages will be spent on money for her lodgings, it doesn't suggest that she is behind on her rent and already owed money to her landlady.

11. **Choice C is the best answer** because the passage explains that as systems of government were developed, they were "framed on the sole idea of man's rights" (lines 33-34). The passage then says that those rights must extend to women equally, and, using the example of the courage and political awareness of women in the American Revolution, explains that they are just as capable of owning those rights. The author quotes Abigail Adams to support her point that women should have equal rights: "We will not obey any laws in which we have no voice or representation" (lines 74-75).
Choice A is incorrect because the idea that free-thinking has been discouraged by both Church and State is touched upon in the second paragraph to explain how, historically, women were given a "crushing free thought" (line 15) as a "subordinate class" (lines 23-24). This point is not the central claim of the whole passage.
Choice B is incorrect because the passage doesn't suggest that revolution is "inevitable" or "unavoidable." It says that if there were a revolution, it would be in a colony of England's.
Choice D is incorrect because the passage is about the necessity that both men and women have an equal stake in both society and government, not about "subjugation" or "bringing one group under the control of another." The author offers that situation in the second and third paragraphs as a reason why it is necessary to pursue equality.

12. **Choice D is the best answer** because the passage suggests that in the "barbarous ages" (line 3), meaning the prehistoric past, "the right of the strongest was the only one recognized" (lines 3-4). In other words, only force or strength "imbued" or "gave" power to the leaders. However, the author continues that "as mankind progressed in the arts and sciences, intellect began to triumph over brute force" (lines 4-6). To paraphrase, over time, "intellect" or "the ability to think and reason" now "holds sway" or "is most important.
Choice A is incorrect because, while the passage states that in the past the authorities were responsible for "crushing free thought, persecuting and torturing those who have dared to speak or act outside of established authority" (lines 15-17), it does not suggest that free thinkers are now being "praised" or "complimented." In fact, in the final paragraph it implies that women are still struggling to gain rights, and are not being "applauded" or "praised" for their ideas and beliefs.
Choice B is incorrect because the passage makes clear that in the past, "our systems of jurisprudence, civil and political theories… have all been framed on the sole idea of man's rights" (lines 30-34). However, the passage does not suggest that these systems are now framed for everyone. Instead it quotes Abigail Adams and other women as "inciting [the] overthrow" (line 91) of systems that are not yet equal.

CONTINUE →

Choice C is incorrect because the passage refers to "the great uprising of women out of the lethargy of the past," which suggests that in the past women did not protest, but now they do. However, the question compares barbarism and the modern age, and the passage claims that brute strength sets barbarism aside from civilization. There is no indication that women were "imprisoned of mind" or felt a desire to protest during that period.

13. **Choice A is the best answer** because the answer to the previous question says that the fundamental difference between the modern age and barbarism is that in the past, brute force ruled, but in the present, intellect is more important. Choice A paraphrases this concept, so it provides solid evidence.
Choice B is incorrect because it refers to a state beyond barbarism, when there were monarchs and popes. It refers to "subjugation" or "bringing someone under control," but does not provide evidence that such rule occurred using force in the past and using reason in the present.
Choice C is incorrect because it only refers to modern rights, not to a difference between barbarism and the present. It also does not provide evidence that the present relies on reason because it shows an imbalance between women and men.
Choice D is incorrect because it only deals with women's voices calling for equality. It does not compare conditions in the past and present.

14. **Choice B is the best answer** because the passage states that progress for women "is hopeless so long as they are taught that their condition is ordained" (lines 44-46). In other words, so long as they are told they must accept an inferior position without the right to vote, they will never gain the equality they deserve. It goes on to say that "Education frees the mind from the bondage of authority and makes the individual self-asserting" (lines 50-53), so education is the key to changing women from being subordinate to "looking within" or "deciding for themselves" that they should have rights as equals.
Choice A is incorrect because the passage refers to the education of women, not men. It says that women's obedience to outside authority has created "a retarding force" (line 43). It does not suggest that educating men will prevent men from holding back civilization.
Choice B is incorrect because the implication is that Church and State already know that individual self-reliance is the first incentive to freedom, which is precisely why they try to suppress it. They don't want people (men or women) to be free-thinkers capable of challenging their authority, so it is not the Church and State that will learn about self-reliance, but the men and women who are obedient and self-sacrificing, or "the subordinate classes," especially women.
Choice D is incorrect because the passage says that when the American Revolution began, women were "as active, earnest, determined, and self-sacrificing as the men" (lines 60-61). Therefore, they did not need education to gain patriotism; they were "endowed with as lofty a patriotism as man" (lines 61-62) despite a lack of education.

15. **Choice B is the best answer** because "established" refers to the type of authority that people were persecuted for speaking out against. Choice B refers to something that is "accepted," so it fits the context of saying that people were persecuted when they spoke out against authority that was generally accepted, such as the Church and State.
Choice A is incorrect because it refers to an act that is "habitual" or "traditional." However, the authority was not something that people did on a regular basis; it existed.
Choice C is incorrect because it refers to a long-established practice, often handed down from generation to generation. The authority described in the passage, though, does not have to continue for generations, as long as most people accept it as valid.
Choice D is incorrect because it refers to something "official" or "ceremonial." However, the authority does not have to be officially recognized as long as everyone accepts its governance and follows its orders.

16. **Choice A is the best answer** because the author is trying to convey the notion that the government of the new United States of America was already carrying a great load on its shoulders, like a train dragging boxcars full of the protests of women demanding fair treatment and equal rights. It did not start with those issues already resolved, so it was "freighted" with the protests of women from revolutionary times.
Choice B is incorrect because although the passage says in (lines 43-44) that women are "a retarding force in civilization," that phrase means that women are not being educated to take an equal part and to speak out for their rights. The reference to being "freighted with the protests" is in an entirely different context and refers to

the "baggage" the new government was carrying from its inauguration.

Choice C is incorrect because "hamstrung" means "crippled." Although the author is explaining that the government had a lot to deal with when it started, it doesn't go so far as to suggest the government was crippled or damaged by the burden of protest, just that it inherited that burden from the moment it was born.

Choice D is incorrect because, although the word "freighted" could suggest a train, the author isn't discussing the revolution.

17. **Choice C is the best answer** because in the previous paragraph, the author writes that "women were as active, earnest, determined, and self-sacrificing as the men… and fully understood the principles upon which the struggle was based" (lines 60-63). She is claiming that women were as politically astute and well-informed as men. The reference to Abigail Adams in the sixth paragraph illustrates this political awareness amongst women as she writes to her husband in Congress imploring him to deal with women fairly as he and his colleague promulgate the new laws of the country.

Choice A is incorrect because, while Abigail Adams is a famous figure, the author is not trying to emphasize a point she thinks no one knows. Instead, she is using a well-known person as an example of her point that women during Revolutionary times were active and earnest.

Choice B is incorrect because "foreshadow" refers to warning about a future occurrence. There is nothing in the description of Adams that warns the reader that the author will then list other famous women.

Choice D is incorrect because the previous paragraph opens with "The American Revolution—that great political rebellion of the ages" (lines 53-54), which clearly establishes the "historical context" or "time frame" for the following discussion of the rights of women. This reference to Abigail Adams, the wife of a founding father, simply continues the context rather than introducing it.

18. **Choice D is the best answer** because "particular to" refers to something that is "specific to" or "only in" the United States. The question is asking for evidence that "contradicts" or "goes against" the claim, so therefore it wants proof that women's suffrage is a struggle that extends beyond the United States. In Choice D, "global society" means society as a concept—all civilized society anywhere. Therefore, the struggle is found in all areas, not just America.

Choice A is incorrect because it refers only to the American Revolution; it does not support the view that the struggle for women's suffrage took place elsewhere, beyond the borders of the new United States.

Choice B is incorrect because, although it refers to England, it does not refer to the struggle for women's rights, only to the history of rebelliousness against authority.

Choice C is incorrect because it refers only to women's suffrage in America, not beyond.

19. **Choice C is the best answer** because both paragraphs focus on "Subjection to the powers that be" (line 13). The difference between the two is that the second paragraph emphasizes how all people are subjugated, and the third paragraph develops this idea by highlighting that men can be included as part of the "powers that be," but women are not. The contrast set up by the two paragraphs is bringing the reader's attention to the disparity between men and women.

Choice A is incorrect because although the second paragraph refers to the conflict between those in "authority" in Church and State, the topic of the subjugation of others is discussed in general: of monarchs to the pope and of nations to the monarch. It refers to a whole subordinate class, but in the third paragraph, the authors stress that this nowhere more manifests itself than in the subjugation of women compared to men.

Choice B is incorrect because while the characteristics of a civilized society are listed in the third paragraph to include "systems of jurisprudence, civil and political theories, trade, commerce, education, religion, friendships, and family life," the main focus is not the characteristics of culture and society or the mechanisms of government and trade. The focus is on explaining that all of them are framed by, and on behalf of, men.

Choice D is incorrect because the struggle for self-determination in the past, while hinted at in the second paragraph, is not emphasized. The passage says that the "powers that be" were responsible for "throttling science, checking invention, crushing free thought" and even of "persecuting and torturing" in the past, but the third paragraph does not bring the struggle forward and say that this is no longer the case. Instead, the third paragraph speaks to the clear and ongoing differences between man and woman.

20. **Choice B is the best answer** because the author clearly sees education as key to improving the position of women, particularly as it pertains to suffrage. In (lines 47-50) she writes, "in the scientific education of woman… lies the hope of the future." The education of men is not brought up, but the concept of equality between genders is implied. Therefore, it could reasonably be assumed that "universal" or "all" suffrage would rest on the same foundation for both men and women.

Choice A is incorrect because "inescapable right" refers to something that is unavoidable. However, the author says that women do not have the right to vote. Since women are citizens, the suffrage could only be inescapable if they were forced to vote, which is not the case.

Choice C is incorrect because the passage mentions "civil disobedience" or "refusing to comply with laws believed to be unjust" in the quotation by Abigail Adams, when she says we "will not obey any laws in which we have no voice or representation" (lines 74-75).

Choice D is incorrect because it suggests that only those who take part in government should be allowed to vote. However, the author implies that all women should be allowed to vote, as should men. Since not every citizen is employed by the government, it can be presumed that the writer would not make participation a qualification for the "privilege" of voting.

21. **Choice A is the best answer** because in the first paragraph, the author says that traditional methods to control invasive species are either ineffective or expensive, but then says that, "Yet there may be a novel, (yet paradoxically traditional) method solution: goats," (lines 13-14) which adds a note of "optimism" or "hope." The author describes this method in more detail in the second and third paragraphs, but then moves on to current research in the fourth paragraph. The tone changes because she says, "but work relates to … specific plants in specific places—not to all 50,000 invasive species" (lines 44-46). She continues by describing more restrictions in the fifth paragraph: "using peripatetic livestock … may not be the panacea that these success stories suggest" (lines 70-73). She concludes that the use of livestock for removing invasive species has not been extensively investigated and that while it may work in Europe, an alternative would be required in the U.S.A.

Choice B is incorrect because the shift from concern over invasive species to relief at a possible solution occurs only in the first to third paragraphs. Choice B does not mention the concerns brought up in the second half of the passage.

Choice C is incorrect because "interest" suggests a mild curiosity, but the author exhibits extreme concern by referring to "nearly half" of America's endangered species being under threat or covering "thousands of acres of land." While it is evident there is an appreciation for goats in "successfully destroying non-native species" (lines 21-22) the general attitude is more cautionary, since the author refers to the limitations of research done so far and the drawbacks of using goats because they "lack discrimination" (line 55).

Choice D is incorrect because, although the author appears to admire the enterprise of Knox and Cash in hiring out their goats, she doesn't express "skepticism" or "doubt" that the academic research has value. She merely acknowledges that the research done so far is incomplete: it does not relate to many species, and it does not offer a management model for using livestock as a means of invasive species control.

22. **Choice C is the best answer** because the quotation explains that the goats like being able to strip an area of vegetation down to the ground, then get moved to another place where they can eat more. The perspective in the quote reflects that of the goats, rather than a scientific or economic view of the problem.

Choice A is incorrect because, while the quote introduces a note of humor, the author isn't ridiculing the solution. If anything, the solution is being praised because even the goats are excited about a magical supply of new food.

Choice B is incorrect because "representative" refers to something which is typical of an entire group of viewpoints. While other goat breeders may feel that their goats are happy, there is no evidence to show that the speaker represents all goat breeders.

Choice D is incorrect because "the matter" or "topic" is the control of invasive species by natural means: livestock. The quotation is about one owner's feelings on what his goats think about clearing unwanted plants rather than the opinion of an "expert" or "established authority" on the issue of controlling the invasive species.

23. **Choice B is the best answer** because this question asks about the difference between Cash's and Knox's methods of eradicating unwanted invasive plants. The central difference is that after Cash's mixed flock has eaten the

CONTINUE ➡

plants down to ground level, he attacks the roots "with a chainsaw" (line 38) and uses a "growth inhibitor" (lines 38-39) to stop them coming back. In contrast, Knox simply lets the goats loose in the targeted area and moves them when they are done.

Choice A is incorrect because, according to the passage, it was Knox who "stumbled upon" or "found by accident" the idea of using livestock as a means of controlling unwanted plants. He originally intended to sell the goats for meat, but could not bear to send them away for slaughter. Cash, on the other hand, "runs a company that hires out a mixed herd in Georgia to clear infestations" (lines 27-28), suggesting that he made a deliberate decision to raise livestock for this purpose.

Choice C is incorrect because the passage says that Knox uses his goats on "plants like poison ivy and bittersweet," but also refers to the fact that the goats "like the variety," suggesting they eat multiple species. The passage also says that Cash set up his business to "clear infestations like the kudzu vine from people's properties" (lines 28-29), but also adds that "other invasive species like English Ivy stop the animals' diet from becoming monotonous" (lines 31-33)." Since both men's animals feast on multiple varieties, this point is not a difference.

Choice D is incorrect because the passage refers to the fact that Knox has been "hiring out his goats for years" (line 22), but that Cash "prefers to mix sheep and goats because while the goats are more gastrically tolerant, the sheep are better behaved" (lines 39-41).

24. **Choice D is the best answer** because the answer to the previous question is that Brian Cash's method of controlling invasive species uses additional means to ensure the plants were eradicated, but Knox's method did not. Choice D supports this claim because it emphasizes that Cash uses other methods than just animals—it uses a chainsaw and growth inhibitor.

None of the other choices support the claim that Cash uses different methods to eradicate weeds but Knox does not. Choice A is incorrect because it refers only to Knox's motivation for using goats to control unwanted plants; it does not refer to what methods both farmers use to ensure weeds do not grow back.

Choice B is incorrect because it only contains Knox's view that his goats like the variety in their diet that comes from moving from place to place.

Choice C is incorrect because it only touches on Cash's business location rather than its methods.

25. **Choice B is the best answer** because the discussion on research by "by universities and research groups" in the fourth paragraph, highlights that only individual species are being targeted, and uses the examples of yellow star-thistle and spotted knapweed. However, the paragraph points out that research isn't looking at "all 50,000" (line 46) invasive species. This claim suggests that the focus of the research is too "narrow" or "limited" to be effective at solving the problem of every invasive species.

Choice A is incorrect because the research examples the author gives are not "inconclusive" or "having no clear results." For example, in the case of yellow star-thistle, the goats achieved the task of removing the unwanted thistle. In the case of the spotted knapweed, the study found that after using the goats at a certain point in the plant's life cycle, "growth the following year is significantly reduced" (lines 59-60), showing that a clear conclusion had been reached. Additionally, while the article does mention the volume "of nutritional food the goats need to eat," this is not a key factor in the main conclusion of the article.

Choice C is incorrect because, although protecting native species is mentioned in reference to the clearing of yellow star-thistle in Idaho, that is not a limitation of the research. The research was conducted properly; protecting species is a limitation of using goats.

Choice D is incorrect because the cost of eradications does not show that the research is "impractical." The research has generated clear results; the problem is that using goats may not ultimately work because "Cattlemen can't pay the thousands of dollars it costs" (lines 85-86).

26. **Choice A is the best answer** because the answer to the previous question is that one conclusion about research into livestock grazing of invasive species infestations is that the research's focus is too "narrow" or "limited." Choice A supports that claim because it says that the research does not address all invasive species, implying that there may only be a solution for the few species that have been studied.

Choice B is incorrect because it does not refer to any limitations in the research itself, only to the possible solution of using goats to solve all invasive species problems.

Choice C is incorrect because it only refers to how much goats need to eat, not to limitations with the research.

Choice D is incorrect because it refers to paying for large-scale grazing, a problem with economics rather than with the studies about how well goats control invasive species.

27. **Choice C is the best answer** because the context uses "discrimination" to describe what goats "lack," or "do not have." The first half of the sentence indicates that goats will eat "everything else," not just the invasive plants. In other words, the goat does not care what it eats, or has no "discrimination" or "judgement" about what it likes or not. Choice C refers to a "liking" or "preference," so fits the context of saying that goats have no preference about what they will eat.

Choices A and B are incorrect because they refer to unfairness or partiality towards one thing; the implication is that they treat something poorly. However, the goats are not deliberately treating some plants poorly; they just eat everything.

Choice D is incorrect because it means acceptance or open-mindedness. The goats are accepting of all food that comes their way, so they do not lack the ability to accept different foods.

28. **Choice B is the best answer** because the passage as a whole explains that goats are useful for cropping unwanted invasive species and that they eat anything, but paragraph five points out that some invasive plant species may not have much nutritional value. The goats would need a far greater volume of something like phragmites than a high-value crop like salad greens of alfalfa. In short, the paragraph is there to remind readers that from the goats' point of view, a diet of invasive species may be insufficient.

Choice A is incorrect because the paragraph, while it does introduce cattle and geese as options for removing alien invasive species, does not primarily focus on cattle and geese. The paragraph is explaining that goats may need more food than invasive species alone can provide.

Choice C is incorrect because, while the final paragraph does introduce the notion of a barter system, paragraph five only discusses the nutritional requirements of goats and not the economics of using them.

Choice D is incorrect because the amount of food goats can eat in a short time is mentioned elsewhere in the passage. (lines 35-36) say, "the flock chomps pests to ground level in a matter of hours," and (line 62) claims that one experiment "took just half a day" to eradicate a troublesome species. Paragraph five is therefore less about the speed at which the goats eat, and more about the nutritional requirements.

29. **Choice C is the best answer** because the map shows the darkened area is in the south and east of the country. The passage refers to Cash's company working in Georgia to eradicate kudzu vine, stating, "The vine is a problem in the warm, damp climate of the southeastern region of the United States" (lines 29-31).

Choice A is incorrect because the map shows the south and east of the country, but the reference to yellow star-thistle in the passage refers to it "in the rocky canyons of Idaho" (line 48), which is in the northwest, not the southeast.

Choice B is incorrect because poison ivy is referred to in (line 20) as one of the plants that Knox's goats were used to eliminate, but the location is not mentioned, so it could be anywhere on the map, not just in the shaded area.

Choice D is incorrect because the passage refers to "the eradication of spotted knapweed in the Pacific Northwest" (lines 56-57), but the map shows the south and east, not the north and west.

30. **Choice B is the best answer** because in terms of the cost benefit, the best result is the least re-growth for the lowest cost, so the least cost-effective would be high re-growth levels and high costs. The two columns for cutting show there is 25% regrowth after three months (the second highest rate) and the cost is around 12 cents per meter (the second highest rate)—making it the least efficient means of control for the price paid.

Choice A is incorrect because, although it is true that removal is the most effective means of eradicating the vine, the cost is about 32 cents per square meter. If all the other means are added together, the total is higher than 32 cents. Therefore, it is not "greater than the other methods combined."

Choice C is incorrect because the chart does not explain how the plants regrow, so it is impossible to determine whether burning "stimulates" or "prompts" new growth. Burning could harm the kudzu and there could be another reason that the plant grows back.

Choice D is incorrect because, although the chart does show that "other" grazers cost the least per meter (2 cents) and that re-growth is higher than for goats (22% rather than 15%), the chart doesn't explain why there is a difference. It is impossible to determine whether goats pull up the roots as they graze or not.

31. **Choice C is the best answer** because the question asks what part of the passage the chart best supports. The chart shows six different means of removing kudzu vine with data on the cost per square meter and the efficiency in terms of re-growth after 4 months. Based on the chart, using goats or goats and sheep to remove kudzu is *not* the best method— complete removal is. Therefore, when the passage says "using peripatetic livestock" may not be the best answer, this is supported by the chart.
    Choice B is incorrect because these lines focus on the use of livestock grazing. Figure 1 does not relate to livestock grazing at all, and that is not the focus of Figure 2. .
    Choice A is incorrect because those lines explain that there is a kudzu vine problem in southeastern America, which is supported by Figure 1, but not necessarily by Figure 2, because the location of Figure 2 is confined to Mississippi.
    Choice D is incorrect because those lines refer to the model of renting out livestock for pest plant control in Europe, but there is no evidence in the passage that kudzu is an issue in Europe, and the chart is not about management or means of ensuring such a system would work in the U.S.A.; instead, the chart shows the relative efficiency and relative costs of six different methods of controlling kudzu vine.

32. **Choice C is the best answer** because the passage explains that Alexander Oparin and John Haldane's idea about a reducing atmosphere spontaneously creating the building blocks of life on earth was revolutionary because it is known that life cannot exist without oxygen, which a reducing atmosphere lacks. The later experiment done by Stanley Miller and Harold Urey which developed this idea "began a branch of science called prebiotic chemistry" (line 29-30). Clearly Alexander Oparin and John Haldane's idea revolutionized the field.
    Choice A is incorrect because "thorough" is a definition of "radical" used to describe a complete change or action, relating to the fundamental nature of something.
    Choice B is incorrect because "belonging to the root of a word" relates to the linguistic definition of the word "radical."
    Choice D is incorrect because "fundamental" means "forming a necessary base or core" and Oparin and Haldane's idea was not previously necessary to the understanding of chemistry.

33. **Choice B is the best answer** because the passage says the theory was first proposed a century ago by Haldane and Oparin, proven to be possible by Miller and Urey, and confirmed by many other experiments since then, which suggests the theory was accepted. However, the conditions under which it took place were disputed. Miller and Urey thought the heat source was lightning, others though it was geothermal heat, or solar power. The composition of the gases was also contested, with some scientists believing that they had to be volcanic. Therefore, the basic principle that life could be created from inorganic materials was agreed upon, but the "conditions" or "specific details" were not.
    Choice A is incorrect because the theory was first proposed independently by two scientists from different countries: Oparin from Russia and Haldane from Britain. Two Americans from Chicago University first proved inorganic materials could form sugars and amino acids, but they didn't "propose" or "suggest" the theory.
    Choice C is incorrect because the passage doesn't tell us how Oparin and Haldane, the people who created the theory, came up with their theory or whether they did any experiments.
    Choice D is incorrect because the 2011 experiments using cerium did not disprove the theory that life on earth developed from inorganic materials, only that it developed from organic materials in the presence of oxygen. Prior theories stated that oxygen was not in the atmosphere at the time life developed.

34. **Choice C is the best answer** because the answer to the previous question is that the theory that life on Earth developed from inorganic materials was widely accepted, although the conditions under which it took place were disputed. Choice C shows that scientists used different mixtures of gases and different sources of energy, indicating that scientists accepted the theory in general but were trying to determine the exact way in which organic matter was created from inorganic materials because that was not agreed upon.
    Choice A is incorrect because it explains Oparin and Haldane's basic theory, but does not say whether the theory was accepted at all.
    Choice B is incorrect because it explains that Miller and Urey's experiments kick-started probiotic chemistry and became a "classic" or "standard model." This claim suggests widespread acceptance of the theory that inorganic materials could create organic life, but does not say that there was disagreement over the exact conditions. If

anything, the idea of a "classic" could imply that the experiments were accepted in their entirety.

Choice D is incorrect because it gives the results of the 2011 experiments showing that there was oxygen on Earth when life began. It does not say whether it was widely accepted among other scientists that that life on Earth developed from inorganic materials.

35. **Choice D is the best answer** because the passage tells us that "under reducing conditions the mineral [cerium] is stable and will not precipitate out in water" (lines 47-48), but the scientists' samples had precipitated out, altering the $Ce^{4+}:Ce^{3+}$ ratio. This fact led them to conclude that the Earth's atmosphere was an oxidizing one. Their conclusions, therefore, were based on the fact that cerium will not dissolve in an atmosphere that lacked oxygen.

Choice A is incorrect because the scientists used samples that matched those that were taken from the Earth's crust, but had just been created in their laboratory. Therefore, the samples were not "almost the same age as the Earth itself."

Choice B is incorrect because the conclusion was that the Earth had oxygen when life emerged; that conclusion was based on the balance of cerium. The scientists replicated the zircon from early Earth because it contained cerium. The source of the zircon was not as important as the chemical content of the mineral.

Choice C is incorrect because the scientists did not need different compositions of $Ce^{4+}:Ce^{3+}$ in zircon; they needed only one that replicated the composition of zircon from when life formed on Earth. Multiple different samples that did not reflect the time period would not explain whether oxygen was present when life formed.

36. **Choice D is the best answer** because the passage explains that while most terrestrial planets had a primary atmosphere containing light gases, Earth's differed because it is close to the Sun. That makes the atmosphere warm up, and as it warmed, the light gases (with their small atomic weights) sped up until they were able to "escape the Earth's gravitational pull" (lines 67-68), meaning they reached "escape velocity."

Choice A is incorrect because the passage suggests that gases usually remain around a planet due to its gravitational pull, as they do around Jupiter. However, Earth is close to the Sun, so the gases are able to escape because they are warm despite the natural tendency to be attracted by Earth's gravity.

Choice B is incorrect because light gases do accrete into primary atmospheres around planets like Jupiter, so Choice B indicates that Earth's atmosphere should have large quantities of light gases of its own rather than supporting the opposite claim.

Choice C is incorrect because although the passage explains that there are gases trapped in chondrites, the chondrites came from meteors, so would introduce more gases as they interacted rather than remove gases from the atmosphere.

37. **Choice B is the best answer** because the answer to the previous question is that the Earth's atmosphere lacks large quantities of light gases because Earth's proximity to the Sun means the gases reach escape velocity. Choice B directly paraphrases this claim because it says that the gases heat up "to the point where they can escape the planet's gravitational pull," meaning that such gases reach escape velocity.

Choice A is incorrect because it explains that most "terrestrial" or "rocky" planets have a lot of light gases. This claim indicates that Earth, a terrestrial planet, should have light gases, so does not support any claim about why it does not.

Choice C is incorrect because it explains that once the light gases had escaped, rocky materials, icy materials and methane were what was left behind, but it doesn't explain why the light gases escaped in the first place.

Choice D is incorrect because it explains that Fegley and Shaefer were able to figure out the chemical makeup of chondrites—the small, icy, rocky meteorites that traveled to Earth from space—but it doesn't suggest that the light gases inside the chondrites once formed Earth's primary atmosphere, or explain why there are few light gases in Earth's atmosphere now.

38. **Choice C is the best answer** because the passage explains that "most icy materials remain in the outer solar system, but some reached Earth in the form of small rocky meteorites" (lines 82-84), and then goes on to say that the scientists "examined masses of these chondrites" (lines 86-87), indicating that the chondrites and the small rocky meteorites are the same. The chondrites therefore form part of the class of icy materials.

Choice A is incorrect because the passage refers to the "interaction" or "contact and reaction" of chondrites with each other, but it doesn't suggest that they "break down" or "decompose" in the Earth's crust. Since the two scientists examined masses of them, at least some remained intact.

Choice B is incorrect because the passage says that "Fegley and Schaefer examined masses of these chondrites from different layers in the Earth's crust" (lines 86-89). "Masses" refers to large clusters, so suggests chondrites are not "rare" or "few and far between."

Choice D is incorrect because the passage refers to methane (CH4) and ammonia (NH3) as the products of interactions between the meteorites, not their original contents.

39. **Choice C is the best answer** because the passage talks about life, which is organic, being created from inorganic matter which is "coming into existence."

Choice A is incorrect because *materialization* means "becoming apparent," usually used in the sense of a ghost appearing, or "occurrence," used in the sense of something happening, but doesn't suggest life slowly evolving from inorganic matter.

Choice B is incorrect because *hatching* means emerging from an egg, like a chicken or a turtle, but not slowly being transformed from one thing to another and that think being life on Earth.

Choice D is incorrect because surfacing means rising or coming up to the surface from below. Organic life was not hiding below a surface, and therefore cannot surface.

40. **Choice A is the best answer** because Passage 1 starts by proposing that life on Earth began in a reducing atmosphere with no oxygen, which Miller and Urey proved in their experiments. However, this conclusion is disputed by Trail, Watson and Tailby, whose experiments with cerium suggest "that the atmosphere on Earth when life began was rich in oxygen, far removed from the toxic swamp previous studies suggested" (lines 53-56). Passage 2, on the other hand, confirms the original theory by looking at chondrites, concluding that Earth had a "reducing atmosphere ...just as Miller and Urey had claimed" (lines 92-95).

Choice B is incorrect because Oparin and Haldane's theory, as Miller and Urey's experiments appeared to confirm, were generally accepted and formed the basis of a new field of science. Therefore, the theories were not "unpopular" or "viewed or received unfavorably by the public."

Choice C is incorrect because Passage 2 does not "question" or "cast doubt upon" the experiments presented in Passage 1 (either Miller-Urey's or Trail, Watson and Tailby's). Instead, it presents another experiment that supplements and helps confirm the reducing atmosphere theory.

Choice D is incorrect because "reconcile" means "to make exist together without conflict." However, Passage 1 presents conflicting views: that the primary atmosphere had no oxygen when life emerged, and that it did have oxygen when life emerged. These theories are mutually exclusive, so are not reconciled by an experiment that shows that oxygen did not exist.

41. **Choice C is the best answer** because the author of Passage 1 says that all the studies before Trail, Watson and Tailby's work suggested that the atmosphere on Earth when life began, a reducing atmosphere, was a "noxious quagmire" (line 55). Since the atmosphere in Passage 2 is described as "reducing atmosphere thick with methane (CH4) and ammonia (NH3)," (lines 93-94), the author would likely describe it as a "toxic swamp," another term for "noxious quagmire."

Choice A is incorrect because the author of Passage 1 suggests that a reducing atmosphere might not provide the elements necessary for the evolution of life, as a more recent theory shows that there was probably oxygen when life emerged

Choice B is incorrect because the author of Passage 1 does not discuss either primary or secondary atmospheres, just ones that are either reducing (lacking oxygen) or oxidizing (full of oxygen).

Choice D is incorrect because an "assumption" is something that is accepted as true without proof, but a "conclusion" is accepted as true with proof. Since the description of the atmosphere in Passage 2 is based on specific research, the author of Passage 1 would call it a conclusion based on experimentation.

42. **Choice C is the best answer** because Oparin and Haldane both suggested life on Earth could begin with a reducing atmosphere, but couldn't prove that Earth actually had one billions of years ago when life began to emerge. In consequence, they would be interested in Fegler and Shaefer's results confirming that Earth really did have a reducing atmosphere, because it would support their theory.

Choice A is incorrect because Fegler and Shaefer's findings support Oparin and Haldane's theory. The latter would be unlikely to feel "dismayed" or "upset" that the findings disprove a theory that contradicted theirs.

Choice C is incorrect because Fegler and Shaefer did not "prove" or "confirm" that life evolved in anaerobic conditions. Their experiments showed that the atmosphere probably did not have oxygen, but do not conclusively show that life originated under those conditions.

Choice D is incorrect because "indifference" refers to a lack of interest. Although Fegler and Shaefer's experiments were based on the chemical makeup of chondrites and Oparin and Haldane were interested in biology, the emergence of organic life from inorganic matter, the two areas overlap. In fact, Passage 1 points out that the field of prebiotic chemistry has arisen to encompass both. The field did not exist when Oparin and Haldane were active, but they would be very interested in following developments in the field.

43. **Choice B is the best answer** because the author begins by suggesting that, against our instincts, reducing congestion isn't solved by building more roads ("the answer to congestion could be reducing capacity"), then suggests imposing charges ("the advantage of these [toll roads] is that they can mitigate demand"), introduces an example of where removing a road reduced congestion, but counters this by saying that congestion will increase because "Americans are simply just too attached to their cars." He concludes, "Pricing our way out of congestion may be the answer after all." This indicates that, although a complex subject and with caveats about indirect tax, the only possible solution to road congestion in America is increasing the cost of using roads so that people use them less often: a "financial means."

    Choice A is incorrect because, although the passage indicates that congestion increases as more roads are built, it does not suggest that road congestion in America is the result of building roads. It is the result of people driving their cars. As capacity increases, more people want to use their cars and so congestion increases, due to "induced demand," but the fundamental problem is "Americans are simply just too attached to their cars."

    Choice C is incorrect because the passage actually implies the opposite. This is clear in (lines 82-84): schemes to reduce traffic through freeway removal "only work, however, in dense urban environments, with good public transport networks, and facilities for pedestrians and cyclists. What about elsewhere?" Clearly, traffic congestion is not just an issue in dense urban environments with public transport systems.

    Choice D is incorrect because, although the author points out than an underlying cause of increased vehicle miles travelled is the fact that Americans love their cars, he does not suggest that the issue is insoluble. He acknowledges that measures like uncapped tolls may be effective.

44. **Choice A is the best answer** because "traditionally" describes the answer that city planners turn to. The answer is "build more roads" (line 3), which is the most intuitive and common response. Choice A means "done in the past" so shows that the solution of building more roads is the usual response to the problem in the past.

    Choice B is incorrect because it refers to something that is real. However, "real" does not fit the context of an answer that does not work well in solving the problem.

    Choice C is incorrect because it refers to something that is correct, and carries a moral judgement that the decision is good. Therefore, it doesn't describe an answer that is not effective.

    Choice D is incorrect because it refers to doing something in a cautious and not extravagant way. However, building more roads is more extravagant than solving the problem without spending tons of money on construction.

45. **Choice B is the best answer** because the passage says that "induced demand" is a phenomenon in which more of a product leads to more demand for it. In the context, the phenomenon manifests as "if more roads are provided, more people are encouraged to drive" (lines 19-20). However, the passage says that the traditional method of addressing the problem of congestion is to build more roads (lines 1-7, "For anyone…in Houston"). The traditional method, therefore, creates induced demand rather than fixing the problem in other ways.

    Choice A is incorrect because according to the theory of induced demand, if more roads are built, then there will be more congestion. Therefore, the theory supports rather than contradicts the belief that congestion is a result of more roads.

    Choice C is incorrect because the passage actually says that the reverse is true. "The phenomenon [of induced demand] has largely been ignored when it comes to transport infrastructure planning" (lines 34-35) .

    Choice D is incorrect because the passage actually says that the reverse is true. In the fourth paragraph, the author refers to the I-405 where uncapped pricing has resulted in no congestion "unlike on the I-5, where the fee on toll lanes is capped, making congestion a daily occurrence" (lines 45-47). This means that "mitigation" or "reduction" of induced demand relies on uncapped tolls, not capped ones.

46. **Choice C is the best answer** because the answer to the previous question is that induced demand is a phenomenon that is rarely taken into account when road systems are being planned. Choice C clearly paraphrases that claim by saying that the "phenomenon" of induced demand has been "ignored" or "not taken into account."

    Choice A is incorrect because it says that it is counterintuitive to reduce congestion by reducing numbers of roads, but does not support the idea that planners largely ignored induced demand.

    Choice B is incorrect because it explains the result of induced demand but does not provide any evidence about whether the concept is used when planning roads.

    Choice D is incorrect because it includes data from the Department of Transport about capped and uncapped toll roads, but does not refer to building more roads or whether induced demand was taken into account when planning roads.

47. **Choice D is the best answer** because in the fifth paragraph the author says that the "burden" or "heaviest load" of the policy would fall unfairly on low-income families, since they typically live further away from their jobs. He concludes, "the burden of paying for roads like a utility would fall most heavily on those least able to afford it" (lines 67-69). "Disapproval" refers to an unfavorable opinion, so this attitude fits in the context of saying he feels the policy is unfair.

    Choice A is incorrect because "dismay" refers to shock and horror. The author is not horrified by the notion of treating roads like other utilities; he just thinks it is unfair for the poorest members of society. They already have lower wages and have further to travel, so making them pay even more to travel to work is unfair.

    Choice B is incorrect because he is certainly not "delighted" or "extremely happy" because of the prospect. Although a financial solution may be viable, he does not want to unfairly make one group of people pay the cost.

    Choice C is incorrect because "disbelief" refers to "incredulity" or an unwillingness to believe in something. The author acknowledges that "such measures would undoubtedly reduce demand" (line 64), so he appears to accept the policy as viable or possible.

48. **Choice A is the best answer** because, while the author says that the example of the Embarcadero Freeway is not an isolated case, he acknowledges that such schemes only work "in dense urban environments, with good public transport networks, and facilities for pedestrians and cyclists" (lines 82-84). The rhetorical question "What about elsewhere?" (line 84) implies that in places that do not have such infrastructure, such systems simply would not work.

    Choice B is incorrect because this is not supported by the passage. While it does say that "the decisions of hundreds of different individuals in dozens of different agencies all play a part," (lines 28-30) it also mentions studies on toll road (line 40)s.

    Choice C is incorrect because this is a misinterpretation of the text, which says that there are many factors involved in studying induced demand, not that there are too many external factors involved in road congestion reduction schemes.

    Choice D is incorrect because the passage does discuss who pays for road reduction schemes. It is implied that the government makes the decision, not "capital markets" or "the people who buy and sell things."

49. **Choice C is the best answer** because the answer to the previous question is that road reduction schemes to reduce traffic have limited use because they will only work in certain places with appropriate infrastructure. Choice C paraphrases this conclusion by giving examples of infrastructure, such as good public transport networks, and facilities for pedestrians and cyclists, that are required for road reduction to work.

    Choice A is incorrect because it discusses variables when studying induced demand, but does not show that road reduction will or will not work in any given place. Therefore, it doesn't support the claim that road reduction only is effective in places with specific infrastructure.

    Choice B is incorrect because it refers to how utilities are funded using a payment strategy that is different than the strategy of road reduction.

    Choice D is incorrect because it only refers to the fact that Americans are very attached to their cars; it does not say that certain infrastructure is required for road reduction to be successful at reducing congestion.

50. **Choice A is the best answer** because "sought-after" refers to the properties on either side of the refurbished

road. The paragraph says that after the new boulevard was opened, not only did traffic get better, but "the neighborhoods through which it flowed became more prosperous" (lines 78-79). Since Choice A means "greatly wanted," it fits the context of describing properties that commanded higher prices and made the area more prosperous.

Choice B is incorrect because it refers to paying special attention to something, but does not specify why. In fact, the phrase is often used in negative situations. Therefore, Choice B does not indicate that the houses are wanted by many buyers.

Choice C is incorrect because although the houses on either side of the new road may have been more "highly esteemed or cherished," that is an opinion, rather than the fact of people seeking them out or their being in demand.

Choice D is incorrect because it refers to being in fashion or up to the minute. While the houses may have been in fashion, Choice D does not indicate that people actually wanted to purchase them.

51. **Choice D is the best answer** because the passage is about how to control traffic congestion. The premise is based on the assumption that congestion is a problem, and the chart shows various routes into one urban area (Los Angeles) and indicates that at peak times people's commuting time rises dramatically. As a result, the author would very likely see the chart as representative of the impact of congestion in urban areas and a good example of the issue the passage is dealing with.

Choice A is incorrect because, while he likely would agree that the chart is accurate, he is unlikely to feel it lacks enough detail to be informative. The chart shows various commuter routes of different lengths into Los Angeles (a good example of an urban area), together with how the journey for a commuter changes depending on whether he or she drives in normal traffic or at peak times, and the average speed taken across all journeys on those routes. The chart contains a lot of details, so he would probably *not* find it uninformative.

Choice B is incorrect because the central argument in the passage is that the most effective way to reduce congestion may be to curb driving using financial measures. Since the chart makes no reference to costs, it does not directly support this argument.

Choice C is incorrect because the only authority cited in the passage is Robert Poole, the author of *Rethinking America's Highways,* and his perspective is that roads should be treated like other utilities in that people should pay for what they use. This chart does not refer to costs or ways to limit congestion, so it is not "representative" or "typical" of his argument.

52. **Choice C is the best answer** because while the trend in terms of miles per hour would be downward overall if the lines were evened out from left to right, there are variations in a number of the routes. For example, in route 4 and route 7 the speed increases in relation to the routes of longer distance from the city

Choice A is incorrect because for the difference between peak flow journey time and freeflow journey time to be directly proportional to length of journey, the columns for routes 7 and 8 should be identical. They are both 13 miles long, and yet it takes much longer at peak times to travel route 8, so it is untrue to say that the longer the journey the greater the difference. In fact, the shortest journey (Route 10) takes three times as long at peak times, while the longest journey (Route 1) only takes less than twice as long.

Choice B is incorrect because while looking at the first and last columns in isolation would lead to this conclusion (the difference between freeflow and peak travel times is greater in column 10 than in column 1), for the *whole* chart this is not true. If it were, there would be no anomalies like it taking roughly the same amount of time during peak travel times for Route 5 as Route 8, despite it being two miles longer.

Choice D is incorrect because while the passage does introduce Los Angeles as an example of *induced demand,* saying that it doubled commuter time on some routes, the chart does not clearly show induced demand because it does not show commuter time before and after the implementation of the Los Angeles road improvement scheme.

1. **Choice B is the best answer** since it introduces what autoethnography is generally. Therefore, by keeping the underlined section we have an effective introductory sentence to frame the following paragraph.
   Choice A is incorrect because there is nothing about the "impact" of the method of autoethnography that is included in this statement. We are simply informed here about what autoethnography is.
   Choice C is incorrect because it clearly contradicts the content of the sentence, which explicitly states that autoethnography falls between anthropology and literary studies.
   Choice D is incorrect. As established above, the sentence does function as a good introduction and deleting it would be detrimental to the flow of the paragraph. If deleted, the reader woud immediately start with "some social science researchers [...]", without having had the opportunity to understand what autoethnography is.

2. **Choice A is the best answer.** The first sentence of a new paragraph – called the topic sentence – should be used to indicate what the following text is about. Since this paragraph is about the questions that are raised about autoethnography, it is appropriate to introduce the paragraph by saying that it is a "contested field."
   Choice B is incorrect. There is nothing in this paragraph to suggest that autoethnography is "revolutionary" in any way. This statement is both extreme and does not accurately reflect the content of the text that follows.
   Choice C is inaccurate because this answer choice contradicts the following material, which explicitly speaks about the concerns surrounding autoethnography.
   Choice D is incorrect. This statement defines autoethnography rather than framing the content of the second paragraph of the essay.

3. **Choice B is the best answer** since this choice makes the same point, while using fewer dependent clauses and extra phrases like "greater or lesser extent." In so doing, this statement is more direct and easier to understand for the reader.
   Choice A, while not incorrect in meaning, is a very long sentence that is grammatically hard to follow. When presented with a choice that is clearer and more concise (like Choice B), it is always the better answer.
   Choice C is incorrect because it is incomplete and a fragment. If the current statement were to be replaced with this choice, there would be no mention of the "questions" that are raised because of the "introspective and subjective" qualities to autoethnography.
   Choice D is incorrect because it is irrelevant in relation to both the context of this paragraph (in specific), and the passage (in general).

4. **Choice B is correct** because the sentence tells us how autoethnography goes past "the writing of selves." The verb "goes" is necessary here, to communicate the idea that this particular method extends beyond specific ideas.
   Choice A is incorrect because the use of "has" in this context makes the sentence grammatically inaccurate and meaningless.
   Choice C is incorrect because of the use of the present continuous tense (is going) when the simple present (goes) is the better choice.
   Choice D is incorrect because the use of the past tense (was) implies that something has changed in the present. From the following sentences, we know that this is not the case, i.e. that autoethnography is being spoken about in the present tense (note the use of "is" after "contemporary performance").

5. **Choice C is the best answer** because we are told in this line how autoethnography is different from autobiography, while also containing some elements that are similar to autobiography. "While" is the only option that captures this particular relationship of something being similar, yet not being the same.
   Choice A is incorrect because "however" only implies difference whereas we are also told about a similarity in this context.
   Choice B is incorrect because "each time" in the context of this sentence would be completely irrelevant and make the sentence meaningless.
   Choice D is incorrect because "whenever" refers to a quality of time – that something happens when something else occurs -- rather than a condition of similarity and difference.

6. **Choice A is the best answer** No change is needed (Choice A) since "it goes beyond the writing of selves" is the independent clause that is qualified by the preceding dependent clause. A comma is appropriate in this particular sentence construction.

Choices B and D are incorrect for the same reason. Colons (:) and hyphens (-) are used to introduce lists and/or additional ideas to a sentence. They are not necessary in a sentence like the one here, where there is no list and/or an added idea that has been included.

Choice C is incorrect because semicolons (;) are only needed when there are two independent clauses – each with their own subject, verb, and object – that need to be separated. Here, the use of the term "while" makes the first part of the sentence a dependent clause, making the semicolon inaccurate.

7. **Choice B is the best answer** because it is the only one that shows a subject-verb agreement between "social and cultural spaces" (plural) and "have" (plural).

   Choice A is incorrect because there is a disagreement between the subject, which is plural, and the verb "has," which is in the singular form.

   Choices C & D are incorrect because of the verb tense inconsistency. The earlier part of the sentence uses the present tense and, therefore, to use the future tense (will have) or the present continuous tense (are having) would cause a grammatical inconsistency.

8. **Choice D is the best answer.** Since this paragraph is in no way related to the content of the previous paragraph, there is no need for the use of a connector word like "in fact," "but," or "however" (the other three answer choices).

   A connector word at the beginning of a new paragraph is only needed if the following content links directly to what came before it. Here, the previous paragraph has to do with the links and differences between autobiography and autoethnography while the current paragraph has to do with different approaches in autoethnography.

9. **Choice A is the best answer** since both the use of the comma (,) and the use of the term "where" to clarify the meaning of evocative and analytical autoethnography are grammatically accurate and contextually relevant.

   Choice B is incorrect because of the use of the word "and," which not does not help transition the reader from the terms (evocative and analytical) to their definitions.

   Choice C is incorrect. The use of the connector "indeed" does not help frame the brief descriptions that follow the previous mention of the terms evocative and analytical.

   Choice D is incorrect. "Unfortunately" implies a following condition that is less than ideal while here, we are simply presented with statements of definition/clarification that have nothing to do with how ideal/not ideal something is.

10. **Choice B is the best answer** because it effectively defines analytical autoethnography, just as evocative autoethnography has been defined before it.

    Choice A is inaccurate because it is misleading in its ambiguity. We are told in the earlier part of the paragraph that the differences being spoken about are between the "personal" and the "social and cultural world." There is no reason given to consider these two ideas as being in opposition to each other.

    Choice C is incorrect because it repeats the use of "personal stories" and associates it inaccurately with analytical autoethnography, when "personal stories" are already associated with evocative autoethnography.

    Choice D is incorrect. Deleting the underlined section without replacing it with something else would render the sentence incomplete and meaningless.

11. **Choice C is the best answer** since all that is needed from the verb here is the simple present conjugation ("This is a methodological decision").

    Choice A is incorrect because the use of "being" makes the sentence grammatically inaccurate.

    Choice B is inaccurate because it uses the past tense, rather than the present tense that has been used in the surrounding text. This would cause a verb-tense inconsistency.

    Choice D is inaccurate because it uses the future tense, rather than the present tense that has been used in the surrounding text. This would cause a verb-tense inconsistency.

12. **Choice B is the best answer** because, later in the same sentence, we see the use of the hyphen (–). This is an immediate indicator that the definition of Partition as "the division of British India into the two separate states of India and Pakistan on August 14-15, 1947" would be best punctuated with hyphens on both sides of the

CONTINUE

phrase. If not, the use of any other punctuation mark in the underlined section, would render the sentence as grammatically incorrect.

Choice A is incorrect. Colons are used to introduce lists and/or to join sentences (like a semicolon). In this case, the use of the later hyphen makes the colon grammatically incorrect – there is no list being introduced, neither is what follows a complete sentence.

Choice C is inaccurate. While the comma would have been a possible option if the punctuation before "was the" was also a comma, the use of the hyphen in that latter instance makes the comma use in the underlined section inaccurate.

Choice D is inaccurate. There is no need to include "Partition" as its own sentence. While some authors might choose to use such a device as a stylistic tool, here, doing so would render what follows as an incomplete and grammatically incorrect sentence.

13. **Choice B is the best answer.** From a general introduction of Partition in the first paragraph, the second paragraph introduces the reader to the "Congress" – a term that has not yet been defined or explained. Adding the suggested sentence, therefore, helps the reader better understand the following information.

Choice A is inaccurate. Structurally, introducing what the Congress is after explaining what it does, would be ineffective – since the reader needs to understand what Congress is, before being able to contextualize its actions/interests.

Choice D is inaccurate. As information that is closely linked to the content of the paragraph, the information in the suggested lines cannot be termed irrelevant.

Choice C is incorrect because there is no information in the suggested sentence that helps clarify/address information that came before (prior) to this paragraph.

14. **Choice A is the best answer.** The underlined section enables the reader to understand who the majority population was and also give specific demographic information about how much of a majority the Hindus were. Choice B is incorrect for two reasons. First, the sentence is more ambiguous and does not allow the reader to understand what is meant by "majority." Second, the use of the conjugation "are," when the paragraph/sentence uses the past tense, also make this choice grammatically incorrect.

Choice C is inaccurate. Although deleting the underlined portion would not affect the grammatical accuracy of the sentence, it would remove relevant information that allows the reader to better understand the context that is being spoken of.

Choice D is inaccurate. This choice makes an assumption that has not been evidenced thus far in the text. So far, all we have been told is that there were concerns about the potential political dominance of the majority over the minorities – we have not been told about the attitude of the majority towards those minorities.

15. **Choice D is the best answer.** In order to determine the best conclusion to this paragraph, we need to also look at the subsequent paragraph and its content. We see that this paragraph mentions World War II, and the next paragraph begins by saying how "Britain took India into the war." Therefore, an effective conclusion to this paragraph would ideally include something to do with World War II.

Choice A is less accurate because it does not allow a connection/flow of ideas between paragraphs (4) and (5).

Choices B and C are inaccurate since they provide information that seems irrelevant in the context of the given text. They do not help the reader better understand anything in paragraph (4), neither do they help introduce the ideas included in paragraph (5).

16. **Choice D is the best answer.** Congress is described as opposing the singular event that is described before it – Britain taking India to war without consultation. Therefore, a singular preposition – like it – is far more accurate.

Choice A is incorrect. "Them" refers to people rather than events; it is also a pronoun that refers to a subject in the plural. Both these qualities make the answer choice incorrect.

Choice B is inaccurate. "It's" is a contraction of "it is" or "it has" – neither of which would be relevant nor grammatically accurate in the given context.

Choice C is inaccurate. "Its" is the possessive form of "it" and there is no need for a possessive use of the word in the underlined section.

17. **Choice A is the best answer.** The sentence is direct, concise, and clear as it is and does not seem to require any change.
Choice B is less suitable because, in comparison to Choice A, this choice is less direct. Note the extra use of words in the phrase "Because of their role in the mass movement against British rule" as compared to "For their role in it." Furthermore, the use of "the mass movement against British rule" is repetitive, since this phrase appears in the previous sentence.
Choice C is inaccurate because it is ambiguous and does not tell us who "those" refers to.
Choice D is inaccurate because deleting the underlined portion would eliminate relevant and useful information that tells us about consequences to those who opposed the British's actions.

18. **Choice B is the best answer.** Notice that the paragraph/passage are written, generally, in the simple past tense. To maintain verb-tense consistency, the verb "to give" should be conjugated in the simple past tense ("gave").
Choice A is incorrect. The current conjugation is in the simple present, rather than the simple past tense.
Choice C is inaccurate both for the use of the simple present tense "gives" and the inclusion of the term "that," which is unnecessary in the current sentence. In fact, the use of "that" would make the sentence incomplete and inaccurate.
Choice D is inaccurate. Although the simple past tense ("gave") is used here, this answer choice also includes an unnecessary "that."

19. **Choice B is the best answer** because by clarifying the term "separate states" and by telling the reader who the separate nations were for, clarity is definitely improved.
Choice A is incorrect. The subsequent paragraph has to do with historians' disagreements and, as such, the function of this sentence has nothing to do with being an effective transition.
Choice B is inaccurate. In order to understand how the Muslim League proposed the separate states' idea, we need to understand what conditions enabled the League to make such a call. Understanding the British's need for wartime allies, therefore, is needed before the underlined section.
Choice D is inaccurate. This choice does not eliminate relevant information. It provides it.

20. **Choice C is the best answer.** Notice the use of "this demand" in the first sentence of this paragraph. Clearly, this links to the demand for a separate state that is mentioned at the end of paragraph (5). Moving this paragraph anywhere else would alter the meaning of the text entirely since we would not be able to understand which demand is being spoken of and in relation to which issue.
Choices A, B, and D, therefore, are easy to eliminate. Because of its clear link to the content in paragraph (5), paragraph (6) cannot function anywhere else.

21. **Choice D is the best answer.** By telling us about what Partition "triggered," this sentence enables us to transition to the following ideas.
Choice A is incorrect. This sentence would help the flow of the paragraph rather than interrupt it.
Choice B is inaccurate. Effective paragraphs flow from more general ideas, to more specific ones. Given that the current sentences are more specific than the one which the author is considering adding, this general outline of Partition's negative consequences belongs before the lines that are currently in the paragraph.
Choice C is inaccurate. There is nothing about this text to make it irrelevant in relation to the surrounding text – they all speak about Partition.

22. **Choice C is the best answer.** The passage goes over both the causes and outcomes of Partition and tells us the many ways in which these factors interacted with each other.
Choice A is incorrect. This sentence is much too ambiguous to accurately capture the specific impact of British colonialism on India/Pakistan that has been described in this passage.
Choice B is less suitable because it only captures one of the main points of the passage (the outcomes) rather than also speaking about the causes/histories that led to those outcomes.
Choice D is inaccurate. This statement contradicts the tone and content of the passage, by suggesting that a complex event is "simple" to understand.

CONTINUE

23. **Choice D is the most suitable answer.** Since there is no other use of a conjugated verb in this sentence, in order to identify verb-tense consistency, look to the use of the conjugated verb in the following paragraph. We immediately see the use of "is" in the first line of the second paragraph: "The first moment of innovation in documentary performance is marked by the work." This is an immediate indicator that the present tense needs to be used throughout the passage.
    Choice A is incorrect because it uses the singular, simple past tense, whereas – as established above – the singular, simple present tense is needed to maintain consistency with the next paragraphs.
    Choice B is inaccurate. This choice uses the plural, simple past tense, whereas – as established above – the singular, simple present tense is needed to maintain consistency with the next paragraphs.
    Choice C is incorrect. "Are," while in the simple present, is the plural conjugation of the verb "to be." Here, the subject is singular ("American documentary theatre) and since there needs to be subject-verb agreement, "are" would be grammatically incorrect.

24. **Choice C is the best answer.** The first line of the following paragraph mentions the idea of a "moment of innovation in documentary performance." As such, the use of this phrase in the suggested sentence would enable an effective transition between the first and second paragraphs.
    Choice A is incorrect. Since there is no information in the prior statements to refer to "moments of innovation," this answer choice is irrelevant.
    Choice B is inaccurate because the current introductory sentence to the paragraph enables the reader to understand what documentary performance is, before then talking about how this genre might be categorized. To talk about the categorization before framing the concept for the readers, therefore, would negatively impact the flow of the paragraph.
    Choice D is incorrect. As information that specifically relates to the topic of the passage, this information cannot be deemed irrelevant.

25. **Choice B is the best answer,** It improves the clarity, tone, and language of the underlined sentence. by being more concise and direct than the current text.
    Choice A is incorrect. Although this information is used to expand on the idea of "living newspapers," it would be an overstatement to say it supports the entire passage. The underlined section helps support one term and not the entire text.
    Choice C is incorrect because we have no reason to think that the presented information might be inaccurate or unsupported.
    Choice D is unsuitable. To label information as "redundant" implies that it has been mentioned before and, as such, is repeating something that has already been said. Since the underlined section does not repeat any previously mentioned information, it would not be correct to call it redundant.

26. **Choice A is the most suitable answer** since "decidedly" – by referring to an obvious adherence in relation to particular aesthetic forms – simply describes the form of the early American documentary plays.
    Choice B is incorrect because "uniformly" alters the meaning of the sentence and suggests that all the different plays were the same in their way of relating to particular aesthetic traditions – information that would require making an assumption that cannot be evidenced by the text.
    Choices C & D are inaccurate. The terms "finally" and "ultimately" would be meaningless in the current contest and using them would make the sentence inaccurate.

27. **Choice D is the best answer** since there is no need for a punctuation mark in this part of the sentence. The ideas in the currently different sentences are clearly linked to each other, without having an independent clause/dependent clause relationship that would necessitate a punctuation mark.
    Choice A is incorrect. The current sentence structure is ineffective since there is no need to break the presented ideas into two different sentences. Clearly "where" refers to the "plays that were sometimes built with the input of communities."
    Choices B & C are incorrect. Semicolons are needed to separate two independent clauses; hyphens are used particularly in long sentences that need extra clarification. Since neither of these is the case here, these particular punctuation marks are not necessary.

CONTINUE

28. **Choice B is the best answer.** Sentence (1) speaks about plays that are built with the input of communities (i.e., the content); the underlined sentence speaks about the tension between content and form; sentence (2) talks about the techniques used to build the piece and the tension between the form and the stories it contains. Therefore, since the underlined sentence begins by speaking to "this tension" – and sentence (2) ends by referring to a particular tension – it makes more logical sense to have the underlined section follow sentence (2). All other answer choices would disrupt the flow of the passage and would not allow the reader to understand what "this" refers to in "this tension."

29. **Choice A is the best answer.** By reiterating information about the 1930s before going on to information about the 1960s, the underlined section helps contextualize/introduce what follows for the reader.
    Choice B is incorrect because it would be an overstatement to call what has been mentioned in this sentence as a "extensive" information about the 1930s.
    Choice C is inaccurate. Since the sentence explicitly refers to what happened in the 1930s, it would be contradictory to state that the highlighted text ignores what happened in the 1930s. That said, this sentence also specifically refers to documentary performance in 1930s' America and this answer choice ambiguously refers to "what happened" in that time period.
    Choice D is incorrect because this information, by being centered around the trends of American documentary performance, is clearly relevant to the theme of the passage and paragraph.

30. **Choice B is the best answer.** It is suitable because the following paragraph begins by mentioning "these subjects"; subjects that have not been mentioned so far in the previous passage. The suggested sentence, by providing examples of "new theatre collectives" and the themes they explored, therefore, help lead the reader into "these" subjects that are mentioned in the following passage.
    Choice A is incorrect. While this underlined information does help give examples that address the "new theatre collectives" mentioned in the current last sentence of the passage, it is not necessary to "clarify" preceding information. Rather, it adds to it.
    Choice C is incorrect. If the names of theatre companies and the themes they address were mentioned at the beginning of the paragraph, the flow of logic in the text would be negatively impacted.
    Choice D is incorrect because this information is clearly extremely relevant in relation to the content being spoken about in the paragraph and the passage.

31. **Choice C is the best answer.** From the following sentence we know that verb-tense consistency requires the use of the past tense (see the use of "were" in describing the "emerging genres of naturalism and realism"). Since plural "subjects" are referred to in the highlighted sentence, using the plural, simple past conjugation of "to be" (i.e., "were") is the best possible answer.
    Choice A is incorrect because it uses the simple present rather than the simple past tense – causing a verb-tense inconsistency within the paragraph.
    Choices B & D are unsuitable for the same reason – the use of "being" following the use of the conjugated verb in this sentence is grammatically incorrect. Choice B additionally uses the present tense.

32. **Choice A is the best answer.** The use of the comma in this sentence effectively follows the introductory, dependent clause ("but in the 1960s and 70s") while also complementing the use of the comma after "fervor" – creating a delineating of the clause "as traditional definitions of home, family, nation, and creation were contested with new fervor."
    Choice B is incorrect. Without an added punctuation after the introductory phrase, the sentence becomes hard to follow.
    Choice C is incorrect. Semicolons are used to separate independent clauses, each with their own subject, verb, and object – since this is not the case here, a semicolon would be grammatically inaccurate.
    Choice D is incorrect. For the hyphen to be used before "as," there should have been a complementary hyphen after the word "fervor." Since that is not the case, this choice would be inaccurate.

33. **Choice B is the best answer** since it specifically states whose physical capacities are being referred to in the text.
    Choices A, C, and D are extremely ambiguous and do not specify whose physical capacities are being referred to in the highlighted section. This ambiguity would negatively affect the clarity, tone, and voice of the text.

34. **Choice B is the best answer.** The sentence here describes what rainwater harvesting is, i.e., the action that is involved in executing it. Here, since the underlined word is preceded by a verb in the simple present tense ("is), the gerund (a verb ending with "ing") would be the only grammatically accurate choice.

    Choices A, C, and D, by using the noun ("collection"), simple past ("collected"), and simple present ("collect"), render the sentence grammatically incorrect.

35. **Choice D is the best answer.** We see that the sentence retains its meaning best when there is no punctuation mark between "as" and "collecting" – "as collecting rain in a [...]" is the same phrase and adding a punctuation mark disrupts the flow of the sentence and makes it less understandable.

    Choices A, B, and C are incorrect since adding any punctuation mark between "as" and "collective" disrupts the flow of logic in the sentence. As a result, they can all be immediately eliminated as possible answer choices.

36. **Choice A is the best answer.** It is most viable since maintaining the underlined section as it is allows separate ideas to be kept in different sentences while also making the flow of logic easy to understand.

    Choice B is less suitable. While the use of "and" would not be grammatically incorrect, it does lead to the creation of a longer sentence than is needed. Strong writing generally opts for strategies that are more concise and direct – like using shorter sentences whenever possible.

    Choices C and D are incorrect since words like "however" and "although" imply a relationship of contrast between ideas. Here, there is no contrast that is included. Instead, we are simply provided with an idea (about rainwater harvesting not being "just for the farm anymore) that complements/adds to the idea that came before it (rainwater harvesting being viable for households and businesses).

37. **Choice C is the best answer.** "They" refers to the variety of names (plural), which is the subject of the previous sentence. Furthermore, the use of "range" in the singular, demonstrates verb tense consistency that is absent in two of the other answer choices.

    Choices A and D can immediately be eliminated because "they" and "the names" use plural forms, which would be grammatically incorrect when used with the verb "ranges."

    Choice B is inaccurate because "their" is a possessive pronoun, which would be grammatically incorrect in the given context.

38. **Choice B is the most suitable answer.** This paragraph explicitly deals with the different names by which rainwater harvesting is known and since the suggested inclusion offers additional terms, it can be said that it provides information that helps clarify/evidence prior information.

    Choice A is incorrect since there is no "new information" that these alternative terms to rainwater harvesting are used to "transition" to.

    Choice C is incorrect. The sentence would be redundant only if the previous sentence also mentioned the same terms that are put forward in the suggested inclusion. Since this is not the case, and this proposed sentence includes names/terms for rainwater harvesting that have not been mentioned before, it cannot be deemed redundant.

    Choice D is incorrect. In sticking to the theme of the passage, there is nothing irrelevant about the information that has been included in the proposed sentence.

39. **Choice B is the best answer.** "This" in the underlined section refers to the process of capturing "the free water falling on your roof and direct[ing] it to a rainwater storage tank." Since the following text describes the consequences of carrying out this process (i.e., that "you can take control of your water supply [...]"), "by doing this" is the best answer. This choice helps connect cause and effect, which is the relationship between the two sentences.

    Choice A is meaningless in this context since it does not help us understand that the following effect is a result of implementing/doing the cause that has been described in the previous sentence.

    Choices C and D use phrases that imply a contradiction of some kind, i.e., where something happens "despite"/ "regardless of" something else being done. Since there is no contradictory relationship that is being described here, these choices would be unsuitable.

40. **Choice C is the best answer.** Notice that the content following the punctuation mark ("Rainwater harvesting systems") talks about a different subject than the preceding one (where the subject is what happens by capturing "free water falling on your roof") – necessitating a period that breaks the ideas up into two different sentences. Choices A, B, and D - by using punctuations that suggest a direction relationship in content between the two sentences - are grammatically incorrect. They would make the sentence difficult to read by disrupting the flow of logic in the statements.

41. **Choice D is the best answer.** Looking at the verb that follows the underlined one, we see the use of the present continuous tense ("need to start looking"). This tells us that the underlined section should also use the same form in order to maintain verb-tense consistency. "Are tapping out," therefore, is the only possible answer. Choice A's use of the simple past, Choice B's use of the simple present, and Choice C's suggestion of deletion would all create grammatical inaccuracies within the highlighted sentence.

42. **Choice A is the best answer.** The use of this introductory, transition phrase helps highlight what the reader can understand as being the implications of the graph (i.e., what can be seen in the graph).
    Choices B & D are incorrect since "however" and "despite" refer to contradictions/contrasts that are not implied in the text.
    Choice C is unsuitable. "Through this" is ambiguous and does not convey to the reader that the "this" being referred to is the information showcased in the graph.

43. **Choice C is the only possible answer.**
    - The grey dotted line (for toilets) shows an increase of 4.8
    - The grey line (for dishwasher) shows an increase of 8
    - The black line (for clothes washers) shows an increase of 30
    Therefore, the only statement that accurately represents the data is that "clothes washers show the steepest increase in the progression of water conservation standards between 1960 and 2005."

44. **Choice B is the best possible answer.** The best way to reach this answer is through a process of elimination. Choice B is the best possible answer.
    Choice A is incorrect there is no concept after the highlighted sentence. Therefore, there is no way for this text to function as a transition "between" ideas.
    Choice C is incorrect. There is no interruption to the flow of the text through the inclusion of this sentence at the end of the paragraph.
    Choice D is incorrect. In being focused on rainwater collection, this information is clearly related to the main focus of the passage.

1. **Easy | Heart of Algebra**

   Choice C is correct. When $x = 3$, one can substitute 3 for x in the equation, which becomes $3(3) + 3 = \dfrac{5y}{2}$. By simplifying the left side of the equation by multiplication and then addition, the equation becomes $9 + 3 = \dfrac{5y}{2}$ and subsequently $12 = \dfrac{5y}{2}$. Multiplying both sides by 2 gives $24 = 5y$ and then dividing by 5 gives $y = \dfrac{24}{5}$. Choices A, B, and D are incorrect because the result of multiplying those values of y by 5 and dividing by 2 does not equal 12, which is the correct result of 3 substituted for x on the left side of the equation.

2. **Difficult | Additional Topics in Math**

   Choice A is correct. In order to rewrite $\dfrac{5 + 3i}{1 + i}$ in the form $x + yi$, one must multiply the numerator and denominator of the original expression by the conjugate of the denominator. The conjugate has the same constants but the opposite sign, i.e., $1 - i$. This simplifies to $\left(\dfrac{5 + 3i}{1 + i}\right)\left(\dfrac{1 - i}{1 - i}\right) = \dfrac{5 - 5i + 3i - 3i^2}{1 - i + i - i^2}$. And because $i^2 = -1$, the equation can be rewritten as $\dfrac{5 - 5i + 3i + 3}{1 - (-1)} = \dfrac{8 - 2i}{2} = 4 - i$. So if $x = 4$ $y = -1$, the sum of x and y is $4 - 1 = 3$ Choices B, C, and D are incorrect because they are the result of errors in multiplying conjugates and simplifying equations.

3. **Medium | Heart of Algebra**

   Choice B is correct. In order to create an expression that represents the data from Sally's snack bar, the variables f and b, for fries and burgers respectively, must be matched and multiplied with their correct prices and constants. The price for fries (f) is matched with the constant 3.50 and the price for a burger (b) is matched with the constant 5, so that the total profit is the sum of each product of the number of items sold multiplied by the unit price. Therefore, the expression must be $5b + 3.50f$. Choices A, C, and D are incorrect because they match the wrong item with the wrong price or incorrectly add or multiply the variables.

4. **Easy | Heart of Algebra**

   Choice A is correct. In the linear equation, $C = 29.99s + 14.99$. Choice B is incorrect because the initial fee is $14.99, and not subject to the number of tickets purchased. Choice C is incorrect because, as the question states, C is the total amount Daniel will make per transaction. Similarly, Choice D is incorrect because, as the question states, s is the number of tickets purchased.

5. **Medium | Passport to Advanced Math**

   Choice D is correct. First, the -2 must be distributed to the second polynomial, which becomes $-2(x^2 + x - 1) = (-2x^2 - 2x + 2)$. The full expression is then $5x^2 + 4x - 15 - 2x^2 - 2x + 2$, and when like terms are simplified it is $(5x^2 - 2x^2) + (4x - 2x) + (-15 + 2) = 3x^2 + 2x - 13$, which is Choice D. Choice B incorrectly distributes the negative sign into the second polynomial, which results in incorrect simplification of like terms. Choices A and D represent errors in simplification and addition.

6. **Easy | Heart of Algebra**

   Choice B is correct. If Martha tutors three individual students for one hour each at the rate of $20 an hour, she will make $3 \times \$20 = \$60$. Alternatively, if Martha tutors three pairs of students for one hour each at the rate of $25 an hour, she will make $3 \times \$25 = \$75$. The difference in the two profits can be found by subtracting $75 - $60 = $15, which is Choice B. Choices A, C, and D represent errors in multiplication of the rates and hours and errors in subtracting to identify the difference between two values.

7. **Medium | Passport to Advanced Math**

   Choice A is correct. In order to rearrange the equation to equal R, begin by multiplying the denominator of the right side of the equation to the left in order to eliminate the fraction, so that $g(R^2) = GM$. Then in order to isolate R, divide g to the right side of the equation $R^2 = \dfrac{GM}{g}$ and then square root both sides, so $R = \sqrt{\dfrac{GM}{g}}$. Choices B, C, and D are incorrect and the result of incorrectly multiplying or dividing variables.

8. **Easy | Heart of Algebra**

   Choice C is correct. If $\dfrac{x+4}{3} = 2$ then $x + 4 = 6$ and $x = 2$. By substituting $x = 2$ in the expression $\dfrac{x+2}{(x-1)^2}$, the expression becomes $\dfrac{2+2}{(2-1)^2} = \dfrac{4}{(1)^2} = 4$. Choice A, B, and D are incorrect because they result in errors in computing the value of x in the first equation and/or the second equation.

9. **Easy | Heart of Algebra**

   Choice B is correct. To eliminate one variable, first multiply the bottom equation by 2 so that the coefficients of y have opposite signs, $-x + 2y = -8$ and $8x - 2y = 50$. By adding both equations together, x is the only variable remaining such that $7x = 42$ so $x = 6$ By plugging $x = 6$ back into one of the original equations, for example the first, $-(6) + 2y = -8$ then $2y = -2$, so that $y = -1$ The solution to the system (x, y) is then $(6, -1)$ Choices A and C are incorrect because they flip the values for x and y, and C also features the incorrect signs of the correct answer. Choice D is incorrect because when $(6, 6)$ is substituted for (x, y) in either equation, it does not equal either -8 or 25.

10. **Medium | Passport to Advanced Math**

    Choice D is correct. In order to find the value of x that makes $f(x) - g(x) = 0$, one has to start by determining what value of x makes $f(x)$ equal to $g(x)$. Start by setting both equations equal to one another $(x - 4)(x + 2) = 4x - 17$ and then expand into a polynomial $x^2 - 2x - 8 = 4x - 17$ then $x^2 - 6x + 9 = 0$ and then factor $(x - 3)^2 = 0$ so $x = 3$ Choices A, B, and C are incorrect because when substituted for x in $f(x)$ and $g(x)$ the equation are not equal.

11. **Medium | Heart of Algebra**

    Choice A is correct. In order to determine which expression represents the situation, add the prices of Irene and Tabitha's lunches $c + (c + 2) = 2c + 2$, which is the total amount they paid for lunch. If they split the bill, the expression becomes $\dfrac{(2c+2)}{2}$, which simplifies to $(c + 1)$. If they each pay a 20% tip then the final expression becomes $2(c +1) + (c + 1) = 1.2(c + 1)$. Choices C and D are incorrect because they multiply the final total by 20% and not 20% in addition to the original total before tip, which then represents the amount paid in tip, not the total. Choice B is incorrect and most likely results in a fraction simplification error.

12. **Medium | Passport to Advanced Math**

    Choice A is correct. To determine the line that is perpendicular to the function, one must first find the slope of the original line. Using the slope formula, $\dfrac{-2-1}{-4-2} = \dfrac{-3}{-6} = \dfrac{1}{2}$. To find the slope of the perpendicular line, one must find the opposite reciprocal of the original slope, which is -2. Choices B, C, and D are incorrect because they feature errors in finding opposite reciprocals of the original slope.

13. **Difficult | Passport to Advanced Math**

Choice D is correct. First, a -1 in the exponent indicates that the right side of the equation can be rewritten as a fraction $\frac{1}{(x+3)} = \frac{1}{x^2 - x - 12}$. Then cross multiply to eliminate the fractions $(x + 3) = x^2 - x - 12$ and then factor the right side of the equation to $(x + 3) = (x - 4)(x + 3)$, which then simplifies to $1 = (x - 4)$ and then to $x = 5$ Choices A, B, and C are incorrect and could be the result of orders of operations errors when simplifying complex fractions.

14. **Difficult | Passport to Advanced Math**

Choice A is correct. In order to divide exponents, they first must have the same base, so that $27^a = 3^{3a}$ And to divide the bases of the exponents means also subtracting the exponents, such that $\frac{3^{3a}}{3^a} = 3^{2a}$ If $a = \frac{1}{2}$, then $3^{2\left(\frac{1}{2}\right)} = 3^1 = 3$. Choices B and C are incorrect and most likely result from mistakes in manipulating expressions with exponents. Choice D is most likely the result of an error in substituting the fraction into the exponent expression.

15. **Medium | Passport to Advanced Math**

Choice A is correct. To determine the values of a, b, c start by multiplying the right side of the equation into a polynomial that matches the format of the left side of the equation, $ax^2 + bx + c = (2x^2 - 9x - 5) - 13$. Simplify the right side of the equation by joining like terms, $ax^2 + bx - 18 = 2x^2 - 9x - 18$. Therefore $a = 2$ $b = -9$, and $b = -9$. Therefore, $a + b + c = 2 - 9 - 18 = -25$ Choices B, C, D are incorrect and most likely result from errors in multiplying factors and simplifying like terms.

16. **Medium | Passport to Advanced Math**

The correct answer is 0. First, one must determine the factors of the equation to find the solutions. The equation $b^2 - \frac{1}{4} = 0$, features one perfect square being subtracted from another, which indicates the equation can be factored into conjugates, so that $\left(b + \frac{1}{2}\right)\left(b - \frac{1}{2}\right) = 0$. The two values of $b = \frac{1}{2}, -\frac{1}{2}$, which when added together, equal 0. Another possible solution would be to add $\frac{1}{4}$ to the right side of the equation and then square root both sides, so that $b^2 = \frac{1}{4}$ and $\sqrt{b^2} = \sqrt{\frac{1}{4}}$ and finally, $b = \pm\frac{1}{2}$. The sum of $b = \frac{1}{2}, -\frac{1}{2}$, also produces 0.

17. **Medium | Additional Topics in Math**

The correct answer is 80. To find the difference between the number of tiles needed to cover 540 square inches, one must first find the area of each triangular tile. The area of triangle ABC can be found by the formula $A = \frac{1}{2}bh$ where b = base and h = height, so $\frac{1}{2}(12)(9) = \frac{1}{2}(108) = 54$ square inches. To find the area of triangle abc, one needs to determine the value of z, or the base of the triangle. In order to find this value, one can use the Pythagorean theorem to find z or use the properties of similar triangles to determine the value of z. Because ABC and abc share an angle and a proportional side 12:4 (or 3:1), the triangles are similar and proportional by a factor of 3. Therefore, $z = 9 \div 3 = 3$, so the area of abc is $\frac{1}{2}(4)(3) = \frac{1}{2}(12) = 6$ square inches. If the area of the floor is 540 square inches, triangle ABC and its area of 54 square inches, and triangle *abc* with its area of 6 square inches, give the following values 540 ÷ 54 = 10 and 540 ÷ 6 = 90, so the difference between the number of tiles needed is 90 - 10 = 80.

18. **Difficult | Heart of Algebra**

    The correct answer is 2. A system of equations with no solution on a coordinate plane is two parallel lines or lines with the same slope. In a system this means that the change in *y*. over the change in *x* in both equations must be equal, so the coefficients for each variable will be proportional by the same amount. The two values the question provides are the coefficients for *x*, 24 and 8, or $\frac{24}{8} = \frac{3}{1} = 3$. The coefficients for *y* must have the same proportional relationship such that $\frac{3}{1} = \frac{-6}{-s}$ so *s* = 2

19. **Difficult | Additional Topics in Math**

    The correct answer is $\frac{5}{13}$ or 0.38. For complementary angles (sum of the angles is 90°), The trigonometric ratios of complementary angles states that the $sin\theta = cos(90°\text{-}\theta)$, or $sinx = cosy$, therefore, the $sin(sin(x)) = \frac{5}{13}$ means that the $cos(cos(x)) = \frac{5}{13}$ as well. For the decimal, 5 ÷ 13 = 0.38.

20. **Easy | Passport to Advanced Math**

    The correct answer is 17. Begin by substituting $f = 2$ into the second equation, so that $\sqrt{g+3} = (2)\sqrt{5}$ and then square both sides to eliminate the radicals $g + 3 = 2^2 (5)$ Simplify $g + 3 = 4(5)$, $g + 3 = 20$, and finally $g = 17$.

1. **Easy | Problem Solving and Data Analysis**

   Choice B is correct. The equation $y = 2^x$ is an exponential function, and the graph in Choice B is the only graph that features exponential growth. Choice A is incorrect because it features a linear equation, Choice C and D are incorrect because they do not feature exponential growth.

2. **Easy | Heart of Algebra**

   Choice D is correct. Begin by translating the text into equation form, so that $y = 3x + 2$ and substitute $x = \dfrac{1}{2}$ so that $y = 3\left(\dfrac{1}{2}\right) + 2$, $y = \dfrac{3}{2} + 2 = \dfrac{7}{2}$. If $x = \dfrac{1}{2}$ and $y = \dfrac{7}{2}$, then the sum of the two values is $\dfrac{1}{2} + \dfrac{7}{2} = \dfrac{8}{2} = 4$. Choices A and C are incorrect because they give the individual values of x and y and not the sum of the two. Choice B is incorrect and most likely features an arithmetic error.

3. **Medium | Problem Solving and Data Analysis**

   Choice A is correct. To find the average temperature, first identify the approximate temperatures of the three cities: New York ≈ 98, DC ≈ 102, Chicago ≈ 87. Find the average $98 + 102 + 87 = 287 \div 3 = 95.67$. Therefore, Choice C is the closest approximate value. Choices B, C, and D are incorrect because they do not represent the average of the temperatures listed in the graph.

4. **Difficult | Passport to Advanced Math**

   Choice B is correct. In order to express the relationship in terms of F, rearrange the equation to equal $C: \dfrac{9}{5}C + 32 = F$ and $\dfrac{9}{5}C = F - 32$ and finally, $C = \dfrac{5}{9}(F - 32)$. Choices A, C, and D are incorrect because when they are rearranged to express the equation in terms of C, they do not equal $\dfrac{9}{5}C + 32 = F$.

5. **Medium | Passport to Advanced Math**

   Choice C is correct. In order to calculate the change in degrees Fahrenheit, modify the equation in order to express an increase in Celsius by two degrees: $\dfrac{9}{5}(C + 2) + 32 = F$. Simplify, $\left(\dfrac{9}{5}C + \dfrac{18}{5}\right) + 32 = F$ and $\dfrac{18}{5} + \left(\dfrac{9}{5}C + 32\right) = F$. The change in Fahrenheit is $\dfrac{18}{5}$ degrees or 3.6. Choices A, B, and D are incorrect and most likely feature arithmetic errors in calculating the change in degrees Fahrenheit.

6. **Medium | Heart of Algebra**

   Choice D is correct. The absolute value indicates that there are two solutions to the equation, which can be found by creating two equations as follows: $x + 3 = \dfrac{11}{5}$ and $x + 3 = -\dfrac{11}{5}$. By solving for x, the two values are then $x = \dfrac{-4}{5}$ and $\dfrac{-26}{5}$ and so the sum of both values is $\dfrac{-4}{5} + \dfrac{-26}{5} = \dfrac{-30}{5} = -6$. Choices A and B are incorrect because they are the separate solutions, not the sum of both. Choice C is incorrect and most likely is the result of errors in solving an equation with an absolute value.

7. **Medium | Problem Solving and Data Analysis**

   Choice A is correct. If Jessica drives 250 miles every day and the total trip is 2,669 miles, then one must divide $2,669 \div 250 = 10.676$. This value represents the number of days it will take her to complete the trip, but to find the number of weeks, divide your answer by 7, so that $10.676 \div 7 = 1.525$. Rounded to the nearest tenth is then 1.5. Choices B is incorrect because it is the number of days the trip would take, not weeks. Choices C and D are incorrect and are mostly likely the result of arithmetic errors.

8. **Medium | Additional Topics in Math**

   Choice B is correct. In order to find the supplementary angle of B, which is $x°$, one must first find the value of B. If the other two angles in the triangle add to $51° + 62° = 113°$, then angle B must equal $180° - 113° = 67°$, and the supplement of $67°$ is $113°$, which is the value of angle x. Choices A and C are incorrect and most likely result from arithmetic errors in finding supplementary angles. Choice D is incorrect and most likely results from a lack of understanding of the characteristics of triangles and interior angle relationships to exterior angles.

9. **Easy | Problem Solving and Data Analysis**

   Choice B is correct. In order to find the slowest speed they hike, one must first identify how speed is represented on the graph itself. If speed can be represented as feet per hour, which is the y-axis of the graph in terms of the x-axis, speed can be identified as the slope of the graph. The slowest speed is therefore the smallest rate of change, which can be identified as the smallest slope on the graph. The interval, therefore, where the slope is at its minimum is between hours 2-3. Choice A, C, and D are all incorrect and most likely result in errors of identifying and understanding speed as the slope on a coordinate plane.

10. **Easy | Heart of Algebra**

    Choice A is correct. First, use the information provided to determine the value of x, before finding the value of $(x)^{-1}$ or $\frac{1}{x}$. Simplify $(x) = \frac{3}{2}x + 2 = 3$ and solve for x, so that $\frac{3}{2}x = 1$ so $x = \frac{2}{3}$. So $\left(\frac{2}{3}\right)^{-1} = \frac{3}{2}$. Choices B, C, and D are all incorrect because they incorrectly simplify and invert the fraction $\frac{3}{2}$.

11. **Medium | Problem Solving and Data Analysis**

    Choice C is correct. To find the median value of the data set, start by finding the total number of students in the school, $74 + 73 + 81 + 90 + 75 + 82 = 475$. The median, or halfway point, would then be half of 475, or 237.5. The 237th student falls in the 5th grade row (students 228 through 318), so the median student is in the 5th grade. Choices A, B, and D are incorrect and most likely result from errors in calculating the total number of students to find the median value.

12. **Easy | Heart of Algebra**

    Choice C is correct. In order to find the equation that is not true, choose a value for x which is greater than 3 and check each answer. Choice C is the only equation where a value greater than three, such as 4, does not solve the equation: $\frac{6}{5}(4) \geq 21$ or $\frac{24}{5} \geq 21$, which is false. Choices A, B, and D are incorrect because when a value greater than 3 is substituted for x, they are all true.

13. **Medium | Problem Solving and Data Analysis**

    Choice D is correct. The probability that Mary will not choose a caramel flavored candy can also be expressed as the probability that Mary will choose a chocolate or a peppermint, which can be expressed as $\frac{16+17}{47} = \frac{33}{47}$.

    Choices A, B, and C are incorrect because they represent the probability that Mary will choose a chocolate, a peppermint, or a caramel candy, respectively.

14. **Medium | Problem Solving and Data Analysis**

Choice A is correct. Because the mean score for Class 1 is lower than the mean for Class 2, and they feature the same median, that indicates that the data points below the median for Class 1 are further away from the median than in Class 2. Choices B, C, and D are incorrect and most likely result from a lack of knowledge about the relationship between median and mean.

15. **Easy | Heart of Algebra**

Choice D is correct. In order to set the two functions equal to each other, combine the information for both functions into one equation, $(x + 2)^2 = (3) + 6$, and simplify: $(x + 2)^2 = 9$, $x + 2 = \pm\sqrt{9}$, $x + 2 = \pm3$. Therefore, $x = 1, -5$ Choices A and B are incorrect because they omit the $\pm$ when taking the square root of 9, and Choice C is incorrect and is likely the result of arithmetic errors after solving for ±3.

16. **Medium | Heart of Algebra**

Choice C is correct. In order to create equations that represents the data from the market, the variables f and s, for 4 square feet spots and 6 square feet spots, respectively, must be matched and multiplied with their correct totals and constants. If the number of spots sold in total is 14, and the number of spots can be represented by the two variables, one equation must be $s + f = 14$, and Choice C is the only answer choice to feature that equation. Choices A, C, and D are incorrect because they match the wrong spot with the wrong area or incorrectly add or multiply the variables.

17. **Medium | Problem Solving and Data Analysis**

Choice C is correct. The function in the table represents an exponential function. When $f(x) = 1$, that indicates that is where the exponent is equal to 0, or alternatively, the value of the graph of x when $y = 1$. On this graph, $x = 0$ when $f(x) = 1$. Choices A, B, and D are incorrect and most likely result from errors in interpreting functions on a coordinate plane.

18. **Easy | Problem Solving and Data Analysis**

Choice C is correct. The y-intercept on the graph represents when the variable on the x-axis is equal to 0. The y-intercept, therefore, must be representative of the initial number of cells when the x-axis (time) is at zero, which is Choice C. Choices A, B, and D are incorrect and most likely result from errors in interpreting functions on a coordinate plane.

19. **Difficult | Passport to Advanced Math**

Choice A is correct. For a system to have infinitely many solutions, the coefficients of both x and y and the constant on the right side of the equation must be proportional between the two equations. Using the coefficients of y, one can identify the proportional relationship as 1:-2 between the two equations. Using this proportion, the relationship between a and c can be found: $-2\left(\dfrac{4}{5}\right) = \dfrac{-8}{5} = a$ and $-2(17) = -34$. The sum of f $a + b + c$ is then $\dfrac{-8}{5} + 2 - 34 = -33.6$. Choices B, C, and D are incorrect and result from errors in finding proportional relationships between the two equations.

20. **Medium | Problem Solving and Data Analysis**

Choice D is correct. If you are choosing a student at random from Grade 10, the total number of students to choose from is 62. If a student has studied at least 6 hours, then he or she has studied anywhere between 6 and 15 hours, so the probability can be expressed as $\dfrac{16+25}{62}=\dfrac{41}{64}$. Choices A, B, and C are incorrect and most likely result from errors in calculating the probability for Grade 10.

21. **Difficult | Problem Solving and Data Analysis**

    Choice B is correct. In order to correctly represent the situation, one must match the correct variable with the correct percentage. The sofa s is 60% off, so the total price is in fact 40% of the original price, or 0.4s . The armchair price is a fixed price of $450, and the sum of 0.4s and $450 is then discounted again by 40%, or 60% of the original price, which can be rewritten as 0.6(0.4s + 450). Choices A, C and D are incorrect because they represent errors in writing discounts as percentages and errors in matching variables and prices with the correct discount.

22. **Medium | Additional Topics in Math**

    Choice B is correct. To find an endpoint of a circle, first one must find the equation of a circle from the center and the radius: $(x-3)^2 +(y-1)^2 =\dfrac{3}{10}$. Choice B is correct because it is the only answer, when inserted into the above equation, to solve the circle equation. Choices A, C, and D are incorrect because when they are inserted into the above equation, they do not solve the equation.

23. **Medium | Heart of Algebra**

    Choice A is correct. In the equation $-m^2 + 27.5m = h$, the two x- intercepts are when the $h = 0$ at 0 minutes and 28 minutes, which are given in the question itself. The maximum value of a parabola lies at the midpoint between the two x- intercepts, so around $m = 14$. Substitute 14 for m in the equation: $-(14)^2 + 27.5(14) = -196 + 385 = 189$ which is ≈ 190 ft. Choices B, C, and D are incorrect and most likely result from errors in calculating the x- value of the vertex of the parabola.

24. **Easy | Problem Solving and Data Analysis**

    Choice A is correct. In order to find the average number of geese in all four cities in the Fall, find the average of the 4th column in the table: $420+701+300+673=2094 \div 4 = 523.5 \approx 524$. Choices B, C, and D are incorrect because they represent the averages of other seasons, not the Fall.

25. **Medium | Problem Solving and Data Analysis**

    Choice D is correct. To find the largest difference, calculate the actual values for each answer choice. That subtraction should yield the following values: City A, spring to summer = 1430; City B, fall to winter = 94; City C, summer to fall = 409; City D, spring the summer = 3771. The largest change is therefore, Choice D. Choices A, B, and C are incorrect because they are less than 3771.

26. **Medium | Problem Solving and Data Analysis**

    Choice B is correct. To calculate the price per oz for each bottle, one must first determine how many oz are in the new bottle of shampoo. If a bottle now has 20% more, it is 120% of the original volume, or 1.2(20) = 24 oz. To calculate price per oz, set up a fraction, of price divided by volume in oz: $\dfrac{15.99}{20}=\$0.79$ per oz and

    $\dfrac{17.99}{24}=\$0.74$ per oz. Therefore, Choice B is correct, because $\$0.74<\$0.79$. Choices A, C, and D are incorrect because when the price is calculated, $\$0.74<\$0.79,$ so other answers are the result of errors in manipulating percentages and proportional fractions.

CONTINUE ▶

27. **Medium | Passport to Advanced Math**

    Choice D is correct. After 9 darts, Jerome has a total of 400 points and Matilda has a total of 290 points. If Jerome throws a 70-point throw, his score increases to 470 points. Because the difference between their two scores is over 100 points, which is the largest single point value, it is therefore impossible for Matilda to beat Jerome with only one more throw. Choices A, B, and C are incorrect because every value added to 290 is still less than 470 points.

28. **Medium | Heart of Algebra**

    Choice C is correct. First, find the solution to the system of equations by graphing the two equations or solving algebraically. The intersection of the two lines is (-2,-1), which lies in the third quadrant. Choices A, B, and D are incorrect and most likely result from graphing or algebraic errors in solving the system of equations.

29. **Medium | Passport to Advanced Math**

    Choice C is correct. When the polynomial is factored into its distinct roots, the polynomial becomes $(x + 2)^2$ $(x - 1) = 0$, so the zeroes are -2 and 1. There are three zeros in total, but because x = -2 is a double solution, the polynomial has only two distinct zeros. Choices A, B, and D are incorrect and most likely result from a lack of knowledge about polynomials and the properties of zeros.

30. **Medium | Passport to Advanced Math**

    Choice B is correct. In order to find the x-value of the vertex, start by finding the midpoint between the two x-intercepts, which is $x = 1$ in this function. The table contains the coordinates for when $x = 1$ so the vertex is actually listed in the table, and is(1,-16). Choices A, C, and D are incorrect because their x-values are not midpoints between -1 and 5.

31. **Easy | Heart of Algebra**

    The correct answer is 6.27. In order to determine the difference in Chris' average speed, one needs to calculate both speeds first. His normal trip of 45 minutes (0.75 hours) can be represented by $\frac{47}{0.75} = 62.66666$ and the unusual day of 50 minutes ($\frac{5}{6}$ hours) can be represented by $\frac{47}{\frac{5}{6}} = 56.4$. The difference is then 62.26666, which rounds to 6.27.

32. **Medium | Heart of Algebra**

    The correct answer is 6. Begin by finding the volumes of the boxes themselves, the $1x1x1 = 1ft^2$ and $2x2x2 = 8\,ft^2$. If there are already 51 $1ft^2$ boxes, the remaining area is$100\,ft^2$ - $51ft^2 = 49ft^2$. The $8ft^2$ boxes are then divided by the remaining space,$49\,ft^2/8\,ft^2 = 6.125$. And because there can be no fractions of boxes, only 6 whole boxes can fit in the space.

33. **Easy | Problem Solving and Data Analysis**

    The correct answer is 3. To find the percent increase from 2010 to 2012, one must start by finding the actual increase from 2010 to 2012 from the graph, which is 340 - 330 = 10. Then, determine what fraction of the original value (330) is 10. So, $\frac{10}{330}$ = 0.030, which is a 3% increase.

34. **Easy | Heart of Algebra**

    The correct answer is 8. If Jerry wants to do two full coats of paint on his fence, then the surface area is essentially doubled: $371 \times 2 = 742 \, ft^2$. If a paint can covers $100 \, ft^2$, then Jerry will need $\dfrac{742}{100} = 7.42$ cans, or 8 full cans to complete the job.

35. **Medium | Additional Topics in Math**

    The correct answer is 36.8. Begin by finding the volume of the piñata itself, using the sphere volume formula:

    $V = \dfrac{4}{3}\pi r^3 = \dfrac{4}{3}\pi \left(7\right)^3 = 457.33333\pi = 1{,}436.755$. The leftover volume inside the piñata is then,

    $1{,}436.755 - 1400 = 36.755 \approx 36.8$.

36. **Easy | Problem Solving and Data Analysis**

    The correct answer is 331. To rent a car for four days, substitute 4 for x in the function: $3^4 + 250 = 81 + 250$ = \$331 for four days. This problem can also be solved by graphing and identifying the point (4, 331) on the coordinate plane.

37. **Medium | Problem Solving and Data Analysis**

    The correct answer is 31. To find the difference, start by calculating the cost from both companies, starting with Company A $3^{(3)} + 250 = 27 = 250 = 277$. Company B however, is $2^x + 300 = 8 + 300 = 308$. The difference in price is then $308 - 277 = 31$.

38. **Medium | Passport to Advanced Math**

    The correct answer is $\dfrac{8}{7}$ or 1.14. To find when a function is undefined, find the value of x where the denominator is equal to 0. Ignoring the numerator of the fraction, set the denominator equal to 0 and simplify:

    $(b + 2)^2 - b(b - 3) + 12 = b^2 + 4x + 4 - b^2 + 3b - 12 = 7x - 8$. Therefore, $x = \dfrac{8}{7}$ or as a decimal, 1.14.

SAT Practice
Test #2

It is recommended that you use a No. 2 pencil. It is very important that you fill in the entire circle darkly and completely. If you change your response, erase as completely as possible. Incomplete marks or erasures may affect your score.

1 A B C D
2 A B C D
3 A B C D
4 A B C D
5 A B C D
6 A B C D
7 A B C D
8 A B C D
9 A B C D
10 A B C D
11 A B C D
12 A B C D
13 A B C D

14 A B C D
15 A B C D
16 A B C D
17 A B C D
18 A B C D
19 A B C D
20 A B C D
21 A B C D
22 A B C D
23 A B C D
24 A B C D
25 A B C D
26 A B C D

27 A B C D
28 A B C D
29 A B C D
30 A B C D
31 A B C D
32 A B C D
33 A B C D
34 A B C D
35 A B C D
36 A B C D
37 A B C D
38 A B C D
39 A B C D

40 A B C D
41 A B C D
42 A B C D
43 A B C D
44 A B C D
45 A B C D
46 A B C D
47 A B C D
48 A B C D
49 A B C D
50 A B C D
51 A B C D
52 A B C D

It is recommended that you use a No. 2 pencil. It is very important that you fill in the entire circle darkly and completely. If you change your response, erase as completely as possible. Incomplete marks or erasures may affect your score.

	A B C D		A B C D		A B C D		A B C D		A B C D
1	○○○○	10	○○○○	19	○○○○	28	○○○○	37	○○○○
2	○○○○	11	○○○○	20	○○○○	29	○○○○	38	○○○○
3	○○○○	12	○○○○	21	○○○○	30	○○○○	39	○○○○
4	○○○○	13	○○○○	22	○○○○	31	○○○○	40	○○○○
5	○○○○	14	○○○○	23	○○○○	32	○○○○	41	○○○○
6	○○○○	15	○○○○	24	○○○○	33	○○○○	42	○○○○
7	○○○○	16	○○○○	25	○○○○	34	○○○○	43	○○○○
8	○○○○	17	○○○○	26	○○○○	35	○○○○	44	○○○○
9	○○○○	18	○○○○	27	○○○○	36	○○○○		

It is recommended that you use a No. 2 pencil. It is very important that you fill in the entire circle darkly and completely. If you change your response, erase as completely as possible. Incomplete marks or erasures may affect your score.

```
   A B C D        A B C D        A B C D        A B C D         A B C D
1  O O O O    4  O O O O    7  O O O O    10 O O O O     13 O O O O

   A B C D        A B C D        A B C D        A B C D         A B C D
2  O O O O    5  O O O O    8  O O O O    11 O O O O     14 O O O O

   A B C D        A B C D        A B C D        A B C D         A B C D
3  O O O O    6  O O O O    9  O O O O    12 O O O O     15 O O O O
```

Only answers that are gridded will be scored. You will not receive credit for anything written in the boxes.

```
16              17              18              19              20
 _____     _____     _____     _____     _____
|  |  |  |  |   |  |  |  |  |   |  |  |  |  |   |  |  |  |  |   |  |  |  |  |

 /   O O         /   O O         /   O O         /   O O         /   O O
 .  O O O O      .  O O O O      .  O O O O      .  O O O O      .  O O O O
 0  O O O O      0  O O O O      0  O O O O      0  O O O O      0  O O O O
 1  O O O O      1  O O O O      1  O O O O      1  O O O O      1  O O O O
 2  O O O O      2  O O O O      2  O O O O      2  O O O O      2  O O O O
 3  O O O O      3  O O O O      3  O O O O      3  O O O O      3  O O O O
 4  O O O O      4  O O O O      4  O O O O      4  O O O O      4  O O O O
 5  O O O O      5  O O O O      5  O O O O      5  O O O O      5  O O O O
 6  O O O O      6  O O O O      6  O O O O      6  O O O O      6  O O O O
 7  O O O O      7  O O O O      7  O O O O      7  O O O O      7  O O O O
 8  O O O O      8  O O O O      8  O O O O      8  O O O O      8  O O O O
 9  O O O O      9  O O O O      9  O O O O      9  O O O O      9  O O O O
```

NO CALCULATOR ALLOWED

CONTINUE ➡

It is recommended that you use a No. 2 pencil. It is very important that you fill in the entire circle darkly and completely. If you change your response, erase as completely as possible. Incomplete marks or erasures may affect your score.

A B C D 1 ○ ○ ○ ○	A B C D 7 ○ ○ ○ ○	A B C D 13 ○ ○ ○ ○	A B C D 19 ○ ○ ○ ○	A B C D 25 ○ ○ ○ ○
A B C D 2 ○ ○ ○ ○	A B C D 8 ○ ○ ○ ○	A B C D 14 ○ ○ ○ ○	A B C D 20 ○ ○ ○ ○	A B C D 26 ○ ○ ○ ○
A B C D 3 ○ ○ ○ ○	A B C D 9 ○ ○ ○ ○	A B C D 15 ○ ○ ○ ○	A B C D 21 ○ ○ ○ ○	A B C D 27 ○ ○ ○ ○
A B C D 4 ○ ○ ○ ○	A B C D 10 ○ ○ ○ ○	A B C D 16 ○ ○ ○ ○	A B C D 22 ○ ○ ○ ○	A B C D 28 ○ ○ ○ ○
A B C D 5 ○ ○ ○ ○	A B C D 11 ○ ○ ○ ○	A B C D 17 ○ ○ ○ ○	A B C D 23 ○ ○ ○ ○	A B C D 29 ○ ○ ○ ○
A B C D 6 ○ ○ ○ ○	A B C D 12 ○ ○ ○ ○	A B C D 18 ○ ○ ○ ○	A B C D 24 ○ ○ ○ ○	A B C D 30 ○ ○ ○ ○

CALCULATOR
ALLOWED

CONTINUE

It is recommended that you use a No. 2 pencil. It is very important that you fill in the entire circle darkly and completely. If you change your response, erase as completely as possible. Incomplete marks or erasures may affect your score.

31 **32** **33** **34** **35**

Only answers that are gridded will be scored. You will not receive credit for anything written in the boxes.

36 **37** **38**

CALCULATOR
ALLOWED

CONTINUE

Reading Test

65 MINUTES, 52 QUESTIONS

Turn to Section 1 of your answer sheet to answer the questions in this section

DIRECTIONS

Each passage or pair of passages below is followed by a number of questions. After reading each passage or pair, choose the best answer to each question based on what is stated or implied in the passage or passages and in any accompanying graphics (such as a table or graph).

Questions 1-10 are based on the following passage.

This passage is adapted from Chapter 1 of *Moby Dick; or The Whale,* copyright 1851 by Herman Melville.

Call me Ishmael. Some years ago—never mind how long precisely—having little or no money in my purse, and nothing particular to interest me on
Line shore, I thought I would sail about a little and see
5 the watery part of the world. It is a way I have of driving off the spleen and regulating the circulation. Whenever I find myself growing grim about the mouth; whenever it is a damp, drizzly November in my soul; whenever I find myself involuntarily
10 pausing before coffin warehouses, and bringing up the rear of every funeral I meet—then, I account it high time to get to sea as soon as I can. This is my substitute for pistol and ball. With a philosophical flourish Cato throws himself upon his sword; I
15 quietly take to the ship. There is nothing surprising in this. If they but knew it, almost all men in their degree, some time or other, cherish very nearly the same feelings towards the ocean with me.

Now, when I say that I am in the habit of
20 going to sea whenever I begin to grow hazy about the eyes, and begin to be over conscious of my lungs, I do not mean to have it inferred that I ever go to sea as a passenger. For to go as a passenger you must need have a purse, and a purse is but
25 a rag unless you have something in it. Besides, passengers get sea-sick—grow quarrelsome—don't

sleep of nights—do not enjoy themselves much, as a general thing;—no, I never go as a passenger; nor, though I am something of a salt, do I ever go to sea as a Commodore, or a Captain, or a Cook. I
30 abandon the glory and distinction of such offices to those who like them. For my part, I abominate all honorable respectable toils, trials, and tribulations of every kind whatsoever. It is quite as much as I can do to take care of myself, without taking care
35 of ships, barques, brigs, schooners, and what not. And as for going as cook,—though I confess there is considerable glory in that, a cook being a sort of officer on ship-board—yet, somehow, I never fancied broiling fowls;—though once broiled,
40 judiciously buttered, and judgmatically salted and peppered, there is no one who will speak more respectfully, not to say reverentially, of a broiled fowl than I will.

No, when I go to sea, I go as a simple sailor, right
45 before the mast, plumb down into the forecastle, aloft there to the royal mast-head. True, they rather order me about some, and make me jump from spar to spar, like a grasshopper in a May meadow. And at first, this sort of thing is unpleasant enough.
50 It touches one's sense of honor, particularly if you come of an old established family in the land, the Van Rensselaers, or Randolphs, or Hardicanutes. But this wears off in time.

Again, I always go to sea as a sailor, because they
55 make a point of paying me for my trouble, whereas they never pay passengers a single penny that I ever heard of. On the contrary, passengers themselves

CONTINUE

must pay. And there is all the difference in the world
between paying and being paid. *Being paid*,—what
60 will compare with it? The urbane activity with
which a man receives money is really marvelous,
considering that we so earnestly believe money to
be the root of all earthly ills, and that on no account
can a monied man enter heaven. Ah! how cheerfully
65 we consign ourselves to perdition!

Finally, I always go to sea as a sailor, because of
the wholesome exercise and pure air of the forecastle deck. For as in this world, head winds are far
more prevalent than winds from astern (that is, if
70 you never violate the Pythagorean maxim), so for
the most part the Commodore on the quarter-deck
gets his atmosphere at second hand from the sailors
on the forecastle. He thinks he breathes it first; but
not so. In much the same way do the commonalty
75 lead their leaders in many other things, at the same
time that the leaders little suspect it. But wherefore
it was that after having repeatedly smelt the sea
as a merchant sailor, I should now take it into my
head to go on a whaling voyage; this the invisible
80 police officer of the Fates, who has the constant
surveillance of me, and secretly dogs me, and
influences me in some unaccountable way—he can
better answer than any one else. It came in as a sort
of brief interlude and solo between more extensive
85 performances.

1

Which choice best summarizes the passage?

A) A whaling captain describes the reasons for
embarking on his career.

B) A sailor reminisces about the impetus for
setting out on a whaling voyage.

C) A merchant sailor develops an argument
against riding a boat as a passenger.

D) An impoverished man explains how he
degenerated to his current condition.

2

Over the course of the passage, the narrator's
focus shifts from

A) why he favors sailing to reasons that other
people choose to go sailing.

B) his desire for sailing to complications that
render sailing a less gratifying experience.

C) an analysis of his motivations to an expression
of contempt for superior officers.

D) reasons for sailing in general to speculation
about embarking on a whaling vessel.

3

What is the effect of the references to "coffin warehouses" and "funeral" in lines 10-11?

A) It indicates that many of the narrator's close acquaintances became deceased.

B) It illustrates an event which frequently occurs in the month of November.

C) It reinforces the bleakness of the narrator's emotions during a certain period.

D) It emphasizes the source of the narrator's despondent sentiments.

4

As used in line 17, "degree" is closest in meaning to

A) rank

B) amount

C) standard

D) diploma

5

The narrator brings up the analogy of a grasshopper to anticipate which of the following arguments?

A) A regular crew member does not receive enough compensation.

B) The duties of a simple sailor are sufficient to occupy that person's time.

C) The narrator comes from a very reputable family in the region.

D) Obeying orders from a superior officer is extremely distasteful.

6

Based on the passage, Ishmael does not travel aboard ship as a passenger because he

A) does not want excessive responsibilities.

B) desires reimbursement for his efforts.

C) sometimes enters periods of deep depression.

D) hungers for recognition for his efforts.

7

Which choice provides the best evidence for the answer to the previous question?

A) Lines 13- 15 ("With a... ship")

B) Lines 23- 25 ("For to... in it")

C) Lines 30- 32 ("I abandon... like them")

D) Lines 54- 57 ("they make... heard of")

8

The narrator repeats the phrase, "I always go to sea as a sailor" (Line 66) most likely to

A) justify his decision to hold a minor role.

B) emphasize his disdain for passengers.

C) reveal a secret longing for luxury.

D) highlight his financial difficulties.

9

With which idea about captains would the narrator most likely agree?

A) They have worked hard to earn their position.

B) They are greatly worthy of respect.

C) They do not understand the needs of simple sailors.

D) They are mistaken about the extent of their power.

10

What role does the final sentence play in the context of the passage?

A) It indicates that whaling was not the narrator's usual occupation.

B) It foreshadows a tragedy that the narrator does not want to repeat.

C) It offers the narrator's rationale for embarking on a whaling voyage.

D) It explains that the narrator could not find longer employment at the time.

CONTINUE

Questions 11-20 are based on the following passages.

Passage 1:

The Government of the United States creates no Slaves; it only recognises as lawful the Slavery existing in the several States, or to use the words of the Constitution, "held to service or labor, under the laws thereof." The *laws* of the several slave-holding States are made the standard for the general government's action upon this subject. No quibble can possibly evade this, for it is not necessary to prove that a runaway Slave justly owes service to his master, but only if he does, under *the laws of his master.* The master has made certain laws, claiming his Slaves as absolute property; the Constitution says, "persons owing service under these laws," shall be returned, thus making the most complete provision for the support of the system.

The recent decision of judge Edmonds in behalf of Belt, the most favorable one on record, fully recognises this principle; and Belt owes his liberty not so much to the humanity of the judge, as to the absence of positive proof that the laws of Maryland uphold Slavery. A copy of the Slave laws of Maryland was produced, but it only said published by authority, and not by the authority of the legislature, therefore Belt was allowed to go free. The omission of one word in a book, saved Belt from the jaws of Slavery, more than any other thing. To be sure, it was proved that the master did not take legal steps after the seizure of Belt, and therefore had no right to him; but the main reason for his discharge was, not the wrongfulness of delivering him up, not because God had given Lee no *bill of sale,* but because a lawyer could not swear that a certain book was the laws of Maryland!

From this decision there is no appeal, until a higher authority has decided differently. All that a slave-hunter has to do, is merely to bring an attested copy of the laws of the State, in which he lives, and prove that in such a State he held the person claimed as his Slave, and there is no redress for the panting fugitive. He *must be* returned to his former bondage, without any power to protect him from the punishment his master may choose to inflict upon him in consequence of his escape. Thus is

Slavery legalized by our laws. What then is necessary to be done to remove this prop from under the colossal statue of Slavery? Plainly, to repeal all laws recognising its existence. Do this, and refuse to obey any of the claims of the South in reference to this matter, and Slavery ceases as soon as the earth would cease to turn upon its axis.

Passage 2:

Now Abolitionists are before the community, and declare that all slavery is sin, which ought to be immediately forsaken; and that it is their object and intention to promote the *immediate emancipation* of all the slaves in this nation.

Now what is it that makes a man cease to be a slave and become free? It is not kind treatment from a master; it is not paying wages to the slave; it is not the intention to bestow freedom at a future time; it is not treating a slave as if he were free; it is not feeling toward a slave as if he were free. No instance can be found of any dictionary, or any standard writer, nor any case in common discourse, where any of these significations are attached to the word as constituting its peculiar and appropriate meaning. It always signifies *that legal* act, which, by the laws of the land, changes a slave to a freeman.

What then is the *proper* meaning of the language used by Abolitionists, when they say that all slavery is a sin which ought to be immediately abandoned, and that it is their object to secure the immediate emancipation of all slaves?

The true and only *proper* meaning of such language is, that it is the duty of every slave-holder in this nation, to go immediately and make out the legal instruments, that, by the laws of the land, change all his slaves to freemen. If their maxim is true, no exception can be made for those who live in States where the act of emancipation, by a master, makes a slave the property of the State, to be sold for the benefit of the State; and no exception can be made for those, who, by the will of testators, and by the law of the land, have no power to perform the legal act, which alone can emancipate their slaves.

To meet this difficulty, Abolitionists affirm, that, in such cases, men are physically unable to emancipate their slaves, and of course are not bound

CONTINUE

to do it; and to save their great maxim, maintain
90　that, in such cases, the slaves are not slaves, and the
slave-holders are not slave-holders, although all
their legal relations remain unchanged.

11

Which choice best states the central idea of
Passage 1?

A) The U.S. government has no binding authority
regarding slavery.

B) Judge Edmonds made a reasonable decision
in the trial involving Belt.

C) Slaveholders should be responsible for
maintaining adequate documents.

D) Any legislation that upholds slavery should be
rescinded.

12

The main purpose of Passage 1 is to

A) formulate a counterargument to an assertion.

B) offer an opinion regarding a solution to a
problem.

C) summarize a current specific occurrence.

D) outline steps the reader should take to
eliminate a problem.

13

As used in line 6, "standard" most nearly means

A) guideline

B) quality

C) ideal

D) worth

14

Stearns uses the decision of judge Edmonds in
behalf of Belt to illustrate his point that

A) most paperwork regarding slavery is
inadequate.

B) laws should be developed to include the
morality of slavery.

C) slavery is upheld by the legal system rather
than ethics.

D) judges should have more freedom to interpret
the laws.

15

It can be reasonably inferred from Passage 2 that Beecher

A) feels that Abolitionists are not adequately concerned with ethics.

B) has many friends who are part of the Abolitionist movement.

C) thinks Abolitionists should write books supporting their views.

D) does not consider herself part of the Abolitionist movement.

16

Beecher italicizes the word "proper" in line 73 most likely to

A) emphasize that she feels a meaning is misinterpreted.

B) indicate that she approves of the Abolitionists' language.

C) show that she disagrees with the goals of the Abolitionists.

D) highlight the ethical nature of arguments regarding slavery.

17

According to Passage 2, kind treatment is not true emancipation because there is no

A) guarantee that owners will treat slaves as promised.

B) documentation supporting that interpretation of the word.

C) example of a slaveholder who behaves humanely.

D) precedent for freeing slaves using any method.

18

Both authors would most likely agree with the assertion that

A) the behavior of slaveholders to fugitive slaves are too extreme.

B) the legal system is the major impediment in the way of abolitionism.

C) slaveholders should immediately declare that their slaves are emancipated.

D) Abolitionists are taking an ineffective course towards ending slavery.

19

Which statement describes how Stearns would most likely react to Beecher's assertion that some slaves are not freed because they live in states that consider emancipated slaves the property of the state?

A) Stearns would argue that such a case is only possible with adequate paperwork.

B) Stearns would argue that is one more reason that all slavery laws should be eliminated.

C) Stearns would argue that slavery is an integral part of the U.S. Constitution.

D) Stearns would argue that if such slaves left the state, they would then be free.

20

Which choice provides the best evidence for the answer to the previous question?

A) Lines 1-3 ("The Government... states")

B) Lines 11-15 ("The master... system")

C) Lines 25-26 ("The omission... thing")

D) Lines 44-47 ("What then... existence")

Questions 21-31 are based on the following passage and supplementary material.

This passage is adapted from "Bogus Business Opportunities," published by the Federal Trade Commission, November, 2011.

Maybe you've seen ads for stuffing envelopes or assembling crafts at home. Perhaps a company says it can help you set up a vending business.
Line Before you sign on the dotted line or send money,
5 find out about the Business Opportunity Rule, enforced by the Federal Trade Commission, the nation's consumer protection agency. The Rule puts safeguards in place to make sure you have the information you need to evaluate whether a business
10 opportunity is risky business.

Under the Rule, sellers have to give you a one-page disclosure document that offers five key pieces of information. Use the information in the disclosure document to fact-check what the seller
15 tells you about the opportunity and what you find out from your own research. The document has to identify the seller and tell you about certain lawsuits or other legal actions involving the seller or its key personnel. It must tell you if the seller has
20 a cancellation or refund policy, and what the terms are. The seller must also give you a list of references.

The Rule says that a seller has to give you the disclosure document at least seven days before you sign a contract or pay them anything. Use that
25 time to check out the information in the disclosure document, including contacting references. Be aware that some questionable business opportunity promoters have been known to name "insiders" who give glowing – but bogus – recommendations.
30 Don't just talk to the few people they suggest. Choose whom to contact. What if what the seller is telling you is different from what's on the disclosure document or what you hear from another buyer? Step on the brake. An inconsistency could be a tell-
35 tale sign of a business opportunity rip-off. However, it is important to remember that many business investments have a wide range of returns, so not all differences in profit are a deliberate attempt to scam a potential buyer. For example, factors such
40 as real estate price may create a large difference in the startup costs of some legitimate franchise opportunities.

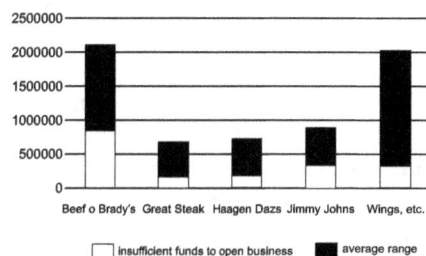

Average Start-Up Costs for Select Legitimate Franchises

Categories: Beef o Brady's, Great Steak, Haagen Dazs, Jimmy Johns, Wings, etc.

Legend: insufficient funds to open business; average range

Data adapted from Franchise Direct, 2019

What if the seller makes a claim about how much money a person can earn? Under the Rule, they have to give you a separate document that says
45 in big type across the top: EARNINGS CLAIM STATEMENT REQUIRED BY LAW. This document has to include many statistics including the specifics of the claim; the start and end date those earnings were achieved; the number and percentage of people
50 who got those results or better, and any information about those people that may differ from you – for example, the part of the country where they live. There must also be a statement that you can get written proof of the seller's earning claims if you ask
55 for it.

Since the Rule gives you the right to see written proof for the seller's earnings claims, savvy buyers exercise that right and study those materials carefully. Like the disclosure document, the earnings
60 claim statement has to be in the same language that the seller used to communicate with you.

The revised Business Opportunity Rule spells out that certain practices are against the law. For example, it's illegal for business opportunity sellers
65 to say anything that contradicts what's in their disclosure document and earnings statement. Under the Rule, sellers can't claim they're offering you a job when they're really promoting a business opportunity. The revised Rule puts new protections
70 in place for prospective buyers. But for added protection, take the time to find out what the Rule requires of *sellers*. If you spot a seller who isn't complying with the law, it's a red flag: You could be in the cross hairs of a business opportunity
75 scammer.

What else can you do to add an extra layer of protection? Before you buy a business opportunity, insist on seeing proof in writing for earnings claims,

CONTINUE

including statements like "Earn up to $10,000 a
80 month!" Phrases like "up to" aren't a way out for
the seller. It's an earning claim and it's your right to
demand proof. You should also interview current
owners of the seller's business opportunity. Ask
the tough questions – like if the information in the
85 disclosure document matches their experience with
the company. Listen to sales presentations with a
critical ear. They are – of course – trying to sell you
something. Finally, if a seller doesn't give you the
information you know they have to provide, walk
away.

21

The main purpose of the passage is to

A) educate the reader about different forms that
franchise scams may take.

B) warn readers against buying into franchise
opportunities.

C) suggest careful research is needed when
considering a franchise opportunity.

D) explain that franchise offers invariably
overstate the true situation.

22

The passage is written in the point of view of

A) an expert addressing a group of franchise
owners.

B) a lawyer outlining redress options to a scam
victim.

C) an advisor giving information to a franchise
seller.

D) a resource person advising an uninformed
buyer.

23

In the overall structure of the passage, the main
purpose of the second paragraph is to

A) outline the key elements of the Business
Opportunity Rule.

B) describe one of the essential documents that
sellers must provide.

C) explain how the Business Opportunity Rule
protects buyers.

D) establish that sellers must give references to
potential buyers.

24

The author includes the information that the
seller must disclose information at least seven
days before signing a contract in order to

A) point out that there is adequate time to make
a decision.

B) emphasize that the buyer is under a lot of
pressure.

C) indicate that honest references take time to
find.

D) offer the reason that sellers secure bogus
recommendations.

25

As used in line 27, "questionable" most nearly means

A) arguable

B) disreputable

C) improbable

D) unresolved

26

The figure supports the author's point that there may be variations in reported costs in legitimate franchises by showing that

A) the cost of opening a Beef o Brady's franchise is significantly higher than opening a Great Steak franchise.

B) the cost of land for building a Wings, etc. franchise is more expensive than for many other franchises.

C) the start-up costs for one franchise, Wings, etc., range from well under $500,000 to about $2,000,000.

D) investors with less than $500,000 can still have enough money to start a legitimate franchise.

27

According to the figure, what is the minimum startup investment that a potential buyer could expect to spend on a Beef o Brady's franchise?

A) about $500,000

B) about $750,000

C) about $2,000,000

D) about $2,500,000

28

Which statement best identifies one of the author's implicit claims about the Earnings Claim Statement Required by Law?

A) Demographic factors may affect a franchise's earnings.

B) The earnings claims must be updated every month.

C) Most sellers do not provide the Statement willingly.

D) The document is required with any franchise purchase.

29

It can reasonably be inferred from the passage that the author feels that

A) franchises do not offer realistic information about their earnings potential.

B) franchise advertisements usually highlight the best possible scenarios.

C) there are insufficient laws for the protection of franchise sellers.

D) with proper research, an investor can ensure that the business will not fail.

30

Which choice provides the best evidence for the answer to the previous question?

A) Lines 4-7 ("Before you… agency")

B) Lines 34-35 ("An inconsistency… rip-off")

C) Lines 70-72 ("But for… *sellers.*")

D) Lines 86-88 ("Listen… something")

31

Based on information from the passage, which of the following would be a warning sign that a business may be a fraud?

A) The seller gives you a written claim that it will be possible for you to earn up to $500 per day.

B) All the references given by the company give very positive reports about their experiences with it.

C) The seller specifically states that you are being offered a business opportunity rather than a job.

D) Your negotiations with a Chinese company have been in English, but the contract contains several portions written in Chinese.

Questions 32-41 are based on the following passage.

Passage is adapted from Andreas Uihlein and Davide Magagna, *Wave and tidal current energy: A review of the current state of research beyond technology,* copyright 2016 by Renewable and Sustainable Energy Reviews 58.

Ocean energy, as all other renewable sources of energy, can contribute to a more sustainable energy supply, but it is not environmentally friendly per se.

Line
5 The activities involved in manufacturing, operation, maintenance, and decommissioning of ocean energy devices will have various effects on the environment. Governments and society need a robust understanding of the environmental implications of ocean energy systems before ocean energy systems
10 are built, and also to reduce or adjust impacts to acceptable levels. While Environmental Impact Assessments (EIA) are performed to ensure that companies consider the environmental implications of their decisions Life Cycle Assessments (LCA)
15 are used to identify and quantify the impact of industrial products on the environment.

The main direct expected environmental impacts of ocean wave and tidal current technology include impact on the deep ocean community (due
20 to alterations in flow patterns, wave structures, and sediment movement), species-specific response to habitat changes, and the entanglement of marine mammals, turtles, larger fish, and seabirds. However, due to limited observations, the significance of
25 environmental impacts of commercial projects cannot fully be determined yet. Further research in the area of environmental impacts should be focused on localized environmental impacts..

A new range of technologies, devices, and
30 sub-systems need in-depth analysis. In addition, competing pressures and uses such as climate change, fishing, and marine transport should be considered when looking at environmental impacts. The literature research shows that only
35 a small number of LCA on wave and tidal energy converters have been performed. The main focus was on devices that are in advanced stages of development, so there is little data for prototype models. So far, most of the studies focused only on
40 the impact of energy and carbon. Existing data are very much dispersed among countries, researchers, and developers. Since wave energy and tidal energy technologies are at an early development stage, no data on environmental effects from large integrated
45 systems called arrays are available.

In general, deep ocean habitats will be affected by tidal current energy systems due to the change of water flows, materials in the ocean floor, and movement of sediment. Potential other effects
50 include mortality of fish passing through turbines (blade-strike) and the collision risk of marine mammals with tidal stream farms. A study showed that change in sediment patterns will most likely follow the installation of tidal arrays, impacting
55 the local underwater habitat. This, in turn, could impact animal and plant species. Species of marine mammals and fish could experience distress and discomfort. However, in their review, Frid et al. conclude that "there is little scientific literature to
60 suggest that operation of underwater tidal stream energy devices will cause elevated levels of mortality to organisms such as fish and marine mammals." Also, Lewis et al. mention that, "while current technologies have moving parts (rotating rotor
65 blades or flapping hydrofoils) that may harm marine life, there is no evidence to date of harm from tidal current devices to marine life, such as whales, dolphins, seals, and sharks."

A critical issue related to tidal energy converters
70 relates to the noise disruption in turbulent waters, affecting in particular marine mammals. Wave energy converters can potentially alter underwater ecosystems because they create new wave patterns both between and beyond the various parts of an
75 array. According to Lewis et al., environmental impact from ocean wave energy devices might include "competition for space, noise and vibration, electromagnetic fields, disruption to biota and habitats, water quality changes, and possible
80 pollution."

As for tidal devices, the environmental impacts are considered comparably small. Wave devices will represent a much lower collision risk compared to offshore wind devices but they could be the risk of
85 underwater collisions for diving birds. According to Lewis et al., "information on the environmental and social impacts is limited mainly due to the lack of experience in deploying and operating ocean technologies, although adverse environmental
90 effects are foreseen to be relatively low."

CONTINUE

In general, environmental impacts will very much depend on the size of installation and the location selected. Potential positive effects such as the creation of roosting sites and habitat
95 enhancement for marine birds might occur as well. The majority of the studies recommend that the first commercial scale installations of ocean energy technology should be accompanied by research studies on the local environmental impacts and for
100 most installations.

32

Which choice best summarizes the main idea of the passage?

A) At present, there is not enough research to establish the full impact of tidal energy systems.

B) Tidal energy systems have more negative environmental effects than anyone foresaw.

C) Because they are in developmental stages, tidal energy systems are relatively inefficient.

D) Most researchers have not focused on important issues related to tidal energy systems.

33

To support and develop the argument, the authors mostly rely on

A) data from original research.

B) opinions of experts in the field.

C) their own empirical observations.

D) information from other studies.

34

As used in line 7, "robust" most nearly means

A) vigorous

B) sturdy

C) strong

D) tough

35

The passage indicates that marine life may be harmed by tidal energy systems because such systems

A) have dangerous moving parts.

B) are located where animals are most plentiful.

C) attract animals with their sounds.

D) provide habitats for marine birds.

36

A developer argues that his company performed an EIA on a test system and that proves it is safe to start building a large tidal system array to generate electricity for a profit. Which of the following would the authors most likely use to counter that argument?

A) Lines 11-16 ("While... the environment")

B) Lines 23-26 ("However... determined yet")

C) Lines 31-34 ("competing... impacts...")

D) Lines 58-62 ("in their... marine mammals")

37

In line 41, by saying that data is "very much dispersed," the authors most nearly mean that

A) the data is very incomplete.

B) the groups are sharing data.

C) the data is comprehensive.

D) the sources are incompatible.

38

In the fourth paragraph, the authors include quotes from Frid et al. and Lewis et al. most likely to

A) show reputable scientists that hold very different views from each other.

B) provide authoritative viewpoints that oppose that of the authors.

C) undermine conclusions which emphasize safety of tidal energy systems.

D) introduce expert opinions that reinforce the authors' primary claim.

39

As presented in the passage, the claim that tidal energy systems may improve some aspects of the local environment is

A) incorrect, because systems change too many aspects of the region.

B) overly optimistic, because there are no examples of improvement.

C) justifiable, because systems may create new habitats for birds.

D) valid, because many systems have revealed unexpected side benefits.

40

According to the passage, which of the following will most determine how much a tidal system alters the environment?

A) The placement in the ocean

B) The number of moving parts

C) The number of research studies about it

D) The total energy it generates

41

Which choice provides the best evidence for the answer to the previous question?

A) Lines 52-55 ("A study... underwater habitat")

B) Lines 63-66 ("current technologies... marine life")

C) Lines 75-80 ("According to... pollution")

D) Lines 91-93 ("In general... selected")

Questions 42-52 are based on the following passage and supplementary material.

This passage is adapted from Julien Koffi Kpinkoun, et al. "Effect of salt stress on flowering, fructification and fruit nutrients concentration in a local cultivar of chili pepper (Capsicum frutescens L.)." copyright 2019 by the International Journal of Plant Physiology and Biochemistry.

Salt stress, too much salt in the soil for plants to thrive, is one of the major environmental constraints limiting agricultural productivity and influencing
Line the concentration of bioactive compounds of
5 vegetables. In this study, we assessed the effect of NaCl salt stress on flowering, fructification and fruit nutritional quality of a local cultivar of chili pepper. Chili (Capsicum spp.) is a spice, a fruit vegetable widely grown in the world as it is very important
10 in human food. Chili pepper belongs to the crops grown throughout the world for their nutraceutical (nutritional and medicinal) and economic virtue. In Benin, chili is the second cash gardening crop after the tomato. Its annual production is about
15 47.162 tons. Pepper plants produce the compound capsaicin, primarily in the fruits, possibly to deter mammalian herbivores. Chili is classified as moderately sensitive to salinity, and some adverse effects of salinity on this species have been reported.
20 In Benin, chili pepper is grown only for food partially in the cultivable lands of the coastal areas, where soil salinity and water irrigation are a reality. Salt stress is known to negatively affect plant growth at all developmental stages, but sensitivity varies
25 greatly at different stages. Crop production in saline areas largely depends on successful germination, seedling emergence and establishment and efficient reproductive phase. Moreover, as environmental stress, it may have a strong influence on the
30 concentration of bioactive compounds of vegetables.

However, despite a substantial amount of literature on responses of plants to salinity stress, data on the effect of salt stress on flowering, fructification and on nutrient contents of fruits are
35 lacking. In a recent study, we demonstrated that salt stress reduced plant growth in five chili cultivars produced in Benin, and that there is a variability in salt tolerance of these cultivars.

The experiment was carried out in a screen
40 house at Center for Agricultural Research of Agonkanmey, Benin, from February to May 2017. Plants were cultivated at a temperature of 26/22°C day/night with natural light and a relative humidity of 55%. Seeds were incubated for germination in
45 tanks filled with potting moistened soil for two weeks. Young seedlings were then transferred to earthen small pots of 5.8 cm diameter and 6 cm height containing a mixture of potting soil and sandy loam soil 50:50 (one plant/pot) and cultivated
50 for one week before stress application. Plants 21 days old were submitted to salt stress in earthen big pots of 11.3 cm diameter and 14 cm height filled with 3 kg of a same mixture for 94 days. Treatments consisted of plant irrigation every two days with 100
55 ml/pot of 0, 30, 60,90 or 120 mM NaCl solution. The experiment was laid out as a completely randomized design (CRD) with one factor (NaCl concentrations) and three replications.

The date of appearance of the first flowers was
60 noted for each treatment; thus, the number of days it took for each plant to make its first flower from the start of the stress application was covered. Fruit ripening, number, size and fresh mass were also evaluated. Ripe fruits were collected and counted
65 for each treatment from their appearance to 45 days after the first fruit ripening (approximately 94 days from the start of stress application). The first ripe fruits samples from each treatment were photographed and two ripe fruits were selected
70 from each plant and weighed. Thus, a total of six (6) fruits were weighed per treatment to determine the average fresh mass of each fruit for each treatment. The average fresh mass of each pepper fruit is obtained for each treatment as the means of
75 the fresh mass of the six (6) fruits. As no fruit was obtained from plants cultivated in the presence of 90 and 120 mM NaCl, only fruits from 0, 30 and 60 mM NaCl were used for nutrients determination. A significant increase was observed in capsaicinoids.
80 These increases were 50 and 389% in comparison with the control respectively at 30 and 60 mM NaCl. Salt effect resulted in a significant decrease for vitamin B6, B12, and C. The decreases were 76, 82 and 65% in comparison with the control respectively
85 for vitamins B6, B12 and C at 60 mM NaCl.

This study indicated that increasing NaCl concentrations delayed significantly flowering and fruit ripening and reduced significantly fruits' number, size, fresh mass and vitamins B6, B12 and C

90 concentrations, but increased capsaicinoids
concentration and consequently fruit tangy
appearance. Thus, salt stress reduced the fruit
yields and deteriorated fruit nutritional quality
by reducing vitamins concentrations. Further
95 study is necessary to check the implication of
capsaicinoid synthetase activity in the increase of
the capsaicinoids concentration under salt stress in
our local chili cultivar fruits.

Figure 1: Chili Peppers Exposed to Salt Stress

NaCl con-centration (mM)	Average days to first flower	Average days to first fruit	Average number of fruit
0	23.66	48	6
30	23.66	52	3
60	31.66	66	2
90	39.66	0	0
120	40.33	0	0

42

The primary purpose of the passage is to

A) recommend an approach for improving chili
   pepper production.

B) discuss the implications of salinity on raising
   chili peppers.

C) compile the results of several studies about
   salt and chili plants.

D) describe efforts to increase the nutritional
   value of chili peppers.

43

As used in line 4, "concentration" most nearly
means

A) attentiveness

B) dedication

C) accumulation

D) centralization

44

According to the passage, the reason that the chili
plant evolved to contain capsaicin in the fruit is
most likely to

A) add flavor to human food dishes.

B) be a part of herbal medicine remedies.

C) increase the plant's salt absorption.

D) protect the plant from predation.

CONTINUE

45

Which choice best supports the answer to the previous question?

A) Lines 8-10 ("Chili (Capsicum... human food")

B) Lines 10-12 ("Chili pepper... virtue")

C) Lines 15-18 ("Pepper... herbivores")

D) Lines 23-25 ("Salt stress... stages")

46

The author's discussion best supports which statement about chili pepper production in Benin?

A) Farmers do not realize the problem of salt stress.

B) It an important source of income for many farmers.

C) It is one of the largest sectors of the economy.

D) Most plants produce no fruits because of salt.

47

The comment in the first paragraph that "soil salinity and water irrigation are a reality" (lines 21-22) primarily serves to

A) emphasize the need for a different crop.

B) show that the environment is suitable for crops.

C) highlight the importance of the study.

D) describe methods to combat salt stress.

48

As used in line 63, "application" most nearly means

A) significance

B) diligence

C) request

D) execution

49

Based on the information in the passage, the experiment is open to the criticism that

A) the fruits selected for measurement may not have been representative of the other fruits in the group.

B) the change in number of capsaicinoids may have been based on variations in temperature rather than amount of salt.

C) fluctuation in humidity as fruits develop can affect the nutritional value of the mature fruit.

D) the results of the experiment may not be applicable to species of plant other than chili peppers.

50

Which choice provides the best evidence for the answer to the previous question?

A) Lines 41-44 ("Plants were... of 55%")

B) Lines 67-70 ("The first... and weighed")

C) Lines 75-78 ("As no... determination")

D) Lines 91-94 ("Thus, salt... concentrations")

51

According to figure 1, how many days did it take the average chili plant with 60 mM of NaCl to bear fruit?

A) 2

B) 31.66

C) 48

D) 66

52

Which statement about chili pepper growth is supported by both figure 1 and the passage?

A) Plants subjected to high NaCl concentrations were highest in capsaicinoids.

B) Plants subjected to high NaCl concentrations had lower nutritional value.

C) Plants with a NaCl concentration of 90 mM or over did not generate viable fruit.

D) Plants with a NaCl concentration of 30 mM or less took about 23.66 days to flower.

STOP
If you finish before time is called, you may check your work on this section only.
Do not turn to any other section.

Writing and Language Test

35 MINUTES, 44 QUESTIONS

Turn to Section 2 of your answer sheet to answer the questions in this section

DIRECTIONS

Each passage below is accompanied by a number of questions. For some questions, you will consider how the passage might be revised to improve the expression of ideas. For other questions, you will consider how the passage might be edited to correct errors in sentence structure, usage, or punctuation. A passage or a question may be accompanied by one or more graphics (such as a table or graph) that you will consider as you make revising and editing decisions.

Some questions will direct you to an underlined portion of a passage. Other questions will direct you to a location in a passage or ask you to think about the passage as a whole.

After reading each passage, choose the answer to each question that most effectively improves the quality of writing in the passage or that makes the passage conform to the conventions of standard written English. Many questions include a "NO CHANGE" option. Choose that option if you think the best choice is to leave the relevant portion of the passage as it is.

Questions 1-11 are based on the following text that has been adapted from The New York Times' What Would Giving Health Care to Undocumented Immigrants Mean?

[1] The United States is facing multiple debates about providing free healthcare for the homeless. People in the country illegally are generally barred from enrolling in Medicaid or Medicare. They are also prohibited from buying insurance through the marketplaces set up by the Affordable Care Act, or Obamacare. Undocumented children do not qualify for the Children's Health Insurance Program, commonly known as CHIP.

[2] But six states and the District of Columbia have expanded their Medicaid programs to cover children through 18 years old (California recently approved coverage through age 25), regardless of immigration status [3] About 16 states cover income-eligible pregnant women, also regardless of residency status.

1

The writer is considering deleting the underlined sentence. Should the sentence be kept or deleted?

A) Kept, because it shows the importance of healthcare.

B) Deleted, because it provides irrelevant information.

C) Deleted, because it disrupts the flow of logic in the paragraph.

D) Kept, because the sentence makes for an effective introduction to the passage.

2

A) NO CHANGE

B) However, this trend

C) However, this trend is changing. Six states and the District of Columbia

D) The District of Columbia and six states

3

A) NO CHANGE

B) About 16 states cover pregnant women

C) About 16 states cover pregnant women, also regardless of residency status.

D) Delete the underlined portion

Many illegal immigrants 4 receiving primary care and prescription drugs for a sliding-scale fee at 1,400 federally funded health care centers spread across 11,000 communities. Those centers are required to treat anyone, regardless of ability to pay, and administrators do not ask patients about their citizenship status. The centers serve some 27 million people, but do not have estimates on how many are undocumented. Of course, when undocumented immigrants arrive at hospitals for medical emergencies, they will be treated.

Some undocumented residents receive coverage through their own or a spouse's employer-provided plan, 5 though they are less likely than legal residents or citizens to have jobs with employer coverage.

If the United States were to begin providing comprehensive health coverage to undocumented 6 immigrants; it would be an outlier, health policy experts say. Even countries with universal, government-run coverage like Norway place tough restrictions on health care for undocumented immigrants. Most immigrants can get emergency care but have to pay other costs.

4

A) NO CHANGE

B) received

C) have received

D) receive

5

A) NO CHANGE

B) while

C) despite

D) furthermore

6

A) NO CHANGE

B) immigrants:

C) immigrants,

D) immigrants -

Thailand, with waves of migrant workers, [7] is considering to offer one of the most generous pro grams, screening immigrants for diseases and allowing them to buy into the national health insurance.

[8] According to the Pew Research Center, in 2017 there were about 10.5 million undocumented immigrants in the United States. According to estimates, 5.5 to 6 million still need coverage.

Neither the Congressional Budget Office nor independent experts have worked up a cost estimate [9] ; some economists say that the expense of providing primary care would eventually pay off, because it would keep people [10] from waiting.

7

A) NO CHANGE
B) has considered
C) is considered
D) considered

8

A) NO CHANGE
B) Despite the
C) In addition to the
D) DELETE the underlined word

9

A) NO CHANGE
B) , some
C) DELETE the underlined word
D) . Some

10

A) NO CHANGE
B) from waiting until they were very sick to seek treatment.
C) from waiting to pay for healthcare.
D) DELETE the underlined section.

CONTINUE

Some studies [11] to find that undocumented immigrants tend to be younger and healthier (therefore potentially cheaper) than the overall American population, particularly because they were able to survive arduous travel for weeks to come to the United States.

Other research suggests that they are disproportionately poor, with high rates of diabetes, obesity and hypertension.

[11]

A) NO CHANGE

B) have found

C) is finding

D) will find

Questions 12-22 are based on the following text that has been adapted from South African History Online's Ngugi wa Thiong'o.

(1)

The academic and social [12] activist Ngugi wa Thiong'o is one of the greatest writers of the 20th century. He was born James wa Thiong'o Ngugi in Limuru, Kenya on 5 January 1938 during the height of British colonialism. He attended Kamandura, Manguu and Kinyogori primary schools before proceeding to Alliance High School. During his education, the background was the Mau Mau war of independence between 1952 and 1963. He obtained a Bachelor of Arts degree from Makerere University in 1963, the same year that Kenya became independent from Britain. The following year he got another Bachelor of Arts degree at the University of Leeds in Britain.

(2)

[13] Thiong'o wrote the play, *The Black Hermit* whilst still an undergraduate at Makerere University. It was [14] done at Kampala National Theatre during the country's independence celebrations in 1962. Thiong'o published his first novel, *Weep Not, Child*, in 1964 and the second, *The River Between*, the following year.

[12]

A) NO CHANGE

B) activist; Ngugi

C) activist - Ngugi

D) activist, Ngugi

[13]

At this point, the author is considering including the following sentence:

"Thiong'o is a prolific writer who has written both plays and novels."

Should the writer make this addition here?

A) Yes, because it provides information that helps clarify prior statements.

B) No, because it would be more effective as a conclusion at the end of the paragraph.

C) Yes, because it provides an effective introduction for the following information.

D) No, because it provides irrelevant information.

[14]

A) NO CHANGE

B) performed

C) DELETE the underlined portion

D) written

(3)

[15] In 1967 he worked as a lecturer in the Department of English at the University of Nairobi and published *A Grain of Wheat* in July the same year. Subsequently, he [16] became a senior lecturer and the chair of the literature department. This led to him being instrumental in a movement that saw the changing of the same department into the Department of Literature, which advantaged African literature. He discarded his English name, James, in favor of Ngugi during this time.

[15]

Which choice provides the best conclusion to this paragraph (2)?

A) NO CHANGE

B) *A Grain of Wheat* became a hugely successful novel.

C) He was part of a movement that focused on African literary traditions.

D) This name was significant and marked Thiong'o's desire to focus on his roots.

[16]

A) NO CHANGE

B) had

C) is

D) was being

(4)

In 1976 Thiong'o co-authored the play, *The Trial of Dedan Kimathi* with a colleague, Micere Githae Mugo. The play was performed in an open-air theatre and ruffled feathers within the country's political [17] leadership. The British settler establishment [18] killed the revolutionary Kimathi in 1957 for being on the forefront of the Mau Mau uprisings.

17

A) NO CHANGE

B) although the

C) leadership. This was because the

D) DELETE the underlined portion

18

A) NO CHANGE

B) will kill

C) kills

D) was killing

(5)

[19] Thiong'o chose to write in the Kikuyu language around this period. He lost his job at the university and, upon release from prison in 1978, he struggled to get any employment in the country. Owing to political challenges at home, wa Thiong'o decided to live in exile. [20]

[19]

At this point, the writer is considering changing the underlined sentence to the following:

"During this period Thiong'o made another significant change, like that of his name, and instead of writing in English, began writing in his native language."

Should the writer make this change here?

A) Yes, because it improves clarity, tone, and voice of the sentence.

B) Yes, because it provides an effective conclusion.

C) No, because it would be more effective as a conclusion at the end of the paragraph.

D) No, because it includes irrelevant information.

[20]

At this point, the writer is considering adding the following sentence:

"As a result, he lived in Britain between 1982 and 1989.

Should the writer make this addition here?

A) No, because it provides information that interrupts the logical flow of the passage.

B) No, because it provides a more effective introduction and should be placed at the beginning of the paragraph.

C) Yes, because it provides relevant information that clarifies a previous statement.

D) Yes, because it is an effective transition.

(6)

[21] The following year Thiong'o published another novel, Petals of Blood, which portrayed the state of the country post-colonialism. The same year, his play, *Ngaahika Ndena (I Will Marry When I Want)*, proved too challenging to the authorities and was consequently banned. He was subjected to an onslaught of political persecutions. Thiong'o's collection of books was confiscated and he spent the rest of 1978 in detention without trial at Kamiti Maximum Prison.

[21]

To make this passage most logical, paragraph (6) should be placed:

A) before paragraph (2)

B) before paragraph (5)

C) where it is now

D) after paragraph (3)

[22]

Which of the following most effectively captures a main point of the passage?

A) Colonialism has long-lasting effects.

B) Ngugi wa Thiong'o lives in exile because he does not like his home country.

C) One should not make art that is political.

D) Thiong'o used his writing to make political statements.

Questions 23-33 are based on the following text that has been adapted from Douglas Cohen's Music: Its Language, History, and Culture.

The human voice 23 <u>has been</u> a natural musical instrument, and singing by people of all ages, alone or in groups, is an activity in all human cultures. The human voice is essentially a wind instrument, with the lungs supplying the air, the vocal cords setting up the vibrations, and the cavities of the upper throat, mouth, and nose forming a resonating chamber. 24 Different pitches are obtained by varying the tension of the opening between the vocal cords.

23

A) NO CHANGE

B) were

C) are

D) is

24

At this point, the author is considering including the following sentence:

"A distinctive potential of the human voice is its ability to attain different pitches."

Should the writer make this addition here

A) Yes, because it provides an effective transition between ideas.

B) No, because it would be more effective as an introduction to this paragraph.

C) Yes, because it provides an effective transition to the following paragraph.

D) No, because it provides irrelevant information.

In the Western tradition, voices are classified according to their place in the pitch spectrum: soprano, mezzo soprano, and alto [25] being the respective designations for the high, middle, and low ranges of women's voices, and tenor, baritone, and bass for men's. A counter tenor or contra tenor is a male singer with the range of an alto. [26] These terms are applied not only to voices and singers but also to the parts they sing.

25

At this point, the writer is considering deleting the underlined text. Should the writer make this change here?

A) Yes, because it is redundant.

B) Yes, because it negatively affects language, clarity, and tone.

C) No, because it provides necessary information.

D) No, because it is an effective transition between ideas.

26

A) NO CHANGE

B) Furthermore, these

C) Finally, these

D) Ultimately, these

---

(1) [27] <u>However,</u> because the vocal cords are muscles, even the most modest singing activity can increase their flexibility and elasticity, and serious training can do so to a remarkable degree.
(2) Singers also work to extend the power of their voices, control pitch, and quality at all dynamic levels, and develop speed and agility. [28] (3) <u>The range of an individual's voice is determined by the physiology of the vocal cords.</u>

27

A) NO CHANGE

B) However

C) However -

D) However;

28

To make this passage most logical, the underlined sentence should be placed:

A) after sentence (2)

B) NO CHANGE

C) before sentence (1)

D) after sentence (1)

Vocal quality and singing technique are other important criteria in the classification of voices. [29] A singer's tone color is determined in part by anatomical features, which include the mouth, nose, and throat as well as the vocal cords. [30] But the cultivation of a particular vocal timbre is also strongly influenced by other factors.

[29]

The writer is considering deleting the underlined sentence. Should the sentence be kept or deleted?

A) Kept, because it provides relevant information.

B) Kept, because it provides extensive information about pitch.

C) Deleted, because it provides redundant information.

D) Deleted, because it provides irrelevant information.

[30]

At this point, the writer is considering changing the underlined section to the following:

"by aesthetic conventions and personal taste."

Should the writer make this change here?

A) No, because it is an ineffective transition.

B) No, because it provides redundant information.

C) No, because it eliminates relevant information.

D) Yes, because it improves clarity and voice.

A tight, nasal tone is associated with many Asian and Arabic traditions, whereas opera and gospel singers [31] <u>employs</u> a chest voice with pronounced vibrato. Even within a single musical tradition there may be fine distinctions based on the character and color of the voice. For example, among operatic voices, a lyric soprano has a [32] <u>light refined</u> quality and a dramatic soprano has a powerful, emotional tone.

Vocal music is often identified as sacred or secular on the basis of [33] <u>their</u> text. Sacred music may be based on a scriptural text or the words of a religious ceremony, or may deal with a religious subject. The words in secular music may express feelings, narrate a story, describe activities associated with work or play, comment on social or political situations, convey a nationalistic message, and so on.

31

A) NO CHANGE

B) employ

C) are employing

D) employed

32

A) NO CHANGE

B) light and refined

C) light, refined

D) light; refined

33

A) NO CHANGE

B) it's

C) they're

D) its

Questions 34-44 are based on the following text that has been adapted from Andrew Kusiak's Renewables: Share Data on Wind Energy

The energy industry has long met demand by [34] varying the rate at which it consumes fuel. Controlling the output of an oil-fired power plant is much like changing the speed of a [35] car press the accelerator pedal and more gas flows to the engine.

[36] Nevertheless, the wind cannot be turned up or down. Smart software can make wind farms more efficient and responsive. Computer models can predict wind speed and control the number and capacity of turbines in operation to meet energy demand. Low-vibration designs and health monitoring would enable turbines to run more smoothly, avoiding expensive failures of gearboxes and other components whose replacement can cost hundreds of thousands of dollars and take days.

34

A) NO CHANGE

B) vary

C) varied

D) varies

35

A) NO CHANGE

B) car, press

C) car - press

D) car : press

36

A) NO CHANGE

B) Despite this,

C) Furthermore,

D) However,

Optimizing renewables requires data: on device performance, energy output and weather predictions, seconds to days in advance. Vast quantities of information are collected by turbine manufacturers, operators and utility companies — yet hidden in [37] its archives. The information is prohibitively difficult for anyone outside to access. The lack of data sharing in the renewable-energy industry is hindering technical progress and squandering opportunities for improving the efficiency of energy markets. [38]

[37]

A) NO CHANGE

B) their

C) the

D) it's

[38]

At this point, the writer is considering adding the following sentence:

"I call on the energy industry to follow the examples of defense, commerce and health care and share its data openly so that researchers can design better solutions for powering our planet."

Should the writer make this addition here?

A) Yes, because it provides an effective transition.

B) Yes, because it provides information that helps clarify prior information.

C) No, because it provides redundant information.

D) No, because it negatively impacts the use of voice in the paragraph.

[39] <u>Perhaps</u> this trend will change if it is known that there is money to be made. Once academic and industrial researchers develop suitable wind-farm management models and prove their value, software companies can sell energy and weather- monitoring and -predicting systems. Large technology companies such as the Hewlett Packard Enterprise or Google could establish wind-energy divisions for planning and balancing energy across different states and countries, as General Electric has done in wind-turbine manufacturing.

[40]

Figure 1

POOR PERFORMANCE
Intermittent faults caused by blade misalignment or electronic problems, for example, can reduce the power produced by a single turbine. (Data taken at 10-minute intervals over 5 days.)

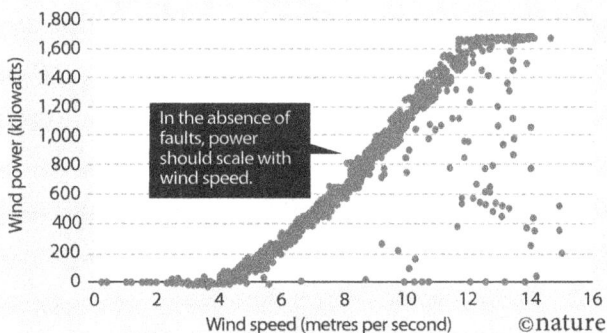

Leveraging renewable-energy data makes economic sense for a product [41] <u>-- like electricity --</u> that is universal. Unlike other commercial industries, energy utilities do not compete on the basis of product quality.

39

A) NO CHANGE

B) Additionally,

C) Possibly

D) It might

40

Which of the following provides the most effective support from Figure 1?

A) In general, wind power does not scale with wind speed.

B) Wind power always scales with wind speed.

C) In general, wind power scales with wind speed.

D) Wind power never scales with wind speed.

41

A) NO CHANGE

B) electricity

C) like, electricity

D) Delete the underlined section

CONTINUE

42 Nevertheless, they depend on generation and distribution processes and business operations, which are the greatest beneficiaries of big-data mining. Efficient renewable-energy plants equipped with software for accurate power prediction and responsive management will be able to take advantage of real-time, or 'spot', energy **43** prices - supplying more when prices and demand are high and less when they are low. This extra profitability will encourage more firms and utility companies to acquire renewable-energy assets.

44 The renewable-energy industry needs to decide which data can be shared and at what risk. Wind speed and direction, for example, could be released given that anyone could measure them. Although data on the real-time energy output of an entire wind farm should be rightfully protected for competitive reasons, sharing power produced by one or a few turbines would not compromise business value. When necessary, data could be transformed or anonymized; for example, by reporting relative percentage changes rather than absolute power values.

42

A) NO CHANGE

B) Rather,

C) Additionally,

D) Despite this,

43

A) NO CHANGE

B) prices; supplying

C) prices: supplying

D) prices supplying

44

The writer is considering deleting the underlined sentence. Should the sentence be kept or deleted?

A) Kept, because it provides an effective transition.

B) Deleted, because it interrupts the flow of the paragraph.

C) Deleted, because it provides information that is not related to the passage.

D) Kept, because it is an effective introduction to the paragraph.

STOP

**If you finish before time is called, you may check your work on this section only.
Do not turn to any other section.**

No Test Material On This Page

Math Test – No Calculator
25 MINUTES, 20 QUESTIONS

Turn to Section 3 of your answer sheet to answer the questions in this section.

DIRECTIONS

For questions 1-15, solve each problem, choose the best answer from the choices provided, and fill in the corresponding circle on your answer sheet. **For questions 16-20,** solve the problem and enter your answer in the grid on the answer sheet. Please refer to the directions before question 16 on how to enter your answers in the grid. You may use any available space in your test booklet for scratch work.

NOTES

1. The use of a calculator **is not permitted.**
2. All variables and expressions used represent real numbers unless otherwise indicated.
3. Figures provided in this test are drawn to scale unless otherwise indicated.
4. All figures lie in a plane unless otherwise indicated.
5. Unless otherwise indicated, the domain of a given function f is the set of all real numbers x for which $f(x)$ is a real number.

REFERENCE

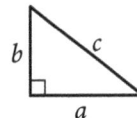
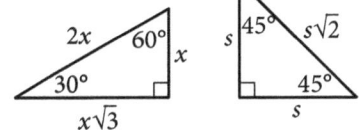

$A = \pi r^2$
$C = 2\pi r$

$A = \ell w$

$A = \frac{1}{2} bh$

$c^2 = a^2 + b^2$

Special Right Triangles

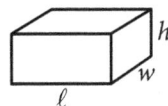

$V = \ell wh$

$V = \pi r^2 h$

$V = \frac{4}{3}\pi r^3$

$V = \frac{1}{3}\pi r^2 h$

$V = \frac{1}{3}\ell wh$

The number of degrees of arc in a circle is 360.

The number of radians of arc in a circle is 2π.

The sum of the measures in degrees of the angles of a triangle is 180.

1

When $\frac{2}{3}x + 4 = 10y$ and $x = 3$, what is the value of y?

A) $\frac{10}{13}$

B) $\frac{3}{5}$

C) 2

D) 6

2

$$6a - 4b = 24$$

$$-a + 2b = -8$$

If (a, b) is the solution to the system of equations above, what is the value of $a + b$?

A) −1

B) 1

C) 0

D) 2

3

A manager is calculating the amount of overtime pay she owes her employees. The equation $y = 20x + 25z$ represents the value of an employee's weekly paycheck in dollars (y), where x represents the number of regular hours worked and z represents the number of overtime hours worked. What is the best interpretation for the value 25 in the equation?

A) Number of total hours worked

B) Number of overtime hours

C) Rate of pay per normal hour of work

D) Rate of pay per overtime hour of work

4

Simplify the following expression: $x(x - 5) + 4(x - 3) - 8$.

A) $(x + 11)^2$

B) $11x - 11$

C) $(x - 5)(x + 4)$

D) $x^2 - x - 8$

5

What is the value of $\left(x + \sqrt{3}\right)^2 + 3$ when $x = 0$?

A) 6

B) 0

C) 3

D) −3

6

$$dx = -7y + 4$$

$$4x + 14y = e$$

In the system of equations above, for what value of d is the system true for all real numbers?

A) 6

B) 2

C) 4

D) –2

7

Which of the following expressions is equivalent to $\dfrac{x^{-1}y^2}{y^3 x^{-2}}$?

A) $\dfrac{y}{x}$

B) y

C) x

D) $\dfrac{x}{y}$

8

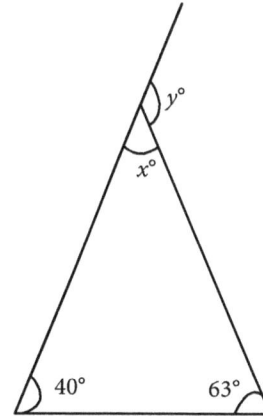

(Note: Figure is not drawn to scale.)

In the figure above, what is the value of $y°$?

A) 103°

B) 77°

C) 13°

D) 90°

9

A line passes through points $\left(2, \dfrac{1}{2}\right)$ and (4, 2).

What is the equation of a line perpendicular to this line, which passes through (3, –2)?

A) $y = -\dfrac{4}{3}x - 2$

B) $y = \dfrac{3}{4}x + 2$

C) $y = \dfrac{3}{4}x - 1$

D) $y = \dfrac{-4}{3}x + 2$

10

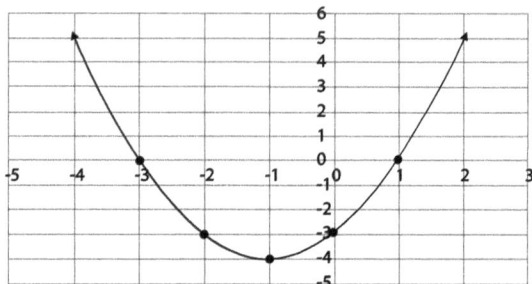

Which of the following equations, when graphed on the (x, y) plane above, expresses the following function in vertex form?

A) $y = \dfrac{1}{2}x - \dfrac{5}{2}$

B) $y = (x+1)^2 - 4$

C) $y = (x-1)(x+3)$

D) $y = (x+1)^2 + 4$

11

Which of the following expressions correctly expresses $\dfrac{-i+2+3i}{4-3i+4i}$ in the form $a+bi$, when $i = \sqrt{-1}$ and a and b are both real numbers?

A) $\dfrac{3}{8} + \dfrac{5i}{8}$

B) $\dfrac{5}{8} + \dfrac{3i}{8}$

C) $\dfrac{10}{17} - \dfrac{6i}{17}$

D) $\dfrac{10}{17} + \dfrac{6i}{17}$

12

The formula for air resistance is can be represented by the equation $F = -cv^2$, where F is the force of air resistance, c is the air constant, and v is the velocity of the object. Which of the following equation represents v in terms of c and F?

A) $v = cF^2$

B) $v = \sqrt{-\dfrac{c}{4F}}$

C) $v = \sqrt{\dfrac{F}{-c}}$

D) $v = \sqrt{\dfrac{F}{c}}$

CONTINUE

13

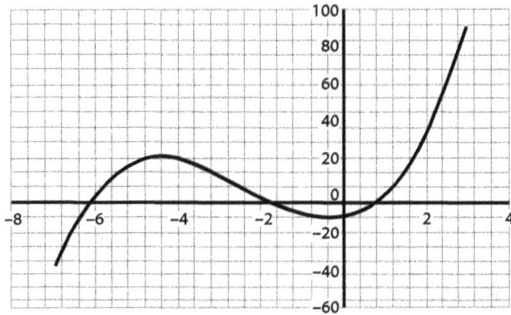

Which equation below represents the graph in the xy-plane above?

A) $y = \left(x^2 + 5x - 6\right)\left(x + 2\right)$

B) $y = \left(x^2 + 5x - 6\right)\left(x + 3\right)$

C) $y = \left(x^2 + 3x + 2\right)\left(x + 1\right)$

D) $y = \left(x^2 + 3x + 2\right)\left(x + 2\right)$

14

A furniture store is having a sale on lamps and rugs. Which function below represents the total purchase (T) after the 20% discount of (l) lamps and (r) rugs if both cost \$75 each?

A) $T = 0.2\left(75rl\right)$

B) $T = 0.8\left(75r + 75l\right)$

C) $T = 1.2\left(75r + l\right)$

D) $T = 0.2\left(l + 75r\right)$

15

Simplify the following expression: $\dfrac{2x+1}{x-3} - \dfrac{x-1}{x+2}$.

A) $\dfrac{x^2 + 9x - 1}{x^2 - x - 6}$

B) $\dfrac{x^2 + 9x - 1}{x^2 + x - 6}$

C) $\dfrac{x^2 - x - 6}{2x - 1}$

D) $\dfrac{x^2 + x - 6}{\left(x+2\right)\left(x-3\right)}$

DIRECTIONS

For questions 16–20, solve the problem and enter your answer in the grid, as described below, on the answer sheet.

1. Although not required, it is suggested that you write your answer in the boxes at the top of the columns to help you fill in the circles accurately. You will receive credit only if the circles are filled in correctly.
2. Mark no more than one circle in any column.
3. No question has a negative answer.
4. Some problems may have more than one correct answer. In such cases, grid only one answer.
5. **Mixed numbers** such as $3\frac{1}{2}$ must be gridded as 3.5 or 7/2. (If | 3 | 1 | / | 2 | is entered into the grid, it will be interpreted as $\frac{31}{2}$, not $3\frac{1}{2}$.)
6. **Decimal answers:** If you obtain a decimal answer with more digits than the grid can accommodate, it may be either rounded or truncated, but it must fill the entire grid.

Answer: $\frac{7}{12}$

Write answer in boxes.

← Fraction line

Grid in result.

Answer: 2.5

← Decimal point

Acceptable ways to grid $\frac{2}{3}$ are:

Answer: 201 – either position is correct

NOTE: You may start your answers in any column, space permitting. Columns you don't need to use should be left blank.

16

Jerry is buying cups and napkins for a party. If he buys twice as many napkins as cups, and napkins cost $2 each and cups cost $3 each, how many cups did he buy if he spends $105 in total? Note: Disregard tax in your answer.

17

What is the value of $-x$ in the function

$$f(x) = \left(\frac{x^2 + x - 12}{x + 4}\right)^2 \text{ when } f(x) = 25?$$

18

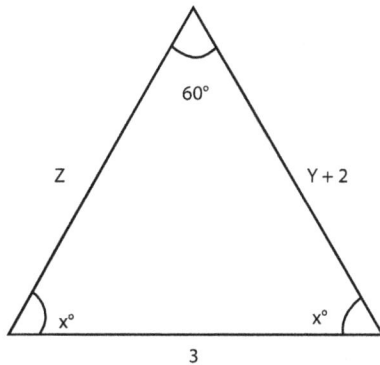

According to the triangle above, what is the value of side Z?

19

In a right triangle, angles $x° + y° = 90°$. If the $cos(cos(x)) = 5/12$, what is the value of $sin(sin(y))$

20

$$3x + y = 9$$
$$-x + 5y = 21$$

According to the system of equations for ordered pair (x, y) above, what is the value of $x + y$?

STOP

**If you finish before time is called, you may check your work on this section only.
Do not turn to any other section.**

Math Test – Calculator

55 MINUTES, 38 QUESTIONS

Turn to Section 4 of your answer sheet to answer the questions in this section.

DIRECTIONS

For questions 1-30, solve each problem, choose the best answer from the choices provided, and fill in the corresponding circle on your answer sheet. **For questions 31-38**, solve the problem and enter your answer in the grid on the answer sheet. Please refer to the directions before question 16 on how to enter your answers in the grid. You may use any available space in your test booklet for scratch work.

NOTES

1. The use of a calculator **is permitted.**
2. All variables and expressions used represent real numbers unless otherwise indicated.
3. Figures provided in this test are drawn to scale unless otherwise indicated.
4. All figures lie in a plane unless otherwise indicated.
5. Unless otherwise indicated, the domain of a given function f is the set of all real numbers x for which $f(x)$ is a real number.

REFERENCE

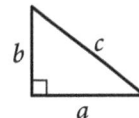
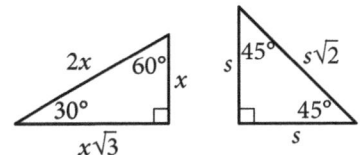

$A = \pi r^2$
$C = 2\pi r$

$A = \ell w$

$A = \frac{1}{2}bh$

$c^2 = a^2 + b^2$

Special Right Triangles

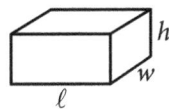
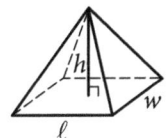

$V = \ell w h$

$V = \pi r^2 h$

$V = \frac{4}{3}\pi r^3$

$V = \frac{1}{3}\pi r^2 h$

$V = \frac{1}{3}\ell w h$

The number of degrees of arc in a circle is 360.

The number of radians of arc in a circle is 2π.

The sum of the measures in degrees of the angles of a triangle is 180.

1

Eliza is moving to a new house. If her living room is 175 square feet and she has a couch and table that measure 10 x 7 feet in total, how much empty space will she have left in her living room once she arranges the couch and table?

A) $70\ ft^2$

B) $105\ ft^2$

C) $150\ ft^2$

D) $175\ ft^2$

2

Jackie is scheduling her next haircut. If her hair is already 10 inches long and she knows her hair grows at least an inch every two months, which equation represents the length of her hair (y) after (x) months?

A) $y \geq 0.5x + 10$

B) $y \leq x + 10$

C) $y \geq 2x - 10$

D) $y \leq 10 - 0.5x$

3

A golfer hits a golf ball at a driving range. If the equation $h = t^2 + 15t$ (t=time in seconds) represents the height of the ball (h) in feet, what is the height four seconds after the ball was hit?

A) $74\ ft$

B) $75\ ft$

C) $76\ ft$

D) $77\ ft$

For questions 4 and 5, refer to the following information:

Thomas writes practice tests for a test prep company at a rate of $2 per question. If he writes 150 questions he earns a bonus of $75.

4

How many questions must Thomas write per day to earn his bonus after one week? Round the number of questions to the next whole number.

A) 20

B) 21

C) 22

D) 23

5

If Thomas writes 150 questions in one week, and earns his bonus, how much money will he make?

A) $383

B) $378

C) $380

D) $375

6

When Jen is x years old, her brother's age can be calculated using the expression $3x - 12$. When Jen is 15 years old, what is the difference between Jen and her brother's age?

A) 12

B) 18

C) 33

D) 45

7

How many real solutions does $y = 2x^2 - 3x + 5$ have?

A) 2

B) 1

C) 0

D) Cannot be determined

8

Doug's car holds 50 gallons of fuel. If he drives 150,000 miles at 35 miles per gallon, how many full tanks of gas will he go through on his journey if he starts with a full tank?

A) 10

B) 25

C) 72

D) 86

9

Jennifer is putting together panels of speakers for a conference. There are two panels, one that is 60 minutes and one is 120 minutes. Jennifer is offering speakers on the 60 minute panel $50 for their time, and the speakers on the 120 minute panel $110 for their time. If Jennifer budgets $900 for 12 total speakers, which of the following systems of equations represents the number of 60 minute panelists (x) and 90 minute panelists (y)?

A) $x + y = 12, 50x + 110y = 900$

B) $x + y = 900, 50x + 110y = 12$

C) $xy = 12, 50y + 110x = 900$

D) $x - y = 900, 50x + 110y = 12$

10

If $f(x) = x^2 + x$, which of the following equations is equal to $f(x + 2)$?

A) $x^2 + 4$

B) $(x + 2)(x + 3)$

C) $x^2 + 5x - 6$

D) $4x + 4$

11

Number of family members	Number of students
1	3
2	10
3	12
4	6
5	2
6	3

The number of family members which students in a class have invited to graduation are listed in the table above. If every invited family member needs a ticket to graduation, how many tickets does the school need to issue?

A) 100

B) 112

C) 113

D) 115

12

Tyrone is creating a study schedule for his midterms over (y) weekend days and (x) weekdays. If he wants to study for at least 50 hours per week, with 10 hours per day over the weekend, then how many hours does he need to study per weekday?

A) 3

B) 4

C) 5

D) 6

13

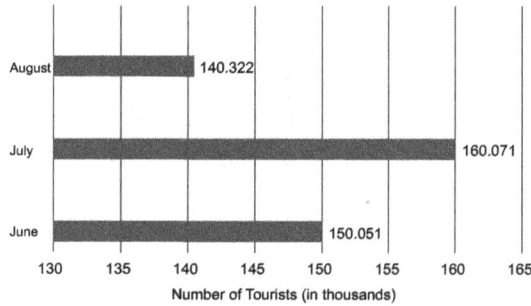

The graph above represents the number of tourists in a city over three months during the summer:

What is the average number of tourists in the city over the three months?

A)   150,020

B)   150,148

C)   145,098

D)   160,333

14

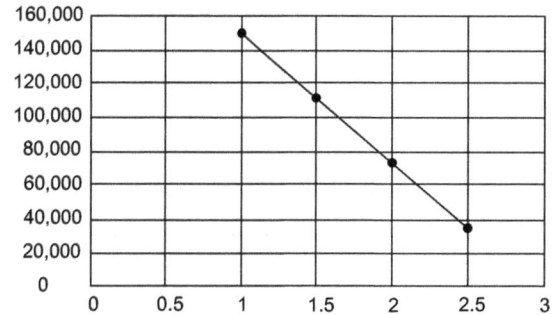

The graph above represents the average salary as it corresponds to distance from the city center:

According to the graph, which value is closest to the average salary at 1.75 miles from the city center?

A) $60,000

B) $70,000

C) $90,000

D) $120,000

15

If Jamie drove 4,154 miles at (x) mph for 62 hours, how many mph under the 70 mph speed limit did he drive?

A)   10 mph

B)   8 mph

C)   5 mph

D)   3 mph

16

	Took a gap year	Did not take a gap year	Total
Freshman	37	75	112
Sophomore	21	62	83
Junior	40	60	100
Senior	15	82	97
Total	113	279	392

The table above includes the results of a survey of students at a school who took a gap year:

If a freshman or sophomore is chosen at random, what is the probability that they took a gap year?

A) $\dfrac{58}{195}$

B) $\dfrac{58}{392}$

C) $\dfrac{112}{392}$

D) $\dfrac{83}{392}$

17

A school is renovated so that it is 15% larger than before. If the school currently holds a maximum of 744 students after the renovation, how many students did it hold before the renovation?

A) 512

B) 647

C) 745

D) 807

18

Cathy is counting the number of cans her students collected for a food drive. Her class of 22 students collected 157 cans. If one student brought 50 cans and five students brought none, how many cans, on average, did each student in the rest of her class bring? Round to the nearest can.

A) 6

B) 7

C) 8

D) 9

Questions 19 and 20 refer to the following table:

The table below represents the number of species of butterfly found in parks over two different seasons:

	Spring	Summer
Park A	32	22
Park B	16	10
Park C	17	20
Park D	40	32
Park E	23	17

19

What is the difference in the average number of butterflies in the parks per season?

A) 5.4

B) 15.1

C) 20.2

D) 25.1

20

Which ratio represents the relationship between Spring and Summer for park B?

A) 8:4

B) 5:8

C) 8:5

D) 4:3

21

Elizabeth needs to write a 25-page paper. If she wants to take a day off in the next 7 days, how many pages must she write per day to finish the paper after one week?

A) 3.5

B) 4.17

C) 5.23

D) 6.5

Questions 22 and 23 refer to the following information:

The equation of the acceleration of an object sinking in water can be represented by

$$a = g\left(1 - \frac{m_w}{m_o}\right)$$

Where (a) is acceleration in meters per second, (g) is the gravitational constant of 9.8 meters per second squared, m_w is the mass of the displaced water and m_o is the mass of the object itself, both in grams.

22

Which of the following expresses the mass of the displaced water (m_w) in terms of the other variables?

A) $m_w = -m_o\left(\dfrac{a}{g} - 1\right)$

B) $m_w = \dfrac{-m_o}{\left(\dfrac{a}{g} - 1\right)}$

C) $m_w = \left(\dfrac{a}{g} + 1\right)(-m_o)$

D) $m_w = \left(\dfrac{am_o}{g} - 1\right)$

23

What is the value of (a) when an object of a mass of 15 grams displaces 10 grams of water?

A) 3.12 m/s^2

B) 3.27 m/s^2

C) 3.5 m/s^2

D) 4.1 m/s^2

24

What is the center of the circle represented by the equation $x^2 - 8x + y^2 - 2x = -8$?

A) (1,4)

B) (4,4)

C) (4,1)

D) (3,3)

25

For the graph of a parabola with a positive lead coefficient, and a vertex at (2,1), which quadrant(s) does the graph not pass through?

i.   Quadrant II

ii. Quadrant III

iii. Quadrant IV

A) i

B) i and ii

C) ii and iii

D) i, ii, and iii

26

If the x-intercepts of the graph of a quadratic function are (−1, 0) and (5, 0), and the graph has not been dilated or reflected from the parent function, what is the distance between the points on the graph intercepted by the line $y = 7$?

A) 3

B) 8

C) 9

D) 10

27

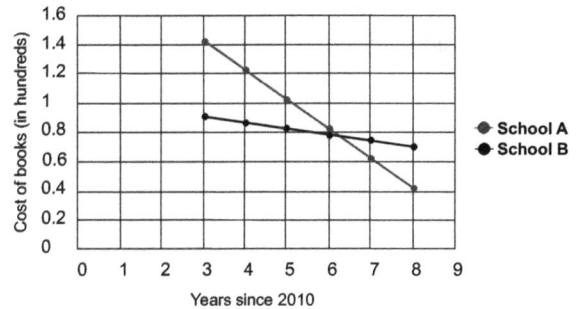

The graph above represents the approximate cost of textbooks in college for two different schools.

Between which years was the cost of textbooks equal at both schools?

A) 2013 – 2014

B) 2014 – 2015

C) 2015 – 2016

D) 2016 – 2017

28

A circle at the origin has a radius of $\sqrt{2}$. Which ordered pair below represents a point on the circle?

A) (2,0)

B) (1,1)

C) $\left(\sqrt{2},1\right)$

D) (0,0)

29

$$-x + 2y = 8.1$$

$$5x - 3y = -\frac{122}{5}$$

The system of equations above can be solved by solution (x, y). What is the value of $2x - y$?

A) −3.5

B) 2.3

C) 7

D) −9.3

30

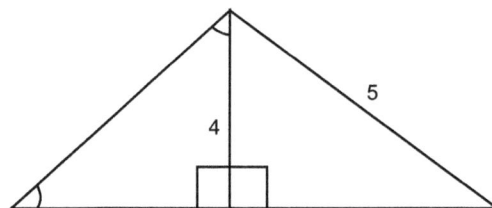

(Note: Figure is not drawn to scale.)

What is the total area of the figure above?

A) 10

B) 11

C) 13

D) 14

DIRECTIONS

For questions 31–38, solve the problem and enter your answer in the grid, as described below, on the answer sheet.

1. Although not required, it is suggested that you write your answer in the boxes at the top of the columns to help you fill in the circles accurately. You will receive credit only if the circles are filled in correctly.
2. Mark no more than one circle in any column.
3. No question has a negative answer.
4. Some problems may have more than one correct answer. In such cases, grid only one answer.
5. **Mixed numbers** such as $3\frac{1}{2}$ must be gridded as 3.5 or 7/2. (If 3 1 / 2 is entered into the grid, it will be interpreted as $\frac{31}{2}$, not $3\frac{1}{2}$.)
6. **Decimal answers:** If you obtain a decimal answer with more digits than the grid can accommodate, it may be either rounded or truncated, but it must fill the entire grid.

Answer: $\frac{7}{12}$

Write answer in boxes.
← Fraction line
Grid in result.

Answer: 2.5

← Decimal point

Acceptable ways to grid $\frac{2}{3}$ are:

Answer: 201 – either position is correct

NOTE: You may start your answers in any column, space permitting. Columns you don't need to use should be left blank.

31

Sea levels are rising by 18 cm every 50 years. How many years will it take for a city currently 5 meters above sea level to be at the water level? Note: 1 meter = 100 cm.

32

A number is four more than 17 times 13. What is the value of $\frac{1}{3}$ of that number?

33

What is the slope of a line perpendicular to the line formed by points (3, 2) and (–6, 4)?

34

Jed bought tickets to the drive-in movie for himself and 2 of his friends. If he paid a total of $34.50 for the tickets and the parking fee, and tickets were $7.50 each, how much was the parking fee in?

35

According to the equation $y = 4a - 0.5b$, what is the value of b when $a = 4$ and $y = -\frac{3}{2}$?

36

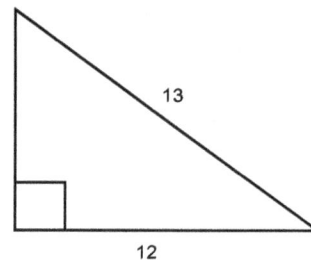

What is the perimeter of a triangle that is twice the size of the triangle above?

Questions 37 and 38 refer to the following information:

A teacher is diluting hydrochloric acid for her chemistry class. She adds 100 mL of a 3% solution to 150 ml of a 4.5% solution.

37

What is the percent of the strength of the resulting 250 ml solution of hydrochloric acid? Omit the % in your answer.

38

The teacher is dividing the resulting 250 ml to pairs of students. If she gives each pair of students 50 ml, how many total students does she have in her class?

STOP
**If you finish before time is called, you may check your work on this section only.
Do not turn to any other section.**

Section #1 – Reading Test

#	Correct Answer	#	Correct Answer	#	Correct Answer	#	Correct Answer	#	Correct Answer	#	Correct Answer
1	B	11	D	21	C	31	D	41	D	51	D
2	D	12	B	22	D	32	A	42	B	52	C
3	C	13	A	23	B	33	D	43	C		
4	B	14	C	24	A	34	C	44	D		
5	D	15	D	25	B	35	A	45	C		
6	B	16	A	26	C	36	B	46	B		
7	D	17	B	27	B	37	A	47	C		
8	A	18	B	28	A	38	B	48	D		
9	D	19	B	29	B	39	C	49	A		
10	A	20	D	30	D	40	A	50	B		

Number of Correct Answers [   ] Reading Test Raw Score

Section #2 – Writing and Language Test

#	Correct Answer	#	Correct Answer	#	Correct Answer	#	Correct Answer	#	Correct Answer
1	B	11	B	21	B	31	B	41	A
2	C	12	A	22	D	32	C	42	B
3	A	13	C	23	D	33	D	43	A
4	D	14	B	24	A	34	A	44	D
5	A	15	D	25	C	35	C		
6	C	16	A	26	B	36	D		
7	C	17	C	27	A	37	B		
8	A	18	A	28	C	38	D		
9	D	19	A	29	A	39	A		
10	B	20	C	30	D	40	C		

Number of Correct Answers [   ] Writing and Language Test Raw Score

Section #3 – Math Test (No Calculator)

#	Correct Answer	#	Correct Answer	#	Correct Answer	#	Correct Answer
1	B	6	B	11	D	16	15
2	A	7	D	12	C	17	2
3	D	8	A	13	A	18	3
4	C	9	D	14	B	19	0.417
5	A	10	B	15	A	20	6

Number of Correct Answers [   ] Math Test (No Calculator) Raw Score

Section #4 – Math Test (Calculator)

#	Correct Answer	#	Correct Answer	#	Correct Answer	#	Correct Answer
1	B	11	C	21	B	31	1389
2	A	12	D	22	A	32	75
3	C	13	B	23	B	33	9/2 or 4.5
4	C	14	C	24	C	34	12
5	D	15	D	25	C	35	35
6	B	16	A	26	B	36	60
7	C	17	B	27	D	37	3.9
8	D	18	B	28	B	38	10
9	A	19	A	29	D		
10	B	20	C	30	D		

Number of Correct Answers [   ] Math Test (Calculator) Raw Score

CONTINUE

```
┌─────────────┐  CONVERT  ┌─────────────┐
│             │    →      │             │──────────┐
└─────────────┘           └─────────────┘          │
 Reading Test              Reading Test             │
 Raw Score (0 - 52)        Score (10 - 40)          │
```

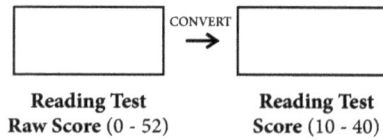

The following is a **Score Conversion Table** (Raw to Scaled) used by the College Board for an SAT® practice test available online. Although each SAT test is scored a bit differently, this table will give you an estimate of your score. Enter your raw scores in the appropriate boxes below, follow the conversion directions and know your estimated SAT scores for this test.

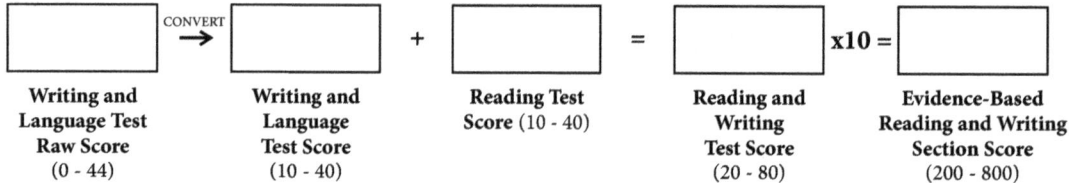

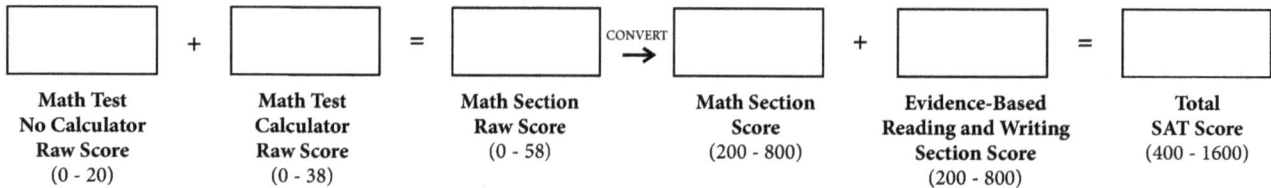

```
┌──────────┐ CONVERT ┌──────────┐       ┌──────────┐       ┌──────────┐        ┌──────────┐
│          │   →     │          │   +   │          │   =   │          │  x10 =  │          │
└──────────┘         └──────────┘       └──────────┘       └──────────┘        └──────────┘
 Writing and          Writing and        Reading Test       Reading and         Evidence-Based
 Language Test        Language           Score (10 - 40)     Writing             Reading and Writing
 Raw Score            Test Score                             Test Score          Section Score
 (0 - 44)             (10 - 40)                              (20 - 80)           (200 - 800)
                                                                                      ↓
┌──────────┐       ┌──────────┐       ┌──────────┐ CONVERT ┌──────────┐       ┌──────────┐       ┌──────────┐
│          │   +   │          │   =   │          │   →     │          │   +   │          │   =   │          │
└──────────┘       └──────────┘       └──────────┘         └──────────┘       └──────────┘       └──────────┘
 Math Test          Math Test          Math Section         Math Section       Evidence-Based      Total
 No Calculator      Calculator         Raw Score            Score              Reading and Writing  SAT Score
 Raw Score          Raw Score          (0 - 58)             (200 - 800)        Section Score        (400 - 1600)
 (0 - 20)           (0 - 38)                                                   (200 - 800)
```

Raw Score Conversion Table: Section and Test Scores

Raw Score (# of correct answers)	Math Section Score	Reading Test Score	Writing and Language Test Score	Raw Score (# of correct answers)	Math Section Score	Reading Test Score	Writing and Language Test Score
0	200	10	10	30	530	27	29
1	200	10	10	31	530	27	30
2	210	10	10	32	540	28	31
3	230	10	10	33	550	28	31
4	250	11	11	34	550	29	32
5	260	12	12	35	560	29	32
6	280	13	12	36	570	30	33
7	290	14	13	37	580	30	34
8	310	15	14	38	590	31	34
9	320	15	15	39	590	31	35
10	330	16	15	40	600	32	36
11	350	17	16	41	610	32	36
12	360	17	17	42	620	33	37
13	370	18	18	43	630	34	39
14	380	18	18	44	640	35	40
15	390	19	19	45	650	35	
16	400	20	19	46	660	36	
17	420	20	20	47	670	37	
18	430	21	21	48	680	37	
19	430	21	22	49	680	38	
20	440	22	22	50	690	39	
21	450	22	23	51	700	39	
22	460	23	24	52	720	40	
23	470	23	25	53	730		
24	480	24	25	54	740		
25	490	24	26	55	760		
26	500	25	26	56	770		
27	510	25	27	57	790		
28	510	26	28	58	800		
29	520	26	29				

1. **Choice B is the best answer** because "impetus" refers to a reason or motivation. The passage begins by explaining that the narrator "take[s] to the ship" (line 15) whenever he is feeling morbid and needs a change. He then clarifies why he does not travel as a passenger or officer, but instead travels as a regular sailor. Finally, he wonders why he chose a whaling boat rather than his regular occupation of merchant sailing, but assumes that it was due to powers beyond his control, "the invisible police officer of the Fates."
    Choice A is incorrect because the narrator is not a captain; he clearly states, "nor…do I ever go to sea as a Commodore, or a Captain, or a Cook." In addition, he is primarily a merchant sailor, not a whaler, as his one whaling voyage was "a sort of brief interlude and solo between more extensive performances." Choice C is incorrect because the narrator does not try to "argue" or "prove" that other people should not be passengers. The discussion about why he does not want to be a passenger is only one part of the development of the reason that he joined a whaling voyage. Choice D is incorrect because, while the narrator indicates that he was "impoverished" with "little or no money in my purse," he only describes why he set out on the whaling voyage. His present situation is not mentioned, so he could now be wealthy.

2. **Choice D is the best answer** because the narrator begins by saying that he feels compelled to go to the sea whenever he is in a dark "November" mood, and then specifies that he goes to sea as a sailor because it is more emotionally and financially rewarding than going as a passenger. In the last paragraph, there is a sudden shift (line 76, "But wherefore…") to a question or "speculation" about why he went on a whaling rather than merchant boat. He indicates that he does not really know the reason for why he did.
    Choice A is incorrect because the narrator discusses other roles on a ship, but he does not analyze why other people want to ride on ships. He only lists the other roles in his justification of why he does not go in those positions. Choice B is incorrect because the narrator discusses drawbacks but implies that his experience is very "gratifying" or "rewarding" because he gets paid, which is "really marvelous," to travel aboard a ship. Choice C is incorrect because, while the narrator does say that he is pushed around and that officers do not get the freshest air, he does not show "contempt" or "disregard and scorn" for them. He says that he is accustomed to his role (line 53, "this wears off in time"), which implies that he tolerates the difference in status. Moreover, he shows deep respect for cooks, whom he considers a type of officer.

3. **Choice C is the best answer** because the "coffin warehouses" and "funerals" are things that the narrator "pauses" at or "follows," meaning that he becomes fascinated with them. Coffins and funerals are strong symbols of death, so they "reinforce" or "strengthen" the description of his mood when he is "grim about the mouth" (line 7). The graphic imagery shows the depth of his depression and explain why he feels compelled to go to sea; his other option is "pistol and ball," referring to suicide by shooting oneself.
    Choice A is incorrect because there is no evidence in the passage that the coffins and funerals belong to friends of the narrator. "Every funeral I meet" (line 11) shows that he is fascinated by any funeral, not just those of people he knew. Choice B is incorrect because "November" is symbolic for a dark, depressed time. It does not literally refer to the time of year that the narrator experiences these feelings; "in my soul" (line 9) shows that the emotions are related to an internal clock rather than the calendar. Choice D is incorrect because the "coffin warehouses" and "funerals" are things he becomes interested in when he is depressed; they are not things that cause him to be depressed in the first place. The "source" or "origin" of his depression is not described in the passage.

4. **Choice B is the best answer** because in the context, "degree" refers to something in which most men cherish feelings towards the ocean. Choice B means "quantity," so it accurately shows that all men have some quantity of desire to go to the sea.
    All of the other choices can be eliminated because they do not describe what most men have in relation to the ocean. Choice A refers to status. Choice C refers to a measurement or level of attainment. Choice D refers to an official document showing that a course of study was completed.

5. **Choice D is the best answer** because the narrator describes his actions on the boat, "jump from spar to spar" (line 47) as similar to the jumping of a grasshopper. This work is because "they rather order me about some" (line 46); presumably "they" are the officers that are not "simple sailors." He says that it is true that he has to hop around obeying orders, but says that "at first, this sort of thing is unpleasant enough" (line 49) but that "this wears off in time" (line 53). Therefore, the analogy "anticipates" or "defends against" the argument that such work is "distasteful" or "unpleasant" because he says he is used to the role.

193   CONTINUE

Choice A is incorrect because "compensations" refers to payment. The narrator refers to payment later, but not in relation to the grasshopper analogy. Choice B is incorrect because the question is asking for an argument that the grasshopper analogy is used to disprove. Since the grasshopper analogy is that sailors are hopping around, or busy, the argument being disproved should be the opposite, that sailors are not busy. Choice C is incorrect because the analogy of the grasshopper does not prove that the narrator does not come from a good family. The list of names at the end of the paragraph only emphasize that it is hard for some elite people to accept orders.

6. **Choice B is the best answer** because "reimbursement" refers to payment, and in the fourth paragraph he explains how much he enjoys getting paid for traveling aboard a ship.
Choice A is incorrect because there is no reference to "excessive" or "too much" responsibilities for passengers. The narrator avoids being an officer because he does not want the "responsibilities" or "tasks" of running a ship. Choice C is incorrect because it only describes why he goes to sea; it does not specify why he prefers to be a sailor rather than a passenger. Choice D is incorrect because the narrator does not want "recognition" or "fame." He indicates that he is happy to leave those "to those who like them" (line 31).

7. **Choice D is the best answer** because the answer to the previous question is that the narrator does not travel as a passenger because he desires "reimbursement" or "payment" for his efforts. Choice D directly supports this claim because it says that he travels as a sailor because passengers do not get paid and he, as a sailor, does.
None of the other choices offer evidence that supports the claim that the narrator does not travel because he wants payment or money for riding a ship. Choice A gives a reason for riding, but not for being a seaman rather than a passenger. Choice B is incorrect because it only says that a passenger needs money to ride. It does not offer solid evidence for the claim that the narrator wants to be paid. Choice C shows why the narrator does not want to be an officer; it does not explain why he does not want to be a passenger.

8. **Choice A is the best answer** because the narrator uses the phrase when introducing reasons that he does not travel in other roles. He first uses it to show why he does not want to be a passenger—they are not paid. He then uses it to show why he does not want to be an officer—they do not get fresh air and exercise. Therefore, he is using the phrase to point out why he wants to be a simple sailor on a boat.
Choice B is incorrect because, while the narrator may have some "disdain" or feel that passengers are not worthy of respect, he does not use the phrase to introduce this idea. The first time he uses it is to show that he likes to get paid for his work. The second time he uses it does not relate to passengers at all; it shows why he prefers to be a simple sailor versus an officer. Choice C is incorrect because there is no hint in the passage that the narrator secretly wants "luxury" or "com fort and money." He does not have money, but he prefers hard exercise to being an officer, which would bring more money and honor. Choice D is incorrect because only the first use of the phrase refers to his lack of money. The second time the phrase is used, it relates to why he likes to work as a sailor rather than be an officer.

9. **Choice D is the best answer** because the narrator says that the simple sailors breathe the fresh air first, and that the captain "thinks he breathes it first; but not so" (line 73). The comparison is expanded to say that "In much the same way do the commonalty lead their leaders in many other things, at the same time that the leaders little suspect it" (lines 74-76). In other words, he is implying that the captain feels he has power, but really the sailors have influence and can lead or have control about many things in a quiet way.
All of the other choices can be eliminated because they are not supported by any evidence from the passage. For Choice A, there is no reference to how captains get appointed. For Choice B, the comment that they breathe second-hand air implies that captains do not deserve as much respect as they think they do. For Choice C, there is no evidence that captains do not understand the needs of sailors. They order sailors about, but they still could take care of sailors well.

10. **Choice A is the best answer** because the narrator is using the analogy of the theater to show that the whaling voyage was "brief" or "short" compared to his "extensive performances" or "longer jobs" as a merchant sailor. The word "solo" hints that he only went on one whaling voyage, so it was not his "usual" or "regular" employment.
Choice B is incorrect because the final sentence does not give any clue that a "tragedy" or "sad story" will follow. It only indicates that the narrator's experiences on the whaling boat, whatever they were, were a short break in

his regular work. Choice C is incorrect because the final sentence does not give a "rationale" or "reason" for going on the voyage. The narrator indicates in the previous sentence that he does not really know why he chose to go; the final sentence explains that he only went once. Choice D is incorrect because, although the final sentence says that the narrator had had longer positions, it does not say that the narrator had no other choices when he decided to go on a whaling voyage.

11. **Choice D is the best answer** because the author begins by saying that the U.S. government does not create slaves, it only recognizes laws that permit people to own slaves. He then gives the example of Belt's trial, in which a person could not be proved to be a slave because of inadequate paperwork related to the laws. His conclusion is that if all slavery-related laws were "removed" or "rescinded," then slavery would no longer exist.
Choice A is incorrect because, while the author feels that laws related to slavery should be revoked, he accepts that the laws are currently "binding" or "can be upheld." Choice B is incorrect because Belt's trial is offered as an example in support of the main claim that slavery could be eliminated if all laws related to it are abolished. Belt's trial is not the main topic of the passage. Choice C is incorrect because the author does not want to continue slavery. He does not want any documents that permit slaveholders to hold slaves, so he is not saying that they should have "adequate" or "sufficient" documents.

12. **Choice B is the best answer** because the writer is addressing the problem of slavery. He gives his opinion or viewpoint that eliminating all laws will get rid of the problem: "What then is necessary to be done to remove this prop from under the colossal statue of Slavery? Plainly, to repeal all laws recognising its existence" (lines 44-47). Choice A is incorrect because a "counterargument" is a set of reasons that attempts to prove that a different claim is untrue. However, the author is just supporting his own view about slavery. There is no claim that he says is wrong. Choice C is incorrect because the author is not summarizing an "occurrence" or "event." Instead, he is discussing the general situation regarding slavery and offering ways to change it. Choice D is incorrect because the author does not give "steps" or "a series of actions" for the reader to do. He says that laws regarding slavery should be eliminated, but offers no practical way to do it.

13. **Choice A is the best answer** because, in the context, "standard" refers to what the laws of the several slave-holding States are in relation to the government's action. Choice A refers to a general rule or requirement. Therefore, it accurately shows that the laws of the states are the rules that the government follows.
None of the other choices adequately establishes the relationship between the laws and the government's action. Choice B refers to the general excellence of something, so does not act as a measure. Choice C refers to the most perfect example, but the laws are not necessarily perfect. Choice D refers to how valuable something is rather than how it is used.

14. **Choice C is the best answer** because judge Edmonds' decision was that Belt was free. It was based on one legal point: there was inadequate paperwork showing Belt was sold as a slave. The decision did not include any consideration about whether it was fair to own a human being. Therefore, the decision was based on a legal technicality rather than "morality" or "ethics."
Choice A is incorrect because the author is not arguing that paperwork should be more complete; he is giving an example of the power of laws related to slavery to show why eliminating them would eliminate slavery. Choice B is incorrect because the author wants slavery eliminated, and feels that the most direct method is to eliminate slavery-related laws. It would defeat his point to create more laws. Choice D is incorrect because the author wants to end slavery. If judge Edmonds had freedom to interpret the laws, he might have agreed that Belt was a slave. He was restricted to the word of the law, so let Belt free. Therefore, the author is not arguing that judges should be able to interpret laws in more flexible ways.

15. **Choice D is the best answer** because Beecher always refers to the Abolitionists in the third person as "they." She also thinks that they have an incorrect interpretation of the situation. In other words, she is not "considering" or "counting" herself as one of them; she has a different way of thinking than they do.
Choice A is opposite of the correct answer because the author says that the Abolitionists are too concerned about whether "all slavery is a sin" (line 52) and that they should focus instead on the legal aspects of the problem. Choice B is incorrect because it cannot be supported by evidence from the passage. There is no clue about who Beecher's friends are or what their opinions are. Choice C is incorrect because, while Beecher says that there are

no documents proving that good treatment or wages make a man free, she does not say that such books should be made. She brings up the lack of documents to show that a different method of approaching the slavery issue is needed.

16. **Choice A is the best answer** because "proper" refers to the meaning of the language of the Abolitionists. Beecher indicates that the language is being used incorrectly, or is not interpreted the way it should be. Her argument is set up in the previous paragraph, that slavery only refers to "that legal act" (line 66) rather than kind treatment, wages, or attitude. She indicates that the Abolitionists are wrong because they "say that all slavery is a sin which ought to be immediately abandoned" (lines 69-70), but in reality, the "proper" or "correct" interpretation is that slavery is a legal act and slaveholders should "by the laws of the land, change all his slaves to freemen" (lines 67-68).

    Choice B is opposite the correct answer because Beecher is trying to show that the Abolitionists are using the language incorrectly, so she does not "approve" or "agree" with them. Choice C is incorrect because Beecher agrees with the goal that slavery should be abolished. She just feels that the Abolitionists are using the wrong method to reach their goal; she feels they should address the laws instead of the morality of slavery. Choice D is incorrect because she is highlighting the legal rather than ethical nature of the issue.

17. **Choice B is the best answer** because the second paragraph explains that no "dictionary, or any standard writer, nor any case in common discourse" (lines 62- 63) "supports" or "provides evidence" to show that "kind treatment" is a form of emancipation. She emphasizes that "that legal act" (line 66) is the only true definition of emancipation.

    None of the other choices are supported by evidence from the text. Choice A is incorrect because there is no reference about the ongoing relationship between owners and slaves. Choice C is incorrect because "humanely" refers to doing things in compassionate ways. Beecher does not say that all slaveholders are cruel. Choice D is incorrect because a "precedent" is a previous case that is used as a justification for future actions. Beecher says that it is possible to free slaves using legal methods, implying that it has been done before, so the words "there is no precedent for freeing slaves using any method" in the answer choice create too strong a claim.

18. **Choice B is the best answer** because Stearns writes, "Thus is Slavery legalized by our laws. What then is necessary to be done to remove this prop from under the colossal statue of Slavery? Plainly, to repeal all laws recognising its existence" (lines 43-47). These sentences show that he thinks that laws are the main "impediment" or "barrier" towards getting rid of slavery. Beecher also agrees on this point. She says that "It always signifies *that legal* act, which, by the laws of the land, changes a slave to a freeman" (lines 66-67). Both authors agree that addressing slavery laws is the only way to eliminate slavery.

    Choice A is not discussed in either passage. Stearns mentions that fugitive slaves may be treated in any way by the former master, but does not say that masters always exert extreme penalties. Beecher does not discuss "fugitive" or "runaway" slaves at all. Choice C is incorrect because Beecher points out that even when some owners emancipate their slaves, the state takes ownership. Therefore, just announcing freedom is not sufficient to make the slave free. Stearns also indicates that paperwork, not just a verbal claim, is necessary to prove freedom. Choice D is incorrect because only Beecher discusses the position of Abolitionists, so it is impossible to determine Stearns' view of the topic.

19. **Choice B is the best answer** because Stearns says that slavery is only possible because laws governing slavery exist. The fact that the slave is owned by the state is one piece of legislation, so it supports the claim that slavery continues due to legislation rather than just the wishes of the slave and owner.

    Choice A is incorrect because Stearns says that the law is the only thing to be considered. Therefore, if the law says that emancipated slaves are state property, it doesn't matter if the former slave has any paperwork showing otherwise. Choice C is incorrect because Stearns says that the U.S. Constitution supports laws of the states, but does not support slavery per se. Choice D is incorrect because Stearns says that the slaves are subjected to the laws of their masters. In the scenario given, the master would be the state, so running away would not protect the slave from the laws of that state.

20. **Choice D is the best answer** because the answer to the previous question is that Stearns would most likely react to Beecher's assertion by saying that it is one more reason that all slavery laws should be eliminated. Choice D

summarizes Stearns' argument that all laws should be eliminated. The "colossal statue of Slavery" is a metaphor to show the extreme size and extent of the problem, which would include cases such as freed slaves being considered the property of the state.

Choices A and B are incorrect because they do not provide evidence that says that laws should be eliminated; they only say that the Constitution supports slavery laws. Choice C is incorrect because it refers to a technicality in a law relating to a case of a runaway slave. Therefore, it does not show how he might react to a scenario involving a freed slave.

21. **Choice C is the best answer** because the passage is discussing the details of the Business Opportunity Rule, a set of regulations that governs the selling of franchises. The passage emphasizes that potential buyers have time to read the documents and should "exercise that right and study those materials carefully" (lines 58-59). The passage lists several different conditions and advises not pursuing the contract if the seller does not meet them. Choice A is incorrect because the passage only lists points related to a specific document to protect against franchise scams in general. The passage starts by giving examples of envelope stuffing and a vending business, but it does not explain "forms" or structures of any specific scam. Choice B is incorrect because the passage is not saying that all franchise opportunities are bad. The passage is giving information that may help detect when a franchise is a scam or not what it initially appears. Choice D is incorrect because, while some franchise offers may overstate the potential earnings, other offers are honest. "Invariably," means "always" or "in every occasion," so does not accurately portray the author's claim.

22. **Choice D is the best answer** because the passage describes the Business Opportunity Rule in detail, so the author is someone who has expertise and can advise about the rule. The explanation is given in simple, broad terms, highlighting the main points of the rule. Therefore, the listener is someone who is "uninformed" or who does not even know the basic rights granted by the rule.

Choice A is incorrect because the audience is not someone who is familiar with franchises or the rights of people buying a franchise. It can be presumed that most franchise owners already have a basic knowledge of an important law regarding their field. Choice B is incorrect because "redress" refers to ways of correcting a problem. However, the passage does not give any advice to someone who bought a scam franchise. It only talks about things to watch for or avoid when deciding whether to buy. Choice C is incorrect because the audience is a possible buyer, not a seller, as clearly indicated by phrases such as "before you buy a business opportunity" (line 77).

23. **Choice B is the best answer** because the second paragraph describes the one-page disclosure document. It suggests that the document can be used to check data and offers some of the main pieces of information that need to be on the document.

Choice A is incorrect because the second paragraph only describes the disclosure document, not all the key points of the Rule. For example, the second paragraph does not even mention the earnings claim document or the seven-day period for reviewing the paperwork. Choice C is weak because the paragraph lists what facts must be included in the document, but it does not "explain" or "clearly describe" how the rule itself protect the buyer. Choice D is incorrect because references are only a small portion of the paragraph, not its main topic. The comment about references only rounds out the larger discussion of what is required on the disclosure document.

24. **Choice A is the best answer** because the reference to the seven-day period is followed by, "Use that time to check out the information in the disclosure document, including contacting references" (lines 24-26). Therefore, the information about the length of time is given to show that buyers have a full week to research the purchase before agreeing to it.

Choice B is incorrect because the author does not give any indication that the amount of time is too short. The time is mentioned to show that one even has leeway to contact references. Choice C is incorrect because the author suggests using the time to check all the information, not just the references. There is no indication that finding honest references is more time-consuming than any of the other portions. Choice D is incorrect because sellers "secure" or "get" bogus recommendations because they want the company to sound good. They do not do it only because of a seven-day period before signing.

25. **Choice B is the best answer** because "questionable" is used to describe the business opportunity promoters who get people to make "glowing – but bogus – recommendations" (line 29). In other words, the sellers who find

people to give fake good reviews. If the reviews are fake, they are dishonest. Choice B refers to something which is dishonest or corrupt, so accurately describes the sellers that do dishonest things.
None of the other choices fits the context of describing a promoter who uses fraudulent methods to convince someone to buy a product. Choice A refers to something that does not have a clear answer. Choice C refers to something that is unlikely. Choice D refers to something that has not been decided or settled.

26. **Choice C is the best answer** because the point is that there are "variations" or "differences" in reported costs. Choice C emphasizes that point because it highlights the extreme differences found in one specific franchise that is legitimate. An investor might be told that one branch cost $500,000 and another cost $2,000,000, but both are true figures.
Choice A is incorrect because it does not show the variations in cost for one franchise. Therefore, it does not explain why the actual data from branches of one company may have a range of different start up investments. Choice B is incorrect because the graph does not provide data about the cost of land at all. Choice D is incorrect because a possible start-up cost of a franchise is not relevant to proving the point that one franchise might have a wide range of start-up investments depending on the conditions related to any given branch.

27. **Choice B is the best answer** because the "average range" for Beef o Brady's starts approximately halfway between $500,000 and $1,000,000 and goes up to just over $2,000,000. The "minimum" or "lowest" amount that an investor would have to spend to set up the restaurant would be the lowest number in this average range. Since $750,000 is halfway between $500,000 and $1,000,000, Choice B is the closest choice.
Choice A is lower than the amount of money needed to start a Beef o Brady's restaurant. Choice C is about the maximum, not minimum, investment. Choice D is the highest number on the y-axis and does not correspond with the average range of Beef o Brady's startup investments at all.

28. **Choice A is the best answer** because the fact that "any information about those people that may differ from you – for example, the part of the country where they live" (lines 50-52) must be included implies that the information is essential for interpreting the data. Since the data is related to earnings claims and the percentage of people who actually reached the earnings, then it can be reasonably inferred that differences in environment affects the earnings. Since "demographic factors" are differences between parts of the population, those are important to estimate if one person will earn the same amount as other investors.
Choice B is not supported by the passage. The earnings claims must include the dates that earnings were achieved, but there is no evidence regarding how often the document is "updated" or "rewritten." It is possible that the same document could be used for a year or more. Choice C is incorrect because, while some sellers may be happy to provide evidence about their claims, there is no indication that "most" do not want to give the document to the buyer. Choice D is incorrect because the paragraph says that any sellers making claims about how much money a person can earn have to give the document. The implication is that sellers not making claims do not have to give the document.

29. **Choice B is the best answer** because the author warns the buyer to do research and be cautious about any purchase. For example, the author points out that references may give bogus glowing recommendations. This is a case of a description of a "good scenario" that is not true. Another implication is that sales claims are also often higher than what an average person is able to earn. Therefore, the sellers are trying to "highlight" or "emphasize" the best possible aspects so that you buy into the scheme.
Choice A is incorrect because the author only warns that some scams try to cover up how much it is possible to earn. However, the implication is that the Earnings Claim document is correctly used—meaning that facts are "realistically" reported—by at least some franchises. Choice C is impossible to determine from the passage because there is no discussion about laws that protect the seller. Choice D is incorrect because the author does not delve into the success or failure of a franchise. The author only indicates that with proper research, an investor may be able to avoid a scam.

30. **Choice D is the best answer** because the answer to the previous question is that the author thinks that franchise advertisements usually highlight the best possible scenarios. Choice D implies the same thing because it says that "sales presentations," which are a form of advertisement, are "trying to sell you something." In other words, they are doing their best to make the product look good. One implication for looking good is offering the best

possible situation, which is true, but not necessarily accessible by other branches of the franchise. The author warns against getting sucked in by the exciting possibilities by advising to use a "critical ear" or "look for weaknesses" in the advertising.

Choice A only says you should become familiar with the Business Opportunity Rule before buying a franchise. It does not say that advertising may make things look better than they really are. Choice B indicates that there may be "inconsistencies," but on its own, does not say if the inconsistencies relate to advertising or if they make things look better or worse. Choice C refers to seller rules and does not provide evidence related to the correct answer of the previous question.

31. **Choice D is the best answer** because the passage says, "Like the disclosure document, the earnings claim statement has to be in the same language that the seller used to communicate with you" (lines 59-61). Therefore, if the document is partly in Chinese, it is not in the language you communicated in, English. This should be taken as a warning sign that the seller is not adhering to the Business Opportunity Rule and may have something to hide.

    Choice A is incorrect because it is acceptable for sellers to make claims. However, if they do make such a claim, there should also be documentation supporting it. Choice B is not necessarily a fraud; legitimate franchises will have many references that had positive experiences and who give good reviews of those experiences. The warning that a fraud exists is when the reviews from the company's references are very different from other people you speak with. Choice C is an example of the correct procedure when a business opportunity rather than a job is offered. Therefore, it is a sign that the business is following rules and may be legitimate.

32. **Choice A is the best answer** because the authors stress the lack of complete information throughout the passage. The second paragraph, for example, says that "due to limited observations, the significance of environmental impacts of commercial projects cannot fully be determined yet" (lines 24-26). The third paragraph concludes, "no data on environmental effects from arrays are available." The final paragraph recommends, "that the first commercial scale installations of ocean energy technology should be accompanied by research studies on the local environmental impacts and for most installations." In other words, the message is that the data is "insufficient" or "not complete enough" to understand all of the impacts of tidal systems now. Choice B is incorrect because, while the passage does outline potential negative effects, there is no indication that there are more effects than first predicted. Choice C is incorrect because the passage does not delve into the efficiency— which would be the energy output compared to the investments—of tidal systems. Choice D is incorrect because the passage is not saying that the research to date is worthless. The authors identify many areas which have not been studied, but the implication is that the parts which have been studied so far are also important.

33. **Choice D is the best answer** because the authors discuss what research has been done related to tidal energy systems. There is an analysis of topics covered and areas that have not been studied. Some conclusions from the studies, such as no reports of harm to marine animals from moving parts, are also presented. Therefore, the authors are not presenting new material, only summarizing the results of other research projects.

    Choice A is incorrect because "original research" refers to facts that the authors collect from their own experiments. Choice B is incorrect because, while statements by experts are given in the passage, they only one method used to present a summary of data from other studies. Choice C is incorrect because it refers to things which are only directly seen or experienced by the authors.

34. **Choice C is the best answer** because in the context, "robust" describes the understanding that governments and society need before ocean energy deployment takes place. Choice C refers to something that is solid and able to withstand outside pressures. It shows that the understanding needs to be complete and not easy to crumble when the pressure of arguments is brought against it.

    None of the other choices are uses of "robust" that describe the understanding that governments and society need. Choice A refers to something that is healthy and full of energy. Choice B refers to something that is physically able to withstand rough treatment. When used to describe something intangible, Choice D refers to something that is strict or uncompromising. It refers to things such as rules rather than the way something is understood.

CONTINUE

35. **Choice A is the best answer** because the passage directly states that "current technologies have moving parts (rotating rotor blades or flapping hydrofoils) that may harm marine life" (lines 63-66). This shows that harm may occur, even though there is no documentation of such accidents.

    All of the other choices can be eliminated because there is no evidence in the passage to support the claims. For Choice B, animals may be present, but there is no indication that they are "most" plentiful. For Choice C, sounds may be harmful, but the passage does not explain why. Choice D is incorrect because it is a benefit rather than a "harmful thing."

36. **Choice B is the best answer** because the argument is that it is safe to build a large array "for a profit," meaning a large "commercial" tidal system array. Choice B acts as a counterargument because it says that there is not enough research to show how big "commercial" or "for profit" systems will affect the environment. In other words, it is not clear if large systems are as safe as smaller test systems have been so far.

    Choice A is incorrect because it only defines types of studies. It does not counter the developer's argument that it is safe to build a large commercial array. Choice C is incorrect because it only suggests aspects of placement that need to be considered. It is possible that the developer has taken these all into account and that the system is perfectly safe, so Choice C does not function as a solid counterargument. Choice D says that some researchers concluded that larger marine organisms are probably not at great risk from tidal energy systems. Therefore, Choice D supports the developer's claim that the system will be safe rather than offers a counterargument against the claim.

37. **Choice A is the best answer** because the paragraph is discussing gaps in the current research. The claim that the data is "dispersed" or "spread out" shows that there are bits of data from sources that are far apart. The authors are trying to show that there needs to be a more comprehensive collection that "fills in the blanks" before conclusions can be drawn.

    Choice B is incorrect because "dispersed" refers to "spread out" rather than "announced to everyone." Choice C is incorrect because "comprehensive" refers to something that is complete, but the authors discuss many areas that are lacking information or "not complete." Choice D is incorrect because "incompatible" means "not able to get along with each other." There is no evidence that the groups are hostile to each other, only that there are many different groups that have pieces of data related to the field.

38. **Choice B is the best answer** because the paragraph is outlining various potential problems to benthic (underwater) habitats. The authors indicate that they feel there are many different potential problems that could impact "the local underwater habitat" (line 55) and "animal and plant species" (line 56). The authors' conclusion is that "Species of marine mammals and fish could experience distress and discomfort" (line 56). The quotations come after this discussion and are preceded with "however," which shows that a contradiction to the previous idea will follow. Therefore, they are included to show the opposite side of the argument. They indicate that as yet, there has been no "elevated levels of mortality" (line 66) or "evidence to date of harm" (line 65).

    Choice A is incorrect because the claims made in the quote support the same idea: very little damage to ocean creatures. Therefore, the views are not different from each other. Choice C is incorrect because "undermine" refers to weakening an argument. However, the quotes strengthen rather than weaken the idea that systems are safe. Choice D is incorrect because the conclusions oppose rather than strengthen the paragraph's main claim that there are risks from tidal energy systems to aquatic habitats and creatures.

39. **Choice C is the best answer** because "justifiable" means that a claim is reasonable because it is possibly true. The passage says, "Potential positive effects such as the creation of roosting sites and habitat enhancement for marine birds might occur as well" (lines 94-95). Therefore, according to the passage, the claim that there may be "improvements" or "potential positive effects" is reasonable.

    Choice A is incorrect because "incorrect" means that the claim is not true. Although tidal energy systems may change many aspects of the region, there may also be some positive changes. Choice B is incorrect because "overly" means "too." Although the claim is optimistic, there is a potential that it is true, so it is not "too optimistic." Choice D is incorrect because, while the claim is valid, the reason that it is valid is not because there are "revealed" or "proven" examples of side benefits. The passage only offers "potential" or "theoretical" advantages.

40. **Choice A is the best answer** because "placement" refers to "location." The passage directly states that "environmental impacts will very much depend on… the location selected" (lines 91-93).
None of the other choices are supported by any evidence from the passage. Choice B is incorrect because, although the passage does say that moving parts can kill wildlife, it does not say that is the most important factor when determining environmental change. Such things as changed water currents, electric fields, and sedimentation changes are also important elements. The passage discusses research studies, but Choice C is incorrect because the studies learn about how the system affects the environment, but do not change how much it does. There is no discussion at all of Choice D, the total energy generated.

41. **Choice D is the best answer** because the answer to the previous question is that the placement of a tidal energy system in the ocean will most determine how much the system alters the environment. Choice D directly supports this claim by including "location" or "placement" as one of the two factors (along with size) that will change the environmental impacts.
Choices A and B are incorrect because they discuss factors that could affect the environment, but they do not say that position is one of the major influences in how much a system will impact the environment. Choice C is incorrect because, though it lists things that impact the environment, it does not include "position" or "location." As a result, it does not support the claim that position is important.

42. **Choice B is the best answer** because the passage focuses on the results of a study that compared how varying salt concentration impacted certain qualities of a chili pepper, including how long it took to grow, the number of fruits per plant, and the nutritional value of those fruits. The main "implication" or "conclusion" is that it is better to raise chilis in an environment with less salt.
Choice A is incorrect because the author does not make any "recommendation" or "suggestion" based on his study. It is implied that farmers should try to avoid growing peppers in salty environments, but there are no suggestions for, for instance, how to improve the soil at a farm that has salty soil. Choice C is incorrect because the passage refers to one study with multiple facets, not "several." Choice D is incorrect because the study was not conducted as a way to make chili pepper nutrition better. Instead, it was designed to monitor the response to see how nutrition varies. How that data is used is not explained.

43. **Choice C is the best answer** because C refers to the gradual amassing or acquisition of something. It fits the context of describing what aspect of bioactive compounds—in this case, nutrients—in vegetables is affected by salt stress. The sentence can be paraphrased by saying that salt changes the rate that bioactive compounds amass. None of the other choices fits the context of describing what aspect of biological compounds is affected by salt. Choice A refers to how well one focuses one's thoughts, so it does not apply to inanimate things. Choice B also does not refer to inanimate things, as it describes the emotion of being committed to a purpose. Choice D is incorrect because it refers to bringing activities, not things, into one place under one form of control or leadership.

44. **Choice D is the best answer** because "evolved" refers to the changes that the plant underwent over time. The first paragraph defines capsaicin and says that it is mostly contained in the fruit. The speculation is "possibly to deter mammalian herbivores." "Herbivores" are animals that eat plants, so the plants that contained capsaicin "stopped" or "deterred" predators that eat the chili. Over time, the plants with more capsaicin survived. Choices A and B are incorrect because they are uses that chilis have been adapted for by humans but are not why chili plants evolved capsaicin in their fruit. Choice C is not mentioned anywhere in the text. Although there is more capsaicin when there is more salt in the soil, the passage does not describe how one affects the other.

45. **Choice C is the best answer** because the answer to the previous question is that the chili plant evolved to contain capsaicin in the fruit in order to protect the plant from predation. Choice C directly supports that claim because it says that capsaicin possibly developed to "deter" or "stop" mammalian herbivores. Herbivores are animals which eat plants; in other words, they are "predators" or "things that eat" plants.
None of the other choices shows that capsaicin may have evolved in chili to protect from predators. Choices A and B refer to how humans use chili, but the pepper plants evolved to protect against all different mammals that eat them, not just against humans. Choice D does not refer to capsaicin or why the plant might need it.

46. **Choice B is the best answer** because the passage states that "in Benin, chili is the second cash gardening crop after the tomato" (lines 13-14). This statement shows that chili is the second largest crop grown to be sold rather than used by the farmer. Without chili, one of the major crops that provides income would be missing, so it is important to many farmers.

    Choice A is incorrect because the passage states that "Salt stress is known to negatively affect plant growth at all developmental stages" (lines 23-24), which indicates that the farmers also know about the negative effect. The study was not trying to prove that an effect exists; it was trying to find out more details related to the effect of different salt concentrations. Choice C is incorrect because there is no discussion of sources of income in Benin. In reality, textiles and cotton are more important than the cash crops sold for food. Choice D is impossible to determine from the text because, while the passage says many plants are raised in areas with salt, it does not say that the plants are very unproductive. Since it is an important cash crop, the implication is that the plants grow and make fruit.

47. **Choice C is the best answer** because the study is about salt stress on chili peppers in Benin. Chili peppers are an important cash crop, but if they were raised in environments that didn't have salt, there would be no need beyond curiosity to see how salt affects the plants. The comment that the soil has salt in it and irrigation is by water (rather than, for example, in controlled hydroponic tanks) shows that the farmers must deal with salt. The study can therefore help them understand ways in which the soil could be amended or growing practices altered to increase crop yield and nutrition.

    Choice A is incorrect because the author does not say that farmers should try growing different crops. The author is just trying to learn more about how the environment affects the crops. Choice B is incorrect because salinity is bad for the crops. Therefore, the comment that the soil salinity "is a reality" or "exists" shows that the environment is less than ideal. Choice D is incorrect because there are no suggestions for how to raise plants in salty conditions.

48. **Choice D is the best answer** because "application" refers to the starting point of the salt stress. Choice D refers to the carrying out of a course of action, so aptly shows that the number of days from the action of creating stress until the appearance of the first flowers was recorded.

    None of the other choices fits the context of indicating when the salt process began. Choice A refers to "meaning" or "importance. Choice B refers to putting in hard effort over a long period. Choice C refers to asking for something.

49. **Choice A is the best answer** because the passage only says that some fruits from each plant were selected to determine the nutritional value. It does not give any information about how the fruits were chosen. For example, if only the largest ones were taken from one plant and the smallest from another, the results might be skewed based on that decision.

    Choices B and C are incorrect because the passage directly states that the temperature and humidity of the greenhouse was kept consistent throughout the experiment (lines 42-44, "Plants were…of 55%"). Therefore, the variations resulted from another cause. Choice D is incorrect because, while it is true that the results may not apply to other plants, the study never claims that they do.

50. **Choice B is the best answer** because the answer to the previous question is that the experiment is open to the criticism that the fruits selected for measurement may not have been representative of the other fruits in the group. The photographed fruits followed a certain standard: the first ripe ones. However, Choice B also says that fruits were selected, but it does not give any details about the selection process, such as "randomly" or "the largest and smallest." The lack of detail leaves open the question that there may have been some bias in which fruit were used for the weighing process.

    Choice A is incorrect because it discusses the conditions of the greenhouse, not the fruits selected. Choice C gives a logical reason for why only the fruits from some plants were used: other plants did not have fruits. It does not show that the ones that were used may not have been similar to the others from the same salinity group. Choice D is incorrect because it only describes the results, not how the results were obtained. Therefore, it does not shed light on whether the fruits were representative or not.

CONTINUE

51. **Choice D is the best answer** because the third row shows the statistics for the chili peppers with a NaCl concentration of 60 mM. The third column shows "average days to first fruit." Choice D is the number where the row and column intersect.
Choice A is the average number of fruit for chili peppers with a NaCl concentration of 60 mM, not the days to first fruit. Choice B is the average days to first flower for chili peppers with a NaCl concentration of 60 mM. Choice C is the average days to first fruit for chili peppers with a NaCl concentration of 0 mM.

52. **Choice C is the best answer** because "viable" means "capable of surviving," so Choice C is referring to plants that did not "generate" or "make" fruit. This claim is supported by the passage, "As no fruit was obtained for plants cultivated in the presence of 90 and 120 mM NaCl, only fruits from 0, 30 and 60 mM NaCl were used for nutrients determination" (lines 75-78). Figure 1 also supports the claim because it lists "0" in the column for "average number of fruit" for the concentrations of 90 and 120 mM.
Choice A is incorrect because only the passage refers to capsaicinoids. Choice B is incorrect because only the passage refers to vitamins and minerals. Nutritional value is impossible to determine from the figure. Choice D is data found only in figure 1. Though the passage indicates that salt stress caused plants to flower later, it does not give an exact number of days.

CONTINUE ▶

1. **Choice B is the best answer** since "free healthcare for the homeless" is irrelevant in relation the theme of the passage, which is about healthcare for "undocumented immigrants" (as mentioned in the title itself).
    Choice A is incorrect because it is vague and inaccurate. This answer choice speaks ambiguously about "free healthcare for the homeless" and there is no mention of "importance" in the underlined text.
    Choice C is incorrect. As established above, the sentence does not function as a good introduction since it has nothing to do with the content of the passage. Therefore, since this answer choice does not highlight anything about the irrelevance of the underlined text, it is not a suitable answer.
    Choice D is incorrect because it suggests an idea that is inaccurate - for an introductory sentence to be effective, it first needs to be related to the following content.

2. **Choice C is the best answer.** The first sentence of a paragraph – called the topic sentence – should be used to indicate what the following text is about. Ideally, the topic sentence should also allow the reader to transition from the ideas in the previou   s paragraph, to what follows. In this case, the term "however" indicates that the following information will contrast what came in the introductory paragraph (allowing a good transition). Furthermore, by speaking about a changing trend, this choice also effectively introduces the subsequent text's focus i.e., states in the US that offer free healthcare to illegal immigrants.
    Choice A is less accurate since there is no introductory phrase/sentence to enable the reader to connect the information that comes before and after.
    Choice B is incorrect. Using this answer would have the sentence state: "However this trend have expanded their Medicaid programs to cover children through 18 years old." Such a sentence would be both meaningless and grammatically inaccurate.
    Choice D is incorrect. This statement simply flips the order in which the "District of Columbia" and "six states" are mentioned, while also removing the word "but." Like Choice A, this choice does not function as an effective connection between the first two paragraphs.

3. **Choice A is the best answer.** The information presented here conveys meaning and maintains grammatical accuracy. There is no need to change it.
    Choices B & C are incorrect since they both delete some information. Choice B does not mention the pregnant women's residency status, while Choice C does not mention that these women are "income-eligible." Since these two options remove information in an arbitrary fashion, they are not suitable answers.
    Similarly, Choice D would involve removing relevant and important information from the given paragraph.

4. **Choice D is the best answer.** Notice the use of the verb "serve" (in the last sentence of the paragraph) in speaking about the centers. This tells us that, for verb-tense consistency, the verb in the underlined section should also be in the simple present tense. "Receive," therefore, is the most suitable answer.
    Note that the use of the simple past in the second line ("are required") is not used as a reference for tense consistency because it refers to specific centers ("those" centers) that are mentioned at the end of the preceding sentence.
    Choice A is in the present continuous tense, Choice B is in the simple past tense, and Choice C is in the present perfect tense: all of these choices would cause a verb-tense inconsistency within the paragraph.

5. **Choice A is the best answer.** Here, the first part of the sentence tells the reader that "undocumented residents receive coverage" through a spouse's plan, while the second part of the sentence provides information that adds a different dimension to the preceding idea (that employer coverage is less likely for such individuals).
    Replacing the underlined word with the remaining options, we would see the following:
    — "Some undocumented residents receive coverage through their own or a spouse's employer-provided plan, <u>while</u> they are less likely than legal residents or citizens to have jobs with employer coverage." The term "while" implies that something different is happening at the same time. Such a term would be out of context in the given sentence.
    — "Some undocumented residents receive coverage through their own or a spouse's employer-provided plan, despite they are less likely than legal residents or citizens to have jobs with employer coverage." The sentence becomes meaningless and grammatically incorrect.

— "Some undocumented residents receive coverage through their own or a spouse's employer-provided plan, <u>furthermore</u> they are less likely than legal residents or citizens to have jobs with employer coverage." The sentence becomes meaningless and grammatically incorrect.

6.   **Choice C is the best answer** since "it would be an outlier, health policy experts say" is qualified by the preceding dependent clause. A comma is appropriate in this particular sentence construction.
    Choice A is incorrect because semicolons (;) are only needed when there are two independent clauses – each with their own subject, verb, and object – that need to be separated. Since we do not have two independent clauses here, a semicolon cannot be a grammatically viable option.
    Choices B and D are incorrect for the same reason. Colons (:) and dashes (-) are used to introduce lists and additional ideas to a sentence, respectively. They are not necessary in a sentence like the one here, where there is no list and/or an added idea that has been included.

7.   **Choice C is the best answer.** This sentence is telling us about a particular status that Thailand has on the global stage, where the nation is seen as offering one of the most generous healthcare programs to immigrants. The current articulation of "is considering," in addition to being grammatically incorrect, alters the meaning of the sentence by suggesting that Thailand <u>might</u> offer these benefits to immigrants (rather than stating that the nation <u>is already</u> taking these steps). Therefore, Choice A is unsuitable.
    Choices B and D are incorrect because they both use the past tense "considered" -- suggesting that Thailand no longer has the specified plans. This would involve making an assumption that cannot be evidenced by the text.

8.   **Choice A is the best answer.** Since the following information tells us what the Pew Research Center has found, it is completely accurate to use "according to" – since "according to" is used to attribute acknowledgment/ownership of what follows.
    Choice B is inaccurate. "Despite" suggests a contrast, where something happens even though something else occurs. Since such a contrast-based relationship would be meaningless in the highlighted sentence, this choice can be easily eliminated.
    Choice C is inaccurate since "in addition to" suggests a connection to a preceding idea that is being augmented/supplement by what follows. Clearly, this is not the case in the highlighted text.
    Choice D is incorrect. Deleting the underlined section would render the sentence incomplete and grammatically inaccurate.

9.   **Choice D is the best answer.** The two clauses refer to related but <u>different</u> information and therefore, would best be structured as two different sentences that are separated by a period.
    While the semicolon has been used between two independent clauses, Choice A is less suitable because it unnecessarily creates an extremely long sentence. Shorter sentences are clearer and more active in their use of voice. When grammatically accurate, therefore, shorter sentences are always preferred.
    Choice B is incorrect since adding a comma would imply an independent clause/dependent clause relationship that does not exist here.
    Choice C is inaccurate. Deleting the underlined text would create a meaningless, run-on sentence.

10.   **Choice B is the best answer** since this sentence effectively tells the reader what people are waiting for/from. Without this clarification, the sentence is ambiguous and hard to understand – making Choice A an unsuitable answer.
    Choice C is incorrect since the suggested text would make the sentence meaningless.
    Choice D is incorrect since deleting the suggested text would make the sentence meaningless.

11.   **Choice B is the best answer.** Notice that the sentence is telling us what some studies have already found. The present perfect ("have found"), therefore, is the only grammatically viable option of the choices that have been presented here.
    Choices A and D are inaccurate because the infinitive form of the verb ("to find") and the future tense "will find" both disrupt the logic of the sentence.
    While the present continuous tense ("finding") by itself would not be inaccurate, notice that the subject is in the plural ("studies"). Therefore, "finding" would have to be preceded by "are" in order to be grammatically accurate.

12. **Choice A is the best answer** since "Ngugi wa Thiong'o" is a restrictive, appositive phrase. An appositive phrase refers to information that renames the subject of the sentence. A restrictive, appositive phrase is one that is necessary to preserve the meaning of the sentence. Here, "Ngugi wa Thiong'o" renames "the academic and social activist," and is necessary for the sentence to function. Therefore, a comma should not to be used after the term "activist."

     Choice B is incorrect. Semicolons are used to separate two independent clauses that each have their own subject, verb, and object. Since that condition would not be met in this case, the semicolon cannot be used.

     Choice C is incorrect. If a dash were to be used before "Ngugi," there would have to be another one that is used after "Thiong'o." Since this is not the case here, the use of one dash creates a grammatical inconsistency.

     Choice D is incorrect because of the use of a comma after an appositive and restrictive introductory phrase.

13. **Choice C is the best answer** since an effective topic sentence to a paragraph gives the reader an idea of the content that is to follow. In this case, since the following content mentions one of Thiong'o's plays and one of his novels, the suggested sentence would indeed make an effective introduction for this paragraph.

     Choice A is incorrect. There is no information presented earlier that would be clarified by stating that Thiong'o writes both plays and novels.

     Choice B is incorrect. Concluding sentences in a paragraph help to sum up the ideas in that text and to lead the reader to the next paragraph. Adding the suggested sentence to the end of the current paragraph is likely to disrupt the flow of the text and as such, cannot be more effective as a conclusion.

     Choice D is incorrect. For information to be irrelevant, it would have nothing to do with the following content. Here, the suggested sentence is explicitly linked to the content of the paragraph and is pertinent to its focus.

14. **Choice B is the best answer** since "perform" is the most accurate verb with which to describe the execution of a play at the theatre.

     Choice A, while not grammatically inaccurate, is not good diction. To say that a play was "done" is far less specific and appropriate than saying that it was "performed."

     Choice C is incorrect since deleting the underlined word would make the sentence incomplete and meaningless.

     Choice D is incorrect. While plays are written by its authors (playwrights), the context here clearly refers to a play being staged at the National Theatre. "Written," therefore, would be inaccurate in this context.

15. **Choice D is the best answer** since the suggested sentence would help wrap up the paragraph by informing the reader as to why the author's name change is significant.

     Choice A is less suitable since the current conclusion to the paragraph, without any change, does not help the reader understand why Thiong'o's change of name has been mentioned. While the current construction is not incorrect, it does negatively affect the flow of logic in the paragraph by not bringing the ideas to a clear conclusion.

     Choice B is incorrect. *A Grain of Wheat* is mentioned in the first line of the paragraph, before other information is presented to the reader. To jump back to this subject in the last line would disrupt the flow of ideas in the text.

     Choice C is incorrect because it is ambiguous. While it is not inaccurate to say that Thiong'o was/is part of a movement that focuses on African traditions, using this sentence as a conclusion to the paragraph does not allow the reader to follow a flow in logic/ideas from the previous sentences.

16. **Choice A is best answer** since it is grammatically accurate and uses the simple past tense to tell us about Thiong'o's position in the literature department.

     Choice B is incorrect since "he had a senior lecturer" would alter the meaning of the sentence and suggest that the text is referring to a lecturer that Thiong'o had (as a student), rather than referring to Thiong'o's position as a lecturer within the department.

     Choice C is incorrect. The paragraph is clearly speaking about the past (around 1967) and using the present tense ("is") would cause a verb-tense inconsistency.

     Choice D is incorrect. The use of the past continuous tense in this sentence would render it grammatically incorrect.

17. **Choice C is the best answer** since the use of a phrase like "This was because the" helps the reader transition between/link the ideas that are being presented in the two sentences. Without the use of such a transition

phrase – as in Choice A – it is more difficult for the reader to follow how the different ideas presented here are connected to each other.

Choice B is incorrect. "Although" suggests a relationship in which something happens despite something else happening – whereas here, the relationship being described is more direct, i.e., the play "ruffled feathers" because of what the "British settler establishment" did to him.

Choice D is incorrect. Deleting the underlined portion would result in a meaningless statement.

18. **Choice A is the only possible answer,** since it is the only choice that uses the past tense in a paragraph that refers to historical events.

    Choices B, C and D, by using the future tense, simple present tense, and the past continuous forms of the verb "to kill," immediately cause verb-tense inconsistencies in the statement.

19. **Choice A is the best answer.** By linking an idea in this paragraph to one that came earlier in the passage, the rewritten sentence would improve clarity and help the reader identify how two seemingly discrete events (the author's decision to change his name and his decision to write in Kikuyu) are linked.

    Choice B is incorrect. This sentence is clearly an introduction rather than a conclusion.

    Choice C is incorrect. Adding this sentence to the end of the paragraph would disrupt the flow of ideas in the text.

    Choice D is incorrect since the information in the suggested rewrite remains extremely relevant to the content of the passage.

20. **Choice C is the best answer** since this additional line provides information that clarifies where Thiong'o lived "in exile" (the previous statement).

    Choice A is incorrect. There is no disruption of logic caused by this sentence – it adds to the topic that is being discussed in the sentence that comes before it.

    Choice B is incorrect. Placing this sentence at the beginning of the paragraph, when the topic of "exile" is only brought up at the end of it, would immediately cause a disruption in the flow of logic in the text.

    Choice D is incorrect since the following paragraph begins with a sentence about *Petals of Blood*, which has nothing to do with the topic of exile that is mentioned in the current and suggested last sentence of the previous paragraph. Therefore, this sentence does not serve as a "transition."

21. **Choice B is the best answer** Because of the chronological nature of the text, the best way to locate this answer would be to look at the timeline of events that are mentioned in each paragraph.

    We see that paragraph 5 mentions Thiong'o's release from prison and paragraph 6 mentions Thiong'o's going into prison – immediately telling us that paragraph 6 belongs before paragraph 5 (Choice B).

    Any other choice would disrupt the flow about events surrounding Thiong'o's imprisonment and release.

22. **Choice D is the best answer** and can be arrived at through a process of elimination.

    Choice A is incorrect since it would be inaccurate to suggest that "colonialism" is a main point of the passage, when it is Thiong'o's response to colonialism through writing that is the explicit focus (hence making choice D the best answer).

    Choice B is incorrect. While the passage does tell us that the author lived in exile, there is nothing to suggest that this is because Thiong'o does not like his country. Instead, we are told that he lived in exile because he feared repercussions for his work.

    Choice C is incorrect. There is qualitative judgment that is presented in the text about whether or not one should make art that is political. All we are told is that Thiong'o did.

23. **Choice D is the best possible answer.** Although "has been" (Choice A) is not grammatically inaccurate, note the use of "is" preceding "an activity" later in the same sentence. In order to maintain verb-tense consistency, throughout the sentence, "is" the most appropriate answer.

    Choices B and C are immediately inaccurate because they are both plural conjugations, while the subject for the sentence (the human voice) is in the singular. In addition, "were" – by being the in the past tense – would cause a verb-tense inconsistency within the sentence.

CONTINUE

24. **Choice A is the best answer.** The first two sentences speak about the nature of the human voice as an instrument. Currently, the last sentence talks about how different pitches are obtained. By making a connection between the ideas of the human voice as instrument and its potential to create different pitches, the addition would indeed help with a transition of ideas.

    Choice B is unsuitable. Since the concept of pitches comes in later in the paragraph, the addition would be disruptive to flow of logic if it were used as an introduction to the paragraph.

    Choice C is incorrect. In order for a sentence to be an effective transition to the following paragraph, it needs to be the last line of the preceding paragraph. Since this would not be the case, the addition cannot be an effective transition to the following paragraph.

    Choice D is incorrect. The information provided by the suggested addition, in being clearly linked to the content of the passage, is clearly relevant.

25. **Choice C is the best answer.** Notice that later in the sentence, we are told that "tenor, baritone, and bass" are the designations for men's voices. Therefore, it would be necessary to clarify that "soprano, mezzo soprano, and alto" are the corresponding designations for women's voices. Without the underlined text, we would miss information that is necessary to understanding the content of the statement.

    Choice A is unsuitable. Information is "redundant" when it is repetitive and thus, useless. In this case, there is nothing repetitive/useless about the underlined information.

    Choice B is inaccurate. The underlined section positively impacts the clarity of the statement.

    Choice D is inaccurate. There is no "transition" that is being achieved by the underlined section, only a clarification and flow of ideas.

26. **Choice B is the best answer.** The information following the underlined text adds to the content that has been provided earlier in the paragraph. "Furthermore," by explicitly referring to added information, is the best conjunctive adverb to use.

    Choice A is less suitable since the use of no conjunctive adverb, while not grammatically incorrect, is less effective in maintaining the flow of the text.

    Choices C and D are incorrect for the same reason. "Finally" and "ultimately" are used to indicate the last point that is being made within a larger argument. Here, the following information is addition rather than being conclusive in any way. As such, neither of these choices is suitable.

27. **Choice A is the best, and only possible answer.** The comma following "are muscles" tells us that the punctuation after "however" needs to be a comma. In addition, conjunctive adverbs like "however" are always followed by a comma when used at the beginning of a sentence.

    Any other choice of punctuation would immediately pose a grammatical inaccuracy.

28. **Choice C is the best answer.** Look at the flow of ideas in the passage:
    — (1) speaks about the muscular qualities of the vocal cords
    — (2) speaks about how singers extend the "power of their voices"
    — (3) speaks about the physiology – the physical characteristics – of the vocal cords

    Mapping out the focus of each sentence in this way, we immediately see that lines (1) and (3) are related in content.

    Once this relationship has been established, the next clue lies in the use of a conjunctive adverb like "however" at the beginning of sentence (1). This indicates that sentence (3) is likely best positioned before sentence (1).

29. **Choice A is the best answer.** The underlined sentence adds relevant information about the factors influencing a singer's tone color i.e., how anatomy and other factors are influential.

    Choice B is inaccurate since there is no "extensive" information about pitch in the underlined sentence.

    Choices C and D are incorrect since there is nothing irrelevant or repetitive about the information in the underlined sentence.

30. **Choice D is the best answer.** The suggested edit would specifically tell the reader what "other factors" are being referred to – and also help transition to the cultural dimensions to vocal qualities that are discussed in the following paragraph.

Choice A is incorrect. The specificity of the addition would in fact help the reader better transition to the next paragraph.

Choices B and C are incorrect since the information is neither irrelevant not repetitive/redundant in relation to the surrounding text.

31. **Choice B is the best answer.** The verb here refers to "a chest voice" in the singular and in order to preserve subject-verb agreement, the verb needs to be in the singular (eliminating Choice A as a possible answer). In addition, in order to maintain the verb-tense agreement in the sentence, notice the use of the simple present earlier on ("is associated"). This tells us that the conjugation of "to employ" would also be most accurate in the simple present form (elimination Choices C and D).

32. **Choice C is the most accurate answer.** Notice how the following descriptions of a "dramatic soprano" are punctuated with a comma between "powerful" and "emotional." This tells us that, in order to maintain grammatical consistency and flow within the earlier part of the sentence, the description of a "lyric soprano" would also be best punctuated with a comma between "light" and "refined."

Any other answer choice would both be grammatically inaccurate and negatively impact the flow of the text.

33. **Choice D is the only possible answer.** The subject being referred to is the vocal music and "text," therefore, belongs to that vocal music and indicates possession. "Its" is the only possible answer to refer to a singular subject and indicate possession.

Choice A is incorrect since "their" would imply possession for a subject in the plural.

Choices B & C include contractions that would render the sentence grammatically inaccurate and meaningless - "it's" is a contraction for "it is," and "they're" is a contraction for "they are."

34. **Choice A is the best answer.** The simple present (vary/varies) is used when there is a fixed action that does not change. In this case, the action of changing the rate – by its very nature – is not fixed. Therefore, the present continuous tense (varying) is the best answer.

Choice B is inaccurate because it is in the simple present, which is not suitable for the reasons mentioned above. Using "vary" in the current sentence structure would also make the text meaningless.

Choice C is inaccurate. The use of the simple past tense would cause a verb-tense inconsistency with the use of "consumes" at the end of the first sentence.

Choice D is unsuitable since "varies" would cause a subject-verb disagreement. The subject here, "the energy industry," is in the singular while "varies" is in the plural form.

35. **Choice C is the best answer** since "press the accelerator pedal and more gas flows to the engine" is a phrase that comes after an independent clause (the previous part of the sentence) and is a non-essential part of the sentence. Since dashes are used in a sentence to highlight a parenthetical remark, it is the perfect choice for a sentence such as this one.

Choice A is incorrect since the lack of punctuation in this instance creates a run-on sentence that cannot be understood.

Choice B is incorrect. Using a comma in the highlighted section would not highlight its parenthetical/non-essential nature. Instead, the comma would make the following clause dependent and make it meaningless.

Choice D is incorrect. Colons are used in a sentence to introduce a list. Since there is no list in this sentence, a colon is a grammatically incorrect choice.

36. **Choice D is the best answer.** "The wind cannot be turned up or down" contrasts the previous sentence, which speaks to how the speed of a car might be changed. "However," by indicating such a contrast, creates an effective transition.

Choice A is unsuitable. 'Nevertheless" – like Choice B -- means that although something happens, something else also occurs. Such a term would alter the meaning of the highlighted phrase.

Choice C is incorrect. "Furthermore" is used to introduce an additional idea of the same nature, rather than a contrasting idea of a different nature.

37. **Choice B is the best answer.** Here, the underlined pronoun refers to the "turbine manufacturers, operators and utility companies" that are hiding vast quantities of information. Therefore, the pronoun needs to be in the plural, making "their" the only possible choice.
Choice A is incorrect since "its" refers to a singular subject.
Choice C is unsuitable since "the" is ambiguous and does not tell the reader what is being referred to.
Choice D is incorrect. "It's" is a contraction for "it is" and this choice would make the sentence meaningless.

38. **Choice D is the best answer.** If added, this would be the only sentence in the paragraph that is written in the first-person voice ("I").
Choice A is incorrect. The use of voice in this sentence does not allow it to serve as transition between this paragraph and what follows, both of which are written in a more depersonalized tone.
Choice B is incorrect. There is no previous information that is clarified by the suggestion addition.
Choice C is incorrect. Although it has been written in a different voice, the content in the sentence has not been discussed before (i.e., a personal call to action in relation to the topic of the passage). Therefore, this choice cannot be deemed redundant.

39. **Choice A is the best answer.** The last line of the previous paragraph describes what the lack of "data sharing" is "hindering" and "squandering". This first sentence/paragraph speaks about what might change (about data sharing trends) if people knew that money could be made from it. "Perhaps" – by underscoring uncertainty and yet putting forward a possibility – is the best possible word to use here.
Choice B is incorrect since "additionally" suggests that the information that follows adds to what came before. Since this is not the case, "additionally" is not a suitable choice.
Choice C is unsuitable. While "possibly" is not grammatically inaccurate per se, it is a less suitable choice of diction when compared to "perhaps".
Choice D is inaccurate. The use of this choice would make the sentence meaningless.

40. **Choice C is the only possible answer.** We see a generally upward trend in the blue dots, showing a direct relationship between power and speed (i.e., when one increases, so does the other). However, we cannot say that this "always" happens since there are some blue dots that fall outside the generally upward sloping line that is formed.
Therefore, to say that "generally" wind power scales with the speed is the only possible correct answer.
Choices that say "always" would be an overstatement; choices that say "does not scale" would misrepresent the data.

41. **Choice A is the best answer.** The phrase "like electricity" is a non-essential, parenthetical statement and dashes on both sides of the phrase is the best way to highlight the role of the enclosed text in serving as an example for the surrounding idea.
Choice B is grammatically inaccurate. Without any punctuations, and no qualifying term such as "like" or "for example" preceding "electricity," the sentence would be impossible to understand.
Choice C is inaccurate. The use of punctuation would disrupt the use of "electricity" as an example and cause the sentence to become meaningless.
Choice D is unnecessary. Since a grammatically accurate option is available to include the additional information, there is no need to delete it (although the sentence would remain grammatically accurate without the underlined section).

42. **Choice B is the best answer.** The text that follows the underlined section contrasts a preceding idea. "Rather" emphasizes this contrast by highlighting that something other than what was explained before occurs.
Choices A and C imply a causal relationship – where something happens despite something else happening. These terms do not capture the contrast that is expressed by a term like "Rather."
Choice D is incorrect since the preceding idea is not simply being added to, it is being contrasted with.

43. **Choice A is the best answer.** Once again, the dash has been used accurately, to introduce non-essential information that helps clarify preceding information but that is not needed for the sentence to be grammatically

accurate or understood.

Choice B is inaccurate. Semicolons are only used to separate two independent clauses, each with their own subject, verb, and object. Since the second clause here is not independent, the semicolon would be grammatically incorrect.

Choice C is incorrect. Colons are used to introduce a list and since there is no list the highlighted sentence, this choice would be grammatically incorrect.

Choice D is incorrect. The absence of punctuation would create a run-on sentence that is difficult to understand.

44. **Choice D is the best answer.** By providing general information that helps the reader understand the following content, the underlined sentence functions as a good topic sentence for this paragraph.

Choice A is incorrect since there is no "transition" between ideas that is supported by the underlined text.

Choice B is incorrect. The flow is enhanced, rather than disrupted, by the underlined text.

Choice C is incorrect. The information is clearly relevant to the topic of the passage.

1. **Easy | Heart of Algebra**

   Choice B is correct. When $x = 3$, one can substitute 3 for x in the equation $\frac{2}{3} x + 4 = 10y$, which becomes $\frac{2}{3} (3) +$ 4 = 10y. By simplifying the left side of the equation by multiplication and then addition, the equation becomes 2 + 4 = 10y and subsequently 6 = 10y. By dividing both sides by 10 gives $\frac{6}{10} = y$, which simplifies to $\frac{3}{5} = y$. Choices A, C,

   and D are incorrect because the result of multiplying those values of y by 10 and subtracting 4, does not equal 2, which is the correct result of 3 substituted for x on the left side of the equation.

2. **Medium | Heart of Algebra**

   Choice A is correct. The system of equations can be solved by either substitution or elimination, but the standard form of the equation indicates elimination is best. Begin by matching the coefficients of one of the variables:

   $6a - 4b = 24$

   $2(-a + 2b = -8)$

   Which simplifies to:

   $6a - 4b = 24$

   $-2a + 4b = -16$)

   Then add the equations, eliminating one variable:

   $4a = 8$

   $a = 2$

   Then substitute a back into one of the original equations, to solve for b:

   $-(2) + 2b = -8$

   $-2 + 2b = -8$

   $2b = -6$

   $b = -3$

   The solution to the system (a, b) is then $(2, -3)$. The sum of $a + b$ is $2 + (3) = -1$. Choices B, C, and D are incorrect and are most likely the result of arithmetic errors in combining the equations.

3. **Easy | Heart of Algebra**

   Choice D is correct. In the equation, the variables $(x + z)$ represent the number of hours worked, and the total pay (y) is determined by the rate of pay. The rate of pay is represented by the coefficients of the variables, $(20,25)$. The coefficient of (z), which is the number of overtime hours worked, is 25 and so, must be the amount paid per overtime hour of work. Choices A, B, and C are incorrect because they represent other variables and coefficients in the equation.

4. **Medium | Passport to Advanced Math**

   Choice C is correct. In order to simplify the expression, distribute and combine like terms:

   $x(x - 5) + 4 (x - 3) - 8$

   $x^2 - 5x + 4x - 12 - 8$

   $x^2 - x - 20$

The equation can be simplified once more by factoring:

$x^2 - x - 20$

$(x - 5)(x + 4)$

The correct answer is therefore, C. Choices A, B, and D are incorrect and are the result of incorrectly distributing values, combining like terms, or factoring polynomials.

5. **Easy | Heart of Algebra**

    Choice A is correct. Begin by substituting $x = 0$ into the equation:

    $$\left(0 + \sqrt{3}\right)^2 + 3$$

    $$\left(\sqrt{3}\right)^2 + 3$$

    $$3 + 3 = 6$$

    Choices B, C, and D are incorrect and are the result of errors in distributing exponents to radicals.

6. **Medium | Passport to Advanced Math**

    Choice B is correct. In order for a system of equations to be true for all real numbers, the equations must be the same line. The coefficients for both variables, as well as the constants, must then match or be proportional to one another. Start by reorganizing the equations into the same form:

    $dx + 7y = 4$

    $4x + 14y = e$

    The coefficients of y reveal that the equations are proportional 1:2, so another equation can be written to represent the value of d: $(2)d = 4$, so $d = 2$. Choices A, C, and D are incorrect and represent arithmetic errors.

7. **Difficult | Passport to Advanced Math**

    Choice D is correct. Start by simplifying the exponents of each variable, by subtracting the exponents of the matching bases being divided: $x^{-1-(-2)}$ and y^{2-3}. These both simplify to xy^{-1}, which according the inverse exponent rules, can be rewritten as $\dfrac{x}{y}$. Choices A, B, and C are incorrect and are the result of incorrectly dividing inverse exponents.

8. **Medium | Additional Topics in Math**

    Choice A is correct. The sum of the interior angles of a triangle is 180°. Therefore, the angles in the figure must be $x° + 40° + 63° = 180$. When simplified, $x° = 180° - 103° = 77°$ Angles $x°$ and $y°$ are supplementary angles, which also have a sum of 180°. Therefore, the value of $y°$ is equal to $180° - 77° = 103°$. Choices B is incorrect because it misidentifies the supplement of angle $x°$, and C and D are most likely the result of errors in calculating supplementary angles.

9. **Medium | Passport to Advanced Math**

    Choice D is correct. In order to find a line perpendicular to the given line, the slope of the original line must be determined:

$$slope = \frac{\frac{1}{2}-2}{2-4} = \frac{\frac{-3}{2}}{-2} = \frac{3}{4}$$

The slopes of perpendicular lines are opposite reciprocals, so the slope of the line perpendicular to $\frac{3}{4}$ is $-\frac{4}{3}$.

Next, to find the equation of the line in slope-intercept form ($y = mx + b$), one must find the y-intercept (b). To find (b), substitute the given point for the new line for (x, y) and solve:

$$(-2) = -\frac{4}{3}(3) + b$$

$$-2 = -4 + b$$

$$b = 2$$

The full equation of the perpendicular line is then: $y = -\frac{4}{3}x + 2$. Choices A is incorrect and features an incorrect y-intercept value. Choice B features a parallel slope to the given slope, not a perpendicular one. Choice C represents the equation of the initial line.

10. **Medium | Passport to Advanced Math**

    Choice B is correct. Start by identifying the function in the graph, $y = (x + 3)(x - 1)$ and the vertex at $(-1, -4)$ Vertex form can be represented as $y - k = (x - h^2)$ where ($h.k$) is the vertex. Therefore, when $(-1, -4)$ is substituted into the vertex form equation, it yields: $y + 4 = (x + 1^2)$. This is equivalent to $y = (x + 1)^2 - 4$ Choices A is incorrect because it represents a linear equation, not a quadratic equation. Choice C is incorrect as it is in x-intercept form, not vertex form. Choice D is incorrect because it includes the opposite sign for the y-value of the vertex.

11. **Difficult | Passport to Advanced Math**

    Choice D is correct. In order to rewrite the expression in the form $a + bi$, one must eliminate the i in the denominator by multiplying both numerator and denominator by the conjugate of the denominator. Begin by joining like terms: $\frac{i - 2 + 3i}{4 - 3i + 4i} = \frac{2 + 2i}{4 + i}$. Then multiply by the conjugate of the denominator:

    $\frac{2 + 2i}{4 + i} \times \frac{4 - i}{4 - i} = \frac{8 - 2i + 8i - 2i^2}{16 - 4i + 4i - i^2}$. In order to simplify further, replace i with $\sqrt{-1}$ and continue to join like terms:

    $\frac{8 - 2i + 8i + 2}{16 - 4i + 4i + 1} = \frac{10 + 6i}{17}$. Choices A, B, and C are incorrect and are most likely the result of errors in simplifying polynomials with i in the denominator.

12. **Medium | Passport to Advanced Math**

    Choice C is correct. In order to rewrite the equation in terms of v, one must isolate that variable on one side of the equation:

    $$F = -cv^2$$

    $$\frac{F}{-c} = v^2$$

$$\sqrt{\frac{F}{-c}} = v$$

Choice A, B, and D are incorrect because when they are rearranged to isolate F, they do not equal. $F = -cv^2$

13. **Medium | Heart of Algebra**

    Choice A is correct. To determine the equation of the polynomial in the graph, one must first recognize that all answers are written in some version of x-intercept. Then identify the x-intercepts of the graph, which lie at $(-6, 0)$ and $(-2, 0)$ and $(1, 0)$. The equation of the graph can then be written as $y = (x+6)(x-1)(x+2)$. This answer can be rewritten as $y = (x^2 + 5x - 6)(x+2)$, by multiplying the first two factors together. Choices B, C, and D are incorrect because when factored into their x-intercept form, they do not match the polynomial $y = (x+6)(x-1)(x+2)$.

14. **Medium | Passport to Advanced Math**

    Choice B is correct. In order to determine the equation of the total purchase, begin by determining the total cost of (l) lamps and (r) rugs before the discount is applied: . $T = 75(r + l)$ When distributed, the equation then becomes: $T = 75r + 75l$. When the 20% discount is applied, the cost is 80% of the original: $T = 0.8(75r + 75l)$. Choices A, C, and D are incorrect and are most likely the result of errors in applying discounts to equations with variables.

15. **Medium | Heart of Algebra**

    Choice A is correct. In order to simplify the expression, the fractions must have a common denominator. To find the common denominator for these fractions, multiply each fraction by the denominator of the other and simplify:

    $$\frac{2x+1}{x-3}\left(\frac{x+2}{x+2}\right) - \frac{x-1}{x+2}\left(\frac{x-3}{x-3}\right)$$

    $$\frac{2x^2 + 4x + x + 2}{x^2 - x - 6} - \frac{x^2 - x - 3x + 3}{x^2 - x - 6}$$

    $$\frac{2x^2 + 5x + 2}{x^2 - x - 6} + \frac{-x^2 + 4x - 3}{x^2 - x - 6}$$

    $$\frac{x^2 + 9x - 1}{x^2 - x - 6}$$

    Choices B, C, and D are incorrect and are the result of arithmetic errors in simplifying polynomials and fractions.

16. **Medium | Heart of Algebra**

    The correct answer is 15 cups. To determine the number of cups Jerry bought, one must write a system of equations, with variables for the number of napkins bought (n) and cups bought (c):

    $2c = n$

    $2n + 3c = 105$

    One can solve by elimination of a variable or by substitution of one variable for another. The simpler option in this case is substitution because of the relationship between (c) and (n) in the first equation:

    $2(2c) + 3c = 105$

$$4c + 3c = 105$$

$$7c = 105$$

$$c = 15$$

17. **Medium | Passport to Advanced Math**

   The correct answer is 2. Begin by substituting 25 for y in the equation:

   $$25 = \left(\frac{x^2 + x - 12}{x + 4} \right)^2$$

   $$\pm 5 = \left(\frac{x^2 + x - 12}{x + 4} \right)$$

   $$\pm 5 (x + 4) = x^2 + x - 12$$

   One can either simplify the left side of the equation or factor the right side of the equation. The latter is represented below:

   $$\pm 5 (x + 4) = (x + 4)(x - 3)$$

   $$\pm 5 = x - 3$$

   Therefore, $x = -2, 8$ and $-x = 2, -8$. There can be no negative answer, so the only correct answer is 2.

18. **Medium | Additional Topics in Math**

   The correct answer is 3. The triangle in the figure represents an equilateral triangle, which has equal angles and equal sides. The interior angles of an equilateral triangle must all be 60°, because $\frac{180°}{3} = 60°$. If the one angle in the triangle is 60° and the other two angles are also equal, the triangle is equilateral. The sides are therefore equal as well, so $z = 3$.

19. **Difficult | Additional Topics in Math**

   The correct answer is $\frac{5}{12}$ or 0.417. If two angles are complementary, the Law of Trig Identities states that the cosine of one is equal to the sine of the other, so $cos\big(cos(x)\big) = sin\big(sin(y)\big) = 5/12$.

20. **Medium | Heart of Algebra**

   The correct answer is 6. In order to solve the system of equations, one must use either substitution or elimination. The standard form of the equations indicates that elimination of one variable is simplest:

   $$3x + y = 9$$

   $$3(-x + 5y = 21)$$

   $$3x + y = 9$$

   $$-3x + 15y = 63$$

   Then, combine the two equations into one, eliminating one variable:

CONTINUE ➡

$16y = 72$

$y = \dfrac{72}{16}$ or 4.5

To determine x, substitute 4.5 for y in one of the original equations:

$3x + 4.5 = 9$

$3x = 4.5$

$x = 1.5$

The sum of $x + y = 1.5 + 4.5 = 6$.

1. **Easy | Problem Solving and Data Analysis**

    Choice B is correct. In order to find the space left in the room, one must find the difference between the area of the room itself and the furniture. The area of the furniture is 10 x 7 feet, so the area of that space is $10 \times 7 = 70 \, ft^2$. Then, subtract this value from the area of the entire room, $175 - 70 = 105 \, ft^2$ Choices A, C, and D are incorrect because when they are subtracted from $175 \, ft^2$ they do not equal the dimensions of the furniture.

2. **Medium | Heart of Algebra**

    Choice A is correct. In order to determine the equation in terms of (x) number of individual months, first determine the length her hair grows per month: $\dfrac{1inch}{2months}$ = 0.5 inches per month. If her hair is already 10 inches long, then the equation for (y) the total length of her hair can be written as $y = 0.5x + 10$. Choices B, C, and D are incorrect and are most likely the result of incorrectly joining variables with the wrong constants.

3. **Medium | Heart of Algebra**

    Choice C is correct. The height of the ball after (t) seconds can be found by substituting 4 seconds for (t) in the equation:

    $h = (4)^2 + 15(4)$

    $h = 16 + 60$

    $h = 76 \, ft$

    Choices A, B, and D are incorrect because when they are substituted for h in the equation, t does not equal 4.

4. **Medium | Passport to Advanced Math**

    Choice C is correct. In one week (7 days), Thomas must write 150 questions. Therefore, he must write $\dfrac{150}{7}, = 21.4.$ Then rounding to the nearest whole number, the number of questions he must write a day is 22.

    Choices A, B, and D are incorrect and are most likely the result of arithmetic and rounding errors.

5. **Easy | Passport to Advanced Math**

    Choice D is correct. If Thomas makes $2 per question, and write 150 questions, he makes a total of $2 \times 150 =$ $300 per week. Including the bonus, he then makes 300 + 75 = $375 in a week.

    Choices A, B, and C are incorrect and are likely the result of arithmetic errors.

6. **Easy | Heart of Algebra**

    Choice B is correct. Begin by calculating the brother's age: 3(15) –12= 33 years old. The difference between Jen's age (15 years old) and her brother's age can be found using subtraction: 33 –15 =18.

    Choices A, C, and D are incorrect and are the result of errors in solving algebraic functions.

7. **Difficult | Passport to Advanced Math**

    Choice C is correct. In order to find the number of solutions a function has, use the discriminant $b^2 - 4ac$. In this function $a = 2$, $b = -3$, $c = 5$. The discriminant, therefore is:

    $(-3)^2 - 4(2)(5)$

    $9 - 4 = -31$

    If the discriminant is a negative number, this indicates the function has no real solutions.

Choices A, B, and D are incorrect and are due to a lack of understanding of the discriminant and its uses in determining the number of real solutions.

8. **Medium | Heart of Algebra**

   Choice D is correct. Create a proportion to express miles per gallon in terms of the total gallons:

   $$\frac{35\,miles}{1\,gallon} = \frac{150,000\,miles}{x\,gallons}$$

   Cross-multiply to solve:

   $35x = 150,000$

   $x = 4285.71\ gallons$

   If his tank can hold 50 gallons per tank, divide to determine how many total tanks are needed:

   $$\frac{4285.71}{50} = 85.71\ tanks$$

   Rounded to nearest whole tank: 86 tanks.

   Choices A, B, and C are incorrect and are most likely the result of rounding errors or errors in creating and solving proportions.

9. **Medium | Problem Solving and Data Analysis**

   Choice A is correct. The word problem describes a system of equations with variables representing the number of 60 minute panelists x and 90 minute panelists y. If Jennifer is offering speakers on the 60 minute panel $50 for their time, and the speakers on the 120 minute panel $110 for their time, one equation must be $50x + 110y = 900$. The other equation represents the total number of panelists $x + y$, which must equal 12. The other equation is therefore $x + y = 12$

   Choices B, C, and D are incorrect and are the result of pairing the wrong variables with constants to create the system.

10. **Medium | Heart of Algebra**

    Choice B is correct. Begin by substituting $(x + 2)$ for x in the equation:

    $(x + 2)^2 + (x + 2)$

    $x^2 + 4x + 4 + x + 2$

    $x^2 + 5x + 6$

    $(x + 2)(x + 3)$

    Choices A, C, and D are incorrect and are the result of errors in simplifying polynomials.

11. **Medium | Problem Solving and Data Analysis**

    Choice C is correct. Find the total number of tickets needed by multiplication:

    $3(1) + 10(2) + 12(3) + 6(4) + 2(5) + 3(6)$

    $3 + 20 + 36 + 24 + 10 + 18 = 113$

    Choices A, B, and D are incorrect and are the result of misinterpretations of the data in the table.

12. **Medium | Problem Solving and Data Analysis**

    Choice D is correct. Begin by creating an equation to represent the total number of hours Tyrone needs to study in terms of x hours per 5 weekdays, if he studies 10 hours per day over the two weekend days:

    $50 = 20 + 5x$

    $30 = 5x$

    $x = 6$ hours per day

    Choices A, B, and C are incorrect and reflect errors in interpreting the value of variables in the word problem.

13. **Medium | Passport to Advanced Math**

    Choice B is correct. To calculate the average of the three values, first set up an equation with the values from the graph:

    $140.322 + 160.071 + 150.051 = 450.444$

    $$\frac{450.444}{3} = 150.148$$

    The graph is in thousands; the average is 150,148.

    Choices A, C, and D are incorrect and are likely the result of arithmetic errors.

14. **Easy | Problem Solving and Data Analysis**

    Choice C is correct. In order to determine the average salary (y), when (x) is 1.75, use the line of best fit. The line of best fit includes the ordered pair (1.75, 90,000), so the average income is approximately $90,000.

    Choices A, B, and D are incorrect and are the result of incorrectly interpreting the data on the graph.

15. **Easy | Heart of Algebra**

    Choice D is correct. Determine Jamie's average speed by dividing the hours he traveled by the total miles he traveled:

    $$\frac{4{,}154 \, miles}{62 \, hours} = 67 \text{ mph}$$

    To find the difference between his average speed and the speed limit, 70 mph, use subtraction: $70 - 67 = 3$ mph.

    Choices A, B, and C are incorrect and are the result of arithmetic errors.

16. **Medium | Problem Solving and Data Analysis**

    Choice A is correct. If a freshman or sophomore is chosen at random, the total number of students that could be chosen is $112 + 83 = 195$. Then, the number of students who took a gap year is $37 + 21 = 58$. The probability is therefore $\frac{58}{195}$.

    Choices B, C, and D are incorrect and reflect errors in isolating totals from the table provided.

17. **Medium | Heart of Algebra**

    Choice B is correct. The size of the school after it's renovation is 15% larger than before, so it is now 115% larger than the original school. Use the value of 744 as 115% to determine the original size, 100%:

$$\frac{744}{115} = \frac{x}{100}$$

$115x = 100 \times 744$

$x = 646.95$

Rounded to the nearest student: 647 students.

Choices A, C, and D are incorrect and are the result in errors in creating and solving a proportion.

18. **Medium | Passport to Advanced Math**

    Choice B is correct. If her class brought 157 cans, but one student brought 50 cans and five students brought none, then 16 students were responsible for 107 cans. The average is therefore: $\frac{107}{16} = 6.7$. Then rounded, 7 cans per student.

    Choice A, C, and D are incorrect and are the result of algebraic errors in creating the equation.

19. **Medium | Problem Solving and Data Analysis**

    Choice A is correct. To find the difference between the averages, one must calculate the averages from the table first: 32 + 16 + 17 + 40 + 23 = 128

    $$\frac{128}{5} = 25.6$$

    22 + 10 + 20 + 32 + 17 = 101

    $$\frac{101}{5} = 20.2$$

    Then, subtract to find the difference: 25.6 – 20.2 = 5.4

    Choices B, C, and D are incorrect because when the averages of the two seasons are subtracted, they are not equal to those values.

20. **Easy | Problem Solving and Data Analysis**

    Choice C is correct. The ratio from Spring to Summer for park B can be found in the second row of the table: 16:10. This value can be simplified to 8:5.

    Choices A, B, and D are incorrect because 16:10 does not simplify to those ratios.

21. **Easy | Problem Solving and Data Analysis**

    Choice B is correct. If Elizabeth wants to take a day off in a week, she must write the paper in 6 days. If she needs to 25 pages in 6 days, she must write $\frac{25\,pages}{6\,days} = 4.17$ pages per day.

    Choices A, C, and D are incorrect because when they are multiplied by 6, they do not equal 25.

22. **Medium | Problem Solving and Data Analysis**

    Choice A is correct. Rearrange the equation to equal m_w:

    $$a = g\left(1 - \frac{m_w}{m_o}\right)$$

$$\frac{a}{g} = 1 - \frac{m_w}{m_o}$$

$$\frac{a}{g} - 1 = -\frac{m_w}{m_o}$$

$$-m_o\left(\frac{a}{g} - 1\right) = m_w$$

Choice B, C, and D are incorrect because then they are rearranged to equal a, they do not equal $a = g\left(1 - \frac{m_w}{m_o}\right)$.

23. **Easy | Problem Solving and Data Analysis**

Choice B is correct. To find the value of $a = g\left(1 - \frac{m_w}{m_o}\right)$, when $m_w = 10$ and $m_o = 15$, substitute the values into the equation and solve:

$$a = 9.8\left(1 - \frac{10}{15}\right)$$

$$a = 9.8\left(\frac{1}{3}\right)$$

$a = 3.27 \ m/s^2$

Choice A, C, and D are incorrect because when those values are substituted for a in the equation, the other variables do not match the values given in the question.

24. **Difficult | Additional Topics in Math**

Choice C is correct. In order to find the center of the circle, complete the square and rewrite the expression in center form: $(x - h)^2 + (y - k)^2 = r^2$

$x^2 - 8x + y^2 - 2x = -8$

$(x^2 - 8x + 16) + (y^2 - 2x + 1) = -8 + 16 + 1$

$(x - 4)^2 + (y - 1)^2 = 9$

Therefore, the center is (4,1).

Choices A, B, and D are incorrect because when (4, 1) is substituted for (x, y) in the equation, they do not equal 9.

25. **Difficult | Problem Solving and Data Analysis**

Choice C is correct. Write the equation of the parabola in vertex form: $y = (x - 2)^2 + 1$ and graph on the calculator. The parabola opens in the positive direction and its vertex is in Quadrant I. Therefore, the graph will never cross into where the y is negative. Therefore, the function will not cross into Quadrant III and IV.

Choices A, B, and D are incorrect and the graph of the function reveals it only occupies Quadrant I and II.

26. **Difficult | Problem Solving and Data Analysis**

    Choice B is correct. To find where the function intercepts the function $y = 7$, one must first write the quadratic function from the given points:

    Points $(-1, 0)$ and $(5, 0)$ form an equation $y = (x + 1)(x - 5)$, which can be set equal to the other function $y = 7$:

    $7 = (x + 1)(x - 5)$

    $7 = x^2 - 4x - 5$

    $0 = x^2 - 4x$

    $0 = (x + 2)(x - 6)$

    $x = -2, 6$

    The two points that intercept the other function are then $(-2, 7)$ and $(6, 7)$, so the distance between the two points is $6 - (-2) = 8$.

    Choices A, C, and D are incorrect and reflect errors in finding solutions and intersections between two functions.

27. **Easy | Problem Solving and Data Analysis**

    Choice D is correct. The value where the costs of textbooks were both equal lies where the lines intersect and the y-values are equal, which lies between 6 and 7 on the x-axis, which is years 2016-2017.

    Choices A, B, and C are incorrect because the intersection of the two lines do not lie between those x-values.

28. **Medium | Problem Solving and Data Analysis**

    Choice B is correct. Start by writing an equation to represent the circle with the center at the origin and a radius of $\sqrt{2} : x^2 + y^2 = 2$. Substitute each ordered pair into the equation, and $(1,1)$ is the only ordered pair that solves the equation:

    $1^2 + 1^2 = 2$

    $2 = 2$

    Choices A, C, and D are incorrect because when substituted into the equation, they do not equal 2.

29. **Medium | Passport to Advanced Math**

    Choice D is correct. Start by solving the system of equations:

    $5(-x + 2y = 8.1)$

    $5x - 3y = -\dfrac{122}{5}$

    $-5x + 10y = 40.5$

    $5x - 3y = -\dfrac{122}{5}$

    $7y = 16.1$

    $y = 2.3$

    Then, substitute this value into the equation and solve for x:

    $-x + 2(2.3) = 8.1$

    $-x + 4.6 = 8.1$

$x = -3.5$

Therefore, (x, y) equals $(-3.5, 2.3)$, so $2x - y = 2(-3.5) + 2.3 = -9.3$

Choices A, B, and C are incorrect and are most likely the result of arithmetic errors in solving the system of equations.

30. **Medium | Additional Topics in Math**

    Choice D is correct. Use the formulas for identifying special right triangles to find the base and height of each triangle. One triangle is isosceles, with equal base angles, so the other leg length is 4. The area of this triangle is $\frac{1}{2}(4 \times 4) = 8$. The other triangle has a hypotenuse of 5 and a leg of 4. This is a 3-4-5 triangle, so the other leg must

    be 3. The area of this triangle is then $\frac{1}{2}(3 \times 4) = 6$. The combined area is $6 + 8 = 14$.

    Choices A, B, and C are incorrect and are most likely the result of errors in identifying special right triangles.

31. **Medium | Heart of Algebra**

    The correct answer is 1389. If sea levels are rising 18 cm every 50 years, the sea must rise a total of 500 cm to reach 5 meters. Use division to find how many cm the sea rises per year, and divide that value by 500 cm:

    $\frac{18 cm}{50 years} = 0.36 \frac{cm}{year}$. $500 cm \div 0.36 \frac{cm}{year} = 1388.89$. Rounded to the nearest whole number, 1389.

32. **Medium | Heart of Algebra**

    The correct answer is 75. Create an equation: $(17 \times 13) + 4 = 225$. Therefore, $\frac{1}{3}(225) = 75$.

33. **Easy | Passport to Advanced Math**

    The correct answer is 9/2 or 4.5. Find the slope of the line formed by the two points: $\frac{(2-4)}{3-(-6)} = -\frac{2}{9}$. The

    perpendicular line is the opposite reciprocal, which is $\frac{9}{2}$.

34. **Medium | Heart of Algebra**

    The correct answer is 12. If Jed spent $34.50 on three tickets that cost $7.50 and an unknown parking fee. Find the difference between the total value and the value of three $7.50 tickets: $34.50 - 3(7.50) = 34.50 - 22.50 = 12$.

35. **Medium | Heart of Algebra**

    The correct answer is 35. Begin by substituting the given values into the equation and solving for b:

    $\left(-\frac{3}{2}\right) = 4(4) - 0.5b$

    $\left(-\frac{3}{2}\right) - 16 = -0.5b$

    $\left(-\frac{3}{2}\right) = 4(4) - 0.5b$

$$-\frac{35}{2} = -0.5b$$

$$b = 35$$

36. **Medium | Additional Topics in Math**

    The correct answer is 60. Find the perimeter of the given triangle using the Pythagorean Theorem:

    $$13^2 = 12^2 + x^2$$

    $$169 - 144 = x^2$$

    $$\sqrt{25} = x$$

    $$x = 5$$

    The perimeter can then be calculated and multiplied by two to find the larger triangle:

    $$5 + 12 + 13 = 30$$

    $$30 \times 2 = 60$$

37. **Difficult | Problem Solving and Data Analysis**

    The correct answer 3.9. Create an equation to represent the percent strength of the mixture:

    $$100(0.03) + 150(0.045) = 250(x)$$

    $$3 + 6.75 = 250x$$

    $$\frac{9.75}{250} = x$$

    $$x = 0.039$$

    Therefore, the percent strength is 3.9%.

38. **Medium | Problem Solving and Data Analysis**

    The correct answer is 10. Create an equation to represent the number of pairs the teacher has in her class (x):

    $$250ml = 50x$$

    $$x = 5$$

    If the class has 5 pairs of students, then the class has 10 total students.

No Test Material On This Page

SAT Practice
Test #3

It is recommended that you use a No. 2 pencil. It is very important that you fill in the entire circle darkly and completely. If you change your response, erase as completely as possible. Incomplete marks or erasures may affect your score.

	A B C D		A B C D		A B C D		A B C D
1	○ ○ ○ ○	14	○ ○ ○ ○	27	○ ○ ○ ○	40	○ ○ ○ ○
2	○ ○ ○ ○	15	○ ○ ○ ○	28	○ ○ ○ ○	41	○ ○ ○ ○
3	○ ○ ○ ○	16	○ ○ ○ ○	29	○ ○ ○ ○	42	○ ○ ○ ○
4	○ ○ ○ ○	17	○ ○ ○ ○	30	○ ○ ○ ○	43	○ ○ ○ ○
5	○ ○ ○ ○	18	○ ○ ○ ○	31	○ ○ ○ ○	44	○ ○ ○ ○
6	○ ○ ○ ○	19	○ ○ ○ ○	32	○ ○ ○ ○	45	○ ○ ○ ○
7	○ ○ ○ ○	20	○ ○ ○ ○	33	○ ○ ○ ○	46	○ ○ ○ ○
8	○ ○ ○ ○	21	○ ○ ○ ○	34	○ ○ ○ ○	47	○ ○ ○ ○
9	○ ○ ○ ○	22	○ ○ ○ ○	35	○ ○ ○ ○	48	○ ○ ○ ○
10	○ ○ ○ ○	23	○ ○ ○ ○	36	○ ○ ○ ○	49	○ ○ ○ ○
11	○ ○ ○ ○	24	○ ○ ○ ○	37	○ ○ ○ ○	50	○ ○ ○ ○
12	○ ○ ○ ○	25	○ ○ ○ ○	38	○ ○ ○ ○	51	○ ○ ○ ○
13	○ ○ ○ ○	26	○ ○ ○ ○	39	○ ○ ○ ○	52	○ ○ ○ ○

It is recommended that you use a No. 2 pencil. It is very important that you fill in the entire circle darkly and completely. If you change your response, erase as completely as possible. Incomplete marks or erasures may affect your score.

	A B C D		A B C D		A B C D		A B C D		A B C D
1	○ ○ ○ ○	10	○ ○ ○ ○	19	○ ○ ○ ○	28	○ ○ ○ ○	37	○ ○ ○ ○
2	○ ○ ○ ○	11	○ ○ ○ ○	20	○ ○ ○ ○	29	○ ○ ○ ○	38	○ ○ ○ ○
3	○ ○ ○ ○	12	○ ○ ○ ○	21	○ ○ ○ ○	30	○ ○ ○ ○	39	○ ○ ○ ○
4	○ ○ ○ ○	13	○ ○ ○ ○	22	○ ○ ○ ○	31	○ ○ ○ ○	40	○ ○ ○ ○
5	○ ○ ○ ○	14	○ ○ ○ ○	23	○ ○ ○ ○	32	○ ○ ○ ○	41	○ ○ ○ ○
6	○ ○ ○ ○	15	○ ○ ○ ○	24	○ ○ ○ ○	33	○ ○ ○ ○	42	○ ○ ○ ○
7	○ ○ ○ ○	16	○ ○ ○ ○	25	○ ○ ○ ○	34	○ ○ ○ ○	43	○ ○ ○ ○
8	○ ○ ○ ○	17	○ ○ ○ ○	26	○ ○ ○ ○	35	○ ○ ○ ○	44	○ ○ ○ ○
9	○ ○ ○ ○	18	○ ○ ○ ○	27	○ ○ ○ ○	36	○ ○ ○ ○		

It is recommended that you use a No. 2 pencil. It is very important that you fill in the entire circle darkly and completely. If you change your response, erase as completely as possible. Incomplete marks or erasures may affect your score.

	A B C D		A B C D		A B C D		A B C D		A B C D
1	○ ○ ○ ○	4	○ ○ ○ ○	7	○ ○ ○ ○	10	○ ○ ○ ○	13	○ ○ ○ ○
2	○ ○ ○ ○	5	○ ○ ○ ○	8	○ ○ ○ ○	11	○ ○ ○ ○	14	○ ○ ○ ○
3	○ ○ ○ ○	6	○ ○ ○ ○	9	○ ○ ○ ○	12	○ ○ ○ ○	15	○ ○ ○ ○

Only answers that are gridded will be scored. You will not receive credit for anything written in the boxes.

16   **17**   **18**   **19**   **20**

(grid-in bubbles for digits . 0 1 2 3 4 5 6 7 8 9 and fraction bar / for questions 16–20)

NO CALCULATOR ALLOWED

It is recommended that you use a No. 2 pencil. It is very important that you fill in the entire circle darkly and completely. If you change your response, erase as completely as possible. Incomplete marks or erasures may affect your score.

	A	B	C	D			A	B	C	D			A	B	C	D			A	B	C	D			A	B	C	D
1	○	○	○	○		7	○	○	○	○		13	○	○	○	○		19	○	○	○	○		25	○	○	○	○
2	○	○	○	○		8	○	○	○	○		14	○	○	○	○		20	○	○	○	○		26	○	○	○	○
3	○	○	○	○		9	○	○	○	○		15	○	○	○	○		21	○	○	○	○		27	○	○	○	○
4	○	○	○	○		10	○	○	○	○		16	○	○	○	○		22	○	○	○	○		28	○	○	○	○
5	○	○	○	○		11	○	○	○	○		17	○	○	○	○		23	○	○	○	○		29	○	○	○	○
6	○	○	○	○		12	○	○	○	○		18	○	○	○	○		24	○	○	○	○		30	○	○	○	○

CALCULATOR ALLOWED

It is recommended that you use a No. 2 pencil. It is very important that you fill in the entire circle darkly and completely. If you change your response, erase as completely as possible. Incomplete marks or erasures may affect your score.

31 32 33 34 35

Only answers that are gridded will be scored. You will not receive credit for anything written in the boxes.

36 37 38

CALCULATOR ALLOWED

Reading Test

65 MINUTES, 52 QUESTIONS

Turn to Section 1 of your answer sheet to answer the questions in this section

---

DIRECTIONS

Each passage or pair of passages below is followed by a number of questions. After reading each passage or pair, choose the best answer to each question based on what is stated or implied in the passage or passages and in any accompanying graphics (such as a table or graph).

Questions 1-10 are based on the following passage.

This passage is adapted from book 1 of *The Beautiful and the Damned,* © 1922 by F. Scott Fitzgerald.

Anthony drew as much consciousness of social security from being the grandson of Adam J. Patch as he would have had from tracing his line over the
Line sea to the crusaders. Now Adam J. Patch left his
5 father's farm in Tarrytown early in sixty-one to join a New York cavalry regiment. He came home from the war a major, charged into Wall Street, and amid much fuss, fume, applause, and ill will he gathered to himself some seventy-five million dollars.

10 This occupied his energies until he was fifty-seven years old. It was then that he determined, after a severe attack of sclerosis, to consecrate the remainder of his life to the moral regeneration of the world. He became a reformer among reformers.
15 Emulating the magnificent efforts of Anthony Comstock, after whom his grandson was named, he levelled a varied assortment of uppercuts and body-blows at liquor, literature, vice, art, patent medicines, and Sunday theatres. From an armchair in the office
20 of his Tarrytown estate he directed against the enormous hypothetical enemy, unrighteousness, a campaign which went on through fifteen years, during which he displayed himself a rabid monomaniac, an unqualified nuisance, and an
25 intolerable bore. The year in which this story opens found him wearying; 1861 was creeping up slowly

on 1895; his thoughts ran a great deal on the Civil War, somewhat on his dead wife and son, almost infinitesimally on his grandson Anthony.

30 Early in his career Adam Patch had married an anemic lady of thirty, Alicia Withers, who brought him one hundred thousand dollars and an impeccable entré into the banking circles of New York. Immediately and rather spunkily she had
35 borne him a son and, as if completely devitalized by the magnificence of this performance, she had thenceforth effaced herself within the shadowy dimensions of the nursery. The boy, Adam Ulysses Patch, became an inveterate joiner of clubs,
40 connoisseur of good form, and driver of tandems—at the astonishing age of twenty-six he began his memoirs under the title "New York Society as I Have Seen It." On the rumor of its conception this work was eagerly bid for among publishers, but as it
45 proved after his death to be immoderately verbose and overpoweringly dull, it never obtained even a private printing.

This Fifth Avenue Chesterfield married at twenty-two. His wife was Henrietta Lebrune, the
50 Boston "Society Contralto," and the single child of the union was, at the request of his grandfather, christened Anthony Comstock Patch. When he went to Harvard, the Comstock dropped out of his name and was never heard of thereafter.

55 Young Anthony had one picture of his father and mother together—so often had it faced his eyes in childhood that it had acquired the impersonality

CONTINUE ➡

of furniture, but every one who came into his
bedroom regarded it with interest. It showed
60 a dandy of the nineties, spare and handsome,
standing beside a tall dark lady with a muff and the
suggestion of a bustle. Between them was a little
boy with long brown curls, dressed in a velvet Lord
Fauntleroy suit. This was Anthony at five, the year of
65 his mother's death.

His memories of the Boston Society Contralto
were nebulous and musical. She was a lady who
sang, sang, sang, in the music room of their house
on Washington Square—sometimes with guests
70 scattered all about her, the men with their arms
folded, balanced breathlessly on the edges of sofas,
the women clapping very briskly and uttering
cooing cries after each song—and often she sang to
Anthony alone, in Italian or French.

75 His recollections of the gallant Ulysses were
much more vivid. After Henrietta Lebrune Patch
had "joined another choir," as her widower huskily
remarked from time to time, father and son lived
up at grampa's in Tarrytown, and Ulysses came
80 daily to Anthony's nursery and expelled pleasant,
thick-smelling words for sometimes as much as
an hour. He was continually promising Anthony
hunting trips and fishing trips and excursions to
Atlantic City, "oh, some time soon now"; but none
85 of them ever materialized. One trip they did take;
when Anthony was eleven they went abroad, to
England and Switzerland, and there in the best
hotel in Lucerne his father died with much sweating
and grunting and crying aloud for air. In a panic
90 of despair and terror Anthony was brought back to
America, wedded to a vague melancholy that was to
stay beside him through the rest of his life.

1

Which choice best summarizes the passage?

A) A young man reminisces about his family.

B) A man's family background is explained.

C) An aristocrat's achievements are outlined.

D) The cause of a tragic event is revealed.

2

As used in line 8, "fume" most nearly means

A) exhaust

B) stench

C) pollution

D) rage

3

According to the passage, who was Anthony
Comstock?

A) Adam J. Patch's close friend who made many
major reforms.

B) An individual who liked to indulge in a
variety of vices.

C) A professional fighter who was an inspiration
to Adam J. Patch.

D) A man who tried changing society and was
revered by Adam J. Patch.

4

The main purpose of including the phrase "1861 was creeping up slowly on 1895" (lines 26-27) is to

A) indicate that the elder Adam Patch was living in the past rather than the present.

B) provide a reason he did not reflect often on the deaths of his wife and son.

C) offer the reason that he dedicated most of his time to campaigning against vices.

D) clarify the previous claim that the elder Adam Patch was an intolerable bore.

5

Based on the passage, Adam J. Patch's wife could best be characterized as

A) powerful.

B) captivating.

C) diffident.

D) animated.

6

Which choice provides the best evidence for the answer to the previous question?

A) Lines 30-34 ("Adam Patch… New York.")

B) Lines 34-35 ("Immediately… a son")

C) Lines 35-38 ("as if… nursery")

D) Lines 66-69 ("his memories… Washington Square")

7

In line 41, the word "astonishing" creates the effect of

A) indicating irony.

B) expressing admiration.

C) highlighting respect.

D) emphasizing talent.

CONTINUE

8

Which choice best supports the claim that Adam Ulysses Patch was an engaging conversationalist?

A) Lines 43-47 ("On the... printing")

B) Lines 59-60 ("It showed... handsome")

C) Lines 75-76 ("His recollections... vivid")

D) Lines 79-82 ("Ulysses came... an hour")

9

The main purpose of including the information about Adam Ulysses Patch continually promising trips to Anthony is to

A) foreshadow the trip in which Adam Ulysses passes away.

B) reinforce the superficial nature of Anthony's father.

C) emphasize the deep interest that Adam Ulysses has for his son.

D) give an indication of Adam Ulysses' vast wealth.

10

The author includes details about the episode in the hotel in Lucerne most likely to

A) show that Adam Ulysses ultimately kept his promises.

B) highlight the pain during Adam Ulysses's last moments.

C) explain why Anthony decided to live in America.

D) provide background for a feature in Anthony's personality.

Questions 11-21 are based on the following passage.

This passage is adapted from a statement by Jefferson Keel, President of the National Congress of American Indians, in "The Indian Reorganization Act—75 Years Later: Renewing our Commitment to Restore Tribal Homelands and Promote Self-determination." Published June 23, 2011 by the U.S. Government Publishing Office. "Carcieri v. Salazar" refers to a Supreme Court decision in 2009 that only tribes recognized in 1934 would be protected by the Indian Reorganization Act.

Our predecessors had a shared vision for our future as Indian people. Indian reservations should be places where the old ways are maintained, our
Line languages are spoken, and our children learn our
5 traditions and pass them on to the next generation. They are places where there are fish in the stream and game in the field, and food and medicines grow wild for harvest; places where our people can live and be Indian. At the same time, this vision includes
10 modern life, economic development to sustain our people; safety and respectful relationships with our neighbors; and the blessings of education, health care and modern technology to help us thrive.

This vision was shared by the U.S. Congress
15 in 1934 when it passed one of the most important Federal laws in the history of our Country, the Indian Reorganization Act. With the IRA, Congress renewed its trust responsibility to protect and restore our tribal homelands and the Indian way of
20 life.

Two years ago, our shared vision and the Federal responsibility to Indian tribes were threatened by the Supreme Court's interpretation of the IRA in Carcieri v. Salazar. Prior to 1934, the Federal
25 Government policy toward Indian tribes was to sell off the tribal land base and assimilate Indian people. "Kill the Indian and save the man" was the slogan of that era.

The Federal Government did everything it
30 could to disband our tribes, break up our families and suppress our culture. Over 90 million acres of tribal land held under treaties were taken, more than two-thirds of the tribal land base, and the remaining lands were often of little value for development
35 or agriculture. But in the 1930s, the assimilation

policies were widely recognized as failures. The policies did little more than inflict great suffering on Indian people and dishonor our Nation.

In 1934, Congress rejected allotment and
40 assimilation and passed the IRA. The clear and overriding purpose of Congress was to reestablish the tribal land base and restore tribal governments that had withered under prior Federal policy. The legislative history and the Act itself are filled with
45 references to restoration of Federal support for tribes that had been cut off and to provide land for landless Indians.

A problem with our legal system is that lawyers sometimes lose sight of the fundamental purpose
50 of the law, debate the meaning of a few words, and suddenly the law is turned on its head. Today, because of the Carcieri decision, we have opponents arguing that tribes are not eligible for the benefits of the IRA if they were not under active Federal
55 supervision by the Bureau of Indian Affairs (BIA) in 1934, or if they did not have lands in trust in 1934. Both of these arguments are contrary to the basic purpose of the law to reestablish Federal support for tribes that had been abandoned or ignored by the
60 BIA and to restore land to tribes that had little or no land.

Today, 75 years later, the IRA is as necessary as it was in 1934. The purposes of the IRA were frustrated first by World War II and then by the
65 termination era. Work did not begin again until the 1970s with the self-determination policy, and since then Indian tribes are building economies from the ground up and they must earn every penny to buy back their own land. Still today, many tribes have no
70 land base and many tribes have insufficient lands to support housing and self-government and culture. We will need the IRA for many more years until the tribal needs for self-support and self-determination are met.

75 Two years have passed since the Carcieri decision and our fears are coming to pass. There are at least 14 pending cases where tribes and the Secretary of the Interior are under challenge. There are many more tribes whose land-to-
80 trust applications have simply been frozen while the Department of the Interior works through painstaking legal and historical analysis. We are seeing harassment litigation against tribes who

were on treaty reservations in 1934 with a BIA
85　superintendent. It is litigation merely for the
purpose of delay. Land acquisitions are delayed.
Lending and credit are drying up. Jobs are lost or
never created. We fear that this will continue to
get worse until Congress acts. Even worse, that
90　this decision will create two classes of Indian
tribes: those who will benefit from Federal trust
responsibility and those who will not.

11

One central idea of the passage is that the Indian
Reorganization Act

A) has been interpreted too strictly so that it no
longer adheres to its original purpose.

B) needs to be replaced by new legislation that is
more in keeping with current times.

C) was created in the effort to deny Native
Americans the basic rights of citizens.

D) has been successful in helping Native
American cultures to thrive since it
was enacted.

12

Over the course of the passage, Keel's focus shifts
from

A) the historical background for the IRA to the
reasons that the IRA should be eliminated.

B) the intentions behind the IRA to the current
application of the legislation.

C) an analysis of the goals of Native Americans
to a discussion of the Carcieri v. Salazar case.

D) the ethics taking land from Native Americans
to a solution for returning that land.

13

Based on the passage, which choice best describes
the government's stance towards Native American
people before 1934?

A) The government encouraged Native
Americans to maintain their traditional
customs as long as they lived on reservations.

B) The government made efforts to ensure that
Native Americans could preserve their
traditional lands and heritage.

C) The government wanted Native Americans
to abandon traditional practices in the effort
of creating a single nation.

D) The government decided that only Native
Americans who owned land would qualify as
United States citizens.

14

Which choice provides the best evidence for the
answer to the previous question?

A) Lines 2-5 ("Indian reservations… generation")

B) Lines 17-20 ("With the… of life")

C) Lines 27-28 ("Kill the… that era")

D) Lines 40-43 ("The clear… policy")

CONTINUE

15

As used in line 54, "active" most nearly means

A) energetic.

B) vigorous.

C) operative.

D) industrious.

16

A student argues that Native Americans no longer need the IRA because they are no longer persecuted. Which choice provides the best evidence to counter that claim?

A) Lines 24-26 ("Prior to… people")

B) Lines 65-69 ("Work did… own land")

C) Lines 69-71 ("Still today… culture")

D) Lines 75-76 ("Two years… to pass")

17

As used in line 60, "frustrated" most nearly means

A) annoyed.

B) unfulfilled.

C) dissatisfied.

D) thwarted.

18

Keel suggests that the Carcieri decision was especially problematic because it

A) did not adhere to the exact wording of the original IRA legislation.

B) asserted that the IRA legislation only applies to specific Native Americans.

C) created new methods by which the Native Americans could regain lands.

D) set precedents that facilitated the establishment of tribal governments.

19

According to the passage, present-day Native Americans can only acquire their tribal lands by

A) applying for a grant to reimburse the property owner.

B) proving to the state that the land was historically theirs.

C) paying money to buy the land from the property owner.

D) exercising their right to become a member of the IRA.

20

In the passage, Keel implies that the Department of the Interior

A) regularly changes its policy regarding Native American land acquisition.

B) has the authority to transfer property from individuals to Native American tribes.

C) does not offer sufficient employment opportunities for Native Americans.

D) is not expediting the process of returning tribal land to Native Americans.

21

Which of the following statements best summarizes a main concern that Keel has about the Carcieri decision?

A) It will lead to a complete repeal of the Indian Reorganization Act.

B) It will create an unfair division among groups of Native Americans.

C) It will legally prevent Native Americans from regaining their tribal lands.

D) It will only protect the rights of tribes on reservations with BIA superintendents.

Questions 22-31 are based on the following passage and supplementary material.

This passage is adapted from the Bureau of Labor Statistics's "Occupational Outlook Handbook: Urban and Regional Planners," 2019.

Becoming an urban or regional planner can be a very satisfying career for individuals who want to positively change the daily lives of people
Line around them. Urban and regional planners develop
5 land, use plans and programs that help create communities, accommodate population growth, and revitalize physical facilities in towns, cities, counties, and metropolitan areas. They typically meet with public officials, developers, and the public regarding
10 development plans and land use; administer government plans or policies affecting land use; gather and analyze data from market research, censuses, and economic and environmental studies; and conduct field investigations to analyze factors
15 affecting community development and decline, including land use. They also review site plans submitted by developers, assess the feasibility of proposals, identify needed changes, and recommend whether proposals should be approved or denied.

20 As an area grows or changes, planners create short- and long-term plans to help communities manage the related economic, social, and environmental issues, such as planning new parks, sheltering the homeless, and making the region
25 more attractive to businesses. When beginning a project, planners need to work closely with public officials, community members, and other groups to identify community issues and goals. Through research, data analysis, and collaboration with
30 interest groups, they formulate strategies to address the issues they have isolated and to meet goals. Planners may also help carry out community plans by overseeing projects, enforcing zoning regulations, and organizing the work of the groups involved.
35 Urban and regional planners use a variety of tools and technology in their work. They commonly use statistical software, data visualization and presentation programs, financial spreadsheets, and other database and software programs.
40 Geographic Information System (GIS) software is used to integrate data, such as population density, with digital maps. Therefore, planners need solid technological and analytical skills as well as excellent communication skills to convey information to the

45 appropriate audiences. Urban and regional planners may specialize in areas such as transportation planning, community development, historic preservation, or urban design, among other fields of interest.

50 Urban and regional planners held about 39,100 jobs in 2018. Planners work throughout the country, but most work in large metropolitan areas. They may travel to inspect proposed changes and their impacts on land conditions, the environment, and
55 land use. Candidates need a master's degree from an accredited planning program to qualify for most positions. Master's degree programs accept students with a wide range of undergraduate backgrounds. However, many candidates who enter these
60 programs have a bachelor's degree in economics, geography, political science, or environmental design.

The median annual wage for urban and regional planners was $73,050 in May 2018. The median
65 wage is the wage at which half the workers in an occupation earned more than that amount and half earned less. The lowest 10 percent earned less than $45,180, and the highest 10 percent earned more than $114,170. Employment of urban and
70 regional planners is projected to grow 11 percent from 2018 to 2028, much faster than the average for all occupations. Demographic, transportation, and environmental changes will drive employment growth for planners. Within cities, urban planners
75 will be needed to develop revitalization projects and address issues associated with population growth, environmental degradation, the movement of people and goods, and resource scarcity. Similarly, suburban areas and municipalities will need
80 planners to address the challenges associated with population changes, including housing needs and transportation systems covering larger areas with less population density. Planners will also be needed as new and existing communities require extensive
85 development and improved infrastructure, including housing, roads, sewer systems, parks, and schools. However, federal, state, and local government budgets may affect the employment of planners in government, because development projects are
90 contingent on available funds.

Figure 1: Median annual wages for urban and regional planners in selected industries in the United States, May, 2019

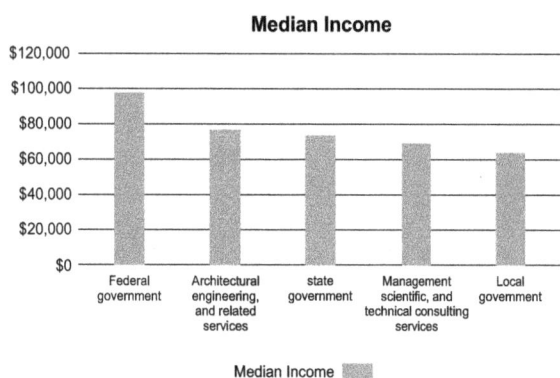

Median Income

Figure 2: Main Employers of Urban and Regional Planners in the United States, 2018

Local government	71%
Architectural, engineering, and related services	11%
State government	9%
Management, scientific, and technical consulting services	3%
Federal government	2%

22

Which choice best describes the structural development of the passage?

A) The author analyzes new research that reveals a potential opportunity.

B) The author makes a claim then provides specific details that reinforce it.

C) The author offers a suggestion then enumerates the suggestion's weaknesses.

D) The author describes the process of entering employment in a certain field.

23

As used in line 25, "attractive" most nearly means

A) charismatic.

B) irresistible.

C) appealing.

D) fascinating.

24

The author suggests that urban and regional planners most need strong skills in

A) creating strong plans and securing funding to complete them.

B) expressing ideas clearly and using specialized technology.

C) negotiating disputes and creating new parks.

D) historic preservation and understanding economic complexities.

25

Which choice provides the best evidence for the answer to the previous question?

A) Lines 4-8 ("Urban… metropolitan areas")

B) Lines 25-28 ("When beginning… and goals")

C) Lines 36-39 ("They commonly… programs")

D) Lines 42-45 ("Therefore… audiences")

26

The author includes the definition of a median wage in lines 63-67 ("The median wage…earned less") most likely to

A) give perspective about some data provided in the passage.

B) point out that the median wage is an insufficient measurement.

C) suggest a possible reason for the wide range in salaries.

D) provide support for the claim that employment is predicted to grow.

27

As used in line 76, "address" most nearly means

A) remit.

B) confront.

C) communicate.

D) approach.

28

According to figure 1, the median income of urban and regional planners

A) is higher for state government employees than for local government employees.

B) is greater for those in architectural, engineering and related fields than for those in any government position.

C) is lower for those working in the government than for those who work in private industries such as engineering or related services.

D) is not as high for management, scientific, and technical consulting service employees as it is for local government employees.

CONTINUE

29

Based on information in the passage, it can be reasonably inferred that the percentage of urban and regional planners employed by the federal government in figure 2

A) is extremely low because there is very little demand for urban planning outside of large cities.

B) does not reflect the actual number of planners employed by the federal government compared to those employed in other sectors.

C) will remain approximately the same level because federal government positions are very stable.

D) has the potential to decrease if the federal government receives fewer tax dollars and revises its spending plans.

30

Which choice provides the best evidence for the answer to the previous question?

A) Lines 69-72 ("Employment... occupations")

B) Lines 72-74 ("Demographic... planners")

C) Lines 83-86 ("Planners... and schools")

D) Lines 87-90 ("However... funds")

31

Which choice best states the relationship between the two figures and the passage?

A) Both figures offer a visual interpretation of data discussed in the passage.

B) Both figures present data that challenge specific points within the passage.

C) Both figures provide specific data to reinforce claims made within the passage.

D) Both figures give data that is only loosely related to the main claim of the passage.

Questions 32-42 are based on the following passages.

Passage 1 is adapted from "Scientists find Southern Ocean removing CO2 from the atmosphere more efficiently," copyright September 10, 2015, by NOAA. Passage 2 is adapted from "Saildrone is first to circumnavigate Antarctica, in search for carbon dioxide," copyright August 5, 2019 by NOAA.

Passage 1:

Since 2002, the Southern Ocean has been removing more of the greenhouse gas carbon dioxide (CO_2) from the atmosphere, according to
Line a new study in the journal *Geophysical Research*
5 *Letters* (GRL).

The global oceans are an important sink for human-released CO_2, absorbing nearly a quarter of the total CO_2 emissions every year. Of all ocean regions, the Southern Ocean below the 35th parallel
10 south plays a particularly vital role. "Although it comprises only 26 percent of the total ocean area, the Southern Ocean has absorbed nearly 40 percent of all anthropogenic CO_2 taken up by the global oceans up to the present," says David Munro,
15 a scientist at the Institute of Arctic and Alpine Research at the University of Colorado Boulder and a co-author on the *GRL* paper.

The *GRL* paper focuses on one region of the Southern Ocean extending from the tip of South
20 America to the tip of the Antarctic Peninsula. "The Drake Passage is the windiest, roughest part of the Southern Ocean," says Colm Sweeney, lead investigator on the Drake Passage study and co-author on the GRL paper, "The critical
25 element to this study is that we were able to sustain measurements in this harsh environment as long as we have—both in the summer and the winter, in every year over the last 13 years. This data set of ocean carbon measurements is the densest ongoing
30 time series in the Southern Ocean."

The team was able to take these long-term measurements by piggybacking instruments on the Antarctic Research Supply Vessel *Laurence M. Gould*, which makes nearly 20 crossings of the
35 Drake Passage each year, transporting people and supplies to and from Antarctic research stations. For over 13 years, it's taken chemical measurements of the atmosphere and surface ocean along the way.

By analyzing more than one million surface
40 ocean observations, the researchers could tease out subtle differences between the CO_2 trends in the surface ocean and the atmosphere that suggest a strengthening of the carbon sink. This change is most pronounced in the southern half
45 of the Drake Passage during winter. Although the researchers aren't sure of the exact mechanism driving these changes, "it's likely that winter mixing with deep waters that have not had contact with the atmosphere for several hundred years plays an
50 important role," says Munro.

These results contrast with previous findings that showed that the Southern Ocean CO_2 sink was stagnant or weakening from the early 1990s to the early 2000s. "Given the importance of the Southern
55 Ocean to the global oceans' role in absorbing atmospheric CO_2, these studies suggest that we must continue to expand our measurements in this part of the world despite the challenging environment," says Sweeney.

Passage 2:

60 It was an audacious idea: To send an unmanned research vehicle called a saildrone on a 13,670-mile journey around Antarctica alone, at the mercy of the most hostile seas on the planet. In winter.

"The assumption was the Southern Ocean
65 would eat the saildrone … and that would be that," said NOAA oceanographer Adrienne Sutton. "But we were willing to try, given the large role the ocean plays in the trajectory of climate change. Getting the Southern Ocean's carbon balance right is urgently
70 important."

Despite a run-in with an iceberg that wrecked some of its sensors, Saildrone 1020 completed its mission on August 3 having successfully collected oceanic and atmospheric carbon dioxide
75 measurements with an instrument developed by NOAA's Pacific Marine Environmental Laboratory. The 196-day voyage was the world's first autonomous circumnavigation of Antarctica — a technological feat that was unfathomable just a
80 decade ago.

Until recently, scientists assumed that the Southern Ocean steadily absorbed large volumes of

CONTINUE

CO2 from the atmosphere — a big contributor to the entire ocean's uptake of up to 40 percent of the
85 greenhouse gases driving global warming. However, scientists also knew shifts in winds and circulation around Antarctica could alter CO2 uptake from the atmosphere, and recent measurements showed that under certain conditions the Southern Ocean could
90 emit CO2 instead of absorbing it. But researchers had yet to sample vast areas, especially during stormy autumn and winter seasons.

Preliminary results suggest that parts of the ocean identified as potential CO2 sources were
95 indeed emitting the greenhouse gas during winter months. "It was a high-risk, high reward kind of deployment," Sutton said. "We weren't sure it was going to make it." Fortunately, the risks paid off with vital data that can help scientists better understand
100 the relationship between the Southern Ocean and the atmosphere.

32

According to Passage 1, the results of the Drake Passage study are unique because they

A) used more complete measurements than any other study of the region.

B) were derived using equipment that had not previously been used.

C) incorporated chemical measurements as well as other forms of data.

D) determined that the Southern Ocean absorbs more CO_2 than other oceans.

33

Which choice provides the best evidence for the answer to the previous question?

A) Lines 18-20 ("The *GRL* paper... Peninsula")

B) Lines 21-22 ("The Drake Passage... Ocean")

C) Lines 28-30 ("This data set... Southern Ocean")

D) Lines 31-36 ("The team... research stations")

34

Passage 1 implies that the Drake Passage study falls short of being definitive because the study

A) did not collect sufficient data to come to a solid conclusion.

B) was unable to collect data during critical time periods.

C) only focused on one region rather than the world's oceans.

D) isolated an effect but not the cause of that effect.

35

In Passage 1, the sixth paragraph (Lines 50-58) mainly serves to

A) emphasize the difficulty of collecting accurate data from the Southern Ocean.

B) illustrate the problems with amassing an adequate data base on the Southern Ocean.

C) place the results of the Drake Passage study in the wider context of other studies.

D) highlight the need to correct the problem of CO_2 absorption before it is too late.

36

According to Passage 2, one of the main goals of launching the saildrone during the winter was to

A) prove that the Southern Ocean was absorbing as much CO_2 as previously estimated.

B) test the limitations of new technology designed to survive harsh conditions.

C) collect data during a time period in which very little research had previously been done.

D) establish whether the Southern Ocean played a vital role in CO_2 absorption.

37

In describing the seas as "hostile" (Line 62), the author of Passage 2 most nearly means that the ocean is

A) aggressive.

B) antagonistic.

C) unforgiving.

D) conflicting.

38

In Passage 2, the phrase "in winter" (Line 62) mainly serves to

A) emphasize the harshness of the conditions that the saildrone faced.

B) inform the reader of the date when the saildrone was launched.

C) indicate that research conducted during the winter season was lacking.

D) explain why the saildrone was not manned during its voyage.

39

Which choice best supports the idea that using the saildrone was a revolutionary method to collect data?

A) Lines 64-65 ("The assumption... be that")

B) Lines 71-77 ("Despite a... Laboratory")

C) Lines 77-80 ("The 196-day... decade ago.")

D) Lines 90-92 ("But researchers... seasons")

40

Which choice best describes the relationship between the two passages?

A) Passage 1 describes important research results and Passage 2 offers details about obtaining the data for the research.

B) Passage 1 describes a barrier to research and Passage 2 shows one solution to help surmount that barrier.

C) Passage 1 outlines a method of collecting data whereas Passage 2 argues that such a method is obsolete.

D) Passage offers historical background about a region whereas Passage 2 discusses conditions in the region today.

41

Based on the research published in the *GRL* paper described in Passage 1 and the data derived from the saildrone in Passage 2, with which claim regarding the Southern Ocean would the authors of the passages most likely agree?

A) The Southern Ocean is absorbing significantly more CO_2 than it did in the past.

B) The CO_2 absorbed by the Southern Ocean is not enough to counteract global warming.

C) The changes in CO_2 absorption are likely based on mixing between water layers.

D) The implications of the Southern Ocean's CO_2 absorption are not fully understood.

42

How would Sweeney in Passage 1 most likely respond to Sutton's claim at the end of Passage 2 (lines 96-98, "It was... make it")?

A) By saying that the imperative for more concrete data justified the risks taken.

B) By saying that the resulting conclusions were not commensurate with the dangers.

C) By saying that the research was redundant after the *Laurence M. Gould* study.

D) By saying that the data could have been gathered using less risky methods.

Questions 43-52 are based on the following passage and supplementary material.

This passage is adapted from "Understanding Images: Identifying a novel gene involved in hair disorders" by Prashant Sharma, Undiagnosed Diseases Program, National Human Genome Research Institute, National Institutes of Health. Copyright July 16, 2019.

Copper is essential for many body functions, and impairment of the management of copper in the body leads to a wide spectrum of impairments,
Line including several genetic diseases. One of the best
5 known of these is Menkes kinky hair syndrome, which is characterized by the presence of a peculiar "kinky hair" trait and degeneration of the brain, bones and connective tissue. Menkes is a rare X-linked disease caused by disruptive mutations
10 in the *ATP7A* gene, which encodes a protein that pumps copper across cellular membranes. How the copper deficiency in Menkes syndrome patients leads to hair abnormalities is not completely understood, but it has been suggested that the low
15 activity of an enzyme which depends on copper for its activity results in fewer of the bridges that provide structural strength and elasticity in hair.

Menkes syndrome is lethal and there is no known cure, so most patients die within the first
20 decade of their lives, most before the age of 3. Because it is so rare, few pharmaceutical companies are investing in research related to the disease. Through the NIH Undiagnosed Diseases program, we evaluated a patient who presented clinically
25 with abnormal hair and cognitive dysfunction. The hair abnormalities observed in our patient resemble those found in Menkes syndrome, but sequence analysis of the *ATP7A* gene and relevant biochemical testing showed that *ATP7A* wasn't
30 involved in causing our patient's clinical features. To identify other variants that might be contributing, we sequenced all of the protein-coding regions of the patient's DNA, along with those of his parents, and identified two deleterious mutations, one
35 from each parent, in the *HEPHL1* gene, located on chromosome 11.

HEPHL1 belongs to a family of proteins known as Multi-Copper Oxidases (MCOs). The main function of *HEPHL1's* two closest relatives,
40 ceruloplasmin and hephaestin, is to catalyze the oxidation of iron so that it can bind to a circulating protein called transferrin which distributes it throughout the body. One unique property of MCOs is the presence of three copper-binding sites that
45 can house six copper atoms. Mutations that alter the structure of these sites are likely to affect their ability to bind copper, and this in turn may alter the activity of the enzyme. Our study demonstrates that each mutation found in the patient led to complete
50 loss of iron-oxidizing activity. As a consequence, we found unexpectedly high levels of iron in skin cells taken from the patient.

To help us explore the physiological consequences of the loss of *HEPHL1* activity more
55 thoroughly, we used a gene targeting approach to make mice with a disrupted *HEPHL1* gene. Interestingly, all mice that had a complete deletion of both copies of their *HEPHL1* gene had short, curled whiskers throughout their life. The curly
60 whisker in Hephl1 knockout mice resemble the hair found in our patient with two different *HEPHL1* mutations. Mice with one copy of the normal *HEPHL1* gene didn't have curly whiskers, showing that complete loss of *HEPHL1* function is needed to
65 affect the structure of the hair.

How *HEPHL1* mechanistically regulates hair growth and development will require further in-depth analysis, and the curly whiskers from *HEPHL1* knockout mice could help these
70 investigations. Our preliminary results showed that *HEPHL1* regulates the activity of an enzyme, lysyl oxidase, which needs copper for its enzymatic activity. This raises the intriguing possibility that, in addition to playing an iron-related role, *HEPHL1*
75 could relate to the copper absorption associated with Menkes syndrome. In conclusion, our study identified *HEPHL1* as a novel gene responsible for hair abnormalities and highlights the importance of exploring the role of *HEPHL1* — and its
80 interconnections with other key regulators — in developing new therapeutic strategies to treat hair disorders and even more insidious genetic diseases.

CONTINUE

Figure 1: Total Increase in Iron Content in Cells

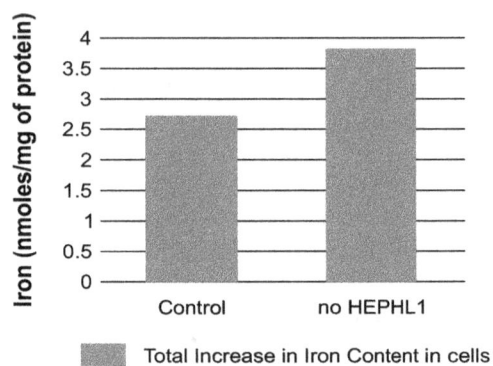

Figure 2: Change in Lysyl Oxidase Activity (as percentage of control)

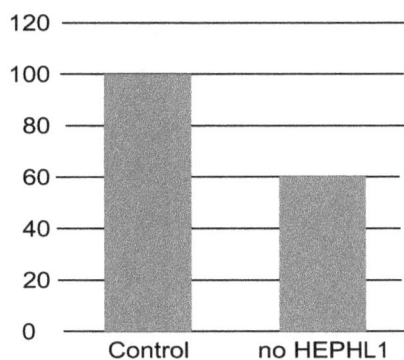

Figures adapted from "Biallelic *HEPHL1* variants impair ferroxidase activity and cause an abnormal hair phenotype" by Prashant Sharma et al., PLOS Genetics, 2019.

43

The primary purpose of the passage is to

A) present a study that proposes a potential cure for Menkes syndrome.

B) discuss research on a gene that may be influential in causing Menkes syndrome.

C) describe the method in which scientists determine how genes cause genetic diseases.

D) analyze the reasons that some mice are born with a gene causing kinky whiskers.

44

Which statement regarding Menkes syndrome can be most reasonably inferred from the passage?

A) Pharmaceutical companies are irresponsible in their attitude towards the disease.

B) Patients are usually not aware that they have the disease until its advanced stages.

C) There are not enough patients to make the development of a cure financially viable.

D) Giving a patient adequate copper supplements can help reduce the effect of the disease.

45

Which choice provides the best evidence for the answer to the previous question?

A) Lines 4-8 ("One of… tissue")

B) Lines 18-20 ("Menkes… age of 3")

C) Lines 21-22 ("Because it… disease")

D) Lines 23-25 ("Through the… dysfunction")

46

As used in Line 43, "house" most nearly means

A) accommodate.

B) quarter.

C) lodge.

D) shelter.

47

According to the passage, which statement best explains the importance of finding a patient who had symptoms of Menkes syndrome but not an *ATP7A* mutation?

A) It allowed the researchers to uncover another gene that could contribute to the symptoms.

B) It permitted scientists to find a treatment that could reverse damage from Menkes syndrome.

C) It proved that an *ATP7A* mutation does not cause Menkes syndrome as previously believed.

D) It indicated that Menkes syndrome probably originated from a mutation found in mice.

48

Which choice best establishes the potential link between *HEPHL1* and the lack of proper copper absorption found in patients with Menkes syndrome?

A) Lines 8-11 ("Menkes is… membranes")

B) Lines 48-50 ("Our study… activity")

C) Lines 59-62 ("The curly… mutations")

D) Lines 70-73 ("Our preliminary… activity")

49

In line 78, the author uses the words "novel" primarily to suggest that

A) *HEPHL1* has never before been classified by researchers.

B) the relationship between *HEPHL1* and hair anomalies has only just been identified.

C) *HEPHL1* is the newest solution in the fight against genetic diseases.

D) no one had realized that *HEPHL1* was closely linked to *ATP7A* mutations.

50

According to figure 1, the difference in the iron uptake increase between the cells of the mouse with no *HEPHL1* and the cells of the control mouse was closest to which value?

A) 1.1 nmoles/mg of protein

B) 2.1 nmoles/mg of protein

C) 2.7 nmoles/mg of protein

D) 3.8 nmoles/mg of protein

51

Figure 2 supports which statement about the change in lysyl oxidase activity caused by altering the *HEPHL1* genes in a mouse?

A) The mouse did not display any lysyl oxidase activity if it had the two *HEPHL1* genes removed.

B) The mouse with two *HEPHL1* genes removed had a decrease but not a total loss of lysyl oxidase activity.

C) The mouse with two *HEPHL1* genes removed had lower lysyl oxidase activity and no iron uptake.

D) The mouse displayed increasingly low lysyl oxidase activity over time if it had the two *HEPHL1* genes removed.

52

Based on the passage and figures, how would the bars in figure 1 most likely change if the second mouse had one viable gene containing *HEPHL1* from its mother as opposed to a complete lack of *HEPHL1* genes?

A) the bar for the second mouse would be shorter than it is on the existing graph, but taller than that for the control.

B) the bar for the second mouse would be shorter than that for the control.

C) the bar for the second mouse would be taller than it is on the existing graph.

D) there would be no change to the graph.

STOP

If you finish before time is called, you may check your work on this section only.
Do not turn to any other section.

Writing and Language Test

35 MINUTES, 44 QUESTIONS

Turn to Section 2 of your answer sheet to answer the questions in this section

---

DIRECTIONS

Each passage below is accompanied by a number of questions. For some questions, you will consider how the passage might be revised to improve the expression of ideas. For other questions, you will consider how the passage might be edited to correct errors in sentence structure, usage, or punctuation. A passage or a question may be accompanied by one or more graphics (such as a table or graph) that you will consider as you make revising and editing decisions.

Some questions will direct you to an underlined portion of a passage. Other questions will direct you to a location in a passage or ask you to think about the passage as a whole.

After reading each passage, choose the answer to each question that most effectively improves the quality of writing in the passage or that makes the passage conform to the conventions of standard written English. Many questions include a "NO CHANGE" option. Choose that option if you think the best choice is to leave the relevant portion of the passage as it is.

CONTINUE ➤

Questions 1-11 are based on the following text that has been adapted from Stanford Social Innovation Review's Social Entrepreneurship: The Case for Definition.

[1] The nascent field of social entrepreneurship is growing rapidly and attracting increased attention from many sectors. The term itself shows up frequently in the media, is referenced by public officials, has become common on university campuses, and informs the strategy of several prominent social sector organizations.

[2] On the most basic level, there's something inherently interesting and appealing about entrepreneurs and the stories of why and how they do what they do. People are attracted to social entrepreneurs like last year's Nobel Peace Prize laureate Muhammad Yunus for many of the same reasons that they find business entrepreneurs like Steve Jobs so compelling — [3] these extraordinary people come up and improve people's lives.

1

The writer is considering deleting the underlined sentence. Should the sentence be kept or deleted?

A) Kept, because it frames the idea of social entrepreneurship.

B) Deleted, because it contradicts the idea of social entrepreneurship.

C) Deleted, because it does not function as an effective topic sentence.

D) Kept, because it defines what social entrepreneurship is.

2

At this point, the author wants to add a sentence that introduces the topic of this paragraph. Which addition should be made?

A) NO CHANGE

B) Social entrepreneurship is beneficial.

C) The reasons behind the popularity of social entrepreneurship are many.

D) The reasons behind the complexities of social entrepreneurship are many.

3

A) NO CHANGE

B) these extraordinary people come up with ideas that dramatically improve people's lives.

C) these extraordinary people come up with ideas.

D) these extraordinary people come up with ideas that negatively impact people's lives.

But interest in social entrepreneurship transcends the phenomenon of popularity and fascination with people. Social entrepreneurship **4** is signaling the imperative to drive social change, and it is that potential payoff, with its lasting, transformational benefit to society, that sets the field and its practitioners apart.

5 However, the potential benefits offered by social entrepreneurship are clear to many of those promoting and funding these **6** activities, the actual definition of what social entrepreneurs do to produce this order of magnitude return is less clear. In fact, we would argue that the definition of social entrepreneurship today is anything but clear. As a result, social entrepreneurship **7** becoming so inclusive that it now has an immense tent into which all manner of socially beneficial activities fit.

4

A) NO CHANGE
B) signal
C) will signals
D) signals

5

A) NO CHANGE
B) Although
C) Furthermore
D) Whenever

6

A) NO CHANGE
B) activities:
C) activities;
D) activities—

7

A) NO CHANGE
B) became
C) has become
D) will become

8 Similarly, this inclusiveness could be a good thing. If plenty of resources are pouring into the social sector, and if many causes that otherwise would not get sufficient funding now get support because they are regarded as social 9 entrepreneurship. Then it may be fine to have a loose definition. We are inclined to argue, however, that this is a flawed assumption and a precarious stance.

Social entrepreneurship is an appealing construct precisely because 10 . If that promise is not fulfilled because too many "nonentrepreneurial" efforts are included in the definition, then social entrepreneurship 11 falls into disrepute, and the kernel of true social entrepreneurship will be lost. Because of this danger, we believe that we need a much sharper definition of social entrepreneurship, one that enables us to determine the extent to which an activity is and is not "in the tent." Our goal is not to make an invidious comparison between the contributions made by traditional social service organizations and the results of social entrepreneurship, but simply to highlight what differentiates them.

8

A) NO CHANGE

B) In addition

C) Despite this

D) In some respects

9

A) NO CHANGE

B) entrepreneurship; then

C) entrepreneurship, then

D) entrepreneurship then

10

A) NO CHANGE

B) it holds such high promise.

C) it encompasses ideas that can dramatically change people's lives.

D) of the abovementioned reasons.

11

A) NO CHANGE

B) fell

C) is falling

A) will fall

Questions 12-22 are based on the following text that has been adapted from Royal Museum Greenwich's "Who was the first woman in space?"

(1)

12 The first woman to travel in space was a Soviet <u>cosmonaut</u> Valentina Tereshkova. On 16 June 1963, Tereshkova was launched on a solo mission aboard the shuttle *Vostok 6*. She spent more than 70 hours orbiting the Earth, two years after Yuri Gagarin's first human-crewed flight in space.

(2)

Tereshkova was born on 6 March 1937 in the village of Bolshoye Maslennikovo in central Russia. 13 At the time of his death on the Finnish front, 14 <u>Tereshkova was two.</u>

12
A) NO CHANGE
B) cosmonaut:
C) cosmonaut,
D) cosmonaut.

13

At this point, the author is considering including the following sentence:

"Her mother was a textile worker, and her father was a tractor driver who was later recognised as a war hero during World War Two."

Should the writer make this addition here

A) Yes, because it provides necessary information.

B) No, because it would be more effective as a conclusion to the passage.

C) Yes, because it provides an effective introduction for the following paragraph.

D) No, because it provides irrelevant information.

14

A) NO CHANGE
B) Tereshkova was very young.
C) DELETE the underlined portion
D) Tereshkova was two years old.

(3)

After leaving school, Tereshkova followed her mother into work at a textile factory. Her first appreciation of flying was going down rather than up when she joined a local skydiving and parachutist club. It was her hobby of jumping out of planes that appealed to the Soviets' space programme committee. **15** On applying to the cosmonaut corps, Tereshkova was eventually chosen from more than 400 other candidates.

(4)

After her selection, Tereshkova received 18 months of training and tests with the Soviet Air Force. **16** They studied her abilities to cope physically under the extremes of gravity, as well as handle challenges such as emergency management and the isolation of being in space alone. At 24 years old, she was honourably inducted into the Soviet Air Force. Tereshkova still holds the title as the youngest woman, **17** and the first member of civil society, to fly in space.

15

Which choice provides the best conclusion to this paragraph?

A) NO CHANGE

B) Tereshkova was eventually chosen from more than 400 other candidates.

C) On applying to the cosmonaut corps, Tereshkova was eventually chosen.

D) On applying, Tereshkova was eventually chosen from more than 400 other candidates.

16

A) NO CHANGE

B) These tests

C) It

D) These

17

A) NO CHANGE

B) and the first civilian

C) and the first lady

D) and the first young person

(5)

While Tereshkova 18 remains the only woman to have flown solo in space, her mission was a dual flight. Fellow cosmonaut Valeriy Bykovsky launched on *Vostok 5* on 14 June 1963. Two days later, Tereshkova launched. The two spacecrafts took different flight paths and came within three miles of each other. The cosmonauts exchanged communications while making 48 orbits of Earth, with Tereshkova responding to Bykovsky via her callsign 'Seagull.' During the flight, the Soviet state television network broadcast a video of Tereshkova inside the capsule, and she spoke with the Russian Premier Nikita Khrushchev over the radio. 19

(6)

20 Today, much after the collapse of the Soviet Union, she holds the position of Deputy Chair for the Committee for International Affairs in Russia. She also remains active within the space community and is quoted as suggesting that she would like to fly to Mars - even if it were a one-way trip.

18

A) NO CHANGE

B) remaining

C) remained

D) will remain

19

At this point, the writer is adding the following sentence:

"And if all these past accomplishments were not enough, Tereshkova is still ambitious and inspiring."

Should the writer add this sentence?

A) Yes, because it improves clarity, tone, and voice of the paragraph.

B) No, because it would be more effective as an introduction at the beginning of the paragraph.

C) Yes, because it provides a more effective transition to the ideas in the next paragraph.

D) No, because it eliminates relevant information.

20

To make this passage most logical, paragraph (6) should be placed:

A) after paragraph (4)

B) after paragraph (7)

C) where it is now

D) after paragraph (3)

(7)

In her later life, Tereshkova was decorated with prestigious medals and has held several prominent political positions both for the Russian and global councils. Before the collapse of the Soviet Union, she was an official head of State and was elected a member of the World Peace Council in 1966. 21 22

21

At this point, the writer is considering adding the following sentence:

"Tereshkova is an inspiring figure to women everywhere.

Should the writer make this addition here?

A) Yes, because it provides information that is essential to the passage.

B) No, because it provides a more effective introduction and should be placed at the beginning of the paragraph.

C) Yes, because it provides information that helps explain what comes next.

D) No, because it provides ambiguous information that does not add substance to the paragraph.

22

Which of the following most effectively summarizes the main point of the passage?

A) Women in science have been ignored for too long.

B) The passage provides an example of a woman who is a pioneer in her field.

C) The passage critiques the creation of the former Soviet Union.

D) The passage highlights the gender dynamics in Russian society.

Questions 23-33 are based on the following text that has been adapted from Thought Economics' "The Role of Film in Society".

Film has a uniquely powerful ubiquity within human culture. In 2009, across major territories, there 23 are over 6.8 billion cinema admissions, creating global box office revenues of over US$30 billion. 24

23

A) NO CHANGE

B) were

C) have

D) is

24

At this point, the author is considering including the following sentence:

"When you start to then consider revenues and audience figures from those who consume digitally, via television and repeat view content that they already own, the figures become truly staggering."

Should the writer make this addition here

A) Yes, because it provides information that further evidences a previous argument.

B) No, because it contradicts a previously made argument.

C) Yes, because it is necessary for an effective transition to the following paragraph.

D) No, because it provides irrelevant information.

[25] Cinema is a tool for culture, education, leisure and propaganda. In a 1963 report for the United Nations Educational Scientific and Cultural Organization looking at Indian Cinema and Culture, the author quoted a speech by Prime Minister Nehru who stated, "…the influence in India of films is greater than newspapers and books combined." [26] When at this early stage in cinema, the Indian film-market catered for over 25 million people a week- considered to be just a 'fringe' of the population.

[25]

At this point, the writer is considering revising the underlined sentence to the following:

"Cinema is a powerful vehicle for culture, education, leisure, and propaganda."

Should the writer make this change here?

A) Yes, because it provides evidence to support the following arguments.

B) No, because it provides inaccurate or unsupported information.

C) Yes, because it improves the tone of the sentence.

D) No, because it provides redundant information.

[26]

A) NO CHANGE

B) While

C) During

D) Even

(1)In a 2005 paper by Noah `27` Uhrig the author describes how "the narrative and representational aspects of film make it a wholly unique form of art. (2) Moreover, the collective experience of film as art renders it a wholly distinct leisure activity." `28` (3) Contemporary research has also revealed more profound aspects to film's impact on society

27

A) NO CHANGE
B) Uhrig —
C) Uhrig:
D) Uhrig,

28

To make the paragraph most logical, sentence (3) should be placed

A) where it is now
B) before sentence (2)
C) before sentence (1)
D) after sentence (1)

[29] Uhrig further states that the unique properties of attending the cinema can have decisively positive effects on mental health. Cinema attendance can have independent and robust effects on mental wellbeing because visual stimulation can queue a range of emotions. Furthermore, the collective experience of these emotions through [30] the cinema provides a safe environment.

29

The writer is considering deleting the underlined sentence. Should the sentence be kept or deleted?

A) Kept, because it provides an effective introduction to the following information.

B) Kept, because it provides extensive information mental health.

C) Deleted, because it ignores the main topic of the paragraph.

D) Deleted, because it would be more relevant in the following paragraph.

30

At this point, the writer is considering changing the underlined sentence to the following:

"the cinema provides a safe environment in which to experience roles and emotions we might not otherwise be free to experience."

Should the writer make this change here?

A) Yes, because it helps clarify preceding information.

B) No, because it is not an effective transition to the next paragraph.

C) Yes, because it improves the clarity, voice, and tone of the sentence.

D) No, because it eliminates relevant information.

The collective nature of the narrative and visual stimulation [31] make the experience enjoyable and controlled, thereby offering benefits beyond mere visual stimulation. Moreover, the cinema is unique in that it is a highly accessible social art form, the participation in which generally cuts across economic lines.

At the same time, attending the cinema allows for the exercise of personal preferences and the human need for distinction. In a nutshell, cinema attendance can be both a personally expressive experience, good [32] fun, and therapeutic at the same time. In a rather ground-breaking study, Konlaan, Bygren and Johansson found that frequent cinema attendees have particularly low mortality risks – those who never attended the cinema had mortality rates nearly 4 times higher than [33] them who visit the cinema occasionally. Their finding holds even when other forms of social engagement are controlled, suggesting that social engagement specifically in an artistic milieu is important for human survival."

31

A) NO CHANGE

B) makes

C) made

D) will make

32

A) NO CHANGE

B) fun

C) fun;

D) fun —

33

A) NO CHANGE

B) they

C) those people

D) those

Questions 34-44 are based on the following text that has been adapted from the International Renewable Energy Agency's Renewable Energy: A Gender Perspective.

Energy access and gender are deeply [34] entwined components of the global development agenda. The transformative effect on women of access to affordable, reliable and sustainable modern energy is well-known. Energy access frees up time for women who otherwise may spend an average of 100 hours a year collecting fuel wood and gives them more flexibility in sequencing [35] tasks; since lighting allows them to do more at night. [36] However, it improves access to public services and opens new opportunities for part-time work and income-generating activities.

The distributed nature of off-grid renewable energy solutions offers tremendous opportunities for women's engagement along multiple segments of the value chain. Many of the skills needed to take advantage of [37] opportunities can be developed locally and women are ideally placed to lead and support the delivery of energy solutions, especially in view of their role as primary energy users and their social networks.

34

A) NO CHANGE
B) entwining
C) entwine
D) entwination

35

A) NO CHANGE
B) tasks:
C) tasks,
D) tasks

36

A) NO CHANGE
B) And
C) Although
D) Furthermore

37

A) NO CHANGE
B) them
C) these opportunities
D) these

Organisations have found it difficult to ignore the value of involving women in the renewable energy supply chain. [38] As women become engaged in delivering energy solutions, they take on more active roles in their communities and [39] consequently facilitate a gradual shift in the social and cultural norms that previously acted as barriers to their agency.

[38]

At this point, the writer is considering adding the following sentence:

"SELCO India, for instance, trained female solar technicians in the early 2000s simply (at least initially) as a means to accomplish its business goals: technicians were needed to enter the homes of customers to repair solar lanterns and cookstoves."

Should the writer make this addition here?

A) Yes, because it provides an effective transition to new information.

B) Yes, because it provides an example to support previous information presented in the paragraph.

C) No, because it provides redundant information.

D) No, because it provides information that contradicts information in presented earlier in the paragraph.

[39]

A) NO CHANGE

B) by doing this,

C) despite this,

D) regardless of this,

Over two-thirds of survey respondents noted that women face barriers to participation in the renewables-based energy access sector. Cultural and social norms were cited by respondents as the most common 40 barrier; followed by lack of gender-sensitive policies and training opportunities and inequity in ownership of assets. Security and the remoteness of field locations were also mentioned 41 as barriers. 42 Through this, cultural and social norms was the barrier selected more often by respondents in Europe and North America, while respondents from other regions were much more likely to select the lack of skills and training as important barriers in the access context.

40

A) NO CHANGE

B) barrier: followed

C) barrier. Followed

D) barrier, followed

41

A) NO CHANGE

B) as other barriers to participation.

C) DELETE the underlined portion

D) too.

42

A) NO CHANGE

B) However,

C) Interestingly,

D) Despite this,

Figure 1

Measures to improve women's engagement in deploying renewables for energy access

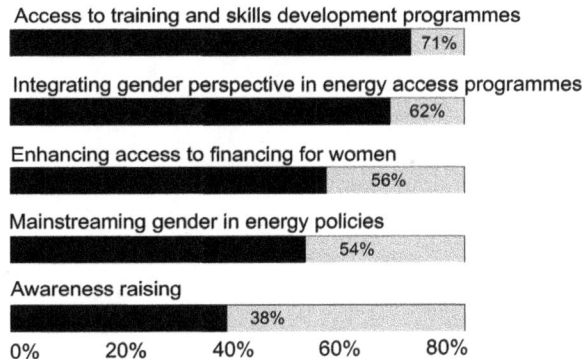

Access to training and skills development programmes
71%

Integrating gender perspective in energy access programmes
62%

Enhancing access to financing for women
56%

Mainstreaming gender in energy policies
54%

Awareness raising
38%

0%   20%   40%   60%   80%

Source: IRENA online gender survey, 2018
Note: The respondents were asked to select three key measures to improve women's engagement in deploying renewables for energy access. The percentages represent the share of respondents who selected a specific measure as one of their top three.

In identifying solutions, respondents highlighted first the importance of access to education and training. Training is often an integral part of energy access programs, **44** but greater efforts are needed to make them more accessible to women. Training sessions must be tailored and scheduled around women's childcare responsibilities and be sensitive to mobility constraints, security concerns and social restrictions that may prohibit women from participating.

43

Which of the following provides the most effective support from Figure 1?

A) Women's engagement can be improved through a number of different measures.

B) Women's engagement can be best improved by enhancing access to financing.

C) Women's engagement can be best improved by raising awareness.

D) Women's engagement can be best improved by integrating gender perspective in energy access programs.

44

The writer is considering deleting the underlined portion of the sentence. Should the sentence be kept or deleted?

A) Kept, because it is an effective conclusion to the passage.

B) Kept, because it provides an effective transition between one sentence and the next.

C) Deleted, because it interrupts the flow of the paragraph.

D) Deleted, because it provides information that is not related to the paragraph.

STOP
**If you finish before time is called, you may check your work on this section only.
Do not turn to any other section.**

Math Test – No Calculator

25 MINUTES, 20 QUESTIONS

Turn to Section 3 of your answer sheet to answer the questions in this section.

DIRECTIONS

For questions 1-15, solve each problem, choose the best answer from the choices provided, and fill in the corresponding circle on your answer sheet. **For questions 16-20**, solve the problem and enter your answer in the grid on the answer sheet. Please refer to the directions before question 16 on how to enter your answers in the grid. You may use any available space in your test booklet for scratch work.

NOTES

1. The use of a calculator **is not permitted.**
2. All variables and expressions used represent real numbers unless otherwise indicated.
3. Figures provided in this test are drawn to scale unless otherwise indicated.
4. All figures lie in a plane unless otherwise indicated.
5. Unless otherwise indicated, the domain of a given function f is the set of all real numbers x for which $f(x)$ is a real number.

REFERENCE

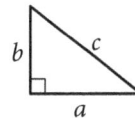 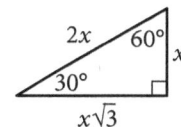 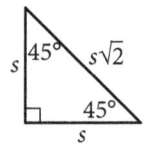

$A = \pi r^2$ $A = \ell w$ $A = \dfrac{1}{2}bh$ $c^2 = a^2 + b^2$ Special Right Triangles
$C = 2\pi r$

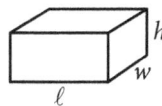 

$V = \ell wh$ $V = \pi r^2 h$ $V = \dfrac{4}{3}\pi r^3$ $V = \dfrac{1}{3}\pi r^2 h$ $V = \dfrac{1}{3}\ell wh$

The number of degrees of arc in a circle is 360.

The number of radians of arc in a circle is 2π.

The sum of the measures in degrees of the angles of a triangle is 180.

1

If $5y + 7y + 15y + 42y = 3y + 14y + z$, what is the value of y?

A) $y = \dfrac{z}{52}$

B) $y = \dfrac{52}{z}$

C) $y = \dfrac{1}{51}$

D) $y = 51$

2

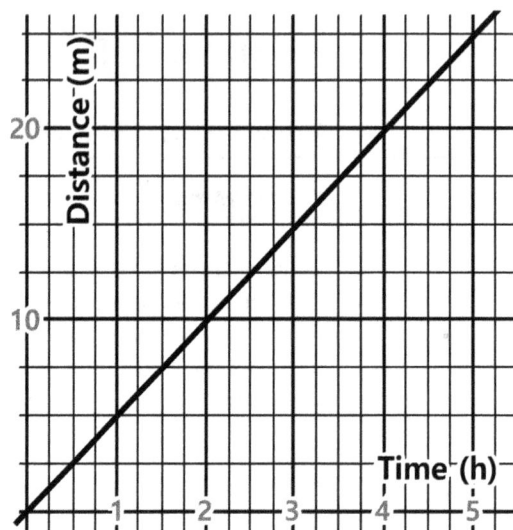

The graph above shows how far Dallas travels on her bike, m, in miles per hour, h, in hours. Which of the following correctly shows a direct variation between m and h?

A) $m = \dfrac{5}{h}$

B) $m = 5 + h$

C) $m = 5h$

D) $m = 5 - h$

CONTINUE

3

The formula for break-even point is $b = \dfrac{f}{s} - c$

where (b) is the break-even point, (f) is fixed costs, (s) is the sales price and (c) is the cost to make each unit. Which of the following correctly expresses (s) in terms of b, f, and c?

A) $s = \dfrac{f}{b+c}$

B) $s = \dfrac{b+c}{f}$

C) $s = \dfrac{f}{b} - c$

D) $s = \dfrac{b+f}{c}$

4

I. $-2x + y = 3$

II. $2y - x = 12$

III. $y = -\dfrac{1}{2}x + 7$

IV. $y = -2x - 7$

Which one of the following statements is true based on the four linear equations above?

A)   Lines I and II are perpendicular

B)   Lines I and IV are parallel

C)   Lines I and III are perpendicular

D)   Lines II and III are parallel

5

The width of a bulletin board being decorated for a football game is (a) meters and the length, (b), is 3 meters shorter than twice the width. Which of the following represents the area of the bulletin board?

A) $a(2a+3)$

B) $a(2a-3)$

C) $2a^2 - 3$

D) $4a + 3$

6

$$x + 2 \le -1$$

$$y < \frac{5}{3}x + 2$$

Which of the following express the x-coordinates that satisfy the system of equations above?

A) $x \le -1$

B) $x \ge -1$

C) $x \ge -3$

D) $x \le -3$

7

If $m + 4 = \sqrt{m + 10}$, what is the solution set of the equation?

A) $\{-6, 1\}$

B) $\{-6\}$

C) $\{-1\}$

D) $\{\varnothing\}$

8

$$f(x) = x^2 + 36$$

$$g(x) = x^3 + 18x^2 + 108x + 216$$

Which of the following expressions is equivalent to $\dfrac{g(x)}{f(x)}$, for $x > 6$?

A) $\dfrac{x^2 + 12x + 36}{x - 6}$

B) $\dfrac{1}{x + 6}$

C) $\dfrac{1}{x - 6}$

D) $(x + 6)^3$

9

$$(x - 2)^2 + (y - 1)^2 = 16$$

A student graphed the equation of the circle above on the coordinate plane. Point O is the center of the circle and Point N is a point on the circle. If $\overline{ON}$ is the radius of the circle, which could NOT be a coordinate for Point N?

A) (2, 3)

B) (6, -1)

C) (-2, -1)

D) (2, -6)

10

A group of 100 students went on a trip for a choir competition and lodged in 20 hotel suites that either held 4 or 6 students. If all of the rooms were filled to capacity, what is the difference between the amount of 4 and 6 person suites?

A) 60

B) 40

C) 10

D) 0

11

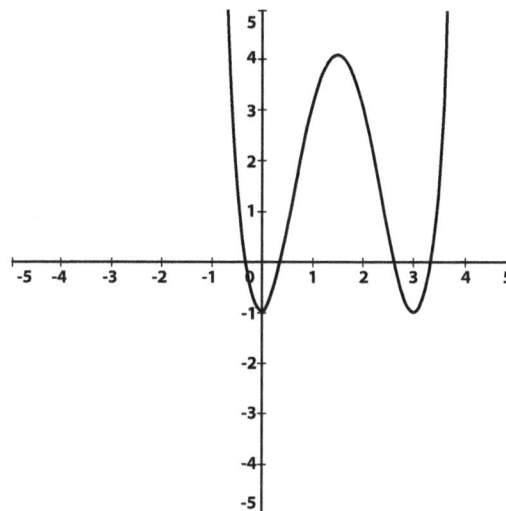

Which of the following could be the equation of the graph above?

A) $x^2(x-3)^2 - 1$

B) $x(x+3)^2 - 1$

C) $x^2(x-3)^2$

D) $x^2(x+3)^2 + 1$

CONTINUE

12

If $\dfrac{4c}{d} = \dfrac{1}{4}$, what is the value of $\dfrac{d}{c}$?

A) 4

B) 16

C) $\dfrac{1}{16}$

D) $\dfrac{1}{2}$

14

$$y - x^3 = 4$$

$$y(x-4) = x^2 + 16$$

How many solutions are there to the system of equations above?

A) 1 solution

B) 2 solutions

C) 3 solutions

D) 4 solutions

13

A car maker operates production plants that saw an increase in production in 2018 to 5.6 million units annually from 5 million units in 2013. If the production of the cars increases at a constant rate, which function, f, in millions of units, best models production x years after 2013?

A) $f(x) = -\dfrac{3}{20}x + 5$

B) $f(x) = -\dfrac{3}{25}x + 5$

C) $f(x) = \dfrac{3}{20}x + 5$

D) $f(x) = \dfrac{3}{25}x + 5$

15

$$p(n) = 2n - 2$$

$$q(n) = 2 - p(n)$$

The functions p and q are defined above. What is the value of $q(2)$?

A) −2

B) −4

C) 2

D) 0

DIRECTIONS

For questions 16–20, solve the problem and enter your answer in the grid, as described below, on the answer sheet.

1. Although not required, it is suggested that you write your answer in the boxes at the top of the columns to help you fill in the circles accurately. You will receive credit only if the circles are filled in correctly.

2. Mark no more than one circle in any column.

3. No question has a negative answer.

4. Some problems may have more than one correct answer. In such cases, grid only one answer.

5. **Mixed numbers** such as $3\frac{1}{2}$ must be gridded as 3.5 or 7/2. (If $3|1|/|2$ is entered into the grid, it will be interpreted as $\frac{31}{2}$, not $3\frac{1}{2}$.)

6. **Decimal answers:** If you obtain a decimal answer with more digits than the grid can accommodate, it may be either rounded or truncated, but it must fill the entire grid.

Answer: $\frac{7}{12}$

Answer: 2.5

Write answer in boxes. ← Fraction line

Grid in result. ← Decimal point

Acceptable ways to grid $\frac{2}{3}$ are:

Answer: 201 – either position is correct

NOTE: You may start your answers in any column, space permitting. Columns you don't need to use should be left blank.

16

$$x^2 + x - 90$$

If c is a solution to the equation above, and $c > 0$, what is the value of c?

17

The difference of $-7x^2 + 4x - 12$ and $3x^2 + 16x + 4$ can be written in the form $ax^2 + bx + c$ where a, b, and c are constants. What is the value of $a \times c$?

18

$$4e + f = 2$$

$$e - f = 3$$

If the point (e,f) satisfies the system of equations above, what is the value of e?

19

A farmer started with 8 rows of corn. He planned to add 3 rows during the summer months of June, July and August for the next 7 years. If an equation is written in the form $y = mx + b$ to represent the number of rows of corn, y, the farmer planted x years after his first summer crop, what is the value of b?

20

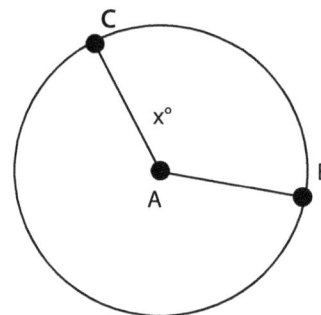

Note: Figure not drawn to scale.

In the circle above, Point A is the center and the length of minor arc BC is $\dfrac{3}{8}$ of the circumference of the circle. What is the difference between the length of minor arc BC and major arc BC?

STOP

If you finish before time is called, you may check your work on this section only.
Do not turn to any other section.

Math Test – Calculator

55 MINUTES, 38 QUESTIONS

Turn to Section 4 of your answer sheet to answer the questions in this section.

DIRECTIONS

For questions 1-30, solve each problem, choose the best answer from the choices provided, and fill in the corresponding circle on your answer sheet. **For questions 31-38**, solve the problem and enter your answer in the grid on the answer sheet. Please refer to the directions before question 16 on how to enter your answers in the grid. You may use any available space in your test booklet for scratch work.

NOTES

1. The use of a calculator **is permitted.**

2. All variables and expressions used represent real numbers unless otherwise indicated.

3. Figures provided in this test are drawn to scale unless otherwise indicated.

4. All figures lie in a plane unless otherwise indicated.

5. Unless otherwise indicated, the domain of a given function f is the set of all real numbers x for which $f(x)$ is a real number.

REFERENCE

$A = \pi r^2$
$C = 2\pi r$

$A = \ell w$

$A = \frac{1}{2}bh$

$c^2 = a^2 + b^2$

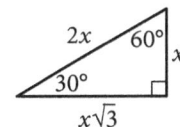

Special Right Triangles

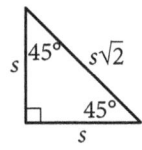

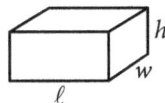

$V = \ell wh$

$V = \pi r^2 h$

$V = \frac{4}{3}\pi r^3$

$V = \frac{1}{3}\pi r^2 h$

$V = \frac{1}{3}\ell wh$

The number of degrees of arc in a circle is 360.

The number of radians of arc in a circle is 2π.

The sum of the measures in degrees of the angles of a triangle is 180.

1

If two pounds of grapes cost $3.96, how much will g pounds of grapes cost?

A) $3.96g$

B) $3.96\left(\dfrac{g}{2}\right)$

C) $3.96 + g$

D) $\dfrac{3.96}{g}$

2

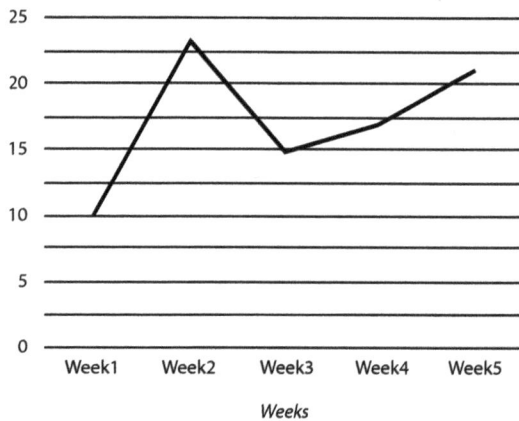

Dan collects baseball cards and tracks the number of baseball cards he has on the graph above.

During which interval did the number of baseball cards increase the fastest?

A) Between 1-2 Weeks

B) Between 2-3 Weeks

C) Between 3-4 Weeks

D) Between 4-5 Weeks

3

In a random sample of 300 widgets, 4 are defective. Under these circumstances, how many of the 12,000 widgets are defective?

A) 160

B) 200

C) 240

D) 280

4

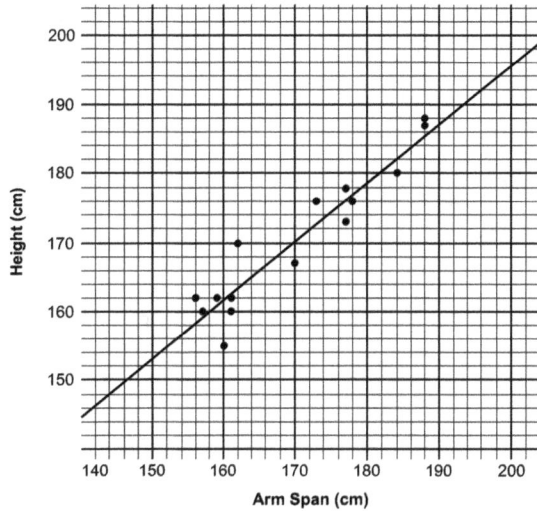

The scatter plot above shows the data collected on the arm span and height of students in a class. A line of best fit, with the equation $y = 0.85x + 25.68,$ where x is arm span in cm and y is height in cm, is calculated for the data. Based on the line of best fit, if the arm span of a student is 166 centimeters, what is the predicted height in centimeters?

A)   169.21

B)   166.78

C)   163.64

D)   168.91

5

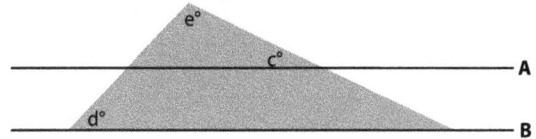

In the figure above, lines A and B are parallel, $c = 35°$, and $d = 55°$. Which best describes the shaded triangle? Note: Figure not drawn to scale.

A)   Isosceles Right Triangle

B)   Scalene Right Triangle

C)   Equilateral Triangle

D)   Scalene Obtuse Triangle

6

What is the value of m in the equation $(2^{m-n})^{m+n} = 128$ if $n^2 = 9$ and $m < 0$?

A) 3

B) 4

C) –3

D) –4

7

Three types of tickets were sold for at a movie theater for a premiere a movie. Adult tickets were $5.75, children's tickets, $9.75, and student tickets, $6.50. The theater reported that they sold 1310 tickets and collected $9732.50 through ticket sales. If A represents the number of adult tickets, S, student tickets, and C, children tickets, write a system of equations to solve for the amount of tickets sold for children, students and adults.

A) $A + C + S = 9732.50$

$5.75A + 9.75C + 6.50S = 1310$

B) $A + C + S = 3$

$5.75A + 9.75C + 6.50S = 1310$

C) $A + C + S = 3$

$5.75 + 9.75 + 6.50 = 9732.50$

D) $A + C + S = 1310$

$5.75A + 9.75C + 6.50S = 9732.50$

8

In the xy-plane, the graph of which of the following equations is a line with a slope of -4?

A) $y = \dfrac{1}{4}x$

B) $y = x - 4$

C) $y = -4x + 7$

D) $y = -4 + 4x$

CONTINUE ➤

9

In the equation $a + 3 = \dfrac{1}{a+3}$, which of the following is a possible value for $a + 3$?

A) 1

B) 3

C) –3

D) $\sqrt{-1}$

10

Which of the following is a value for b for which the expression $\dfrac{2b^2 + 30b + 52}{b^2 - 169}$ is undefined?

A) –2

B) 2

C) 13

D) 0

11

John wants to put new carpet in his movie room. The movie room is 6.25 yard long and 4.37 yards wide. The carpet costs $9.75 per square foot. What will John pay to put new carpet in his movie room?

A) $266.30

B) $2396.67

C) $27.35

D) $245.81

Use the table below for questions 12-15.

A random sample of students, male and female, were asked if they had a smart phone and the answers were recorded in the table below.

Number of Middle School Students with Smartphones

	Smart Phone	No Smartphone	Total
Male	153	47	200
Female	180	20	200
Total	333	67	400

12

What percentage of males in the sample have a smartphone?

A) 50%

B) 76.5%

C) 23.5%

D) 45.95%

13

What percentage of middle school students in the sample do not have smartphones?

A) 83.25%

B) 45.95%

C) 16.75%

D) 50%

14

What is the proportion of female students in the sample who do not have smartphones?

A) 9:10

B) 20:67

C) 1:2

D) 1:10

15

How many students were surveyed?

A) 200

B) 400

C) 67

D) 333

Use the table below for questions 16-19.

Number of Questions Correct on Math Exam

Number Correct	Frequency
31-40	3
41-50	6
51-60	7
61-70	9
71-80	3
81-90	4
91-100	2

16

Which values in this set have the highest value?

A)   Median and Mean

B)   Median and Mode

C)   Mode and Mean

D)   Cannot be determined

17

What is the estimated median?

A)   41-50 Points

B)   51-60 Points

C)   61-70 Points

D)   71-80 Points

18

What percentage of students scored between 0 and 70?

A)   26.5%

B)   73.5%

C)   25%

D)   75%

19

How many students took the test?

A)   7

B)   34

C)   25

D)   27

20

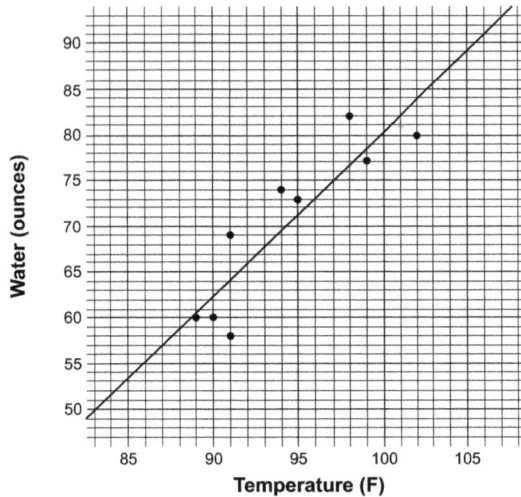

The scatterplot above shows the relationship between outdoor temperature and water consumption for a camper on a 10-day camping trip.

One day is not included in the scatter plot where the temperature was $97°F$. Based on the line of best fit, which of the following is closest to the amount of water consumed by the camper on that day?

A)   68 ounces

B)   73 ounces

C)   75 ounces

D)   82 ounces

21

The range of the function $g(x)$ is the set of real numbers greater than or equal to $-\dfrac{9}{4}$. If the zeros of the function $g(x)$ are -3 and 0, which of the following could be the function of $g(x)$?

A) $(x+5)(x-2)+1$

B) $(x+5)(x-2)+10$

C) $(x+5)(x-2)+5$

D) $(x+5)(x-2)+2$

22

$$2^x \cdot 2^y = 1024$$

In the equation above, what is the value of $x + y$?

A)   2

B)   5

C)   7

D)   10

CONTINUE

23

A bag contains 20 marbles. If there are 5 blue, 8 purple and 7 orange, what is the minimum number of marbles one must pick from the bag to be assured one blue, one purple, and one orange?

A) 16

B) 9

C) 8

D) 6

24

Point A has coordinates of (6,4) and Point B has coordinates of (0,-8). C is the midpoint of $\overline{AB}$. Which one of the following lines does C lie on?

A) $y = x + 4$

B) $y = x + 3$

C) $y = x - 5$

D) $y = x - 2$

25

What is the circumference of a circle that has a square inscribed with an area of 128 $units^2$?

A) 4π

B) 8π

C) 16π

D) 32π

26

A high school basketball arena has 40 bleachers where 600 people can sit. Some of the bleacher benches sit 10 fans while the others seat 20 fans. What is the ratio of the number of 20 fan bleachers to the number of 10 fan bleachers?

A) 4 to 1

B) 1 to 2

C) 2 to 1

D) 1 to 1

27

Which of the following is NOT equal to $sin\dfrac{\pi}{3}$?

A) $sin\dfrac{2\pi}{3}$

B) $cos\dfrac{\pi}{6}$

C) $cos\dfrac{11\pi}{6}$

D) $sin\dfrac{4\pi}{3}$

28

A vacuum can empty the water in a pool in x hours. How much of the pool can it drain in 4 hours?

A) $\dfrac{4}{x}$

B) $4x$

C) $\dfrac{x}{4}$

D) $x - 4$

29

Every year, Ron adds twice the number of model airplanes to his collection from the year before. Which of the following types of functions best describes the number of model airplanes Ron has in his collection with respect to time?

A)   Increasing exponential

B)   Decreasing exponential

C)   Increasing linear

D)   Decreasing linear

30

Year	Drivers Licenses
2000	141,000
2002	137,000
2005	133,000
2006	127,000
2011	102,000
2014	91,800

Using the table above, a regression analysis between the number of drivers licenses issued in Humble, Texas and the year resulted in the following equation: $\hat{y} = -3725x + 7,596,500$.

According to the regression equation:

A)   there is a decrease in the number in the number of drivers licenses issued since the year 2000.

B)   there is an increase the number in the number of drivers licenses issued since the year 2000.

C)   there is no evidence of an increase or decrease in the number in the number of drivers licenses issued since the year 2000.

D)   there is a decrease in the number of drivers licenses issued since the year 2000.

CONTINUE ➡

DIRECTIONS

For questions 31–38, solve the problem and enter your answer in the grid, as described below, on the answer sheet.

1. Although not required, it is suggested that you write your answer in the boxes at the top of the columns to help you fill in the circles accurately. You will receive credit only if the circles are filled in correctly.
2. Mark no more than one circle in any column.
3. No question has a negative answer.
4. Some problems may have more than one correct answer. In such cases, grid only one answer.
5. **Mixed numbers** such as $3\frac{1}{2}$ must be gridded as 3.5 or 7/2. (If $\boxed{3\,1\,/\,2}$ is entered into the grid, it will be interpreted as $\frac{31}{2}$, not $3\frac{1}{2}$.)
6. **Decimal answers:** If you obtain a decimal answer with more digits than the grid can accommodate, it may be either rounded or truncated, but it must fill the entire grid.

Answer: $\frac{7}{12}$ Answer: 2.5

Write answer in boxes. ← Fraction line
Grid in result. ← Decimal point

Acceptable ways to grid $\frac{2}{3}$ are:

Answer: 201 – either position is correct

NOTE: You may start your answers in any column, space permitting. Columns you don't need to use should be left blank.

31

Of 30 students, exactly 15 are athletes, 10 are on student council, and 8 are in the band. Only 3 of the athletes are in the band and only 4 non-athletes are in the band. In this group, a person who is an athlete may be in the band and in the student council but not in one or the other alone. How many of the 30 students are not athletes, in student council, or band?

32

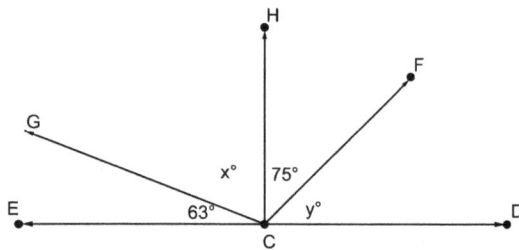

In the figure above, assuming E, C, and D are collinear, what is the sum of $x + y$?

33

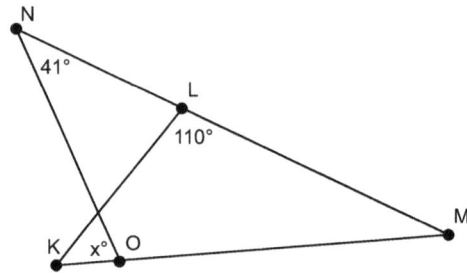

In the figure above, $\overline{KL} = \overline{ML}$. What is the value of x?

34

If 15 team members make an average of 80% of their shots and 10 make an average of 90% of their shots, what is the average percentage of shots made by all 25 team members?

CONTINUE

35

$$b - \frac{1}{4}c = 0$$

If $b = 2$ in the equation above, what is the value of c?

36

Julie rides her bike up the hill at an average speed of 8 miles per hour and down the same hill at an average speed of 11 miles per hour. What is her average biking speed, in miles per hour?

37

Amanda bakes a cake in 4 hours and 45 minutes. Danielle bakes the same cake in 5 hours and 15 minutes. How much time would it take for them to bake 3 cakes if they are working together?

38

At 9:00AM, train X left the New York train station and an hour later, train Y left the same station on a different track going in the same direction. If train X traveled at a constant speed of 70 miles per hour and train Y at 90 miles per hour, how many hours did it take for train Y to pass train X after train Y left?

STOP

If you finish before time is called, you may check your work on this section only.
Do not turn to any other section.

Section #1 – Reading Test

#	Correct Answer	#	Correct Answer	#	Correct Answer	#	Correct Answer	#	Correct Answer	#	Correct Answer
1	B	11	A	21	B	31	C	41	D	51	B
2	D	12	B	22	B	32	A	42	A	52	D
3	D	13	C	23	C	33	C	43	B		
4	A	14	C	24	B	34	D	44	C		
5	C	15	C	25	D	35	C	45	C		
6	C	16	C	26	A	36	C	46	A		
7	A	17	D	27	B	37	C	47	A		
8	D	18	B	28	A	38	A	48	D		
9	B	19	C	29	D	39	C	49	B		
10	D	20	D	30	D	40	B	50	A		

Number of Correct Answers [   ] **Reading Test Raw Score**

Section #2 – Writing and Language Test

#	Correct Answer	#	Correct Answer	#	Correct Answer	#	Correct Answer	#	Correct Answer
1	A	11	D	21	D	31	B	41	B
2	C	12	C	22	B	32	A	42	C
3	B	13	A	23	B	33	D	43	A
4	D	14	D	24	A	34	A	44	B
5	B	15	A	25	C	35	C		
6	A	16	B	26	D	36	D		
7	C	17	B	27	D	37	C		
8	D	18	A	28	C	38	B		
9	C	19	C	29	A	39	A		
10	B	20	B	30	C	40	D		

Number of Correct Answers [   ] **Writing and Language Test Raw Score**

Section #3 – Math Test (No Calculator)

#	Correct Answer	#	Correct Answer	#	Correct Answer	#	Correct Answer
1	A	6	D	11	A	16	9
2	C	7	C	12	B	17	160
3	A	8	A	13	D	18	1
4	C	9	D	14	D	19	8
5	B	10	D	15	D	20	90

Number of Correct Answers [   ] Math Test (No Calculator) Raw Score

Section #4 – Math Test (Calculator)

#	Correct Answer	#	Correct Answer	#	Correct Answer	#	Correct Answer
1	B	11	B	21	B	31	7
2	A	12	B	22	D	32	42
3	A	13	C	23	A	33	76
4	B	14	D	24	C	34	84
5	B	15	B	25	C	35	8
6	D	16	D	26	D	36	9.26
7	D	17	C	27	D	37	7.5
8	C	18	B	28	A	38	3.5
9	A	19	B	29	A		
10	C	20	C	30	A		

Number of Correct Answers [   ] Math Test (Calculator) Raw Score

Reading Test
Raw Score (0 - 52)
CONVERT →
Reading Test
Score (10 - 40)

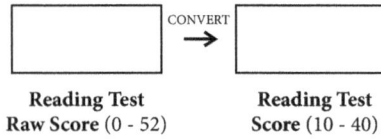

The following is a **Score Conversion Table** (Raw to Scaled) used by the College Board for an SAT® practice test available online. Although each SAT test is scored a bit differently, this table will give you an estimate of your score. Enter your raw scores in the appropriate boxes below, follow the conversion directions and know your estimated SAT scores for this test.

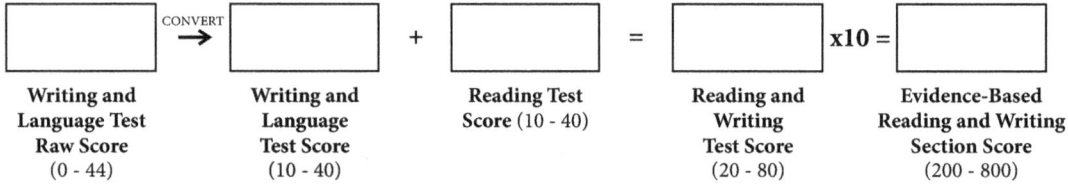

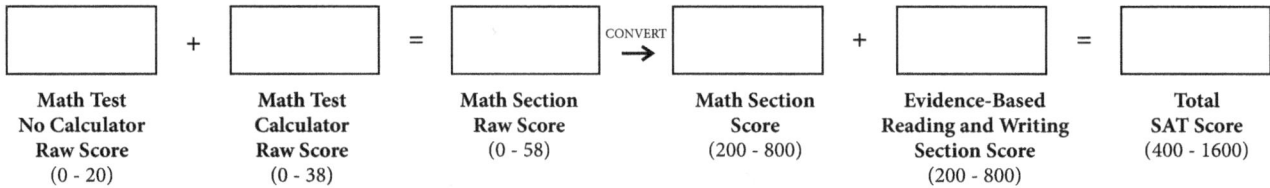

Writing and Language Test Raw Score (0 - 44)
CONVERT →
Writing and Language Test Score (10 - 40)
+
Reading Test Score (10 - 40)
=
Reading and Writing Test Score (20 - 80)
x10 =
Evidence-Based Reading and Writing Section Score (200 - 800)

Math Test No Calculator Raw Score (0 - 20)
+
Math Test Calculator Raw Score (0 - 38)
=
Math Section Raw Score (0 - 58)
CONVERT →
Math Section Score (200 - 800)
+
Evidence-Based Reading and Writing Section Score (200 - 800)
=
Total SAT Score (400 - 1600)

Raw Score Conversion Table: Section and Test Scores

Raw Score (# of correct answers)	Math Section Score	Reading Test Score	Writing and Language Test Score	Raw Score (# of correct answers)	Math Section Score	Reading Test Score	Writing and Language Test Score
0	200	10	10	30	530	27	29
1	200	10	10	31	530	27	30
2	210	10	10	32	540	28	31
3	230	10	10	33	550	28	31
4	250	11	11	34	550	29	32
5	260	12	12	35	560	29	32
6	280	13	12	36	570	30	33
7	290	14	13	37	580	30	34
8	310	15	14	38	590	31	34
9	320	15	15	39	590	31	35
10	330	16	15	40	600	32	36
11	350	17	16	41	610	32	36
12	360	17	17	42	620	33	37
13	370	18	18	43	630	34	39
14	380	18	18	44	640	35	40
15	390	19	19	45	650	35	
16	400	20	19	46	660	36	
17	420	20	20	47	670	37	
18	430	21	21	48	680	37	
19	430	21	22	49	680	38	
20	440	22	22	50	690	39	
21	450	22	23	51	700	39	
22	460	23	24	52	720	40	
23	470	23	25	53	730		
24	480	24	25	54	740		
25	490	24	26	55	760		
26	500	25	26	56	770		
27	510	25	27	57	790		
28	510	26	28	58	800		
29	520	26	29				

1. **Choice B is the best answer** because the passage is about the relatives of Anthony and how they affected his life. The passage begins with a detailed description of his grandfather, who selected the name for Anthony. The third paragraph touches on Anthony's grandmother and the birth and personality of his father. The following two paragraphs describe Anthony's mother, whom he barely remembers. The final paragraph goes into more detail about his relationship with his father and the impact that the father's death had on him.
    Choice A is incorrect because the passage is written from the point of view of a third-person narrator. Anthony does not "reminisce" or "nostalgically talk about" the people himself. Choice C is incorrect because, while several of the characters might be "aristocrats" or "upper class," the passage does not focus on the "achievements" or "successes" of only one. It describes several people and, if anything, touches upon weaknesses of character rather than goals reached. Choice D is incorrect because, while the father's death might be called "tragic" or "sad," the cause of his death is not "revealed" or "shown." The passage does say that Anthony has a tragic aspect to his personality, but that is not an "event" or "occasion."

2. **Choice D is the best answer** because "fume" refers to one of the things relating to the way that Adam amassed millions of dollars in Wall Street. The other things are "fuss" or "commotion," "applause" or "praise," and "ill will" or "hard feelings." Choice D refers to anger that is often related to a conflict, so aptly shows that he was very aggressive or hurt others as he "charged in" and made money.
    None of the other choices fits the list of emotional qualities reflecting what happened to Adam on Wall Street. Choice A refers to waste gasses, Choice B to an unpleasant smell, and Choice C to waste products.

3. **Choice D is the best answer** because the passage describes Adam J. Patch as "Emulating the magnificent efforts of Anthony Comstock, after whom his grandson was named, he levelled a varied assortment of uppercuts and body-blows at liquor, literature, vice, art, patent medicines, and Sunday theatres" (lines 14-19). In other words, Adam "emulated" or "tried to copy" the things that Anthony Comstock did. Adam "revered" or "admired" Anthony so much that he gave his grandson the same name. Anthony attacked a variety of vices such as liquor, which shows that he was a reformer who was trying to change society.
    Choice A is incorrect because there is no evidence that Adam was a "close friend" or that he even knew Anthony personally. Adam only "emulated" or "tried to copy" Anthony's ways. Choice B is incorrect because Anthony "levelled a varied assortment of uppercuts and body-blows" (lines 17-18) at different "vices" or "wicked behaviors," showing that he attacked rather than "indulged" or "participated in and enjoyed" them. Choice C is incorrect because, while the passage refers to fighting terms, it does not mean that the attacks were literal moves of a professional boxer or wrestler. Instead, "uppercuts and body-blows" (lines 17-18) are symbolic of an aggressive campaign.

4. **Choice A is the best answer** because the phrase implies that the elder Adam Patch still felt he was living in 1861, whereas really years had passed and the times were changing. The phrase gives a reason for him to "weary" and become tired…he had been so wrapped up in reforms, but his causes were not current or relevant ones anymore. His thoughts were still focused on events such as the Civil War rather than on everyday life or raising his grandson.
    Choice B is incorrect because the passage implies that Adam focused on things that interested him. The fact that the wife and son died in the past is not the reason that he thinks about them infrequently; he doesn't really care about them as much as he does about things that happened earlier like the Civil War. Choice C is incorrect because the fact that the times changed was the reason that his campaign against vices started to fade. The changing times is not why he started to fight against vice. Choice D is incorrect because someone can be interesting even if the times change. The reason that Adam was a bore was his actions during that time.

5. **Choice C is the best answer** because Adam's wife, Alicia Withers, is described as "anemic" (line 31), which refers to someone who lacks vitality or spirit. She spent her time raising her son out of sight of the general public: "she had thenceforth effaced herself within the shadowy dimensions of the nursery" (lines 36-38) rather than take an active interest in society or her husband's activities. Choice C means "withdrawn" or "not confident," and therefore describes Alicia well.
    Choice A is incorrect because, while Alicia had some valuable connections, the passage does not indicate that she used them to her advantage. Therefore, she was not "influential" or "dominant" in manipulating her connections for her own good. Choice B refers to being able to attract and hold attention and Choice D refers to being very

lively, neither of which are consistent with the description of an "anemic" lady who does not leave the nursery.

6. **Choice C is the best answer** because the previous question is that Adam J. Patch's wife could best be characterized as "diffident" or "withdrawn and not confident." Choice C supports this claim because it shows that Alicia "effaced" or "made herself appear inconspicuous" in her son's nursery rather than taking an active part in society or her husband's activities.

    Choice A is weak because, while it does say Alicia is "anemic," it could refer to a wan appearance rather than a desire to keep out of the public eye. Choice A also indicates that Alicia had considerable wealth and connections, so could indicate that she was influential in certain circles. Choice B is incorrect because it shows an energetic, determined act rather than highlights a passive, weak nature. Choice D is incorrect because it does not refer to Alicia, Adam J. Patch's wife. Instead, the section refers to Henrietta Lebrune, the wife of Adam Ulysses Patch.

7. **Choice A is the best answer** because "astonishing" is used to describe the age, 26, that Adam Ulysses started his memoirs. Memoirs are typically a person's reflections on life that draw upon extensive experience, often as the person approaches old age. Therefore, the fact that a 26-year-old is writing about New York society is relatively presumptuous. The author is highlighting the "irony" or "incongruity" that the person has not seen much of life by that age, let alone enough to write a detailed analysis on a complex portion of society. The use of "astonishing" is further explained by showing that the book was "dull" or "boring," indicating that it did not capture the excitement or depth that Adam Ulysses was trying to achieve.

    Choices B and C are incorrect because the author is not trying to say that people have a high opinion—"admire" or "respect"—Adam Ulysses. They may be curious about his views, but do not necessarily think that he is a great person for writing memoirs. Choice D is incorrect because the book was not published because it was boring; this shows that Adam Ulysses was not a "talented" or "skilled" writer. Therefore, the author is not highlighting Adam's abilities, only the fact that he chose to write at a young age.

8. **Choice D is the best answer** because "engaging" refers to something that is "charming and attractive." Choice D shows that Anthony found Ulysses' conversations "pleasant" or "appealing." His conversation was "thick-smelling" or "enticing." The idea that it might last for up to an hour implies that Anthony wanted the conversation to continue longer. Therefore, Choice D supports the idea that Adam Ulysses was an engaging "conversationalist" or "speaker."

    Choice A is incorrect because, although it shows that publishers were interested in the book, it does not explain why. It does not say that Adam Ulysses spoke in an attractive way. The claim that the book was boring also implies that Ulysses did not have a good way with words. Choice B shows that Ulysses was physically handsome or attractive, but it does not give any evidence about how pleasing he was when he spoke. Choice C says that Anthony remembered Ulysses, but does not give any reasons supporting why he did.

9. **Choice B is the best answer** because despite promising trips, "none of them ever materialized" (lines 84-85). This shows that Ulysses was more interested in talking than in following through with his word. That is the action of a "superficial" or "shallow" personality: saying one thing but not caring enough to do it.

    Choice A is incorrect because "foreshadowing" involves giving a clue of something that will happen in the future. However, the promised trips never happened, so they do not give any hint that Ulysses would take his son on a trip or that Ulysses would die. Choice C is incorrect because, if Ulysses really took an interest in his son, he would follow through on promises and spend time with the boy rather than getting the boy's hopes up and breaking those hopes. Choice D is incorrect because the trips would cost a lot of money if the father and son really took them all, but the trips never happen. Therefore, it is possible that the father has very little money and is just talking about places he can only dream of visiting.

10. **Choice D is the best answer** because the description of Ulysses's death in the hotel gives a valid reason for Anthony to have a "panic of despair and terror" (lines 89-90). The scene implies that Anthony saw his father die in an unpleasant way, and provides a logical reason that he had a "vague melancholy" (line 91) or "uncertain, self-absorbed sadness" for the rest of his life. Without knowing about the traumatic event, the reader might wonder why Anthony took his father's death so hard.

    Choice A is incorrect because Ulysses promised many trips, but only took one. Therefore, the death scene is a somewhat paradoxical image because it shows that Ulysses did not even keep the promise of completing one whole trip with his son; he died before it was over. Choice B is incorrect because, while the scene indicates that Ulysses had a painful death, that is not the reason that the author included the information. If there was no need to establish why Anthony had terror and panic that stayed with him for life, it would be sufficient to know only that his father died. Choice C is incorrect because the passage does not say that Anthony chooses to live in America. He was "brought back" (line 90), which implies that others made the decision for him when he was too panicked to think for himself.

11. **Choice A is the best answer** because Keel claims in (lines 48-51) that "a problem with our legal system is that lawyers sometimes lose sight of the fundamental purpose of the law, debate the meaning of a few words, and suddenly the law is turned on its head." He makes this claim about the Carcieri decision, which limits the application of the IRA to only the Native Americans who had land in 1934. This means that the legislation does not apply to groups such as "tribes who were on treaty reservations in 1934 with a BIA superintendent" (lines 83-85). Keel's point is that the intent of the law was to include all Native Americans, so the "strict" or "rigid" restriction to ones with land in 1934 is going against the "spirit" or "purpose" of the law.
Choice B is incorrect because Keel does not say that a new law is needed. In fact, he says, "We will need the IRA for many more years until the tribal needs for self-support and self-determination are met" (lines 72-74). He simply indicates that a wider interpretation of the law that includes all Native Americans is needed. Choice C is incorrect because the law was meant to protect rather than "deny" or "refuse" the rights: "With the IRA, Congress renewed its trust responsibility to protect and restore our tribal homelands and the Indian way of life" (lines 17-20). Choice D is incorrect because the IRA has not been successful "since" or "from the time" that it was enacted. (lines 63-65) point out that "the purposes of the IRA were frustrated first by World War II and then by the termination era," showing that at times the law was not successful in reaching its goal.

12. **Choice B is the best answer** because the first paragraph begins with a description of the ideal situation for Native Americans; it explains that they should retain cultural traditions while still thriving in the modern world. The second paragraph asserts that the IRA had the same "intention" or "vision" (lines 14-17, "This vision… Reorganization Act"). Background about the policies prior to 1934 explain why those intentions were important. Starting with paragraph 6, the focus changes from the original purpose of the law to how it is administered now: only Native Americans who held land in 1934 qualify. The final two paragraphs discuss the problems with this new policy: it does not allow tribes who did not have land to develop fully. They suffer from legal battles, a lack of land, and poor tribal economies.
Choice A is incorrect because, while the passage gives historical background, it never says that the IRA should be eliminated. Instead, it says that there is still a great need for the protection it provides (lines 72-74, "We will… are met"). Choice C is incorrect because the passage describes the goals of Native Americans, but accepts them as given rather than "analyzing" or "examining" them in detail. In addition, the repercussions of the Carcieri v. Salazar case are given, but there is no discussion about the content of the case itself. Choice D is incorrect because Keel discusses the importance of land as a place to maintain customs, but does not describe the "ethics" or "morality" of taking away that land. Furthermore, he does not come up with a good solution to the problem of land; he says that it is hard and requires money and government support.

13. **Choice C is the best answer** because the question is asking about the government's position before 1934, and the passage says that "prior to 1934, the Federal Government policy toward Indian tribes was to sell off the tribal land base and assimilate Indian people" (lines 24-26). In other words, the government tried to get Native Americans "abandon" or "get rid of" the traditional tribal system and "assimilate" them, meaning that it tried to "absorb them into mainstream culture." The goal was to create a single nation" or "make a nation without divisions" based on traditional tribal practices.
Choice A is incorrect because the government prior to 1934 tried to "sell off" tribal lands, not to create reservations. In addition, the government did not encourage the continuance of traditional customs because it wanted all people to be "assimilated" or "following the same system." Choice B is incorrect because it is the government's stance after 1934 with the introduction of the IRA. Choice D is incorrect because there is no discussion of which Native Americans "qualified" or "were eligible to become" citizens.

14. **Choice C is the best answer** because the answer to the previous question is that the government wanted Native Americans to abandon traditional practices in the effort of creating a single nation. Choice C gives the "slogan" or "memorable saying" of the "era," which refers to the time before 1934. The slogan is "kill the Indian," meaning that Native American traditions and customs should be eliminated. "Save the man" refers to becoming part of mainstream society rather than maintaining "barbaric" Native American ways separate from the regular society. Choice A is incorrect because it describes the opposite view from what was prevalent in 1934: it says that Native Americans should retain and preserve rather than abandon traditional practices. Choice B refers to "renewing a promise," which could imply that prior to the IRA, the government thought it important to maintain the "way of life" or "traditions," which is not accurate. Choice D is incorrect because it says that tribal governments had "withered" or "gotten weaker," under Federal policy, but it does not provide solid evidence showing why. Choice D does not say that the Federal policy was to eliminate the traditions in an effort of creating a single nation. For example, the tribes could have withered because there was not sufficient funding.

15. **Choice C is the best answer** because "active" is an adjective that describes the "Federal supervision by the Bureau of Indian Affairs in 1934" that was necessary to qualify tribes to be covered by the IRA. Choice C refers to something that is functioning or in effect. In other words, it shows that the Federal supervision needed to be in effect in 1934 for the IRA to apply.
Choices A and B are incorrect because they refer to something that is healthy, strong, or lively. The Federal supervision, however, did not need to be "full of energy" or "healthy;" it needed to be present and working or not. Choice D is incorrect because it refers to something that is hard-working and productive. Choice D contains an emotional quality of an effort to do well that does not fit the context.

16. **Choice C is the best answer** because the question is asking for a quote that "counters" or "goes against" the claim that the IRA is not needed. Choice C shows that, despite a lack of "persecution" or direct aggression against Native Americans, there are still areas that need the type of help that the IRA provides: regaining land, establishing self-government, and ensuring that traditional culture continues.
Choice A is incorrect because it refers to a past government policy, so it does not provide support that the IRA is not needed now, in the present time. Choice B is incorrect because it only says that the effort to rebuild is difficult. It does not provide evidence that the services of the IRA are needed. Choice D is incorrect because it says that there are "fears," but does not explain what those fears are. The fears could be completely unrelated to the services of the IRA.

17. **Choice D is the best answer** because "frustrated" refers to what World War II and the termination era did to the purposes of the IRA. Choice D means "blocked" or "prevented," which fits the context of showing that events prevented the goals of the IRA from being completely fulfilled.
Choices A and C can be eliminated because they are emotional responses, but "the purposes of the IRA" are inanimate and cannot experience emotions. Choice A means "irritated" and Choice D means "not happy with something." Choice B is incorrect because the "fulfilling" refers to something doing the act of making another thing happen. However, it does not fit the context because World War II and the termination era were not things that could "fulfill" or make the IRA's goals happen. They were obstacles that stopped other things from fulfilling the purposes of the IRA.

18. **Choice B is the best answer** because Keel complains in the last sentence, "this decision will create two classes of Indian tribes: those who will benefit from Federal trust responsibility and those who will not" (lines 90-92). In other words, he feels that the decision has problems because some Native Americans qualify and some do not, so the "classes" or "groups" will be unequal in how they are treated.
Choice A is incorrect because it is the opposite of Keel's claim. He feels that the decision was too rigid because "lawyers sometimes lose sight of the fundamental purpose of the law, debate the meaning of a few words, and suddenly the law is turned on its head" (lines 48-51). He feels that the intent of the law was ignored in reading the specific words of the law too exactly. Choice C is incorrect because the decision did not make any "new" methods or laws. It only restricted which groups of people the law applied to. Choice D is incorrect because "precedents" are legal cases that act as a guide for deciding future cases. The Carcieri decision, however, did not "facilitate" or "make easier" the process of "establishing" or "creating" tribal governments.

19. **Choice C is the best answer** because Keel directly says in (lines 68-69), "they must earn every penny to buy back their own land." In other words, the tribes must earn the money to buy back land from the people who currently own it.

    None of the other choices are supported by evidence from the passage. For Choice A, there is no discussion of "grants" or "money given by an organization to use for a specific purpose." For Choice B, the passage refers to proof of prior land ownership: "There are many more tribes whose land-to-trust applications have simply been frozen while the Department of Interior works through painstaking legal and historical analysis" (lines 79-82). However, the burden of proof belongs to the Department of Interior, not to the Native Americans. For Choice D, there is no indication that the IRA is an organization that tribes can join or not. Therefore, no one is a "member" of the IRA. Rather, the IRA is legislation that applies to some tribes and not others.

20. **Choice D is the best answer** because Keel states that "there are many more tribes whose land-to-trust applications have simply been frozen while the Department of Interior (DOI) works through painstaking legal and historical analysis" (lines 79-82). He also says that there is "harassment litigation against tribes who were on treaty reservations in 1934 with a BIA superintendent. It is litigation merely for the purpose of delay" (lines 83-86). These quotes indicate that the DOI just "freezing" or "delaying" the procedure of proving ownership rather than trying hard to "expedite" or "speed up" the process of helping Native Americans reclaim their lands. Choice A is incorrect because there is no evidence to support "regular" or "frequent" changes in the DOI policies. The passage does say that there have been changes in the overall view of the government over time, but there is no indication that the methods used by the DOI to prove ownership are any different than they were in the past. Choice B is not supported by the passage. There is evidence that the DOI helps prove historical ownership, but there is no indication of how that information is used. The DOI may not have "authority" or "power" to force anyone to sell lands at all. Choice C is incorrect because, while Keel says that "jobs are lost or never created" (line 84), he does not say that the jobs are specifically ones working for the DOI.

21. **Choice B is the best answer** because Keel says that the worst part of the decision is that it "will create two classes of Indian tribes: those who will benefit from Federal trust responsibility and those who will not" (lines 86-88). In other words, there will be an arbitrary or unjust "division" or "split" between the groups who had land in 1934 and those who did not.

    Choice A is incorrect because Keel never says that the IRA will be "repealed" or "ended." He only discusses what will happen if the strict interpretation set by the Carcieri decision continues to be upheld. Choice C is incorrect because the final paragraph indicates that it is difficult to get back tribal lands, but indicates that it is still possible after "painstaking legal and historical analysis" (line 82). Therefore, it is not "against the law" or "legally prevented." Choice D is incorrect because the final paragraph says that there is now "harassment litigation against tribes who were on treaty reservations in 1934 with a BIA superintendent" (lines 83-85). This claim implies that there is doubt that the tribes are protected by the IRA because they might not have been "under (question 15) active Federal supervision by the Bureau of Indian Affairs in 1934" (lines 54-56). Therefore, that group is not the only one protected by the IRA. Native Americans with "lands in trust in 1934" (line 56) are possibly more inclined to receive protection.

22. **Choice B is the best answer** because the author starts the passage with the claim that "becoming an urban or regional planner can be a very satisfying career for individuals who want to positively change the daily lives of people around them" (lines 1-4). The rest of the passage "reinforces" or "supports" that claim by describing the skills needed and what they are used for, such as communicating with others and analyzing data. The passage also shows that the career involves positive change because planners "develop land use plans and programs that help create communities, accommodate population growth, and revitalize physical facilities in towns, cities, counties, and metropolitan areas" (lines 4-8). The final paragraph also indicates that the career can be "satisfying" because there is a high growth rate for jobs and a good average income.

    Choice A is incorrect because the author discusses a "potential opportunity" or "possible chance" of a good career and gives data showing why the career choice can be a good one. However, the author does not "analyze" or "evaluate" any research that generated the data. In fact, even the source of the data is not revealed in the text. Choice C is incorrect because the author does not "enumerate weaknesses" or "list problems" about the suggestion of becoming a planner. The author only gives one possible weakness about one type of employer at the end: "federal, state, and local government budgets may affect the employment of planners in government, because development projects are contingent on available funds" (lines 87-90). Choice D is incorrect because the passage only refers to qualifications (a master's degree) and skills needed to be a planner. There is no explanation of the "step by step method" or "process" to become trained, search for jobs, and get hired as a planner.

23. **Choice C is the best answer** because "attractive" describes how businesses view the region that the planner is helping. Choice C refers to something that is desirable. The resulting sentence therefore indicates that the planner helps make the region desirable to businesses so that more businesses move there and the economy gets stronger. None of the other choices adequately shows how the businesses view the region. Choice A refers to a personal quality that inspires others. It does not refer to something inanimate like a region. Choice B refers to something that is impossible to avoid the effect of. The businesses, though, are not forced to move to the region. Instead, they just are more interested in doing so. Choice D refers to something that is extremely interesting so that it is impossible to stop paying attention to.

24. **Choice B is the best answer** because the passage says that planners need to "meet with public officials, developers, and the public regarding development plans and land use" (lines 8-10). Therefore, they need to "convey" or "express" what they mean to a wide range of listeners. In addition, planners "commonly use statistical software, data visualization and presentation programs, financial spreadsheets, and other database and software programs" (lines 36-39). Therefore, they are using technology that is "specialized" or "requires specific knowledge to use."
Choice A is incorrect because, while planners need to create strong plans, there is no discussion of how they "secure funding" or "get money" to pay for the plans to be completed. Choice C is incorrect because, while it may be assumed that planners "negotiate disputes" because they must sometimes enforce regulations or deny proposals, the passage does not emphasize "creating new parks" as a main skill. Planners will be needed to help with "extensive development and improved infrastructure, including housing, roads, sewer systems, parks, and schools" (lines 84-86), but planners in general do not necessarily have to be very good at making new parks.

25. **Choice D is the best answer** because the answer to the previous question is that planners most need strong skills in expressing ideas clearly and using specialized technology. Choice D supports that claim because it shows that planners need to be good at "conveying information" or "expressing ideas." Choice D also supports the second portion of the answer, "using specialized technology," by showing that "technological and analytical skills" are also important.
Choice A is weak because it only describes what planners do. It does not provide any evidence to say what skills are needed to accomplish the goals. Choice B is incorrect because it only implies that planners need good communication skills to work with different groups of people. There is no evidence to support the claim that technological and analytical skills are important. Choice C is incorrect because it only provides evidence to show that planners need technological skills. Choice C does not relate at all to communication skills.

26. **Choice A is the best answer** because the definition explains what a median wage is. This definition clarifies that not all planners earned the median figure of $73,050. It also explains why a total of 20% of the planners earned less than $45,180 or more than $114,170. If the reader did not know the definition of median wage, then the reason for the wide range in salaries might not make much sense.
Choice B is incorrect because the author does not imply that the median wage is "insufficient" or "not good enough." The median wage does not give all the necessary detail to know the range of salaries, but offers a valid middle point to use as a point of reference. The definition shows how the data can be used to better understand the salary that could be earned as a planner. Choice C is incorrect because there is no "reason" or "cause" given to explain why planners earn different amounts of money. Choice D is incorrect because there is no link drawn between salary earned and number of jobs. Therefore, a definition of how the salary in the passage was calculated does not support or prove that there will be more jobs in the future.

27. **Choice B is the best answer** because "address" is used to show what urban planners will be needed to do with different types of issues. Choice B refers to "dealing with" or "solving" a problem or difficulty. Therefore, it fits the context of saying that in cities, urban planners will have to deal with problems such as population growth. None of the other choices effectively explains what the planners do with issues. Choice A refers to cancelling

or sending something rather than solving something. Choice C refers to sharing information. However, the planners do not just need to talk about issues, they need to solve issues. Choice D is incorrect because it refers to starting or beginning to do something, but it does not include the idea of following through until the problem is solved.

28. **Choice A is the best answer** because the graph shows that the median income for state government employees is slightly under the $80,000 mark, at about $75,000. The bar for the median income for local government employees is shorter, closer to $70,000, which is halfway between the $60,000 and $80,000 lines. Therefore, the median income for state government employees is "higher" or "larger" than that for local government employees. All of the other choices can be eliminated because they are not supported by the data from figure 1. Choices B and C are incorrect because the bar for "architectural, engineering and related fields" at just under $80,000 is lower, not greater, than the bar for "federal government employees" at just under $100,000. Choice D is incorrect because the bar for "management, scientific, and technical consulting service" is slightly higher than the bar for "local government," though both are between $60,000 and $80,000.

29. **Choice D is the best answer** because figure 2 only includes data for the year 2018. The passage warns that "federal, state, and local government budgets may affect the employment of planners in government, because development projects are contingent on available funds" (lines 87-90). In other words, employment may increase or decrease if available "funds" or "money" changes. "Budgets" are "spending plans," so if the federal government revises or changes its plan due to "fewer tax dollars," the amount of money for employing planners may be lower. Therefore, there is a "potential" or "chance" that there will be fewer planners in the future than listed in figure 2. Choice A is incorrect because neither the figure nor the passage explains where federal planners work; it is possible that they work in large cities. Therefore, there is not enough evidence to say that the percentage is low because of "need" or "demand" in one area or another. Choice B is incorrect because, while no exact numbers are given, figure 2 does show the percentages of the total number of planners. Therefore, it is possible to determine which sectors hire more planners than others. The actual number is "reflected" or "indicated" as a comparison. Choice C is incorrect because the passage does not say that federal government positions are stable. On the contrary, the passage says that employment in government positions is variable depending upon budgets, so if the budget changes in any of the levels of government, the percentage of people employed by each sector may also change. In addition, it says that planning jobs as a whole are expected to increase, so the percentages hired by different sectors may change.

30. **Choice D is the best answer** because the answer to the previous question is that the percentage of urban and regional planners employed by the federal government in figure 2 has the "potential" or "chance" to decrease if the federal government receives fewer tax dollars and revises its spending plans. Since a "budget" is a "spending plan," Choice D clearly supports the answer to the previous question. It says that any employment of planners in any level of government is "contingent on" or "happens only given" available funds. Therefore, it shows that a change in the budget due to lower tax dollars could lead to fewer planners getting jobs.
Choice A is incorrect because it could, if anything, weaken the claim that the percentage of planners employed will decrease. Choice A says that there will be more planners overall, so it could suggest that all the percentages would remain similar but the actual number of planners they represent would be larger. Choices B and C also give reasons for hiring planners, but do not show which sector of employment would increase. Therefore, Choices B and C do not give not reasons that the percentage represented by the federal government would decrease.

31. **Choice C is the best answer** because figure 1 shows the median annual wages for certain types of urban and regional planners, which gives a more detailed breakdown expanding on the passage's description of wages in (lines 64-69) ("The median…than $114,170"). Figure 2 gives the specific percentages of planners employed by different sectors. The sectors are not directly referred to in the passage, so the figure gives the reader a better idea of employment than vague claims such as, "planners work throughout the country, but most work in large metropolitan areas" (lines 51-52) or "suburban areas and municipalities will need planners" (lines 79-80). Choice A is incorrect because a "visual interpretation" is a way of showing data using pictures or illustrations. Figure 1 is "visual" because it offers bars to compare the relative wages. However, figure 2 only uses words and numbers. Choice B is incorrect because the figures do not "challenge" or "bring into question" any points from

CONTINUE

the passage. Instead of opposing the passage, they add more information. Choice D is incorrect because, while figure 2 is arguably "loosely" or "not directly" related to any claim in the passage, figure 1 provides an expansion of the discussion of median wage given in (lines 64-69) ("The median…than $114,170").

32. **Choice A is the best answer** because, according to Sweeney, "The critical element" or "important point" of the study was that the researchers "were able to sustain measurements in this harsh environment as long as [they] have—both in the summer and the winter, in every year over the last 13 years" (lines 25-28). In other words, the results of the study were "unique" or "one of a kind" because they relied on "measurements" or "data" that did not lack large blocks of time. No previous study had such complete data to work with: the Drake Passage data "is the densest ongoing time series in the Southern Ocean" (lines 29-30).
Choice B is incorrect because there is no discussion of what equipment or methods the scientists used to collect their data. They could have used very common tools. Choice C is incorrect because there is no evidence that previous studies did not "incorporate" or "use" chemical measurements. The only difference brought up is that the period of collection in the Drake Passage study was unbroken for 13 years. Choice D is incorrect because it is implied that researchers already knew that the Southern Ocean absorbs more CO_2 than other oceans; they just did not know the exact rate or whether the rate is changing.

33. **Choice C is the best answer** because the answer to the previous question is that the results of the Drake Passage study are unique because they used more complete measurements than any other study of the region. Choice C supports that claim because it says that the data is "the densest ongoing time series," meaning that it "has the most measurements over a period of time." In other words, no other study had as "dense" or "complete" information to work with for the region of the Southern Ocean.
Choice A is incorrect because it only describes the region covered by the study. It does not offer evidence that the data from the study was more complete than data from any other study done in the area. Choice B is incorrect because it only indicates that the Drake Passage is a hard place to conduct research. Choice D is weak because it describes the number of times the boat that carried the research equipment travels per year, but does not say that the research was done every time. The research could have been done, for example, once a year. Choice D also contains no evidence to show that other research was not more thorough.

34. **Choice D is the best answer** because "definitive" means "conclusive" or "final." The data was complete enough to determine that "since 2002, the Southern Ocean has been removing more of the greenhouse gas carbon dioxide (CO_2) from the atmosphere (lines 1-3), so the "effect" of removing CO_2 was "isolated" or "identified." However, the cause of the removal of CO_2 is still unknown: "the researchers aren't sure of the exact mechanism driving these changes" (lines 46-47). Therefore, the study does not conclusively answer all questions.
Choice A is incorrect because the researchers were able to collect "sufficient" or "enough" data to come to the "solid" or "well-supported" conclusion that the Southern Ocean has recently been removing more CO_2 from the atmosphere. Choice B is incorrect because the passage says that the research took place on a boat that traveled "both in the summer and the winter, in every year over the last 13 years" (lines 27-28). Therefore, it is implied that the research was not missing any "critical" or "important" time periods. Choice C is incorrect because there is no indication that the results are missing important information because they focused on one region—the Southern Ocean—rather than a wider area. The conclusion drawn from that data about CO_2 absorption is valid.

35. **Choice C is the best answer** because the main point of the paragraph is that "these results contrast with previous findings" and emphasize that more studies are needed, indicating that the Drake Passage study did not provide all the answers. Therefore, the paragraph shows how the results of the Drake Passage study fits into "the wider context" or "bigger picture" of other studies.
Choice A is incorrect because the paragraph does not suggest that any of the data gathered so far is "inaccurate" or "not correct." Therefore, the paragraph is not being used to show how difficult it is to get correct data. Choice B is incorrect because the paragraph does not "illustrate" or "explain" why it is hard to "amass" or "gather" enough data. The paragraph mentions that the conditions are "challenging," but does not give any detail about why. Choice D is incorrect because, though the paragraph says that CO_2 absorption is important, it does not talk about "correcting" or "fixing" the problem. It only says that there needs to be more research done to understand the process better.

36. **Choice C is the best answer** because (lines 90-92) say that "researchers had yet to sample vast areas, especially during stormy autumn and winter seasons," indicating that the results from the saildrone would fill in the missing information by taking samples during the autumn and winter.
Choice A is incorrect because the saildrone was not launched to prove a point about CO_2 absorption. It was to collect data in order to determine patterns in the times or places that had not previously been studied much. If anything, the statement that "preliminary results suggest that parts of the ocean identified as potential CO_2 sources were indeed emitting the greenhouse gas during winter months" (lines 93-96) hint that the saildrone was expected to find less absorption than previously estimated. Choice B is incorrect because the saildrone was sent to collect data, not to "test limitations." Of course, researchers hoped that it would survive the harsh conditions and did not know if it would, but the main point of the journey was not to see if the saildrone would make it. Choice D is incorrect because the passage implies that it was already known that the Southern Ocean played a vital role. The details of that role were not known, so the winter launch was to determine certain details, not to see if it had a role at all.

37. **Choice C is the best answer** because C is used to describe a place that is harsh and severe. It fits the context of saying that the Southern Ocean contains some of the most harsh and severe water conditions on the planet. None of the other choices fits the context of describing a harsh environment. Choice A refers to something that is ready to attack or confront something else. It is not used to describe something which is not deliberately trying to inflict harm. Choice B refers to an emotional state in which someone feels hostility towards something; it is not used to describe an inanimate object. Choice D refers to things which are at variance with each other. However, "hostile" is only referring to the "seas," not to more than one thing that could be incompatible with each other.

38. **Choice A is the best answer** because the paragraph is all about the "audacious" or "daring" idea. The description in the previous sentence shows how hard the conditions were: the journey was long (13,670 miles), through hostile waters, and there was no backup because the saildrone was "alone." By mentioning "in winter," the author stresses another point that makes the previous claims appear even more daring: the weather was colder and might have worse storms than if it were sent at other times of the year.
Choice B is incorrect because, while "in winter" does explain in general when the saildrone was launched, that is not the purpose of including the detail at that point. The exact date—not even the month—of the launch is not explained, so the reader only gets a vague idea of when the launch occurred. Choice C is incorrect because the discussion of a lack of data from winter is discussed in a later paragraph (lines 90-92, "But researchers... winter seasons"). Therefore, the phrase "in winter" is related to a different topic, the audacious idea. Choice D is incorrect because the fact that the saildrone was launched in winter does not give a reason why it was unmanned. If anything, the harder conditions might make it more logical to send along, for example, a boat to monitor its progress.

39. **Choice C is the best answer** because "revolutionary" refers to something that is "new" or "pioneering." Choice C supports the idea because the saildrone was able to do something that was "unfathomable" or "impossible even to imagine" happening even 10 years ago. The saildrone was the "first" to collect data in an "autonomous circumnavigation of" or "unmanned trip around" Antarctica, so it was pioneering or new in its field.
Choice A is incorrect because it only suggests that the trip was anticipated to be difficult. It does not say that the saildrone was "revolutionary" or "new;" it could have been old technology that was predicted not to survive the conditions. Choice B is incorrect because it only indicates that the saildrone collected data with newly invented instruments. It does not say that the saildrone itself was an innovative way to gather data. Choice D is incorrect because it only says that other people had not done research in the area; it does not provide any evidence related to the saildrone at all.

40. **Choice B is the best answer** because Passage 1 introduces the idea of conducting research in the "challenging environment" (line 58) of the Southern Ocean and says that it is important, though dangerous. The "barrier" or "obstacle" is therefore the severe weather conditions. Passage 2 gives one solution or possible way to get by the barrier: to use unmanned research vessels. That way there is less risk of harm to humans, but the data still gets collected.
Choice A is incorrect because, while Passage 1 describes important research results, Passage 2 offers details about obtaining the data for a completely different research project. Choice C is incorrect because, though Passage

CONTINUE

1 "outlines" or "describes" a method of collecting data by putting instruments on board a vessel sailing for a different purpose, Passage 2 does not call that method "obsolete" or "outdated." Passage 2 describes a specific study and does not "argue" or "try to persuade" that other methods are not as good. Choice D is incorrect because both passages describe the "historical" or "past" view of the role of the Southern Ocean in absorbing CO_2. They both also give current analyses of data about the topic. Therefore, the passages do not focus on only one element each.

41. **Choice D is the best answer** because Passage 1 concludes that "we must continue to expand our measurements" (lines 56-57), which indicates that the "implications" or "potential effects" are not completely known yet. For example, "the researchers aren't sure of the exact mechanism driving these changes" (lines 45-47), so that finding more about the mechanism might help better understand "the importance of the Southern Ocean to the global oceans' role in absorbing atmospheric CO_2" (lines 54-56). Passage 2 also indicates that the complete "implications" or "effects" are not well understood because so far there are only "preliminary results" (line 93), which implies that there will be more complete results or a better understanding later after other results are released.

Choice A is incorrect because, while Passage 1 identifies that "since 2002, the Southern Ocean has been removing more of the greenhouse gas carbon dioxide (CO_2) from the atmosphere" (lines 1-3), Passage 2 does not support the same conclusion. Its preliminary results show that "parts of the ocean identified as potential CO_2 sources were indeed emitting the greenhouse gas during winter months" (lines 91-94). Therefore, it could be absorbing less CO_2 than previously estimated. Choice B is incorrect because neither passage discusses the amount of CO_2 that needs to be absorbed to "counteract" or "prevent" global warming. Although it is indicated in both passages that the Southern Ocean plays an important role, they do not say whether it is sufficient. Choice C is incorrect because only Passage 1 offers the theory of mixing water as a reason for variable CO_2 absorption.

42. **Choice A is the best answer** because Sweeney claims that "we must continue to expand our measurements in this part of the world despite the challenging environment" (lines 56-58). In other words, the data needs to be collected even though the environment is "challenging" or "dangerous." He would therefore most likely say that the risks were "justified" or "acceptable" because there was an "imperative" or "great need" for more measurements, and the unmanned research vehicle was not endangering any human lives.

Choice B is incorrect because "commensurate" means "corresponding in degree." However, Sweeney acknowledges both the great need for data and the potential great danger. Therefore, he would consider them both to have a similar degree. Choice C is incorrect because Sweeney would not call additional research "redundant" or "repetitive and not needed." He points out that "we must continue to expand our measurements" (lines 55-56), meaning he thinks more measurements are needed despite the ones collected from the *Laurence M. Gould* study. Choice D is unsupported by any evidence because Sweeney does not compare various methods of collecting data. Therefore, it is impossible to tell his opinion of the risk level of the saildrone project.

43. **Choice B is the best answer** because the passage starts by explaining that Menkes syndrome is associated with a specific gene, *ATP7A*. However, the researchers found a patient who "presented clinically" or "showed" the signs of Menkes syndrome but who did not have mutations of *ATP7A*. Instead, he had mutations "in the *HEPHL1* gene, located on chromosome 11" (lines 35-36). Therefore, the researchers did experiments with mice that had changes to their *HEPHL1* genes and observed the results. The conclusions of the study were that the "study identified *HEPHL1* as a novel gene responsible for hair abnormalities" (lines 76-87) and that it might "relate to the copper absorption associated with Menkes syndrome" (lines 75-76).

Choice A is incorrect because the study does not "present" or "give" a possible cure for Menkes syndrome; it only says that more research might lead to possible treatments. Choice C is incorrect because the passage is not teaching about how scientists work in general. The passage summarizes the results of one study but does not even outline the steps to achieve those results. Choice D is incorrect because the reason for the mice to be born with kinky whiskers was clear: the mice had genetic modifications. The passage explains the range of effects caused by the genetic modification.

44. **Choice C is the best answer** because the passage establishes that the disease does not have many patients: "Menkes is a rare X-linked disease" (lines 8-9). As a direct result of that rarity, "few pharmaceutical companies are investing in research related to the disease" (lines 21-22). In other words, the companies are not "investing"

Practice Tests for the SAT   **304**   CONTINUE ▶

or "putting money" into research because it is rare. The logical implication is that the companies will not get enough profits back from their investment; the process of creating a cure is "not financially viable" or "will lose money."

Choice A is incorrect because the passage does not condemn the decision of the pharmaceutical companies. The tone is neutral and stating a fact that companies have not done research on Menkes syndrome rather than saying that the company should invest money even though they will not be able to recoup their losses. Choice B is incorrect because the passage does not discuss the stages of the disease or when the disease can be diagnosed. It is possible that the disease could be diagnosed from right after birth or even through prenatal testing before any symptoms have appeared. Choice D is incorrect because, while the passage says that the disease is linked to copper absorption, it does not indicate whether increasing amounts of copper will change the effects or allow the body to absorb more.

45. **Choice C is the best answer** because the answer to the previous question is that it can be inferred from the passage that there are not enough patients to make the development of a cure "financially viable" or "profitable." Choice C supports that claim because it says that the disease is rare—meaning that there are not many patients— and that the rarity is why companies are not "investing" or "spending money" on research. It is reasonable to assume that the rarity means that there are not enough patients who would use a cure if one is developed, so the company would lose money and not recoup its investment.

Choice A is incorrect because it only describes Menkes syndrome. It does not say that the syndrome is rare or that developing a cure would not be profitable. Choice B is incorrect because it only says that there is no cure. It does not say that creating a cure would probably lead to a financial loss. Choice D is incorrect because it introduces some research related to the topic of Menkes syndrome. The fact that research is being done could weaken the claim that it is not financially viable to do research.

46. **Choice A is the best answer** because it means "hold" or "provide sufficient space for." It fits the context of saying that MCOs have three copper-binding sites that can provide space for or hold six copper atoms.

None of the other choices sufficiently fits the context of explaining what the three copper-binding sites do to the six copper atoms. Choice B refers to providing space for a person or people to stay; it does not apply to inanimate objects such as atoms. Choice C refers to providing a person a room to stay in for a rental fee. Choice D refers to protecting something from something harmful, but there is no evidence that the copper-binding sites are trying to help the copper atoms remain safe.

47. **Choice A is the best answer** because the passage says that the patient did not have an *ATP7A* gene mutation, so the researchers "sequenced all of the protein-coding regions of the patient's DNA, along with those of his parents" (lines 32-33) in order to "identify other variants that might be contributing" (line 31). They found mutations in another gene, *HEPHL1*, and performed tests on mice to see what symptoms might appear in the mice afflicted with that mutation. In other words, the researchers were able to "uncover" or "find" another gene that could "contribute to" or "cause" the symptoms found in Menkes syndrome.

Choice B is incorrect because there is no discussion of success in "reversing the damage" or "curing" the symptoms, though there is an implication that the study might help scientists find a cure in the future. Choice C is incorrect because the passage does not say that the *ATP7A* gene is not involved in Menkes syndrome. It only indicates that there are more factors involved than may have previously been realized. Choice D is incorrect because there is no indication that the mutation originally came from mice. The scientists genetically engineered mice with the mutation, but there is no indication that mice naturally have the condition.

48. **Choice D is the best answer** because the question is asking for evidence that shows that *HEPHL1* might be responsible for an inability to absorb copper properly. Choice D shows that *HEPHL1* "regulates" or "controls" an enzyme that needs copper. That point indicates that if the enzyme is not turned on and off properly, it might use copper in different ways or amounts. *HEPHL1* could therefore cause the "lack" or "absence" of proper absorption because it turns off an enzyme that absorbs copper.

Choice A is incorrect because it does not refer to *HEPHL1* at all. It only shows that a different gene is related to copper absorption. Choice B is incorrect because it refers to iron oxidation, but not to copper use at all. Choice C is incorrect because it only establishes a link between the distinctive hair shape when *HEPHL1* is absent. It does not indicate that the hair shape is a result of copper absorption.

49. **Choice B is the best answer** because "novel" is used to describe the gene *HEPHL1* and how it is responsible for hair abnormalities. The gene itself is a natural part of the human chromosome, so has presumably been around for a long time. Therefore, "novel" is referring to the newly-discovered relationship with hair abnormalities rather than to the existence of the gene itself. "Novel" can refer to something that is "groundbreaking" or "innovative," so using this word shows that the gene is an innovative answer for why hair abnormalities occur.

Choice D is incorrect because the passage does not establish a "link" or "connection" between *HEPHL1* and *ATP7A* mutations. If anything, the passage shows that a patient and mice with normal *ATP7A* still could display Menkes syndrome symptoms, which could weaken the link between the two genes.

50. **Choice A is the best answer** because the question is asking about the "difference in the iron uptake increase." Therefore, the correct answer is derived by subtracting the smaller column from the larger. The smaller column is the control mouse, which has a value of about 2.7. The larger is the mouse with no *HEPHL1* genes, which has a value of about 3.8. The difference is 3.8-2.7=1.1. Even if the values are changed by a few decimal points, Choice A is the closest approximate.

None of the other choices shows the "difference in the iron uptake increase." Choice B would represent a difference larger than 2 of the lines on the y-axis, but there is only one line (the one for 3 nmoles) between the two bars. Choice C refers to the total increase for the control mouse, not the difference between the control mouse and the mouse with no *HEPHL1*. Choice D refers to the total increase of the mouse with no *HEPHL1*.

51. **Choice B is the best answer** because figure 2 is given as a percentage of the activity shown in a "control" or "normal" mouse. The figure for the control is therefore 100%, or complete activity. If the figure for the mouse with two *HEPHL1* genes removed was 0, then it would be no activity. However, the bar reaches about 60%, which means that it demonstrates 60% of the activity that the normal mouse does; that means a decrease, but not all activity stopped.

None of the other choices are supported by figure 2. Choice A is incorrect because "no activity" would be 0%. Choice C is impossible to determine because figure 2 has no reference to iron uptake. Choice D is incorrect because there is no discussion of change over time in the figure.

52. **Choice D is the best answer** because the first graph refers to the increase in iron content in cells of mice that had normal *HEPHL1* and mice that had no *HEPHL1*. It might be presumed that mice with one functional *HEPHL1* would lead to partial absorption of iron. However, the passage directly says that the "study demonstrates that each mutation found in the patient led to complete loss of iron-oxidizing activity" (lines 48-50). In other words, if only one mutation existed and one *HEPHL1* were normal, there would still be a complete loss of iron-oxidizing activity. The effect would be the same for both mutations as it would be for one mutation, so there is no change to the graph.

All of the other choices can be eliminated because they show that the graph for the mouse with one *HEPHL1* would be different than the graph for a mouse with no *HEPHL1*, though both cases would represent a scenario in which all activity is shut down.

1. **Choice A is the best answer.** The second sentence begins with the words "the term," and since the previous sentence would need to clarify this term (i.e., the topic of the passage), the underlined sentence is necessary.
    Choice B is incorrect. There is no contradiction that has been put forward in this sentence.
    Choice C is incorrect. By framing the topic of the passage for the reader, the underlined sentence is indeed an effective topic sentence to introduce the idea of "social entrepreneurship" for the reader.
    Choice D is unsuitable because there is no definition for "social entrepreneurship" in the underlined sentence. In fact, the very point of the passage is to make a case for definition, as indicated by the title of the passage.

2. **Choice C is the best answer.** The paragraph describes the reasons why social entrepreneurship is "interesting" or "appealing," and both of these terms can be used to define "popularity." Therefore, using this choice as a topic sentence for this paragraph would be an effective choice.
    Choice A is incorrect. Currently, there is no topic sentence in the paragraph that helps transition the reader into the following content.
    Choice B is incorrect. The suggested answer here is extremely ambiguous and does not effectively encapsulate what follows in the paragraph.
    Choice D is incorrect. The "complexities" of social entrepreneurship are not mentioned or explained in the following text. Therefore, this topic sentence would be misleading.

3. **Choice B is the best answer** since this choice would tell the reader how these extraordinary people might "improve people's lives."
    Choice A is incorrect. The sentence as it is now is incomplete, since it does not tell readers what it is that "these extraordinary people come up with."
    Choice C is incorrect since the sentence is incomplete. We are not told why the ideas are significant.
    Choice D is incorrect since it contradicts the main premise of this paragraph, which is to speak about why social entrepreneurship is popular and interesting, rather than its "negative impact."

4. **Choice D is the best answer.** The following verb "is" is conjugated in the simple present tense. This tells us that for verb-tense consistency to be maintained, "signal" should also be conjugated as such.
    Since social entrepreneurship is a singular subject, we need the singular verb "signals."
    Choice A is incorrect since the verb is in the present continuous tense.
    Choice B is incorrect. While the simple present tense is used, the use of the plural verb "signal" would cause a grammatical error in the sentence.
    Choice C is incorrect. The use of the simple future tense would cause a verb-tense inconsistency.

5. **Choice B is the best answer.** Notice that the first part of the sentence points to visible benefits, while the second part of the sentence presents a problem, i.e., that the definition is unclear. Since contrasting ideas are being presented, a term like "although" would be the best answer.
    Choice A is incorrect. "However," is used when there is a contradicting/contrasting idea that is presented immediately after the use of that word. Since that is not the case here, "however" would be inaccurate.
    Choice C is inaccurate. "Furthermore" is used to refer to an idea that is being added to a particular argument. It does not capture the contrasting quality that has been described above.
    Choice D is unsuitable since "whenever" refers to a temporal quality (related to time), which is absent in the highlighted sentence.

6. **Choice A is the best answer.** The use of the comma is accurate and allows the reader to follow the flow of ideas in the highlighted text.
    Choice B is incorrect. Colons are used to introduce lists and since there is no list here, this punctuation mark would be inaccurate.
    Choice C is inaccurate. Semicolons can only be used between two independent clauses, each with their own subject, verb, and object.
    Choice D is incorrect. The dash is used to lend emphasis to a statement and the use of this punctuation in this particular sentence would disrupt its flow of logic.

7. **Choice C is the best answer.** Notice that the following verb has been conjugated as "has," immediately indicating that "has become" is the best possible answer.
    Choice A is incorrect. The present continuous tense in this sentence causes a verb-tense inconsistency in this statement.
    Choices B & D, similarly to Choice A, cause an inconsistency by using the past and future tense respectively.

8. **Choice D is the best answer.** The last sentence of the previous paragraph speaks about the challenges that stem from the lack of clarity surrounding social entrepreneurship. The highlighted sentence mentions how this same inclusiveness "could be a good thing." Therefore, "in some respects" would be the best way to transition between the two ideas.
    Choice A is incorrect. The argument that follows highlights a contrasting idea rather than a similar one.
    Choice B is unsuitable. Like "similarly," "in addition" would contradict the shift in ideas that occurs between this sentence and the one that came before it.
    Choice C is incorrect. "Despite this," while not incorrect in meaning, would negatively impact the sentence since it is followed by "this inclusiveness" which would lead to a repetition of the word "this."

9. **Choice C is the best answer.** Using the comma after "entrepreneurship" would maintain the logic of the sentence and allow it to reach a conclusion.
    Choice A is incorrect. As it is now, the sentence is broken up into two fragments, neither of which makes sense by itself.
    Choice B is unsuitable. The semicolon would be inaccurate since it does not separate two independent clauses.
    Choice D is incorrect. The lack of any punctuation would make this long sentence difficult to understand.

10. **Choice B is the best answer.** Notice the use of "that promise" in the second line. This is in indication that "promise" is either directly mentioned, or implied, in the correct answer. None of the other choices include the mention or implication of a "promise."

11. **Choice D is the best answer.** Note that the sentence begins with a conditional statement beginning with the word "if." The conjugation of the verb, therefore, should highlight this conditional quality and given the options, the future tense would be the only one to meet this particular requirement.
    The use of the simple present, simple past, or present continuous tense would cause an inconsistency with the conditional quality of the subject in this sentence.

12. **Choice C is the best answer.** Here, the name of the cosmonaut is an appositive phrase that provides useful information without being necessary for the sentence to be grammatically correct. Therefore, a comma needs to precede this appositive phrase.
    Choice A is incorrect since there is no punctuation mark before the nonrestrictive appositive phrase, "Valentina Tereshkova."
    Choice B is incorrect. Semicolons can only be used between two independent clauses that each have their own subject, verb, and object.
    Choice D is incorrect. Splitting the sentence into two at the underlined section would create a sentence that has only the cosmonaut's name, and this would not function as an independent clause.

13. **Choice A is the best answer.** In the sentence that follows the suggested addition, we see reference to "his death on the Finnish front." Without the suggested addition, there would be no context for us to understand who "his" is being used in reference to.
    Choice B is incorrect. If placed at the end of the paragraph, the abovementioned reference to "his death" would still remain meaningless.
    Choice C is irrelevant. As a sentence that is placed in the middle of this paragraph, this text would not serve to introduce content in the following paragraph.
    Choice D is incorrect. The information here, by speaking to biographical information about Tereshkova, is clearly relevant to the paragraph and passage.

14. **Choice D is the best answer** for its clarity and formality.
Choice A is incorrect since ending the sentence at "two," without mentioning the context for this number as being the cosmonaut's age, is too informal for a passage of this nature.
Choice B is incorrect for its ambiguity. When possible, specific information is preferable to generic statements.
Choice C is incorrect. Deleting the underlined section would create an incomplete phrase.

15. **Choice A is the best answer.** Compared to all the other answers, this one is most suitable for the following reasons because it <u>both</u> (1) creates a transition to the following idea by using the introductory phrase "on applying to the cosmonaut corps" <u>and</u> (2) mentions the number of candidates from which Tereshkova was chosen.
All the other answer choices only do one or the other.

16. **Choice B is the best answer,** since it clarifies what is being referred to from the previous sentence. The first sentence mentions "training," "tests," and the "Soviet air force." Term like "they," "it," or "these" would be ambiguous and not clarify the context for the reader. Therefore, the remaining choices are less suitable.

17. **Choice B is the best answer.** "Civilian" is a more efficient and direct way of saying "member of civil society" — making this choice preferable to Choice A.
This sentence highlights three aspects that set this woman apart from her peers: her age, her gender, and her status in society (civilian = not military). The remaining answer choices eliminate one of these pieces of information and, instead, create redundancies by repeating information. Choice C repeats the fact that she is a woman; Choice D repeats the fact that she was young.

18. **Choice A is the only possible answer** since the sentence speaks about what is true until the present moment (when the article was written).
The use of the gerund in Choice B would be grammatically incorrect.
Choice C is incorrect. If the past tense is used in this sentence, it would have to be qualified with more information, i.e., she remained the first woman to fly solo in space until something else happened. Since there is no additional context here, the past tense would render this sentence meaningless.
Choice D is incorrect. We have no way of saying that Tereshkova will remain the only woman to have ever flown solo in space.

19. **Choice C is the best answer.** Notice that the current paragraph speaks about Tereshkova's past accomplishments, while the next paragraph speaks about her current accomplishments. Adding the suggested sentence would allow the reader to make a more fluid transition between the different time periods that are mentioned in these two paragraphs.
Choice A is unsuitable. Although this sentence would make the transition more effective, it does not necessarily improve the clarity or tone of the text itself.
Choice B is inaccurate. This sentence would be meaningless as an introduction to this paragraph, since it clearly marks a transition between past and future accomplishments.
Choice D is inaccurate. There is no relevant information that would be eliminated by the inclusion of this sentence.

20. **Choice B is the best answer.** Notice that Paragraph (6) speaks of events "much after the collapse of the Soviet Union," while Paragraph (7) mentions events "before the collapse of the Soviet Union." The identification of this information, in relation to the linear timeline that has been followed by the rest of the passage immediately tells us where Paragraph (6) should be placed.

21. **Choice D is the best answer.** The suggested addition does not connect to the ideas in the previous sentences; it does not provide the reader with any new information. Therefore, there is no need for its inclusion at the end of this paragraph. Adding this generic statement here only serves as a forced, ambiguous conclusion to an otherwise fact-based paragraph.
Choice A is incorrect. There is nothing in this sentence that makes it "essential" to the passage.
Choice B is incorrect. The sentence would be as meaningless at the beginning of the paragraph as it would be at the end.

Choice C is incorrect since there is no information that follows this suggested addition, which it would help clarify.

22. **Choice B is the only answer** that effectively captures the focus of the passage on being on one woman who has accomplished an incredible feat in her field.
All of the other answer choices speak to lofty ideas that are not directly mentioned anywhere in the text. While issues related to gender dynamics and the politics of representation are not irrelevant to a passage of this nature, it would be an overstatement to summarize the passage's main point as having to do — generally — with the role of women in science, or pre/post-Soviet Union politics, or the gender dynamics in Russia.
Choice B is incorrect. Placing this sentence at the beginning of the paragraph, when the topic of "exile" is only brought up at the end of it, would immediately cause a disruption in the flow of logic in the text.
Choice D is incorrect since the following paragraph begins with a sentence about Petals of Blood, which has nothing to do with the topic of exile that is mentioned in the current and suggested last sentence of the previous paragraph. Therefore, this sentence does not serve as a "transition."

23. **Choice B is the best answer.** The verb here is referring to the number of cinema admissions (in the plural), and to something that took place in the past (requiring the simple past conjugation). "Were" is the only answer choice that fits both these conditions.
Choice A is incorrect. "Are" is the present tense conjugation of the verb "to be".
Choice C is incorrect. "Have" is a different verb that would be meaningless in the highlighted section.
Choice D is incorrect. "Is" is both singular and in the present tense form.

24. **Choice A is the best answer.** By telling us how large the market for film is, the information in the suggested addition functions as effective evidence to support the point being made in the previous sentence.
Choice B is incorrect. There is no contradiction between this sentence and the one that comes before it — both function as information to support the popularity of the medium of film.
Choice C is incorrect. The following paragraph goes on to talk about the specific example of India vis-à-vis film. The information in this suggested addition is, therefore, not necessary to transition to the following content.
Choice D is incorrect. The information in this suggested addition is extremely pertinent in relation to the focus of the passage.

25. **Choice C is the best answer.** While "tool" and "vehicle" could be used as synonyms for each other in the context presented here, the difference in the revision lies in the inclusion of the adjective "powerful," which helps support the impact of film that is further discussed in this paragraph. The adjective, therefore, heightens the positive tone of the sentence.
Choice A is incorrect. The sentence is used to introduce the importance of film in India but does not contain any direct reference to the Indian market. Therefore, this sentence cannot be said to function as "evidence." It simply serves to set up the following ideas.
Choice B is incorrect. There is no unsupported information in this sentence. In fact, the following information helps support this sentence's claim of cinema being a vehicle for culture.
Choice D is incorrect. The previous sentence speaks about the economics of film, while this sentence speaks about film's other benefits. Therefore, there is no repetition or redundancy here.

26. **Choice D is the best answer.** The "stage" being referred to is time during which the report about Indian film was written i.e., the 1960s. The sentence seeks to make the point that despite this early stage in the development of film technology, over 25 million people went to watch films in India. "Even" is the only answer choice that captures this meaning.
All the remaining choices would make the sentence grammatically inaccurate and/or meaningless.

27. **Choice D is the best answer.** In this sentence, "In a 2005 paper by Noah Uhrig" is an introductory phrase that is necessary to help the reader understand the following information. Therefore, this dependent clause needs to be followed by a comma.
Choice A is inaccurate since the complete lack of punctuation in this sentence makes the ideas harder for the reader to follow.

Choice B is incorrect. A dash would be grammatically inappropriate in this context since this punctuation is usually utilized in order to provide special emphasis to the following idea. Here, there is no need for such a special emphasis.

Choice C is incorrect since a colon is used to introduce a list and/or a quotation. In the highlighted location, a colon would be completely misplaced.

28. **Choice C is the best answer.** Notice that sentences (1) and (2) describe a quotation by Noah Uhrig. The paragraph following this one moves on to a different topic (mental health) and the content of this sentence (3) is therefore not necessary at its current location for purposes of transition. Since this paragraph currently does not have a topic sentence, therefore, sentence (3) would probably be best placed before sentence (1), to introduce the findings of Noah Uhrig.

29. **Choice A is the best answer.** The underlined text functions as an effective topic sentence that frames the following content for the reader. The sentence tells us, explicitly, that the following text will focus on the subject of mental health in relation to attending cinema.

    Choice B is incorrect. There is no "extensive information" about mental health that is provided in this sentence.

    Choice C is incorrect. The sentence is closely related to the main topic of the paragraph.

    Choice D is incorrect. The next paragraph goes on to speak about a different topic, i.e., the collective nature of the film viewing experience. Therefore, this sentence would not be more relevant in that paragraph.

30. **Choice C is the best answer.** The suggested revision would indeed help the reader better understand what the author means by the term "safe environment."

    Choice A is incorrect. The sentence provides new information vis-à-vis the ways in which cinema can function as a "safe environment." To say that it clarifies previous information would therefore be inaccurate.

    Choice B is incorrect. While this sentence is not necessarily the most effective transition to the following paragraph, it cannot be eliminated simply for this reason — since there is useful information/clarification that would be provided by the revised text.

    Choice D is incorrect. Relevant information is provided in this revised text; it is not eliminated.

31. **Choice B is the best answer.** The subject being referred to in this sentence is "the collective nature" of film (as a singular entity) and verb-tense consistency with the following text requires the use of the present tense (see "is unique in the following sentence). "Makes" is the only one of the provided choices that addresses both these requirements.

32. **Choice A is the best answer.** When there are three or more items in a list, they are separated by commas. Here, the three items in the list are "personally expressive experience," "good fun," and "therapeutic." Given the nature of this list, a comma would be the only grammatically accurate punctuation mark to use after the word "fun."

33. **Choice D is the best answer.** Since the people who never attended cinema are referred to as "those," it would be entirely appropriate to refer to the people who "visit the cinema occasionally" also with the same term. "Them" and "they" — Choices A and B — would be grammatically inaccurate.

    "Those people"— as in Choice C — is not necessary since it has already been established that "those" refers to people.

34. **Choice A is the best answer.** "Deeply entwined" is an idiomatic expression that refers to two things (people, ideas, concepts) being closely connected/interrelated to each other.

    Given that this is a particular turn of phrase, rather than a grammatical condition that can be explained, none of the other answer choices would be accurate.

35. **Choice C is the best answer.** "Since lighting allows them to do more at night" is a dependent clause that helps contextualize the preceding information i.e., why freeing up time for women and giving them flexibility in sequencing tasks is important. Given that the information following "tasks" directly relates to it, a comma is the best choice for punctuation.

    Choice A is incorrect. Semicolons can only be used between two independent clauses.

    Choice B is incorrect. Colons are used to introduce a list or a quotation, neither of which are present in the given sentence.

Choice D is incorrect. Not using a punctuation mark would make the sentence hard to follow.

36. **Choice D is the best answer.** The last line in this paragraph provides an additional reason for the important links between energy access and gender. "Furthermore," by referring to such an addition without adding any other implication, is the best choice.

    Choices A and C are incorrect for the same reason. The terms "However" and "Although" refer to a relationship that includes a contrast of some kind. Since there is no contrast that is mentioned/implied in the subsequent text, these two options are unsuitable.

    Choice B is incorrect. It is not a good choice to begin a sentence with a conjunction like "and."

37. **Choice C is the best answer.** By using "these," this choice clarifies that it is the opportunities being mentioned in the previous sentence that are being addressed here (rather than other opportunities). Furthermore, restating the word "opportunities" helps the reader better understand the subject is being referred to in the highlighted text, since there are many ideas that are included in the previous sentence.

    Choices A, B and D are incorrect because "opportunities," "them," and "these" are ambiguous terms that do not as effectively clarify the subject that is being referred to.

38. **Choice B is the best answer.** This suggested addition provides a specific example that helps explain how one organization has tried to involve women in the "renewable energy chain."

    Choice A is incorrect. There is no "transition —" link between ideas — that would be afforded by the addition of this sentence.

    Choice C is incorrect since the information provided by this addition has not been mentioned anywhere else.

    Choice D is incorrect. This information does not contradict anything that has been presented earlier.

39. **Choice A is the best answer.** The text that follows the underlined section explains a consequence of women becoming "engaged in delivering energy solutions" and taking on "more active roles in their communities." Therefore, "consequently" is an appropriate word choice.

    Choice B is incorrect. Although "by doing this" is not grammatically incorrect, it is less suitable for a couple of reasons. First, this choice takes more words than needed to make the same point as "consequently." Second, the use of a comma after "this" requires that there be a comma before "by."

    Choices C and D are incorrect. "Despite" and "regardless" refer to conditions that have been overcome in order for something else to happen. Since this is not the context in this case, neither of these answer choices would be appropriate.

40. **Choice D is the best answer.** The text that begins with "followed by" is a dependent clause that directly relates — and furthers — information that comes before it. A comma would be an accurate choice to capture this particular flow of ideas.

    Choice A is incorrect since a semicolon would require that there are two independent clauses that need to be separated.

    Choice B is incorrect. Given that there is no list or quotation that would follow the use of a colon, this punctuation mark would be grammatically inaccurate.

    Choice C is incorrect. Since one part of the sentence is a dependent clause, separating the text into two different sentences would be grammatically inaccurate

41. **Choice B is the best answer.** By using the term "other" and reiterating "to participation," this sentence is the most effective choice for the clarity of the sentence. Since the "most common barrier" is mentioned much before "security and the remoteness of field locations" are mentioned, the reader benefits from the added clarity that the articulation in this answer choice affords.

    Choice A is less suitable since "as barriers" is not as clear as the text in Choice B.

    Choice C is incorrect. Deleting the underlined section would not allow the reader to have any context with which to understand "security and the remoteness of field locations."

    Choice D is incorrect for the same reasons as above. "Too" is ambiguous and does not allow the reader to effectively understand the ideas that are being presented here.

42. **Choice C is the best answer.** The text that follows the underlined conjunctive adverb presents an interesting observation from the data, that does not extend/contrast with a previously mentioned idea. Therefore, "interestingly," is the best possible answer.

    Choices like "through this," "however," and "despite this" create a causal connection between the stated ideas — a connection that does not exist.

43. **Choice A is the only possible answer.**

    Reading the notes below the graph, we see that respondents were asked to select "three key measure to improve women's engagement." To qualify any one of the stated options as the "best," therefore, would require making assumptions from the data that simply shows us which answer most respondents chose more often than others.

    What we are provided with in the graph is a range of measures, as suggested by a small group of respondents. This is not a definitive list of how "women's engagement can be <u>best improved.</u>"

44. **Choice B is the best answer.** The underlined section connects the idea of "training" that is mentioned in the first sentence, with that of adapting training sessions based on women's needs in the following sentence. Therefore, since it helps link preceding and following ideas, the underlined text can certainly be considered an effective transition.

    Choice A is incorrect. Since the paragraph goes on to talk about how training sessions "must be tailored and scheduled," there would be no need to talk about "greater efforts" as a concluding line to the paragraph.

    Choice C is incorrect. There is no interruption to the flow of the paragraph with the underlined section remaining where it is.

    Choice D is incorrect. The information is clearly related to the content of both the paragraph and the passage.

CONTINUE

1. **Easy | Passport to Advanced Math**

   Choice A is correct. To solve for y, combine like terms on both sides of the equation; $5y+7y+15y+42y=3y+14y+z \Rightarrow 69y=17y+z$. Move all y terms to one side and z terms to the other side of the equal sign; $69y=17y+z \Rightarrow 52y=z$. Divide both sides by 52; $52y=z \Rightarrow y=\dfrac{z}{52}$. Choices B, C, and D are incorrect and are likely the result of arithmetic errors.

2. **Easy | Heart of Algebra**

   Choice C is correct. Direct variation is represented by an equation in the form of y=kx where k is a constant. The graph shows that in one hour, Dallas rides 5 miles. If $k = 5$, therefore $y = kx$ and $y = 5x$. Choices A, B, and D are incorrect and are the result of errors in manipulating equations with multiple variables.

3. **Medium | Passport to Advanced Math**

   Choice A is correct. To solve for s, add c to both sides:

   $$b=\frac{f}{s}-c$$

   $$b+c=\frac{f}{s}.$$

   $$b+c=\frac{f}{s}$$

   $$s=\frac{f}{b+c}.$$

   Choices B, C, and D are incorrect and are the result of errors in rearranging equations with multiple variables.

4. **Medium | Additional Topics in Math**

   Choice C is correct. Lines I and III are perpendicular and perpendicular lines have opposite reciprocal slopes. Therefore, for line I, $m = 2$ and for line III, $m=-\dfrac{1}{2}$. Choices A, B, and D are incorrect and reflect errors in identifying relationships between parallel and perpendicular lines and slopes.

5. **Medium | Passport to Advanced Math**

   Choice B is correct. The formula to find the area rectangle multiply $length \times width$. Since $a = width$ and $b = length$, and b "is 3 meters shorter than twice the width" can be expresses to $2a-3$, then $A=a \times b=a \times (2a-3)=a(2a-3)$. Choices A, C, and D are incorrect and are the result of errors in calculating the area.

6. **Easy | Heart of Algebra**

   Choice D is correct. Subtracting 2 from both sides of the first inequality produces $x \leq -3$; the y-coordinates are irrelevant. Choices A, B, and C are incorrect and are likely the result of arithmetic errors.

7. **Medium | Heart of Algebra**

   Choice C is correct To solve for m, begin by squaring both sides of the equation to remove the square root:

   $$m+4=\sqrt{m+10}$$

$$(m+4)^2 = m+10$$

Then foil the left side:

$$(m+4)^2 = m^2 + 8m + 16$$

$$m^2 + 8m + 16 = m + 10$$

$$m^2 + 7m + 6 = 0.$$

$$(m+6)(m+1) = 0$$

Therefore, $m = -1, -6$. When -6 is substituted for m in the original equation, there is a negative number under the square root, so that is not a solution. Therefore, $m = -1$ is the only solution. (Note: $\varnothing$ means *no solution*). Choices A, B, and D are incorrect and are the result of arithmetic errors and incompletely solving the equation to eliminate the extraneous solution.

8. **Medium | Passport to Advanced Math**

   Choice A is correct. Place $g(x)$ in the numerator and $f(x)$ in the denominator. Factor both numerator and denominator, then cancel any like terms. Finally, multiply the numerator to get the solution:

   $$\frac{x^3 + 18x^2 + 108x + 216}{x^2 + 36}$$

   $$\frac{(x+6)(x+6)(x+6)}{(x+6)(x-6)}$$

   $$\frac{(x+6)(x+6)}{x-6}$$

   $$\frac{x^2 + 12x + 36}{x-6}.$$

   Choices B, C, and D are incorrect and reflect errors in simplifying complex functions.

9. **Medium | Additional Topics in Math**

   Choice D is correct. The equation of a circle is $(x-h)^2 + (y-k)^2 = r^2$, with the center at (h, k) and r being radius. Therefore, the center of the circle for $(x-2)^2 + (y+1)^2 = 16$ is (2, -1) and the radius is 4. Subtracting 4 from the x coordinate gives us the point (2, –5) which would be the minimum y value. Since the answer choice gives a y coordinate of –6, This point is outside of the circle and cannot be point N since Point N is on the circle. Choices A, B, and C are incorrect and reflect errors in solving equations of circles.

10. **Medium | Heart of Algebra**

    Choice D is correct. Let x represent the number of 4 person suites and let y represent the number of 4 person suites 6 person suites. Set up a system of equations where $x + y = 20$ (number of rooms) and $4x + 6y = 100$ (number of people). Solve for x in the first equation; $x + y = 20, x = 20 - y$. Substitute the value for x into the second equation; $4(20-y) + 6y = 80 - 4y + 6y = 80 + 2y = 100$. Therefore, $80 + 2y = 100, 2y = 20; y = 10$. Since $y = 10$, solve for x by substituting the value for y into one of the equations:

    $$x + y = 20, x + 10 = 20, x = 10$$

    The difference between the x and y is 10 – 10 = 0 Choices A, B, and C are incorrect and reflect errors in solving systems of equations.

11. **Medium | Passport to Advanced Math**

    Choice A is correct. The function $y = x^2(x-3)^2 - 1$ has a vertical shift down 1 from the graph meeting the x-axis at the points $(0,0)$ and $(0,3)$, resulting in the equation $(x-0)^2(x-3)^2 - 1$. Choices B, C, and D are incorrect and reflect errors in interpreting functions on graphs.

12. **Easy | Passport to Advanced Math**

    Choice B is correct. Cross multiply and divide:

    $4c \times 4 = d$

    $16c = d$

    $\dfrac{d}{c} = 16.$

    Choices A, C, and D are incorrect and reflect errors in simplification.

13. **Medium | Heart of Algebra**

    Choice D is correct. The function can be written in the form of $f(x) = mx + b$ where m is the slope and b is the y-intercept. There are 5 million units in 2013; this is the y intercept. There was a .6 million unit increase over 5 years which indicates a slope of $\dfrac{0.6}{5} = \dfrac{3}{25}$. Therefore, the function is $f(x) = \dfrac{3}{25}x + 5$. Choices A, B, and C are incorrect and are the result of errors in writing linear functions.

14. **Medium | Passport to Advanced Math**

    Choice D is correct. By solving for y in the top equation, one finds that $y = x^3 + 4$. Substituting y into the second equation; $(x^3 + 4)(x-4) = x^2 + 16$. Simplify:

    $x^4 - 4x^3 - 4x - 16 = x^2 + 16$

    $x^4 - 4x^3 - x^2 - 4x - 32 = 0$

    Therefore, since the fundamental theorem of algebra states that there are equal number of solutions as the degree of any polynomial, there are 4 solutions.

15. **Easy | Heart of Algebra**

    The correct answer is D. Combining the two equations and simplifying yields

    $q(n) = 2 - p(n) = 2 - (2n-2) = 4 - 2n$

    $q(2) = 4 - 2(2) = 4 - 4 = 0.$

    Choices A, B, and C are incorrect and reflect errors in simplification.

16. **Difficult | Passport to Advanced Math**

    The correct answer is 9. The function $x^2 + x - 90$ can be factored:

    $(x+10)(x-9) = 0$

    $x = \{-10, 9\}$

Therefore, $c = 9$.

17. **Medium | Passport to Advanced Math**

    The correct answer is 160. Subtract the two equations and simplify:

    $$-7x^2 + 4x - 12 - \left(3x^2 + 16x + 4\right)$$

    $$-7x^2 + 4x - 12 + \left(-3x^2\right) + \left(-16x\right) + \left(-4\right)$$

    $$-10x^2 - 12x - 16$$

    Therefore, $a = -10, b = -12, c = -16$. The product of a, b is $-10 \cdot -16 = 160$.

18. **Easy | Heart of Algebra**

    The correct answer is 1. Solve for e in the second equation by adding f to both sides:

    $$e - f = 3$$

    $$e = 3 + f$$

    Substitute this value for e into the first equation and solve for f:

    $$4e + f = 2$$

    $$4\left(3 + f\right) + f = 12 + 5f = 2$$

    $$12 + 5f = 2$$

    $$5f = -10$$

    $$f = -2$$

    It follows that $e - \left(-2\right) = e + 2 = 3; e = 1$. You may also solve using elimination. Start by combining the two equations, which will leave the variable e and eliminate f.

    $$e - f = 3$$

    $$4e + f = 2$$

    $$5e = 5 \Rightarrow e = 1$$

19. **Difficult | Heart of Algebra**

    The correct answer is 8. Since the equation is written in the form of $y = mx + b$, where m represents the change of rows of corn in x years after he planted his first 8 rows, these 8 rows at the start represent b. Therefore, $b = 8$.

20. **Difficult | Additional Topics in Math**

    The correct answer is 90. Start by finding the degrees of the major and minor arcs:

    $$\text{Minor Arc } BC: \quad \frac{3}{8} = \frac{x}{360}; x = 135°$$

    $$\text{Major Arc } BC: \quad 360° - 135° = 225°$$

    $$\text{Major Arc } BC - \text{Minor Arc } BC = 225° - 135° = 90°$$

1. **Easy | Heart of Algebra**

   Choice B is correct. If 2 pounds of grapes cost \$3.96, then one pound is $\dfrac{\$3.96}{2}$. Multiplying $\dfrac{\$3.96}{2} \times g$ results in

   the cost of g pounds of grapes. Choices A, C, and D are incorrect and are the result of arithmetic errors.

2. **Easy | Problem Solving and Data Analysis**

   Choice A is correct. Between weeks 1 and 2, there was the steepest increase. There is an increase of over 12 baseball cards. Choices B, C, and D are incorrect and are the result of incorrectly interpreting the data in the graph.

3. **Easy | Problem Solving and Data Analysis**

   Choice A is correct. Set up a proportion; $\dfrac{\textit{defective sample widgets}}{\textit{total sample widgets}} = \dfrac{\textit{defective widgets}}{\textit{total widgets}} \Rightarrow \dfrac{4}{300} = \dfrac{x}{12,000}$. Cross

   multiply then divide both sides by 300 to solve for x:

   $300x = 4(12,000)$

   $300x = 48,000$

   $x = 160$.

   Choices B, C, and D are incorrect and are the result of arithmetic errors.

4. **Medium | Problem Solving and Data Analysis**

   Choice B is correct. Substitute 166 for x in the equation:

   $y = 0.85x + 25.68$

   $y = 0.85(166) + 25.68 = 166.78$.

   Choices A, C, and D are incorrect and reflect errors in simplification.

5. **Medium | Additional Topics in Math**

   Choice B is correct. If angle $\angle c = 35°$ and $\angle d = 55°$ then $\angle e$ is $180° - 90° = 90°$. Since $\angle e$ is a right angle and $\angle d = 55°$ the remaining angle is $180° - (90 + 55)° = 35°$. Since all of the angles are different values, this is a scalene right triangle. Choices A, C, and D are incorrect and are the result of errors in finding supplementary and complementary angles within triangles.

6. **Medium | Passport to Advanced Math**

   Choice D is correct. Use exponent rules to raising a power to a power and factor $(m-n)(m+n) = m^2 - n^2$. It follows that $(2^{m-n})^{m+n} = 2^{m^2-n^2} = 128$. Because $2^7 = 128$, $2^7 = 2^{m^2-n^2} = 128$. Since $n^2 = 9$, substitute 9 for n^2 is the equation and solve for m:

   $2^7 = 2^{m^2-n^2}$

   $2^7 = 2^{m^2-9}$

   $7 = m^2 - 9$

   $m^2 = 16$

   $m = \pm 4$.

The question states that $m < 0$ therefore $m = -4$. Choices A, B, and C are incorrect and reflect errors in using exponent rules.

7. **Medium | Heart of Algebra**

   Choice D is correct. The equations $A + C + S = 1310$ and $5.75A + 9.75C + 6.50S = 9732.50$ represent the sum of tickets sold (1310) and the total sum of the product of number of tickets sold and cost per ticket ($9732.50). Choices A, B, and C are incorrect and are the result of incorrectly writing a system of equations from the given situation.

8. **Medium | Heart of Algebra**

   Choice C is correct. Slope-intercept form of a linear equation is written as $y = mx + b$ where m is the slope and b is the y intercept. The slope is -4, so m is -4. Choices A, B, and D are incorrect and reflect errors in identifying the slope in a linear function.

9. **Medium | Passport to Advanced Math**

   Choice A is correct. The equation $a + 3 = \dfrac{1}{a+3}$ can be solved by multiplying both sides by $a + 3$ and solving:

   $(a+3)^2 = 1$

   $\sqrt{(a+3)^2} = \sqrt{1}$

   $a + 3 = \sqrt{1} = 1$

   Choices B, C, and D are incorrect and are the result of arithmetic errors.

10. **Difficult | Passport to Advanced Math**

    Choice C is correct. Simplify the expression by factoring and simplifying like terms:

    $\dfrac{2b^2 + 30b + 52}{b^2 - 169}$

    $\dfrac{2\left(b^2 + 15b + 26\right)}{\left(b+13\right)\left(b-13\right)}$

    $\dfrac{2\left(b+13\right)\left(b+2\right)}{\left(b+13\right)\left(b-13\right)}$

    $\dfrac{2\left(b+2\right)}{b-13}.$

    Because a denominator equal to zero is undefined, set the denominator to zero and solve for b to determine the value where the expression is undefined; $b - 13 = 0$, so $b = 13$. Choices A, B, and D are incorrect and are the result of arithmetic errors in setting the denominator equal to zero.

11. **Easy | Additional Topics in Math**

    Choice B is correct. Convert yards to feet by multiplying by 3; $l = 6.25\,yds \times 3 = 18.75\,ft, w = 4.37\,yds \times 3 = 13.11\,ft$. Find the area using the formula $A = lw = 18.75 \times 13.11 = 245.81\,ft^2$. Find the cost by multiplying the area by the cost per square foot, $245.81\,ft^2 \times \$9.75 = \$2396.67$. Choices A, C, and D are incorrect and are likely the result of arithmetic errors in manipulating units.

12. **Easy | Problem Solving and Data Analysis**

Choice B is correct. Create a proportion and solve:

$$\frac{Males\,with\,Smart\,Phones}{Total\,Males} = \frac{153}{200} = 76.5\%.$$

Choices A, C, and D are incorrect and are the result of incorrect proportions.

13. **Easy | Problem Solving and Data Analysis**

Choice C is correct. Create a proportion and solve:

$$\frac{Students\,with\,No\,Smart\,Phone}{Total\,Students} = \frac{67}{400} = 16.75\%.$$

Choices A, B, and D are incorrect and are the result of incorrect proportions.

14. **Medium | Problem Solving and Data Analysis**

Choice D is correct. The correct answer represents the simplified ratio of females students with smart phones out of the 200 female students. Choices A, B, and C are incorrect and are the result of incorrect proportions.

15. **Easy | Problem Solving and Data Analysis**

Choice B is correct. There were 200 males and 200 females surveyed, which, in total, is 400. Choices A, C, and D are incorrect and are the result of incorrectly interpreting the data in the table.

16. **Difficult | Problem Solving and Data Analysis**

Choice D is correct. Although the frequency table reveals where the median of the data set lies and one can estimate the mean, the mode cannot be determined based on a frequency chart. Choices A, B, and C are incorrect and are the result of errors in interpreting frequency charts.

17. **Difficult | Problem Solving and Data Analysis**

Choice C is correct. Between 61-70 Points; The average of the 17th and 18th data points will give the median. The 17th and 18th points lie in the interval 61-70. Choices A, B, and D are incorrect and are the result of errors in interpreting frequency charts.

18. **Medium | Problem Solving and Data Analysis**

Choice B is correct. There are 25 out of 34 scores between 0 and 70. Set up a proportion and solve:

$$\frac{25}{34} = 73.5\%.$$

Choices A, C, and D are incorrect and are the result of errors in interpreting frequency charts.

19. **Easy | Problem Solving and Data Analysis**

Choice B is correct. Find the sum of the frequencies to get the total number of students that took the test:

$$3 + 6 + 7 + 9 + 3 + 4 + 2 = 34.$$

Choices A, C, and D are incorrect and are the result of errors in interpreting frequency charts.

20. **Medium | Problem Solving and Data Analysis**

    Choice C is correct. Identify $97°\,F$ on the x-axis. Then identify the intersection on the line of best fit at $y = 75$. Choices A, B, and D are incorrect and are the result of errors in interpreting lines of best fit.

21. **Difficult | Passport to Advanced Math**

    Choice B is correct. Expand $(x+5)(x-2)$ to $x^2 + 3x - 10$. Choice B is the only option with zeros of $x = 0$ and $x = -3$. Choices A, C, and D are incorrect and are the result of errors in factoring polynomials to find solutions.

22. **Medium | Passport to Advanced Math**

    Choice D is correct. Using exponent rules for multiplication with the same base, find that $2^x \cdot 2^y = 2^{x+y} = 1024$. Therefore, $2^{10} = 1024$, $2^{x+y} = 1024 = 2^{10}$ and $x + y = 10$. Choices A, B, and C are incorrect and are the result of errors in manipulating exponents.

23. **Difficult | Problem Solving and Data Analysis**

    Choice A is correct. If 15 marbles are picked from the bag, they could be only orange and purple. On the 16th pick, there must be one of every color, for only other colors are left in the bag after the 15th pick. Choices B, C, and D are incorrect and are the result of errors in interpreting probabilities.

24. **Easy | Heart of Algebra**

    Choice C is correct. The midpoint of $\overline{AB}$ is $\left(\dfrac{6+0}{2}, \dfrac{4+(-8)}{2}\right) = (3, -2)$. One can substitute the midpoint into the

    equation:

    $-2 = 3 - 5$

    Therefore, the midpoint lies on the line $y = x - 5$. Choices A, B, and D are incorrect and are the result of errors in interpreting interpreting midpoint or in substituting points into equations.

25. **Medium | Additional Topics in Math**

    Choice C is correct.

    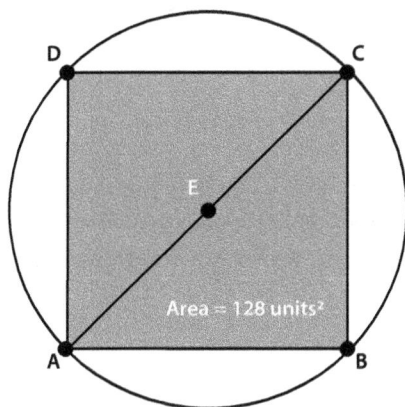

    The area of the square is $128\,units^2$ and the formula for the area of a square is $A = s^2$ where s is equal to the side length of the square. Therefore, $s = \sqrt{128}$. The diagonal of the square is equal to the side length times the square root of 2, so the diameter of the circle is $\sqrt{128} \times \sqrt{2} = \sqrt{256} = 16$. Use the formula for circumference $C = \pi \times d = 16\pi$. Choices A, B, and D are incorrect and are the result of errors in calculating the area of a square or the circumference of a circle.

26. **Difficult | Heart of Algebra**

    Choice D is correct. Let a be the number of bleachers 10 fans can sit in, and b be the number of bleachers 20 fans can sit in. There are 40 bleachers in the arena, so $a + b = 40$. $10a$ represents the number of fans sitting in 10 person bleachers, and $20b$ represents the number of fans sitting in 20 person bleachers. Since the arena can seat 600 fans, $10a + 20b = 600$. Solve the system by solving for a in the first equation, $a + b = 40, a = 40 - b$. Substitute the expression for a in terms of b, into the first equation to solve for b:

    $$10a + 20b = 600$$

    $$10(40 - b) + 20b = 600$$

    $$400 - 10b + 20b = 600$$

    $$10b = 200, b = 20$$

    Substitute the value for b into either equation and solve for a; $a + b = 40, a + 20 = 40, a = 20$. There are 20 bleachers that sit 20 fans each and there are 20 bleachers that seat 20 fans each. It follows that the ratio is 20 to 20 which is 1 to 1. Choices A, B, and C are incorrect and are the result of arithmetic errors in solving systems of equations.

27. **Medium | Additional Topics in Math**

    Choice D is correct. Using the Unit Circle or the Calculator (in radians), $sin\dfrac{\pi}{3} = \dfrac{\sqrt{3}}{2}$. Since $sin\dfrac{4\pi}{3} = \dfrac{-\sqrt{3}}{2}$ then $sin\dfrac{4\pi}{3} \neq sin\dfrac{\pi}{3}$. Choices A, B, and C are incorrect and are the result of errors in interpreting Trig Identities.

28. **Medium | Problem Solving and Data Analysis**

    Choice A is correct. Because it takes the hose x hours to drain the pool, it will drain $\dfrac{1}{x}$ part each hour. In 4 hours it will drain $4\left(\dfrac{1}{x}\right) = \dfrac{4}{x}$. Choices B, C, and D are incorrect and are the result of errors in interpreting algebraic rates.

29. **Easy | Passport to Advanced Math**

    Choice A is correct. Ron is adding planes to his collection, resulting in an increase. Since his collection does not increase at a constant rate each year, this is considered an exponential increase. Choices B, C, and D are incorrect and are the result of errors in interpreting functions.

30. **Easy | Problem Solving and Data Analysis**

    Choice A is correct. The regression equation is written in the form of $y = mx + b$ where m is the slope and b is the y-intercept. In the regression equation $y = -3725x + 7,596,500$ the slope (-3725) is negative which indicates that as the years increase, the number of driver's licenses decrease. Choices B, C, and D are incorrect and are the result of interpreting linear functions.

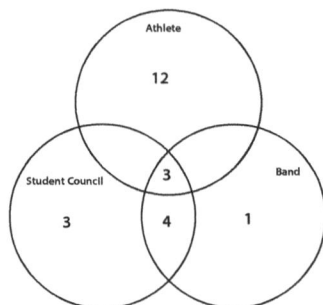

31. **Difficult | Problem Solving and Data Analysis**

    The correct answer is 7. The total number of students was 30 and 23 are represented on the Venn Diagram therefore 30 – 23 = 7 is the number of students that are neither an athlete, band or student council member.

32. **Medium | Additional Topics in Math**

    The correct answer is 42. Simplify:

    $$63 + x + 75 + y = 180$$

    $$x + y + 138 = 180$$

    $$x + y = 42.$$

33. **Difficult | Additional Topics in Math**

    The correct answer is 76. First we find $\angle M$ & $\angle K$. Since ΔKLM is an isosceles triangle with $\angle K$ & $\angle M$ congruent, $180 - 110 = 70 \Rightarrow 70 \div 2 = 35$: $\angle K$ & $\angle M$ are both $35°$. To find $\angle O$ find the sum of $\angle M$ and $\angle N$ and subtract the sum from $180; 180 - (41 + 35) = 104°$. $\angle x$ is the supplement of $\angle O$; $180 - 104 = 76°$.

34. **Difficult | Problem Solving and Data Analysis**

    The correct answer is 84. To find the weighted average, multiply the number of team members by their shot percentage then divide by the total number of team members. $15 \times 0.80 = 12$ & $10 \times 0.90 = 9, 12 + 9 = 21, 21 \div 25 = 84\%$.

35. **Easy | Heart of Algebra**

    The correct answer is 8. Simplify:

    $$2 - \frac{1}{4}c = 0$$

    $$-\frac{1}{4}c = -2$$

    $$c = 8.$$

36. **Difficult | Problem Solving and Data Analysis**

    The correct answer is 9.26. Find the LCM and use as distance; $LCM(8,11) = 88$. Julie biked 88 miles up hill at 8 miles an hour; this would take 11 hours. Julie biked 88 miles downhill at 11 miles an hour; this would take 8 hours. 88 miles uphill + 88 miles downhill = 176 miles total. 11 hours+8 hours =19 hours total. The average biking speed is $Speed = \dfrac{distance}{time} = \dfrac{176\,miles}{19\,hours} \approx 9.26\,miles\,per\,hour$.

37. **Difficult | Problem Solving and Data Analysis**

    The correct answer is 7.5. First find the work rate for Amanda and Danielle; Amanda = $\dfrac{t}{4.75}$, Danielle = $\dfrac{t}{5.25}$.

    It follows that $\dfrac{t}{4.75} + \dfrac{t}{5.25} = 1 \Rightarrow \dfrac{4t}{19} + \dfrac{4t}{21} = 1 \Rightarrow 399\left(\dfrac{4t}{19} + \dfrac{4t}{21} = 1\right) \Rightarrow 84t + 76t = 160t = 399; t = \dfrac{399}{160}$. It takes

    Amanda and Danielle $\dfrac{399}{160} \approx 2.49$ hours to bake one cake together. To bake 3 cakes, it takes $3\left(\dfrac{399}{160}\right) = \dfrac{1197}{160} = 7.48$ hours, which rounds to 7.5.

38. **Difficult | Heart of Algebra**

The correct answer is 3.5 hours. Let x be the length of time train 2 travels, so $x+1$ is the time train 1 travels. Create equations and simplify:

$$70(x+1)=90x$$

$$70x+70=90x$$

$$70=20x$$

$$\frac{70}{20}=3.5.$$

Train 2 will catch train 1 in 3.5 hours.

SAT Practice
Test #4

It is recommended that you use a No. 2 pencil. It is very important that you fill in the entire circle darkly and completely. If you change your response, erase as completely as possible. Incomplete marks or erasures may affect your score.

	A B C D		A B C D		A B C D		A B C D
1	○○○○	14	○○○○	27	○○○○	40	○○○○
2	○○○○	15	○○○○	28	○○○○	41	○○○○
3	○○○○	16	○○○○	29	○○○○	42	○○○○
4	○○○○	17	○○○○	30	○○○○	43	○○○○
5	○○○○	18	○○○○	31	○○○○	44	○○○○
6	○○○○	19	○○○○	32	○○○○	45	○○○○
7	○○○○	20	○○○○	33	○○○○	46	○○○○
8	○○○○	21	○○○○	34	○○○○	47	○○○○
9	○○○○	22	○○○○	35	○○○○	48	○○○○
10	○○○○	23	○○○○	36	○○○○	49	○○○○
11	○○○○	24	○○○○	37	○○○○	50	○○○○
12	○○○○	25	○○○○	38	○○○○	51	○○○○
13	○○○○	26	○○○○	39	○○○○	52	○○○○

It is recommended that you use a No. 2 pencil. It is very important that you fill in the entire circle darkly and completely. If you change your response, erase as completely as possible. Incomplete marks or erasures may affect your score.

	A B C D		A B C D		A B C D		A B C D		A B C D
1	○○○○	10	○○○○	19	○○○○	28	○○○○	37	○○○○
2	○○○○	11	○○○○	20	○○○○	29	○○○○	38	○○○○
3	○○○○	12	○○○○	21	○○○○	30	○○○○	39	○○○○
4	○○○○	13	○○○○	22	○○○○	31	○○○○	40	○○○○
5	○○○○	14	○○○○	23	○○○○	32	○○○○	41	○○○○
6	○○○○	15	○○○○	24	○○○○	33	○○○○	42	○○○○
7	○○○○	16	○○○○	25	○○○○	34	○○○○	43	○○○○
8	○○○○	17	○○○○	26	○○○○	35	○○○○	44	○○○○
9	○○○○	18	○○○○	27	○○○○	36	○○○○		

It is recommended that you use a No. 2 pencil. It is very important that you fill in the entire circle darkly and completely. If you change your response, erase as completely as possible. Incomplete marks or erasures may affect your score.

	A B C D		A B C D		A B C D		A B C D		A B C D
1	○○○○	4	○○○○	7	○○○○	10	○○○○	13	○○○○
2	○○○○	5	○○○○	8	○○○○	11	○○○○	14	○○○○
3	○○○○	6	○○○○	9	○○○○	12	○○○○	15	○○○○

Only answers that are gridded will be scored. You will not receive credit for anything written in the boxes.

16

17

18

19

20

CONTINUE ➤

It is recommended that you use a No. 2 pencil. It is very important that you fill in the entire circle darkly and completely. If you change your response, erase as completely as possible. Incomplete marks or erasures may affect your score.

	A B C D		A B C D		A B C D		A B C D		A B C D
1	○○○○	7	○○○○	13	○○○○	19	○○○○	25	○○○○
2	○○○○	8	○○○○	14	○○○○	20	○○○○	26	○○○○
3	○○○○	9	○○○○	15	○○○○	21	○○○○	27	○○○○
4	○○○○	10	○○○○	16	○○○○	22	○○○○	28	○○○○
5	○○○○	11	○○○○	17	○○○○	23	○○○○	29	○○○○
6	○○○○	12	○○○○	18	○○○○	24	○○○○	30	○○○○

CALCULATOR ALLOWED

CONTINUE

It is recommended that you use a No. 2 pencil. It is very important that you fill in the entire circle darkly and completely. If you change your response, erase as completely as possible. Incomplete marks or erasures may affect your score.

31 **32** **33** **34** **35**

Only answers that are gridded will be scored. You will not receive credit for anything written in the boxes.

36 **37** **38**

CALCULATOR
ALLOWED

Reading Test

65 MINUTES, 52 QUESTIONS

Turn to Section 1 of your answer sheet to answer the questions in this section

---

DIRECTIONS

Each passage or pair of passages below is followed by a number of questions. After reading each passage or pair, choose the best answer to each question based on what is stated or implied in the passage or passages and in any accompanying graphics (such as a table or graph).

Questions 1-10 are based on the following passage.

This passage is adapted from *White Nights and Other Stories* by Fyodor Dostoevsky, originally published in 1848.

I took long walks, succeeding, as I usually did, in quite forgetting where I was, when I suddenly found myself at the city gates. Instantly
Line I felt lighthearted, and I passed the barrier and
5 walked between cultivated fields and meadows, unconscious of fatigue, and feeling only all over as though a burden were falling off my soul. All the passers-by gave me such friendly looks that they seemed almost greeting me, they all seemed so
10 pleased at something. And I felt pleased as I never had before. It was as though I had suddenly found myself in Italy—so strong was the effect of nature upon a half-sick townsman like me, almost stifling between city walls.
15 And yet my night was better than my day! This was how it happened.

I came back to the town very late, and it had struck ten as I was going towards my lodgings. My way lay along the canal embankment, where
20 at that hour you never meet a soul. It is true that I live in a very remote part of the town. I walked along singing, for when I am happy I am always humming to myself like every happy man who has no friend or acquaintance with whom to share his
25 joy. Suddenly I had a most unexpected adventure. Leaning on the canal railing stood a woman with

her elbows on the rail, she was apparently looking with great attention at the muddy water of the canal. She was wearing a very charming yellow hat and a
30 jaunty little black mantle. "She's a girl, and I am sure she is dark," I thought. She did not seem to hear my footsteps, and did not even stir when I passed by with bated breath and loudly throbbing heart. "Strange," I thought; "she must be deeply absorbed
35 in something," and all at once I stopped as though petrified. I heard a muffled sob. Yes! I was not mistaken, the girl was crying, and a minute later I heard sob after sob. Good Heavens! My heart sank. And timid as I was with women, yet this was such
40 a moment!... I turned, took a step towards her, and should certainly have pronounced the word "Madam!" if I had not known that that exclamation has been uttered a thousand times in every Russian society novel. It was only that reflection stopped me.
45 But while I was seeking for a word, the girl came to herself, looked round, started, cast down her eyes and slipped by me along the embankment. I at once followed her; but she, divining this, left the embankment, crossed the road and walked along the
50 pavement. I dared not cross the street after her. My heart was fluttering like a captured bird. All at once a chance came to my aid.

Along the same side of the pavement there suddenly came into sight, not far from the girl,
55 a gentleman in evening dress, of dignified years, though by no means of dignified carriage; he was staggering and cautiously leaning against the wall. The girl flew straight as an arrow, with the timid

haste one sees in all girls who do not want any one
60 to volunteer to accompany them home at night.
Suddenly, without a word to any one, the gentleman
set off and flew full speed in pursuit of my unknown
lady. She was racing like the wind, but the staggering
gentleman was overtaking—overtook her. The
65 girl uttered a shriek, and... I bless my luck for the
excellent knotted stick, which happened on that
occasion to be in my right hand. In a flash I was on
the other side of the street; in a flash the obtrusive
gentleman had taken in the position, had fallen back
70 without a word, and only when we were very far
away protested against my action in rather vigorous
language.

"Give me your arm," I said to the girl. "And he
won't dare to annoy us further."

75 She took my arm without a word, still
trembling with excitement and terror. Oh, obtrusive
gentleman! How I blessed you at that moment! I
stole a glance at her, she was very charming and
dark—I had guessed right.

On her black eyelashes there still glistened a
80 tear—from her recent terror or her former grief—I
don't know. But there was already a gleam of a smile
on her lips. She too stole a glance at me, faintly
blushed and looked down.

1

Which choice best summarizes the passage?

A) A man recounts an incident from his
experiences.

B) A young woman is placed in an alarming
predicament.

C) Two characters are searching for change in
their lives.

D) An old man shares an anecdote about his
youth.

2

The passage indicates that the narrator takes a
walk because

A) he wants to spend time with new people.

B) he is displeased with his daily life.

C) he hopes to have an exciting adventure.

D) he is trying to forget a sad event.

3

Which choice provides the best evidence for the
answer to the previous question?

A) Lines 3-6 ("Instantly... fatigue")

B) Lines 7-10 ("All the... something")

C) Lines 11-14 ("It was... city walls")

D) Lines 25 ("Suddenly... adventure")

4

According to the passage, the narrator was
walking along the embankment late at night
because he

A) wanted to avoid meeting other people.

B) was escaping the pressures of the city.

C) was returning to his quarters.

D) sought more excitement in his life.

5

In the fourth paragraph, the words "charming" and "jaunty" primarily serve to

A) show that the girl's true age belied her outward appearance.

B) establish that the girl was not suitably clad for the weather.

C) identify the reason for the narrator's interest in the girl.

D) highlight a contrast between the girl's appearance and her actions.

6

The passage suggests that the narrator does not initially approach the woman because he

A) was afraid of insulting her by using an inappropriate title.

B) realized that she did not want to be disturbed.

C) felt that his conversation might be considered trite.

D) did not want to intrude on the girl's privacy

7

Which choice provides the best evidence that the stranger following the girl was probably a coward?

A) Lines 53-57 ("Along… the wall")

B) Lines 61-63 ("Suddenly… unknown lady")

C) Lines 67-69("In a flash… position")

D) Lines 70-72("only when… language")

8

The passage indicates that the narrator viewed the girl's encounter with the stranger as

A) providential, because it gave him an opportunity to interact with the girl.

B) abominable, because there was a perceptible change in the girl's response.

C) intrusive, because it interrupted his first attempt to talk with the girl.

D) foreboding, because the man may return to exact revenge.

9

As used in line 76, "obtrusive" most nearly means

A) obvious.

B) conspicuous.

C) deplorable.

D) inevitable.

10

The last paragraph mainly serves to

A) indicate that the girl feels more than just gratitude for her savior.

B) emphasize the acuteness of the narrator's perceptions.

C) highlight the girl's fear at the encounter with the undignified man.

D) offer the rationale for the narrator's daring intervention.

Questions 11-21 are based on the following passage.

This passage is adapted from a speech made by Mother Jones to coal miners picketing in Charlestown, West Virginia, on August 15, 1912. The miners were striking to gain better working conditions, but the situation had escalated to martial law.

This, my friends, is a day that will mark history in the long ages to come. What is it? It is an uprising of the oppressed against the master class.

Line
5 To me, I think, the proper thing to do is to read the purpose of our meeting here today - why these men have laid down their tools, why these men have come to the statehouse. The guards of the mining companies beat, abuse, maim, and hold up citizens without process of law; deny freedom of speech, a
10 provision guaranteed by the Constitution; deny the citizens the right to assemble in a peaceable manner for the purpose of discussing questions in which they are concerned. Said guards also hold up a vast body of laboring men who live at the mines, and
15 so conduct themselves that a great number of men, women, and children live in a state of constant fear, unrest, and dread. We hold that the stationing of said guards along the public highways and public places is a menace to the general welfare of the State.
20 That such action on the part of the companies in maintaining such guards is detrimental to the best interests of society and an outrage against the honor and dignity of the State of West Virginia.

They wouldn't keep their dog where they keep
25 you fellows. You know that. They have a good place for their dogs and a slave to take care of them. The mine owners' wives will take the dogs up, and say, "I love you, dea-h." My friends, the day for petting dogs is gone; the day for raising children to a nobler
30 manhood and better womanhood is here! You have suffered; I know you have suffered. I was with you nearly three years in this State. I went to jail. I went to the Federal courts, but I never took any back water!

35 Now, brothers, not in all the history of the labor movement have I got such an inspiration as I have got from you here to-day. Your banners are history; they will go down to the future ages, to the children unborn, to tell them the slave has risen, children
40 must be free.

I hope, my friends, that you and the mine owners will put aside the breach and get together before I leave the State. But I want to say, make no settlement until they sign up that every bloody murderer of
45 a guard has got to go. This is done, my friends, beneath the flag our fathers fought and bled for, and we don't intend to surrender our liberty.

I want to show you here that the average wages you fellows get in this country is $500 a year. Before
50 you get a thing to eat there is $20 taken out a month, which leaves about $24 a month. Then you go to the "pluck-me" stores** and want to get something to eat for your wife, and the child comes back and says, "Papa, I can't get anything."

55 "Why," he says, "there is $24 coming to me?"

The child says, "they said there was nothing coming to you." And the child goes back crying without a mouthful of anything to eat. The father goes to the "pluck-me" store and says to the
60 manager, "there is $24 coming to me," and the manager says, "Oh, no, we have kept $26 for rent."

That is honesty? Do you wonder these women starve? Do you wonder at this uprising? And you fellows have stood it entirely too long! It is time now
65 to put a stop to it! We will give the Governor until to-morrow night to take them guards out of Cabin Creek.

Here on the steps of the Capitol of West Virginia...I want to tell you that the Governor will
70 get until tomorrow night, Friday night, to get rid of his bloodhounds, and if they are not gone, we will get rid of them! It is freedom or death, and your children will be free. We are not going to leave a slave class to the coming generation, and I want to
75 say to you that the next generation will not charge us for what we've done; they will charge and condemn us for what we have left undone.

** A "pluck-me" store is a slang term for a store with extremely inflated prices operated by
80 the mining company and where the miners are supposed to buy all their goods.

11

The main purpose of the passage is to

A) describe the working conditions suffered by miners.

B) encourage miners to avoid making compromises.

C) convince the government to change conditions of miners.

D) initiate negotiations with the owners of mines.

12

The main purpose of the discussion of the mine owners' pet dogs is to

A) offer one point of consolation for the mine workers.

B) point out one of the adversaries faced by the miners.

C) illustrate that some mine owners can be compassionate.

D) emphasize the sordid conditions of the mine workers.

13

As used in line 10, "provision" most nearly means

A) allocation.

B) arrangement.

C) contingency.

D) requirement.

14

Over the course of the passage, Mother Jones anticipates and addresses which counterargument about her credibility?

A) She is not qualified to speak for the miners because she is not a miner herself.

B) Her involvement could harm the miners' cause because she had been in jail.

C) She does not have adequate contacts in the government to enforce her demands.

D) She does not have a sufficient proxy to continue her crusade after she leaves the state.

15

According to the passage, the wages of the mine workers are

A) lower than the income of mine workers around the country.

B) periodically being reduced without explanation.

C) not consistent with the minimum wages of other jobs.

D) insufficient because of the policies of the mine owners.

16

Which choice best supports the claim that Mother Jones will not remain with the miners to the conclusion of their negotiations with the mine owners?

A) Lines 31-32 ("I was… to jail")

B) Lines 41-43 ("I hope… the State")

C) Lines 62-64 ("Do you… too long")

D) Lines 68-71 ("Here on… bloodhounds")

17

The main effect of the phrase "bloody murderer" in line 44 is to

A) describe the tactics used by certain guards.

B) offer the reason that guards must be removed.

C) suggest that guards overreached the orders of the mine owners.

D) emphasize the inhumanity exhibited by the guards.

18

The passage most strongly suggests that Mother Jones believes that

A) the working conditions will not significantly change in the immediate future.

B) one of the primary impediments to progress is the presence of armed guards.

C) the mine owners are not truly aware of the abysmal conditions of the workers.

D) the miners are not interested enough in protecting their own interests.

19

Which choice provides the best evidence for the answer to the previous question?

A) Lines 7-9 ("The guards… of law")

B) Lines 13-17 ("Said guards… and dread")

C) Lines 51-54 ("Then you… anything")

D) Lines 65-72 ("We will… of them")

20

Including a quote from the miner's child in line 56 primarily serves to

A) illustrate the point that there is insufficient money to pay bills.

B) indicate that the miners are too busy to do their own shopping.

C) highlight the cruelty of the practice being described.

D) emphasize that children are also forced to work in the mines.

21

As used in lines 75 and 76, "charge" most nearly means

A) accuse.

B) demand.

C) impose.

D) assault.

CONTINUE ➡

Questions 22-31 are based on the following passage and supplementary material.

This passage is adapted from *World Regional Geography: People, Places, and Globalization,* copyrighted by the University of Minnesota, 2016.

Most of the population in Sub-Saharan Africa works in subsistence agriculture to make a living and feed their typically large families. In recent decades, there has been enormous rural-to-urban
5 migration to the major cities, which are extremely overcrowded. At the center of the main business districts are modern high-rise business offices well connected to the global economy, but outside are slums with no services and miserable, unsanitary
10 conditions. The informal sector of the economy— that which is not regulated, controlled, or taxed— has become the primary system of doing business.

The lack of government regulation prevents taxes from being assessed or collected, which in
15 turn diminishes support for public services or infrastructure. The formal sector of the economy is forced to foot the bill to operate the government and support public services such as education, security, and transportation. In spite of the misery and
20 unhealthy conditions of the slums where millions of people already live, more migrants from the countryside continue to shift to the city in search of jobs and opportunities. African cities are growing rapidly, many without organized planning.

25 The populations of West African countries are increasing rapidly and will double in about thirty years at the current rate. This trend places an extra burden on the economy and on the environment. It is fueling one of the fastest rural-to-urban shifts in
30 the world. Personal income levels in West African countries are among the lowest in the world— Sub-Saharan Africa has over 750 million people, and most earn the US equivalent of only $1–3 per day—and few economic opportunities exist for the
35 millions of young people entering the employment market. However, if Africa can manage its resources and provide a safe environment for travelers, tourism could have a strong impact on Africa's economic growth and play a significant role in its
40 future.

Tourism is a growing sector of the global economy. Travel and tourism jobs are increasing worldwide, but Africa as a whole attracts less than 5 percent of total world tourists and accounts for only
45 a small percentage of international tourism income. However, Sub-Saharan Africa has a strong supply-side potential to attract tourists. Beach resorts alone create a large draw. The coastal waters of the Indian Ocean boast some of the finest beaches in
50 the world, with plenty of opportunities for sailing, diving, or other water sports. Other well-known coastal tourist destinations include Zanzibar in Tanzania, Benguerra Island in Mozambique, and the Seychelles.

55 Even now, Africa excels in attracting tourists to its wildlife and game reserves. Safari tourism highlights exotic creatures, including elephants, lions, rhinos, hippos, and big game. The region is also replete with natural features or attractions
60 that tourists gravitate toward, particularly those in search of outstanding scenic sites or who desire an environmental adventure. There are dozens of awe-inspiring national parks throughout Africa like Mt. Kilimanjaro in Tanzania and Zuma Rock in Nigeria.
65 Furthermore, cultural locations with a rich heritage of historical significance such as Timbuktu in Mali have been growing in their attractiveness to and accessibility for world travelers in recent years.

Every African country, urban center, or rural
70 village could be, in fact, its own unique tourism magnet. The tourism business, though, is broader than just the sites themselves. Considerations need to be made for transportation, hotels and guest accommodations, and services that link the various
75 components of a trip, such as guide services in national parks or city bus tours. The attractiveness and competitiveness of each tourism destination will depend on the site's quality and accessibility.

A serious financial investment is needed to
80 bring Sub-Saharan Africa up to par with the global marketplace. Africa has huge potential for growth in its tourism market, but heavy tourism traffic might have a negative impact on the environment, cultural stereotypes could be exploited, and the disparity
85 between wealthy tourists and service workers earning a modest wage may lend itself to divisions and social friction. Tourism demands higher levels of security and public health at all levels. Money spent on tourism development is money not spent
90 on schools or clinics. On the other hand, without tourism income, there are no jobs. To be successful, Africa will need to balance out the economic need

for tourism with its willingness to comply with the requirements of the tourism industry.

Figure 1: Number of Tourists to Select African Countries (2016)

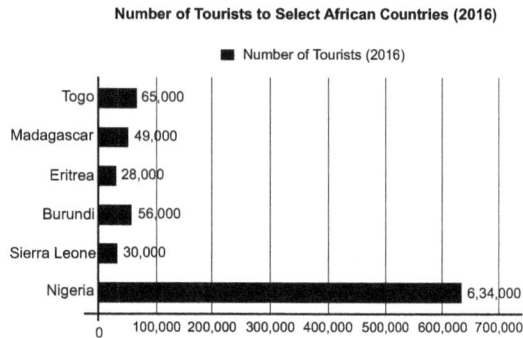

Number of Tourists to Select African Countries (2016)

■ Number of Tourists (2016)

Togo	65,000
Madagascar	49,000
Eritrea	28,000
Burundi	56,000
Sierra Leone	30,000
Nigeria	6,34,000

0   100,000 200,000 300,000 400,000 500,000 600,000 700,000

Figure 2: Increase in Tourism from 2015-2016 for Select African Countries

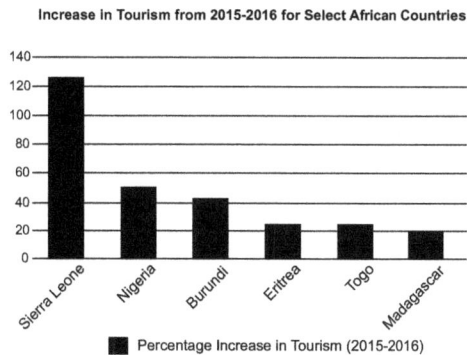

Increase in Tourism from 2015-2016 for Select African Countries

Sierra Leone, Nigeria, Burundi, Eritrea, Togo, Madagascar

■ Percentage Increase in Tourism (2015-2016)

Data for figures is adapted from African Development Bank Group, 2016

22

The main purpose of the passage is to

A) compare strategies for resolving an ongoing problem.

B) analyze reasons for a demographic change.

C) discuss the economic situation in a specific region.

D) argue that a population is not aware of its natural resources.

23

Which choice best describes the overall structure of the passage?

A) A complex social situation is described, a deficient attempt to remedy the problem is mentioned, and a potential solution is offered.

B) A major problem is outlined, several obstacles to solving it are described, and a way to eliminate those obstacles is presented.

C) An impending crisis is outlined, a list of available resources is given, and a potential solution is proposed.

D) A worrisome trend is presented, a possible solution is introduced, and caveats regarding that solution are mentioned.

24

Based on information from the passage, which of the following would best illustrate a transaction that occurs in the informal sector of the Sub-Saharan economy?

A) A farmer trades several chickens for enough wood to build a house for his newly-married son.

B) An international corporation from Denmark invests money in erecting a new school in a rural area.

C) A governor uses tax money to build a bridge, but hires a construction company owned by a good friend.

D) A young man from a rural area moves into a large city because he wants to find a better job.

25

As used in line 48, "draw" most nearly means

A) haul.

B) persuasion.

C) appeal.

D) connection.

26

Which choice best supports the claim that it would be difficult to establish a strong tourism industry in Sub-Saharan Africa without specifically making major changes?

A) Lines 36-40 ("if Africa… future")

B) Lines 43-45 ("Africa as… income")

C) Lines 76-78 ("The attractiveness… accessibility")

D) Lines 87-88 ("Tourism… all levels")

27

As used in line 71, "broader" most nearly means something that is more

A) pronounced.

B) general.

C) spacious.

D) extensive.

28

One conclusion that can be drawn about the negative impact of tourism in Africa is that

A) jobs created may not provide adequate employment for all community members.

B) most of the income will be taxed and therefore not benefit the local communities.

C) an increase in tourism would result in a loss of local culture and traditions.

D) individuals who work in the industry may become resentful of visitors.

CONTINUE

29

Which choice provides the best evidence for the answer to the previous question?

A) Lines 83-84 ("cultural... exploited")

B) Lines 84-87 ("the disparity... friction")

C) Lines 88-90 ("Money... or clinics")

D) Lines 90-91 ("without... no jobs")

30

According to figure 1, the number of tourists in Togo in 2016 was

A) the highest of the selected countries represented in the figure.

B) greater than that of either Burundi or Nigeria.

C) lower than that of Nigeria but higher than that of Eritrea.

D) higher than it had been in the previous year.

31

Which of the following claims about tourism in 2016 is best supported by the data from figure 1 and figure 2?

A) Nigeria has one of the best infrastructures to cater to tourists, which is why it had one of the greatest numbers of tourists.

B) Although Sierra Leone only had 30,000 tourists in 2016, that was over a 120% increase compared to the number from 2015.

C) Burundi had an increase of 56,000 visitors from 2015 to 2016, which was an increase of over 40 percent.

D) Madagascar had a greater percentage of tourists who visited in 2016 than Eritrea did in the same year.

Questions 32-41 are based on the following passage and supplementary material.

This passage is adapted from *Antibodies Reverse Synthetic Opioid Overdoses in Mice,* by Tien Nguyen, copyright October 2019 by ACS Publications.

In a potential advance in treating opioid overdose, researchers have developed long-lasting monoclonal antibodies that selectively bind potent
Line synthetic opioids and reverse their effects in mice.
5 The researchers propose that the antibodies could one day be administered as a stand-alone treatment or as part of a more effective combination treatment against opioid overdoses.

Medical professionals have only one treatment
10 option, a drug called naloxone, against acute opioid overdoses, which is a growing problem that in 2017 killed more than 47,000 people in the US. The fast-acting treatment, sold as Narcan, races towards the brain where it blocks opioid receptors, denying
15 the drugs access to them. But naloxone breaks down after about an hour, which allows a relapse into overdose unless the drug is re-administered. Naloxone's short lifetime also makes it less effective against powerful synthetic opioids like fentanyl and
20 carfentanil, which are 100- and 10,000-fold stronger than morphine, respectively.

An antibody-based drug is one candidate for a more effective, longer lasting overdose treatment. To explore this possibility, a team at Scripps Research
25 Institute led by Kim D. Janda first treated mice with a vaccine developed by their group in 2016 that stimulates the animals to produce a slew of different antibodies against fentanyl, some of which help protect the mice from overdoses.

30 In the new work, the team recovered antibodies from the mice, purified them, and screened them for their ability to bind fentanyl. Although vaccines work by building up these antibodies for the next time opioids enter the body, in this case the
35 researchers extracted the antibodies for direct use against an overdose. The team further evaluated six of these antibodies against nine fentanyl analogs commonly confiscated by law enforcement. One antibody, 6A4, demonstrated the best fentanyl
40 binding affinity and had a six-day half-life in mice.

The team then compared 6A4 and naloxone's ability

to rescue mice from fentanyl and carfentanil's effects. Mice received an opioid dosage expected to completely block pain followed half an hour later
45 by an intravenous dose of either 6A4 or naloxone. To evaluate each treatment's effectiveness, the team measured the animals' response to pain using standard tests.

Both drugs reversed the opioid's effects
50 compared with mice that didn't receive any treatment but naloxone's effects kicked in earlier than 6A4, after about 1 hour, which the researchers attribute to naloxone's faster distribution through the body as a small molecule. Notably, 6A4 proved
55 more effective than naloxone around 2 hours after delivery, likely due to its longer half-life.

Naloxone works fast because it makes a beeline for opioid receptors in the brain, whereas antibodies like 6A4 can't cross the barrier that separates the
60 brain from the rest of the bloodstream. So Janda and colleagues propose that 6A4 sequesters synthetic opioids in the blood, creating an equilibrium imbalance that pulls more opioids from the brain into the bloodstream, where more antibodies await.

65 Combining 6A4 and naloxone could offer treatment that is both fast and long acting, Janda says. He adds that the antibody's specificity for synthetic opioids avoids unwanted off-target binding to drugs like buprenorphine, which is used to help
70 people reduce their opioid use.

Allegheny Health Network Research Institute's Saadyah Averick, who has worked on extending naloxone's lifetime using nanoparticles, says the work offers a "unique and orthogonal approach
75 to sequester the potent synthetic opioids." He says the antibodies' specificity and longer circulation is interesting but wonders about the antibodies' practicality as a treatment: biological therapies are much more expensive to make than small molecules,
80 because they require special manufacturing facilities and storage, he says.

Although an antibody-based overdose drug would be more expensive than a drug like naloxone, the authors say, it would cost less than cancer
85 immunotherapy, which is now routinely used to treat patients. Janda adds that the costs of making antibodies has significantly decreased over the past 10 years.

In the coming weeks, the team will test the antibod
90 ies' ability to counter synthetic opioids' effects in
nonhuman primates, Janda says.

Figure 1: Deaths from Drug Overdoses in the
United States by Year

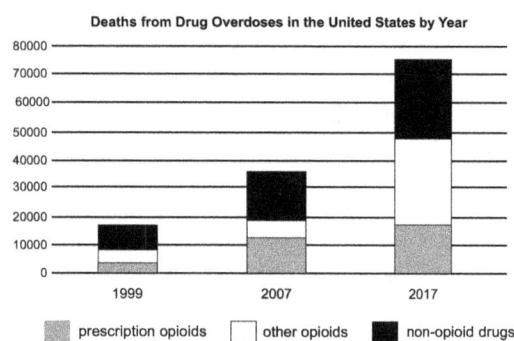

**Data from National Institute on Drug Abuse,
2019.**

32

The main purpose of the passage is to

A) explore the methods with which several drugs
counteract the effects of opiate overdoses.

B) explain why naloxone is the preferred method
for treating patients with drug overdoses.

C) discuss the implications on the medical
industry of a scientific study about opiates.

D) introduce research on a promising drug for
overcoming the effects of opiate overdoses.

33

Which choice best explains why naloxone is not
completely desirable as a solution for patients
who have overdosed on opiates?

A) Naloxone is only able to protect a patients for
a limited period.

B) Naloxone is more expensive than other
available treatment options.

C) Naloxone offers no results for overdoses of
many opiate drugs.

D) Naloxone has harmful side effects which can
injure the patient.

34

Which choice provides the best evidence for the
answer to the previous question?

A) Lines 9-12 ("Medical… the US")

B) Lines 12-15 ("The fast-acting… to them")

C) Lines 15-17 ("But naloxone… re-
administered")

D) Lines 49-54 ("Both drugs… molecule")

35

The author most likely includes the information that the drugs were "commonly confiscated by law enforcement" (line 38) in order to

A) explain how the researchers obtained drugs for experimentation.

B) indicate that the research would apply to overdoses in authentic cases.

C) eliminate the argument that the trials were improperly conducted.

D) establish why special permits were needed to experiment with the drugs.

36

The fact that 6A4 does not bind to drugs like buprenorphine is significant because

A) it demonstrates that 6A4 will not interfere with other treatments that the patient is receiving.

B) buprenorphine can reduce various symptoms that the patient is experiencing which 6A4 does not reduce.

C) buprenorphine is less inclined to trigger a severe drug overdose than other forms of opiates are.

D) patients taking buprenorphine are more likely to survive a drug overdose than patients who do not.

37

As described in the passage, which choice best describes the relationship between Kim D. Janda and Saadyah Averick?

A) Averick is a researcher in the same field who has reservations about Janda's work.

B) Both researchers are working to create antibody treatments for opiate overdoses.

C) Janda is pursuing research based on preliminary tests conducted by Averick.

D) Averick's research generated different results when duplicating Janda's tests.

38

One doctor says that the antibody 6A4 is a perfect solution for curing overdose patients in third-world countries. Which choice provides the most effective counterargument to his claim?

A) Lines 54-56 ("Notably...half-life")

B) Lines 57-60 ("Naloxone...bloodstream")

C) Lines 78-81 ("biological...storage")

D) Lines 86-88 ("Janda...10 years")

39

As used in line 90, "counter" most nearly means

A) rebuff.

B) parry.

C) contradict.

D) negate.

40

According to the data presented in figure 1, what was the approximate number of deaths in the United States caused by drug overdoses using any opiate in 2017?

A) 18,000

B) 35,000

C) 48,000

D) 75,000

41

The data in figure 1 best support which statement about drug overdoses in the United States?

A) A greater number of individuals misused all types of opiates in 2017 than did so in 1999.

B) There was a greater increase in deaths from prescription opiates than from other opiates between 2007 and 2017.

C) In 2017, more people died of overdoses from non-prescription opiates than from prescription opiates.

D) The percentage of prescription drug users who die of drug overdoses has increased since 1999.

Questions 42-52 are based on the following passages.

Passage 1 is adapted from Cathal O'Connell, *Why the Idea of Alien Life Now Seems Inevitable and Possibly Imminent,* published April 30, 2019 by Cosmos Conversation. Passage 2 is adapted from *Astronomy,* by Andrew Fraknoi et al., published by OpenStax.

Passage 1:

Extraterrestrial life, that familiar science-fiction trope, that kitschy fantasy, that CGI nightmare, has become a matter of serious discussion, a "risk
Line factor," a "scenario." How has ET gone from sci-fi
5 fairytale to a serious scientific endeavour modelled by macroeconomists, funded by fiscal conservatives and discussed by theologians? Because, following a string of remarkable discoveries over the past two decades, the idea of alien life is not as far-fetched as
10 it used to seem. Discovery now seems inevitable and possibly imminent.

While life is a special kind of complex chemistry, the elements involved are nothing special: carbon, hydrogen, oxygen and so on are among the most
15 abundant elements in the universe. Complex organic chemistry is surprisingly common. Amino acids, just like those that make up every protein in our bodies, have been found in the tails of comets. There are other organic compounds in Martian soil.
20 And 6,500 light years away a giant cloud of space alcohol floats among the stars. Habitable planets seem to be common too. The first planet beyond our Solar System was discovered in 1995. Since then astronomers have catalogued thousands.

25 Based on this catalogue, astronomers from the University of California, Berkeley worked out there could be as many as 40 billion Earth-sized exoplanets in the so-called "habitable zone" around their star, where temperatures are mild enough for
30 liquid water to exist on the surface. There's even a potentially Earth-like world orbiting our nearest neighbouring star, Proxima Centauri. At just four light years away, that system might be close enough for us to reach using current technology. With the
35 Breakthrough Starshot project launched by Stephen Hawking in 2016, plans for this are already afoot. It seems inevitable other life is out there, especially considering that life appeared on Earth so soon after the planet was formed. The ancient question "Are we

40 alone?" has graduated from being a philosophical musing to a testable hypothesis. We should be prepared for an answer.

Passage 2:

Our observations suggest increasingly that Earth-size planets orbiting within the habitable zone
45 may be common in the Galaxy—current estimates suggest that more than 40% of stars have at least one. But are any of them inhabited? With no ability to send probes there to sample, we will have to derive the answer from the light and other radiation
50 that come to us from these faraway systems.

We need to look for robust biospheres (atmospheres, surfaces, and/or oceans) capable of creating planet-scale change. Presently, Earth is the only body in our solar system with a biosphere
55 detectable by its light spectrum, despite the possibility that habitable conditions might prevail in the subsurface of Mars or inside the icy moons of the outer solar system. Even if life exists on these worlds, it is very unlikely that it could yield planet-
60 scale changes that are both telescopically observable and clearly biological in origin.

What makes Earth "special" among the potentially habitable worlds in our solar system is that it has a photosynthetic biosphere. This requires
65 the presence of liquid water at the planet's surface, where organisms have direct access to sunlight. The habitable zone concept focuses on this requirement for surface liquid water—even though we know that subsurface habitable conditions could prevail at
70 more distant orbits—exactly because these worlds would have biospheres detectable at a distance.

If we manage to separate out a clean signal from the planet and find some features in the light spectrum that might be indicative of life, we will
75 need to work hard to think of any nonbiological process that might account for them. "Life is the hypothesis of last resort," noted astronomer Carl Sagan. This requires some understanding of what processes might operate on worlds that we will
80 know relatively little about; what we find on Earth can serve as a guide but also has potential to lead us astray.

We also might not be able to detect biospheres even if they exist. Life has flourished on Earth for
85 perhaps 3.5 billion years, but the atmospheric

"biosigna tures" that, today, would supply good
evidence for life to distant astronomers have not
been present for all of that time. Oxygen, for
example, accumulated to detectable levels in our
90 atmosphere only a little over 2 billion years ago.
Could life on Earth have been detected before that
time? Scientists are working actively to understand
what additional features might have provided
evidence of life on Earth during that early history,
95 and thereby help our chances of finding life beyond.

42

The author of Passage 1 builds his argument using

A) personal anecdotes.

B) comprehensible analogies.

C) unsubstantiated theories.

D) summaries of findings.

43

In Passage 1, the author most likely uses the
phrases "science-fiction trope," "kitschy fantasy"
and "CGI nightmare" (lines 1-2) in order to

A) point out the ever-changing image of how
   extraterrestrial creatures appear.

B) encourage readers to imagine the possible
   variety of extraterrestrial life.

C) interject a lighthearted note into an otherwise
   serious passage.

D) emphasize that there is credibility in
   something that once was believed impossible.

44

As used in line 12, "kind" most nearly means

A) model.

B) variety.

C) version.

D) design.

45

What is implied in Passage 1 about Stephen
Hawking's Breakthrough Starshot project?

A) It was designed to search for Earth-sized
   planets in the "habitable zone."

B) It intends to send spacecraft to the Proxima
   Centauri system in the future.

C) It wants to prove that life appeared in the
   Proxima Centauri system soon after it
   formed.

D) It is trying to show that humans can survive
   on a planet circling Proxima Centauri.

46

Passage 2 most strongly suggests that

A) even if life is present on other planets, we may not be able to recognize it.

B) life on other planets probably only exists in regions that sustain surface water.

C) it is impossible to find life on other planets using currently available technology.

D) theories about life on other planets have not considered the practicality of finding it.

47

As used in line 56, "prevail" most nearly means

A) exist.

B) triumph.

C) overcome.

D) endure.

48

Which choice provides the best evidence to support the claim that it may be impossible to detect subsurface life on distant planets?

A) Lines 58-61 ("Even if… origin")

B) Lines 62-66 ("What makes… sunlight")

C) Lines 72-76 ("If we… them")

D) Lines 84-88 ("Life has … time")

49

Which hypothetical situation is Carl Sagan most likely warning to avoid in his quote in Passage 2?

A) A rover that was sent to Mars discovers a bacteria-like organism when it drills deep into the core of the planet.

B) An astronomer realizes that the atmosphere of a planet is too hot to sustain life even though it has oxygen.

C) A scientist finds a planet with a large amount of oxygen in its atmosphere so claims that the oxygen is produced by living creatures.

D) A new telescope finds a new planet orbiting a star that was previously believed to have no planets.

50

One point that the authors of the passages would most likely agree upon is that

A) if it were possible to travel there, life most likely could be found on the surface of Mars.

B) it may not be possible to determine whether a planet hosts life based only on its biosphere.

C) the most probable location for finding extraterrestrial life is on planets with surface water.

D) positive identification of extraterrestrial life will occur in the immediate future.

51

The author of Passage 2 would most likely respond to the claim in Passage 1 that encountering extraterrestrial life is now a testable hypothesis by saying that the claim is

A) farfetched, as there is no method of exploring places where life might exist.

B) fallacious, as the only planet with a detectable biosphere is Earth.

C) plausible, as many planets could contain life in subsurface regions.

D) inconceivable, as there is no evidence that extraterrestrial life exists.

52

Which choice provides the best evidence for the answer to the previous question?

A) Lines 47-50 ("With no… systems")

B) Lines 51-53 ("We need… change")

C) Lines 53-55 ("Presently… spectrum")

D) Lines 66-71 ("The habitable… distance")

STOP

If you finish before time is called, you may check your work on this section only.
Do not turn to any other section.

Writing and Language Test

35 MINUTES, 44 QUESTIONS

Turn to Section 2 of your answer sheet to answer the questions in this section

DIRECTIONS

Each passage below is accompanied by a number of questions. For some questions, you will consider how the passage might be revised to improve the expression of ideas. For other questions, you will consider how the passage might be edited to correct errors in sentence structure, usage, or punctuation. A passage or a question may be accompanied by one or more graphics (such as a table or graph) that you will consider as you make revising and editing decisions.

Some questions will direct you to an underlined portion of a passage. Other questions will direct you to a location in a passage or ask you to think about the passage as a whole.

After reading each passage, choose the answer to each question that most effectively improves the quality of writing in the passage or that makes the passage conform to the conventions of standard written English. Many questions include a "NO CHANGE" option. Choose that option if you think the best choice is to leave the relevant portion of the passage as it is.

Questions 1-11 are based on the following text that has been adapted from Deloitte's "Catch the wave: The 21st-century career."

In an age where skill sets can become obsolete in just a few years, many workers are scrambling just to stay current. [1] How can organizations encourage continuous learning, improve individual mobility, and foster a growth mind-set in every employee, year after year?

[2] You'd hire a bright young person out of college, plug him into an entry-level role, and then watch him climb the corporate ladder over the years as he progressed toward retirement. The company could plan for this continuous process — hire people based on their degrees, help them develop slowly and steadily, and [3] expect leaders, specialists, and plateaus.

1

The writer is considering deleting the underlined sentence. Should the sentence be kept or deleted?

A) Kept, because it effectively sets up the main question being addressed in the passage.

B) Deleted, because it does not provide an effective introduction.

C) Deleted, because it ignores essential information.

D) Kept, because the sentence helps clarify the preceding sentence.

2

At this point, the author is considering adding a clause to better introduce the following text. Which addition should they make?

A) NO CHANGE

B) A rewarding career used to be easy;

C) Offering employees a rewarding career used to be easy:

D) Careers have rewards:

3

A) NO CHANGE

B) expect some to become leaders, some to become specialists, and some to plateau.

C) expect different results.

D) Delete the underlined section.

Today this model 4 is shattered. As research suggests, the days of a steady, stable career are over. 5 Therefore, organizations have become flatter and less ladder-like, making upward progression less common (often replaced by team or project leadership). Young, newly hired employees often have skills not found in experienced hires, leaving many older people to work for young leaders. And the rapid pace of technology makes many jobs, crafts, and skills go out of date in only a few years.

The training department used to offer a stable and well-architected career. Today, many training departments are struggling to keep 6 up, often pointing us to online courses and programs, telling us that it's our job to "reskill ourselves." And while they try to give us what we need to stay ahead, research 7 are showing that they are also falling behind: Employees rate their Learning & Development departments a dismal -8 in net promoter score, lower than almost any product in the consumer landscape.

4

A) NO CHANGE

B) shattered

C) shattering

D) is being shattered

5

A) NO CHANGE

B) Although

C) Because

D) Delete the underlined word.

6

A) NO CHANGE

B) up; often

C) up: often

D) up — often

7

A) NO CHANGE

B) shows

C) showed

D) will show

As technology evolves apace and more of us work part-time, these trends are only accelerating. [8] But LinkedIn co-founder Reid Hoffman believes that careers are now simply "tours of duty," prompting companies to design organizations that assume people will only stay a few years. And data bears this out: 58 percent of companies believe their new employees will stick around less than 10 years; LinkedIn research shows that, on average, new degree-holders have twice as many jobs in their first five post-college years now as they did in the mid-1980s.

But hold on. The world of careers doesn't have to be so difficult and unforgiving. Organizations [10] their career strategies and help people learn faster and continue to stay engaged. It just takes a rethinking of the problem, and a need to be aware of how jobs, careers, and skills are rapidly changing.

The bottom-line question is this: How can organizations build career models that [11] encourage continuous learning, improve individual mobility, and foster a growth mind-set in every employee, year after year? This is the opportunity for today; companies that figure this out will outperform, out-innovate, and out-execute their peers.

8

A) NO CHANGE
B) However,
C) For instance,
D) Although

9

A) NO CHANGE
B) years, LinkedIn
C) years. LinkedIn
D) years: LinkedIn

10

A) NO CHANGE
B) can adapt their career strategies
C) should not adapt their career strategies
D) DELETE the underlined section.

11

A) NO CHANGE
B) encouraged
C) encouraging
D) encourages

Questions 12-22 are based on the following text that has been adapted from The Conversation's "Fanon continues to resonate more than half a century after Algeria's independence."

(1)

Algeria marks its 53rd year of independence from France this [12] month, the bitter struggle for freedom in the late 1950s and early 1960s became a central focus of the global movement against colonialism. It also influenced the evolving forms of repression and resistance in apartheid South Africa.

(2)

Independence followed a hard-fought revolutionary war that began in late 1954 and ended six years later. [13] Massacres were common, extending in 1961 to the mass killing of unarmed Algerian civilians in Paris. Torture and rape were routine [14] features of French military operations.

[12]

A) NO CHANGE

B) month— the

C) month: the

D) month. The

[13]

At this point, the author is considering including the following sentence:

"It cost hundreds of thousands of lives."

Should the writer make this addition here?

A) Yes, because it provides information that helps clarify prior statements.

B) No, because this information is not essential in communicating the main ideas of the paragraph.

C) Yes, because it provides an effective introduction for the following information.

D) No, because it provides irrelevant information.

[14]

A) NO CHANGE

B) features.

C) military operations.

D) Delete the underlined portion.

CONTINUE

(3)

Alongside the revolution in Cuba in 1959, the Algeria war for national liberation inspired struggles against racism and colonialism around the world. After the war, grand figures on the global stage – such as Malcolm X and Che Guevara – made their way to Algeria. [15]

(4)

In 1961, Nelson Mandela, in search of military training, was hosted by the Algerian army in exile in Morocco. He went on to spend some time with guerrillas in the mountains of Algeria. He declared [16] it to be: "... the closest model to our own in that the rebels faced a large white settler community that ruled the indigenous majority [17] of Black South Africans."

[15]

Which added sentence would provide the best conclusion to this paragraph?

A) NO CHANGE

B) Malcom X is a controversial figure in the United States.

C) Guevara declared Algiers "one of the most heroic capitals of freedom."

D) Che Guevara is known as a revolutionary figure.

[16]

A) NO CHANGE

B) them

C) these

D) the Algerian context

[17]

A) NO CHANGE

B) DELETE the underlined portion

C) in these countries.

D) of people.

(5)

The apartheid state also 18 seeks to learn from the war in Algeria. By 1963, activists in South Africa were being subjected to methods of torture learnt from the French in Algeria. 19 Today, the most visible legacy of the Algerian war in South Africa is the ubiquity of the event's name and, arguably, to a lesser extent, ideas of one of the major intellectuals whose thought was forged, in large part, in the crucible of that war: Frantz Fanon.

(6)

Frantz Fanon's name is mobilized in the service of all kinds of political projects, some of which are in obvious contradiction to both the books that he wrote as well as what we know of his biography.

18

A) NO CHANGE

B) will seek

C) sought

D) was seeking

19

At this point, the writer is considering changing the underlined sentence to the following:

"Today, the most visible legacy of the Algerian war in South Africa is the ubiquity of the event's name. To a lesser extent, one can recognize the ideas of one of the major intellectuals to emerge from that war: Frantz Fanon"

Should the writer make this change here?

A) Yes, because it provides an effective transition.

B) Yes, because it improves clarity, tone, and voice of the sentence.

C) No, because it would be more effective as an introduction at the beginning of the paragraph.

D) No, because it eliminates relevant information.

(7)

[20] All these years later, it remains a foundational text in the growing body of literature in the field of critical race studies. It had an explosive impact on South Africa in the late 1960s and early 1970s, when, along with thinkers like James Cone, Aimé Césaire and Jean-Paul Sartre, Fanon became an important part of the intellectual foundation of the black consciousness movement. [21]

[20]

To make this passage most logical, paragraph (7) should be placed:

A) after paragraph (8)

B) after paragraph (5)

C) where it is now

D) before paragraph (3)

[21]

At this point, the writer is considering adding the following sentence:

"Fanon is a significant figure in history."

Should the writer make this addition here?

A) No, because it provides redundant information.

B) No, because it provides a more effective introduction and should be placed at the beginning of the paragraph.

C) Yes, because it provides irrelevant information.

D) Yes, because it provides information that helps explain what comes next.

(8)

Fanon, born on the Caribbean island of Martinique in 1925, published his first book, *Black Skin, White Masks,* in 1952 at the precociously young age of 27. The book deals with the lived experience of racism in the Caribbean and France. 22

22

Which of the following most effectively summarizes the main point of the passage?

A) Colonialism has long-lasting effects.

B) Algeria's war of independence was different from that of South Africa's.

C) Mandela wanted to create stronger relationships between Algeria and South Africa.

D) Algeria's war of independence — and Fanon's work — were greatly influential in South Africa.

Questions 23-33 are based on the following text that has been adapted from the Los Angeles Review of Books' "It Has Happened. So, it Can Happen Again:" Philip Gourevitch on Genocide.

We live in an era of genocides. Author Philip Gourevitch [23] was one of the experts, probing how genocide happens, how the murderers rationalize their participation, and how they live with themselves later. [24] With his new research, he reports on the survivors, who now continue their lives alongside those who have murdered their friends and families.

[23]

A) NO CHANGE

B) is

C) are

D) will be

[24]

At this point, the author is considering including the following sentence:

"Gourevitch undertakes new research projects."

Should the writer make this addition here

A) Yes, because it provides information that helps clarify prior statements.

B) No, because it would be more effective as an introduction to this paragraph.

C) Yes, because it provides an effective transition to the following sentence.

D) No, because it restates information that can be understood from the next sentence.

We Wish to Inform You That Tomorrow We Will Be Killed with Our Families: Stories from Rwanda was named by The Guardian as one 100 greatest non-fiction books. Gourevitch is now working on a sequel, *You Hide That You Hate Me and I Hide That I Know,* [25] describing the aftermath of the 1994 genocide, in which Hutus slaughtered 800,000 of their Tutsi neighbors in a hundred days. [26] Therefore, the new book considers how people continue their lives under impossible conditions, and the nature of evil.

25

At this point, the writer is thinking of revising the underlined sentence to the following:

"which describes the aftermath of the Rwandan genocide."

Should the writer make this change here?

A) Yes, because it provides more effective support for the paragraph.

B) Yes, because it is a more effective transition to the next sentence.

C) No, because it eliminates information that is necessary for a reader who might be unfamiliar with the topic.

D) No, because it would disrupt the flow of logic in the sentence.

26

A) NO CHANGE

B) Delete the underlined word.

C) Finally,

D) However,

(1) Gourevitch has been a staff writer at *The New Yorker* for over two decades, and from 2005 to 2010 served as editor of *The Paris Review*. (2) In his 2016 Entitled Opinions [27] conversation, Gourevitch discusses multiple timely and complex issues. (3) He then goes on to critically consider the complexity of truth and how justice can be a backward-looking concept that rationalizes the thirst for revenge. [28] (4) He begins that conversation by elaborating upon the history of Rwanda and contextualizes the events of 1994. (5) Finally, Gourevitch elaborates upon how self-comforting notions of "never again" lead us to believe that we are immunized from the repeated cycles of the past.

27

A) NO CHANGE
B) conversation
C) conversation:
D) conversation —

28

To make this passage most logical, the underlined sentence should be placed:

A) Where it is now
B) before sentence (1)
C) before sentence (3)
D) after sentence (5)

[29] *Entitled Opinions* host, Robert Harrison, draws from Dante's *Inferno* to propose how a disconnect between past and future events might enable Rwanda to move forward from the genocide without reconciliatory efforts. However, in Rwanda, reconciliation was a national necessity. [30] "How on earth do you live with this — both in the local sense, and in the broader sense of all the stories we tell ourselves about our common humanity?" Gourevitch asks.

[29]

The writer is considering deleting the underlined sentence. Should the sentence be kept or deleted?

A) Kept, because it provides extensive information about *Entitled Opinions*.

B) Deleted, because it would be more effective as a conclusion to this paragraph.

C) Deleted, because it provides irrelevant information.

D) Kept, because it provides a necessary introduction to the following information.

[30]

At this point, the writer is considering changing the underlined sentence to the following:

As Gourevitch asks us to consider: "How on earth do you live with this — both in the local sense, and in the broader sense of all the stories we tell ourselves about our common humanity?"

Should the writer make this change here?

A) Yes, because it helps clarify a preceding term.

B) Yes, because it provides a more effective transition from the previous sentence.

C) No, because it would be more effective as an introduction at the beginning of the paragraph.

D) No, because it eliminates relevant information.

He also discusses the new genre of his work, creating "books that [31] are being based on reporting, that are fact-checkable, that are drawn from intensely close [32] observation, and a lot of interviews." Gourevitch tries to write in a way that captures not just the facts, but the human pathos he faces as [33] he returns again and again to the land that was the site of what has been one of the greatest genocides since World War II.

[31]

A) NO CHANGE

B) will be

C) were

D) are

[32]

A) NO CHANGE

B) observation. And

C) observation and

D) observation; and

[33]

A) NO CHANGE

B) Gourevitch

C) it

D) the feeling

Questions 34-44 are based on the following text that has been adapted from the Environmental Protection Agency's (EPA) "Facts and Figures about Materials, Waste and Recycling."

EPA began <u>34 collected</u> and reporting data on the generation and disposition of waste in the United States more than 30 years ago. The Agency uses this information to measure the success of materials management programs across the country and to characterize the national waste stream.

EPA is also thinking beyond <u>35 waste, and</u> we have transitioned from focusing on waste management to focusing on Sustainable Materials Management (SMM), which refers to the use and reuse of materials across their entire life cycle. <u>36 However,</u> SMM conserves resources, reduces waste and minimizes the environmental impacts of materials we use. In an era of limited resources, the sustainable management of natural capital is increasingly at the forefront of international dialogue about how to achieve economic growth without compromising human health and the environment.

34

A) NO CHANGE

B) collecting

C) collection

D) collect

35

A) NO CHANGE

B) waste; and

C) waste and

D) waste — and

36

A) NO CHANGE

B) Finally,

C) Although the

D) Delete the underlined word.

CONTINUE

37 <u>EPA</u> refers to trash, or municipal solid waste (MSW), as various items consumers throw away after they are used. These items include bottles and corrugated boxes, food, grass clippings, sofa, computers, tires and refrigerators. However, MSW does not include everything that is landfilled in MSW, or nonhazardous, landfills, such as construction and demolition (C&D) debris, municipal wastewater sludge, and other non-hazardous industrial wastes. 38

37

A) NO CHANGE

B) They

C) It

D) The people

38

At this point, the writer is considering adding the following sentence:

"It only includes the items mentioned earlier."

Should the writer make this addition here?

A) Yes, because it provides an effective transition to new information.

B) Yes, because it provides information that helps clarify prior information presented in the paragraph.

C) No, because it provides redundant information.

D) No, because it provides information that would be more effective as an introduction to the paragraph.

Management of MSW continues to be a high priority for states and local governments. [39] Ultimately, the concept of integrated solid waste management is increasingly being used by states and local governments as they plan for the future. This management practice includes the source reduction of wastes before they enter the waste stream and the recovery of generated waste for recycling or composting. It also includes environmentally sound management through combustion with energy [40] recovery and landfilling practices that meet current standards or newly emerging waste conversion technologies.

EPA has endorsed the concept of integrated waste management, which allows municipalities to manage MSW through different pathways and practices that can be tailored to the needs of a particular community. EPA's integrated waste management hierarchy [41] include the following pathways: source reduction (or waste prevention), [42] additionally the reuse of products and the on-site (or backyard) composting of yard trimmings; recycling; composting, including off-site (or community) composting; combustion with energy recovery; and disposal through landfilling.

[39]

A) NO CHANGE
B) However,
C) Regardless,
D) Consequently,

[40]

A) NO CHANGE
B) recovery; and
C) recovery, and
D) recovery. And

[41]

A) NO CHANGE
B) includes the following
C) is including
D) DELETE the underlined portion

[42]

A) NO CHANGE
B) in addition to
C) plus
D) including

The total generation of municipal solid waste in 2015 was 262.4 million tons (U.S. short tons, unless specified) of MSW, approximately 3.5 million tons more than the amount generated in 2014. MSW generated in 2015 increased to 4.48 pounds per person per day. [43] This is an increase from the 259 million tons generated in 2014 and the 208.3 million tons in 1990.

[44]

Figure 1

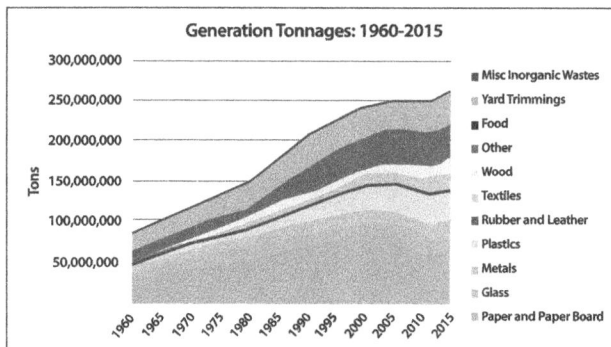

Generation Tonnages: 1960-2015

[43]

The writer is considering deleting the underlined sentence. Should the sentence be kept or deleted?

A) Kept, because it provides an effective transition between one concept and the next.

B) Kept, because it summarizes preceding information in the paragraph.

C) Deleted, because it interrupts the flow of the paragraph.

D) Deleted, because it provides information that is not related to the passage.

[44]

Which of the following provides the most effective support from Figure 1?

A) The generation of paper and paperboard has both increased and decreased over time.

B) The generation of glass has increased over time.

C) The generation of plastics has stayed constant over time.

D) The generation of yard trimmings has decreased over time.

STOP

If you finish before time is called, you may check your work on this section only.
Do not turn to any other section.

Math Test – No Calculator

25 MINUTES, 20 QUESTIONS

Turn to Section 3 of your answer sheet to answer the questions in this section.

DIRECTIONS

For questions 1-15, solve each problem, choose the best answer from the choices provided, and fill in the corresponding circle on your answer sheet. **For questions 16-20**, solve the problem and enter your answer in the grid on the answer sheet. Please refer to the directions before question 16 on how to enter your answers in the grid. You may use any available space in your test booklet for scratch work.

NOTES

1. The use of a calculator **is not permitted.**
2. All variables and expressions used represent real numbers unless otherwise indicated.
3. Figures provided in this test are drawn to scale unless otherwise indicated.
4. All figures lie in a plane unless otherwise indicated.
5. Unless otherwise indicated, the domain of a given function f is the set of all real numbers x for which $f(x)$ is a real number.

REFERENCE

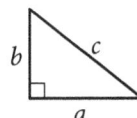 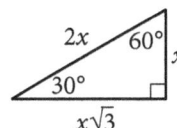 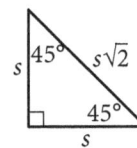

$A = \pi r^2$
$C = 2\pi r$

$A = \ell w$

$A = \frac{1}{2}bh$

$c^2 = a^2 + b^2$

Special Right Triangles

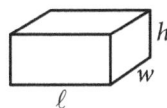 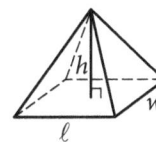

$V = \ell wh$

$V = \pi r^2 h$

$V = \frac{4}{3}\pi r^3$

$V = \frac{1}{3}\pi r^2 h$

$V = \frac{1}{3}\ell wh$

The number of degrees of arc in a circle is 360.

The number of radians of arc in a circle is 2π.

The sum of the measures in degrees of the angles of a triangle is 180.

1

If $\dfrac{a-1}{2} = b$ and b=2, what is the value of $a+1$?

A) 4

B) 5

C) 6

D) 7

2

What is the difference of $(7-2x)-(-8+10x^2)$?

A) $10x^2 - 2x + 15$

B) $-10x^2 - 2x + 15$

C) $10x^2 - 2x - 1$

D) $-10x^2 - 2x - 1$

3

On Sunday morning, Courtney sent x text messages each hour for 4 hours, and Lauren sent y text messages each hour for 6 hours. Which of the following represents the total number of messages sent by Courtney and Lauren on Sunday morning?

A) $10xy$

B) $24xy$

C) $6x + 4y$

D) $4x + 6y$

4

Leslie is a technician for a cable company. Each day, she receives multiple locations with cable boxes that need repair. The number of boxes that she has left to fix at the end of each hour can be estimated with the equation $C = 12 - 8h$ where C is the number of cable boxes left and h is the number of hours worked that day. What is the meaning of the value 12 in this equation?

A) Leslie will complete the repairs within 12 hours.

B) Leslie starts each day with 12 boxes to fix.

C) Leslie repairs cable boxes at a rate of 12 boxes per hour.

D) Leslie repairs cable boxes at a rate of 12 per hour.

CONTINUE ⮕

5

$$\left(a^2b - 3a^2 + 10ab^2\right) - \left(-2a^2b - 2ab^2 - 3b^2\right)$$

Which of the following is equivalent to the preceding expression?

A) $3a^2b - 3a^2 + 3b^2 - 12ab^2$

B) $3a^2b - 12ab^2$

C) $3a^2b - 3a^2 + 3b^2 + 12ab^2$

D) $15a^2b^2 - 3a^2 + 3b^2$

6

Jenna deposits an initial amount of money into an account with simple interest. If she accumulates 3% of her original deposit every year and originally deposited $1000, which equation represents $Y the value of her account after t years?

A) $y = 30t + 1000$

B) $\dfrac{y}{x} = 30t$

C) $y = 1000 - 30t$

D) $y = 1000t - 30$

7

The formula for specific resistance can be expressed as $A = R\dfrac{1}{p}$, where p is a constant and A is the cross-sectional area. Which of the following gives A in terms of R and p?

A) $A = R\dfrac{1}{p}$

B) $A = \dfrac{p}{R}$

C) $A = pR$

D) $A = \dfrac{1}{pR}$

8

If $\dfrac{m}{n} = 3$, what is the value of $\dfrac{6n}{m}$?

A)   0

B)   1

C)   2

D)   6

9

$$2x - 4y = -17$$

$$-x + 3y = \frac{27}{2}$$

What is the solution to the system of equations above?

A) (–5, 1.5)

B) (15, 5)

C) (3, –3)

D) (1.5, 5)

10

$$f(x) = ax^2 - 22$$

For the function $f(x)$, a is a constant and $f(-2) = -14$. What is the value of $f(3)$?

A) –2

B) –4

C) 2

D) 4

11

Quentin's sales: $T_Q = 5b + 48$

Alice's sales: $T_A = 5.5b + 159$

Quentin and Alice sell bagels before school. The equations above represent the number of bagels (b) they sell on a given day. How many bagels did they sell on a given day if Alice made twice as much money as Quentin?

A) 15

B) 14

C) 13

D) 12

12

A line is formed by points (3,8) and (–1, –4). What is the equation of the line that forms a right angle that also passes through (3,3)?

A) $y = 3x - 1$

B) $y = 3x + 4$

C) $y = \frac{1}{3}x - 4$

D) $y = -\frac{1}{3}x + 4$

13

If $m > 4$ which of the following is equivalent to

$$\dfrac{1}{\dfrac{1}{m+2}+\dfrac{1}{m+4}}?$$

A) $\dfrac{1}{(2m+6)}$

B) $2m+6$

C) m^2+6m+8

D) $\dfrac{m^2+6m+8}{2m+6}$

14

If $6m-n=24$, what is the value of $\dfrac{64^{2m}}{4^n}$?

A) 4^{24}

B) 64^6

C) 2^8

D) The value cannot be determined from the information given.

15

If $(px+3)(qx+8)=6x^2+rx+24$ for all values of x and $p+q=5$, what are the two possible values for p?

A) 2 and 3

B) 6 and 1

C) 8 and 2

D) −1 and −6

DIRECTIONS

For questions 16–20, solve the problem and enter your answer in the grid, as described below, on the answer sheet.

1. Although not required, it is suggested that you write your answer in the boxes at the top of the columns to help you fill in the circles accurately. You will receive credit only if the circles are filled in correctly.
2. Mark no more than one circle in any column.
3. No question has a negative answer.
4. Some problems may have more than one correct answer. In such cases, grid only one answer.
5. **Mixed numbers** such as $3\frac{1}{2}$ must be gridded as 3.5 or 7/2. (If $3\,1\,/\,2$ is entered into the grid, it will be interpreted as $\frac{31}{2}$, not $3\frac{1}{2}$.)
6. **Decimal answers:** If you obtain a decimal answer with more digits than the grid can accommodate, it may be either rounded or truncated, but it must fill the entire grid.

Answer: $\frac{7}{12}$ Answer: 2.5

Write answer in boxes. → Fraction line ← Decimal point

Grid in result.

Acceptable ways to grid $\frac{2}{3}$ are:

Answer: 201 – either position is correct

NOTE: You may start your answers in any column, space permitting. Columns you don't need to use should be left blank.

16

If $d > 0$ and $d^2 - 16 = 0$, what is the value of d?

17

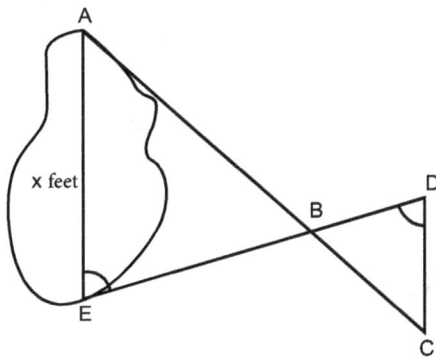

A camp is preparing for competition where a person has to swim across river x feet as denoted by segment $\overline{AE}$ then run along a path collecting flags from Point A to Point B to Point C to Point D, back to point B then ending at Point E. The camp would like to determine the difference between the length of the swim and the length of the run in feet. The lengths represented by $\overline{AB}, \overline{EB}, \overline{BD},$ and $\overline{DC}$ on the sketch were determined to be 1200 feet, 1000 feet, 500 feet, and 550 feet, respectively. Segments AC and DE intersect at B, and $\angle AEB$ and $\angle CBD$ have the same measure. What is the difference between the length of the swim and the length of the run in feet?

18

According to the preceding system of equations, what is the value of y?

$$y - 2x = -6$$

$$2y - x = 5$$

19

In a right triangle, one angle measures $x°$ where $\tan x° = 1$ What is $\sin(90° - x°)$?

20

If $x = 7\sqrt{2}$ and $2x = \sqrt{2y}$ what is the value of y?

STOP

If you finish before time is called, you may check your work on this section only.
Do not turn to any other section.

No Test Material On This Page

Math Test – Calculator

55 MINUTES, 38 QUESTIONS

Turn to Section 4 of your answer sheet to answer the questions in this section.

DIRECTIONS

For questions 1-30, solve each problem, choose the best answer from the choices provided, and fill in the corresponding circle on your answer sheet. **For questions 31-38**, solve the problem and enter your answer in the grid on the answer sheet. Please refer to the directions before question 16 on how to enter your answers in the grid. You may use any available space in your test booklet for scratch work.

NOTES

1. The use of a calculator **is permitted.**

2. All variables and expressions used represent real numbers unless otherwise indicated.

3. Figures provided in this test are drawn to scale unless otherwise indicated.

4. All figures lie in a plane unless otherwise indicated.

5. Unless otherwise indicated, the domain of a given function f is the set of all real numbers x for which $f(x)$ is a real number.

REFERENCE

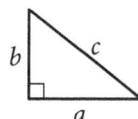
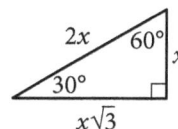
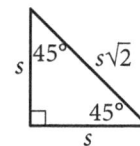

$A = \pi r^2$
$C = 2\pi r$

$A = \ell w$

$A = \frac{1}{2}bh$

$c^2 = a^2 + b^2$

Special Right Triangles

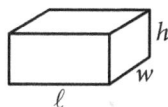

$V = \ell wh$

$V = \pi r^2 h$

$V = \frac{4}{3}\pi r^3$

$V = \frac{1}{3}\pi r^2 h$

$V = \frac{1}{3}\ell wh$

The number of degrees of arc in a circle is 360.

The number of radians of arc in a circle is 2π.

The sum of the measures in degrees of the angles of a triangle is 180.

1

There are 36 students at a statistics camp. If two thirds of the students are girls and three fourths of the girls are under 5.5 feet, how girls are under 5.5 feet tall?

A) 24

B) 18

C) 12

D) 6

2

If the circumference of a circular region equals exactly 6π inches, which is the area of the region?

A) 3π

B) 36π

C) 12π

D) 9π

3

	3	
4	L	K
	J	

In the figure above, the sum of the values in the horizontal row equals the sum of the values in the vertical row. If K equals 4, what is the value of J?

A) 5

B) 6

C) 8

D) 10

4

$a + b = p + rq$ and $q \neq 0$ then r is represented by which expression?

A) $\dfrac{a+b+p}{q}$

B) $a - b + \dfrac{p}{q}$

C) $a - b + \dfrac{p}{q}$

D) $\dfrac{a+b-p}{q}$

5

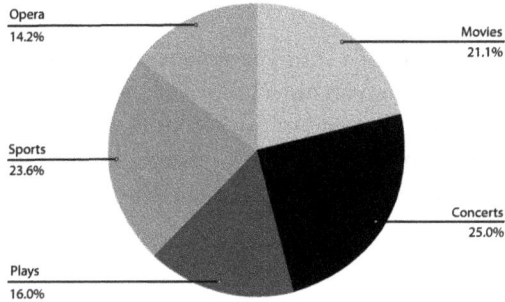

Opera
14.2%

Movies
21.1%

Sports
23.6%

Concerts
25.0%

Plays
16.0%

In 2017, approximately 5842 people were surveyed about preferred weekend activities. How many people preferred opera or concerts?

A) 1460

B) 830

C) 3550

D) 2209

6

Using the pie chart above, approximately what percent of people did not like sports?

A) 76.4

B) 23.6

C) 25

D) 14.2

7

$$-3x + 4y = s$$

$$rx - 8y = -28$$

What values of (r, s) make the system of equations above have infinitely many solutions?

A) (6, 14)

B) (14,6)

C) (3, 4)

D) (9, 5)

8

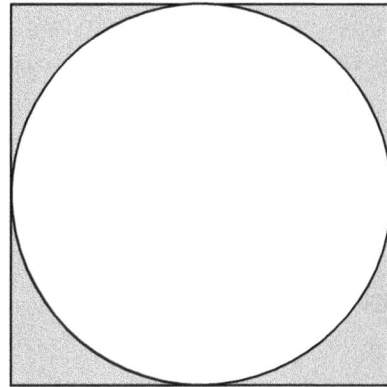

In the figure above, the circle is inscribed within the square. If the diameter of the circle is 12, what is the area of the shaded region?

A) 144

B) 36π

C) $144 - 36\pi$

D) $36 - 9\pi$

9

An author sells the rights to her book to a publishing house. If she sold the book for an initial fee of $1500 and she makes $18.50 for every purchase of the book (x), which expression represents her total profit from sales of the book?

A) $1500 - 18.5x$

B) $18.5x - 1500$

C) $18.5x + 1500$

D) $-18.5 + 1500$

10

A manager at a widget factory inspects 8 widgets out of every 200 produced. At this rate, how many widgets will be inspected if the factory produces 40,000 widgets?

A) 8

B) 200

C) 1600

D) 5000

11

$$y = 22 + 3.9x$$

One end of a slinky is attached to the top of the tent. When an object of mass x grams is attached to the other end of the slinky, the slinky stretches to a length of y inches as shown in the equation above. What is x when y is 69?

A) 47

B) 12.05

C) 23.33

D) 17.69

Questions 12 and 13 refer to the following information.

A school requires that there be, at most, a 20:1 student to teacher ratio.

12

If the school has a total population of 623 students, how many teachers must be employed for the school year?

A) 18

B) 19

C) 30

D) 32

13

The school also sells school supplies to students before the beginning of the year. If 70% of the student body purchases school supplies for $25 each, how much does the school make in total?

A) $9,486

B) $10,902.50

C) $12,543

D) $15.575

14

When 3 times the number m is added to 12, the result is 33. What number results when 15 times m is added to 9?

A) 105

B) 114

C) 135

D) 396

15

Which of the following expresses the parabola $y = (x+3)(x-1)$ in vertex form?

A) $y = x^2 + 2x - 3$

B) $y = (x-1)^2 + 4$

C) $y = (x+1)^2 - 4$

D) $y = x^2 - 2x + 3$

16

Students in a geography bee score 10 points for every correctly answered question and lose 5 points for every incorrectly answered question. If a student answers 14 questions correctly, but misses the final question, what is his final score?

A) 150

B) 145

C) 140

D) 135

17

If $g(n) = 2n + 4$, what has the same value as $g(4) + g(6)$?

A) $g(8)$

B) $g(10)$

C) $g(12)$

D) $g(28)$

18

Number of hours Blake plans to study for the SAT per day	4
Number of parts in the SAT Study Guide	8
Number of chapters in the SAT Study Guide	27
Number of problems Blake works per minute	2
Number of pages in the SAT Study Guide	1,020
Number of problems in the SAT Study Guide	5,000

Blake is planning to study for the SAT. The table above shows information about the SAT Study Guide, Blakes problem solving speed, and the amount of time he plans to spend reading the SAT Study Guide each day. If Blake solves problems at the rates given in the table, which of the following is closest to the number of days it would take Blake to solve all of the problems in the SAT Study Guide?

A) 3

B) 10

C) 11

D) 12

19

Jane is knitting scarves and hats for her family as presents. If each scarf takes 15 feet of yarn to make and each hat takes 12 feet of yarn to make, and she purchases 425 feet of yarn, which inequality represents the maximum number of hats (h) and scarves (s) she can make for her family?

A) $425 \geq 15h + 12s$

B) $425 \geq 15s + 12h$

C) $425 \leq 15h + 12s$

D) $425 \leq 15s + 12h$

20

A company conducted a survey to determine whether students at a school prefer to buy books or borrow them from the library. They surveyed 340 students at the entrance to the library on campus, and 12 refused to answer. Which of the following factors directly affects the reliability of the conclusions drawn from this survey?

A)   Size of the sample

B)   Number of students who refused to answer

C)   Location where survey was given

D)   Size of student population

21

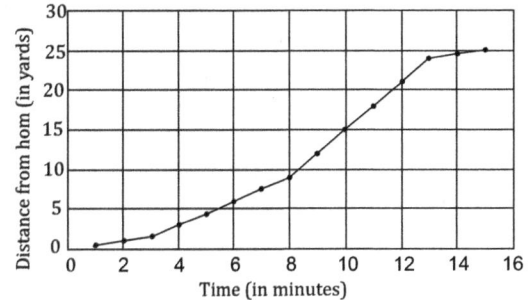

The scatterplot above represents Janet's walk to her friend's house from her home. According to the graph, at approximately what time does Janet walk the fastest?

A)   2 minutes

B)   5 minutes

C)   10 minutes

D)   14 minutes

22

A flock of geese flies south for the winter. If their journey is 2,365 miles and they take 3.75 days to complete the journey, what was their average speed in miles per hour? Round your answer to the nearest tenth.

A) 26.3 mph

B) 260.2 mph

C) 315.3 mph

D) 630.7 mph

23

If a person's weight on the Moon is 16.5% than his or her weight on Earth, what is a person's weight on Earth if they weigh 32 kg on the Moon? Round to the nearest tenth.

A) 44.3 kg

B) 56 kg

C) 193.9 kg

D) 200.1 kg

Questions 24 and 25 refer to the following information.

	Declared Pre-Med Majors	Non-Majors	Total
Passed Biology 101	204	150	354
Did Not Pass Biology 101	32	55	87
Total	236	205	441

The table above shows the pass/fail results of a class of Biology 101 students, which includes Pre-Med majors and some Non-Major students.

24

If a single student is chosen from the full class, what is the probability that they are a Non-Major student who passed the exam?

A) $\dfrac{150}{441}$

B) $\dfrac{204}{441}$

C) $\dfrac{32}{441}$

D) $\dfrac{87}{441}$

25

Of the Pre-Med students who passed the exam, 2.91% of those students achieved a perfect score on the test, while only one Non-Major student received a perfect score. How many total students achieved a perfect score?

A) 2

B) 3

C) 8

D) 10

Questions 26 and 27 refer to the following information.

Number of Days Taken Off	Company A	Company B
0	240	280
1	162	220
2	118	60
3	60	20
4	20	20

A statistician chose 600 employees at random from each of two companies and asked each employee at random how many days they had taken off since the first day of the year. The results are shown in the table above.

26

There are a total of 2,500 employees at Company A and 3,600 at Company B. What is the median number of days taken off in the survey?

A) 0

B) 1

C) 2

D) 3

27

Based on the survey data, which of the following most accurately compares the two companies for employees taking 3 days off?

A) The total number of employees that have taken 3 days off is the same at Company A and Company B.

B) Of the total number of employees that have taken 3 days off Company A is expected to be 60 more than at Company B.

C) Of the total number of employees that have taken 3 days off Company B is expected to be 60 more than at Company A.

D) The total number of employees that have taken 3 days off at Company B is expected to be 1800 more than at Company A.

28

A hardware company is selling a new kind of picture hanging hardware that can hold up to 12 pounds. If a painting is x pounds and the frame is y pounds, which of the following inequality correctly expresses the amount of weight the hardware (h) can hold?

A) $h \geq y - x$

B) $h \geq y + x$

C) $h \leq y - x$

D) $h \leq y - x$

29

For function $f(x) = 4x + x^2 - 12$, what is the value of (x) when (y) is at its minimum?

A) -2

B) 2

C) -4

D) -6

30

A circle with a diameter of 4 cm is transcribed in a square, with the circumference of the circle tangent to the edges of the square. What is the difference between the area of the square and the transcribed circle? Round answer to nearest hundredth,

A) $16 \ cm^2$

B) $12.57 \ cm^2$

C) $4.34 \ cm^2$

D) $3.43 \ cm^2$

DIRECTIONS

For questions 31–38, solve the problem and enter your answer in the grid, as described below, on the answer sheet.

1. Although not required, it is suggested that you write your answer in the boxes at the top of the columns to help you fill in the circles accurately. You will receive credit only if the circles are filled in correctly.
2. Mark no more than one circle in any column.
3. No question has a negative answer.
4. Some problems may have more than one correct answer. In such cases, grid only one answer.
5. **Mixed numbers** such as $3\frac{1}{2}$ must be gridded as 3.5 or 7/2. (If $3|1|/|2$ is entered into the grid, it will be interpreted as $\frac{31}{2}$, not $3\frac{1}{2}$.)
6. **Decimal answers:** If you obtain a decimal answer with more digits than the grid can accommodate, it may be either rounded or truncated, but it must fill the entire grid.

Answer: $\frac{7}{12}$

Write answer in boxes.
← Fraction line
Grid in result.

Answer: 2.5

← Decimal point

Acceptable ways to grid $\frac{2}{3}$ are:

Answer: 201 – either position is correct

NOTE: You may start your answers in any column, space permitting. Columns you don't need to use should be left blank.

31

A limnologist believes that the lakes in the Muskoka Region are eroding by 1.21 meters per year. According to the limnologist's estimate, how long will it take, in years, for the lakes in the Muskoka Region to erode by 20 kilometers?

32

If a hours and 20 minutes is equal to $4\frac{1}{2}$ hours, what is the value of a in quarter hours?

33

In the xy-plane, the point (0, -12) lies on the graph of the function $f(x) = 2x^2 - b$. What is the value of b?

34

In two semesters, Ashley and Danielle spent a combined 480 hours in the center that supports mathematics and statistics on campus. If Ashley spent 60 more hours in the lab than Danielle did, how many hours did Danielle spend in the center each semester?

35

Jerome drove for 15 hours at an average speed of 65 miles per hour. If his car uses 35 miles per gallon, how many gallons did he use on his trip? Round to the nearest whole number.

36

If a sector's interior angle is 72° and the radius is 5 cm, what is the area of the sector? Round your answer to the nearest tenth.

37

A parabolic function can be written in the terms of $f(x) = ax^2 + bx + c$. What is the value of $-c$ after simplifying the function

$$(7x^2 + 3x - 18) - (-3x^2 - 17x + 19)?$$

38

Three cars are traveling 336 miles but breaking up the trip. Car A traveled 3 times as far as Car B, and Car C traveled twice as far as Car B. How many miles did Car C travel?

STOP

**If you finish before time is called, you may check your work on this section only.
Do not turn to any other section.**

No Test Material On This Page

Section #1 – Reading Test

#	Correct Answer	#	Correct Answer	#	Correct Answer	#	Correct Answer	#	Correct Answer	#	Correct Answer
1	A	11	B	21	A	31	B	41	C	51	A
2	B	12	D	22	C	32	D	42	D	52	A
3	C	13	D	23	D	33	A	43	D		
4	C	14	A	24	A	34	C	44	B		
5	D	15	D	25	C	35	B	45	B		
6	C	16	B	26	D	36	A	46	A		
7	D	17	D	27	D	37	A	47	A		
8	A	18	B	28	D	38	C	48	A		
9	C	19	D	29	B	39	D	49	C		
10	A	20	C	30	C	40	C	50	C		

Number of Correct Answers [　　　] **Reading Test Raw Score**

Section #2 – Writing and Language Test

#	Correct Answer	#	Correct Answer	#	Correct Answer	#	Correct Answer	#	Correct Answer
1	A	11	A	21	A	31	D	41	B
2	C	12	D	22	D	32	C	42	D
3	B	13	B	23	B	33	A	43	B
4	D	14	A	24	D	34	B	44	A
5	D	15	C	25	C	35	A		
6	A	16	D	26	B	36	D		
7	B	17	B	27	A	37	A		
8	C	18	C	28	C	38	C		
9	C	19	B	29	D	39	D		
10	B	20	A	30	B	40	A		

Number of Correct Answers [　　　] **Writing and Language Test Raw Score**

Section #3 – Math Test (No Calculator)

#	Correct Answer	#	Correct Answer	#	Correct Answer	#	Correct Answer
1	C	6	A	11	B	16	4
2	B	7	B	12	D	17	2750
3	D	8	C	13	D	18	5.33
4	B	9	D	14	A	19	0.7071
5	C	10	B	15	A	20	196

Number of Correct Answers ☐ Math Test (No Calculator) Raw Score

Section #4 – Math Test (Calculator)

#	Correct Answer	#	Correct Answer	#	Correct Answer	#	Correct Answer
1	B	11	B	21	C	31	16,528.93
2	D	12	D	22	A	32	62.5
3	A	13	B	23	C	33	12
4	D	14	B	24	A	34	105
5	D	15	C	25	C	35	28
6	A	16	D	26	B	36	15.7
7	A	17	C	27	B	37	37
8	D	18	B	28	B	38	112
9	C	19	B	29	A		
10	C	20	C	30	D		

Number of Correct Answers ☐ Math Test (Calculator) Raw Score

CONTINUE

Reading Test
Raw Score (0 - 52)

CONVERT →

Reading Test
Score (10 - 40)

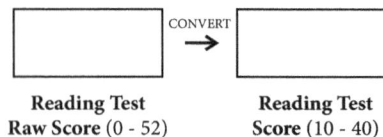

The following is a **Score Conversion Table** (Raw to Scaled) used by the College Board for an SAT® practice test available online. Although each SAT test is scored a bit differently, this table will give you an estimate of your score. Enter your raw scores in the appropriate boxes below, follow the conversion directions and know your estimated SAT scores for this test.

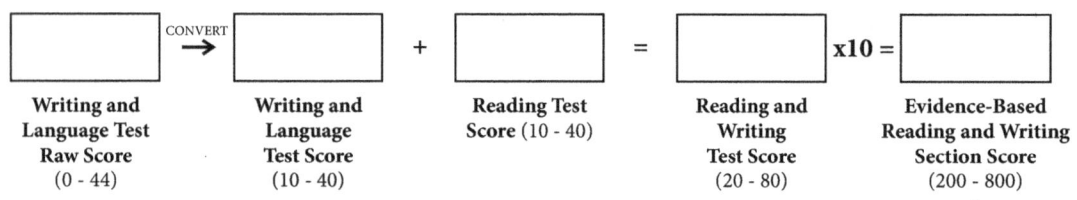

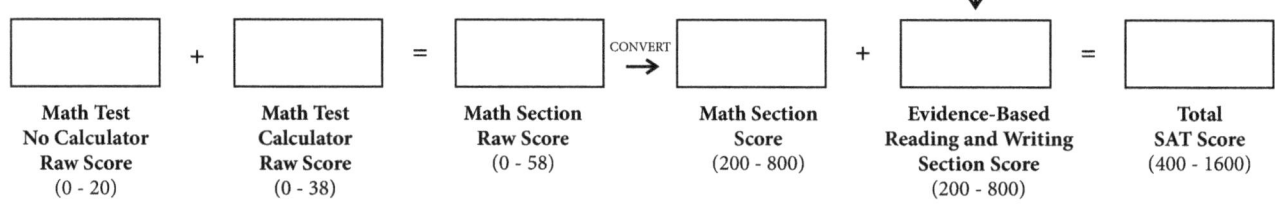

Writing and
Language Test
Raw Score
(0 - 44)

CONVERT →

Writing and
Language
Test Score
(10 - 40)

+

Reading Test
Score (10 - 40)

=

Reading and
Writing
Test Score
(20 - 80)

x10 =

Evidence-Based
Reading and Writing
Section Score
(200 - 800)

↓

Math Test
No Calculator
Raw Score
(0 - 20)

+

Math Test
Calculator
Raw Score
(0 - 38)

=

Math Section
Raw Score
(0 - 58)

CONVERT →

Math Section
Score
(200 - 800)

+

Evidence-Based
Reading and Writing
Section Score
(200 - 800)

=

Total
SAT Score
(400 - 1600)

Raw Score Conversion Table: Section and Test Scores

Raw Score (# of correct answers)	Math Section Score	Reading Test Score	Writing and Language Test Score	Raw Score (# of correct answers)	Math Section Score	Reading Test Score	Writing and Language Test Score
0	200	10	10	30	530	27	29
1	200	10	10	31	530	27	30
2	210	10	10	32	540	28	31
3	230	10	10	33	550	28	31
4	250	11	11	34	550	29	32
5	260	12	12	35	560	29	32
6	280	13	12	36	570	30	33
7	290	14	13	37	580	30	34
8	310	15	14	38	590	31	34
9	320	15	15	39	590	31	35
10	330	16	15	40	600	32	36
11	350	17	16	41	610	32	36
12	360	17	17	42	620	33	37
13	370	18	18	43	630	34	39
14	380	18	18	44	640	35	40
15	390	19	19	45	650	35	
16	400	20	19	46	660	36	
17	420	20	20	47	670	37	
18	430	21	21	48	680	37	
19	430	21	22	49	680	38	
20	440	22	22	50	690	39	
21	450	22	23	51	700	39	
22	460	23	24	52	720	40	
23	470	23	25	53	730		
24	480	24	25	54	740		
25	490	24	26	55	760		
26	500	25	26	56	770		
27	510	25	27	57	790		
28	510	26	28	58	800		
29	520	26	29				

1. **Choice A is the best answer** because the first paragraph starts by setting the mood with a description of a man walking outside a city during the day, then shifts to an "incident" or "event" that happened the same evening. The remainder of the passage explains both what happened and how he felt when he rescued a strange woman. Choice B is incorrect because, while the woman is in the "alarming predicament" or "worrisome situation" of being chased by a strange man, she is not the main character of the story. The story is about the narrator's experiences and how he felt during those experiences. Choice C is incorrect because there is no indication that both characters are "searching" or "actively looking" for change. It is possible that they are basically content with their situations and did not plan to make any alterations. Choice D is incorrect because there is no indication about the age of the narrator at the time the story is told. He could be a young man talking about a recent event.

2. **Choice B is the best answer** because the narrator says he felt "lighthearted" (line 4) when he saw the city gates and felt "as though a burden were falling off my soul" (lines 6-7) when he left the city. Later he refers to the walk as making him feel better because he had been "half-sick" (line 13) and "stifling between city walls" (lines 13-14). Therefore, it can be presumed that he was "displeased" or "not happy" with being in town all the time, which would have been his "daily" or "regular" life since he was a "townsman" (line 13). He was discontent with his conditions, feeling trapped within a city, rather than with a specific event.
Choice A is incorrect because, while the narrator greets people on his walk, there is no indication that meeting them was the purpose of his going for the walk. Choice C is incorrect because there is no indication that the narrator was trying to find adventure, only that he was trying to relax. Choice D is incorrect because there is no reference to the narrator having a "sad event." He does not refer to a specific occurrence that bothered him, only the stifling nature of living in the city.

3. **Choice C is the best answer** because the answer to the previous question is that the narrator takes a walk because he is "displeased" or "not happy" with his daily life. Choice C shows the reason that the narrator was not feeling good: he was a "half-sick townsman" who was "stifling" or "not getting enough air" in the city, so going on a walk was a tremendous relief. His relief is an analogy to finding himself in Italy, presumably a lovely place to be. Choice A is incorrect because it says that the narrator felt better going on the walk, but does not explain why. Choice B says that the people were friendly, but does not support any claim about why the narrator went for a walk. Choice D indicates something that happened on the walk, but does not offer the reason for going on a walk.

4. **Choice C is the best answer** because the passage says that the narrator's "way lay along the canal embankment" (line 19), which shows that he was on the embankment because it was the "route" or "way" he needed to go. He says the reason he was taking that route was, "I was going towards my lodgings" (line 18). "Quarters" and "lodgings" both refer to the place where one lives, so he was headed towards his quarters after walking during the day.
None of the other choices are supported by evidence from the passage. Choice A is incorrect because, although the embankment was usually deserted, "at that hour you never meet a soul" (line 20), there is no proof that he was trying to avoid other people. Choice B is incorrect because he went on his walk to escape the pressures of the city, but the embankment was on his return trip as he was going home to his lodgings. Choice D is incorrect because the embankment was usually deserted, so that is not a place that he would have looked for excitement or adventure.

5. **Choice D is the best answer** because the words "charming" and "jaunty" are often associated with cute, fun things. They imply that the yellow hat and black mantle were sweet or endearing things that a happy young girl might wear, for example, to a party. However, the girl is crying on an embankment at night, so her cheerful clothes form a "contrast" or "opposite" impression.
Choice A is incorrect because the passage indicates that the girl is relatively young; the narrator starts by calling her a "woman" (line 26) and shifts to "girl" (line 30) after he gets a closer look. Clothes described as "charming" and "jaunty" are suitable for a younger person, so do not "belie" or "contradict" that she is young. Choice B is not supported by the passage because there is no description of the temperature or that her clothing was inappropriate; for example, she was not shivering because she was too cold. Choice C is incorrect because the narrator became interested in the woman when he noticed her in a place that usually was deserted. Her clothing is described as he takes a closer look.

CONTINUE

6. **Choice C is the best answer** because the narrator was thinking about "approaching" or "talking to" the woman by saying "madam" and continuing. He did not use this approach because "that exclamation has been uttered a thousand times in every Russian society novel" (lines 42-44). In other words, he stopped at first because the word was "trite" or "overused."
None of the other choices are supported by evidence from the passage. Choice A is incorrect because the narrator stopped because "madam" was overused, not because it was "inappropriate" or "incorrect." Choices B and D are incorrect because the narrator wanted to talk to the girl and "took a step towards her" (line 40), so he intended to speak. He just could not find the right words to say before she ran away.

7. **Choice D is the best answer** because the question is asking for evidence that shows that the stranger was a "coward" or "had no courage." Choice D supports that claim because it says that the man only "protested" or "yelled back" after the narrator was "very far away" (line 70). The man probably was too scared to yell sooner because he did not want to enter a real fight with the narrator, so he waited until there was distance between them before using "vigorous language" or "swearing."
Choice A is incorrect because it only shows that the man was "undignified" or "acting drunk." However, drunk people sometimes get into fights, so Choice A does not show that the man was scared of fighting. Choice B is, if anything, provides evidence opposite of showing cowardice because it shows that the man was aggressive enough to run after the lady. Choice C is incorrect because it only refers to the action of the narrator and the fact that the man realized the narrator's intent. It does not give any clue about the man's response to the narrator.

8. **Choice A is the best answer** because the narrator wanted a chance to talk with the girl, but she ran away when she noticed him. At first he "dared not cross the street after her" (line 50), showing that he still wanted to meet her. The narrator views the appearance of the man as "a chance [that] came to my aid" (line 52). He is able to ward off the man and not only talk to the girl, but also hold her arm. Therefore, the man's appearance was "providential" or "advantageous" because it helped the narrator reach his goal.
Choice B is incorrect because, while he does appear to find the man "abominable" or "hateful," the narrator does not necessarily find the encounter hateful because it gave him a chance to talk to the girl. In addition, Choice B is incorrect because the girl's response to the man was the same as the initial response to the narrator: she ran away. After the narrator scared the man off, she did have a "perceptible" or "noticeable" change in her response because she became appreciative, but that is not a cause to view the encounter as hateful. Choice C is incorrect because the encounter with the man happened after the girl ran away from the narrator. Therefore, it was not "intrusive" or "interrupting" them. Choice D is incorrect because the narrator says "he won't dare to annoy us further" (lines 73-74) which indicates that he feels that the encounter is over. There is no evidence in the passage to show that the narrator is covering a feeling of "foreboding" or "anxiety" that the man might in fact come back for any reason.

9. **Choice C is the best answer** because "obtrusive" refers to the gentleman who startled and chased the woman; a "deplorable" act. None of the other choices adequately describe the gentleman. Choice A refers to something easily perceived. Choice B refers to attracting attention. Choice D refers to being unavoidable.

10. **Choice A is the best answer** because the final paragraph begins by saying that she still had a tear from crying, but then it says that there was "already a gleam of a smile on her lips" (lines 81-82). Therefore, she was starting to feel "gratitude" or "appreciation" at being saved. However, the girl then looks at her "savior," the narrator, and blushes and looks away. This implies some embarrassment, possibly because she finds him handsome. Therefore, she is feeling something more than just appreciation.
Choice B is incorrect because, while the narrator might have "acute perceptions," meaning that he is "observant," saying so is not the purpose of the paragraph. The author is not trying to show that the narrator is sharp-eyed because he sees the blush; the author is showing that the girl is reacting to the presence of the narrator. Choice C is incorrect because only the first sentence refers to fear; the second sentence indicates that the girl is smiling and feeling relief that the encounter is over. Choice D is incorrect because it does not give the "rationale" or "reason" that the narrator helped the girl.

11. **Choice B is the best answer** because Mother Jones is addressing the miners. She describes the conditions they suffer in order to show why change is needed. She emphasizes that they should not "compromise" or "accept lower terms" when they negotiate with mine owners: "But I want to say, make no settlement until they sign up that every bloody murderer of a guard has got to go" (lines 43-45). Her goal is to convince the miners not to "leave a slave class to the coming generation" (lines 73-74).
Choice A is incorrect because Mother Jones is not trying to "describe" or "explain" working conditions because her audience is the miners who undergo the conditions. She gives examples of conditions to support her argument that complete change is needed. Choice C is incorrect because she is not addressing members of the government. She is telling the miners not to give up when they request help from the government. Choice D is incorrect because she is not talking to the owners of the mines, nor is she trying to "initiate" or "start" negotiations. The passage indicates that failed negotiations have been going on for a while.

12. **Choice D is the best answer** because pet dogs are brought up to show that there is a contrast between the way that the dogs are treated and the way that the miners are treated. The dogs have "a good place" (line 25) and "a slave to take care of them" (line 26), as well as attention from the wives of the mine owners. These conditions are contrasted with the conditions of the miners: "They wouldn't keep their dog where they keep you fellows" (lines 24-25). In other words, the conditions that the miners live in are more "sordid" or "foul" than the conditions that dogs live in.
Choice A is incorrect because "consolation" is "comfort for a loss." However, the idea of dogs having better living conditions is not comforting to the miners. Choice B is incorrect because an "adversary" is an "opponent." The guards are adversaries and are referred to as "bloodhounds," but they are not the pet dogs cared for by the miner owners' wives. Choice C is incorrect because the description of the dogs does not show any "compassion" or "caring" on the part of the mine owners. The owners keep the miners in conditions worse than they keep their dogs. The wives may be compassionate towards the dogs, but Choice C refers to the mine owners.

13. **Choice D is the best answer** because "provision" is something that is guaranteed by the Constitution, freedom of speech. Choice D refers to something that is necessary or must happen, so it fits the context of saying that freedom of speech is a right or need guaranteed by the highest law of the country.
None of the other choices adequately shows what is guaranteed by the Constitution. Choice A refers to the process of sharing something. Choice B refers to plans or preparations, but does not include the idea that they must occur. Choice C is a future event that might occur but cannot be accurately predicted.

14. **Choice A is the best answer** because a counterargument is an attack against the writer's main argument. The prompt is asking about a counterargument related to Mother Jones's "credibility" or "believability." Mother Jones "addresses" or "faces" the possible attack that she is not qualified to speak because she is not a miner by saying that she has undergone similar conditions that miners live in and suffer through: "I was with you nearly three years in this State. I went to jail. I went to the Federal courts" (lines 31-33).
Choice B is incorrect because Mother Jones uses her experience in jail as a reason that she can empathize with the miners. It supports her argument of understanding hard conditions rather than weakens her ability to speak for miners. Choice C is incorrect because there is no discussion about how many government contacts she has, so she does not "anticipate" a counterargument on that topic. Choice D is incorrect because Mother Jones does not discuss who will lead the campaign for freedom after she is gone; she implies that the miners will work together to achieve their goal. She does indicate that even if she is not there in person, the miners can carry on the plan of changing their conditions to its completion. However, that argument is referring to her presence in the state rather than to any specific person taking over after she is gone.

15. **Choice D is the best answer** because Mother Jones says that the average wage is $500 a year, but that "before you get a thing to eat there is $20 is taken out a month" (lines 49-50), presumably because the mine owners "take out" the money. Then the "pluck-me" stores, which are owned by the mine owners, take the remaining money for rent. Therefore, the wages are "insufficient" or "not high enough" because the mine owners have the policies of deducting wages and unfairly charging too much.
Choice A is incorrect because the passage says that the "average wages you fellows get in this country is $500 a year" (lines 48-49), which indicates that the wages of the miners Mother Jones is addressing is typical of the rest in the country. Choice B is incorrect because there is no indication that the wages are "periodically" or

"sometimes" being reduced. The income is the same at about $500 per year; the problem is that the amount of money is not enough for expenses. Choice C is incorrect because there is no reference to the amount of money people earn in other jobs; it could be that miners earn more, but that their expenses are too high to survive.

16. **Choice B is the best answer** because it includes the phrase "before I leave the State," which implies that Mother Jones is not planning on staying. She is hoping that the miner and mine owners will "put aside the breach" or "come to an agreement" before she leaves, but does not say that she will stay until after they come to the agreement. Therefore, she is not planning to stay until the negotiations are concluded; she just hopes to do so. Choice A is incorrect because it talks about Mother Jones's past experiences, not her plans for the period until the negotiations are complete. Choice C is incorrect because it only says that the miners are justified in rebelling; it does not outline Mother Jones's plans. Choice D is incorrect because she sets a deadline for the Governor, but does not indicate whether she will be present or not.

17. **Choice D is the best answer** because "inhumanity" refers to actions that are extremely cruel or brutal. The passage says that the "guards of the mining companies beat, abuse, maim, and hold up citizens without process of law" (lines 7-9), which are all cruel or bad acts. The phrase "bloody murderer" shows that Mother Jones feels that the guards are not just "bad," but have reached the worst possible level of crime and brutality.
Choice A is incorrect because the passage does not say that the guards actually murder anyone, only that they "beat, abuse, maim, and hold up citizens without process of law" (lines 8-9). Therefore, "bloody murderer" is not a literal description of the methods they use. Choice B is incorrect because, while murder would be a reason to remove the guards, there is no evidence that the guards murdered. The phrase only shows the extent of Mother Jones's contempt for the guards. Choice C is incorrect because the passage implies that the mine owners approve of the guards' tactics. There is no evidence to show that the mine owners think that the guards have gone too far in their actions.

18. **Choice B is the best answer** because Mother Jones discusses many problems with the system from the living conditions that are worse than that of pet dogs and wages that are not sufficient to feed a family. However, she stresses multiple times that the first step to solve the problem is to eliminate the guards who are terrorizing the miners and their families. In the first paragraph, she attests that the guards are a danger to the security of the state (lines 17-23, "We hold that...West Virginia"). She establishes her argument again in (lines 43-45), "But I want to say, make no settlement until they sign up that every bloody murderer of a guard has got to go." Finally, she sums up with, "I want to tell you that the Governor will get until tomorrow night, Friday night, to get rid of his bloodhounds, and if they are not gone, we will get rid of them!" (lines 69-72). Her main concern is to eliminate the guards, so she feels that one of the biggest "impediments" or "obstacles" to better conditions is the presence of the guards.
Choice A is incorrect because Mother Jones does not say how long it will take to have "significant" or "major" change. She says that change will happen after the first step, removing the guards, is done. Choice C is incorrect because she never says whether the mine owners are aware of the conditions or not; if anything, she implies that they are and condone the behavior of the guards. Choice D is incorrect because she says in (lines 35-37), "not in all the history of the labor movement have I got such an inspiration as I have got from you here to-day." This claim shows that she is proud of the efforts that the miners are making.

19. **Choice D is the best answer** because the answer to the previous question is that one of the primary "impediments" or "obstacles" to progress is the presence of armed guards. Choice D supports this claim because it shows Mother Jones's requirement to remove the guards. The requirement is strong enough that if the government does not follow through, the miners will. Therefore, she feels that it is important enough to remove the guards that it is worth taking any measures necessary. The guards, therefore, are one of the main obstacles to get rid of before the miners will get justice.
Choices A and B are weak because they only show that the guards hurt and intimidate the miners and the miners' families. However, they do not show that the guards are one of the "primary" or "main" obstacles to progress; there could be other, more important obstacles such as changing a dangerous health issue. Choice C is incorrect because it appears that the pluck-me stores, not the guards, are a more serious problem.

20. **Choice C is the best answer** because the child says that there is not enough money for food and he is hungry. The quote emphasizes that not only the miners are affected by the problem at hand; the families, including little children, are also suffering. Mother Jones could have introduced the fact that pluck-me stores take more than the monthly wage using statistics. However, using the voice of a child makes the issue seem more personal and pitiful, highlighting the cruel or inhumane aspect of the practice rather than just the financial aspect.
Choice A is incorrect because Mother Jones could show that there is not enough money using many different methods, such as quoting statistics. Therefore, she deliberately uses the voice of a child to emphasize a point other than just the lack of money. Choice B is incorrect because the description says that the miner goes shopping; it appears that the family goes together because the miner talks to the manager after the child reports that there is not enough money. Choice D is incorrect because the speaker is a child of a miner, but there is no reference that the child also works.

21. **Choice A is the best answer** because "charge" is what the next generation will not do to the miners. Choice A means "blame," so it fits the context of saying that the next generation will not blame the miners for what they have done. They will only blame the miners for what is "undone," meaning that they will blame the miners if the working conditions are still terrible.
None of the other choices fits the context of explaining what the next generation will do or not do to the miners. Choice B refers to a strong order or request, but the actions in "what we've done" (line 76) and "what we have left undone" (line 77) are in the past. Choice C refers to forcing something rather than commenting on something, and Choice D refers to a physical attack rather than a verbal complaint.

22. **Choice C is the best answer** because the passage begins with a discussion of the current conditions in Sub-Saharan Africa: the population is mostly poor and agrarian, the cities are overcrowded with unhealthy conditions, and the government does not have sufficient funds from the formal sector. There is a turning point at (lines 36-40)("However…in its future") to the suggestion that tourism could help that problem. The suggestion is backed up with information about appealing places that could be developed for tourism. The passage ends with a few qualifications, showing that the current situation will have to change for the economy to improve via the method suggested.
Choice A is incorrect because only one strategy—tourism—is proposed to help "resolve" or "fix" the "ongoing" or "continuing" problem of a poor economy with low standards of living. Choice B is incorrect because, although the passage "analyzes" or "discusses" the demographic change of moving from rural areas to urban ones, that is not the focus of the passage. About half of the passage discusses tourism, which is not a reason for the change. Choice D is incorrect because there is no indication that people in Sub-Saharan Africa are "not aware" or "do not see" the possibility of using its cultural and natural sites to attract tourists; there is just inadequate infrastructure to use the resources to the fullest. In fact, (lines 55-56) ("Even now…reserves") shows that the potential of animals to attract visitors is already known.

23. **Choice D is the best answer** because the passage begins with a discussion of the "worrisome trend" of a sharp increase in people moving to cities that are unable to accommodate the residents. The trend includes the poor quality of living and economic outlook for the region of Sub-Saharan Africa. After describing the problem, the passage introduces the possible solution of increasing tourism, and says that there are ample reasons that tourists would want to visit. The final section gives "caveats" or "warnings" that establishing the infrastructure for tourism will cost money and could cause various problems such as "a negative impact on the environment" (line 82).
Choice A is incorrect because the passage does not refer to a "deficient attempt" or "insufficient effort" to "remedy" or "solve" the economic problems. Choice B is incorrect because the passage does not describe "obstacles" or "problems in the way" of improving the economy other than to imply that more formal business would increase government tax bases to help with infrastructure. The passage offers one idea, tourism, that could help, but does not explain specific ways that the tourism will get rid of the informal business or bolster the economy. Choice C is incorrect because, while the increasing population and poor economic outlook could be considered an "impending crisis" or "disaster close at hand," the middle of the passage is not a list of resources to fight that problem. The only resources listed are reasons why tourism might flourish, and are presented after the suggestion of tourism is given.

CONTINUE

24. **Choice A is the best answer** because the passage defines the informal sector of the economy as "that which is not regulated, controlled, or taxed" (line 11). Therefore, a situation where goods are bartered between people would count as "informal" because there is no money changing hands and no taxes paid on the exchange.
Choice B is incorrect because the projects sponsored by a foreign investor would most likely need to go through an approval process and the school would need to pass at least a basic inspection. Choice B would include regulations and controls, so would be considered formal. Choice C is incorrect because, while it might not be completely honest, there would still need to be nominal proof about how much tax money was spent and what it was used for. Choice D is weak because there is no evidence in the example to elaborate on the young man's situation. For example, he could have filed all the correct paperwork, moved into a new apartment and be paying income taxes from his new salary.

25. **Choice C is the best answer** because in the sentence, "draw" is what beach resorts create. Choice C refers to the trait of being attractive and interesting. It fits the context of saying that even if there were no other tourist destinations, beach resorts are very attractive and interesting to tourists.
Choice A is incorrect because it refers to a large number of things collected by someone, but the beach resorts do not have a lot of things that they bought or amassed. Choice B refers to the act of convincing someone to do something. However, the beaches do not try to make people come; they are just interesting enough that people want to visit. Choice D relates to a link or attachment rather than something that pulls from afar.

26. **Choice D is the best answer** because the question is asking for evidence that shows that major changes need to be made in order to build a tourist industry. Choice D directly states that changes need to be made to security and public health so they are at higher levels than they are now because tourism "demands" or "requires" the changes.
Choice A is weak because it only says that tourism will grow if Africa offers a safe environment and manages its resources. However, it does not directly say that changes need to be made. It is possible that the resources are managed effectively and that the area is safe already; Choice A could then indicate that the conditions need to continue for tourism to flourish. Choice B is incorrect because it only says that Africa has a small amount of tourism compared to the rest of the world. It does not indicate that changes need to be made to increase the tourism. Choice C is incorrect because it only shows that some sites are more appealing as tourist destinations. It does not say that any need to change to increase tourism.

27. **Choice D is the best answer** because "broader" is a comparative adjective that shows the difference between the tourism business and the sites. The paragraph shows that the tourism business contains many different aspects than just the sites: it also includes "transportation, hotels and guest accommodations, and services that link the various components of a trip" (lines 73-75). Choice D refers to something that covers a wide range of topics or deals with many elements of something, so accurately shows that tourism deals with many more elements than just the sites.
None of the other choices effectively establishes the relationship between the tourism business and the sites. Choice A refers to something that is more noticeable or clear. Choice B refers to something that is not detailed or only covers the main points. Choice C refers to something that is wide in physical space.

28. **Choice D is the best answer** because the passage says that one problem of tourism is that there could be "divisions and social friction" (lines 86-87), which are conflicts, as a result of the "disparity" or "difference" between tourists and the workers who get lower pay. In other words, the local workers become "resentful" or "dissatisfied" because of the difference in wages.
None of the other choices are supported by evidence from the passage. Choice A is incorrect because there is no indication about what members of the community are employed are not. The implication is that enough people will be employed that the entire community will benefit. Choice B is incorrect because, while it is presumed that the income from tourism would be "formal" and taxed, there is no discussion about how much of the income would go to the government and how much would stay in the community. There is also no reference as to how the government would use the tax money; it could benefit the community in terms of better services such as schools and medical facilities. Choice C is incorrect because there is no discussion of replacing local cultures and traditions with new ones. If anything, there could be a preservation of rites that visitors want to watch.

29. **Choice B is the best answer** because the answer to the previous question is that one negative impact of tourism in Africa is that individuals who work in the industry may become resentful of visitors. Choice B supports that claim because it says that the "disparity" or "difference" in income between the visitors with more money and workers with less money could lead to "divisions" or "conflict." Presumably that conflict arises from "resentment" or "dissatisfaction" because the income levels are so different.
Choice A gives one negative effect of tourism, but is incorrect because it does not show that industry workers may become resentful of visitors. Choice C is weak because it does not directly say that locals could be resentful of tourists. It gives a reason that a community may not decide to develop tourism, but does not say that locals are angry at the tourists. Choice D is incorrect because it weakens the claim that locals resent tourists. Choice D gives a very positive reason that locals would appreciate having tourists visit.

30. **Choice C is the best answer** because the number of tourists in Togo in 2016 was 65,000. That number is lower than the one for Nigeria, 634,000, but higher than the number for Eritrea, 28,000.
Choice A is incorrect because, although Togo is the top row on the figure, it does not have the highest number of tourists. The country with the highest number of tourists is Nigeria in the bottom row, which had almost ten times as many visitors as Togo did. Choice B is incorrect because the number for Togo is greater than that for Burundi, 56,000, but lower than that for Nigeria. Choice D is impossible to determine only from figure 1 because the figure does not give the number of tourists for the previous year.

31. **Choice B is the best answer** because figure 1 shows the number of tourists in 2016, and the data for Sierra Leone, the second bar from the bottom, is 30,000. Figure 2 shows the percentage of increase from the previous year, 2015. The data for Sierra Leone, in the far left-hand column, is just over 120%, around 123%.
Choice A is incorrect because the figures do not give any detail about "infrastructure" or the facilities and services needed for tourism. Therefore, it is impossible to determine which country had the best infrastructure based on the data. Choice C is incorrect because it says that Burundi had an "increase" of 56,000 visitors from 2015 to 2016, which misinterprets the data from figure 1. Figure 1 lists the total number of visitors in 2016 rather than the difference or "increase" between 2015 and 2016. Choice D is incorrect because figure 1 shows that Madagascar had a greater number—not percentage—of tourists who visited in 2016 than Eritrea did. Figure 2 shows a percentage increase in numbers of tourists, but the percentage for Madagascar, about 20%, is lower than that of Eritrea, about 25%.

32. **Choice D is the best answer** because the passage begins by saying that researchers have developed an antibody that "could one day be administered as a stand-alone treatment or as part of a more effective combination treatment against opioid overdoses" (lines 5-8). Paragraph 2 describes the currently-available drug for treatment, and paragraph 3 introduces the possibility of an alternative. Paragraphs 4 and 5 describe the methodology of the experiment. The remainder of the passage discusses how the new drug compares to the currently-available treatment and offers possibilities for how it might be used in a treatment program.
Choice A is incorrect because, while the antibody 6A4 is compared to naloxone, the passage focuses on the development of 6A4 rather than the methods in which the drugs work. Choice B is incorrect because the reason naloxone is preferred is given briefly at the start: it is the only available drug now. The negative aspects of naloxone are summarized and a drug that surmounts those problems is introduced. Choice C is incorrect because the "implications on the medical industry" are not really described. It is possible that 6A4 will replace naloxone, but there is no analysis about how that will change the manufacture, distribution, and use of the drugs.

33. **Choice A is the best answer** because the passage says that naloxone breaks down quickly, "after about an hour." This is "not completely desirable" or "unwanted" because it means that the drug needs to be carefully administered and the progress of the patient watched or the patient could "relapse" or "return to the original condition."
Choice B is incorrect because the passage says that "biological therapies are much more expensive to make than small molecules" (lines 78-79), so that implies that the small molecule naloxone is cheaper to make. (lines 52-54) confirm that naloxone is small: "the researchers attribute to naloxone's faster distribution through the body as a small molecule." Choice C is incorrect because the passage does not say that naloxone has "no results" for some drugs. It only claims that it is less effective, meaning it has results that are not as strong, for "powerful synthetic opioids like fentanyl and carfentanil" (lines 19-20). Choice D is incorrect because there is no evidence of side

effects related to naloxone. The only negative effect discussed is that it needs to be reapplied often because it wears off soon.

34. **Choice C is the best answer** because the answer to the previous question is that naloxone is not a completely desirable solution for opiate overdoses because it is only able to protect a patient for a limited period. Choice C supports that claim because it says that the drug "breaks down" or "lasts" for only about an hour, a short period. That is a problem, or "not desirable," because the patient could relapse again.
Choice A says that naloxone is the best option available for treating opiate overdoses; it does not provide any evidence that there is any problem with using it. Choice B is incorrect because it only explains how the drug works. It does not offer any reason that the drug is not "desirable" or "advantageous." Choice D is incorrect because, if anything, it makes naloxone look more desirable than 6A4 because it helps patients faster.

35. **Choice B is the best answer** because the phrase is used to describe the "fentanyl analogs" or "drugs comparable to fentanyl." The fact that they were "commonly confiscated" or "often seized" by law enforcement shows that the drugs are ones in common use, and therefore are likely to be illegal drugs that overdose patients had access to and used. If this is true, the research on the drugs is likely to "apply" or "be relevant" to "authentic cases" or "real situations" in which a patient overdoses on an illegal drug.
Choice A is incorrect because the method of "obtaining" or "getting" the drugs is not mentioned. The researchers could have gotten the drugs from a variety of sources. Choice C is incorrect because the fact that the drugs were the kind seized by officers does not show that the trials were not "improperly" or "incorrectly" done. The research could have been faulty in areas unrelated to the type of drug used. Choice D is incorrect because there is no indication that the research required special permits to use the drugs. Therefore, the quote is not included to "establish" or "provide a reason" for a point that is not even mentioned.

36. **Choice A is the best answer** because the passage says that buprenorphine is "used to help people reduce their opioid use" (lines 69-70). Presumably, it is common in patients who are in treatment for opiate abuse and the patients should continue to use it. If 6A4 bound to buprenorphine, the drug would then not be effective and its good work at reducing opiate use would be negated. If 6A4 does not bind to buprenorphine, then the drug can continue to function normally.
Choice B is incorrect because buprenorphine is not a treatment for drug overdose, so there is no indication that it reduces symptoms of overdoses. Choice C is incorrect because, while buprenorphine is an opioid and can trigger overdoses when misused, that is not a reason that it is good that 6A4 does not bind to it. If anything, Choice C could provide a reason that it might be useful to bind to buprenorphine in extreme cases. Choice D is not supported by evidence from the passage. The passage only says that buprenorphine helps reduce opioid use. It does not say whether people have a greater chance of survival when using it.

37. **Choice A is the best answer** because Averick says that Janda's approach is "unique and orthogonal," meaning that it is interesting and unusual. However, he has "reservations" or "doubts" that it will be a usable option for most patients: he "wonders about the antibodies' practicality as a treatment" (lines 77-78). Since Averick "has worked on extending naloxone's lifetime using nanoparticles" (lines 72-73), he is also in the field of drug research.
Choice B is incorrect because both researchers are working to treat opiate overdoses, but only Janda is using antibodies. Averick is using nanoparticles to improve the drug naloxone. Choice C is incorrect because both researchers are pursuing different lines of treatment; one is not building on the work of the other. Choice D is incorrect because Averick's research was unrelated to Janda's. He did not "duplicate" or "repeat" Janda's tests.

38. **Choice C is the best answer** because the question is asking for a "counterargument" or "evidence against" the claim that 6A4 is a perfect solution for overdose patients in third-world countries. Choice C says that 6A4 is "more expensive" than other solutions because of special facilities to make and store the drug. Therefore, 6A4 may not be useful in places that do not have a lot of financial resources to pay for the drug. In addition, if the countries do not have proper storage facilities (such as refrigeration), the drug may not last long enough to be given to patients in need.
Choice A gives a positive effect of 6A4, which would strengthen rather than weaken the claim that it is a good solution for curing opiate overdoses anywhere. Choice B is incorrect because it only describes a detail about the method that 6A4 works; there is no indication that crossing the blood-brain barrier is a good or bad thing.

Therefore, Choice B does not eliminate the possibility that 6A4 is an ideal solution for opiate overdose patients in third-world countries. Choice D is incorrect because it, if anything, suggests a reason that 6A4 is becoming a better treatment option: manufacturing processes are cheaper than in the past, making it more accessible to people with limited incomes.

39. **Choice D is the best answer** because "counter" is what the antibodies' ability does to the synthetic opioids' effects. Choice D refers to nullifying or making something ineffective, so accurately shows that the researchers are trying to determine how well the antibodies do at making the opioids ineffective.
Choice A refers to refusing something in a way that is not gracious. It describes a deliberate action in response to an offer or request. Choice B refers to evading or deflecting something, so does not show that the opioids are stopped from working. Choice D refers to a conflict in which two things are in disagreement. However, the antibodies do not say that the opioids are wrong or do the opposite action; they stop the effect from occurring.

40. **Choice C is the best answer** because "any opiate" would include both users of prescription opiates and users of non-prescription opiates. In figure 1, any opiate refers to the combination of the bottom and middle sections of the column. The right-hand column for 2017 has a combined amount of about 48,000 deaths since the second section of the bar reaches to just under the 50,000 line.
None of the other choices is supported by data from the graph. Choice A is the combined number of opiate deaths in 2007 or the prescription opiate deaths for 2017. Choice B is the number of deaths for "other opiates" and does not include prescription opiates. Choice D is the total for all overdose deaths in 2017, so it includes deaths caused by drugs other than opiates.

41. **Choice C is the best answer** because in figure 1, there are three division of drugs that caused deaths: prescription opiates, other opiates, and non-opiate drugs. "Non-prescription opiates" applies to the second category because it includes opiates that are not given for prescriptions. According to the data in the far right-hand column for 2017, the center portion for "other opiates" is larger—meaning that more people died in that category—than the bottom section for prescription opiates.
Choice A is incorrect because, while there were more deaths in 2017 than in 1999, figure 1 does not give any data about the number of people who "misused" drugs. It does not show, for example, people who got sick from overdosing but did not die. Choice B is incorrect because the bottom section for "prescription opiates" increases only slightly between 2007 and 2017, from about 13,000 to about 18,000. By contrast, there was a large increase in the number of deaths in the middle section of the bar, from about 6,000 in 2007 to about 30,000 in 2017. Choice D is incorrect because figure 1 does not give information about the percentage of users who die of overdoses, it only gives the total number of deaths. It is possible that a vast number of people got prescription opiates in 2017, but only a few had overdoses, and in the past, only a few people used prescription opiates but almost all died.

42. **Choice D is the best answer** because the author gives many scientific reasons that life may exist, but does not describe the research that went into determining the "findings" or "results." For example, he says, "Amino acids, just like those that make up every protein in our bodies, have been found in the tails of comets" (lines 16-18), giving the findings of experiments on comets but not explaining how the amino acids were found. The same is true for his discussion of organic compounds in Martian soil, a giant cloud of space alcohol, and the discovery of thousands of habitable planets.
Choice A is incorrect because "anecdotes" refers to stories from the author's experience, but the author does not discuss any details from his life. Choice B is incorrect because there are no "analogies" or "comparisons used to teach" in the passage. Choice C is incorrect because "unsubstantiated" means that there is no evidence to support the theories. However, the facts that the author brings up, such as the presence of organic compounds in Martian soil, are based on research and supported by facts that are not discussed in the passage.

43. **Choice D is the best answer** because the author follows the phrases about extraterrestrial life with a question that asks how such life has changed from "sci-fi fairytale to a serious scientific endeavor" (lines 4-5). The author is emphasizing the transition in how people perceive extraterrestrial life. In the past, it was viewed as something "impossible" or "not real," and the phrases highlight that image. The phrases provide a strong contrast to the "credible" or "believable" nature of extraterrestrial life today, which the author summarizes in the concept that

CONTINUE

the search for life is "modelled by macroeconomists, funded by fiscal conservatives and discussed by theologians" (lines 5-7).

Choice A is incorrect because the author never describes the appearance of extraterrestrial life. The phrases may evoke images, but they do not act as a contrast for the current beliefs about what life outside Earth might look like. Choice B is incorrect because the images evoked by the phrases are all theatrical forms of aliens. They do not necessarily reflect what scientists think actual extraterrestrial life might look like, and do not "encourage" or "suggest" that the reader think about anything other than the stereotypes. Choice C is incorrect because, while the phrases may be "lighthearted," the purpose is not to make the reader laugh. The purpose is to emphasize the important point that the new view of extraterrestrial life is very serious compared to views of such life in the past.

44. **Choice B is the best answer** because "special kind of complex chemistry" is what "life" is. Choice B refers to a class or category, so fits the context of saying that life is a category of chemistry that uses simple elements. Choice A is incorrect because it refers to a replica, an original that replicas are made from, or an ideal. None of these fit the context because there are no copies of the general concept of life. Choice C is incorrect because it refers to one form of something that is different from others. It does not fit the context because it is used to describe things that are created or revised to be different from each other, not to a natural process such as chemistry. Choice D refers to a pattern for something. However, life is a changing process that does not follow a specific set of guidelines or blueprint.

45. **Choice B is the best answer** because the Breakthrough Starshot project is introduced in a sentence with "with" showing that it is the method of achieving the main part of the sentence. The main clause is "plans for this are already afoot" (line 36), and "this" refers to the previous sentence, "that system might be close enough for us to reach using current technology" (lines 33-34). Therefore, the Breakthrough Starshot project is the method that may be possible for reaching the start system of Proxima Centauri. Reaching the star system would presumably require a spacecraft of some sort.

Choice A is incorrect because other projects, including one conducted by astronomers from the University of California, are involved in trying to search for Earth-sized planets in the "habitable zone." There is no indication that the Breakthrough Starshot project is looking for new planets, only that it is trying to use current technology to go to one that is close. Choice C is incorrect because, while the project is designed to look for life, it is not trying to prove that life appeared at a certain time period. The project would presumably be a success if it proved that life appeared at any time, even very recently. Choice D is incorrect because there is no evidence to support the claim that the project wants to send humans to a different planet, only that it wants to look for life. It is most likely that if current technology is used, a spacecraft that can reach a planet orbiting Proxima Centauri would be unmanned.

46. **Choice A is the best answer** because the passage begins by saying that many planets might potentially host life, but we only can use "light and other radiation" (line 44) to find out if they do. The second paragraph says that using current technology, we can only find life on planets with specific biospheres that have water such as on Earth. However, the passage continues to warn that what "we find on Earth can serve as a guide but also has potential to lead us astray" (lines 80-82), meaning that we may misinterpret signs because we only know about what life looks like on Earth. The last paragraph further warns that "we also might not be able to detect biospheres even if they exist" (lines 83-84). Therefore, the passage is saying that many types of subsurface life may never be detected, and that even surface life might not appear to be life when we are looking at the radiation patterns. In other words, we may not find life, even in places where it exists.

Choice B is incorrect because the passage only says that we need to focus on searching for planets with surface water because they are easier to identify. The statement that "habitable conditions might prevail in the subsurface of Mars or inside the icy moons of the outer solar system" (lines 56-58) show that it is possible that life exists in places other than the surface. Choice C is incorrect because, while the passage points out that identifying life will be hard, it is still possible to do so using light and other radiation detectable by current equipment. Choice D is incorrect because the passage does not critique theories about extraterrestrial life; it does not complain that the theories make it appear easy to find.

47. **Choice A is the best answer** because "prevail" is used to describe what the "habitable conditions" (line 56) do in the "subsurface of Mars or inside the icy moons of the outer solar system" (lines 57-58). Choice A means "occur"

or "be found," so shows that the habitable conditions may occur in places like under the surface of Mars or inside icy moons.

Choices B and C are incorrect because they refer to having a victory or success over something else. However, the habitable conditions do not win in a contest against places like inside Mars or icy moons. Choice D refers to lasting or continuing, often despite hardship. However, the habitable conditions do not continue on despite problems; the habitable conditions just occur.

48. **Choice A is the best answer** because the question is asking for a reason that life that is not on the outside layer of a planet may not be "detected" or "noticed." Choice A offers such a reason: it shows that life may not change the planet enough that the changes could be seen through a telescope as having a "biological origin" or "caused by life." The signs of life may be too small to affect the overall appearance of the planet from afar. Therefore, no matter where the life is found, scientists may not be able to see the signs.

Choice B is incorrect because it says why it is possible to detect life on Earth from afar. It does not show why life under the surface of a different planet may not be noticeable. Choice C is incorrect because it only says that there may be causes of seemingly biological signs other than life. It does not say that subsurface life forms cannot be detected. Choice D is incorrect because it gives a reason why it might be hard to detect life similar to that which was on the surface of Earth billions of years ago. It does not address the question of how to find life under the surface.

49. **Choice C is the best answer** because Sagan's quote is a warning that before assuming that there is life, "we will need to work hard to think of any nonbiological process" (lines 74-76) that could explain "some features in the light spectrum that might be indicative of life" (lines 73-74). Choice C is a case that Sagan would warn against because it assumes that oxygen is caused by living creatures rather than considering and eliminating all other possible reasons that there may be oxygen present.

Choice A is incorrect because it offers tangible proof of an organism rather than just guessing that there is life based on secondary signs. Choice B is incorrect because it shows that the scientist does not rashly assume that oxygen means there is life. Sagan would approve because the scientist indicates there are other options to explain the oxygen. Choice D is incorrect because it does not show that anyone is jumping to the conclusion that there is life before enough facts exist to prove that there is life.

50. **Choice C is the best answer** because Passage 1 identifies a planet as "habitable" or "capable of hosting life" on planets "where temperatures are mild enough for liquid water to exist on the surface" (lines 29-30). Passage 2 acknowledges that life could occur in many different places, but says that to find life, it is best to look in the habitable zone, which "focuses on this requirement for surface liquid water" (lines 67-68), because "these worlds would have biospheres detectable at a distance" (lines 70-71).

Choice A is incorrect because both passages indicate that life may exist under the surface of Mars, but not on the surface. Choice B is incorrect because Passage 2 says that it may not be possible to determine whether life exists based only on a biosphere, but Passage 1 does not delve into the topic of biospheres at all. Choice D is incorrect because Passage 1 suggests that life will be found in the immediate future: "discovery now seems inevitable and possibly imminent" (lines 10-11). Passage 2 also agrees that life probably exists. However, it does not offer a timeline for finding life, and, if anything, implies that the search is so difficult that it may take a lot of time or not happen at all with currently available technology.

51. **Choice A is the best answer** because "farfetched" means "very unlikely." The author of Passage 2 says that there is "no ability to send probes there to sample" (lines 47-48), so there is no way of "encountering" or "meeting" extraterrestrial life in person. Instead, Passage 2 indicates we can only learn about life through second-hand methods such as scanning the "light and other radiation" (line 49) from systems that may contain life. Therefore, the author of Passage 2 would say it is not "testable" now to meet or identify specific types of life, though it may be possible to detect signs of life.

Choice B is incorrect because "fallacious" means "based on a mistaken belief." The author of Passage 2 might say the idea was fallacious because it is impossible to go somewhere to meet the organisms, but would not say it is fallacious because Earth is the only planet with a detectable biosphere. The passage indicates that it is possible to find other biospheres similar to that of Earth. Choice C is incorrect because "plausible" means "reasonable" or "likely." However, the author of Passage 2 suggests that it might be impossible to find life under the surface of

CONTINUE

planets. Therefore, the reason it would be plausible to find life would be if the life is on a surface with water where scientists are searching for life. Choice D is incorrect because the author of Passage 2 indicates that life could exist, though we do not have evidence of it yet. Therefore, meeting life is not "inconceivable," or "not possible," just "not likely."

52. **Choice A is the best answer** because the answer to the previous question is that the author of Passage 2 would most likely respond to the claim in Passage 1 that encountering extraterrestrial life is now a testable hypothesis by saying that the claim is farfetched, as there is no method of exploring places where life might exist. Choice A supports that answer because it shows that there is no way to "send probes" or "explore" planets in other solar systems. The quote says that the only available way now is to analyze light and other radiation. Therefore, it is "farfetched" or "unlikely" that we will "encounter" or "meet" organisms anytime soon; it is not currently "testable."

Choice B is incorrect because it only says what types of planets may contain life. It does not say that the author of Passage 2 would say that encountering extraterrestrial life is not a testable hypothesis; it is farfetched. Choice C explains why Earth is unique in our solar system, but does not say that it farfetched to encounter life on other planets with similar biospheres. Choice D identifies what planets may have life, but does not say that it is a farfetched claim to encounter the life.

1. **Choice A is the best answer.** The underlined text poses the main question that is explored in the passage. Its inclusion at the highlighted location, therefore, helps frame the focus of the following text for the reader. Choice B is incorrect since the underlined text does, indeed, provide an effective introduction. Choice C is incorrect. There is no essential information that has been ignored by the underlined text. Choice D is incorrect. There is no preceding information that is clarified by the underlined text.

2. **Choice C is the best answer.** Notice that the current first sentence of the paragraph includes a list of ideas. A colon is the best punctuation mark to precede such a list of items. Between Choices C and D — which are the only two options to include a colon — Choice C is far more specific and relevant to the following text. Choice A is incorrect. The current paragraph construction excludes a topic sentence, and this affects the reader's understanding of the following ideas.
Choice B is less suitable. Although the semicolon has been accurately used to separate two independent clauses, this choice would make the sentence less active/direct than using the colon to introduce a list of ideas.
Choice D is incorrect not only because it is more ambiguous than Choice C, but also because it uses the present tense ("have"), when the following list begins with "you'd" (i.e., you would).

3. **Choice B is the best answer.** This answer choice very clearly sets out the expectations that are being described in relation to the hiring and development that are described earlier in the sentence. Choice A is less suitable because this answer choice is ambiguous and does not tell the reader how the described expectations relate to the preceding content. Furthermore, the phrase "expect plateaus" is meaningless without more clarification as to what is being referred to. Choice C is incorrect because "expect different results" is also ambiguous and does not allow the reader to understand the link between this phrase and its preceding ideas. Choice D is incorrect. Deleting the underlined section would lead to an incomplete sentence.

4. **Choice D is the best answer** since it is the only option that accurately places the present tense of "is" alongside the present continuous tense of "being shattered —" maintaining both grammatical accuracy in its conjunction and in verb-tense agreement (present tense and present perfect tense) in this paragraph. Choice A, B, and C are incorrect. All three options are grammatically inaccurate and make the sentence meaningless.

5. **Choice D is the best answer.** None of the proposed conjunctive adverbs are appropriate in the given context, where the following text helps explain why "the days of a steady, stable career are over." Choice A is incorrect since "therefore" alters the nature of the relationship to cause and effect — suggesting that the cause (flatter organizational structures) are actually the effect. Choice B is incorrect. "Although" suggests a conditional relationship that does not exist in the highlighted text. Choice C is incorrect. Starting the sentence with "because" would make it a dependent clause and thus, unable to be a standalone sentence.

6. **Choice A is the best answer.** The comma use here effectively helps separate the different items/ideas that are being presented here. Choice B is incorrect since a semicolon can only be used to separate independent clauses that each have their own subjects, verbs, and objects. Choice C is incorrect. Since there is no list of items following the word "up," a colon would be grammatically inaccurate. Choice D is incorrect. The dash is used to add special emphasis to a particular part of a sentence. Since such emphasis is not needed in the highlighted text, this punctuation choice would not be appropriate.

7. **Choice B is the best answer.** The use of the simple present tense in the preceding verbs ("give" and "need") suggest that the simple present tense would be the best choice here as well. Choice A is incorrect. While the present continuous tense would not be incorrect (since the following verb uses this conjugation), it is the use of "are" that makes the current use of "showing" incorrect. Since

"research" is a singular subject, the only accurate way of using the present continuous tense would be to say, "is showing."

Choices C & D are incorrect since the past and future tense conjugations would cause a verb-tense inconsistency within the sentence.

8. **Choice C is the only possible answer.** Notice that the following information with Hoffman's quote is used to substantiate the preceding idea about part-time work trends "only accelerating."

    Terms like "but," "however," and "although" all point to relationships of contrast and as such, would be inappropriate in the given context.

9. **Choice C is the best answer.** Separating the sentences into two independent clauses retains the meaning, while also preventing the use of an unnecessarily long sentence.

    Choice A is incorrect. Although the semicolon separates two independent clauses, its use here would cause an extremely long sentence.

    Choice B is incorrect since the use of a comma would make the sentence hard to follow for the reader.

    Choice D is incorrect. There is no list in the highlighted section that would need to be preceded by a colon.

10. **Choice B is the best answer.** This is the only answer choice that is both grammatically accurate and is in keeping with the main premise of the paragraph, i.e., that companies need to rethink their approach to the problem (in the following sentence).

    Choice A is unsuitable since the current sentence is grammatically incorrect.

    Choice C is incorrect. This sentence would contradict the following ideas by suggesting that companies should "not" adapt their strategies. The article clearly states that organizations should evolve and adapt in response to shifting approaches to work.

    Choice D is incorrect. Deleting the underlined section would make the sentence grammatically incorrect.

11. **Choice A is the best answer.** Notice the use of the simple present tense in the following verbs ("improve" and "foster"). This immediately tells us that the simple present tense is the only way to maintain verb-tense consistency in this sentence.

    While Choices B and C can be eliminated for not using the simple present tense, Choice D is incorrect because this use of the simple present tense would be appropriate only for a singular subject. Here, the subject is plural ("organizations"), making "encourage" the only grammatically accurate choice.

    Choice A is incorrect since a semicolon would require

12. **Choice D is the best answer.** Notice that there are two independent clauses on either side of the highlighted section. A period or a semicolon, therefore, would be the only possible punctuation options.

    Since a semicolon is not given as a possible choice, Choice D is the only accurate answer.

13. **Choice B is the best answer.** The suggested addition is ambiguous and does not add any insight to ideas that have already been presented in the text. For instance, "massacres" and "mass killing" are terms that already communicate an extensive loss of life. If the suggested addition were more specific in the number of people whose lives were lost, it could have been a more informative addition.

    Choice A is incorrect. No prior information is clarified through this suggested addition.

    Choice C is incorrect. The suggested sentence is not needed to introduce the following information.

    Choice D is incorrect. Although the information is not necessary, it is not irrelevant to the content of the passage.

14. **Choice A is the best answer.** Since the French occupation is only mentioned in the previous paragraph, restating whose military operations used "rape and torture" as features helps clarify the ideas for the reader. Deleting parts or the entirety of the highlighted section would negatively affect the reader's understanding of the ideas being presented here.

15. **Choice C is the best answer.** It is the only one that both expands on why these globally renowned figure made their way to Algeria (unlike Choice A) and retains the focus of the text on Algeria (unlike Choices B & D, which shift focus onto Malcolm X and Guevara).

16. **Choice D is the best answer** since it specifically clarifies what "it" refers to. The previous sentence refers to guerillas, mountains, and Algeria.
Without a specific mention of the subject that is being referred to as "the closest model," the reader stands the risk of misunderstanding what exactly is being referred to.

17. **Choice B is the best answer.** In this quotation, Mandela is comparing the contexts of Algeria and South Africa — both had a large white settler community that ruled over an indigenous majority.
Given that idea remains clear when the sentence ends with "indigenous majority," no following clarifications as presented in Choices A, C, and D are necessary.

18. **Choice C is the only answer** choice that maintains verb-tense consistency with the past tense that has been used in the following sentences ("were," "learnt").
Since all the other answer choices use verb forms in the present tense (Choice A), future tense (Choice B), and past continuous tense (Choice C), they can be eliminated as options.

19. **Choice B is the best answer.** Currently, the sentence is long and hard for the reader to follow. By spitting the ideas that have been presented into two independent clauses, the clarity, tone, and voice are improved.
Choice A is incorrect. The content of this sentence focuses on South Africa, while the following text focuses on Fanon. Therefore, this sentence does not serve as a transition per se.
Choice C is incorrect. There is no reason for this information to be replaced as the introduction to this paragraph.
Choice D is incorrect. Despite some edits, the suggested version of the sentence does not eliminate any relevant information.

20. **Choice A is the only possible answer.** Notice that paragraph (7) refers to "a foundational text" and paragraph (8) is the only one that ends with a description of "the book" i.e., "Black Skin, White Masks." Therefore, in order to preserve the flow of ideas in the passage, it would make the most sense for paragraph (7) to follow paragraph (8).

21. **Choice A is the best answer.** We are already told that Fanon is "an important part of the intellectual foundation of the black consciousness movement — " a statement that speaks of his significance. Restating this information, more ambiguously, is not necessary since it would repeat something that we have already been told.
Choice B is incorrect. The paragraph begins by speaking about a foundational text and using the suggested sentence as an introduction would be detrimental to the flow of ideas in the paragraph.
Choice C is incorrect. Although not necessary, this information — in being centered on Fanon's significance — cannot be deemed irrelevant.
Choice D is incorrect. There is no following information that would require the addition of this sentence.

22. **Choice D is the best answer** since it is the only one of the provided options that mentions the importance of Fanon in the passage (noted from the title of the text itself).
Choices A, B, and C, while related to ideas in the passage do not capture its "main point." The main point is explicitly stated as being the significance of Fanon's work.

23. **Choice B is the nest answer.** Notice the use of the present tense in the verb "reports" in the following sentence, when referring directly to Gourevitch. This tells us that Gourevtich is alive and as such, "is" an expert.
Choice A is incorrect because the use of the past tense would imply either that Gourevtich is dead, or that he is no longer an expert in this field — neither of which is accurate in this case.
Choice C is incorrect. "Are," while in the present tense, would only be accurate to refer to a plural subject.
Choice D is incorrect for the use of the future tense, which would cause a verb-tense inconsistency within the paragraph.

24. **Choice D is the best answer.** The suggested inclusion is vague and its primary content — that Gourevitch has new research — is mentioned in the beginning of the following sentence i.e., "With his new research."

Choice A is incorrect since there is nothing in the suggested addition that would clarify a prior statement.
Choice B is incorrect. There would be no reason to use this sentence as an introduction to the paragraph.
Choice C is incorrect. As established above, this suggested inclusion is not needed in relation to the following sentence.

25. **Choice C is the best answer.** Replacing the current sentence with the terms "the Rwandan genocide" would eliminate necessary information to help the reader better understand that event. Without the description as currently included, the text would assume knowledge that the reader might not have.
Choice A is incorrect. There is no "support" that is provided by the suggested edits that is not already given by the existing text.
Choice B is incorrect. The suggested edits do not provide a better or worse transition than the text that already exists.
Choice D is incorrect. There is nothing in the suggested edits to create a disruption in the flow of logic.

26. **Choice B is the best answer.** The sentence following the highlighted term describes the content of Gourevitch's new book, linking this text to the "sequel" that is mentioned in the previous sentence. Besides that, there is no relationship of cause or contrast that is presented as existing between this sentence and the one that comes before it — making all the three conjunctive adverbs inappropriate in connecting the sentences.

27. **Choice A is the best answer.** A comma is the best choice to follow an introductory and dependent clause.
Choice B is incorrect since a lack of punctuation after an introductory, dependent clause would be grammatically incorrect.
Choice C is incorrect. A colon would only be used if what followed it was a list of items, or a quotation.
Choice D is incorrect. A dash would be appropriate only if what follows it is a phrase/clause that deserves special emphasis.

28. **Choice C is the best answer.** Notice that sentence (2) speaks about a conversation that happened in 2016. Sentence (4) speaks about how Gourevitch "begins that conversation," while sentence (3) uses "then," which implies that something occurred after something else.
Therefore, sentence (4) would best be located before sentence (3) i.e., "begins" comes before "then."

29. **Choice D is the best answer.** Since the following clause begins with the term "however," and since both sentences focus on "reconciliation," the preceding section needs to be kept so as to maintain the flow of logic in the paragraph.
Choice A is incorrect. There is no extensive information about *Entitled Opinions* in the highlighted text.
Choice B is incorrect because this sentence would not make sense if placed at the end of this paragraph, as its conclusion.
Choice C is incorrect. The information is clearly linked to the idea of the passage, since it uses Dante's *Inferno* to introduce an idea about Rwanda.

30. **Choice B is the best answer.** By using the word "as" to create a link with the previous sentence, and by introducing the quote with the name of the speaker, this sentence does indeed function as a more effective transition between the ideas that have been mentioned in this paragraph.
Choice A is incorrect. There is no preceding term that is clarified by this sentence.
Choice C is incorrect. This sentence would not be effective as an introduction to this paragraph, since the current introduction helps set up the need for this quotation.
Choice D is incorrect. There is no relevant information that is eliminated by the suggested edits.

31. **Choice D is the best answer.** The plural nature of the subject ("books") and the use of the present tense in the following phrases ("are fact-checkable" and "are drawn"), make "are" the only possible answer to this question.
The present continuous tense (Choice A), the future tense (Choice B), and the past tense (Choice C) would all cause a verb-tense inconsistency in the statement.

32. **Choice C is the best answer.** Notice that "and" is used to link a list of two items: "intensely close observations" and "a lot of interviews". Since there are only two items in this list, no punctuation is needed to separate them (eliminating Choice A).
Choice B is incorrect since what follows "and" is not an independent clause. This also rules out the use of a semicolon (Choice D).

33. **Choice A is the best answer.** Since "Gourevitch" is explicitly stated as the subject of this sentence, the pronoun "he" is the best term to use.
Choice B is incorrect since it would repeat the subject's name soon after it has already been stated.
Choice C is incorrect. "It" would only be used if the pronoun referred to a non-human subject.
Choice D is incorrect since it inaccurately suggests that it is "the feeling" (of pathos) that returns again and again to Rwanda, rather than Gourevitch himself.

34. **Choice B is the best answer.** The use of the verb "began" before the underlined verb suggests the need for a following gerund.
Using the simple past tense (Choice A), the noun form of the verb (Choice B), or the simple present tense (Choice D) would all cause a grammatical error after the use of the simple past verb, "began."

35. **Choice A is the best answer.** Notice that there are two parts to this sentence: "EPA is also thinking beyond waste" and "we have transitioned from focusing on waste management to focusing on Sustainable Materials Management (SMM)." The two parts of the sentence are independent clauses and, therefore they are joined with the coordinating conjunction "and." Additionally, there should always be a comma before a coordinating conjunction.
Choice B is incorrect since semicolons can only be used to separate independent clauses when there is no coordinating conjunction.
Choice C is incorrect since a comma is always needed before a coordinating conjunction, mentioned above.
Choice D is correct. A dash would only be used if what follows needs special emphasis, which is not the case here.

36. **Choice D is the best answer.** "However," and "although" suggest relationships of contrast between this sentence and the one that comes before it. Therefore, Choices A and C cannot be suitable options.
Choice B is unsuitable since "finally" implies an order of items/ideas in the content. However, here, the ideas following the underlined world simply add to a preceding idea and are not the final items on a list of any sort.

37. **Choice A is the best answer.** Since this marks the beginning of a new paragraph, it is useful to restate the subject that is being referred to — hence this answer being preferable to Choice C.
Choices B and D is incorrect since they both use a plural subject when the use of "refers" (immediately following the underlined term) immediately indicates a singular subject.

38. **Choice C is the best answer.** The added sentence simply repeats an inclusion of "the items mentioned earlier" and as such, is repetitive and useless. The items are clearly mentioned in the second sentence and this is sufficient in communicating the same idea that is being addressed in this suggested addition.
Choice A is incorrect. There is no transitionary quality that is provided by this suggested addition to the topic of the next paragraph.
Choice B is incorrect. No prior information is clarified by this suggested addition.
Choice D is incorrect. There is no use for this sentence as the introduction to the paragraph.

39. **Choice D is the best answer.** The information following the highlighted word indicates a relationship of consequence — because the management of MSW is a high priority, the concept of integrated solid waste management is being used.
Choice A is incorrect since "ultimately" suggests a finality that is not needed in the given context.
Choice B is incorrect. "However," suggests a relationship of contrast that is not needed in the given context.
Choice C is incorrect. "Regardless," suggests a relationship of conditionality that is not needed in the given context.

CONTINUE

40. **Choice A is the best answer.** Since only two items are being separated here ("recovery and landfilling practices"), there is no need for a comma (Choice C).
Choice B is incorrect since a semicolon would only be needed to separate two independent clauses.
Choice D is incorrect. Splitting the sentence at this point would lead to the content being meaningless.

41. **Choice B is the best answer.** The subject being referred to is singular (waste management hierarchy"). Therefore, "includes" is the only grammatically accurate choice.
All the other answer choices would cause a grammatical error in the sentence.

42. **Choice D is the best answer.** Terms like "addition" and "plus" imply that something is being added onto something else, rather than speaking to what is included in the use of a particular term (like "source reduction"). This eliminates Choices A, B, and C.
Furthermore, notice the use of "including" following the use of the term "composting." Since parallelism is generally preferred in a list of items, "including" is the most suitable choice.

43. **Choice B is the best answer.** The sentence does provide an effective summary of previously explained information.
Choice A is incorrect since there is no next concept to transition to.
Choice C is incorrect. The sentence, in being completely in agreement with the content and structure of the paragraph, cannot be said to disrupt its flow.
Choice D is incorrect. The information in this sentence is completely related to the content of the passage.

44. **Choice A is the only possible answer,** since it is the only one that accurately depicts a trend that has been shown in the graph.
All the other choices misrepresent the nature of change in the generation of that material over time.

1. **Easy | Heart of Algebra**

   Choice C is correct. Substitute 2 for b and solve:

   $$\frac{a-1}{2} = 2$$

   $$a-1 = 4$$

   $$a = 5.$$

   It follows that $a+1 = 5+1 = 6$. Choices A, B, and D are incorrect and reflect arithmetic errors.

2. **Medium | Additional Topics in Math**

   Choice B is correct. Combine like terms to find the difference:

   $$(7-2x)-(-8+10x^2)$$

   $$7-2x+8-10x^2$$

   $$-10x^2 - 2x + 15.$$

   Choices A, C, and D are incorrect and reflect arithmetic errors.

3. **Easy | Passport to Advanced Math**

   Choice D is correct. The amount of text messages Courtney sent on Sunday morning was $4x$. The amount of text messages Lauren sent on Sunday morning was $6y$. To find the total amount we find the sum of Courtney's and Lauren's text: $4x+6y$. Choices A, B, and D are incorrect and reflect arithmetic errors.

4. **Difficult | Heart of Algebra**

   Choice B is correct. Leslie starts each day with 12 cable boxes to fix since C is the number of boxes left and h is the number of hours worked that day. Therefore, you start with 12 and each hour subtract how many boxes have been repaired. Choices A, C, and D are incorrect and reflect errors in interpreting functions in word problems.

5. **Medium | Passport to Advanced Math**

   Choice C is correct. Start by distributing the negative to the parentheses of the second term:

   $$(a^2b - 3a^2 + 10ab^2) - (-2a^2b - 2ab^2 - 3b^2)$$

   $$a^2b - 3a^2 + 10ab^2 + 2a^2b + 2ab^2 + 3b^2$$

   Then, combine like terms:

   $$a^2b - 3a^2 + 10ab^2 + 2a^2b + 2ab^2 + 3b^2$$

   $$3a^2b - 3a^2 + 3b^2 + 12ab^2.$$

   Choices A, B, and D are incorrect and reflect errors in simplifying complex polynomials.

6. **Easy | Heart of Algebra**

   Choice A is correct. In order to create an equation that represents the linear relationship, first identity the amount that the deposit increases per year, or the slope of the linear equation: Interest = 3% of original deposit.

   $$1000 (0.03) = \$30$$

If her deposit increases by $30 every t years and she originally deposited $1000, the equation is as follows:

$$y = 30t + 1000$$

Choices B, C, and D are incorrect and are likely the result of incorrect combination of variables.

7. **Medium | Passport to Advanced Math**

   Choice B is correct. In order to express the equation in terms of A, isolate variable A using order of operations:

   $$R = p\frac{1}{A}$$

   $$\frac{R}{p} = \frac{1}{A}$$

   $$RA = p$$

   $$A = \frac{p}{R}$$

   Therefore, B is correct. Choices A, C, and D are incorrect because when they are rearranged to isolate R, they do not equal $R = p\frac{1}{A}$.

8. **Medium | Heart of Algebra**

   Choice C is correct. If $\frac{m}{n} = 3$ then it follows that $\frac{n}{m} = \frac{1}{3}$. Since $\frac{n}{m} = \frac{1}{3}$, and $6 \times \frac{n}{m} = \frac{6n}{m}$, one can conclude that

   $\frac{6n}{m} = 6 \times \frac{1}{3} = 2$. Choices A, B, and D are incorrect and reflect errors in arithmetic.

9. **Medium | Heart of Algebra**

   Choice D is correct. Eliminate one of the variables and solve.

   $$2x - 4y = -17$$

   $$2\left(-x + 3y = \frac{27}{2}\right)$$

   $$2x - 4y = -17$$

   $$-2x + 6y = 27$$

   $$2y = 10$$

   $$y = 5$$

   Then substitute this value for y in one of the original equations and solve for x.

   $$2x - 4(5) = -17$$

   $$2x - 20 = -17$$

   $$2x = 3$$

$x = \dfrac{3}{2}$ or 1.5.

10. **Medium | Heart of Algebra**

    Choice B is correct. Start by determining the value for a by replacing x with -2 and $f(x)$ with -14.

    $-14 = a(-2)^2 - 22$

    $8 = a \times 4$

    $2 = a$

    Then, replace a with 2 and x with 3 to find the value of $f(3)$.

    $f(3) = 2(3)^2 - 22 = 2 \times 9 - 22 = 18 - 22 = -4$. Choice C is the value of a and reflects misunderstanding of the question. Choices A and D are incorrect and reflect errors in arithmetic or solving algebraic equations.

11. **Medium | Heart of Algebra**

    Choice B is correct. First multiply Quentin's sales by two, in order to set the entire equation equal to Alice's sales:

    $2\left(5b + 48\right) = 5.5b + 159$

    $10b + 96 = 5.5b + 159$

    $4.5b = 63$

    $b = 14$

    Choices A, C, and D are incorrect because when they are substituted for b in the original equations, Alice's sales are the double of Quentin's.

12. **Medium | Passport to Advanced Math**

    Choice D is correct. Start by determining the slope of the line formed by the two points: $\dfrac{y}{x} = \dfrac{8 - \left(-4\right)}{3 - \left(-1\right)} = \dfrac{12}{4} = 3.$

    The slope of the line that forms a right angle is the perpendicular line, so then determine opposite reciprocal of the slope, or $-\dfrac{1}{3}.$ Use this slope and the point given to calculate the new equation:

    $3 = -\dfrac{1}{3}(3) + b$

    $3 = -1 + b$

    $b = 4$

    The equation is therefore $y = -\dfrac{1}{3}x + 4.$ Choices A, B, and C are incorrect because when they are graphed, they are not perpendicular to the line formed by the original points.

13. **Difficult | Passport to Advanced Math**

    Choice D is correct. Firstly, find the LCM for the denominators of $m+2$ and $m+4$. The LCM is $(m+2)(m+4)$ therefore $\dfrac{1}{\dfrac{1}{m+2} + \dfrac{1}{m+4}} \Rightarrow \dfrac{1}{\dfrac{m+4}{(m+2)(m+4)} + \dfrac{m+2}{(m+4)(m+2)}}.$ Now add the denominator and get

$$\frac{1}{\dfrac{m+4}{(m+2)(m+4)}+\dfrac{m+2}{(m+4)(m+2)}}=\frac{1}{\dfrac{m+4+m+2}{(m+4)(m+2)}}=\frac{1}{\dfrac{2m+6}{(m+4)(m+2)}}.$$ Then find the reciprocal;

$$\frac{1}{\dfrac{2m+6}{(m+4)(m+2)}}=1\div\frac{2m+6}{(m+4)(m+2)}=1\times\frac{(m+4)(m+2)}{2m+6}.$$ Lastly we will expand the multiply the numerator;

$$\frac{(m+4)(m+2)}{2m+6}=\frac{m^2+6m+8}{2m+6}.$$ Choices A, B, and C are incorrect and reflect errors in manipulating complex

fractions with different denominators.

14. **Difficult | Passport to Advanced Math**

Choice A is correct. Use $6m - n = 24$ and $\dfrac{64^{2m}}{4^n}$, to solve as a system. Solving for n in the first equation, one finds

that $6m - n = 24$, $-n = 24 - 6m$, $n = -25 + 6m$. Then substitute the value for n in terms of n into the expression

$\dfrac{64^{2m}}{4^n}$ and evaluate; $\dfrac{64^{2m}}{4^n}=\dfrac{64^{2m}}{4^{(-25-6m)}}$. Then change the base in the numerator to match the base of 4 in the

denominator; $\dfrac{64^{2m}}{4^{(-24+6m)}}=\dfrac{(4^3)^{2m}}{4^{(-24+6m)}}=\dfrac{4^{6m}}{4^{(-24+6m)}}$. Lastly, we follow our quotient rule for exponents;

$\dfrac{4^{6m}}{4^{(-24+6m)}}=4^{6m-(-24+6m)}=4^{6m+24-6m}=4^{24}$. Choices B, C, and D are incorrect and reflect errors in using exponent

rules to simplify equations.

15. **Medium | Passport to Advanced Math**

Choice A is correct. By FOILING $(px+3)(qx+8)$, find that $(pq)x^2+8px+3qx+24$. If pq represents 6, and $p + q = 5$, the sum of the factors of 6 must be 2 and 3. Choices B, C, and D are incorrect and reflect errors in factoring polynomials.

16. **Easy | Passport to Advanced Math**

The correct answer is 4. Since $d^2-16=0$, solve for d:

$d^2-16=0, d^2=16, d=\{-4,4\}$.

The question states $d > 0$, so therefore, the answer is 4.

17. **Medium | Additional Topics in Math**

The correct answer is 2750. Since $\angle AEB$ and $\angle CDB$ have the same measure and $\angle ABE$ and $\angle CBD$ have the same measure because they are vertical angles and vertical angles are congruent. It follows that the remaining angles of $\triangle ABE$ and $\triangle CBD$ are congruent, therefore the corresponding sides of the triangle are proportional;

therefore $\dfrac{\overline{AB}}{\overline{BC}}=\dfrac{\overline{BE}}{\overline{BD}}=\dfrac{\overline{AE}}{\overline{CD}}\Rightarrow\dfrac{1200}{BC}=\dfrac{1000}{500}=\dfrac{x}{550}$ and $x=1100$, and the length of side $\overline{BC}=600$. The part the

participant is running is $\overline{AB}+\overline{EB}+\overline{CB}+\overline{DB}+\overline{CD}=1200+1000+600+500+550=3850$ and the part the

participant is swimming is $x=1100$. To find the difference, subtract; $Swimming - Walking = 3850 - 1100 = 2750$.

18. **Difficult | Heart of Algebra**

    The correct answer is 5.33. Take the first equation and solve for y; $y - 2x = -6$ therefore $y = -6 + 2x$. We now substitute the value for y in terms of x into the second equation and solve for x; $2y - x = 5 \Rightarrow 2(-6 + 2x) - x = 5$ $\Rightarrow -12 + 4x - x = 5 \Rightarrow -12 + 3x = 5 \Rightarrow 3x = 17 \Rightarrow x = \dfrac{17}{3} \approx 5.667$. Now we find y by substituting the value for x into either equation; $y - 2x = -6 \Rightarrow y - 2\left(\dfrac{17}{3}\right) = -6 \Rightarrow y - \dfrac{34}{3} = -6 \Rightarrow y = \dfrac{16}{3} \approx 5.333$.

19. **Medium | Additional Topics in Math**

    The correct answer is 0.7071 or $\dfrac{\sqrt{2}}{2}$. If $\tan x° = 1$ it follows that this is a $45° - 45° - 90°$ right triangle with the opposite and adjacent sides congruent, it follows that $x° = 45$. The question asks for $sin(90° - x°)$ therefore we take the value for $x°$ and substitute it into the expression $sin(90° - x°)$; $sin(90° - x°) = sin(90° - 45°)$ $= sin 45° = \dfrac{\sqrt{2}}{2} \approx 0.7071$.

20. **Easy | Passport to Advanced Math**

    The correct answer is 196. To find the value of y, we will take the value for x, substitute it into the equation and solve for y; $2(7\sqrt{2}) = \sqrt{2y}, 14\sqrt{2} = \sqrt{2y}, \sqrt{2} \times 14 = \sqrt{2} \times \sqrt{y}, 14 = \sqrt{y}, y = 196$.

1. **Easy | Problem Solving and Data Analysis**

   Choice B is correct. Since there are 36 kids in the camp and two thirds are girls we multiply $36\left(\dfrac{2}{3}\right)=24$ girls at statistics camp. Of the 24 girls, three fourths are under 5.5 feet; $24\left(\dfrac{3}{4}\right)=18$ girls under 5.5 feet. Choices A, C, and D are incorrect and reflect arithmetic errors.

2. **Medium | Additional Topics in Math**

   Choice D is correct. If the circumference is exactly 6π inches, we can find the radius because circumference is represented by the formula $C=2\pi r$ therefore $6\pi=2\pi r \Rightarrow r=3$. To find the Area, use the formula $A=\pi r^2; A=\pi(3)^2=9\pi$. Choices A, B, and C are incorrect and reflect errors in calculating circumference and area of a circle.

3. **Medium | Heart of Algebra**

   Choice A is correct. Since the sum of the horizontal row and vertical row is congruent and K=4, it follows that $4+L+4=3+L+J$. The Ls will cancel out which leaves us with $8=3+J; J=5$. Choices B, C, and D are incorrect and reflect arithmetic errors.

4. **Medium | Passport to Advanced Math**

   Choice D is correct. Since $a+b=p+rq$, we solve for r by isolating it; $a+b=p+rq \Rightarrow a+b-p=rq \Rightarrow \dfrac{a+b-p}{q}=r$. Choices A, B, and C are incorrect and reflect errors in analyzing multiple equations with the same variables.

5. **Medium | Problem Solving and Data Analysis**

   Choice D is correct. We find the number of people preferring opera or concerts by multiplying the total percent by the total number of people; $(14.2\%+23.6\%)(5842)=37.8\%(5842)=0.378(5842)=2209$. Choices A, B, and C are incorrect and reflect errors analyzing pie charts.

6. **Easy | Problem Solving and Data Analysis**

   Choice A is correct. Since 23.6% of the 100% of people surveyed liked sports, to find the percentage of people that do not like sports find the difference between the total and those that did like sports; $100\%-23.6\%=76.4\%$. Choices B, C, and D are incorrect and reflect errors in arithmetic and interpreting data in graph form.

7. **Difficult | Passport to Advanced Math**

   Choice A is correct. Systems of equations that have infinitely many solutions are essentially the same line, so the constants and the coefficients must be proportional to one another. Using the coefficients of the y-values, the proportion is $1:-2$:

   $-3x+4y=s$

   $rx-8y=-28$

   Therefore, one can set the coefficients of the other variables and constants equal by that ratio:

   $-3(-2)=r$

$$s(-2) = -28$$

$$6 = r$$

$$-2s = -28$$

$$s = 14$$

The solution is therefore (6,14). Choices B, C, and D are incorrect because when they are graphed along with the original line, they are not the same line.

8. **Difficult | Additional Topics in Math**

   Choice D is correct. Find the area of the circle by using the formula $A = \pi r^2; A = \pi 6^2 = 36\pi$. Next, find the area of the square by using the formula $A = s^2; A = 12^2 = 144$. Now subtract the area of the circle from the area of the square; $144 - 36\pi$. Last we divide by four; $\dfrac{144 - 36\pi}{4} = 36 - 9\pi$. Choices A, B, and C are incorrect and reflect errors in calculating the area of both circles and squares.

9. **Easy | Problem Solving and Data Analysis**

   Choice C is correct. Since the author sold the book for $1500, she has an initial profit of $1500. Thereafter, each book sale adds $18.50 to her profits, or $1500 + 18.5x$, where x is the number of book sold. Answer Choice C is the same expression, although written backwards. Choice A would be if she loses $18.50 per book sale. Choice B would be if she paid $1500 initially, rather than gaining $1500. Choice D would be if she only sold one book, as there is no variable x in the expression.

10. **Medium | Problem Solving and Data Analysis**

    Choice C is correct. Set up a proportion to solve for the number of widgets inspected if the factory produces 40,000 widgets; $\dfrac{widgets\,inspected}{widgets\,produce} = \dfrac{widgets\,inspected}{widgets\,produce} \Rightarrow \dfrac{8}{200} = \dfrac{x}{40,000}$. To solve for x cross multiply then divide by 200; $200x = 8(40,000) \Rightarrow 200x = 320,000 \Rightarrow x = 1600$. Choices A, B, and D are incorrect and reflect errors in creating proportions.

11. **Easy | Heart of Algebra**

    Choice B is correct. Substitute 69 into the equation for y; $y = 22 + 3.9x, 69 = 22 + 3.9x$. Solve for x by isolating x; $69 = 22 + 3.9x, 47 = 3.9x, x = 12.05$. Choices A, C, and D are incorrect and reflect errors in arithmetic

12. **Medium | Problem Solving and Data Analysis**

    Choice D is correct. If the school has 623 students, one must create a proportion to represent the situation:

    $$\frac{1}{20} = \frac{x}{623}$$

    $$x = \frac{623}{20}$$

    $$x = 31.15$$

    One must then round to the next whole number, because the question states there is, at most, a 20:1 ratio. The number of teachers needed is 32. Choices A, B, and C are incorrect and are likely the result of arithmetic errors in solving a ratio and proportions.

13. **Medium | Problem Solving and Data Analysis**

    Choice B is correct. First, determine what 70% of the student body is: $(0.7)623 = 436.1$. Then, multiply this value by the price per pack of school supplies: $436.1 \times \$25 = \$10,902.50$. Choices A, C, and D are incorrect and are likely the result of arithmetic errors in calculating the percentage of the student body.

14. **Medium | Heart of Algebra**

    Choice B is correct. An equation can be set up and solved with the first sentence as such:

    $$3m=21$$
    $$m=7$$

    The second sentence asks: $15m+9=15 \cdot 7+9=105+9=114$.

    Choice A forgets to add nine at the end. Choices C and D are a result of setting up or solving the problem incorrectly.

15. **Easy | Problem Solving and Data Analysis**

    Choice C is correct. Begin by identifying the vertex of the parabola by graphing. The graph reveals the vertex is at $(-1, -4)$. The vertex form of the line must be $y = (x+1)^2 - 4$. Choices A, B, and D are incorrect because, when graphed, they do not represent the same line as the given function in the question.

16. **Easy | Problem Solving and Data Analysis**

    Choice D is correct. Begin by creating an expression to represent the situation of x, correct answers, and y, incorrect answers:

    $10x - 5y$

    Then substitute the number of correctly and incorrectly answered questions:

    $10(14) - 5(1) = 140 - 5 = 135$

    Choices A, B, and C are incorrect and are likely the result of arithmetic errors.

17. **Medium | Passport to Advanced Math**

    Choice C is correct. $g(4)$ means to plug in 4 as the value of n, and likewise for $g(6)$. Therefore, the value of $g(4)$ $+g(6)=[2(4)+4]+[2(6)+4]=[8+4]+[12+4]=12+16=28$.
    The question asks which has the same value as 28, so we set up the equation equal to 28 and solve for n.
    $$2n+4=28$$
    $$2n=24$$
    $$n=12$$
    Therefore, $g(12)=g(4)+g(6)$
    Choice A is following the pattern 4, 6, 8. Choice B adds 4 and 6 together. Choice D finds the value of $g(4)+g(6)$ but fails to find the value for n.

18. **Difficult | Problem Solving and Data Analysis**

    Choice B is correct. To find the number of days it would take Blake to solve all of the problems in the SAT Study Guide, we divide the number of problems by the rate of problems Blake works per minute;
    $$\frac{5000 \ problems}{2 \ problems \ per \ minute} = 2500 \text{ minutes to complete all problems. Since he studies 4 hours daily, he studies for 240}$$

minutes daily. Since it takes 2500 minutes to complete all problems, $\dfrac{2500\,minutes}{240\,minutes\,studying\,per\,day}$ will give us

approximately 10.4167 days. The closest answer choice is 10. Choices A, C, and D are incorrect and reflect errors in arithmetic and interpreting data in graph form.

19. **Easy | Passport to Advanced Math**

   Choice B is correct. The inequality must be less than or equal to 425 feet of yarn, as that is the maximum value Jane purchased. The values 15 and 12 must be the coefficients of the variables (*s*) and (*h*), respectively. Choices A, C, and D are incorrect and are likely the result of errors in interpreting the values in the given question.

20. **Medium | Problem Solving and Data Analysis**

   Choice C is correct. The location of the survey, outside the library, directly conflicts with the neutrality of the survey, and will unnecessarily skew the results. Choices A, B, and D are incorrect and reflect errors in interpreting popular opinion polls.

21. **Easy | Problem Solving and Data Analysis**

   Choice C is correct. Speed can be calculated as *yards / minute*, which on this graph is $y\,/\,x$ or the slope. The fastest speed is therefore where the slope is the largest or steepest, which is between minute 8 and 13. The answer is, therefore, choice C. Choices A, B, and D are incorrect because the speeds at those times is less than the speed at 10 seconds.

22. **Medium | Problem Solving and Data Analysis**

   Choice A is correct. Begin by calculating the total time traveled by the geese in hours:

   $3.75\,days \times \dfrac{24\,hours}{1\,day} = 90\,hours$. Then use the total time in hours and the total distance in miles to calculate the

   average speed: $\dfrac{2365\,miles}{90\,hours} = 26.2777\,mph$. Then rounded to the nearest tenth, the speed is 26.3 mph. Choices B,

   C, and D are incorrect and are the result of incorrectly calculating the equivalent number of hours form 3.75 days.

23. **Medium | Problem Solving and Data Analysis**

   Choice C is correct. Begin by setting up a proportion to represent the situation and solving for *x*:

   $\dfrac{16.5}{100} = \dfrac{32\,kg}{x\,kg}$

   $16.5x = 100(32)$

   $x = \dfrac{3200}{16.5}$

   $x = 193.9\,kg$

   Choices A, B, and D are incorrect because when they are substituted into the proportion, the result is not 16.5%.

24. **Easy | Problem Solving and Data Analysis**

   Choice A is correct. The probability is a fraction of the total class, so the denominator of the fraction must be

441. Next, identify which value on the table represents Non-Majors who passed the exam, which is 150. The probability is therefore, $\dfrac{150}{441}$. Choices B, C, and D are incorrect and reflect errors in creating probabilities from data sets.

25. **Medium | Problem Solving and Data Analysis**

   Choice C is correct. Begin by calculating the number of Pre-Med students who achieved a perfect score: $0.0291(204) = 6.984$, rounded to 7 students. If only one other student achieved a perfect score, then 8 total students achieved a perfect score. Choices A, B, and D are incorrect are the result of arithmetic errors in calculating fractions with percent values.

26. **Medium | Problem Solving and Data Analysis**

   Choice B is correct. The median is the middle number. Since there are 600 data points for each Company A and B, the median or middle would be the data point 300 and 301 when ordered from least to greatest. Data point 300 and 301 lie in the category of one day. Choices A, C, and D are incorrect and reflect errors in interpreting data sets.

27. **Medium | Problem Solving and Data Analysis**

   Choice B is correct. Since Company A has 2500 employees and $\left(\dfrac{60}{600}\right)(2500) = 250$ gives us the number of

   employees there that took 3 days off and Company B has 3600 employees and $\left(\dfrac{20}{600}\right)(3600) = 120$, we can

   subtract $250 - 120 = 130$. Choices A, C, and D are incorrect and reflect errors in arithmetic.

28. **Easy | Passport to Advanced Math**

   Choice B is correct. If the frame can hold up to 12 pounds, the variable (h) must be greater than or equal to the sum of the other variables. Therefore, B must be correct. Choices A, C, and D are incorrect and are the result of errors in creating inequalities.

29. **Difficult | Heart of Algebra**

   Choice A is correct. When graphed, the vertex of the parabola is clearly the minimum y-value. To calculate the x-value of the vertex, find the midpoint of the zeroes of the function by factoring:

   $$f(x) = 4x + x^2 - 12$$

   $$f(x) = (x + 6)(x - 2)$$

   The midpoint of -6 and 2 is -2. Choices B, C, and D are incorrect because when they are substituted in the function and graphed, they do not represent the minimum y-value.

30. **Medium | Additional Topics in Math**

   Choice D is correct. Begin by finding the area of both figures:

   Square: $A = bh$

   $$A = (4)(4)cm^2$$

   $$A = 16\,cm^2$$

Circle: $A = \pi r^2$

$A = \pi \left(2\right)^2$

$A = 4\pi \, cm^2$

Subtract to find the difference: $16 cm^2 - 4\pi cm^2 = 3.43 \, cm^2$. Choices A, B. and C are incorrect because when they are added to the area of circle, they do not equal the area of the square.

31. **Difficult | Passport to Advanced Math**

    The correct answer is 16,528.93. Since the lakes erode 1.21 meters per year this means they erode .00121 kilometers per year. To erode 20 kilometers, we set up the equation $20 = 0.00121\left(x\right) \Rightarrow 16,528.93 \, years$.

32. **Difficult | Passport to Advanced Math**

    The correct answer is 62.5. Let a hours be rewritten as $60a$ minutes and $4\frac{1}{2} hours \times 60 = 270 \, mins$. Therefore $60a + 20 = 270 \Rightarrow 60a = 250 \Rightarrow a \approx 4.167 \, hours \approx 62.5 \, quarter \, hours$.

33. **Easy | Passport to Advanced Math**

    The correct answer is 12. Start by substituting in the values for $f(x)$ and x; $-12 = 2\left(0\right)^2 - b, -12 = -b$. Therefore, $b = 12$.

34. **Medium | Heart of Algebra**

    The correct answer is 105. We start by writing our first equation $A + D = 480$ to represent the total hours spent by Ashley and Danielle in the center for two semesters. Since Ashley spent 60 more hours in the lab than Danielle did, it would follow that the second equation is $A = D + 60$. To find how many hows Danielle spent, we will substitute the value for A in terms of D into the second equation; $D + 60 + D = 480 \Rightarrow 2D + 60 = 480 \Rightarrow 2D = 420 \Rightarrow D = 210$. Since we are looking for the number of hours Danielle spent on average a semester, divide 210 by 2; $210 \div 2 = 105$.

35. **Medium | Heart of Algebra**

    The correct answer is 28. Begin by calculating the total number of miles Jerome traveled: $15 \, hours \times 65 \, mph = 975 \, miles$. If his car can go 35 miles per gallon, create a proportion to calculate the total number of gallons used: $\frac{975 \, miles}{x \, gallons} = \frac{35 \, miles}{1 \, gallon} = \frac{975}{35} = 27.857$. Rounded, the total number of gallons is 28.

36. **Medium | Additional Topics in Math**

    The correct answer is 15.7 cm². First, use the degree measure of the interior angle to determine the fraction relationship between the sector and the full circle: $\frac{72}{360} = \frac{1}{5}$. Then, find the area of the full circle:

    $A = \pi \left(5\right)^2 = 25\pi$. The area of the sector is therefore, $\left(\frac{1}{5}\right) 25\pi = 15.7 cm^2$.

37. **Easy | Passport to Advanced Math**

    The correct answer is 37. Simplify $\left(7x^2 + 3x - 18\right) - \left(-3x^2 - 17x + 19\right)$ by combining like terms, to get $10x^2 + 20x - 37$ where the value of $-c = 37$.

38. **Medium | Heart of Algebra**

   The correct answer is 112. Create an equation to reflect the relationship between the cars, if the distance Car B traveled is (x): $3x + x + 2x = 336$

   $6x = 336$

   $x = 56$

   Car C traveled $2x$, so the correct answer is $52 \times 2 = 112$.

SAT Practice
Test #5

It is recommended that you use a No. 2 pencil. It is very important that you fill in the entire circle darkly and completely. If you change your response, erase as completely as possible. Incomplete marks or erasures may affect your score.

	A B C D		A B C D		A B C D		A B C D
1	○ ○ ○ ○	14	○ ○ ○ ○	27	○ ○ ○ ○	40	○ ○ ○ ○
2	○ ○ ○ ○	15	○ ○ ○ ○	28	○ ○ ○ ○	41	○ ○ ○ ○
3	○ ○ ○ ○	16	○ ○ ○ ○	29	○ ○ ○ ○	42	○ ○ ○ ○
4	○ ○ ○ ○	17	○ ○ ○ ○	30	○ ○ ○ ○	43	○ ○ ○ ○
5	○ ○ ○ ○	18	○ ○ ○ ○	31	○ ○ ○ ○	44	○ ○ ○ ○
6	○ ○ ○ ○	19	○ ○ ○ ○	32	○ ○ ○ ○	45	○ ○ ○ ○
7	○ ○ ○ ○	20	○ ○ ○ ○	33	○ ○ ○ ○	46	○ ○ ○ ○
8	○ ○ ○ ○	21	○ ○ ○ ○	34	○ ○ ○ ○	47	○ ○ ○ ○
9	○ ○ ○ ○	22	○ ○ ○ ○	35	○ ○ ○ ○	48	○ ○ ○ ○
10	○ ○ ○ ○	23	○ ○ ○ ○	36	○ ○ ○ ○	49	○ ○ ○ ○
11	○ ○ ○ ○	24	○ ○ ○ ○	37	○ ○ ○ ○	50	○ ○ ○ ○
12	○ ○ ○ ○	25	○ ○ ○ ○	38	○ ○ ○ ○	51	○ ○ ○ ○
13	○ ○ ○ ○	26	○ ○ ○ ○	39	○ ○ ○ ○	52	○ ○ ○ ○

It is recommended that you use a No. 2 pencil. It is very important that you fill in the entire circle darkly and completely. If you change your response, erase as completely as possible. Incomplete marks or erasures may affect your score.

	A B C D		A B C D		A B C D		A B C D		A B C D
1	○○○○	10	○○○○	19	○○○○	28	○○○○	37	○○○○
2	○○○○	11	○○○○	20	○○○○	29	○○○○	38	○○○○
3	○○○○	12	○○○○	21	○○○○	30	○○○○	39	○○○○
4	○○○○	13	○○○○	22	○○○○	31	○○○○	40	○○○○
5	○○○○	14	○○○○	23	○○○○	32	○○○○	41	○○○○
6	○○○○	15	○○○○	24	○○○○	33	○○○○	42	○○○○
7	○○○○	16	○○○○	25	○○○○	34	○○○○	43	○○○○
8	○○○○	17	○○○○	26	○○○○	35	○○○○	44	○○○○
9	○○○○	18	○○○○	27	○○○○	36	○○○○		

It is recommended that you use a No. 2 pencil. It is very important that you fill in the entire circle darkly and completely. If you change your response, erase as completely as possible. Incomplete marks or erasures may affect your score.

```
     A B C D        A B C D        A B C D        A B C D        A B C D
1  ○ ○ ○ ○     4  ○ ○ ○ ○     7  ○ ○ ○ ○    10 ○ ○ ○ ○    13 ○ ○ ○ ○

     A B C D        A B C D        A B C D        A B C D        A B C D
2  ○ ○ ○ ○     5  ○ ○ ○ ○     8  ○ ○ ○ ○    11 ○ ○ ○ ○    14 ○ ○ ○ ○

     A B C D        A B C D        A B C D        A B C D        A B C D
3  ○ ○ ○ ○     6  ○ ○ ○ ○     9  ○ ○ ○ ○    12 ○ ○ ○ ○    15 ○ ○ ○ ○
```

Only answers that are gridded will be scored. You will not receive credit for anything written in the boxes.

```
16                17                18                19                20

   / ○ ○            / ○ ○            / ○ ○            / ○ ○            / ○ ○
 . ○ ○ ○ ○        . ○ ○ ○ ○        . ○ ○ ○ ○        . ○ ○ ○ ○        . ○ ○ ○ ○
0 ○ ○ ○ ○        0 ○ ○ ○ ○        0 ○ ○ ○ ○        0 ○ ○ ○ ○        0 ○ ○ ○ ○
1 ○ ○ ○ ○        1 ○ ○ ○ ○        1 ○ ○ ○ ○        1 ○ ○ ○ ○        1 ○ ○ ○ ○
2 ○ ○ ○ ○        2 ○ ○ ○ ○        2 ○ ○ ○ ○        2 ○ ○ ○ ○        2 ○ ○ ○ ○
3 ○ ○ ○ ○        3 ○ ○ ○ ○        3 ○ ○ ○ ○        3 ○ ○ ○ ○        3 ○ ○ ○ ○
4 ○ ○ ○ ○        4 ○ ○ ○ ○        4 ○ ○ ○ ○        4 ○ ○ ○ ○        4 ○ ○ ○ ○
5 ○ ○ ○ ○        5 ○ ○ ○ ○        5 ○ ○ ○ ○        5 ○ ○ ○ ○        5 ○ ○ ○ ○
6 ○ ○ ○ ○        6 ○ ○ ○ ○        6 ○ ○ ○ ○        6 ○ ○ ○ ○        6 ○ ○ ○ ○
7 ○ ○ ○ ○        7 ○ ○ ○ ○        7 ○ ○ ○ ○        7 ○ ○ ○ ○        7 ○ ○ ○ ○
8 ○ ○ ○ ○        8 ○ ○ ○ ○        8 ○ ○ ○ ○        8 ○ ○ ○ ○        8 ○ ○ ○ ○
9 ○ ○ ○ ○        9 ○ ○ ○ ○        9 ○ ○ ○ ○        9 ○ ○ ○ ○        9 ○ ○ ○ ○
```

NO CALCULATOR ALLOWED

It is recommended that you use a No. 2 pencil. It is very important that you fill in the entire circle darkly and completely. If you change your response, erase as completely as possible. Incomplete marks or erasures may affect your score.

	A B C D		A B C D		A B C D		A B C D		A B C D
1	○○○○	7	○○○○	13	○○○○	19	○○○○	25	○○○○
2	○○○○	8	○○○○	14	○○○○	20	○○○○	26	○○○○
3	○○○○	9	○○○○	15	○○○○	21	○○○○	27	○○○○
4	○○○○	10	○○○○	16	○○○○	22	○○○○	28	○○○○
5	○○○○	11	○○○○	17	○○○○	23	○○○○	29	○○○○
6	○○○○	12	○○○○	18	○○○○	24	○○○○	30	○○○○

CALCULATOR ALLOWED

It is recommended that you use a No. 2 pencil. It is very important that you fill in the entire circle darkly and completely. If you change your response, erase as completely as possible. Incomplete marks or erasures may affect your score.

31 32 33 34 35

Only answers that are gridded will be scored. You will not receive credit for anything written in the boxes.

36 37 38

CALCULATOR
ALLOWED

CONTINUE

Reading Test

65 MINUTES, 52 QUESTIONS

Turn to Section 1 of your answer sheet to answer the questions in this section

DIRECTIONS

Each passage or pair of passages below is followed by a number of questions. After reading each passage or pair, choose the best answer to each question based on what is stated or implied in the passage or passages and in any accompanying graphics (such as a table or graph).

Questions 1-10 are based on the following passage.

This passage is adapted from Jane Austin, *Sense and Sensibility,* first published in 1811. Mrs. Dashwood and her daughters, Elinor and Marianne, have been living in the family home which now belongs to her son-in-law John and his wife. Edward is the brother of John's wife, and he has developed a romantic relationship with Elinor.

No sooner was her answer dispatched, than Mrs. Dashwood indulged herself in the pleasure of announcing to her son-in-law and his wife that she was provided with a house, and should incommode
5 them no longer than till every thing were ready for her inhabiting it. They heard her with surprise. Mrs. John Dashwood said nothing; but her husband civilly hoped that she would not be settled far from Norland. She had great satisfaction in replying that
10 she was going into Devonshire. Edward turned hastily towards her, on hearing this, and, in a voice of surprise and concern, which required no explanation to her, repeated, "Devonshire! Are you, indeed, going there? So far from hence! And to what
15 part of it?" She explained the situation. It was within four miles northward of Exeter.

"It is but a cottage," she continued, "but I hope to see many of my friends in it. A room or two can easily be added; and if my friends find no difficulty
20 in travelling so far to see me, I am sure I will find none in accommodating them."
She concluded with a very kind invitation to Mr. and Mrs. John Dashwood to visit her at Barton; and

to Edward she gave one with still greater affection.
25 Though her late conversation with her daughter-in-law had made her resolve on remaining at Norland no longer than was unavoidable, it had not produced the smallest effect on her in that point to which it principally tended. To separate Edward and
30 Elinor was as far from being her object as ever; and she wished to show Mrs. John Dashwood, by this pointed invitation to her brother, how totally she disregarded her disapprobation of the match.

Mr. John Dashwood told his mother again and
35 again how exceedingly sorry he was that she had taken a house at such a distance from Norland as to prevent his being of any service to her in removing her furniture. He really felt conscientiously vexed on the occasion; for the very exertion to which he had
40 limited the performance of his promise to his father was by this arrangement rendered impracticable. The furniture was all sent around by water. It chiefly consisted of household linen, plate, china, and books, with a handsome pianoforte of Marianne's.
45 Mrs. John Dashwood saw the packages depart with a sigh: she could not help feeling it hard that as Mrs. Dashwood's income would be so trifling in comparison with their own, she should have any handsome article of furniture.

50   Mrs. Dashwood took the house for a twelvemonth; it was ready furnished, and she might have immediate possession. No difficulty arose on either side in the agreement; and she waited only for the disposal of her effects at Norland, and to
55 determine her future household, before she set off

for the west; and this, as she was exceedingly rapid in the performance of everything that interested her, was soon done. The horses which were left her by her husband had been sold soon after his death,
60 and an opportunity now offering of disposing of her carriage, she agreed to sell that likewise at the earnest advice of her eldest daughter. For the comfort of her children, had she consulted only her own wishes, she would have kept it; but the
65 discretion of Elinor prevailed. Her wisdom too limited the number of their servants to three; two maids and a man, with whom they were speedily provided from amongst those who had formed their establishment at Norland.

70   In a very few weeks from the day which brought Sir John Middleton's first letter to Norland, every thing was so far settled in their future abode as to enable Mrs. Dashwood and her daughters to begin their journey.

75   Many were the tears shed by them in their last adieus to a place so much beloved. "Dear, dear Norland!" said Marianne, as she wandered alone before the house, on the last evening of their being there; "when shall I cease to regret you!—when
80 learn to feel a home elsewhere! Oh! happy house, could you know what I suffer in now viewing you from this spot, from whence perhaps I may view you no more! And you, ye well-known trees!—but you will continue the same. No leaf will decay because
85 we are removed, nor any branch become motionless although we can observe you no longer! No; you will continue the same; unconscious of the pleasure or the regret you occasion, and insensible of any change in those who walk under your shade!
90 But who will remain to enjoy you?"

1

The main purpose of the passage is to

A) offer the motivations for Mrs. Dashwood's sudden decision to move.

B) describe the events surrounding the departure of Mrs. Dashwood to her new home.

C) express the regret of the family members regarding Mrs. Dashwood's departure.

D) indicate the challenges faced when moving to a distant location.

2

Which choice provides the best evidence that the relationship between Mrs. Dashwood and her family is strained?

A) Lines 1-6 ("No sooner... inhabiting it")

B) Lines 22-24 ("She concluded... affection")

C) Lines 75-76 ("Many were... beloved")

D) Lines 90 ("But who... enjoy you")

3

As used in line 37, "removing" most nearly means

A) transferring.

B) detaching.

C) dismissing.

D) separating.

4

It can reasonably be inferred from the passage that Mr. John Dashwood

A) had given his father a pledge regarding his mother's care.

B) is too busy to assist with the details of his mother's move.

C) feels that his mother is taking too many belongings.

D) wishes that his mother would remain at Norland.

5

The passage indicates that Mrs. John Dashwood feels that Mrs. Dashwood is

A) suffering unduly from grief.

B) extremely pitiful in her situation.

C) unappreciative of her family.

D) overstepping her social position.

6

Which choice provides the best evidence for the answer to the previous question?

A) Lines 34-36 ("Mrs. John Dashwood... Norland")

B) Lines 25-29 ("Though her... tended")

C) Lines 31-33 ("she wished... the match")

D) Lines 34-38 ("Mrs. John Dashwood saw... furniture")

7

Based on the passage, what is the relationship between Mrs. Dashwood and her oldest daughter?

A) Mrs. Dashwood defers to her daughter's decisions.

B) Mrs. Dashwood usually tells her daughter what to do.

C) Both would prefer living apart from each other.

D) Both feel that the other is acting in error.

8

It can most reasonably be inferred from the passage that Mrs. Dashwood and her daughters

A) are moving because they miss the presence of Mrs. Dashwood's deceased husband.

B) have decided to move because they cannot maintain their social position at Norland.

C) are not moving because they feel that the premises at Norland are too small.

D) decided to move because they wanted to live closer to their friends' homes.

9

As used in line 88, "insensible" most nearly means

A) comatose.

B) negligible.

C) unaware of.

D) insentient.

10

In line 90, Marianne's question primarily serves to

A) highlight her fear at moving to an unknown location.

B) stress the tension she feels between family members.

C) lament that her new home will be very different.

D) hint that she feels alone in appreciating her old home.

Questions 11-20 are based on the following passage.

This passage is adapted from Abraham Lincoln's last public address, given April 11, 1965. It refers to the recent acceptance of Louisiana to the United States and the surrender of Gen. Robert E. Lee at the end of the American Civil War.

We all agree that the seceded States, so called, are out of their proper relation with the Union; and that the sole object of the government, civil and military, in regard to those States is to again get
5 them into that proper practical relation. I believe it is not only possible, but in fact, easier to do this, without deciding, or even considering, whether these States have ever been out of the Union, than with it. Finding themselves safely at home, it would
10 be utterly immaterial whether they had ever been abroad. Let us all join in doing the acts necessary to restoring the proper practical relations between these States and the Union; and each forever after, innocently indulge his own opinion whether, in
15 doing the acts, he brought the States from without, into the Union, or only gave them proper assistance, they never having been out of it.

The amount of constituency, so to speak, on which the new Louisiana government rests, would
20 be more satisfactory to all, if it contained fifty, thirty, or even twenty thousand, instead of only about twelve thousand, as it does. It is also unsatisfactory to some that the elective franchise is not given to the colored man. I would myself prefer that it were now
25 conferred on the very intelligent, and on those who serve our cause as soldiers. Still the question is not whether the Louisiana government, as it stands, is quite all that is desirable. The question is, "Will it be wiser to take it as it is, and help to improve it; or to
30 reject, and disperse it?" "Can Louisiana be brought into proper practical relation with the Union *sooner* by *sustaining*, or by *discarding* her new State government?"

Some twelve thousand voters in the heretofore
35 slave-state of Louisiana have sworn allegiance to the Union, assumed to be the rightful political power of the State, held elections, organized a State government, adopted a free-state constitution, giving the benefit of public schools equally to
40 black and white, and empowering the Legislature

to confer the elective franchise upon the colored man. Their Legislature has already voted to ratify the constitutional amendment recently passed by Congress, abolishing slavery throughout the
45 nation. These twelve thousand persons are thus fully committed to the Union, and to perpetual freedom in the state--committed to the very things, and nearly all the things the nation wants--and they ask the nation's recognition and its assistance to make
50 good their committal. Now, if we reject, and spurn them, we do our utmost to disorganize and disperse them. We in effect say to the white men, "You are worthless, or worse--we will neither help you, nor be helped by you." To the blacks we say, "This cup
55 of liberty which these, your old masters, hold to your lips, we will dash from you, and leave you to the chances of gathering the spilled and scattered contents in some vague and undefined when, where, and how." If this course, discouraging and paralyzing
60 both white and black, has any tendency to bring Louisiana into proper practical relations with the Union, I have, so far, been unable to perceive it. If, on the contrary, we recognize, and sustain the new government of Louisiana the converse of all this is
65 made true. We encourage the hearts, and nerve the arms of the twelve thousand to adhere to their work, and argue for it, and proselyte for it, and fight for it, and feed it, and grow it, and ripen it to a complete success. The colored man too, in seeing all united
70 for him, is inspired with vigilance, and energy, and daring, to the same end. Grant that he desires the elective franchise, will he not attain it sooner by saving the already advanced steps toward it, than by running backward over them? Concede that
75 the new government of Louisiana is only to what it should be as the egg is to the fowl, we shall sooner have the fowl by hatching the egg than by smashing it? Again, if we reject Louisiana, we also reject one vote in favor of the proposed amendment to the
80 national Constitution. To meet this proposition, it has been argued that no more than three fourths of those States which have not attempted secession are necessary to validly ratify the amendment. I do not commit myself against this, further than to
85 say that such a ratification would be questionable, and sure to be persistently questioned; while a ratification by three-fourths of all the States would be unquestioned and unquestionable.

I repeat the question, "Can Louisiana be brought
90 into proper practical relation with the Union

CONTINUE

sooner by *sustaining* or by *discarding* her new State Government?

11

What is the role of the first paragraph (lines 1-17) in the context of the passage as a whole?

A) It introduces the passage's main argument.

B) It dismisses one point as irrelevant to the issue.

C) It defines key terms that are used in the passage.

D) It concedes a minor point from an opponent's criticism.

12

According to the passage, one of the controversies regarding Louisiana is that

A) relatively few people reside within the state.

B) the state is much larger than many others in the Union.

C) the proportion of freed slaves is higher than in other states.

D) the state has not agreed to policies accepted elsewhere.

13

Based on the passage, Lincoln would most likely agree with which statement regarding former slaves?

A) Most of them are not qualified to vote.

B) They have an inalienable right to vote.

C) Some should be granted the privilege of voting.

D) They are not capable of voting effectively.

14

Which choice provides the best evidence for the answer to the previous question?

A) Lines 22-24 ("It is also… colored man")

B) Lines 24-26 ("I would… soldiers")

C) Lines 34-42 ("Some twelve… colored man")

D) Lines 54-59 ("To the blacks… and how")

15

As used in line 47, "committed" most nearly means

A) engaged.

B) performed.

C) dedicated.

D) consigned.

16

In the context of the passage, the imagery of a cup of liberty mainly serves to emphasize

A) the generosity of the Union in giving freed slaves certain benefits.

B) the advances made by the Union in protecting the rights of former slaves.

C) the unconscious way in which many people accept their freedoms.

D) the precarious nature of the freedoms granted to former slaves in Louisiana.

17

As used in line 68, "recognize" most nearly means

A) identify.

B) accept.

C) realize.

D) appreciate.

18

It can be reasonably inferred from the passage that Lincoln considers Louisiana

A) crucial in the upcoming decision to amend the Constitution.

B) grievously in error and deserving of punishment.

C) irrational in the policies it has resolved to enact or not.

D) progressive in its handling of blacks who were formerly slaves.

19

Which choice provides the best evidence for the answer to the previous question?

A) Lines 50-52 ("Now, if… disperse them")

B) Lines 71-74 ("Grant that… over them")

C) Lines 78-80 ("Again, if… Constitution")

D) Lines 80-83 ("To meet… amendment")

20

What is Lincoln's purpose in repeating the question in lines 89-92 ("I repeat… Government")?

A) To confirm in case the listeners did not hear the first message clearly.

B) To emphasize the immediacy of the decision to be made.

C) To highlight the inherent difficulty of the question at hand.

D) To summarize the most important aspect of his argument.

CONTINUE

Questions 21-31 are based on the following passage and supplementary material.

This passage is adapted from "More than Just a Diet: An Inquiry into Veganism," by Sarah E. Mann, published 2014 by Scholarly Commons.

The vegan diet has gained momentum in recent years, with more people transitioning to the diet, whether for health or more ethically-based reasons. The vegan diet, often characterized as
5 very restrictive, is associated with health benefits but raises concerns. Controversy regarding the diet exists within the public sphere, with those actively supporting and advocating for it, and others questioning its purpose and proposed benefits, even
10 disparaging its existence, perhaps because of a lack of knowledge about the diet.

A study led by Sarah Mann aimed to provide a fuller picture of the vegan diet in which no animal products are eaten, encompassing both the nutrition
15 and health of the vegan diet as well as related ethical beliefs by studying scientific and popular literature in tandem. Furthermore, the study aimed to provide an insider's perspective of the vegan diet as a means of combating stereotypes and making the diet more
20 relatable/understandable to those who are not vegan. By combining all three sources, the project aims to educate the public regarding a diet and lifestyle that is often perceived, at least partially, in a negative manner.

25 The research was conducted in two parts – literature review and interview study. A literature review of both the scientific and the popular literature was conducted and reviewed from August to November, 2013. *Pubmed* database was
30 used to research the scientific findings while food blogs, vegan websites, and newspaper articles comprised the popular literature. The interview study involved semi-structured, one-time, in-person private interviews conducted during February and
35 March, 2013. Twenty vegans (10 students from the University of Pennsylvania and 10 Philadelphia residents) were interviewed, and questions targeted personal history of veganism, related health beliefs, factors influencing the decision to become vegan,
40 and diet composition. Once all data was obtained, it was analyzed in tandem.

Findings suggest that a well-rounded vegan diet is healthy and such is evidenced by the variety of whole foods and increased vegetable and fruit
45 intake. Health benefits include a decrease in cholesterol, lipid levels, blood pressure, weight, and a reduced risk for a variety of diseases including obesity, diabetes, cardiovascular disease, and cancer. Despite the benefits, health concerns do exist,
50 especially in regard to nutrient deficiencies, without a well-planned and varied diet. Nutrient concerns include calcium, vitamin D, iron, and particularly vitamin B-12, for which supplements should be taken. The nature of the interviews conducted
55 for this paper was such that a comprehensive but diverse collection of information was obtained, precisely because the interviewees have chosen the vegan diet for a multitude of reasons, and approach their diet and lifestyle in varied ways. However,
60 there are some commonalities that were revealed. Results of the interview studies demonstrate that about half of the vegans are potentially at risk for vitamin D deficiency because most are taking neither vitamin D supplements nor a multivitamin.
65 Comparing the scientific literature with the interview results reveals that most of the vegans include working out within their daily routines, implying they place emphasis upon physical fitness. This suggests that the vegan lifestyle has benefits
70 beyond merely nutrition. Finally, comparing popular literature to the information gleaned through the interviews conducted establishes that many of the stereotypes regarding the vegan diet are unfounded.

The vegan diet is one that is chosen by
75 individuals for various reasons, including health and/or ethical reasons. While many health benefits exist, it is essential for those who are vegan or are planning to become vegan to be educated about potential nutrient deficiencies to prevent
80 adverse outcomes. In addition, it is evident that the vegan diet is much more than a diet itself, but has developed into a lifestyle, often associated with animal rights and environmental advocacy as well as a greater concern for physical activity and
85 mindfulness. Further research begs the question of whether the health benefits associated with the diet are solely attributable to the diet or in conjunction with a greater physical activity level and mindful living. With regard to providing an accurate picture
90 of veganism in the popular literature, it is essential to combat negative unsubstantiated stereotypes and myths by providing vegans with an unbiased voice with which to share their own stories and beliefs.

Lastly, the popularity of the vegan diet and the
95 question of whether it is nutritionally sound, raise
issues of anthropologic significance. Specifically, it
prompts consideration of whether our ancestral diet
was vegetarian in nature, or depended upon meat
for evolutionary progress.

Nutrients Found Primarily in Animal Tissues

Nutrient	Function	Natural source	Alternate Source
B12	Used by nervous and circulatory systems	Fish, meat, dairy, eggs	Enriched grain products; some nutritional yeast
Creatine	Increases muscle performance	Animal tissue	Supplements; the body naturally makes small amounts
DHA	Mental health and brain development, especially in children	Fatty fish, fish oil	Microalgae
Taurine	Muscle function, bile production	Fish, meat, poultry, dairy products	Synthetic supplements

21

The main purpose of the passage is to

A) present rationale for adopting an increasingly popular diet.

B) challenge a popular stereotype regarding a certain diet.

C) discredit the supposed benefits of a popular diet.

D) describe a study that analyzes different facets of a diet.

22

The first paragraph (lines 1-11) mainly serves to

A) define key terms in the passage.

B) provide background for a study.

C) establish the author's side of a debate.

D) explain the rationale for a decision.

23

According to the passage, one of the main objectives of Sarah Mann's study was to

A) encourage others to adopt a vegan lifestyle.

B) examine why people are opposed to a vegan diet.

C) teach others about the nature of veganism.

D) determine the anthropological origins of a vegan diet.

CONTINUE ➡

24

Based on the passage, it can be reasonably assumed that Mann included personal interviews in her study because she

A) assumed she would find a conflict between interviews and scientific studies.

B) expected to resolve an outstanding debate about the health benefits of veganism.

C) decided that most of the current literature was biased against the subject of veganism.

D) hoped to better understand the viewpoint of people who opted to become vegan.

25

As used in line 39, "composition" most nearly means

A) arrangement.

B) disposition.

C) constitution.

D) amalgam.

26

As used in line 59, "revealed" most nearly means

A) uncovered.

B) betrayed.

C) confessed.

D) circulated.

27

The passage suggests that Mann's conclusions about the health benefits of veganism are open to the criticism that

A) it is not clear whether the results are solely due to partaking in a vegan diet.

B) the diet is sometimes adopted for ethical rather than health purposes.

C) the study relied on a literature review opposed to obtaining firsthand data.

D) it is important to include additions which are not directly deprived from plants.

28

Which choice provides the best evidence for the answer to the previous question?

A) Lines 51-54 ("Nutrient... taken")

B) Lines 85-89 ("Further... living")

C) Lines 89-93 ("With regard... beliefs")

D) Lines 86-89 ("Specifically... progress")

29

In line 81, what point is the author trying to make by saying that "the vegan diet is much more than a diet itself"?

A) People who are concerned about protecting animals should consider veganism.

B) Adopting veganism is a good way for people to help the environment.

C) Many vegans consider factors other than food to be part of being a vegan.

D) People who are vegans have healthier lifestyles than non-vegans do.

30

According to the figure, a vegan who does not want to take man-made supplements is most likely to suffer from what type of problem?

A) Mental health disorders

B) Insufficient levels of bile

C) Heart diseases

D) Circulatory system disorders

31

Data from the figure most strongly supports which claim from the passage?

A) Lines 45-48 ("Health benefits… and cancer")

B) Lines 60-64 ("Results of… multivitamin")

C) Lines 76-80 ("While many… outcomes")

D) Lines 94-96 ("Lastly, the popularity... anthropologic significance")

Questions 32-42 are based on the following passage and supplementary material.

This passage is adapted from "Ancient Pollen Yields Insight into Forest Biodiversity," published by the Office of Legislative and Public Affairs, 2003.

By analyzing data on tree pollen extracted from ancient lake sediments, ecologists have sharpened the understanding of how forests can maintain a diversity of species. Their findings indicate that
5 stabilizing processes have been more important than previously thought, and that the human-caused loss of species could upset that stability in ways that remain poorly understood.

"Quantifying the link between stability and
10 diversity, and identifying the factors that promote species diversity, have challenged ecologists for decades," said Saran Twombly, program director in the National Science Foundation (NSF)'s division of environmental biology, which funded the research.
15 "The contribution of this study is unique, as the scientists used a clever blend of long-term data and statistical modeling to test the opposing hypotheses of neutrality and stability as key factors promoting community assembly and diversity."

20 Scientist James Clark and graduate student Jason McLachlan of Duke University published their findings in this week's issue of the journal *Nature*. According to Clark, the purpose of their study was to address a central scientific problem
25 in explaining the diversity of tree species in a forest. "In the mathematical models ecologists use to describe how different species compete for resources such as light, moisture and nutrients, it can be difficult to get species to coexist," he said.
30 "In models, slight advantages allow one species to 'out-compete' the other, leading to extinction, that is, loss of biodiversity. And so, ecologists have put a lot of effort into trying to understand the differences among species that would allow one species to
35 coexist with another species."

Explaining such coexistence is critical, if ecologists are to truly understand forest biodiversity and the forces that sustain or reduce it. According to Clark, two basic hypotheses have arisen to explain
40 forest biodiversity. One theory holds that stabilizing forces are required for many species to coexist.

"For example, one might imagine that, if

one species is limited by light, and another by moisture, they could coexist because they're not
45 really competing that much," said Clark. "An alternative 'neutral model' hypothesizes that species are so similar it just takes a long time for winners and losers to be sorted out by competition, but eventually the better competitor would drive the
50 other to extinction."

Direct observations to distinguish which model is correct would take centuries, said Clark, "So in this study we came up with a way to test the neutral model based on long-term changes in species
55 abundance that are evident in the pollen record."

So, Clark and McLachlan examined existing data on pollen from red maple, birch, beech, ash, oak, hemlock and elm trees isolated from cores of lake sediments in southern Ontario.

60 "This record covers about 10,000 years, so if we look at the relative abundance of different species over that time—which encompasses perhaps several hundred generations of trees—we can estimate long-term growth rates," said Clark.

65 According to Clark, the neutral model would predict that the variation among the sites would increase over time, as random chance caused different species to go extinct in some areas but not others. Some sites, just by chance, should come to be
70 dominated by one species, while others would come to be dominated by another species.

However, the researchers found that variance among the sites did not increase over the millennia, leading them to conclude that stabilizing forces were
75 maintaining forest diversity.

"Our findings indicate there are factors that regulate populations at relative abundances that are consistent from one place to another," said Clark. "The variation from place to place is not 'neutral.'
80 Ecologists have long known that, within a region, some species tend to be more abundant and some species less abundant. Our study doesn't identify what those stabilizing forces are, but it clearly shows they do not arise from neutral dynamics." Indeed,
85 said Clark, a major challenge for ecologists is to attempt to understand what the stabilizing forces are in forest biodiversity. "A long-held view that there are tradeoffs among species, in which each has a unique set of competitive advantages and

90 disadvantages that determines its abundance, is often not supported by data."

"What we are seeing is huge variability within populations," said Clark. "And this variability means they overlap in ways that determine who's going to

95 win and who's going to lose. And that variability might itself represent a stabilizing mechanism."

Clark emphasized, however, that even though the role of stabilizing mechanisms remains unknown, the results from his and McLachlan's

100 studies offer cautionary lessons. "Our findings suggest that forest biodiversity has probably been stabilized in some important ways, so extinction of species should cause us greater concern than if we believed that biodiversity was maintained in the past

105 by continual replenishment of random extinction by generation of new species," he said.

Figure 1

Trees in Southern Ontario
(10,000 years before present)

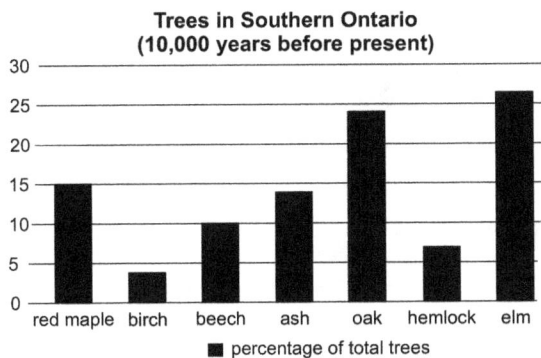

■ percentage of total trees

Figure2

Trees in Southern Ontario
(5,000 years before present)

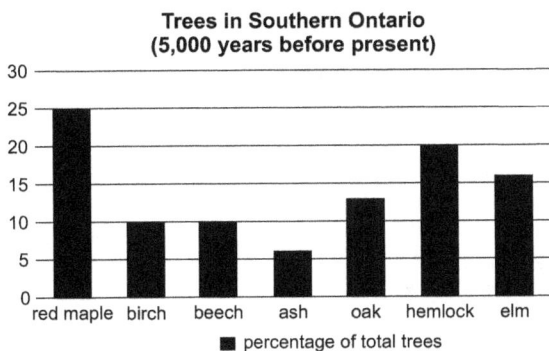

■ percentage of total trees

32

According to the passage, what was the primary purpose of analyzing tree pollen extracted from ancient lake sediments?

A) To explore the ramifications of a phenomenon

B) To confirm whether a specific theory was valid

C) To identify the causes of an unusual incident

D) To isolate the flaws in two common theories

33

Which choice provides the best evidence for the answer to the previous question?

A) Lines 1-4 ("By analyzing… species")

B) Lines 23-26 ("According… forest")

C) Lines 32-35 ("ecologists… species")

D) Lines 52-55 ("So in… pollen record")

34

In the context of the passage as a whole, the quote by Saran Twombly mainly serves what purpose?

A) Clarifying a key term used throughout the passage.

B) Presenting a counterargument that is refuted by the passage.

C) Offering an expert opinion about the study described in the passage.

D) Highlighting one limitation of the methodology described in the passage.

35

As used in line 36, "critical" most nearly means

A) essential.

B) perilous.

C) condemning.

D) analytical.

36

According to Clark, mathematical models are insufficient to study biodiversity because

A) they do not account for changes that take place over the course of centuries.

B) their results do not accurately reflect observations in the natural world.

C) they do not include enough different species of plants from a specific area.

D) their calculations are based on obsolete data that needs to be updated.

37

As used in line 77, "regulate" most nearly means

A) supervise.

B) manage.

C) balance.

D) administer.

38

Which hypothetical data, if true, would most weaken Clark's claim that stabilizing forces control biodiversity in a given region?

A) Scientists determine that there is now significantly greater variation between species in three nearby sites than there was 7,000 years ago.

B) A complex study determines that the reason that plant diversity did not greatly alter in one region was because of a local herbivore.

C) Archaeological evidence shows that early humans ate the nuts from a tree that has subsequently gone extinct in a given area.

D) Several researchers conducted a study that determined that one species of tree is extremely susceptible to temperature changes.

39

Which choice provides the best evidence for the answer to the previous question?

A) Lines 65-69 ("According... others")

B) Lines 69-70 ("Some sites... species")

C) Lines 82-84 ("Our study... dynamics")

D) Lines 97-100 ("Clark emphasized... lessons")

40

Based on the passage, one implication of Clark's study is that due to biodiversity stabilization,

A) there is a smaller chance of ecosystems collapsing than previously theorized.

B) extinction is a random event that is compensated for by evolution of new species.

C) as time progresses, fewer new species will evolve than did in the past.

D) an extinction could indicate a larger-scale collapse of the region's equilibrium.

41

According to figures 1 and 2, which species experienced the least percentage change in numbers of trees in the total population between 10,000 and 5,000 years ago?

A) Red maple

B) Beech

C) Ash

D) Hemlock

42

Taken together, the passage and figures most clearly support which statement about the biodiversity of trees in Southern Ontario?

A) A greater percentage of species went extinct 10,000 years ago than did 5,000 years ago.

B) Elm was the dominant species 10,000 years ago, but lower rainfall favored other tree species 5,000 years ago.

C) Environmental factors changed so that the oak flourished better 5,000 years ago than it did 10,000 years ago.

D) Due to various environmental pressures, the red maple became the dominant species 5,000 years ago.

Questions 43-52 are based on the following passages.

Passage 1 is adapted from "Behavioral Activation: Treatment of Adolescent Depression" copyright November 30, 2018, by Kathryn DeLonga. Passage 2 is adapted from "Side Effects Mild, Brief with Single Antidepressant Dose of Intravenous Ketamine" copyright November 18, 2019 by Elia Acevedo-Diaz. Both articles were published by the National Institute of Mental Health.

Passage 1:

Depression is an illness of brain circuitry and chemistry that causes and is caused by changes in mood, thinking, motivation and behavior. When one reviews the scientific research on most effective
5 treatments for depression in adolescents, what comes up again and again is that the behaviors we engage in make a difference and can help us feel better or can lead to feeling worse. Take, for example, Sally, a hypothetical 15-year-old girl who
10 had a fight with a friend. She's failing in school while her parents are separating. These are some of the stressful events and the daily hassles that she's been dealing with. She feels sad, worthless, overwhelmed and angry. She copes with these big feelings in a
15 pretty natural way. She skips classes because she is overwhelmed by school and she avoids her friends so not to be as anxious. She starts spending a lot of time alone in her room listening to sad music. The ways that she is coping have some negative
20 consequences as well. Her friends stop calling, she gets further behind in school, her parents are upset and severely criticize her.

Behavioral activation is a type of talk therapy that helps teens get unstuck from negative mood
25 spirals by noticing a connection between what they do and how they feel, and gradually adding more small and enjoyable actions back into life. Behavioral activation has the goal of decreasing avoidance, bolstering peer connection, and
30 improving engagement in rewarding activities. It also incorporates parent involvement, so parents gain tools for supporting their adolescents.

Through behavioral activation, a client could work with his counselor to start looking at actions
35 that could help boost his mood. For Sally, at the start of her treatment her goal was to get out of her pajamas and to shower every morning. She

noticed that she actually felt a little bit better, more like herself, just by taking that step. Then, with her
40 parents' support, she reached out to her counselor to get extra support catching up in subjects where she had fallen behind. She started spending more time outside her room and reduced the number of hours she spent on her phone and signed up for a
45 rec basketball league through which she ended up making some new friends. Overall, Sally learned that through taking small, incremental steps, she could do things that would lead to feeling better, more resilient, more like herself, and that she again
50 felt hopeful about the future.

In behavioral activation, the focus is on goal-directed action. Even though a participant might be feeling bad, he will do something because he set the goal to do it. Rather than waiting to feel better,
55 doing things that align with one's values will lead to feeling better.

Passage 2:

Studies have shown that a single, subanesthetic-dose (a lower dose than would cause anesthesia) ketamine infusion can often rapidly relieve
60 depressive symptoms within hours in people who have not responded to conventional antidepressants, which typically take weeks or months to work. However, widespread off-label use of intravenous subanesthetic-dose ketamine for treatment-resistant
65 depression has raised concerns about side effects, especially given its history as a drug of abuse.

"The most common short-term side effect was feeling strange or loopy," said Acevedo-Diaz, of the Section on the Neurobiology and Treatment
70 of Mood Disorders, part of the NIMH Intramural Research Program (IRP) in Bethesda, Maryland. "Most side effects peaked within an hour of ketamine administration and were gone within two hours. We did not see any serious, drug-related
75 adverse events or increased ketamine cravings with a single administration."

The researchers compiled data on side effects from 163 patients with major depressive disorder or bipolar disorder and 25 healthy controls who
80 participated in one of five placebo-controlled clinical trials conducted at the NIH Clinical Center over 13 years. While past studies have been

based mostly on passive monitoring, the NIMH
IRP assessment involved active and structured
85 surveillance of emerging side effects in an inpatient
setting and used both a standard rating scale and
clinician interviews. In addition to dissociative
(disconnected, unreal) symptoms, the NIMH IRP
assessment examined other potential side effects –
90 including headaches, dizziness, and sleepiness. The
study did not address the side effects associated with
repeated infusions or long-term use.

Out of 120 possible side effects evaluated, 34
were found to be significantly associated with the
95 treatment. Eight occurred in at least half of the
participants: feeling strange, weird, or bizarre;
feeling spacey; feeling woozy/loopy; dissociation;
floating; visual distortions; difficulty speaking; and
numbness. None persisted for more than four hours.
100 No drug-related serious adverse events, cravings,
propensity for recreational use, or significant
cognitive or memory deficits were seen during a
three-month follow-up. To overcome the limitations
associated with side effects and intravenous delivery,
105 ongoing research effort are necessary to develop
a more practical rapid-acting antidepressant that
works in the brain similarly to ketamine.

43

According to Passage 1, behavioral activation can
be successful in treating depression in adolescents
because it

A) encourages the patient to do what feels most
comfortable at the time.

B) uses incremental steps to form patterns of
behavior that alter emotions.

C) focuses on solving the problems that triggered
the depressed behavior.

D) emphasizes long-term goals that can be
attempted when the patient is healthy.

44

In lines 14-15 ("She copes… way"), the author
of Passage 1 makes which statement about
depression?

A) Many people respond to depression in the
same way that Sally does.

B) Sally is coping with more stressful feelings
than many people do.

C) Sally's reaction is out of proportion to the
emotions Sally feels.

D) Most people experience periods of depression
as deep as Sally's.

45

As used in line 25, "connection" more nearly
means

A) relevance.

B) bond.

C) correspondence.

D) attachment.

46

Which choice best supports the idea that focusing on positive goals can physically alter the body's composition?

A) Lines 1-3 ("Depression... behavior")

B) Lines 3-8 ("When one ... worse")

C) Lines 33-35 ("Through... your mood")

D) Lines 54-56 ("Rather than... better")

47

According to Passage 2, why is ketamine a preferred drug for treating serious depressive symptoms?

A) Because it acts faster than traditional medications for depression.

B) Because it has fewer side effects that most other depression medications do.

C) Because there is no apparent risk of addiction when administered long-term.

D) Because it can be administered to the patient in multiple different ways.

48

Which choice provides the best evidence for the answer to the previous question?

A) Lines 57-62 ("Studies... to work")

B) Lines 72-74 ("Most side... two hours")

C) Lines 74-76 ("We did... administration")

D) Lines 100-103 ("No drug-related... follow-up")

49

As used in line 79, "controls" more nearly means

A) authorities.

B) restraints.

C) benchmarks.

D) commands.

50

It can be reasonably inferred from Passage 2 that doctors have what major concern about using ketamine to control depression for long periods of time?

A) It may not be effective when used repeatedly.

B) It has serious side effects in conjunction with other drugs.

C) Patients could become addicted to the drug.

D) Patients who take the drug sometimes relapse.

51

Which choice best describes the relationship between the two passages?

A) Passage 1 describes a particular form of treatment that is undermined by the evidence given in Passage 2.

B) Passage 1 explains the symptoms of a problem and Passage 2 describes the most effective way to treat the problem.

C) Passage 2 describes a course of action that can be taken if the methods described in Passage 1 are insufficient.

D) Passage 2 describes complications caused by the course of action proposed in Passage 1 to treat a problem.

52

Based on information from Passage 1, the author of Passage 1 would most likely respond to the conclusion of Passage 2 in the final sentence (lines 103-107, "to overcome…to ketamine") with

A) agreement, because she knows most depression treatments are insufficient.

B) reservation, because she promotes less invasive ways to address depression.

C) confusion, because she feels that the drug does not need any modification.

D) disapproval, because she contends that drug therapies are unacceptable.

STOP

If you finish before time is called, you may check your work on this section only.
Do not turn to any other section.

No Test Material On This Page

Writing and Language Test

35 MINUTES, 44 QUESTIONS

Turn to Section 2 of your answer sheet to answer the questions in this section

DIRECTIONS

Each passage below is accompanied by a number of questions. For some questions, you will consider how the passage might be revised to improve the expression of ideas. For other questions, you will consider how the passage might be edited to correct errors in sentence structure, usage, or punctuation. A passage or a question may be accompanied by one or more graphics (such as a table or graph) that you will consider as you make revising and editing decisions.

Some questions will direct you to an underlined portion of a passage. Other questions will direct you to a location in a passage or ask you to think about the passage as a whole.

After reading each passage, choose the answer to each question that most effectively improves the quality of writing in the passage or that makes the passage conform to the conventions of standard written English. Many questions include a "NO CHANGE" option. Choose that option if you think the best choice is to leave the relevant portion of the passage as it is.

CONTINUE ➡

Questions 1-11 are based on the following text that has been adapted from Social Work Degree Center's Becoming a Social Worker: An Introduction to Careers in Social Work.

The gap between the rich and the poor continues to grow in the United States. [1] As poverty and unemployment continue to rise, so too do other chronic social ills like substance abuse, mental illness, and violence. Civilizations are often measured by how they tend to these problems. And social workers are on the front lines, working for solutions to society's ills and giving of their time and energy to provide resources and life improvements to these most vulnerable members of our communities. [2] If you feel a strong desire to make a difference in your community and in the life of someone in need, than perhaps a career in social work is the right fit for you.

1

The writer is considering deleting the underlined sentence. Should the sentence be kept or deleted?

A) Kept, because it shows the impact of alcoholism in the United States.

B) Deleted, because it would be more effective as the conclusion to this paragraph.

C) Deleted, because it blurs the clarity and tone of the paragraph.

D) Kept, because the sentence is a necessary transition between the preceding and following sentences.

2

Which choice best concludes this paragraph?

A) NO CHANGE

B) Making a difference in our communities is necessary to make the world a better place.

C) The rise in poverty and unemployment is an issue that deserves attention.

D) The most vulnerable in a society are those who are unable to fend for themselves.

Social work is not easy work. [3] You need to be willing to work odd hours, to working with people who are often deemed difficult, and bearing the burdens of the most vulnerable members of your community. Social work can take a toll, but it [4] is deeply rewarded when you can see positive change in someone else's life. There are many different career paths in social work. [5] However, there are some administrative roles, most all social workers deal directly with clients. So regardless of the field you choose, you are most likely to interact with people.

[3]

A) NO CHANGE

B) You need to be willing to do many time-consuming things.

C) You need to be willing to work odd hours, to work with people who are often deemed difficult, and to bear the burdens of the most vulnerable members of your community.

D) You need to be willing to: work odd hours, and with people who are difficult, bearing burdens of the most vulnerable.

4

A) NO CHANGE

B) is deeply rewarding

C) is deep rewarding

D) is deeply reward

5

A) NO CHANGE

B) While

C) Nevertheless

D) Therefore,

The first step toward becoming a social worker 6 is obtaining a Bachelor's degree in social work (BSW). The BSW 7 is opening doors to both further education (like a Master's in Social Work or a Doctorate in Social Work: MSW or DSW) and to entry level job opportunities as a social worker.

8 Although if after completing your BSW you are interested in pursuing further education, the next step is to obtain a Masters' of Social Work degree. The MSW opens up the possibility of moving into higher paying and more long-term social work careers. It also will allow you to move into entry level administrative and managerial roles. There are both good online and traditional MSW 9 programs, but so make sure to look for a program that best fits your goals and life needs.

6
A) NO CHANGE
B) is: obtaining
C) is — obtaining
D) is; obtaining

7
A) NO CHANGE
B) has opened
C) will open
D) will be opening

8
A) NO CHANGE
B) Whenever
C) Given that
D) DELETE the underlined word.

9
A) NO CHANGE
B) programs, so
C) programs, but
D) programs. And

[10] Though it is absolutely necessary in order to have a successful career in social work, there are some social work jobs that require a doctorate. There are two paths the doctorate can take: Doctorate in Social Work (DSW) or Doctorate in Philosophy (PhD). The DSW is aimed at practitioners and will open up further career opportunities working in the field of social work. The PhD is a research degree and [11] prepare you to be able to train the next generation of social workers.

10

A) NO CHANGE

B) Although it is not necessary in order to have a successful career in this field,

C) Despite the lack of necessity,

D) DELETE the underlined section.

11

A) NO CHANGE

B) is preparing

C) has prepared you

D) will prepare

CONTINUE

Questions 12-22 are based on the following text that has been adapted from Harvard University Press Blog's A History of Tahrir Square.

(1)

The recent revolution in Cairo has made Tahrir Square a household name. [12] No one not even a historian who has written a book on the city, could have imagined that this aptly named public space would nurture a spark that would set the entire Middle East ablaze. [13]

[12]

A) NO CHANGE

B) No one –

C) No one,

D) No one. Not

[13]

At this point, the author is considering including the following sentence:

The history of Tahrir Square is insignificant in understanding recent happenings in this symbolic location.

Should the writer make this addition here

A) No, because it provides information that contradicts the central premise of the passage.

B) No, because the sentence is ineffectively constructed and would affect the clarity of the paragraph.

C) Yes, because it provides a necessary transition to the following paragraph.

D) Yes, because it provides evidence to help substantiate a point that was made earlier in the paragraph.

(2)

The 500-acre open space housed cultivated fields, gardens and many royal family palaces [14] during the reign. Ismail, the grandson of Mohamed Ali, came to be known as the founder of modern Cairo. Having lived in Paris during the remake of the city by Baron Haussmann, Ismail embarked on the project of modernizing the city in many ways, one of which was to build a district later named after him. [15] Ismail, therefore, is significant in Egypt's history.

[14]

A) NO CHANGE

B) during the reign of Ismail

C) during the reigning of Ismail

D) Delete the underlined portion.

[15]

Which choice provides the best conclusion to this paragraph?

A) NO CHANGE

B) Therefore, Paris was significant in shaping Ismail's architectural ideas.

C) Thus, all hailed Ismail, the founder of modern Cairo.

D) In the center of this district was a square that carried the same name, Ismailia square.

(3)

The square, however, had an undefined form until the Egyptian Museum was built in [16] their north-eastern corner. Ismail's modernization projects plunged the country into great debt, and he was the first ruler of modern Egypt to be removed from power—in this case, foreign forces did the [17] ousting. The British occupation of Egypt ensued into the waning years of the nineteenth century. The British stationed their troops west of the square in Ismailia, in what Egyptians often called the English Barracks.

[16]

A) NO CHANGE

B) it is

C) its

D) it's

[17]

A) NO CHANGE

B) breaking

C) thinking

D) power

(4)

During the early part of the twentieth century, the Ismailia district emerged as the downtown of modern Cairo and it expanded toward the square, which had to be [18] the re-plan to facilitate the newly introduced vehicular traffic in Cairo. The roundabout in the southern part of the square was consequently built. A few decades later, during the reign of King Farouk, the space acquired the statue-less pedestal. Farouk had commissioned a statue of his grandfather, Khedive Ismail, to be built for the pedestal. [19] The eastern side of the square — with the Arab League headquarters — was also built during this time.

[18]

A) NO CHANGE

B) re-planning

C) being re-planned

D) re-planned

[19]

At this point, the writer is considering changing the underlined sentence to the following:

"The Arab League headquarters were also built during this time, thus defining the eastern side of the square."

Should the writer make this change here?

A) No, because it contains a grammatical error.

B) Yes, because it improves clarity, tone, and voice of the sentence.

C) Yes, because it provides a more effective transition between this paragraph and the following one.

D) No, because it eliminates relevant information.

(5)

Tahrir, which means *liberation* in Arabic, is one of the oldest squares in modern Cairo. [20] Therefore, the images of the square that aired during the recent broadcast coverage of the uprising — images now engraved in the minds of people all over the globe —were taken from the rooftops of the few high-rise buildings situated south of the square. Just beyond this location, looking west and north, is a collection of overlooked buildings that capture the history of modern Egypt and render the revolutionary happenings in Tahrir Square all the more poignant. [21]

Question [22] asks about the passage as a whole.

[20]

A) NO CHANGE
B) Although
C) Then,
D) Delete the underlined word.

[21]

To make this passage most logical, paragraph (5) should be placed:

A) where it is now.
B) after paragraph (1)
C) after paragraph (2)
D) after paragraph (3)

[22]

Which of the following most effectively summarizes the main point of the passage?

A) Tahrir Square has a rich history that relates to its current standing as a site of liberation.
B) Tahrir Square is architecturally fascinating.
C) Egypt is a complex nation.
D) The news, in their coverage of the recent uprising, did not do justice to the history of Tahrir Square.

Questions 23-33 are based on the following text that has been adapted from Medium's Entertainment Law Mythbusters: Your Questions about Legally Sampling Music Answered

The rules around sampling music 23 are mystifying musicians since the enactment of the Copyright Act of 1976. Copyright laws regarding how to clear a sample often seem straightforward when discussed in the 24 abstract. The ability to tell wrong from right when you're experiencing a situation first-hand seems to take a perplexing turn for many musicians. And failing to adhere to copyright laws has proven to evolve into an expensive mistake even the most seasoned of musicians have been known to overlook, including De La Soul, Robin Thicke, and Led Zeppelin.

23

A) NO CHANGE

B) were

C) have been

D) will be

24

What choice best combines the two sentences at the underlined portion?

A) abstract, however, the

B) abstract — the

C) abstract; ability

D) abstract; therefore, the

At the same time, [25] fans will have noticed the decades-long trend of Billboard-topping tracks that directly incorporate inspiration from their predecessors in the form of sampling. [26] Ultimately, Drake sampled Ms. Lauryn Hill, who sampled Wu Tang Clan, who sampled Gladys Knight and the Pips. This points to the fact that sampling is indeed possible to do legally and in good faith; but failing to do so can be detrimental to both your bank account and career.

[25]

At this point, the writer is revising the underlined part of the sentence to the following:

"those who pay attention to the music industry are likely to have noticed."

Should the writer make this change here?

A) No, because it eliminates a necessary piece of information.

B) Yes, because it improves the clarity of the sentence.

C) No, because it adds information that contradicts the focus of the paragraph.

D) Yes, because it provides strong justification for the consideration of copyright laws in sampling.

[26]

A) NO CHANGE

B) In addition,

C) Despite this,

D) For example,

[1]Think of it [27] this way. [2] If you go to the store and steal a pack of gum, is it not considered stealing regardless of the amount or price tag? [3] Keeping this logic in mind will always steer you straight when it comes to the legalities of sampling music. [28] [4] Whether we're discussing a $1 pack of gum or a few songs of someone else's original track, stealing is stealing — regardless of the amount.

27

A) NO CHANGE

B) this way if

C) this way;

D) this way, if

28

To make this passage most logical, sentence 4 should be placed:

A) where it is now.

B) after sentence [1]

C) after sentence [2]

D) before sentence [1]

[29] Copyright issues are complex and need to be paid careful attention to. When you sample another artist's music without obtaining their permission, you're infringing on the copyright to that work, no matter how big or small of a portion you actually use. If the owner of that work registered it with the U.S. Copyright Office, he or she would then have every right to sue you for statutory damages — which can be substantial. Therefore, if you want to legally use a sample from [30] a work of art in your work, you have to obtain permission, every single time.

29

The writer is considering deleting the underlined sentence. Should the sentence be kept or deleted?

A) Kept, because it is an effective topic sentence for this paragraph.

B) Deleted, because it contradicts information that has been provided earlier in the passage.

C) Kept, because it helps evidence the main claim of the passage.

D) Deleted, because it contains information that is ambiguous and would disrupt the specific focus of the following paragraph.

30

A) NO CHANGE

B) a piece of music

C) the creation

D) Delete the underlined portion.

You 31 have also heard that using such a small sample is protected by the concept of "fair use." However, fair use is simply a defense to a claim of copyright 32 infringement, and it will not prevent you from being sued over 33 you're potentially infringing work. Regardless, fair use would be difficult to prove in the case of sampling music. Under fair use, sampling must be for the purpose of criticism, comment, news reporting, teaching, scholarship, or research.

31

A) NO CHANGE

B) having

C) had

D) may have

32

A) NO CHANGE

B) infringement; and it

C) infringement: and it

D) infringement and

33

A) NO CHANGE

B) your

C) their

D) Delete the underlined word.

Questions 34-44 are based on the following text that has been adapted from Amanda Sia's What is Big Data & Predictive Analytics?

Despite being such a buzzword recently, big data is still a pretty nebulous term. While datasets 34 have always exist, with recent advances in 35 technology we have more ways than ever to capture huge amounts of data (such as through embedded systems like sensors) and better ways to store them. 36 Furthermore, big data encompasses the processes and tools used to analyze, visualize, and utilize this huge volume of data in order to harness it and help people make better decisions.

"Predictive analytics" is another term that is often seen with big data. In essence, 37 the term refers to the use of historical data and statistical techniques such as machine learning to make predictions about the future.

34

A) NO CHANGE

B) have always existing

C) may always exist

D) have always existed

35

A) NO CHANGE

B) technology, we

C) technology. We

D) technology;

36

A) NO CHANGE

B) Although

C) In order to achieve this,

D) Delete the underlined word.

37

A) NO CHANGE

B) that

C) this

D) Delete the underlined word.

38 It is also important to note that data doesn't just refer to rows and columns in a spreadsheet, but also to more complex data files such as videos, images, sensor data and so forth.

39 Firstly, it might appear that data analytics in the food industry is often related to **40** marketing — to mining consumer data to understand consumer's behavior, or stocking products at the right time to give companies a competitive edge. However, big data is also a major player in food quality and safety that is not often talked about.

38

At this point, the writer is considering adding the following sentence:

"An example might be how Netflix knows what you want to watch (predictions) before you do, based on your past viewing habits (historical data)."

Should the writer make this addition here?

A) Yes, because it provides a necessary transition to new information.

B) Yes, because it provides a concrete example to help the reader better understand previously mentioned concepts.

C) No, because it disrupts the flow of logic in the paragraph.

D) No, because this example would be better placed in the following paragraph.

39

A) NO CHANGE

B) First of all,

C) First,

D) At first glance,

40

A) NO CHANGE

B) marketing — by

C) marketing. For

D) marketing — for

CONTINUE

The best example for this use of big data is Yelp, a [41] <u>crowding sourced</u> review website that allows users to submit reviews of local businesses, including restaurants. Columbia University's Computer Science department developed a script that uses text classification to dig through Yelp reviews for keywords such as "sick" or "vomit." [42] <u>First,</u> epidemiologists and investigators tried to interview some of the reviewers to find out what their symptoms were, what the incubation period was, and what else they might have eaten.

[41]

A) NO CHANGE

B) crowding sourcing

C) crowd-sourced

D) DELETE the underlined portion

[42]

A) NO CHANGE

B) Second,

C) However,

D) Then,

43

Outbreak	Month of meal	Likely food vehicle	No. of persons ill/ No. in reviewer's party	Environmental findings
	TABLE: Unreported outbreaks of foodborne illness identified by investigation of online restaurant patron reviews. Pilot project, New York City, July 1, 2012-March 31, 2013			
Outbreak A	December 2012	House salad	7/9	Cross contamination in refrigerator Bare-hand contact with ready-to-eat food Improperly sanitized work surfaces No washing of ready-to-eat vegetables
Outbreak B	January 2013	Shrimp and lobster cannelloni	3/5	Improper cold food storage Improper thawing procedures Unhygienic food contact surface Improper storage of food dispensing utensils Mouse activity present Live roaches present
Outbreak C	March 2013	Macaroni and cheese spring rolls	6/6	Bare-hand contact with ready-to-eat food Cold storage temperatures not taken during cold holding of pre-prepared food

Table 1 is from CDC's Using Online Reviews by Restaurant Patrons to Identify Unreported Cases of Foodborne Illness — New York City, 2012–2013

43

Which of the following provides the most effective support from Table 1?

A) One of the three documented outbreaks involved rodent activity.

B) Two of the three documented outbreaks involve the same likely food vehicle.

C) All the documented outbreaks took place within a month of each other.

D) All the documented outbreaks show a 100% rate of infection in the reviewer's party.

44 The NYC Department of Health works with Columbia University to aggregate data from both Yelp and Twitter, and based on the locations and restaurant names mentioned, matches these complaints to specific restaurants. Establishments with multiple complaints are flagged and investigated by the Department of Health. The table above showcases data from one such study that was published on the Centers for Disease Control and Prevention's website, showcasing the identification of foodborne illnesses through online patron reviews in New York City.

44

The writer is considering deleting the underlined sentence. Should the sentence be kept or deleted?

A) Deleted, because it contradicts data that has been provided in the figure.

B) Kept, because it provides evidence for a following concept.

C) Deleted, because this information is not related to preceding content.

D) Kept, because it helps connect information that comes before and after the included figure.

STOP
**If you finish before time is called, you may check your work on this section only.
Do not turn to any other section.**

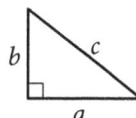
Math Test – No Calculator

25 MINUTES, 20 QUESTIONS

Turn to Section 3 of your answer sheet to answer the questions in this section.

DIRECTIONS

For questions 1-15, solve each problem, choose the best answer from the choices provided, and fill in the corresponding circle on your answer sheet. **For questions 16-20**, solve the problem and enter your answer in the grid on the answer sheet. Please refer to the directions before question 16 on how to enter your answers in the grid. You may use any available space in your test booklet for scratch work.

NOTES

1. The use of a calculator **is not permitted.**

2. All variables and expressions used represent real numbers unless otherwise indicated.

3. Figures provided in this test are drawn to scale unless otherwise indicated.

4. All figures lie in a plane unless otherwise indicated.

5. Unless otherwise indicated, the domain of a given function f is the set of all real numbers x for which $f(x)$ is a real number.

REFERENCE

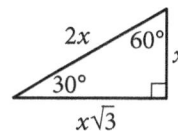 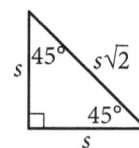 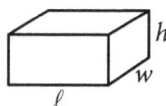 

$A = \pi r^2$
$C = 2\pi r$

$A = \ell w$

$A = \frac{1}{2}bh$

$c^2 = a^2 + b^2$

Special Right Triangles

$V = \ell wh$

$V = \pi r^2 h$

$V = \frac{4}{3}\pi r^3$

$V = \frac{1}{3}\pi r^2 h$

$V = \frac{1}{3}\ell wh$

The number of degrees of arc in a circle is 360.

The number of radians of arc in a circle is 2π.

The sum of the measures in degrees of the angles of a triangle is 180.

1

The sum of which of the following combinations of numbers must be odd?

A) Two odd numbers

B) Three odd numbers

C) Two even numbers

D) Three even numbers

2

If x is a prime number, then $4x$ must be which of the following?

A) odd

B) prime

C) a multiple of 2

D) a multiple of 12

3

$$-3, -15, -75, -375, ...$$

Based on the sequence above, which of the following gives a possible rule for finding each term after the first?

A) Subtract -12 from the preceding term.

B) Multiply the preceding term by 5.

C) Divide the preceding term by 5.

D) Add -12 from the preceding term.

4

The function f is defined by $f(x) = 2x - 2$. Which of the following is equal to $f(x) + 2$?

A) $2x + 2$

B) $2x - 2$

C) $-2x$

D) $2x$

5

If $12n < 49$ and $7n > 22$, which of the following is a possible value of n?

A) 5

B) 4

C) 3

D) 2

6

The cost of a bicycle rental on Beautiful Island is $20, plus $7 per hour for each hour that the bike is rented. If a bike is rented for x hours, which of the following functions f models the total cost in dollars to rent the bike?

A) $f(x) = 20 + 7x$

B) $f(x) = 7 - 20x$

C) $f(x) = 7x - 20$

D) $f(x) = -7x + 20$

7

What is the value of t if t is an integer and $|2t - 2| < 1$?

A) -1

B) 0

C) 1

D) 2

8

In a carnival game, there are bean bags in a sack that are red and yellow. If the probability of choosing a red bean bag at random from the sack is 60%, which of the following represents the number of red bean bags in the sack bags?

A) $\dfrac{6n}{10}$

B) $6n$

C) $\dfrac{10n}{6}$

D) $60n$

9

If $6 \cdot 6^{(s-1)} = 1296$ what is the value of s?

A) 1

B) 2

C) 3

D) 4

10

The diameter of a circle is $2x^3$. What is the area of the circle?

A) πx^2

B) πx^3

C) πx^5

D) πx^6

11

In the xy-coordinate plane, point O is a distance of 7 from the point $(1, 1)$. Which of the following could be the coordinates of point O?

A) $(1, 7)$

B) $(9, 1)$

C) $(-6, 1)$

D) $(1, -7)$

12

M   2x-5   N   x-1   o

6

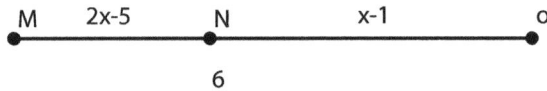

In the figure shown above, $\overline{MO} = 6$ What is the length of segment $\overline{MN}$?

A) 3

B) 4

C) 5

D) 6

13

In the xy-plane, the lines $4x - 2y = 6$ and $y = mx + b$ are perpendicular. Which of the following is the value of m?

A) 2

B) –2

C) $\dfrac{1}{2}$

D) $\dfrac{-1}{2}$

14

The volume of a particular cube is 27 cubic inches. What is the area of the base of the cube, in square inches?

A) 6

B) 9

C) 18

D) 54

15

○ Vanilla
● Chocolate
◐ Strawberry
◕ Cookie Dough

84   63   147   126

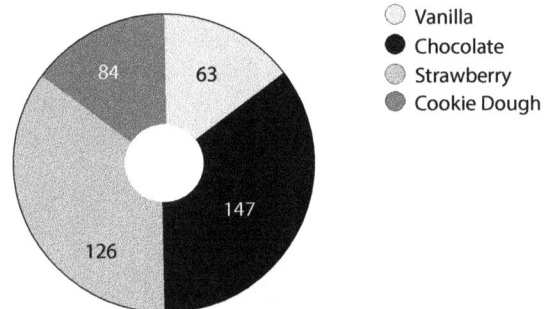

The pie chart above shows the results of a school survey. In the survey, people were asked to choose their favorite ice cream from among a group of four choices. Which of the following was chosen as favorite ice cream by approximately 35% of the students surveyed?

A) Vanilla

B) Chocolate

C) Strawberry

D) Cookie Dough

DIRECTIONS

For questions 16–20, solve the problem and enter your answer in the grid, as described below, on the answer sheet.

1. Although not required, it is suggested that you write your answer in the boxes at the top of the columns to help you fill in the circles accurately. You will receive credit only if the circles are filled in correctly.
2. Mark no more than one circle in any column.
3. No question has a negative answer.
4. Some problems may have more than one correct answer. In such cases, grid only one answer.
5. **Mixed numbers** such as $3\frac{1}{2}$ must be gridded as 3.5 or 7/2. (If $3|1|/|2$ is entered into the grid, it will be interpreted as $\frac{31}{2}$, not $3\frac{1}{2}$.)
6. **Decimal answers:** If you obtain a decimal answer with more digits than the grid can accommodate, it may be either rounded or truncated, but it must fill the entire grid.

Answer: $\frac{7}{12}$

Write answer in boxes. → ← Fraction line

Grid in result. ←

Answer: 2.5

← Decimal point

Acceptable ways to grid $\frac{2}{3}$ are:

Answer: 201 – either position is correct

NOTE: You may start your answers in any column, space permitting. Columns you don't need to use should be left blank.

16

How many integers between 11 and 99 have an odd tens digit and an even ones digit?

17

If k is a positive integer and $2k^3 - 2k = 0$ what is the value of k?

18

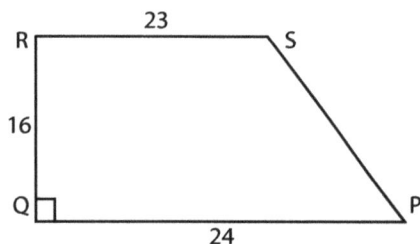

For trapezoid PQRS shown above, $\overline{PQ} = 24$, $\overline{RS} = 23$, and $\overline{QR} = 16$. What is the length of segment $\overline{PS}$? Round to the nearest whole number.

19

At Smartpets, 60% of the 20 dogs have blue eyes. The fraction of hamsters at the store with brown eyes is equal to the fraction of dogs at the store with brown eyes. What is the ratio of hamsters that have brown eyes if the dogs only have brown and blue eyes?

20

$$-4,\ 12,\ y,\ 108,\ -324$$

A sequence of 5 integers is shown above, where y represents the median value. What is the average of the first 4 integers?

STOP

If you finish before time is called, you may check your work on this section only.
Do not turn to any other section.

Math Test – Calculator

55 MINUTES, 38 QUESTIONS

Turn to Section 4 of your answer sheet to answer the questions in this section.

DIRECTIONS

For questions 1-30, solve each problem, choose the best answer from the choices provided, and fill in the corresponding circle on your answer sheet. **For questions 31-38,** solve the problem and enter your answer in the grid on the answer sheet. Please refer to the directions before question 16 on how to enter your answers in the grid. You may use any available space in your test booklet for scratch work.

NOTES

1. The use of a calculator **is permitted.**
2. All variables and expressions used represent real numbers unless otherwise indicated.
3. Figures provided in this test are drawn to scale unless otherwise indicated.
4. All figures lie in a plane unless otherwise indicated.
5. Unless otherwise indicated, the domain of a given function f is the set of all real numbers x for which $f(x)$ is a real number.

REFERENCE

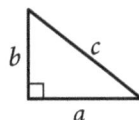 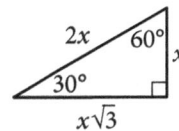 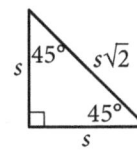

$A = \pi r^2$ $A = \ell w$ $A = \frac{1}{2}bh$ $c^2 = a^2 + b^2$ Special Right Triangles
$C = 2\pi r$

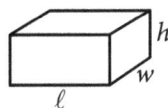 

$V = \ell wh$ $V = \pi r^2 h$ $V = \frac{4}{3}\pi r^3$ $V = \frac{1}{3}\pi r^2 h$ $V = \frac{1}{3}\ell wh$

The number of degrees of arc in a circle is 360.

The number of radians of arc in a circle is 2π.

The sum of the measures in degrees of the angles of a triangle is 180.

1

A negative integer is subtracted from its square and the resulting difference is 6. Which is the integer?

A) – 2

B) 0

C) – 3

D) – 6

2

$$y = 28.2 - 2.5x$$

What are the coordinates of the y-intercept of the above equation?

A) (0, 28.2)

B) (2.5, 0)

C) (0.8, 0)

D) (28.2, 0)

3

$$x, 3x, 9x, \ldots$$

The first term in the sequence above is x, and each term thereafter is equal to three times the previous term. If x is equal to 13, what is the sum of the 5th term and the 4th term?

A) 121

B) 484

C) 363

D) 1,404

4

If $\dfrac{b}{3} - \dfrac{3}{b} = 0$ where $b \neq 0$, then which of the following could not be the value of b?

A) – 3

B) 3

C) 9

D) All of the above.

5

If $\dfrac{m}{0.5} + \dfrac{n}{0.2} = 18$ where m and n are positive integers, then what is the value of n?

A) 1

B) 2

C) 3

D) 4

6

When $\dfrac{1}{3}$ is divided by the reciprocal of a particular number, the result is 16 more than the number. The number is which of the following?

A) –24

B) 16

C) 24

D) –12

7

If $(d + 2)^2 - (d^2 - 4) = 32$, what is the value of d?

A)   14

B)   6

C)   4

D)   2

8

If $pq < 100$ and q is a positive multiple of 6, what is the greatest possible integer value of p?

A)   6

B)   16

C)   30

D)   96

9

In the x-y plane, the line $-9x + 3y = 81$ intersects the y-axis at $y = b$, for some number b. What is the value of b ?

A)   3

B)   9

C)   27

D)   –9

10

1, 2, 3, 4, 5, 6, 7

A data set is shown above. Each number in the set is equal to a third of a value in a similar set of data. What is the average of the numbers in this new data set?

A)   84

B)   28

C)   12

D)   4

11

The median of 20 integers is an odd integer. Which of the following could **not** be true?

I.   The integers of the set are all identical.

II. The integers are consecutive.

III. The 10th largest and 11th largest integers of the set are odd.

A)   I only

B)   II only

C)   I and II only

D)   I and III only

12

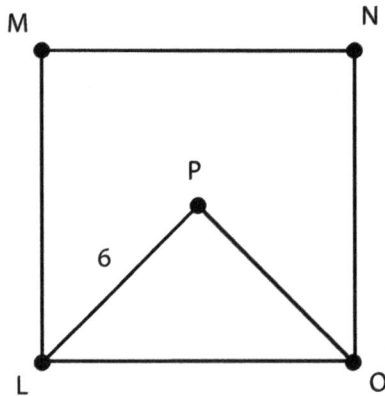

In the figure above, LMNO is a square and triangle LPO is an isosceles triangle. If $\overline{LP} = 6$, what is the area of the square?

A)   36

B)   72

C) $24\sqrt{2}$

D)   24

13

Marcus makes an octagon by arranging 8 equilateral triangles, each of which has a vertex at the center of the octagon. If the length of one side of a triangle is 6, what is the area in square units of the octagon?

A)   48

B)   144

C) $144\sqrt{3}$

D) $72\sqrt{3}$

14

If $x = \dfrac{7y - 4}{4}$, what is the value of y?

A) $\dfrac{x}{y}$

B) $\dfrac{4x}{7}$

C) $\dfrac{x+1}{7}$

D) $\dfrac{4x+4}{7}$

15

If x is a number such that $(x-4)(x+6) = 0$, then what is the smallest possible value of x^2?

A)   4

B)   16

C)   -6

D)   -36

16

A large circular frisbee has a diameter of 2 feet and a height of 3 inches. If Jennifer stacks 15 frisbees on top of each other to prepare for field day, what is the volume of the stack in feet?

A) $\dfrac{15\pi}{4}$

B) 45π

C) $\dfrac{\pi}{4}$

D) 6π

CONTINUE

17

Variables *r* and *s* are real numbers. If $20 < r < 30$ and $40 < s < 60$, which expression represents all possible values of for the difference of *r* and *s*?

A) $-20 < r - s < -30$

B) $-30 < r - s < -20$

C) $-30 < r - s < 20$

D) $-20 < r - s < 30$

18

Jacob went for an 11-mile bike ride and his chain came off after he completed $\frac{4}{9}$ of his trip. How many more miles of the trip does Jacob have to complete after he fixes his chain?

A) $\frac{4}{9}$

B) $\frac{5}{9}$

C) $4\frac{8}{9}$

D) $6\frac{1}{9}$

19

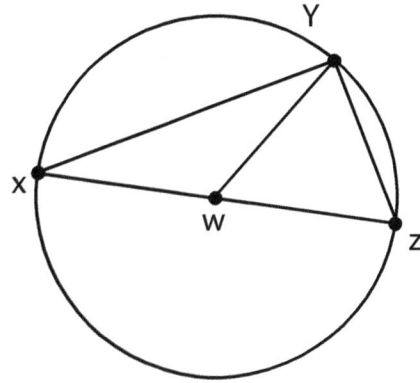

In the figure above, triangle XYZ is inscribed in the circle with center W and diameter $\overline{XZ}$. If $\overline{YZ} = \overline{YW}$, how many degrees is $\angle XWY$?

A) 30°

B) 60°

C) 90°

D) 120°

20

What is the solution to the inequality $-8(a + 3) \leq 2(-2a + 10)$?

A) $a \geq -11$

B) $a \leq -11$

C) $a \leq 11$

D) $a \geq 11$

21

Line p goes through points E and F, whose coordinates are (0, 2) and (x, 0), respectively. For which of the following values of x is the slope of line p less than $\dfrac{-1}{2}$?

A) 3

B) 4

C) 5

D) 6

22

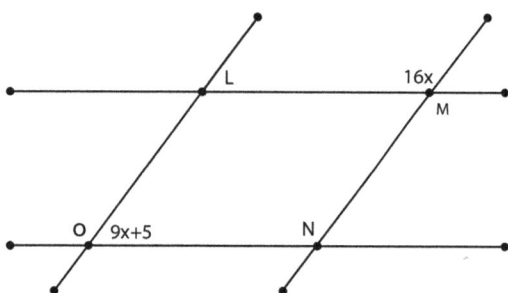

If LMNO is a parallelogram, what is the difference between the measure of $\angle MNO$ and $\angle LMN$?

A) 7°

B) 44°

C) 68°

D) 80°

23

Which of the following parabolas has its vertex in quadrant IV of the coordinate plane?

A) $y = (x - 1)^2 - 2$

B) $y = -(x + 2)^2 + 1$

C) $y = (x + 1)^2 - 2$

D) $y = -(x + 1)^2 - 2$

24

What is the value of $\dfrac{\sqrt{x+13}}{x} \, x\sqrt{x}$ if $x = 36$.

A) 36

B) 42

C) 49

D) 294

25

Triangles PQR and TUV are similar. $\overline{PQ}$ of $\triangle PQR$ corresponds to side $\overline{TU}$ of triangle $\triangle TUV$. If the length of $\overline{PQ}$ is 20 units and the length of $\overline{TU}$ is 8 units, then the area of $\triangle PQR$ is equal to which of the following?

A) $\dfrac{5}{2}(Area\triangle TUV)$

B) $\dfrac{2}{5}(Area\triangle TUV)$

C) $\dfrac{1}{2}(Area\triangle TUV)$

D) $\dfrac{25}{4}(Area\triangle TUV)$

26

The area of a particular equilateral triangle is equal to the perimeter of the triangle. What is the area of the triangle?

A) 3

B) $2\sqrt{3}$

C) 6

D) $12\sqrt{3}$

27

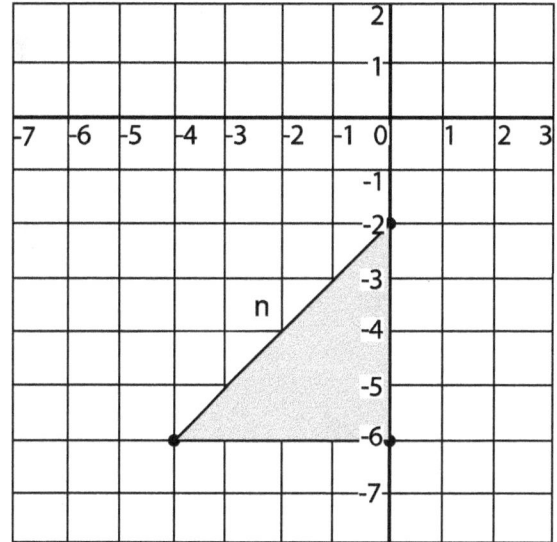

In the graph above, a right triangle is formed with one leg tangent to the y-axis. What is the length of n, the hypotenuse of the triangle?

A) $2\sqrt{2}$

B) 4

C) $4\sqrt{2}$

D) 2

28

Angle X of $\triangle XYZ$ measures 30° and $\angle Z$ measures 60°. If the length of $\overline{YZ}$ is $9\sqrt{3}$, what is the length of $\overline{XZ}$?

A) 9

B) $9\sqrt{3}$

C) $18\sqrt{3}$

D) 27

29

The first term of a sequence is x, and each following term is 3 less than the term before. Which of the following is the mean of the first six terms in the sequence?

A) $6x - 45$

B) $\dfrac{6x + 45}{6}$

C) $\dfrac{2x - 15}{2}$

D) $x - \dfrac{15}{4}$

30

The mean of a data set of eight numbers is 32. When one of the numbers is replaced by 38, the mean increases to 36. What is the number that was replaced?

A) – 5

B) – 8

C) 7

D) 6

DIRECTIONS

For questions 31–38, solve the problem and enter your answer in the grid, as described below, on the answer sheet.

Answer: $\frac{7}{12}$

Write answer in boxes. → Grid in result.

← Fraction line

Answer: 2.5

← Decimal point

1. Although not required, it is suggested that you write your answer in the boxes at the top of the columns to help you fill in the circles accurately. You will receive credit only if the circles are filled in correctly.

2. Mark no more than one circle in any column.

3. No question has a negative answer.

4. Some problems may have more than one correct answer. In such cases, grid only one answer.

5. **Mixed numbers** such as $3\frac{1}{2}$ must be gridded as 3.5 or 7/2. (If $3|1|/|2$ is entered into the grid, it will be interpreted as $\frac{31}{2}$, not $3\frac{1}{2}$.)

6. **Decimal answers:** If you obtain a decimal answer with more digits than the grid can accommodate, it may be either rounded or truncated, but it must fill the entire grid.

Acceptable ways to grid $\frac{2}{3}$ are:

Answer: 201 – either position is correct

NOTE: You may start your answers in any column, space permitting. Columns you don't need to use should be left blank.

31

If x, y and z are positive integers with a mean of 100, which of the following is a possible value for x if $z = 297$?

A)   1

B)   100

C)   297

D)   298

32

Keasha can run 4200 feet in 10 minutes. If she runs at the same rate, how many inches can Keasha run in 15 seconds?

33

When a positive real number is subtracted from its square, the resulting number is equal to zero. What is the value of this number multiplied by 3?

34

What is the y coordinate of the vertex for the parabola defined by the function $y = 2x^2 - 8x + 11$

35

$$4^4 + 4^4 + 4^4 + 4^4 = 2^t$$

In the equation above, what is the value of t?

36

$$2y + 3x = 38$$

$$y - 2x = 12$$

The two equations above define the functions f and g. What value of a makes $f(a)$ equal to $g(a)$?

37

A square has sides with length x. The perimeter of the square is equal to the area. What is the perimeter of the square?

38

The area of all the faces of a cube is the same as the volume of the cube. What is the surface area?

STOP

If you finish before time is called, you may check your work on this section only.
Do not turn to any other section.

No Test Material On This Page

Section #1 – Reading Test

#	Correct Answer	#	Correct Answer	#	Correct Answer	#	Correct Answer	#	Correct Answer	#	Correct Answer
1	B	11	B	21	D	31	C	41	B	51	C
2	A	12	A	22	B	32	B	42	D	52	B
3	A	13	C	23	C	33	D	43	B		
4	A	14	B	24	D	34	C	44	A		
5	D	15	C	25	C	35	A	45	C		
6	D	16	D	26	A	36	B	46	A		
7	A	17	B	27	D	37	C	47	A		
8	C	18	A	28	A	38	A	48	A		
9	C	19	C	29	C	39	A	49	C		
10	D	20	D	30	B	40	D	50	C		

Number of Correct Answers ☐ **Reading Test Raw Score**

Section #2 – Writing and Language Test

#	Correct Answer	#	Correct Answer	#	Correct Answer	#	Correct Answer	#	Correct Answer
1	D	11	D	21	B	31	D	41	C
2	A	12	C	22	A	32	A	42	D
3	C	13	A	23	C	33	D	43	A
4	B	14	B	24	A	34	D	44	D
5	B	15	D	25	B	35	B		
6	A	16	C	26	D	36	D		
7	C	17	A	27	A	37	C		
8	D	18	D	28	C	38	B		
9	B	19	B	29	D	39	D		
10	B	20	D	30	B	40	B		

Number of Correct Answers ☐ **Writing and Language Test Raw Score**

Section #3 – Math Test (No Calculator)

#	Correct Answer	#	Correct Answer	#	Correct Answer	#	Correct Answer
1	B	6	A	11	C	16	24
2	C	7	C	12	A	17	1
3	B	8	A	13	D	18	16
4	D	9	D	14	B	19	0.40
5	A	10	D	15	B	20	20

Number of Correct Answers [   ] **Math Test (No Calculator) Raw Score**

Section #4 – Math Test (Calculator)

#	Correct Answer	#	Correct Answer	#	Correct Answer	#	Correct Answer
1	A	11	B	21	A	31	A
2	A	12	B	22	B	32	1260
3	D	13	D	23	A	33	3
4	C	14	D	24	B	34	3
5	B	15	B	25	D	35	10
6	A	16	A	26	D	36	2
7	B	17	B	27	C	37	16
8	B	18	D	28	C	38	216
9	C	19	D	29	C		
10	C	20	A	30	D		

Number of Correct Answers [   ] **Math Test (Calculator) Raw Score**

CONTINUE ➤

```
┌──────────┐  CONVERT  ┌──────────┐
│          │    ──→    │          │──────────┐
└──────────┘           └──────────┘          │
 Reading Test           Reading Test         │
Raw Score (0 - 52)      Score (10 - 40)      │
```

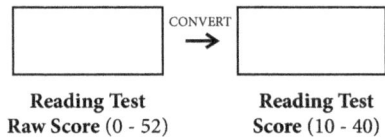

The following is a **Score Conversion Table** (Raw to Scaled) used by the College Board for an SAT® practice test available online. Although each SAT test is scored a bit differently, this table will give you an estimate of your score. Enter your raw scores in the appropriate boxes below, follow the conversion directions and know your estimated SAT scores for this test.

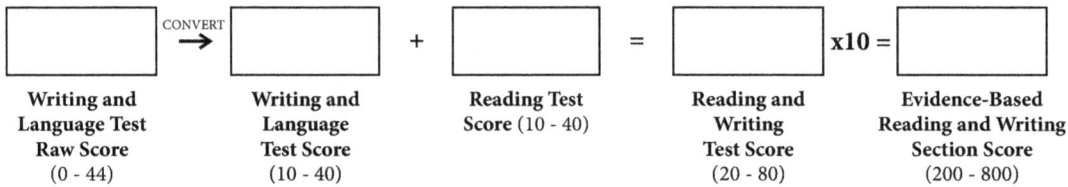

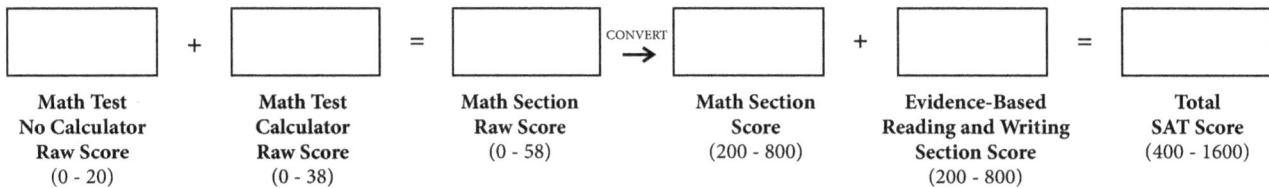

```
┌──────────┐  CONVERT  ┌──────────┐    ┌──────────┐    ┌──────────┐         ┌──────────┐
│          │    ──→    │          │ +  │          │ =  │          │  x10 =  │          │
└──────────┘           └──────────┘    └──────────┘    └──────────┘         └──────────┘
 Writing and            Writing and     Reading Test     Reading and         Evidence-Based
Language Test           Language       Score (10 - 40)     Writing        Reading and Writing
 Raw Score             Test Score                        Test Score          Section Score
 (0 - 44)               (10 - 40)                         (20 - 80)           (200 - 800)
                                                                                  ↓
┌──────────┐    ┌──────────┐    ┌──────────┐ CONVERT ┌──────────┐    ┌──────────┐    ┌──────────┐
│          │ +  │          │ =  │          │  ──→    │          │ +  │          │ =  │          │
└──────────┘    └──────────┘    └──────────┘         └──────────┘    └──────────┘    └──────────┘
 Math Test       Math Test       Math Section          Math Section    Evidence-Based        Total
No Calculator    Calculator      Raw Score               Score       Reading and Writing   SAT Score
 Raw Score       Raw Score        (0 - 58)             (200 - 800)      Section Score      (400 - 1600)
 (0 - 20)        (0 - 38)                                                (200 - 800)
```

Raw Score Conversion Table: Section and Test Scores

Raw Score (# of correct answers)	Math Section Score	Reading Test Score	Writing and Language Test Score	Raw Score (# of correct answers)	Math Section Score	Reading Test Score	Writing and Language Test Score
0	200	10	10	30	530	27	29
1	200	10	10	31	530	27	30
2	210	10	10	32	540	28	31
3	230	10	10	33	550	28	31
4	250	11	11	34	550	29	32
5	260	12	12	35	560	29	32
6	280	13	12	36	570	30	33
7	290	14	13	37	580	30	34
8	310	15	14	38	590	31	34
9	320	15	15	39	590	31	35
10	330	16	15	40	600	32	36
11	350	17	16	41	610	32	36
12	360	17	17	42	620	33	37
13	370	18	18	43	630	34	39
14	380	18	18	44	640	35	40
15	390	19	19	45	650	35	
16	400	20	19	46	660	36	
17	420	20	20	47	670	37	
18	430	21	21	48	680	37	
19	430	21	22	49	680	38	
20	440	22	22	50	690	39	
21	450	22	23	51	700	39	
22	460	23	24	52	720	40	
23	470	23	25	53	730		
24	480	24	25	54	740		
25	490	24	26	55	760		
26	500	25	26	56	770		
27	510	25	27	57	790		
28	510	26	28	58	800		
29	520	26	29				

1. **Choice B is the best answer** because the first three paragraphs describe Mrs. Dashwood's announcement about moving and her family's reaction to it. The fourth and fifth paragraphs detail the belongings she took, how they were sent, some things she left behind, and the servants she sent ahead to prepare the new house. The sixth paragraph states that the preparations were ready. The sixth paragraph gives Marianne's reactions to leaving. Therefore, the passage focuses on the events "surrounding" or "related to" Mrs. Dashwood's "departure" or "leaving" for a new home.

    Choice A is incorrect because "motivations" are "reasons." Although there is an indication of a conflict between Mrs. Dashwood and her daughter-in-law, the passage does not explain why Mrs. Dashwood decided she should move. Choice C is incorrect because Mr. and Mrs. John Dashwood do not express "regret" or "sorrow" about the departure; if anything, they appear glad that she is going. Marianne is upset about leaving her home, but not necessarily sad that her mother is going because she will be traveling with her mother. Choice D is incorrect because, while a few challenges are mentioned (friends have to travel to visit and furniture has to be specially shipped), the passage does not focus on those details.

2. **Choice A is the best answer** because "strained" means "tense" or "awkward." Choice A says that Mrs. Dashwood "indulged herself in the pleasure" or "allowed herself to enjoy" announcing that she found a house. This indicates that she is very glad to get away from them. Her staying with her son is referred to using "incommode," which means "inconvenience." That word choice indicates that the family finds her presence a problem, hinting that she is not welcome in the house. Finally, Choice A shows that she plans to leave as soon as possible, "no longer" than when everything is ready, indicating that she does not like the idea of staying with her relatives more than necessary.

    Choice B is incorrect because, while the invitation may not have been genuine, there is nothing in the quoted words to indicate that Mrs. Dashwood had a tense relationship with her relatives. If anything, Choice B appears that the family is on good terms. Choice C is incorrect because it only says that the family loved the place and did not want to leave. Choice D is incorrect because it hints that the remaining family may not care much about the place, but it does not refer to their feelings about Mrs. Dashwood.

3. **Choice A is the best answer** because "removing" is a verb that shows what Mr. Dashwood cannot do to the furniture. Choice A refers to carrying from one place to another, which fits the context of saying that Mr. Dashwood cannot "be of service" or "help" his mother move the furniture to a new house that is too far away. None of the other choices fits the context of explaining that Mr. Dashwood cannot help take the furniture to a faraway place. Choices B and D refer to disconnecting something, such as removing a part that is fastened in some way. Choice C refers to ordering or sending something away. None of these choices contain the idea of taking the belongings to a new location.

4. **Choice A is the best answer** because (lines 39-41) say, "the very exertion to which he had limited the performance of his promise to his father was by this arrangement rendered impracticable." Therefore, it can be determined that Mr. Dashwood had made a "promise" or "pledge" to take care of his mother, but could not because she was moving too far away.

    Choice B is incorrect because Mr. Dashwood is "vexed" (line 38) that he cannot help due to the distance, not due to a lack of time. Choice C is incorrect because, while Mrs. John Dashwood may feel that Mrs. Dashwood is taking too many nice things, there is no indication that her husband feels the same way. Choice D is incorrect because, if anything, Mr. John Dashwood appears relieved that she will be leaving; the tension between his mother and his wife will ease.

5. **Choice D is the best answer** because as Mrs. John Dashwood watches the furniture leave, she thinks that it is "hard that as Mrs. Dashwood's income would be so trifling in comparison with their own, she should have any handsome article of furniture" (lines 46-49). In other words, Mrs. Dashwood will have "trifling" or "small" income, which puts her in a lower social class than Mrs. John Dashwood. Even so, Mrs. Dashwood has "handsome" or "beautiful" furniture that would normally be too expensive to buy with the amount of money she receives. Mrs. John Dashwood feels her mother-in-law is "overstepping" or "going beyond" what is expected of her social position.

    None of the other choices are supported by evidence from the passage. There is no reference of grief to support

CONTINUE

Choice A. "Pitiful" refers to "pathetic," but Mrs. John Dashwood does not feel sorry because she thinks that Mrs. Dashwood is taking too much. Choice C is incorrect because "unappreciative" means "not showing thanks," but there is no clue that Mrs. John Dashwood expects more shows of thanks.

6. **Choice D is the best answer** because the answer to the previous question is that Mrs. John Dashwood feels that Mrs. Dashwood is "overstepping" or "going beyond" her social position. Choice D supports that claim because it shows that Mrs. Dashwood will have a "trifling" or "small" income, which means that she is of a lower social class than Mrs. John Dashwood. Even so, she is taking with her "handsome" or "attractive" furniture that she would not be able to afford. Since Mrs. John Dashwood feels this situation is "hard" or "inappropriate," it can be assumed that she considers the furniture a sign of going beyond what should be done at the social level.
Choice A is incorrect because it only indicates that Mrs. John Dashwood does not want to comment on the move; the reason for not commenting is not given. Choices B and C gives clues about how Mrs. Dashwood feels about her daughter-in-law, but they do not show that the daughter-in-law thinks Mrs. Dashwood is going beyond what is appropriate for her social level.

7. **Choice A is the best answer** because (lines 58-69) ("The horses...at Norland") explain that Elinor, the oldest daughter, suggests that Mrs. Dashwood sell the carriage and limit their household to three servants. Mrs. Dashwood "defers to" or "allows (someone else) to decide or choose" these decisions.
Choice B is opposite to the relationship portrayed in the passage. Choices C and D are not supported by any evidence. These choices would reflect the relationship between Mrs. Dashwood and her daughter-in-law, Mrs. John Dashwood.

8. **Choice C is the best answer** because the new place is presumably smaller than Norland (lines 17-19, "It is but... be added" and (lines 65-69, "*Her* wisdom...at Norland"), so the reason for moving is not to find larger "premises" or "places." They are moving due to an undescribed conflict with Mrs. John Dashwood, as indicated by (lines 25-27), "her late conversation with her daughter-in-law had made her resolve on remaining at Norland no longer than was unavoidable."
Choice A is incorrect because there is no reference to missing Mr. Dashwood, only to missing Norland. Choice B is incorrect because there is no mention that they cannot "maintain" or "keep up" their "social position" or "status." Although Mrs. Dashwood will have a smaller household in her new home than that at Norland, there is no evidence that her status is declining. Choice D is incorrect because the passage indicates that the new home is farther from friends (lines 17-21, "I hope...accommodating them").

9. **Choice C is the best answer** because "insensible" is a verb that shows what the trees do to the "any change in those who walk" (lines 88 - 89) under them. Choice C means "not notice," so it correctly shows that the trees do not notice that different people are present.
Choice A means "in a state of unconsciousness, especially as a result of injury or illness" and therefore does not apply to the trees and does not reflect Marianne's point that the trees will not notice anything. Choice B means "trivial" or "unimportant," so it does not fit the context of describing what the trees do to a change in people under them. Choice D is incorrect because it refers to a lack of thinking or perception of the environment around something. Although trees do not think, Marianne is talking to them as if they were animate creatures. Choice D therefore does not emphasize that the trees are unable to notice she is gone from Norland; it implies that trees never notice anything.

10. **Choice D is the best answer** because the question asks who will appreciate the trees after Marianne is gone from Norland. This question implies that she thinks that she is the only one who "appreciates" or "feels thankful for" the trees and property; the people who remain will not notice and enjoy things like the trees around them.
Choice A is incorrect because the final question does not include any fear or discussion of where Marianne is moving. The question only indicates concern about the place she is leaving. Choice B is incorrect because the question does not refer to problems between different people. The question just shows that people will react differently to the trees. Choice C is incorrect because Marianne does not refer to her new home at all. It is possible she will enjoy walking under trees there, too.

11. **Choice B is the best answer** because the paragraph asserts that it is not important to determine "whether these States have ever been out of the Union, than with it" (lines 7-8). Lincoln argues that it is more important to return the states to "the proper practical relations" (line 12). Therefore, the first paragraph raises one concern that critics bring up, but then "dismisses" or "gets rid of" that concern because it is "irrelevant" or "not related" to the main discussion of whether Louisiana should retain its government or not.
Choice A is incorrect because the passage's main argument is that Louisiana should retain its government, but that issue is not mentioned in the first paragraph. Choice C is incorrect because no terms are "defined" or "explained in different words." Choice D is incorrect because Lincoln does not "concede a point" or "admit a point is true." Instead, he says that the point confuses the issue (lines 5-9, "I believe it is not only possible, but in fact, easier to do this, without deciding, or even considering, whether these States have ever been out of the Union, than with it.").

12. **Choice A is the best answer** because a "controversy" is a "dispute." One point that clouds the debate is that there are only twelve thousand residents. If there were more, the proper actions might be easier. In Lincoln's words, "The amount of constituency, so to speak, on which the new Louisiana government rests, would be more satisfactory to all, if it contained fifty, thirty, or even twenty thousand, instead of only about twelve thousand, as it does" (lines 18-22).
None of the other choices are supported by evidence from the passage. Choice B is incorrect because the physical size of the state is not mentioned. As for population, the state is presumably smaller than others in the Union. Choice C is incorrect because it is only established that freed slaves live in the state; no number or percentage is given. Choice D is incorrect because the state has "sworn allegiance to the Union" (lines 35-36), indicating that it follows the policies or laws dictated by the Union.

13. **Choice C is the best answer** because Lincoln expresses his personal opinion in (lines 24-26): "I would myself prefer that it were now conferred on the very intelligent, and on those who serve our cause as soldiers." This quote indicates that he feels that some former slaves, such as intelligent men and soldiers, should be "granted" or "given" the right to vote.
Choice A is incorrect because "most" implies over half. Lincoln expresses his view that some former slaves should be able to vote, suggesting that others are not capable of doing so capably. However, there is no indication that the "incapable" or "not qualified" group is over half of the former slave population. Choice B is incorrect because "inalienable" means "absolute" or "inherent." Lincoln, though, does not say that all former slaves should be given the right to vote. He limits his suggestion to giving voting rights to intelligent men and soldiers. Choice D is incorrect because Lincoln indicates that some freed slaves would be capable of voting effectively; otherwise, he would not suggest allowing intelligent men and soldiers to vote.

14. **Choice B is the best answer** because the answer to the previous question is that Lincoln would most likely agree that some former slaves should be granted the privilege of voting. Choice B directly supports that claim because it gives Lincoln's personal opinion that at least certain former slaves should be allowed to vote: intelligent men and soldiers.
Choice A is incorrect because it gives the opinion of "some" that former slaves should be allowed to vote, but Lincoln does not necessarily hold the same opinions. Choice C is incorrect because it describes what voters in Louisiana did; it does not refer to Lincoln's opinions of former slaves voting. Choice D is incorrect because it refers to hypothetically removing the current gains of former slaves; as of the time of the passage, former slaves were not allowed to vote. Therefore, Choice D is not related to the issue.

15. **Choice C is the best answer** because "are committed" is the action that "these twelve thousand persons" does to "the Union." The sentence goes on to say that the people intend to do "nearly all the things the nation wants" (line 48). Choice C means "faithful to," so fits the context that the people are faithful to the Union.
Choice A refers to being busy with something else rather than a promise to follow the orders of a governing body. Choice B refers to doing an action, but does not specify what kind. Choice D refers to something that is sent to a place, but the people choose to enter the Union rather than being sent there by a different authority.

16. **Choice D is the best answer** because the cup of liberty is something that "your old masters" (line 55), or people of Louisiana, holds for slaves. The imagery shows that the cup can be "dash[ed] from you" (line 56) so that it is

CONTINUE

unclear when the "scattered contents" (lines 57-58) or "freedoms" will be given back. In other words, the imagery emphasizes the "precarious" or "unstable" nature of the freedoms. It is very easy to throw aside or break the gains that have been made.

Choice A is incorrect because Lincoln is not saying that the Union is "generous" or "willing to give a lot." He is saying that a poor decision will remove everything that has been given so far. Choice B is incorrect because the cup of liberty is what "your old masters" (line 55), or people of Louisiana, holds for slaves. The cup of liberty is not the advances of the Union, only of Louisiana. Choice C is incorrect because the imagery does not include the reaction of people accepting the cup; it says the cup is easy to break.

17. **Choice B is the best answer** because "recognize" is what "we," the Union, could do to the new government of Louisiana that would make the "converse" or "opposite" of the previous discussion true. The previous discussion is about what happens if the Union does not support Louisiana. Choice B refers to welcoming or integrating something, in this case, Louisiana, so it fits the context of showing the opposite of rejecting Louisiana. None of the other choices show the opposite of rejection. Choice A refers to indicating what something is or naming it. Choice C refers to either fully understanding something or achieving a goal. Choice D refers to knowing the value of something.

18. **Choice A is the best answer** because Lincoln says that Louisiana is "one vote in favor of the proposed amendment to the national Constitution" (lines 78-80). He claims that only "a ratification by three-fourths of all the States would be unquestioned and unquestionable" (lines 87-88), because there would be continued debate if only the states that had not attempted secession were included in the vote. It is implied in the first paragraph that Louisiana tried to secede, so its vote would be extremely useful in ensuring a three-fourths ratification by all states.

Choice B is incorrect because the first paragraph shows Lincoln's view that states that tried to secede should be accepted without question as part of the Union. He is not trying to punish any states for doing so, which means that the attempt to do so is not necessarily a "grievous" or "extremely serious" mistake. Choice C is incorrect because Lincoln implies that many of the policies (lines 35-42, "sworn allegiance to… upon the colored man") are reasonable. They are not "irrational" or "done without thought." Choice D is incorrect because Lincoln doesn't necessarily say that Louisiana is "progressive" or "forward-thinking," as there are still some questions such as voting which are still being debated.

19. **Choice C is the best answer** because the answer to the previous question is that Lincoln considers Louisiana "crucial" or "extremely important" in the upcoming decision to amend the Constitution. Choice C supports that claim because it says that rejecting Louisiana means losing one vote. That suggests that one vote could be enough to change the outcome, so whether Louisiana participates or not could significantly affect the results. Choices A and B are incorrect because they refer to the situation of freed slaves. These choices do not show why Louisiana is important to the vote about the constitutional amendment. Choice D is incorrect because it shows a situation in which Louisiana's vote is not important: if only states that did not try to secede counted, Louisiana would not be included at all.

20. **Choice D is the best answer** because Lincoln is "summarizing" or "condensing" the main idea of his argument in the sentence. He brings up many points to support his view, but he wants to leave the reader with a clear reminder of the main question to be solved rather than focus too closely on any of the details and lose the point. Choice A is incorrect because there is no other indication in the passage that Lincoln is concerned about the acoustics of the area or whether the listeners can hear or not. Choice B is incorrect because there is no reference to a deadline or getting the problem solved at once, so "immediacy," which means "urgency," is inapplicable. "Sooner" in the quote refers to whether the process of uniting Louisiana to other states is faster with one solution or the other, not to the speed that the decision needs to be made. Choice C is incorrect because Lincoln makes the question appear "inherently" or "in its most basic way" simple. He indicates there are too many problems with discarding the state government, so it is easy to see that sustaining it is most important.

21. **Choice D is the best answer** because the passage is describing a study by Sarah Mann that is "aimed to provide a fuller picture of the vegan diet" (lines 12-13). The study reviews different "facets" or "aspects" of veganism, such as its nutritional value, associated lifestyle, and motivations for adopting the diet.

Choice A is incorrect because, while the passage indicates that veganism is increasing in popularity (lines 1-2, "The vegan diet has gained momentum in recent years"), the main point is not just to discuss "rationale" or "reasons" to become a vegan. The passage covers many aspects, such as the risk of nutritional deficiencies, so is not just arguing that people should become vegan. Choice B is incorrect because the passage says that there are stereotypes regarding the diet, but it does not specifically attempt to show that one is wrong. The passage looks into a range of positive and negative aspects of the diet. Choice C is incorrect because the passage does not try to "discredit" or "prove something wrong." It shows that the diet is associated with a healthy lifestyle (lines 64-70, "Comparing the scientific literature…beyond merely nutritional"), supports the claim that there are benefits and "establishes that many of the stereotypes regarding the vegan diet are unfounded" (lines 72-73).

22. **Choice B is the best answer** because "background" refers to the context and circumstances related to the study. The first paragraph explains that the vegan diet is gaining "momentum" (line 1) or "popularity" for various reasons. The paragraph also explains that there is "controversy" (line 6) or "argument" about many aspects of the diet, including its "purpose and proposed benefits" (line 9). Therefore, the paragraph gives the context so the reader knows the situation and offers a reason that Mann decided to conduct a study clarifying points about the diet, including why people choose to become vegan and whether it is nutritionally sound.
Choice A is incorrect because no terms are "defined" or "explained" in the first paragraph. "Vegan diet" is best explained in the second paragraph as "in which no animal products are eaten" (lines 13-14); the first paragraph only says that it is considered "restrictive" (line 5). Choice C is incorrect because the author's view is not given in the first paragraph, which only introduces the fact that there is a lot of controversy. Choice D is incorrect because "rationale" refers to the reasons behind something. There are general statements in the paragraph about why someone might become vegan (lines 3-4, "for health or more ethically-based reasons") and for opposing veganism (lines 10-11, "perhaps because of a lack of knowledge about the diet"). However, the paragraph does not delve into complete reasons for any specific decision or course of action regarding the matter.

23. **Choice C is the best answer** because (lines 21-24) summarize the purpose of the study: "By combining all three sources, the project aims to educate the public regarding a diet and lifestyle that is often perceived, at least partially, in a negative manner." In other words, Mann is trying to "educate" or "teach" people about the "nature" or "basic features" of the diet.
Choice A is incorrect because the passage does not try to "encourage" or "persuade" anyone to become a vegan. Choice B is incorrect because, while the study was trying to fight stereotypes (lines 17-21, "Furthermore, the study…are not vegan"), it did not specifically try to analyze why people are "opposed" or "against" it. It just tried to get a better idea of why people choose to become vegan and explain those reasons to others. Choice D is incorrect because the study did not delve into "anthropological origins" or "historical causes" of the diet. The passage specifically states that such questions are raised rather than answered by Mann's study (lines 94-99, "Lastly, the popularity…evolutionary progress").

24. **Choice D is the best answer** because the passage says that Mann used personal interviews to "to provide an insider's perspective" (lines 17-18). She was trying to get a clearer understanding of veganism from vegans themselves.
Choice A is incorrect because there is no evidence that Mann expected to find a "conflict" or "opposing views" between the interviews and scientific research. She was trying to blend the two to get a more rounded view of the topic as a whole. Choice B is incorrect because the health benefits were analyzed through scientific studies found in the literature review, rather than through data obtained from interviews.. The data provided by research projects is better to "resolve" or "find an answer" to the debate than opinions drawn from interviews. Choice C is incorrect because there is no evidence that "most" or "the largest percentage" of literature is "biased against" or "opposing" veganism. The passage implies that Mann used a range of sources, so did not use interviews for one side of the debate and literature for the other.

25. **Choice C is the best answer** because "composition" refers to an aspect of the diet that Mann questioned twenty vegans about. Choice C refers to the make up or structure of something, so fits the context of explaining that Mann asked about the make up or balance of parts in the diet.
None of the other choices adequately show what part of the diet Mann discussed with the twenty vegans. Choice A refers to how things are spaced and organized rather than the balance of things. Choice B refers to the inherent

personality of someone. Choice D refers to a mixture.

26. **Choice A is the best answer** because "revealed" is what happened to the "commonalities" or "similarities." Choice A refers to detecting or discovering something, which fits the context of explaining that the study discovered some similar points.
Choices B and C are incorrect because they refer to telling a secret, but the study did not decide to share information that it was supposed to keep hidden. Choice D refers to flowing continuously through a closed system, which would imply that the commonalities moved around between members of a certain group of people.

27. **Choice D is the best answer** because Mann concludes that states that "a well-rounded vegan diet is healthy and such is evidenced by the variety of whole foods and increased vegetable and fruit intake" (lines 42-45). However, she also admits that certain nutrients, such as "calcium, vitamin D, iron, and particularly vitamin B-12" (lines 52-53) are insufficient from a plant-based diet, so that "supplements" or "additions" need to be taken. Since plants do not provide all the nutrients humans need, then the conclusion that veganism is sufficient to survive on may be brought into doubt.
Choice A is incorrect because Mann's conclusions are based on people and research into people who "partake" or "follow" a vegan diet. That is not a reason to question that her results may be in error. Choice B is incorrect because even if the diet is "adopted" or "started" for ethical reasons, it still can have health benefits. Choice C is incorrect because Mann used both a literature review and firsthand data in the form of interviews with vegans.

28. **Choice A is the best answer** because the answer to the previous question is that Mann's conclusions about the health benefits of veganism are open to the criticism that it is important to include "additions" or "supplements" which are not directly deprived from plants. Choice A supports this claim because it says that supplements should be taken for certain nutrients that cannot be provided only in a vegan diet. Without supplements, a person could get suffer from deficiencies, which seriously affects Mann's conclusions that veganism by itself is healthy.
None of the other choices address the point that Mann's study is open to the criticism that it is important to include "additions" or "supplements" which are not directly deprived from plants. Choice B refers to a different criticism of the study: it does not prove that the vegans' overall good health is due to the diet; it could be caused by other lifestyle choices. Choice C only offers a way to combat negative stereotypes; it does not address a problem with Mann's study. Choice D questions whether veganism existed in the distant past or not.

29. **Choice C is the best answer** because the author expands on the quote by saying that veganism "has developed into a lifestyle" (line 82) that incorporates other beliefs, such as animal or environmental activism and concern for physical activity. Therefore, the author is trying to say that the vegan diet includes factors or beliefs that are not only related to a "diet" or "food."
Choices A and B are incorrect because, while concern for animals and environmental advocacy are often aspects of veganism, on their own, they are not the only reason to become a vegan. Choice D is incorrect because the quote is not comparing vegans and non-vegans. It is broadening the scope of veganism to include aspects that create a lifestyle, not just the food a person eats.

30. **Choice B is the best answer** because the "alternate source" column on the right-hand side lists only taurine as requiring a "synthetic" or "man-made" supplement. The other nutrients can be at least partly replaced by other sources. The second column of the chart lists "function." The functions of taurine are given as "Muscle function, bile production." Someone who does not have enough taurine would therefore have problems with muscles and bile. Choice B refers to "insufficient levels" or "not enough" bile, which relates to problems with producing or making bile.
None of the other choices are related to the function of taurine. Choice A could be caused by a lack of DHA, which could be replaced using microalgae. Choices C and D could both be caused by a lack of B12, but that can be replaced using nutritional yeast.

31. **Choice C is the best answer** because it says that vegans need to learn about potential nutrient deficiencies to prevent "adverse" or "bad" outcomes. The figure presents nutrients that are "primarily" or "mainly" found in

animal tissues, which are not eaten by vegans, and explains the "function" or "role" of the nutrient. It can be presumed that a "deficiency" or "lack" will cause problems with the normal role, such as poor mental health development in children who do not get DHA. Therefore, the vegan needs to be careful to find sources of those nutrients to avoid negative outcomes.

Choice A is incorrect because it discusses health benefits of veganism. It does not indicate that vegans may be missing some essential nutrients if they do not eat animal products. Choice B is incorrect because it refers to a nutrient that is not in the figure, so data from the figure does not support it. Choice D is incorrect because it indicates that there is a question about whether veganism is nutritionally "sound" or "complete," but does not actually say that there are possible deficiencies. The topic of "anthropologic significance" or "historical importance" is not mentioned in the figure.

32. **Choice B is the best answer** because the study was set up as "a way to test the neutral model based on long-term changes in species abundance that are evident in the pollen record" (lines 53-55). In other words, the study was set up to "confirm" or "test" whether the specific theory of a neutral model was "valid," meaning "correct." Choice A is incorrect because "ramifications" are "consequences." The study does not establish what the consequences or results of biological diversity are; it establishes that there are stabilizing forces on diversity. Choice C is incorrect because an "incident" refers to a specific event or occurrence, not an ongoing process. In addition, the study does not determine the "causes" or "reasons;" the researchers specifically state that they do not know what the forces are (lines 82-83, "Our study doesn't identify what those stabilizing forces are"). Choice D is incorrect because the study does not point of "flaws" or "errors" in the balanced theory. It only shows that the neutral theory is not substantiated by evidence.

33. **Choice D is the best answer** because the answer to the previous question is that the primary purpose of analyzing tree pollen extracted from ancient lake sediments was to "confirm" or "check" whether a specific theory was "valid" or "correct." Choice D directly supports that claim because it specifically says that the purpose of the study was to "test the neutral model."

Choice A is incorrect because it says that the study resulted in a better understanding of biodiversity, but does not explain why the study was conducted. Choice B is vague because it says that the study was to "address a specific scientific problem," but not to test whether a theory was true or not. "Addressing a problem" can refer to solving something that is wrong. Choice C is incorrect because it says that a problem is hard to solve, but does not say what the study was designed to test.

34. **Choice C is the best answer** because Saran Twombly is described as being the program director in the National Science Foundation's division of environmental biology, which implies that she is an "expert" or "authority" on the subject. Twombly's opinion is that the contributions are "unique" or "one-of-a-kind" because they use a creative method of matching different types of data. Twombly indicates that the study's methods have helped solve a problem that has "challenged ecologists for decades" (lines 11-12).

Choice A is incorrect because Twombly's quote does not "clarify" or "define" any vocabulary. Choice B is incorrect because Twombly praises the study rather than giving a "counterargument" or "point that goes against" the premise of the study. Choice D is incorrect because, while Twombly talks about the "methodology" or "techniques" of the study, she does not mention "limitations" or "restrictions" that make the data less applicable.

35. **Choice A is the best answer** because "critical" is the author's view of what "explaining such coexistence" (line 36) is. The sentence continues to say that the explanation is needed to "truly understand forest biodiversity and the forces that sustain or reduce it" (lines 37-38). Choice A refers to something absolutely necessary, so fits the context in saying that explaining coexistence is necessary to understand biodiversity.

None of the other choices accurately describes the essentialness of "explaining such coexistence" (line 36). Choice B means "dangerous." Choice C refers to expressing criticism and disapproval. Choice D refers to using logic and reasoning.

36. **Choice B is the best answer** because Clark says that in mathematical models, "slight advantages allow one species to 'out-compete' the other, leading to extinction, that is, loss of biodiversity" (lines 30-32), but the passage indicates that in real life, species coexist with each other. Therefore, the mathematical models do not accurately "reflect" or "demonstrate" what is observed in natural systems.

CONTINUE

Choice A is incorrect because it is a problem with direct observations (lines 51-52, "Direct observations to distinguish which model is correct would take centuries"), not mathematical models. Choices C and D are not supported by any evidence from the passage. There is no indication that the problem with mathematical models is the number of plants included nor the age of the data.

37. **Choice C is the best answer** because "regulate" is what the factors do to the populations so that the populations are "at relative abundances that are consistent from one place to another" (lines 76-77). Choice C refers to making something stable, so it fits the context of saying that the populations are relatively the same. None of the other choices fit the context of describing what the factors do to the populations. The other choices all refer to a deliberate action of overseeing the actions of someone or something else, but "factors" are inanimate and cannot decide to direct anything else.

38. **Choice A is the best answer** because Clark bases his claim on the concept that there are few overall changes in the biodiversity of an area. He believes that the neutral model, which is the case if no stabilizing factors exist, would result in more variation because chance is the only thing that affects extinction and replacement of species. Therefore, Choice A gives the scenario in which chance takes a large part, weakening Clark's claim that other forces than chance are at work.
Choice B can be eliminated as strengthening rather than weakening Clark's claim that stabilizing forces exist. Choice B offers a "stabilizing force" that controls the biodiversity; Clark did not name the forces, but Choice B shows that at least one exists. Choice C does not greatly affect Clark's data in any way. Even if early humans ate nuts, or one species went extinct, the overall biodiversity can remain the same. Clark's theory accounts for contingencies such as extinction as it only shows that stabilizing forces ensure that biodiversity in the region remains approximately rather than exactly the same. Choice D does not disprove Clark's theory. If one species is susceptible to heat, it could decrease in number or go extinct, but overall, the plants in a region will still remain in the same balance.

39. **Choice A is the best answer** because the answer to the previous question is that if scientists determine that there is now significantly greater variation between species in three nearby sites than there was 7,000 years ago, that fact would weaken Clark's theory of stabilizing forces. Choice A supports that claim because it shows that the scientists' findings are compatible with the neutral case in which random chance exists: variations would increase. The findings oppose Clark's theory.
Choice B is incorrect because it says that chance changes the dominant species in an area, but it does not say that such a case weakens Clark's stabilization theory. Choice C is incorrect because it only says that the stabilizing forces are not known. It does not say how stabilizing forces relate to variation in an area. Choice D is incorrect because it does not relate to variation between regions. It says that the forces are not known and there are lessons to be learned, but provides no specifics.

40. **Choice D is the best answer** because in (lines 102-106), Clark claims, "extinction of species should cause us greater concern than if we believed that biodiversity was maintained in the past by continual replenishment of random extinction by generation of new species." In other words, he feels that if one species goes extinct, it would show that the biodiversity is not being maintained as it should be; the stabilizing forces would no longer be functioning properly. That could indicate a "collapse" or "failure" of the entire system.
Choice A is incorrect because Clark implies that because of stabilization, ecosystems remain in balance, but if one part of the balance is disrupted, the entire system may collapse. Therefore, a total collapse is more likely than if the system is random. Choice B is incorrect because it refers to the situation in the neutral theory, not the biodiversity stabilization theory. Choice C is incorrect because the stabilization theory proposes that the number of species remains about the same. It is implied that the rate of addition and extinction would therefore be about the same.

41. **Choice B is the best answer** because the "least percentage change" refers to the smallest difference between the percentage of trees 10,000 years ago (as shown in Figure 1) and the percentage of trees 5,000 years ago (as shown in Figure 2). In both figures, "beech," the third column from the left, is 10%, so there is no change at all.
All of the other choices can be eliminated as having more change than the beech did. For Choice A, the red maple increased from 15% to 25%, a difference of 10%. For Choice C, the ash decreased from about 14% to about

6%, a difference of 8%. For Choice D, the hemlock increased from about 7% to 20%, a difference of 13%.

42. **Choice D is the best answer** because the passage describes. "stabilizing forces," a general term to describe factors in the environment that keep the balance of organisms in check. Figure 1 shows that 10,000 years before the present, only 15% of the trees were red maple, whereas Figure 2 shows that 5,000 years ago, 25% of the trees were red maple. Red maple became the "dominant" or "main" species, as no other species had more than 20% of the trees. Therefore, it can reasonably be concluded that some of the stabilizing factors or environmental conditions changed so that red maple became more prevalent.
Choice A is incorrect because the two figures show the same trees present, though in different proportions. None of the trees in the figures "went extinct" or "completely died off." Choice B is incorrect because, although elm was dominant 10,000 years ago at over 25% of the trees according to Figure 1, there is no reason given for the reduction to just over 15% as shown in Figure 2. The passage says that the stabilizing forces are unknown, so it is impossible to say from the data that the cause was rainfall. Choice C is incorrect because the opposite is true: the oak "flourished" or "thrived" better 10,000 years ago (at just under 25% of the trees in Figure 1) than it did 5,000 years ago (at under 15% of trees in Figure 2).

43. **Choice B is the best answer** because the process of behavioral activation is described as beginning with simple activities to boost one's mood, such as taking a shower. As the patient improves, more advanced steps can be taken, such as joining club activities. "Incremental" refers to a series of additions, so accurately describes additional steps taken to alter behavior. The passage says that "depression is an illness of brain circuitry and chemistry that causes and is caused by changes in mood, thinking, motivation and behavior" (lines 1-3), so the changes to behavior alter the brain chemistry and subsequent emotions.
Choice A is incorrect because patients are encouraged to do something positive even when they do not feel comfortable about doing it: "Rather than waiting to feel better, doing things that align with one's values will lead to feeling better." (lines 54-56). Choice C is incorrect because the passage does not refer to solving the problems, only to fixing the negative behaviors to get out of a spiral of depression. Choice D is incorrect because behavioral activation focuses on a series of short-term goals, such as brushing one's teeth. The short-term goals may be aligned with a larger, long-term goal, but the process of reaching that goal is through the small steps and is not put off until the patient is healthy.

44. **Choice A is the best answer** because "natural" means "logical" to "to be expected." It indicates that Sally's responses are to be expected given her "big feelings." It can therefore be assumed that other people would also react in the same, expected way given similar circumstances.
Choice B is incorrect because there is no indication that Sally has more stress than others, only that her response is not out of the ordinary. Choice C is incorrect because something "out of proportion" is too great or too small given the circumstances. If that were the case, her response would be "overdone" rather than "natural." Choice D is incorrect because the sentence does not say whether Sally's stress levels are typical of most people or not; the sentence only addresses the way she "copes" or "responds" to the stress.

45. **Choice C is the best answer** because "connection" is something that is noticed which helps "teens get unstuck from negative mood spirals" (lines 24-25). The "connection" is something "between what they do and how they feel" (lines 25-26). Choice C refers to a close similarity or equivalence, so it shows that what they do is equivalent to how they feel and vice versa.
None of the other choices adequately explain the relationship "between what they do and how they feel" (lines 25-26). Choice A refers to the state of being closely connected or important to the subject of the sentence or topic at hand; it is not typically used with "between" and two objects. Choices B and D refer to joining or uniting two things together rather than showing a parallel between two ideas.

46. **Choice A is the best answer** because a "physical" change is a measurable change that can be documented. Choice A supports the idea that the body's "composition" or "make-up" can be changed because it says that changes in mood and thinking can change brain circuitry and chemistry. Therefore, if one focuses on positive goals, this can change the brain chemistry and circuitry in real ways.
Choice B is incorrect because it indicates that behaviors, which would include focusing on goals, can affect emotions. The result is feeling better or worse, but there is no proof that the body structure is changed by those

emotions. Choices C and D are incorrect because they only explain the method used by behavioral activation; they do not explain any results.

47. **Choice A is the best answer** because Passage 2 says that "ketamine infusion can often rapidly relieve depressive symptoms within hours in people who have not responded to conventional antidepressants, which typically take weeks or months to work" (lines 59-62), which indicates that ketamine is "preferred" or "often used" because it works more quickly.

    Choice B is incorrect because the passage lists many side effects of ketamine, but does not compare the number of side effects with those of other drugs. Choice C is incorrect because the long-term risks are not assessed in Passage 2 (lines 90-92, "The study did not address the side effects associated with repeated infusions or long-term use"). There are no apparent short-term risks of addiction when applied once. Choice D is incorrect because the passage addresses only "intravenous subanesthetic-dose ketamine" (lines 63-64). Other forms of administration are not mentioned in the passage.

48. **Choice A is the best answer** because the answer to the previous question is that ketamine is a preferred drug for treating serious depressive symptoms because it acts faster than traditional medications for depression. Choice A supports that claim because it says that ketamine "rapidly" relieves symptoms "within hours," whereas traditional medications "typically take weeks or months to work." In other words, ketamine is much more rapid or faster than other methods of treatment.

    Choice B is incorrect because it refers to the side effects rather than the benefits of the drug, so it does not explain that the drug works faster to help control symptoms of depression than other drugs. Choices C and D are incorrect because they only say that there were no serious side effects from one dose. They do not refer to speed of effect at all.

49. **Choice C is the best answer** because it refers to something that is used as a standard of comparison. It fits the context of saying that 25 healthy people were used as comparisons for the 163 patients with major depressive disorder or bipolar disorder.

    None of the other choices describe the 25 healthy patients. Choice A refers to "experts," but the experts on the subject were conducting the experiment, not taking placebos as part of the test. Choice B refers to limitations rather than comparisons. Choice D refers to orders.

50. **Choice C is the best answer** because (lines 63-66) say, "widespread off-label use of intravenous subanesthetic-dose ketamine for treatment-resistant depression has raised concerns about side effects, especially given its history as a drug of abuse." "Especially" indicates that the main concern is that ketamine is associated with drug abuse or addiction problems. The study in question specifically tested to see whether the patients had "increased ketamine cravings with a single administration" (lines 75-76) or "propensity for recreational use...during a three-month follow-up" (lines 101-103). These factors show that the researchers were particularly trying to determine if users developed addictions to the drug.

    None of the other choices are supported by evidence from the passage. Choice A is incorrect because "the study did not address the side effects associated with repeated infusions or long-term use" (lines 90-92). Choice B is incorrect because, while there is a concern of side effects, the documented effects are not "serious" because they include minor reactions such as short-term "feeling strange, weird, or bizarre; feeling spacey; feeling woozy/loopy; dissociation; floating; visual distortions; difficulty speaking; and numbness" (lines 96-99). Furthermore, there is no discussion of side effects when used "in conjunction with" or "at the same time as" other drugs. Choice D is incorrect because a "relapse" is a return to a former condition. There is no discussion in the passage about whether the patients become depressed again or not.

51. **Choice C is the best answer** because Passage 2 is about ketamine, which is used "for treatment-resistant depression" (lines 64-65), which means it is used to control depression when other methods fail. Passage 1 describes a treatment for depression that may or may not be "sufficient" or "enough" to help some patients. If behavioral activation does not work, ketamine might.

    Choice A is incorrect because, while Passage 1 describes a treatment for depression, Passage 2 does not "undermine" or "weaken" the claim that the treatment works. Passage 2 only offers an alternative for the inevitable cases when the first treatment is not successful. Choice B is incorrect because, while Passage 1 describes what depression is and gives examples of the negative spiral caused by it, Passage 2 does not offer the "most effective" or "best" way to treat the problem. Passage 2 offers a drug that is administered when other treatments fail, indicating that other treatments may be ultimately better for long-term control of the condition. Choice D is incorrect because Passage 1 describes a course of action, behavioral activation, but Passage 2 describes the "complications" or "problems associated with" a completely different course of action, using ketamine.

52. **Choice B is the best answer** because the conclusion of Passage 2 is that researchers need to develop a new drug to treat depression. The author of Passage 1 would probably respond with "reservation" or "some doubt" because she promotes behavioral activation, a method that does not use any medications at all, to retrain the brain into positive patterns. She probably would agree that safer drugs are needed in worst-case scenarios but would encourage avoiding invasive methods like introducing drugs into the body if possible.
Choice A is incorrect because the author of Passage 1 indicates that behavioral activation is successful. She does not discuss any other method of treatment, so it is impossible to tell if she would say that "most" treatments do not work. Choice C is incorrect because the author of Passage 1 does not refer to drug performance at all. She feels that a different type of treatment is satisfactory. Choice D is incorrect because there is not enough information to tell whether the author of Passage 1 "contends" or "argues" that drugs are "unacceptable" or "not allowable." She may agree that drug therapies should be attempted when other methods fail.

CONTINUE ⟶

1. **Choice D is the correct answer.** The line that comes before the underlined sentence refers to the rising gap between the rich and the poor (<u>one</u> problem), while the sentence following the underlined text refers to "these problems" i.e., more than one problem. Therefore, there is a need for a transition between the two, that speaks to multiple problems.
   Choice A is incorrect, since there is nothing about alcoholism that is mentioned in this sentence. Although this topic might be categorized under "substance abuse," its specific impact is not the focus here.
   Choice B is incorrect since this sentence would not be appropriate as the conclusion to this paragraph. Placing this sentence at the end would negatively affect the flow of logic in the text.
   Choice C is incorrect. By adding the sentence in the underlined location, there is no blurring of clarity or tone that is created. The sentence does connect with the ideas that precede and follow it.

2. **Choice A is the best answer.** This answer choice, by focusing on the career choice of social work, is the best way to both conclude this paragraph and to transition to the next one.
   Choices B, C, and D speak to topics that are related to social work, generally, but do not specifically speak about the pursuit of social work as a career. Since this specific theme is the focus of the content that follows — and is the specific topic that the introductory paragraph has led up to — none of these three choices are appropriate.

3. **Choice C is the best answer.** It uses accurate punctuation and maintains parallelism, where all the ideas that have been listed in the sentence show the same grammatical pattern: "to work odd hours," "to work with people," and "to bear the burdens."
   Choice A is incorrect. There are parallelism errors in this sentence structure. Notice the differences between "to work," "to working," and "bearing."
   Choice B is incorrect since it is ambiguous and does not specifically articulate the tasks that social workers need to engage with.
   Choice D is incorrect. In this sentence structure "bearing burdens of the most vulnerable" is crafted as a dependent clause rather than an item on a list. This choice immediately makes the use of the colon after "willing to" grammatically incorrect.

4. **Choice B is the best answer.** Notice that the sentence is in the present tense, making "is" the accurate choice to precede the description of the benefits of the profession. Additionally, when speaking of such benefits that are ongoing, the present progressive tense (made of the helping verb "to be" verb, in the present tense, plus the present participle of the verb, which has an -ing ending) "deeply rewarding" is the only accurate phrasing. Any other choice would be grammatically incorrect.
   Choice A is incorrect because of the use of "rewarded" when referring to benefits that are ongoing in the present.
   Choice C is incorrect. Notice the use of "deep" rather than "deeply;" this choice would make the sentence meaningless and grammatically incorrect.
   Choice D is incorrect. Although "reward" is in the present tense, it does not capture the ongoing, continuous nature of the benefits being described because it is not in the present progressive tense.

5. **Choice B is the best answer.** Notice that there is a contrast that is being referred to in this sentence, where it is pointed out that although some "administrative roles" might exist, social works have to "deal directly with clients." Of all the given choices, "while" comes closest to capturing the implications of "although."
   Choices A and C do not capture the relationship of contrast that is alluded to in this sentence.
   While "nevertheless" (Choice C) can capture the necessary tone, given the current sentence structure, this choice would lead to the sentence becoming meaningless.

6. **Choice A is the best answer.** There is no punctuation that is needed at the underlined location.
   Choice B is incorrect since a colon would only be necessary if what followed was a list, rather than one idea about the Bachelor's degree.
   Choice C is incorrect. Dashes are only needed if what follows is an idea that needs special emphasis, which is not necessary in a sentence that is as direct as this one.
   Choice D is incorrect. Semicolons are only needed when separating two independent clauses, each with

their own subject, verb, and object.

7. **Choice C is the best answer.** Notice that the sentence refers to "further education," i.e., it directly refers to future possibilities. Therefore, the future tense is the most appropriate choice to capture this allusion to what can happen with a BSW.
Choices A, B, and D, by using the present continuous tense, the past tense, and the future continuous tense create verb-tense inconsistencies between the conjugation of the verb and the "further education" that is being referred to.

8. **Choice D is the best answer.** There is no need for a conjunctive adverb in the underlined location since the sentence functions, grammatically and in meaning, without it.
Choice A is incorrect. "Although" refers to a relationship of condition/contrast, that is unnecessary in this sentence. Furthermore, for it to be used accurately, there would need to be a comma that follows the use of this conjunctive adverb.
Choice B is incorrect. "Whenever" would be grammatically or contextually inaccurate in the given sentence.
Choice C is incorrect. Adding "given that" to the beginning of this sentence would make it grammatically inaccurate and meaningless.

9. **Choice B is the best answer** since what follows after the comma directly relates to the preceding part of the sentence.
The use of conjunctions like "and" or "but" would be necessary only if the first idea was being enhanced with a similar/different addition. Since there is no such additional idea that is being included, but just one that directly relates to the first clause, conjunctions like "and" or "but" are not necessary.

10. **Choice B is the best answer.** Notice that the second part of the sentence states that "some" social work jobs require a doctorate — implying that a doctorate is not necessary in order to have a successful career in this field. Therefore the use of "Although" is necessary to show the contrasting ideas in the sentence.
Choice A is incorrect since it contradicts the need for the following clause.
Choice C is incorrect since it is ambiguous with its use of the preposition "the."
Choice D is incorrect since it eliminates relevant information surrounding the necessity, or lack thereof, of a doctorate degree in social work.

11. **Choice D is the best answer.** Notice that the "next generation" is explicitly referred to in this sentence, making the future tense (will prepare) the best possible conjugation of the verb.
Choices A, B, and C are incorrect since the use the present tense, present continuous tense, and the past perfect tense would all cause verb-tense inconsistencies in the sentence.

12. **Choice C is the best answer.** "Not even a historian who has written a book on the city" is a clause that describes "no one" and eliminating this clause would still enable the sentence to make grammatical sense ("No one could have imagined [...]"). Therefore, there needs to be a comma that precedes "not," to clarify the non-essential nature of this clause.
Choice A is incorrect since without a comma, the sentence would not carry meaning.
Choice B is incorrect. For a dash to be used after no one, there would also need to be a dash that is used after "city."
Choice D is incorrect. There is no grammatical or contextual need to split "No one," resulting in it becoming an incomplete sentence.

13. **Choice A is the best answer.** The passage tells us how the history of Tahrir Square helps us better understand the larger significance of this location. Therefore, this sentence contradicts the central premise of the passage.
Choice B is incorrect. It is the content, not the sentence construction, that makes this addition unnecessary.
Choice C is incorrect. The suggested addition does not function as a transition to the content in the next paragraph.
Choice D is incorrect. There is no evidence that is offered here, to substantiate a point that was made earlier in the paragraph.

14. **Choice B is the best answer.** The following sentence tells the reader who Ismail is, and therefore, it is necessary to contextualize the name of the ruler in the previous sentence (i.e., Ismail).
Additionally, the time during which a ruler is in power is considered to be their "reign." Any other version of the verb "to reign" would be grammatically inaccurate.
None of the other choices address both these aspects accurately. Choices A and D do not mention the name of Ismail; Choice C says "reigning" rather than reign.

15. **Choice D is best answer.** Notice that the next paragraph speaks about Ismailia square, beginning with the phrase "the square." Therefore, it would be most appropriate for the concluding sentence of this paragraph to refer to the specific square. Else, the following text would not make sense.
None of the other choices mention "the square" that is discussed at the beginning of the next paragraph. As such, all of them would affect the clarity and flow of logic in the text.

16. **Choice C is the best answer,** since what is being referred to is the north-eastern corner of a singular, non-human entity, "the Egyptian Museum."
Choice A is incorrect, since "their" would only be used to refer to plural, human subjects.
Choice B and D are incorrect. "It's," as a contraction of "it is," would cause the sentence to become meaningless.

17. **Choice A is the best answer.** "Oust" refers to expel someone from a position or place, accurately capturing the removal of power that is being described in the sentence.
None of the other choices capture the meaning of the events being described in the text.

18. **Choice D is the best answer.** Notice the use of the past tense in the preceding verb ("expanded"). "Re-planned," therefore, would be the only choice that preserves verb-tense consistency in the sentence.
All the other choices — of using "re-plan" as a noun (Choice A), in the present continuous tense (Choice B), or the past continuous tense (Choice C) — would render the sentence meaningless.

19. **Choice B is the best answer.** When possible, it is recommended to avoid including additional dependent/non-essential clauses in a sentence. In this case, the suggested edit would make the sentence more active (rather than passive), thus making it the preferred choice for clarity, tone, and voice.
Choice A is incorrect. There is no grammatical error in this sentence.
Choice C is incorrect. Since this sentence contains the same content, it cannot be said to be "more" or "less" effective than the current sentence.
Choice D is incorrect since no information is deleted in this particular sentence construction.

20. **Choice D is the best answer.** While the sentence that follows the underlined word adds an idea to the preceding sentence, the ideas it contains are not related to the preceding content in a way that would necessitate the use of the presented choices.
"Therefore" alludes to a relationship of causality; "although" implies a relationship of contrast; "then" suggests a relationship based on time — none of these relationships exist between the two sentences.

21. **Choice B is the best answer.** Notice that paragraph (1) ends by referring to how the square is "aptly named." By beginning with the meaning of "Tahrir," this text would best follow the first paragraph. Furthermore, this paragraph introduces why the history of the square is important in understanding the poignancy of the contemporary "happenings" that are also referenced toward the end of paragraph 1.
All other answer choices, including the current structure of the passage, cause a break in logic between the ideas contained in the paragraphs.

22. **Choice A is the best answer,** since it accurately summarizes the link between the past and present of the square that is underlined in this passage.
Choice B is incorrect since it suggests an inaccurate emphasis on the architecture of Tahrir Square.
Choice C is incorrect. While the passage's information does describe a nation with a complex history, it would be inaccurate to call this the main point of the passage.
Choice D is incorrect. The coverage of the news is not the main point of the passage. The news is referred to

as a way to describe widely known images of Tahrir Square.

23. **Choice C is the best answer.** Notice that the date/event that is being referenced is introduced by the word "since." This immediately indicates that the present perfect tense (have + the verb) is the best choice. Present perfect tense is used for actions that began in the past and continue to the present.
All of the other choices would create a grammatical inconsistency within the sentence.

24. **Choice A is the best answer.** The first sentence speaks about how copyright laws seem "straightforward," while the second sentence points to an additional condition that contrasts the previous idea (when the same thing that was described as being "straightforward" is then described as "perplexing"). Given this relationship, "however" is the best conjunctive adverb to connect the two sentences and the ideas in them.
Choice B is incorrect. A dash would only be necessary if what follows needs special emphasis, rather than being a complete sentence as is the case here.
Choice C is incorrect. With "the" being removed before "ability," the sentence following the punctuation mark would no longer be complete.
Choice D is incorrect. "Therefore" points to a relationship of consequence rather than contrast.

25. **Choice B is the best answer.** The term "fans" is ambiguous whereas clarifying who these fans are ("those who pay attention to the music industry") is a much clearer choice.
Choice A is incorrect. There is no detail that has been eliminated in the edited text.
Choice C is incorrect. There is no contradictory information in the edited text.
Choice D is incorrect. The sentence does not justify anything to do with copyright laws in sampling.

26. **Choice D is the best answer** since what follows the underlined text are examples of how sampling is used by contemporary, well-known artists.
Choice A is incorrect since "ultimately" refers to a final condition/statement in a list.
Choice B is incorrect. There are no preceding ideas that are being "added" to in the text that follows.
Choice C is incorrect. "Despite" refers to a conditional argument, which is not included here.

27. **Choice A is the best answer.** Of the given choices, separating the two sentences into separate ones is the most grammatically accurate answer.
Choice B is incorrect. Without any punctuation between "way" and "if", the sentence would be impossible to follow.
Choice C is incorrect. While a semicolon can indeed be used to separate two independent clauses, the deletion of the word "if" in the second sentence would make the latter incomplete.
Choice D is incorrect. Using a comma in a sentence like this one would create dependent clauses that make the sentence difficult to follow.

28. **Choice C is the best answer.** The underlined sentence provides a specific example that relates to the ideas in sentence 2 (i.e., referencing the gum and that the monetary value of the thing being stolen doesn't matter). Therefore, to maintain the flow of logic in this paragraph, the text would be best placed after the second sentence.
All the other choices would disrupt the flow of logic in the paragraph.

29. **Choice D is the best answer.** This sentence is vague; it repeats an idea that has already been introduced (about the complexity of copyright issues) and does not mention what the paragraph specifically deals with (registering any use of another artist's music).
Choice A is incorrect. An effective topic sentence would more specifically introduce the content that is contained in the following text.
Choice B is incorrect. There is no preceding information that is contradicted by the underlined sentience.
Choice C is incorrect. The main claim of the passage is the complexity and need of copyright issues, specifically in relation to music sampling (rather than copyright issues in general).

30. **Choice B is the best answer.** The paragraph, and the passage, refer to pieces of music rather than all works of art (Choices A and C).

CONTINUE ➤

Choice D is incorrect since deleting the underlined phrase would make the sentence grammatically incorrect and meaningless.

31. **Choice D is the best answer.** Since the writer is addressing "you" and we do not know what "you" has/has not heard of, a conditional phrase like "may have" is the best possible choice.
Choice A is incorrect since "have" communicates a certainty that is less appropriate (though grammatically accurate).
Choices B and C would create verb-tense inconsistencies within the sentence (notice the following use of "is").

32. **Choice A is the best answer.** A comma is the best way to offset the clause — notice that is preceded by a comma; the text following the "and" is also an independent clause.
Choice B is incorrect. Semicolons are not followed by conjunctions like "and."
Choice C is incorrect. A colon would only be used if the following content includes a list or a quotation, or a colon could be used between independent clauses if the second clause explains, illustrates, paraphrases, or expands on the first sentence.
Choice D is incorrect. Since the text following "and" is an independent clause, a comma is grammatically necessary before "and.

33. **Choice D is the best answer.** Given that the subject, "you," has been referenced directly before the underlined text, there is no need to include another pronoun here. The sentence retains its grammatical accuracy and meaning without it.

34. **Choice D is the best answer.** Since the underlined text refers to something that has always been there (in reference to the past, continuing to the present,") the answer choice in the present perfect tense is the best possible answer. The present perfect tense is made up of the present tense conjugation of "to have" followed by the past tense of "to exist."
None of the other choices would capture this temporal quality of something from the past continuing into the present.

35. **Choice B is the best answer.** "With recent advances in technology" is a dependent clause that is used to introduce the following ideas. A comma is the most accurate punctuation to use in such a case.
Choice A, without a punctuation mark, makes the sentence difficult to follow.
Choice C is incorrect. Using a period to separate the clauses would result in two incomplete sentences.
Choice D is incorrect. Semicolons can only be used between two independent clauses.

36. **Choice D is the best answer.** What follows the underlined word is a clarification of a term that has already been introduced ("big data"). Therefore, the sentence cannot be said to add an additional concept (Choice A) or showcase a relationship of contrast (Choice B), or conditional causation (Choice C).

37. **Choice C is the best answer.** The "term" being referred to is one that has been mentioned in the immediately preceding sentence ("predictive analytics"). "This," therefore, is the best way to refer to the previously mentioned term.
Choice A is incorrect since "the" is more ambiguous and does not accurately pinpoint the subject being referred to.
Choice B is incorrect. "That" does not contain the accuracy of referring to a term in the previous sentence.
Choice D is incorrect. Deleting the underlined word would make the sentence grammatically inaccurate and meaningless.

38. **Choice B is the best answer.** This additional sentence explicitly allows the reader to understand "predictions" and "historical data" in relation to a contemporary example that they are likely to be familiar with (i.e., Netflix).
Choice A is incorrect. While this additional example is useful, it is not "necessary" to transition between the sentences that precede and follow the indicated location.
Choice C is incorrect. There would be no disruption that is caused by including an example at this point.

Choice D is incorrect. There would be no place for an example like this one in the following paragraph.

39. **Choice D is the best answer.** "At first glance" is the clearest way of communicating the idea that, when first looking at this topic in relation to the food industry, its manifestation might seem most likely in the described ways.

All the other choices suggest that this is the first of a number of ranked conditions (first, second, third, and so on), which is not the case in this paragraph.

40. **Choice B is the best answer.** The word "by" is the only preposition that captures the process-based quality that is being described here, i.e., the process in which marketing occurs by mining consumer data.

Choices A and D are incorrect since "to mining" and "for mining" would make the following text meaningless.

Choice C is incorrect since it unnecessarily separates the two clauses, when the latter is not an independent clause.

41. **Choice C is the best answer.** The term refers to the way in which reviews are sourced, i.e., from a crowd. "Crowd" and "sourced" are the only two possible versions of the words that would be grammatically accurate; needing to be separated by a hyphen since it refers to a particular phenomenon that includes both concepts (of the crowd being the source).

Choice A is incorrect because of the use of "crowding." There is no need to use the gerund here.

Choice B is incorrect since both words are in gerund form, which is grammatically incorrect.

Choice D is incorrect since it would eliminate relevant information that is important to include.

42. **Choice D is the best answer.** The sentence following the underlined verb refers to what happened (the interview) <u>after</u> something else occurs (the text classification). "Then" is the only one of the given choices that captures this relationship.

Choices A and B are incorrect. "First" and "second" refer to a ranked process, rather than a continuity that is implied by a term like "then."

Choice C is incorrect because "however" implies a contrast that is not necessary here.

43. **Choice A is the best answer.** "Rodents" is a term that is used to refer to mice and only one of the three outbreaks mentioned in the table mentions mouse activity under "environmental findings."

Choice B is incorrect. No two of the outbreaks include the same food vehicle.

Choice C is incorrect. Given that one of the events took place in December and another in March, there is a time frame greater than one month here.

Choice D is incorrect. Only one of the highlighted outbreaks shows a 100% infection rate, i.e., where all the members of the party contracted the infection.

44. **Choice D is the best answer.** Notice that the paragraph before the figure mentions the study from Columbia University; the underlined sentence helps build on that information in order to then introduce the table. Therefore, the sentence helps connect information that comes before and after the figure.

Choice A is incorrect. The sentence in question does not contradict any of the information included in the figure.

Choice B is incorrect. There is no following concept that is "evidenced" by the underlined sentence.

Choice C is incorrect. The information is clearly related to preceding content.

1. **Medium | Heart of Algebra**

   Choice B is correct. The sum of two odd numbers is even (3+5=8) but the sum of 3 odd numbers is odd (3+5+7=15). The sum of two even numbers is even (2+4=6) and the sum of three even numbers is also even (2+4+6=12). Choices A, C, and D are incorrect and are the result of arithmetic errors.

2. **Medium | Heart of Algebra**

   Choice C is correct. By multiplying by a multiple of 4 (which is a multiple of 2) x cannot be odd or prime. However, since 4 is a multiple of 2, we have the answer; $4x = 2(2x)$ Although $4x$ could be a multiple of 12, this is not always the case. Choices A, B, and D are incorrect and are the result of arithmetic errors in finding multiples.

3. **Easy | Heart of Algebra**

   Choice B is correct. Multiply the first term by 5 and continue to multiply each term afterwards, to get -3, $-3 \times 5 = -15$, $-15 \times 5 = -75$, $-75 \times 5 = -375$. Choices A, C, and D are incorrect and are the result of arithmetic errors.

4. **Easy | Heart of Algebra**

   Choice D is correct. Since $f(x) = 2x, -2$, the expression $f(x) + 2 = 2x - 2 + 2 = 2x$. Choices A, B, and C are incorrect and are the result of arithmetic errors.

5. **Medium | Heart of Algebra**

   Choice A is correct. Since $12n < 49$ we know $n < \dfrac{49}{12} = 4\dfrac{1}{12}$ and $7n > 22, n > \dfrac{22}{7} = 3\dfrac{1}{7}$ then $3\dfrac{1}{7} < n < 4\dfrac{1}{12}$.

   Therefore n can only be 4. Choices B, C, and D are incorrect and are the result of arithmetic errors.

6. **Easy | Heart of Algebra**

   Choice A is correct. Start with the initial $20 to rent the bike, which is the intercept. One then pays $7 per hour, which can be expressed as $7 \times x = 7x$. Therefore, the function is defined by $f(x) = 20 + 7x$. Choices AB C, and D are incorrect and are the result of errors in creating linear equations.

7. **Medium | Passport to Advanced Math**

   Choice C is correct. One is the only answer that yields a value less than 1. Here, one can plug in the values and you will find that $|2(1)-2| = 0$ which is less than 1. Choices A, B, and D are incorrect and are the result of errors in evaluating absolute value inequalities.

8. **Easy | Passport to Advanced Math**

   Choice A is correct. Since $60\% = 0.60 = \dfrac{6}{10}$ then $\dfrac{6}{10}$ of n bean bags will be red. Therefore, multiply

   $\dfrac{6}{10} \times n = \dfrac{6}{10}n$, which translates to $\dfrac{6n}{10}$. Choices B, C, and D are incorrect and are the result of arithmetic errors.

9. **Easy | Passport to Advanced Math**

   Choice D is correct. Using exponent rules for multiplication, one can find that $6 \cdot 6^{s-1} = 6^1 \cdot 6^{s-1} = 6^{1+s-1} = 6^s = 1296$. It follows that $s = 4$ because $6^4 = 1296$. Choices A, B, and C are incorrect and are the result of errors in solving equations with exponents.

10. **Easy | Additional Topics in Math**

    Choice D is correct. If the diameter of a circle is $2x^3$ then the radius is $\dfrac{2x^3}{2} = x^3$. The formula for area of a circle is $A = \pi r^2$ where r is the radius therefore, using the exponent power rule, we find that $A = \pi(x^3)^2 = \pi x^6$. Choices A, B, and C are incorrect and are the result of errors in calculating the area of a circle with algebraic expressions.

11. **Easy | Additional Topics in Math**

    Choice C is correct. $(-6,1)$ could be the coordinates of point O because 7 units to the left of point $(1,1)$ is the point $(-6,1)$. Choices A, B, and C are incorrect and are the result of errors in interpreting data without a graphic aid.

    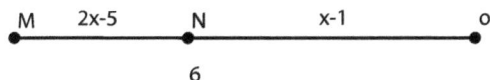

    M ——2x-5—— N ——x-1—— o

    6

12. **Easy | Additional Topics in Math**

    Choice A is correct.. Find the sum of $\overline{MN} + \overline{NO} = \overline{MO}$, $(2x - 5) + (x - 1) = 6$, $3x - 6 = 6$, $3x = 12$, $x = 4$. Substituting this value into MN shows: $\overline{MN} = 2(4) - 5 = 3$. Choices B, C, and D are incorrect and are the result of errors in interpreting data on a number lines.

13. **Medium | Heart of Algebra**

    Choice D is correct. To find the slope of $4x - 2y = 6$, express the linear equation in slope intercept form; $4x - 2y = 6$, $-2y = -4x + 6$, $y = 2x - 3$. The slope is 2, so a perpendicular line would have the opposite reciprocal slope. Therefore, change the sign from negative to positive and flip the fraction; $m = 2, perpendicular\ m = -\dfrac{1}{2}$. Choices A, B, and C are incorrect and are the result of errors in identifying slopes of perpendicular lines.

14. **Medium | Additional Topics in Math**

    Choice B is correct. To find the area of the base, find the length of one of the edges of the cube. Since the volume is $s^3 = 27$, it follows that $s = \sqrt[3]{27} = 3$. Since the length of one of the edges of the cube is 3 then the we use the formula for area of a square: $A = s^2 = (3)^2 = 9$. Choices A, C, and D are incorrect and are the result of errors in evaluating volume and area of a cube and square.

15. **Medium | Passport to Advanced Math**

    Choice B is correct. To find the one that is approximately 35% we find the ratio of $\dfrac{flavor}{total\,number\,surveyed}$; adding up all the numbers finds 420 total people were surveyed, so:

    $\dfrac{chocolate}{total\,number\,surveyed} = \dfrac{147}{420} = .35 = 35\%$. Choices A, C, and D are incorrect and are the result of errors in creating proportions from a pie chart.

16. **Medium | Passport to Advanced Math**

    The correct answer is 24. Generating the table below, one can determine that there are 24 integers between 11 and 99 have an odd tens digit and an even ones digit.

Range	Integers	Number of Integers
11-19	12,14,16,18	4
30-39	30,32,34,36,38	5
50-59	50,52,54,56,58	5
70-79	70,72,74,76,78	5
90-99	90,92,94,96,98	5
Total: 24		

17. **Medium | Heart of Algebra**

The correct answer is 1. To find k isolate the variable in the equation $2k^3 - 2k = 0$, $2k(k^2 - 1)$, $2k(k + 1)(k - 1) \Rightarrow k = \{-1, 0, 1\}$. Since k is a positive integer, then $k = 1$.

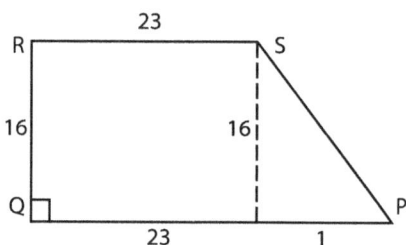

18. **Difficult | Additional Topics in Math**

The correct answer is 16. We draw an altitude from vertex S to $\overline{QP}$. We know the length of the vertex is 16 because $\overline{QR} = 16$. Now we find the distance from the altitude to vertex P which is 1 because $\overline{PQ} = 24$, $\overline{RS} = 23$ therefore $24 - 23 = 1$. We can now use the Pythagorean theorem ($a^2 + b^2 = c^2$) to solve for $\overline{PS}$ because $1^2 + 16^2 = x \Rightarrow 1 + 256 = x^2 \Rightarrow 257 = x^2 \Rightarrow \sqrt{257} = x \approx 16.03$. Round to 16.

19. **Medium | Passport to Advanced Math**

The correct answer is 0.40. To find out the ratio of hamsters that have brown eyes, we determine the fraction of dogs with brown eyes. Since 60% of the 20 dogs have blue eyes and dogs only have brown or blue eyes, we know that 40% have brown eyes. Therefore, the ratio of hamsters is 40:100 which is .40 or $\frac{2}{5}$.

−4, 12, y, 108, −324

20. **Medium | Passport to Advanced Math**

The correct answer is 20. Looking at the sequence, each integer is being multiplied by -3 to get the following integer. If we multiply $12 \times -3 = -36$. Therefore, the median is −36. Use this value to find the average of the first four integers: $-4 + 12 + -36 + 108 = 80, \frac{80}{4} = 20$.

1. **Medium | Problem Solving and Data Analysis**

   Choice A is correct. Let x be the negative integer; $x^2 - x = 6$, $x^2 - x - 6 = 0$, $(x - 3)(x + 2) = 0$

   $x = \{-2, 3\}$ Since x is a negative integer then $x = -2$. Choices B, C, and D are incorrect and are the result of arithmetic errors.

2. **Medium | Heart of Algebra**

   Choice A is correct. The y-intercept is the y-value where x is equal to 0. Substitute and solve: $y = 282 - 2.5x$, $y = 282 - 2.5(0)$, so $y = 28.2$ when $x = 0$. The coordinates are therefore $(0, 28.2)$. Choices B, C, and D are incorrect and reflect errors in interpreting linear functions.

3. **Medium | Problem Solving and Data Analysis**

   Choice D is correct. First, use the pattern to determine the 4th and 5th integers: $27x$, $81x$. Since x is 13, substitute that value for the expression to find the sum of the 4th and 5th terms: $27(13) + 81(13) = 351 + 1053 = 1,404$. Choices A, B, and C are incorrect and reflect arithmetic errors.

4. **Medium | Heart of Algebra**

   Choice C is correct. Since $\dfrac{b}{3} - \dfrac{3}{b} = 0$ where $b \neq 0$, we can solve for b; $\dfrac{b}{3} - \dfrac{3}{b} = 0 \Rightarrow \dfrac{b^2}{3b} - \dfrac{9}{3b} = 0 \Rightarrow \dfrac{b^2 - 9}{3b} = 0 \Rightarrow$

   $\dfrac{(b + 3)(b - 3)}{3b} = 0 \Rightarrow (b + 3)(b - 3) = 0$. Therefore $b = \{-3, 3\}$. Answer Choice C can not be a value of b.

5. **Difficult | Heart of Algebra**

   Choice B is correct. We can change the equation $\dfrac{m}{0.5} + \dfrac{n}{0.2} = 18$ to $\dfrac{m}{1/2} + \dfrac{n}{1/5} = 18 \Rightarrow 2m + 5n = 18$. Since m and n are both positive integers, we check the answer choices and find that $n = 2$ when $m = 4$. If $n = 1$ or 3 we get a fraction. If $n = 4$ then this makes m a negative integer. Choices A, C, and D are incorrect and reflect errors in evaluating fraction equations.

6. **Medium | Problem Solving and Data Analysis**

   Choice A is correct. Let's let the number be x therefore $\dfrac{1}{3} \div \dfrac{1}{x} = x + 16 \Rightarrow \dfrac{x}{3} = x + 16 \Rightarrow x = 3x + 48 \Rightarrow -2x$

   $= 48 \Rightarrow x = -24$. Choices B, C, and D are incorrect and reflect errors in evaluating fraction equations.

7. **Medium | Passport to Advanced Math**

   Choice B is correct. Since $(d + 2)^2 - (d^2 - 4) = 32$ we solve for d; $(d + 2)^2 - (d^2 - 4) = 32 \Rightarrow (d + 2)^2 - (d + 2)(d - 2) = 32 \Rightarrow (d + 2)(d + 2 - (d - 2)) = 32 \Rightarrow (d + 2)(d + 2 - d + 2) = 32 \Rightarrow (d + 2)(4) = 32 \Rightarrow d + 2 = 8 \Rightarrow d = 6$. Choices A, C, and D are incorrect and reflect arithmetic errors.

8. **Medium | Heart of Algebra**

   Choice B is correct. If q is a positive multiple of 6 then the greatest possible integer value q can be for $pq < 100$ is 16 because if we multiply 16 by the smallest multiple of 6 we get 16; $6 \times 16 = 96$. Choices A, C, and D are incorrect and reflect arithmetic errors.

9. **Medium | Heart of Algebra**

   Choice C is correct. We take the linear equation $-9x + 3y = 81$ and change it to slope intercept form; $-9x + 3y =$

$81 \Rightarrow 3y = 9x + 81 \Rightarrow y = 3x + 27$. We find that when the line crosses the y-axis $b = 27$. Choices A, B, and D are incorrect and reflect errors in interpreting linear functions.

10. **Medium | Problem Solving and Data Analysis**

    Choice C is correct. If the numbers in this set are one third of the other set, multiply each number in this set by 3 to get the second set; $1 \times 3 = 3, 2 \times 3 = 6, 3 \times 3 = 9, 4 \times 3 = 12, 5 \times 3 = 15, 6 \times 3 = 18, 7 \times 3 = 21 \Rightarrow New\ Set =$ 3, 6, 9, 12, 15, 18, 21. To find the average, find the sum and divide by 7; $(3 + 6 + 9 + 12 + 15 + 18 + 21) \div 7 = 12$. Choices A, B, and D are incorrect and reflect arithmetic errors.

11. **Difficult | Problem Solving and Data Analysis**

    Choice B is correct. If the median of 20 integers is an odd integer then this could be true only if the two middle numbers are both even, both odd, or the same number. If one is even and the other is odd, the median will not be an integer. Therefore, the integers cannot be consecutive (which means counting numbers). Choices A, C, and D are incorrect and reflect arithmetic errors.

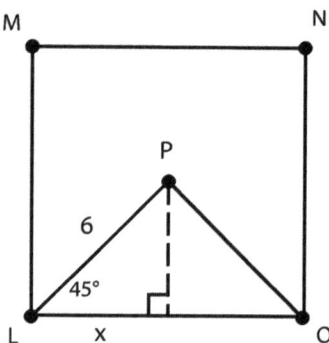

12. **Difficult | Additional Topics in Math**

    Choice B is correct. In the figure LMNO is a square and triangle LPO is isosceles therefore if $\overline{LP} = 6$, and a 45°

    angle represents angle PLO then side x is $cos\,45° = \dfrac{x}{6} \Rightarrow 6(cos\,45°) = x \Rightarrow \dfrac{6\sqrt{2}}{2} = x \Rightarrow 3\sqrt{2} = x$. Since x is half the

    length of one of the sides of the square we find $2x; 2x = 2(3\sqrt{2}) = 6\sqrt{2}$. To find the area of the square, we use the

    formula $Area = s^2$ where s represents the side of the square; $Area = (6\sqrt{2})^2 = 72$. Choices A, C, and D are

    incorrect and reflect errors in interpreting linear functions.

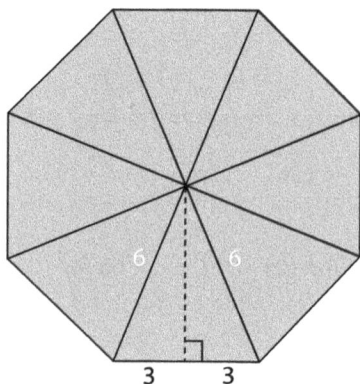

13. **Difficult | Additional Topics in Math**

    Choice D is correct. The area of a regular polygon is equal to $Area = \frac{1}{2}Pa$ where P is the Perimeter and a is the apothem (shortest length from the center to the side). We know the perimeter is equal to $6 \times 8 = 48$ because there are 8 sides with a length of 6. To find the apothem we know that we have a $30° – 60° – 90°$ triangle with side of ratio $1:\sqrt{3}:2$ which in this case, this right triangle has sides $3:3\sqrt{3}:6$. Therefore, the apothem is $3\sqrt{3}$. Therefore, if the formula for area is the area is $Area = \frac{1}{2}Pa; Area = \frac{1}{2}(48)(3\sqrt{3}) = 72\sqrt{3}$. Choices A, B, and C are incorrect and reflect errors in calculating areas of triangles.

14. **Medium | Passport to Advanced Math**

    Choice D is correct. Since $x = \frac{7y-4}{4}$, we can solve for y by isolating the variable; $x = \frac{7y-4}{4} \Rightarrow 4x = 7y - 4 \Rightarrow$ $4x + 4 = 7y \Rightarrow \frac{4x+4}{7} = y$. Choices A, B, and C are incorrect and reflect errors in manipulating algebraic functions.

15. **Easy | Passport to Advanced Math**

    Choice B is correct. Since $(x-4)(x+6) = 0$, it follows that $x = 4$ or $x = -6$. Squaring each gives $4^2 = 16$ and $(-6)^2 = 36$. The smallest value of the two is 16. Choices A and C are the two possible values of x rather than x^2. Answer Choice D is the incorrect squaring of -6, and is therefore not the smallest possible value of x^2.

16. **Difficult | Additional Topics in Math**

    Choice A is correct. First we find the volume of one frisbee by using the formula $Volume = \pi r^2 h$. The diameter is $2ft$ therefore the $r = 1$ ft and since the height is $3in$ we convert it to feet by dividing $h = 3in \div 12 = \frac{1}{4}$ ft. It follows that the volume of one frisbee is $Volume = \pi 1^2 \left(\frac{1}{4}\right) = \frac{\pi}{4}$. Since there are 15 frisbees then the $Volume = \frac{15\pi}{4}$.

    Choices B, C, and D are incorrect and reflect errors manipulating units.

17. **Difficult | Heart of Algebra**

    Choice B is correct. Since $20 < r < 30$ and $40 < s < 60$, we find the range of the difference of $r - s$; $20 - 40 < r - s$ $< 30 - 60 \Rightarrow - 20 < r - s$ and $r - s > - 30$. It follows that $-30 < r - s < -20$. Choices A, C, and D are incorrect and reflect errors in interpreting inequalities.

18. **Easy | Problem Solving and Data Analysis**

    Choice D is correct. If Jacob completed $\frac{4}{9}$ of his 11 mile trip, he has $\frac{9}{9} - \frac{4}{9} = \frac{5}{9}$ of his trip to go. It follows that $\frac{5}{9}$ of 11 is $\frac{5}{9} \times 11 = \frac{55}{9} = 6\frac{1}{9}$. Choices A, B, and C are incorrect and reflect arithmetic errors

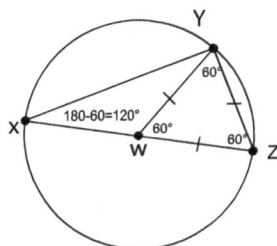

CONTINUE ▶

19. **Medium | Additional Topics in Math**

Choice D is correct. Since the figure above shows triangle XYZ is inscribed in the circle with center W and diameter $\overline{XZ}$ and $\overline{YZ} = \overline{YW}$, we know that $\overline{YW} = \overline{ZW}$ because they are both radii. It follows that ΔWYZ is an equilateral triangle which means all sides and all angles are congruent. Since the total degree measure of a triangle is 180° therefore each angle is 60°. Since $\angle XWY$ is the supplement of $\angle ZWY$ then $\angle XWY = 180 - 60 = 120°$. Choices A, B, and C are incorrect and reflect errors in interpreting angle relationships between triangles and circles.

20. **Medium | Heart of Algebra**

Choice A is correct. To solve the inequality we isolate the variable a; $-8(a + 3) \le 2(-2a+10) \Rightarrow -8a - 24 \le -4a + 20 \Rightarrow -4a \le 44 \Rightarrow a \ge -11$ (Remember to flip the inequality when you multiply or divide both sides by a negative number). Choices B, C, and D are incorrect and reflect errors in interpreting inequalities.

21. **Medium | Heart of Algebra**

Choice A is correct. The slope of line p is $m = \dfrac{y_1 - y_2}{x_1 - x_2} = \dfrac{2-0}{0-x} = \dfrac{2}{-x} = -\dfrac{2}{x}$. To find where the slope of line p is less than $\dfrac{-1}{2}$ we set $\dfrac{-2}{x} < \dfrac{-1}{2} \Rightarrow -x > -4 \Rightarrow x < 4$. The only answer less than 4 is A. 3. Choices B, C, and D are incorrect and reflect errors in interpreting inequalities.

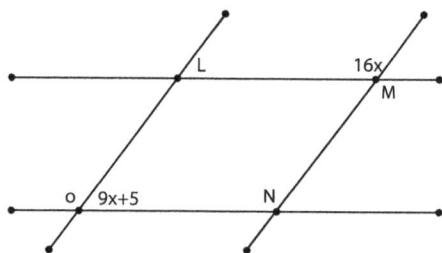

22. **Difficult | Additional Topics in Math**

Choice B is correct. Since LMNO is a parallelogram we know we have two sets of parallel lines being cut by two parallel transversals. Since $16x$ is a supplement to $9x + 15$ we set them equal to 180 and solve for x; $16x + 9x + 5 = 180 \Rightarrow 25x + 5 = 180 \Rightarrow 25x = 175 \Rightarrow x = 7$. It follows that $\angle MNO = 16x = 16(7) = 112$ and $\angle LMN = 9x + 5 = 9(7) + 5 = 63 + 5 = 68$. Therefore the difference between the two is $112 - 68 = 44$. Choices A, C, and D are incorrect and reflect errors in interpreting angle relationships.

23. **Difficult | Passport to Advanced Math**

Choice A is correct. Since the vertex form of a quadratic is $y = a(x - h)2 + k$, where (h, k) is the vertex of the parabola we can check each answer choice by finding the vertex. In answer choice a the vertex is (1, –2) which is in quadrant IV while the vertex in choice b is (–2, 1) which is in quadrant II, choice c (–1, –2) which is in quadrant III and choice d is (–1, –2) which is also in quadrant III. Recall the quadrants go in a "c" shape from the upper right = I and lower right = IV. Choices B, C, and D are incorrect and reflect errors in interpreting quadratic functions.

24. **Medium | Passport to Advanced Math**

Choice B is correct. Since $x = 36$ we can evaluate $\dfrac{\sqrt{x+13}}{x} \times \sqrt{x}; \dfrac{\sqrt{x+13}}{x} \times \sqrt{x} = \dfrac{\sqrt{36+13}}{36} 36\sqrt{36} = \dfrac{\sqrt{49}}{36}(36)\sqrt{36}$

$= \sqrt{49} \cdot \sqrt{36} = 7 \cdot 6 = 42$. Choices A, C, and D are incorrect and reflect arithmetic errors in simplifying expressions.

25. **Difficult | Additional Topics in Math**

    Choice D is correct. Since Triangles PQR and TUV are similar and $\overline{PQ}$ corresponds to side $\overline{TU}$ then

    the scale factor from $\overline{PQ}$ to $\overline{TU}$ is 20:8 or $\dfrac{5}{2}$. If a side of ΔPQR is $\dfrac{5}{2}$ (side of ΔTUV) then the area of

    $\Delta PQR = (\dfrac{5}{2})^2 (Area\Delta TUV) = \dfrac{25}{4}(Area\Delta TUV)$. Choices A, B, and C are incorrect and reflect errors in

    interpreting characteristics of triangles.

26. **Difficult | Additional Topics in Math**

    Choice D is correct. Let's draw a diagram.

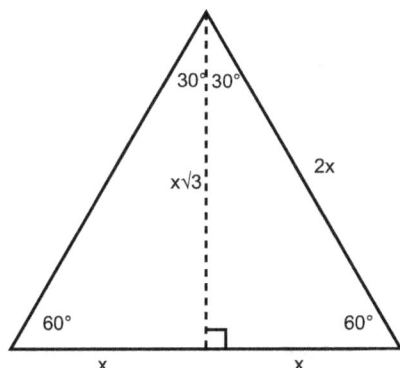

    First we start with the formulas for area and perimeter of an equilateral triangle; $Perimeter = 3x$ and $Area = x^2\sqrt{3}$
    where x is one of the sides. The perimeter was found by adding all three sides; $2x + 2x + 2x = 6x$. To
    find the area we have to find the height of the triangle first. Since the height forms two right triangles
    of ratio $x : x\sqrt{3} : 2x$ we find the height of the triangle to be $x\sqrt{3}$ and the base to be $x\sqrt{3}$ and the

    area to be $Area = \dfrac{bh}{2} = \dfrac{2x \cdot x\sqrt{3}}{2} = \dfrac{2x^2\sqrt{3}}{2} = x^2\sqrt{3}$. Since the perimeter and area are equal we set

    $6x = x^2\sqrt{3} \Rightarrow \dfrac{6x}{x^2} = \sqrt{3} \Rightarrow \dfrac{6}{x} = \sqrt{3} \Rightarrow x = 2\sqrt{3}$. We now find the $Area = \dfrac{bh}{2} = x^2\sqrt{3} = (2\sqrt{3})^2\sqrt{3} = 12\sqrt{3}$.

    Choices A, B, and C are incorrect and reflect errors in interpreting angle and side relationship of triangles.

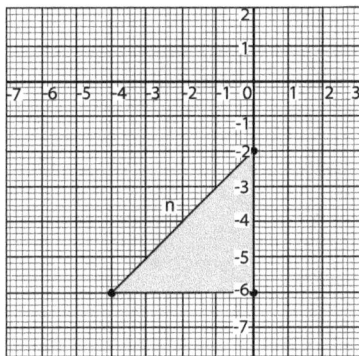

27. **Difficult | Additional Topics in Math**

    Choice C is correct. We know this is an isosceles right triangle, which means this is a 45° – 45° – 90° triangle with a ratio of $x : x : x\sqrt{2}$ and since the lengths of the legs are 4 units, we know that $n = 4\sqrt{2}$. Choices A, B, and D are incorrect and reflect errors in interpreting angle and side relationship for geometric shapes on a graph.

28. **Medium | Additional Topics in Math**

    Choice C is correct. Let's draw a diagram.

    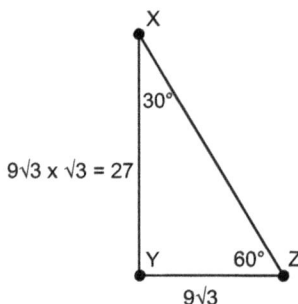

    Since this is a 30° – 60° – 90° triangle with sides ratio $x : x\sqrt{3} : 2x$ we set $x = 9\sqrt{3}$. It follows that $\overline{XZ} = 2 \cdot \overline{YZ} = 2 \cdot 9\sqrt{3} = 18\sqrt{3}$. Choices A, B, and D are incorrect and reflect errors in interpreting characteristics of right triangles.

29. **Difficult | Problem Solving and Data Analysis**

    Choice C is correct. If first term of a sequence is x, and each following term is 3 less than the term before then those terms are as follows: x, $x - 3$, $x - 6$, $x - 9$, $x - 12$, $x - 15$. To find the mean, we find the sum of the terms and divide by six; $(x + x - 3 + x - 6 + x - 9 + x - 12 + x - 15) \div 6 = \dfrac{6x - 45}{6} = \dfrac{3}{3} \cdot \dfrac{2x - 15}{2} = \dfrac{2x - 15}{2}$. Choices A, B, and C are incorrect and reflect errors in interpreting sequences.

30. **Difficult | Problem Solving and Data Analysis**

    Choice D is correct. Since the mean of the data set is 32 we can find the sum of the numbers in the data set by multiplying $32 \times 8 = 256$. If the mean increases to 36 when a number is replaced then this means the sum of the numbers is now 288. Two find what number was replaced, we subtract $288 - 38 = 250$. Our last step is to subtract $256 - 250 = 6$. Choices A, B, and C are incorrect and reflect errors in interpreting data sets.

31. **Difficult | Problem Solving and Data Analysis**

    Choice A is correct. Since x, y and z are positive integers with a mean 100, then the sum of $x + y + z = 300$. It follows that $x + y + 297 = 300 \Rightarrow x + y = 3$. Therefore x and y can only be the sum of integers 1 and 2. Choices A, B, and C are incorrect and reflect errors in interpreting angle and side relationship for geometric shapes on a graph.

32. **Medium | Problem Solving and Data Analysis**

    The correct answer is 1260. First we convert minutes to seconds; $10\ mins \times 60 = 600\ secs$. If Keasha runs 4200 ft in 600 secs then she runs 7 ft in 1 sec because $4200 \div 600 = 7$. It follows that in 15 secs, Keasha runs $15\ sec \times 7 = 105\ ft$. Convert feet to inches by multiplying $105\ ft \times 12 = 1260 in$.

33. **Medium | Problem Solving and Data Analysis**

    The correct answer is 3. The positive real number will be called x therefore $x^2 - x = 0 \Rightarrow x(x-1) = 0 \Rightarrow x = \{0, 1\}$. Since it is a non-zero integer then the answer is 1. Therefore, 1 multiplied by 3 is 3.

34. **Medium | Passport to Advanced Math**

    The correct answer is 3. Vertex form of a quadratic function is $f(x) = a(x-h)^2 + k$ where $h = \dfrac{-b}{2a}$ and $k = f(h)$.

    Here, a and b are represented $y = ax^2 + bx + c$. In the function $f(x) = 2x^2 - 8x + 11, a = 2, b = -8$ therefore the

    vertex is $h = \dfrac{-(-8)}{2(2)} = \dfrac{8}{4} = 2$ and $k = f(2) = 2(2)^2 - 8(2) + 11 = 3$. The vertex is $(2, 3)$ and the y coordinate is 3.

35. **Difficult | Passport to Advanced Math**

    The correct answer is 10. We take the equation $4^4 + 4^4 + 4^4 + 4^4 = 2^t$ and change the bases of 4^4 to $(2^2)^4 = 2^8$. It follows that $4^4 + 4^4 + 4^4 + 4^4 = 2^t \Rightarrow 2^8 + 2^8 + 2^8 + 2^8 = 2^t \Rightarrow 4(2^8) = 2^t \Rightarrow 2^{10} = 2^t \Rightarrow t = 10$.

    $2y + 3x = 38$

    $y - 2x = 12$

36. **Difficult | Passport to Advanced Math**

    The correct answer is 2.

    $2y + 3x = 38 \Rightarrow 2(2x + 12) + 3x = 38 \Rightarrow 4x + 24 + 3x = 38 \Rightarrow 7x + 24 = 38 \Rightarrow 7x = 14 \Rightarrow x = 2$.

    Since we are looking for where $f(a) = g(a)$, and $x = 2$ satisfies the system of equations, $a = x = 2$

37. **Medium | Problem Solving and Data Analysis**

    The correct answer is 16. The formula for the area of a square is $Area = x^2$ and the formula for the perimeter of a square is $Perimeter = 4x$. We set the perimeter equal to the area and solve for s; $x^2 = 4x \Rightarrow x = 4$. Therefore the $perimeter = 4(4) = 16$

38. **Medium | Problem Solving and Data Analysis**

    The correct answer is 216. Since the area of all the faces of a cube is equal to the volume, we set the formula for both equal to each other to solve for an edge. The formula for the area of a cube is $Area = 6x^2$ and the formula for

    the volume of a cube is $Volume = x^3$ where x represents the an edge. It follows that $x^3 = 6x^2 \Rightarrow \dfrac{x^3}{x^2} = 6 \Rightarrow x = 6$.

    Since $x = 6$ the area is $Area = 6x^2 = 6(6)^2 = 216$.

CONTINUE ▶

NOTES

9 781636 510873